ROYAL NAVAL AIR SERVICE

OPERATIONS REPORTS

17th October 1917
to 16th March 1918

Parts 44 to 53

The Naval & Military Press Ltd

Published by

The Naval & Military Press Ltd
Unit 5 Riverside, Brambleside
Bellbrook Industrial Estate
Uckfield, East Sussex
TN22 1QQ England

Tel: +44 (0)1825 749494

www.naval-military-press.com
www.nmarchive.com

In reprinting in facsimile from the original, any imperfections are inevitably reproduced and the quality may fall short of modern type and cartographic standards.

No. 44.

CONFIDENTIAL.

ROYAL NAVAL AIR SERVICE.

OPERATIONS REPORT

(with Royal Flying Corps Reports attached).

17th to 31st OCTOBER 1917.

NAVAL STAFF,
OPERATIONS DIVISION
31st October 1917.

ROYAL NAVAL AIR SERVICE.

REPORT OF OPERATIONS

Completed from Reports during period
17th to 31st October 1917.

CONTENTS.

	PAGE
HOME STATIONS - - - - - -	2
DUNKIRK - - - - - -	9
R.N.A.S. SQUADRONS WITH ROYAL FLYING CORPS REPORTS ATTACHED - - - - - -	26
EASTERN MEDITERRANEAN - - -	28
ROYAL FLYING CORPS COMMUNIQUÉS - - -	39

HOME STATIONS.

WEATHER.

During the latter part of this period flying operations have been impeded owing to unfavourable weather conditions generally.

SUBMARINE PATROL WORK.

October 18th.

Scilly.—Large America Seaplane 8686 (pilot Flight Lieut. McGill, observer Flight Sub-Lieut. Morgan Smith, J. A. Hopkins, Air Mechanic (1) E., and W/T Operator Newbold) left on patrol during the afternoon.

The seaplane left the water at 1328, and when 20 miles out sighted a merchant ship, the s.s. "Madura," in a sinking condition, and which subsequently sunk, with two destroyers and two trawlers in attendance. The seaplane continued the patrol, and after altering course to avoid rain, sighted a submarine ahead breaking surface on the starboard bow. The seaplane prepared to attack and opened out the engines in order to climb and get the sun behind, but when in a position to attack up wind, course was altered, and the seaplane put her nose down to gain speed.

Two red Very's lights were fired when over the submarine, and four 100-lb. bombs were dropped and seen to explode in close proximity to one another and just ahead of the periscope, which was just awash. The seaplane then circled round the position and large quantities of oil and bubbles were observed on the surface, about 200 yards from where the submarine had submerged, the oil covering an area of about 150 to 200 square yards and gradually increasing.

A calcium flare was dropped to mark the position.

The seaplane then proceeded to the position of the two destroyers and trawlers which had been sighted on the outward journey.

The seaplane wireless having broken down, the destroyers were notified by Aldis lamp that the submarine had been bombed about 12 miles S.W. from them.

October 18th.

Portland.—At 1520 Seaplane 9848, with Flight Sub-Lieut. R. Jarman as pilot and S. M. Laycock as observer, left Portland Harbour on patrol, steering a true south course.

At 1540 a small wake was observed on the surface, which gradually increased in size as the seaplane approached. When within half a mile it was seen to be a submarine just awash with the conning tower above water. It commenced to dive, and two 100-lb. bombs were dropped on its port bow, 50 feet off. The seaplane turned and dropped a third 100-lb. bomb into the centre of the wash caused by the disappearing propeller, then a fourth bomb was dropped just a few feet in front of the last one, and oil commenced to come to the surface, which increased until there was quite a large patch. The seaplane then returned to the harbour.

October 18th.

Bembridge.—At 0740, while on "B" patrol in Seaplane N. 1613, Flight Commander A. MacLaurin with observer A.M.I.W/T. Dore sighted a wash on the starboard quarter about 10 miles distant, in a north-westerly direction. The seaplane was then at a height of 3,000 feet; the wind velocity was about 25 miles from the north-east.

The pilot immediately changed course towards the wash, until within three miles, then the engine was shut off, and the machine planed towards the disturbance. When a quarter of a mile away, and at an altitude of 1,000 feet, a submarine between 250 and 300 feet long was observed to come to the surface, and was apparently stationary. One 100-lb. bomb was dropped, which exploded about 25 to 30 feet abaft the conning tower on the starboard side. The seaplane turned to attack again, and observed the submarine disappearing with about a 30-degree list to port, and apparently not under way. Thirty seconds later another 100-lb. bomb was dropped on the spot where the submarine had disappeared, and a few minutes later a patch of oil about 150 feet along and 12 feet wide appeared on the surface. Owing to the rough state of the sea it was impossible to observe any swirl or bubbles; the seaplane remained in the vicinity for two hours and a half, but observed nothing further.

October 22nd.

Calshot.—An attack was carried out by Large America Seaplane (Flight Lieut. Ellis and Flight Sub-Lieut. Mackworth) on a black object resembling the conning tower of a submarine awash on the starboard beam in position 50° 25" N., 1° 40' W., 15 miles south of the Needles.

The object was first sighted at 1355, and, after getting into position, the seaplane attempted to drop her starboard bomb (260-lb.), which, however, failed to release. The seaplane turned, and the port bomb was dropped, and exploded 20 yards short of the target. Several circuits were made in the vicinity of the spot where the submarine had been seen, but beyond a swirl and disturbance of the water nothing further was observed. No shipping was seen in the vicinity.

October 23rd.

Westgate.—Seaplane N. 1203 (pilot Flight Sub-Lieut. F. C. Lander) left on patrol at 0800, and steered a zigzag course for 30 minutes. The pilot then sighted the periscope and wash of a hostile submarine in a position estimated to be 25 to 30 miles east of North Foreland.

Two 65-lb. bombs were dropped, which exploded 100 feet in front of the wash, after which the area was searched for 20 minutes, but nothing further was observed.

Owing to the wind becoming strong from N.N.W., the pilot lost his bearings and finally landed at Calais.

It is remarked that on previous occasions, from reports received, submarines have been traced practically back to Germany, but on this occasion no further signals of this submarine were received, and it is thought that she was destroyed by the bombs.

AIRSHIP ATTACK ON HOSTILE SUBMARINE.

October 22nd.

Pembroke.—Whilst on patrol in Airship C5A (pilot Flight Lieut. J. F. Hart) a submarine was sighted on the surface eight miles south of Caldy, at 0855, and steering south. At this time the airship was about eight miles W. (mag.) of the submarine and course was immediately altered. She started to submerge rapidly, and had completely submerged by the time the airship had reached the position. One 100-lb. contact bomb (which bumped the airship heavily but did no damage) and one 65-lb. delay-action bomb were dropped well ahead at a height of 400 feet.

There was a heavy sea running, and the sun being directly ahead, local objects were difficult to distinguish.

The airship then turned head to wind and stern to the sun and climbed to 900 feet, and after a short search the patch was again sighted. This time one 100-lb. delay-action bomb and one 65-lb. contact bomb were dropped on the swirl, falling within 15 and 20 feet respectively on the target.

It is interesting to note that from the time the submarine was first sighted she submerged in less than a minute, and when first sighted appeared to have a small sail rigged aft.

FORCED LANDING OF H.M. S.S. Z. 14 AT MONTREUIL.

October 22nd.

Mullion.—H.M. S.S. Z. 14 left on patrol at 0820, the crew consisting of Flight Lieut. A. S. Elliot, W. P. Gooding, A.M.I.E., and W. E. Russell, Act.A.M.I.W/T.

At 1200 the S.S. Z. 14 developed engine trouble and at 1205 the engine stopped altogether. In spite of every effort on the part of the crew it refused to start again.

The airship came down from 2,500 to 2,000 feet, during which time endeavours were made to keep pressure in the ship by the hand blower, but this was found to be quite impossible. All petrol was drained from the tanks into the ballast bag and used as required.

At 1540, at 150 feet high, endeavours were again made to get pressure with the hand blower, but without success, and one 100-lb. bomb was dropped to prevent the ship from hitting the water, followed by a second one, a 100-lb. bomb, at 1555, after which the S.S. Z. 14 started to rise slowly.

By 1635 all water ballast, petrol, and bombs had been dropped and the crew commenced to take adrift the wireless gear, radiator, magneto, to use as ballast. A rifle, revolver, and compass were also thrown over.

At 1700 the sun went down, and as darkness came on the ship began to rise slowly, and at 1835 had reached 6,500 feet, after which she started to descend slowly without valving gas.

At 1910, at 50 feet, all possible ballast having been used, boots were removed and thrown over the side; also codes (in weighted cover, and observed to sink) and map box without maps.

At 1940, there being no more loose gear left, the bottom boards of the car were thrown overboard, and one flying coat. The airship was now trailing at about 10 feet, and a moderate sea was running.

At 2100 the S.S. Z. 14 commenced to rise slowly to 1,200 feet, and at 2135 passed over the coast at 1,000 feet; at 2140 she struck some trees and landed at 2200 about three miles from the village of St. Josse.

Four Very's lights which had been saved were then fired, but apparently they were not seen.

The airship was deflated and removed later on lorries supplied by the principal Naval Transport Officer, G.H.Q., France, and on Thursday, October 25th, the S.S. Z. 14 was taken to Boulogne and put aboard the transport "Sultan" bound for Southampton.

The airship eventually arrived back at Mullion on Saturday the 27th, the only damage done being three small holes in the envelope.

ZEPPELIN RAID.

October 19th–20th.

A raid of approximately 7½ hours duration was carried out during the night by 11 hostile airships over the Eastern Counties, from Yorkshire to Kent, the Midlands, including the Birmingham district, and London.

The airships approached the coast in two groups; the first, consisting of four airships, made for the Yorkshire coast between Flamborough Head and Spurn Head. The second group, consisting of six airships, made for the Lincolnshire coast. One other airship participated in the attack, but there are no details to hand regarding its movements.

Of the first group, one airship crossed the Yorkshire coast at 2000, passed east of Lincoln and west of Peterborough, and dropped six high-explosive bombs at Kempston and Elstow, near Bedford Junction, at 2240. She was next heard of to the N.W. of London, and having apparently drifted with the N.W. wind dropped one bomb at Dollis Hill, one at Finchley, and one at Piccadilly Circus at 2330, where there were a number of casualties and some damage done. She also dropped incendiary bombs at New Cross and an explosive bomb at Catford, after which she moved at a great height over Kent, and out to sea over Dungeness. A second airship of the first group passed over the boom at the mouth of the Humber at 1908 and dropped three bombs at Cleethorpes a few minutes later. She then crossed Lincolnshire, passed east of Lincoln, and dropped three bombs at Stainford at 2100, after which she appears to have passed over East Anglia, and crossed out to sea by Clacton shortly before 2300. A third airship of the former group crossed the coast at Withernsea at 1914, and after circling over the mouth of the Humber appears to have made off to sea.

It has not been determined at what point the fourth airship of this group crossed the coast, but she was located traversing north, crossing over Thetford at about 2230, and out to sea over Frinton in Essex.

Of the second group, one airship crossed the coast on the north side of the Wash and passed inland by Anderby, Alford, and Spilsby at about 2000.

From this point her course is very uncertain, but it is reported that she dropped incendiary bombs to the north-west of Birmingham at about 2300, after which she appears to have departed over Towcester and Ware, crossing the county of Essex to sea by the Crouch Estuary at 0100. Another airship passed over Wainfleet and Kirton in Lincolnshire at about 1945. She was located 15 miles east of Lincoln at 1957, and then appears to have turned south. At 2100 she passed 20 miles west of Bedford, and turned gradually south-east, skirting the London defences, after which she crossed Kent, passing over Ashford at 2300, and across the Channel at 2315.

The third airship of the second group came in over the Wash, and was 15 miles west of Peterborough at 2030. She then turned south and dropped bombs in the vicinity of Bedford, Hitchin, and Stevenage, after which she passed the north-east of London, and went out over the Thames Estuary. When clear of the Isle of Sheppey she turned southward over Kent, and passed over Dover at about 2350. Another airship of the group came over the Norfolk coast at 1850, passed to the west of Norwich, and dropped bombs at Costessy at 2020. More bombs were dropped at Hadley and Little Clacton in Essex, after which the airship passed out to sea at about 2115.

The fifth airship came in over Cromer at 1915 and headed south-west, dropping bombs near Aylesham, in Norfolk. She crossed Suffolk, and was over Braintree at 2115, then turned east and went out to sea over Mersea Island at about 2215.

The last airship of this group did not come in overland, but skirted the Norfolk coast. R.N.A.S. machines went up from Frieston, Cranwell, Bacton, Burgh Castle, Yarmouth, and Manstone, but owing to the thick mist prevailing only one of the hostile airships was sighted. A pilot from the Burgh Castle Station, when at an altitude of 8,800 feet, sighted a Zeppelin 3,000 to 4,000 feet below him near the coast, 10 miles north of Yarmouth, at 2330. He dived to attack the Zppelin, but was unable to get into a firing position owing to the superior speed of the airship, which he pursued out to sea for 20 minutes, but could not overtake it.

In all, the total number of bombs reported dropped over the area attacked are:—

High explosive - - - - - 112
Incendiary - - - - - 54

The total casualties reported are:—

Killed - - - - - - 27
Injured - - - - - - 54

No damage of any consequence was caused outside the Metropolitan Police District, where the majority of the casualties also occurred.

RAIDS BY HOSTILE AIRCRAFT.

October 21st.

One or two hostile aeroplanes crossed the Kentish Coast at 0430 between Dover and Deal, and attempted to approach Dover from the north, but on being engaged by the anti-aircraft defences, dropped seven bombs near West Cliffe and three at Guston.

Three more bombs were dropped just outside Dover Harbour; no damage or casualties were caused.

October 31st—November 1st.

A raid by hostile aircraft, probably 20 in number, was carried out during the night and early morning of the dates given above over the area Thames Estuary, Essex, Kent, and London. The raid, which lasted for a period of approximately $4\frac{1}{2}$ hours, commenced with an attack on Dover by the first group of machines at about 2235, where 16 bombs were dropped, a large majority of which were incendiary.

These machines then attempted to approach London via Folkestone, Ashford, and Maidstone, but did not get further than the last-named place. Bombs were dropped at various places in Kent. The second group crossed the Kentish coast near the North Foreland at about 2300 and proceeded towards London by way of the south bank of the Thames, passing Herne Bay, Whitstable, and Tilbury. They were heavily engaged by the guns of the Chatham and outer London defences, and did not reach further west than Erith, where they turned back after dropping some bombs at about 2340.

After a short interval the second group of machines were followed by a third group, which steered a course a few miles more to the south of the river; when in the neighbourhood of Dartford they were dispersed by anti-aircraft gun-fire and turned eastward. Some bombs were dropped at Erith at about 2348.

A fourth group which proceeded up the Thames Estuary turned back near Canvey Island at 2340.

At 0015 a fifth group of raiders were reported off Foulness; this group skirted the Essex coast and steered up the Thames via Shoeburyness, Southend, and Canvey Island. Some of them were turned back, but one or more proceeded to London via Rainham, Chadwell, and Ilford. They were reported over Liverpool Street Station at 0051, after which they turned and proceeded east across the dock area, and dropped bombs near Millwall.

A sixth group crossed the mouth of the Crouch shortly after 0100 and steered towards London, passing Rochford, Billericay, and Brentwood. Here they turned south-west towards Woolwich, and bombs were dropped near Blackwall at about 0145.

One or more enemy machines whose course cannot be determined passed right across London from north to south, but did not drop any bombs until they reached Wandsworth at 0130. Other bombs were dropped at Tooting and Streatham.

A seventh group of hostile machines crossed the coast over the North Foreland at 0045 and proceeded along the south bank of the Thames via Herne Bay and Whitstable, after which they passed over the Nore Light Vessel, and turned back when south of Southend at about 0120.

Meanwhile individual machines were reported along the Kentish coast between Dover and North Foreland from midnight until 0130. R.N.A.S. machines went up in pursuit from Eastchurch and Manstone, and Sopwith machine N. 5617 observed one hostile machine with a white light in front between Southend and Sheerness at 2350. The Sopwith fired a tray of ammunition into the hostile machine; the white light went out, and the machine disappeared from view at 0015. The same pilot observed five hostile aircraft in formation off Whitstable all carrying white lights forward. He fired all his remaining ammunition into the nearest machine, which was replied to by the hostile machine. Having no ammunition left, the Sopwith then returned.

DUNKIRK.

PHOTOGRAPHIC RECONNAISSANCE.

October 18th.

No. 1 Wing (2nd Squadron).—A photographic reconnaissance was carried out and photos exposed over the four bridge-heads over the twin canals of Leopold and De la Lys at Zeebrugge.

Visibility, however, was poor.

October 21st.

No. 1 Wing (2nd Squadron). — A special photographic reconnaissance was carried out over Ostende and in the vicinity of Breedene. The photographs show no signs of the reported aerodrome at the latter place. Photographs of Vlisseghem Aerodrome were also taken during the progress of a bombing raid.

October 27th.

No. 1 Wing (2nd Squadron).—A photographic reconnaissance was carried out between 1210 and 1415 over Zeebrugge and Bruges. Photographs were also obtained of the Lengenboom gun position, Engel Railway Sidings and gun positions, and Sparappelhoek Aerodrome.

Photographs of Zeebrugge Mole show great activity around the Seaplane Base. Seven medium size and one very big seaplane on railway trucks are shown at the south end of main shed. Five empty trucks are joined up to the above. Several spare trucks are observed on the loop line. This is the first time that photographs have shown seaplanes on their trucks as forming a train.

A big reconstruction of and addition to Sparappelhoek Aerodrome is taking place. It appears that the northern half of the aerodrome has been moved to the late position of the Aertrycke Aerodrome. A landing "T" is seen on both aerodromes.

It appears that there are about 15 Bessoneaux in the south-west corner of the Sparappelhoek Aerodrome and five Bessoneaux instead of 14 in the northern section of this aerodrome. Ten enemy aircraft are outside the south-west sheds. One enemy aircraft is also on aerodrome.

Three sheds and two other sheds are also visible behind the group of five Bessoneaux.

At Aertrycke Aerodrome, in the corner where the original south-west group of sheds stood, there are now 14 Bessoneaux with 10 enemy aircraft ranged outside, also a good deal of building material.

Around the two farmhouses a little to the north there are six Bessoneaux, and an enemy aeroplane and 10 Bessoneaux in the second group. Three enemy aeroplanes are shown on the aerodrome, thus giving a total of 24 enemy aeroplanes on both aerodromes, and approximately 28 Bessoneaux on Aertrycke Aerodrome and 20 Bessoneaux on Sparappelhoek Aerodrome, giving a total of 48 Bessoneaux on both aerodromes.

October 31st.

No. 1 Wing (2nd Squadron).—A photographic reconnaissance was carried out during the afternoon, and plates were exposed over Uytkerke, Donerblok (S.E. Blankenburghe—X 5), Houttave Aerodrome, Vlisseghem Aerodrome, and Jacobinessen and Turkyen batteries.

RECONNAISSANCE.

October 24th.

No. 1 Wing (2nd Squadron).—A coastal reconnaissance was carried out between 1230 and 1400 over Ostende, Blankenburghe, Zeebrugge, and Bruges. Owing to the haze over Bruges Harbour no observations could be made.

October 29th.

No. 1 Wing (2nd Squadron).—A special reconnaissance was carried out between 1587 and 1635 in search of enemy mines. The area was successfully located, but no enemy mines were seen.

SPOTTING.

October 20th.

(No. 1 Wing (2nd Squadron).—Spotting was carried out for a monitor firing on Ostende, and the first round was observed to fall in the water in the outer harbour. Immediately dense smoke screens were put up, rendering further spotting impossible. The monitor fired a second round and then ordered the spotting machine to return.

SPOTTING, AND ENGAGEMENT WITH ENEMY.

October 21st.

No. 1 Wing (2nd Squadron).—Spotting was carried out for the monitor firing on Ostende at 1130. The spotting machine reported "all ready" at 1100, but it was decided to delay operations for half an hour.

After the first spot had been given the formation was attacked by hostile machines putting one spotting machine out of action, and slightly wounding the observer. The second machine then attempted to carry on spotting, but smoke screens rendered this impossible. The spotting machine was then ordered to return.

The monitor fired 19 shots, only one of which could be observed, the shot falling alongside the Quai des Paquebot.

OFFENSIVE PATROL—ENGAGEMENTS WITH ENEMY.

October 17th.

No. 4 Wing (4th Squadron).—At 0810 a patrol of five Sopwith F. 1 machines encountered five hostile two-seater machines circling round Thourout at 8,000 feet. They were apparently acting as a decoy, as above the Sopwith at 15,000 feet three V. Strutters were observed, and still higher, and in the sun, were seven other hostile aircraft. The first formation of five machines were attacked, and the Sopwith patrol was then attacked by the Albatross machines from above. Flight Sub-Lieut. Gossip fired 540 rounds, but without any decisive results Upon the arrival of four Sopwith Scouts the hostile aircraft withdrew in the direction of Ghistelles, and avoided engagement by diving away. On the return journey two pilots fired 300 rounds each into the roads near Middelkerke.

October 17th.

No. 4 Wing (9th Squadron).—Whilst on patrol a formation of Sopwith machines encountered a number of hostile aircraft, probably 10 to 15, in the vicinity of Ghistelles, and several combats took place.

Flight Sub-Lieut. Redgate attacked a single-seater enemy machine and fired about 100 rounds into his fuselage from about 106 yards range, after which the hostile machine went into a spin, which increased in speed as it went down. The machine was spinning so fast that it is the opinion of the Sopwith pilot that the enemy pilot must have been out of action, and when last seen at 4,000 feet the hostile machine was still spinning.

Flight Commander Fall attacked one hostile machine at about 13,000 feet over Nieuport, and opened fire from about 800 feet below. The hostile machine dived eastward very steeply, followed by the Sopwith, and all the ammunition—600 rounds—was fired into the enemy machine at ranges of 160 to 75 yards. Many tracers apparently went into the fuselage; the hostile machine continued in a steep dive, and was last seen, still diving, at under 800 feet just east of Middelkerke.

Other combats of an indecisive character took place.

October 21st.

No. 4 Wing (4th Squadron).—A patrol was carried out by five Sopwith F. 1 machines, during which a good many hostile aircraft were encountered to the S.E. of Ghistelles at a height of 17,000 feet, consisting of Albatross, two-seater, Albatross Scouts, and one machine which appeared to be an Aviatik.

These were attacked for a short time without any decisive results. Still further south a formation of hostile scout machines was observed.

The Sopwith formation dived on these from 10,000 feet, but was in turn attacked from above by a type of scout not previously seen, a biplane with a rotary engine.

In the fighting which ensued Flight Commander Shook sent down an Albatross Scout D. 111 type, but was wounded by a shot from one of the other hostile machines.

Flight Sub-Lient. Keirstead shot the port wings off another of the Albatross Scouts, and then sent down one which was among those being attacked by Flight Commander Shook. A fourth was observed to go down in flames. This must be attributed to Flight Sub-Lieut. Eyre, who was seen just afterwards by Flight Commander Shook to turn away to the left, and failed to return from the patrol.

In all it is estimated that nearly 30 hostile aircraft were encountered.

October 21st.

No. 4 Wing (9th Squadron). — A patrol of six Sopwith machines encountered two hostile two-seater machines east of Slype, and were chased down to 3,000 feet east of Slype Wood by Flight Commander Fall and Flight Sub-Lieut. Wood, who attacked from 200 to 150 yards range, each firing about 300 rounds.

The enemy aircraft were last seen diving eastward at about 1,000 feet, and one of the hostile machines was observed by the Royal Flying Corps going down in flames.

The Sopwiths were compelled to break off the engagement owing to anti-aircraft fire and the presence of enemy scouts diving towards them from Ostende.

October 22nd.

No. 4 Wing (9th Squadron).—A patrol was carried out by five Sopwith machines at 15,000 feet, and two hostile machines were observed about 2,000 feet above the formation. When over Middelkerke Flight Sub-Lieut. Haler, who was above the Sopwith formation, fired about 250 rounds into one hostile machine, without result. One hostile machine was observed to go down spinning, as far as could be seen after being attacked by Sopwith Scouts.

October 27th.

No. 4 Wing (9th Squadron).—Whilst on a patrol over the north-east of Nieuport, Flight Commander Edwards, in a

Sopwith F. 1, observed a two-seater Aviatik flying east, which he pursued, and getting within 100 yards range, the Sopwith pilot fired a total of 1,200 rounds. The hostile machine flew straight east for some time, and then went down in a vertical dive.

During the same patrol nine hostile machines were observed diving on four Camels above Flight Commander Edwards' flight in the locality of Slype.

In the short combat that ensued one hostile machine went down in a turning vertical dive, and appeared to be altogether out of control. It fell into clouds and could not be observed further.

October 28th.

No. 4 Wing (9th Squadron).—A patrol was carried out by five Sopwith machines near Pervyse, during which some Spads were observed being attacked by hostile aircraft.

During the encounter one hostile machine was seen to nose-dive down from 9,000 feet, and was still falling out of control at 1,000 feet.

The Sopwith formation attacked one kite balloon at Mariakerke and another east of Slype; both were forced down.

A formation of seven hostile machines were attacked near Pervyse, resulting in one of the machines being sent down and destroyed at Schoore. This is confirmed by 48 Squadron, Royal Flying Corps.

With reference to the latter attack, upon further investigation it has been satisfactorily proved the two hostile aircraft were brought down in this combat, and the evidence shows that the hostile machine confirmed by the 48th Squadron, Royal Flying Corps, as having crashed at Schoore was brought down by Flight Sub-Lieutenant Banbury. Another hostile machine was observed by the Belgian advanced post near Pervyse to fall to within 50 feet of the ground and disappear, probably destroyed, and is attributed to Flight Commander Brown.

October 31st.

No. 4 Wing (9th Squadron).—Whilst on patrol in the vicinity of Nieuport, Flight Commander Fall and his flight attacked a two-seater Albatross returning to his lines. One of the flight leader's guns jammed, so he fired all the ammunition from the other gun, and the remainder of the flight, five machines, each fired about 130 rounds at close range.

The enemy observer fired about 50 rounds, after which he stopped, and was seen later to be lying in the bottom of the cockpit.

The hostile machine was last seen at about 1,000 feet, the other side of Middelkerke, emitting a stream of black smoke.

Later, between Pervyse and Dixmude, Flight Commander Fall and his flight picked up Flight Sub-Lieut. Stackard, after which three formations of hostile scouts were observed patrolling between Leke and Zarren. One flight of five hostile machines were above the Sopwith formation and two other flights of seven machines were below.

The Sopwith formation was attacked from long range, and in the engagement which ensued one hostile machine rolled on its back for some time, and then nose-dived east of Dixmude. When last seen the hostile machine was still nose-diving at under 1,000 feet.

HOSTILE ARTILLERY, AEROPLANE PATROL.

October 23rd.

No. 4 Wing (3rd Squadron).—A patrol of five Sopwith Camels swept Sectors 3 and 4 on receipt of a signal that two hostile planes were registering in these sectors at 4,000 feet. The patrol observed two hostile two-seaters near Middelkerke.

Flight Lieut. Rochford, in Sopwith Camel B. 3808, and Flight Lieut Ireland, in B. 6257, dived down on one and opened fire at about 100 yards range, as a result of which the hostile machine dived down steeply.

The other hostile machine then turned towards Lieutenant Rochford, so he left the first enemy machine and attacked the second one, which then dived steeply away.

The Sopwith pilot continued firing and got in a good burst, whilst the enemy machine did a very steep bank to the left, then dived down beneath the Sopwith machine and was lost sight of.

In all, 700 rounds were fired at the two machines.

FLEET PROTECTIVE PATROL—ENGAGEMENT WITH ENEMY.

October 17th.

Seaplanes.—Whilst on a patrol over the fleet, two Sopwith Camels encountered two hostile seaplanes about 15 miles north-east of Zeebrugge, with the result that one of the enemy machines was driven down out of control into the sea, where it sank. The attack on the other machine had to be abandoned owing to it being within one mile of the Mole.

October 28th.

Seaplane Defence Squadron.— Flight Lieut. Lawson, in Sopwith Camel B. 6212, whilst on patrol about eight miles north of Ostende, saw an engagement between two enemy ships and three British T.B.D.'s.

An enemy seaplane approached from the direction of the engagement, and the Sopwith, climbing into the sun above the hostile machine, attacked at 300 yards, firing a burst of 30 rounds, when the gun jammed. After clearing the jam the attack was resumed, and 100 rounds were fired, when the gun jammed again.

Before the gun could be cleared the hostile machine, after dropping three bombs in the sea, made off and disappeared from view.

HOSTILE AIRCRAFT PATROL—ENGAGEMENT WITH ENEMY.

October 27th.

Seaplane Defence Squadron.—Whilst on patrol north of Malo Flight Lieut. Slatter, in Sopwith Camel B. 3936, observed gun flashes to seaward approximately 15 miles north west of Ostende, and upon investigating discovered an action taking place between five large destroyers and three enemy vessels. A hostile machine then appeared travelling approximately south four miles west of the enemy ships at a height of 11,000 feet. The enemy aircraft seemed unaware of the presence of the Sopwith Camel, which reserved its fire until within 100 yards range, and after the Camel had fired a short burst from both guns the hostile machine rolled over and spun downwards on its back. The pilot then observed other hostile machines, probably 20, extending over the area of the action, and well out to sea.

The Sopwith Camel engaged another isolated hostile machine at about 10,000 feet, and after the Sopwith pilot had emptied both guns, the hostile machine turned sharply to the left and dived towards the enemy ships.

BOMB ATTACKS.

Remarks.—The noteworthy feature of the bomb raids during this period are an attack on Antwerp and an attempted attack on Cologne. Owing to unfavourable weather conditions the Handley-Page machine did not succeed in reaching Cologne, but got to Duren, which is about 20 miles west of the original objective, and dropped bombs, then returned, having covered a distance of 400 miles, occupying $7\frac{1}{2}$ hours.

Antwerp was successfully reached and attacked by Handley-Page machines. A considerable number of bombs were dropped, some of which damaged the railway and started fires.

BOMB ATTACKS.

(Carried out during the period between the dates given.)

*Varsenuaere Aerodrome	Oct. 18th	1,775 lbs.	D.H. 4. (A.)
Bruges Docks	„ 19th–20th	2,364 „	H.P. (A.)
*Engel Aerodrome	„ 20th	1,518 „	D.H. 4. (A.)
Bruges Docks	„ 21st	1,020 „	H.P. (A.)
*Vlisseghem Aerodrome	„ „	986 „	D.H. 4. (A.)
*Houttave Aerodrome	„ „	1,260 „	„
*Zeebrugge Mole	„ 22nd	1,368 „	„
*Melle Railway Sidings	„ „	2,364 „	„
*Thourout Station	„ 26th	452 „	„
*Varssenaere Aerodrome	„ „	64 „	
Lichtervelde Junction and Sidings.	„ 26th–27th	6,696 „	H.P. (A.)
Thourout Junction	„	9,496 „	
Cortemarcke Junction and Station.	„	1,792 „	
*Sparappelhoek Aerodrome	„ 27th	1,078 „	D.H. 4. (A.)
*Engel Aerodrome	„ „	516 „	„
*Ostende-Thourout Railway	„ „	258 „	„
Engel Aerodrome	„ 27th–28th	2,576 „	H.P. (A.)
Cortemarck Junction	„ „	896 „	„
Lichtervelde Junction	„ „	3,360 „	„
St. Denis Westrem Aerodrome.	„ „	6,438 „	„
*Varssenaere Aerodrome	„ 28th	1,181 „	D.H. 4. (A.)
*Stalhillebrugge Station	„ „	82 „	„
Antwerp	„ 28th–29th	6,644 „	H.P. (A.)
Ghent (Railway)	„ „	1,020 „	„
Bruges Docks	„ „	1,020 „	„
Duren (Factory)	„ „	1,344 „	„
Sparappelhoek Aerodrome	„ 29th–30th	1,568 „	„
Varssenaere Aerodrome	„ „	2,740 „	„
Lichtervelde Station	„ 30th–31st	7,756 „	„
Thourout Station	„ „	6,480 „	„
*Sparappelhoek Aerodrome	„ 31st	1,183 „	D.H. 4. (A.)
*Beerst (shed)	„ „	128 „	„
	Total	77,423 lbs.	

* Daylight raid.   (A) Aeroplanes.   (S) Seaplanes.

October 18th.

No. 5 Wing (5th Squadron).—A bombing raid was carried out during the morning at 1142 on Varssenaere Aerodrome by seven D.H. 4 machines, during which eleven 65-lb., two 50-lb., and sixty 16-lb. bombs were dropped at heights varying from 13,000 to 15,000 feet.

Excellent shooting appears to have been made, and many bombs were seen to fall among the sheds and hangars on the east side of the aerodrome, from which clouds of smoke were seen to arise. Three direct hits are claimed as follows :—

> One on shed No. 3 ; one on hangar No. 12 ; and one on a hut close to hangar No. 12.

Bombs were also well placed among the sheds and eight machines standing by them on the west side of the aerodrome.

No. 48 Squadron, Royal Flying Corps, who provided the escort, confirm the claims of the R.N.A.S. pilots as to the direct hits and good shooting generally.

Anti-aircraft fire was very intense and accurate, most of the machines being hit.

The visibility throughout the raid, excepting for occasional clouds, was good.

October 19th-20th.

No. 5 Wing (7th and 7a Squadrons.)—A bombing attack was carried out during the night by two Handley-Pages on Bruges Docks, during which two 250-lb., twelve 112-lb., and eight 65-lb. bombs were dropped.

Visibility was poor, and the prevalence of low clouds rendered observation of results difficult, but bombs were seen to burst in the vicinity of the docks.

October 20th.

No. 5 Wing (5th Squadron).—A bombing raid was carried out during the morning by six D.H. 4 machines on Engel Aerodrome, during which ten 65-lb., two 50-lb., and forty-eight 16-lb. bombs were dropped from a height of from 13,800 to 15,000 feet. Visibility was fair, but the target was in some instances obscured by clouds, making it difficult to observe results.

Both groups of hangars and sheds were well straddled. Direct hits were made on both eastern and western hangars, and other bombs were observed to burst on buildings alongside the road. A large fire was observed among these buildings south of the western hangars and sheds. All machines returned safely.

October 21st.

No. 5 Wing (7th and 7a Squadrons).—Two Handley-Pages left at 2025 to carry out a bombing raid on Bruges Docks, but one of the machines failed to find the objective owing to almost complete absence of visibility, and the bombs were dropped well out to sea. The other machine reached the objective when visibility happened to be just possible yet extremely poor. The docks were straddled and the bombs appeared to burst in a good line. One bomb which failed to release was eventually dropped in the neighbourhood of Ghistelles without results being observed.

In all, two 250-lb. and eight 65-lb. bombs were dropped on the two objectives.

BOMB ATTACK—ENGAGEMENT WITH ENEMY.

October 21st.

No. 5 Wing (5th Squadron).—A bombing raid was carried out during the afternoon by D.H. 4 machines on Vlisseghem and Houttave Aerodromes.

The former objective was attacked by four machines, and two 50-lb., six 65-lb., and thirty-one 16-lb. bombs were dropped from heights of 13,000 to 14,000 feet. Many bombs were seen to burst close to and among the sheds in the south-west corner, and from one of these smoke was seen to arise. Other bombs were seen to explode among sheds and hangars on the north-east side of the aerodrome.

Houttave Aerodrome was attacked by five machines, and two 50-lb., eight 65-lb., and forty 16-lb. bombs were dropped. Good shooting appears to have been made, and smoke was seen to arise from one of the southern sheds after a direct hit.

Direct hits are also reported on huts and sheds north-west of the aerodrome. One bomb exploded close to an enemy machine which was getting off the ground at the time, and this was shortly afterwards seen to crash.

Flight Lieut. Sproatt, D.S.C., with a camera, but no bombs, was late in starting owing to engine trouble, but succeeded in picking up the formation and took two photographs of Vlisseghem and one of Houttave.

The visibility was good on the whole, but owing to continuous attacks by enemy aircraft while our machines were over the objective, details of observations were more difficult to make than usual. Nearly all the bombing machines had encounters with enemy aircraft, and in several cases were rather badly shot about.

Enemy aircraft were also engaged by the Royal Flying Corps escort, and one hostile machine was observed by the crews of two of the bombing machines to go down in a spin.

Anti-aircraft fire was intense and accurate, and some of the D.H. 4's suffered considerably from shell fire, but all returned safely.

October 22nd.

No. 5 Wing (5th Squadron).—Eight D.H. 4 machines left at 1233 to carry out a bomb raid, but two were obliged to return owing to engine trouble.

St. Denis, Westrem, was the original objective, but the formation leader, Flight Commander Le Mesurier, D.S.C., when near Knocke found the whole of the country inland to be completely obscured by clouds, and therefore gave the signal to attack Zeebrugge Mole instead, over which the visibility was excellent.

Six 65-lb., four 50-lb., forty-eight 16-lb. and one 10-lb. bombs were dropped on the objective from heights of 13,000 to 15,000 feet.

The shooting appears to have been good, and a number of bombs were observed to explode on the Mole. Two direct hits are reported on a vessel lying inside the Mole, causing a fire to break out, and smoke was also seen arising from the sheds on the outer end of the Mole. One of the barges moored at the east end of the objective was hit by a 65-lb. bomb and set on fire.

Bombs were also seen to burst round a cargo vessel which was entering the Zeebrugge-Bruges canal, and among the buildings to the east of the shore end of the Mole.

All machines returned safely.

October 22nd.

No. 5 Wing (7th and 7a Squadrons).—An attack was carried out by two Handley-Pages on Melle Railway sidings during the evening.

Two machines were despatched at 1830, and both reached the objectives, on which two 250-lb., twelve 112-lb., and eight 65-lb. bombs were dropped.

Visibility was poor, but lights were showing in the vicinity of the junction, and the bombs were dropped in three good straddles over the railway lines, and were seen to burst on and near to these.

October 26th.

No. 5 Wing (5th Squadron).—Owing to the exceptionally variable weather conditions it was found impossible to carry out the day's bombing programme. Machines were kept in readiness all day, and at the last moment two (of which the crews volunteered for the work) were despatched at 1550 to attack Thourout Station.

The attack was carried out by Flight Sub-Lieut. Dockson with observer Sub-Lieut. Pattison on D.H. 4 N 5962 and Flight Sub-Lieut. Lupton with Aerial Gunlayer Smith on D.H. 4 N 6009.

Four 65-lb. and twelve 16-lb. bombs were dropped at 1610 from 7,000 to 9,000 feet. One direct hit was observed on the railway junction north-east of Thourout and a cloud of smoke was seen to rise in the southern part of the town. Other observations were impossible on account of the clouds. Heavy anti-aircraft fire and a rain storm were encountered whilst the machines were over the target.

Flight Sub-Lieut. Lupton, after dropping two 65-lb. and four 16-lb. bombs on Thourout, lost his bearings in the clouds and drifted over Varssenaere Aerodrome, where he dropped his remaining four 16-lb. bombs.

This attack was carried out in conjunction with military operations to which General Headquarters attached very great importance. The weather was extremely unfavourable and the pilots occasionally encountered snow as well as rain.

The machines returned and landed in the dark by the aid of flares.

In connection with this and other raids the officers and men of these two machines have been recommended for awards.

October 26th–27th.

No. 5 Wing (7th and 7a Squadrons).—A bombing raid was carried out during the night by 10 Handley-Page machines on the railway stations and junctions at Lichtervelde and Thourout. The former target was frequently straddled with twelve 250-lb. and thirty-three 112-lb. bombs, and many direct hits were registered on the railway lines. A heavy explosion was caused close to the south-east junction, followed by a large column of smoke, and numerous flashes which were clearly observed in the moonlight, and it is considered that either ammunition or rolling stock was hit.

Clear visibility allowed an excellent view of the latter target, which was attacked with twelve 250-lb. and fifty-eight 112-lb. bombs, the majority of which were seen to explode on and in close proximity to the railway lines. Two bombs were seen to fall close to a moving train north-east of Thourout, which at once became stationary. A large explosion was caused close to the northern junction.

One machine was unable to reach the objective to which it was allocated, so attacked Cortemarck Junction and Station, on which sixteen 112-lb. bombs were dropped, all well within the limits of the junction.

Visibility was excellent, and it is estimated that considerable damage has been caused and that railway traffic in the vicinity of the objectives has been hindered.

Anti-aircraft fire was intense and very accurate, several machines being hit, but all returned safely.

October 27th.

No. 5 Wing (5th Squadron).—A bombing attack was carried out during the day on Sparappelhoek Aerodrome by eight D.H. 4 machines, during which four 65-lb., four 50-lb., thirty-eight 16-lb., and one 10-lb. bombs were dropped at 1430 from heights of 14,000 to 15,000 feet.

The hangars on the north and south-west sides were well straddled, but no direct hits were observed on account of some machines of the formation passing below. When over Sparappelhoek, four 65-lb. and sixteen 16-lb. bombs were dropped on Engel Aerodrome, but no direct results were observed.

Two 65-lb. and eight 16-lb. bombs were released on the Ostende–Thourout railway, south of Engel.

Visibility was good, but observations difficult to make owin to the presence of numerous enemy aircraft; none of the machines were seriously attacked, however, except D.H. 4 N. 5968 with Flight Sub-Lieut. Pownall and Aerial Gunlayer Wilkinson. The pilot of the machine was wounded in the leg and was forced to land on the beach between Coxyde and La Panne.

Anti-aircraft fire was very heavy and accurate.

October 27th–28th.

No. 5 Wing (7th and 7a Squadrons).—An attack was carried out during the night on active enemy aerodromes, moving trains and railways in the Naval area and St. Denis Westrem, by Handley-Page machines.

Two machines attacked the aerodrome at Engel with twenty-three 112-lb. bombs, which were seen to fall well within the area of the aerodrome and in close proximity to the hangars.

Cortemarck and Lichtervelde Junction and sidings were attacked by three machines. On the former target, eight 112-lb. bombs were seen to burst close together right on the junction. On the latter target, thirty 112-lb. bombs were dropped; the station was hit and the junction was well straddled.

A large fire was observed two miles west of Cortemarck, north of the railway lines.

Four machines attacked the aerodrome at St. Denis Westrem with fifteen 250-lb. and twenty-four 112-lb. bombs, which were seen to explode on the aerodrome and close to the railway line and hangars on the south and west portions of the aerodrome.

Visibility was good throughout the attack.

Eight machines returned safely, but Handley-Page 3122, pilot Flight Sub-Lieut. Andrews, observer Second Lieut. Hutton, R.F.C., with L.M. Gunlayer Kent, failed to return, and must therefore be considered lost.

October 28th.

No. 5 Wing (5th Squadron).—A bombing raid was carried out by six D.H. 4 machines at 1200 on Varssenaere Aerodrome, during which seven 65-lb., one 50-lb., forty-one 16-lb., and two 10-lb. bombs were dropped from heights of 13,500 to 15,000 feet.

Visibility was fair but the target was partially obscured by clouds.

A direct hit on a shed on the east side, and one on a shed on the west side, of the aerodrome are reported. Other sheds were well straddled, and bombs observed to explode close to two machines, supposed to be Gothas, on the ground.

One 50-lb. and two 16-lb. bombs which failed to release over the target were dropped on the railway station at Stalhillebrugge, but no direct results could be observed.

Anti-aircraft fire was heavy and accurate, and the bombing formation was followed, after leaving the objective, by enemy aircraft, which were dispersed by a formation of Camels, which attacked the hostile machines when about four miles from the lines.

Two of the enemy aircraft were observed to go down in a steep nose-dive.

October 28th–29th.

No. 5 Wing (7th and 7a Squadrons).—Eight Handley-Page machines left at 1745 to attack Antwerp, Ghent (railway traffic and sidings), and Bruges Docks. Antwerp was attacked by six machines, and six 250-lb., thirty-two 112-lb., and twenty-four 65-lb. bombs were dropped. Visibility was very good, although heavy banks of clouds and rainstorms were encountered in the vicinity, and bombs were seen to explode on the Cockerill Works at Hoboken, the Station du Sud, and network of adjacent sidings, and the docks and railway sidings to the north of the town. Big explosions were caused, resulting in several fires, and these were seen to be still burning as long as Antwerp was in sight. Three trains running south-west from Ghent were attacked with two 250-lb. and eight 65-lb. bombs, which were observed to burst on the railway lines and in close proximity to the trains.

Bruges Docks were attacked with two 250-lb. and eight 65-lb. bombs, and a good line was taken over the objective, but no results could be observed.

A ninth machine, Handley-Page 3125 (pilot Flight Lieut. Gardner, observer Flight Lieut. Terrell and A.C.M. 1 G/L Beaver) left at the same time with the intention of carrying out an attack on Cologne. When about half way very bad weather was encountered and the machine was forced down to a height of 2,500 feet. The journey was continued at this height until the town of Duren, approximately 20 miles from Cologne, was reached. The machine was then at a height of 2,000 feet; heavy rain was falling and the weather conditions were altogether too bad to proceed further. It was therefore decided to abandon the original objective and to attack a very large factory, which was seen about three miles east of Duren, and was brilliantly lit up. Twelve 112-lb. bombs were dropped on this from a height of 1,500 feet in heavy rain.

One direct hit was made on the factory road, and the remainder of the bombs mostly fell within the walls surrounding the factory. The homeward journey was made under exceedingly trying conditions, and for $2\frac{1}{2}$ hours no land was sighted. The lines were eventually crossed at 0150 at a height of 2,000 feet, the machine being heavily attacked by machine-gun fire when near the German trenches, and a landing was eventually made at 0215 without landing lights at the Drogland Royal Flying Corps Aerodrome, which is an exceedingly difficult aerodrome. The machine was flown back to the Condekerque the next day. The distance covered was approximately 400 miles and occupied 7½ hours.

There are several large factories in the vicinity of Duren devoted to the manufacture of explosives, and it is hoped that it is one of these which was attacked.

Previous to this occasion Flight Lieut. R. G. Gardner had been recommended for the D.S.C. for his fine work, and his observer, Sub-Lieut. Thomas Terrell, is now recommended for the D S.C.

October 29th-30th.

No. 5 Wing (7th and 7a Squadrons).—Three Handley-Pages were despatched at 2115 to carry out a bombing attack on Sparappelhoek Aerodrome and Varssenaere Aerodrome. The former objective was attacked by one machine, and a line was taken from north-north-east to south-south-west, with fourteen 112-lb. bombs over the two principal groups of hangars. The bombs were seen to fall in the proximity of the sheds in both groups.

Four runs in all were made over the latter target, on which two 250 lb. and twenty 112-lb. bombs were dropped, the western group of sheds and hangars being principally attacked. The visibility was excellent and good shooting appears to have been made.

October 30th-31st.

No. 5 Wing (7th and 7a Squadrons).—A bombing attack was carried out during the night by nine Handley-Page machines on the Lichtervelde and Thourout stations and lines.

The visibility was very clear, enabling accurate results to be observed, and it is estimated that considerable damage was caused.

Lichtervelde station and lines were attacked with fourteen 250-lb. bombs and thirty-eight 112-lb. bombs, which were seen to explode in the vicinity of the station, and many direct hits were made on the railway lines. A large explosion was caused on the track west of the north junction and a still larger one on the sidings south of the north junction. After the explosion a dense column of smoke was seen to arise, obscuring the line.

Forty 112-lb. and eight 250-lb. bombs were dropped on the target at Thourout. Excellent shooting was made and many direct hits were scored on the track. The junctions were frequently straddled, and bombs were observed to fall on buildings close to the northern junction.

October 31st

No. 5 Wing (5th Squadron).—A bombing raid was carried out during the day by six D.H. 4 machines on Sparappelhoek Aerodrome, on which seven 65-lb., four 50-lb, and thirty-three 16-lb. bombs were dropped at 1311 from heights of 13,000 to

15,000 feet. Visibility was fairly good, but the target was partially obscured by clouds. In addition to this the formation was attacked by six or seven enemy aircraft when over the objective. These were driven off without any decisive results being obtained. These two circumstances made it rather difficult to observe the results of bombs dropped, but three were observed to explode among sheds in the north-east corner of the aerodrome.

Flight Lieut. Cleghorn dropped eight 16-lb. bombs on a large shed south of the main roads and about three miles east of Beerst; on the return journey, as the aerodrome was completely obscured by clouds just after his two 65-lb. bombs had been released.

Anti-aircraft fire was light and inaccurate and all machines returned safely.

Honours Awarded between October 16th and 31st.

Name.	Unit.	Awarded.
Acting Flt. Comdr. R. Grahame, D.S.C.	Seaplane Defence Squadron	D.S.O.
Acting Flt. Comdr. P. S. Fisher, D.S.C.	No. 4 Squadron	D.S.O.
Acting Flt. Comdr. S. T. Edwards	No. 9 Squadron	D.S.C.
Acting Flt. Comdr. E. R. Brown	No. 9 Squadron	D.S.C.
Flt. Sub-Lieut. F. R. Johnson	No. 7 Squadron	D.S.C.
Flt. Comdr. G. E. Hervey	Dover	D.S.C.
Flt. Lieut. L H. Slatter	Seaplane Defence Squadron	D.S.C.
Flt. Lieut. V. R. Gibbs	No. 7A Squadron	D.S.C.
Aircraftsman 1st Class J. Conley, O. No. F. 16254.	No. 7A Squadron	D.S.M.
Air Mechanic (Gunlayer) J. R. Barber, O. No. F. 3771.	No. 7 Squadron	D.S.M.

Casualties.
Missing.

Name.	Rank.	Squadron.	Date.
Eyre, E. G. A.	Flt Sub-Lieut.	No. 4	21.10.17
Andrews, G.	Flt. Sub-Lieut.	No. 7A	27.10.17
Oakley, W. E. B.	Flt. Sub-Lieut.	No. 9	15.10.17
Kent, G. A.	Leading Mechanic (Gunlayer) O. No. J. 5381.	No. 7A	27.10.17

Wounded.

Name.	Rank.	Squadron.	Date.
Shook, A. M.	Flight Commander	No. 4	21.10.17
Stennett, W. R.	Observer Sub-Lieut.	No. 2	21.10.17
Pinchen, S. H.	Air Mechanic 1 (Gunlayer) F. 2932.	No. 2	31.10.17

BOMB ATTACK BY HOSTILE AIRCRAFT ON BRITISH AND FRENCH WARSHIPS OFF THE BELGIAN COAST.

October 27th.

During a naval engagement between a combined force of British and French destroyers, viz., the "Mentor," "Botha," "Mehl," and "Magnon," and three enemy destroyers in positions Nos. 4 and 5 B. B. Buoys, at 1500 an enemy seaplane dropped three bombs very close to H.M.S. "Botha."

Following this, at about 1520, about 17 hostile aircraft flying in formation were seen approaching the allied ships. It being apparent that the enemy destroyers had been used as a decoy to involve the allied vessels in a concentrated attack from the air, principal attention was devoted to dealing with the enemy aircraft with anti-aircraft gun-fire. Fire was also maintained at the enemy destroyers, who, however, by this time had turned away. The anti-aircraft gun-fire had the effect of breaking up the enemy formation, and although all individual machines dropped bombs very close, there was no concerted attack.

Bombs were dropped from about 4,000 feet, and two of the crew of the "Botha" were slightly wounded by splinters as well as four men in the French destroyer "Magnon," which was also slightly holed on the water line by splinters.

H.M.S. "M. 25" also engaged the enemy aircraft with anti-aircraft gun-fire. A salvo of bombs was dropped, which fell quite close to M. 25, splinters falling on board.

The following day similar tactics were carried out by hostile destroyers, during which nine hostile aircraft made a determined attack on the allied vessels, dropping 20 to 30 bombs without result.

Anti-aircraft gunfire and scattering tactics appeared to be successful in spoiling their aim, as all bombs fell very wide of their mark. The attack lasted about 30 minutes.

Later, a single hostile seaplane attacked with their bombs, one of which fell very close to the "Phœbe." This machine was driven off by fire from the destroyers and M.'s 21 and 24.

NAVAL SQUADRONS WITH THE ROYAL FLYING CORPS.

(PERIOD, 7TH TO 20TH OCTOBER 1917.)

NAVAL SQUADRON No. 1.

This squadron has been attached to the Second Brigade Royal Flying Corps, and during this period has carried out 40 offensive patrols and eight special missions in pursuit of hostile aircraft, amounting in all to 290 hours flying.

During this period two enemy aeroplanes were brought down in our lines, and four more driven down out of control.

October 17th.

Hostile Aircraft.—Flight Commander Minifie, D.S.C., fired 350 rounds from very close range into a two-seater over our lines. The enemy aircraft turned over on its back and crashed on the ground this side of the lines.

Flight Sub-Lieut. Rosevear engaged a two-seater at 15,000 feet, firing 200 rounds at close range. The enemy machine fell completely out of control and crashed close to the one brought down by Flight Commander Minifie.

Flight Lieut Kinkead fired 200 rounds into a two-seater, D.F.W., and drove it down completely out of control.

October 18th.

Flight Lieut. Kinkead and Flight Sub-Lieut. Forman after firing 400 rounds into a hostile two-seater drove it down out of control.

A patrol led by Flight Commander Minifie encountered 15 Gothas escorted by 10 Scouts. These they attacked, Flight Commander Minifie firing 250 rounds into one of the retreating Gothas, which nose-dived vertically for over 2,000 feet into the clouds and was lost to sight.

October 20th.

Flight Commander Minifie, together with some Nieuports, engaged nine enemy Scouts south of Comines. One of these was driven down out of control after 100 rounds had been fired into it from close range.

During the infantry attacks on the 9th and 12th instant, pilots of this squadron fired 2,050 rounds at ground targets, including machine gun emplacements, gun emplacements, blockhouses, troops in trenches, and in the open as follows :—

    Flight Lieut. Kinhead, 200 rounds from 800 feet.
    Flight Lieut. Everitt, 600 rounds from 100 feet.
    Flight Sub-Lieut. Simpson, 50 rounds from 1,000 feet.

Flight Sub-Lieut. de Wilde, 100 rounds from 1,000 feet.
Flight Sub-Lieut. Binks, 350 rounds from 800 feet.
Flight Sub-Lieut. Rosevear, 450 rounds from 100 feet.
Flight Sub-Lieut. Spence, 300 rounds from 300 feet.

Casualties.—

Injured.—Flight Sub-Lieut. W. H. Sneath, 11.10.17. Flight Sub-Lieut. A. J. Binks, 13.10.17.

Hostile Machines driven down out of control - - 4
,, ,, destroyed - - - - - 2.

NAVAL SQUADRON No. 8.

This squadron has been attached to the 1st Brigade, R.F.C., and has carried out 14 offensive patrols and 21 special missions in pursuit of enemy aircraft.

Hostile Aircraft.—Four combats have taken place all of which were indecisive, although in each case the enemy machine was driven east. Many flights were made on receipt of warnings from the compass station that enemy two seaters were ranging for their artillery. On nine of these occasions the enemy machines were discovered and driven east.

Eight 20-lb. bombs were dropped on various billets.

A total of 3,350 rounds have been fired from low altitudes into the enemy's trenches.

Casualties :—Nil.

NAVAL SQUADRON No. 10.

This Squadron has been attached to the Fourth Brigade, Royal Flying Corps, and has carried out 22 offensive patrols, making a total of 195 hours 30 minutes flying.

Hostile Aircraft.—Ten combats have taken place. In one of these Flight Lieut. FitzGibbon led his flight in pursuit of a formation of 14 Gothas, protected by a large number of scouts. Having become separated from his patrol, he attacked this large formation alone and continued until his ammunition was exhausted.

October 15th.

Flight Sub-Lieut. Curtis with his patrol attacked three enemy two-seater observation machines, one of which was driven down out of control.

October 20th.

Flight Commander Saint attacked two enemy aircraft at 10,000 feet, and followed one down to 6,000 feet. He then fired 80 rounds into it from 30 yards, after which the enemy machine went down in a vertical dive, and, when nearing the ground, the left plane folded back and the machine crashed.

Casualties.

Wounded. — Flight Sub-Lieut. Sutherland, 15th October 1917.

Injured. — Flight Sub-Lieut. Cumming, 20th October 1917.

Hostile Machines. — Driven down out of control - - 1
"   "   Destroyed - - - - 1

SUMMARY.

Hostile Machines. — Driven down out of control - 5
"   "   Destroyed - - - - 3

                                     Total - 8

EASTERN MEDITERRANEAN STATION.

(Compiled from Report, No. 81 and 82, dating from September 30th to October 15th, 1917.)

THASOS AIR STATION.

"A" SQUADRON AND "Z" SQUADRON (GREEK).

September 30th—October 6th.

Patrol Work. — On 30th September the area between Thasos and Stavros was searched for minefields, and a similar patrol was made in the vicinity of Thasos on the following day.

On the 2nd and 3rd October the weather was unsuitable for flying.

On the 4th local patrols were made by the Greek Squadron, and on the 5th the area near the coast between Cape Deuthero and Port Lagos was examined for submarines and mines.

On 6th October a submarine patrol was made between Thasos and Mount Athos.

No flying reports for the current week have yet been received and details are therefore lacking.

On 5th October a Sopwith Bomber for the Greek Squadron arrived by air from Mudros.

Work from this station is still reduced to its lowest limits as there is only one British pilot fit for service, and since 5th October there are four Greek pilots.

October 7th–15th.

Patrol Work. — On the 7th October a patrol between Thasos and Samothraki for a submarine was carried out, also one in the vicinity of Thasos. A patrol to Mount Athos was carried out on the 9th.

On the 10th a patrol to Mount Athos was undertaken and a large amount of wreckage was seen to the N.E. of Mount Athos.

This was possibly wreckage of sailing vessel "Ayios Antonios" sunk by submarine "12 miles off Lemnos" on the 6th, the prevailing wind having been from south to south-east. No written report has yet been received.

On the 11th another patrol to Mount Athos was carried out.

Weather prevented flying on the 12th October.

STAVROS AIR STATION.

"D" Squadron.

September 30th—October 6th.

Reconnaissance.—In the morning of 30th September a reconnaissance of the swept channel was made and a minefield was located in lat. 40° 37′ N., long. 23° 52′ E., and reported both by W/T and by firing two Very's lights. A second patrol again observed the minefield previously reported and could find no further minefield in the neighbourhood.

Photographic Reconnaissance. — At the request of 80th Brigade an escorted photographic reconnaissance was made in the afternoon over the Dedeballi district.

On October 1st a machine flew over the minefield, dropped a Calcium buoy in the position and then directed motor launches to the exact spot. The enemy front lines on the lower Struma were reconnoitred later in the day.

Patrol and Spotting Work.—A submarine and mine patrol of the approaches to Stavros was made on October 2nd and on 3rd the Angista Valley was examined, but no movement of importance on the part of the enemy could be seen. A spotting flight for the army was also carried out.

Reconnaissance.—On October 4th a reconnaissance of the enemy front line was again made and the position of guns reported by the duty monitor was definitely located. In consequence of a report from motor launch No. 506, sighting an object resembling a submarine off Cape Deuthero, apparently making for Thasos Strait, a submarine patrol to Thasos was undertaken in the afternoon. The machine landed at Thasos and returned to Stavros, again searching the area on the following day.

As Stavros was reduced to one pilot fit for service, two other pilots from Mitylene have been sent and Royal Flying Corps have kindly lent two other pilots with their machines temporarily to enable the station to undertake the work required.

October 7th–15th.

On the 7th October an attempt was made by aeroplane to locate remainder of the mines in the field reported by aeroplane on 30th September, but owing to bad visibility they could not be found.

On the 8th a photographic reconnaissance of the front line was attempted, but owing to weather had to be abandoned.

New trenches were observed during this flight in 48 F. 3 and 48 F. 6 (Reference Map D. 9).

An escorted reconnaissance was carried out up the Angista Valley.

One machine took the brigade major, Eightieth Brigade, to examine new works reported on Pilav Tepe.

On the 9th a patrol launch was successfully led by aeroplane to the remainder of the minefield which could not be found on the previous day.

Reconnaissance and Spotting Work.—One escorted spotting flight was successfully carried out for the army on to dug-outs in 37 R. 2, four direct hits being obtained. A reconnaissance of the Struma-Orfano area was also carried out. Nothing unusual being observed.

On 10th October machine again patrolled minefield. A front line reconnaissance and three hostile aircraft patrols were also carried out.

On the 11th motor launch was again led to the minefield. Low clouds prevented further work.

On 13th a further mine patrol was attempted, but was abandoned owing to bad weather.

THERMI AIR STATION.

"B" SQUADRON.

September 30th—October 6th.

Reconnaissance.—As the sound of enemy aircraft had been reported both on 29th and 30th September it was thought possible that a concentration of enemy machines had been effected in the neighbourhood with a view to a night raid on Thermi. Accordingly a reconnaissance was made on 30th September of the Menimen Plain by one Sopwith two seater escorted by two "Camels," but no aerodromes nor hangars could be located.

On 5th October a Bristol Scout, a Sopwith Bomber, and a Nieuport were flown to Mudros, and 4 "Camels" were packed and despatched to Mudros in "Elpiniki," leaving the station reduced to two pilots, one of whom was on the sick list, and two Sopwith two seaters and two Sopwith Bombers, one of each being under repair.

This course had been rendered necessary in view of the small number of pilots and other personnel on the Station who are fit for service at present, the Thermi contingent being split up among other stations where work of more immediate importance is being carried out.

Meanwhile work is proceeding rapidly on the new aerodrome at Kalloni where a machine has already landed safely as an experiment.

October 7th–15th.

The week has been spent in transporting hangars, stores, &c., to the new aerodrome at Port Kalloni.

On 9th October enemy commenced shelling Thermi Aerodrome from Tuz Burnu. Shelling continued until the morning of the 11th.

Detailed reports have not yet been received, but there were no casualties and practically no damage.

One hangar is now ready at Kalloni and two machines have been flown there. All stores, bomb, and petrol, &c., have been removed from Thermi.

IMBROS AIR STATION.

"C" SQUADRON.

September 30th—October 6th.

The part played by "C" Squadron in the engagement with the three enemy seaplanes on the morning of 30th September, has been sufficiently detailed under the Mudros report. After Flight Lieut. Alcock had landed at Imbros and reported that two enemy machines had been shot down between Imbros and Tenedos, three aeroplanes, one flown by Flight Lieut. Alcock went out to search for the enemy machines which were still on the surface, and render any assistance in their power. They were unable, however, to find any trace of the enemy machines.

At midday an enemy aeroplane flew over Imbros probably searching for the missing seaplanes. Two Sopwith two-seaters were sent up in pursuit, and proceeded to Gaba Tepe and Helles to intercept the enemy machine, which, however, took another course and was not sighted.

A submarine patrol was carried out in the afternoon over the triangle—Imbros—Samothraki—Suvla.

Search for Handley Page No. 3124.—At dawn on 1st October a machine was sent to search the Gulf of Imbros for the Handley Page aeroplane which was missing from Mudros, and which had intended to cross the enemy coast at the head of the Gulf of Xeros. Nothing was observed of the machine or of any wreckage. Destroyers were also sent to search the Gulf, and as these were fired on by guns on the coast, a second machine was sent to locate the guns, which, however, ceased fire in the interval before the machine arrived and were not located. On the return journey the Dardanelles were patrolled and the shipping reported on.

Patrol Work.—In consequence of a submarine having been reported by "Edgar" south of Pyrgos proceeding east, five flights were made, maintaining a continuous patrol over the quadrilateral Pyrgos-Tenedos-Helles-and-Aliki Bay, while machines from Mudros maintained a patrol to the westward of the Imbros machines.

During one of these patrols the opportunity was taken of examining the British minefields between Rabbit Island and the mainland. Two lines of mines were observed to be intact.

A scout was also sent up from Tenedos to intercept enemy aircraft, which were reported but were not seen from the scout. After dark an enemy machine was reported over Pyrgos; she did not drop bombs and had possibly been sent out to assist the submarine which was being hunted at the time.

On the following morning, 2nd October, submarine patrols were maintained over the same area as on the previous day. On 3rd, 4th, and 5th October reconnaissances of the Straits disclosed no unusual shipping activity.

Nagara nets were examined, and both lines found to be intact.

The seaplane sheds at Nagara were closed and no machines were standing on the slipway.

October 7th-15th.

Patrol and Reconnaissance Work.—A submarine patrol was carried out on the 7th in the triangle Imbros-Suvla-Samothraki, also a reconnaissance of the Straits.

Two patrols of the same area were made on the 8th.

On the 9th and 10th stores, &c., were removed from Kephalo Aerodrome to the new aerodrome at Gliki.

A reconnaissance of the Straits and two submarines patrols in the area Suvla-Imbros-Samothraki were made on the 11th.

Usual small shipping was observed in the Straits.

At 0825 L.T. a hostile machine was seen over Kephalo, three machines went in pursuit, but did not get into touch as the enemy retired rapidly over the Peninsula.

MUDROS.

September 30th—October 6th.

Engagement with Hostile Aircraft.—The event of the greatest interest in the current week has been the successful engagement on the morning of 30th September 1917 between enemy seaplanes which reconnoitred Mudros and the British machines which were sent in pursuit.

At about 0740 L.T. three enemy seaplanes were observed from headquarters, Ispatho Island, approaching from the south. A Sopwith, Type F. 1 ("Camel"), piloted by Flight Lieut. J. W. Alcock; a Sopwith Triplane, No. N. 5431, piloted by

Flight Lieut. H. T. Mellings, D.S.C.; and a Sopwith Scout (Pup) were sent in pursuit from Mudros. Three aeroplanes from Imbros were sent out to endeavour to intercept the enemy on their return journey, and on Sopwith Scout (Pup), piloted by Flight Sub-Lieut. P. K. Fowler was sent up from Tenedos with the same object.

The Sopwith Scout from Mudros and the three Imbros machines were unable to find the enemy and took no part in the engagement.

Two of the enemy machines were single-seater seaplane scouts of the type known as "Blue Birds," capable of a speed of 90 knots flying level, and one two-seater seaplane, a little larger than the scouts, and capable of doing 85 knots when flying level.

The triplane was the first to get into touch with the enemy when they were flying in "V" formation at 12,000 feet, crossing the coast of Lemnos and steering eastward.

The triplane got above the enemy and attacked the two-seater seaplane from in front and was himself attacked by one of the "Blue Birds" diving on to his tail. The triplane, however, shook her off and attacked the other "Blue Bird."

The enemy machine, whose formation had for the time been broken, got into formation disposed quarterly to starboard, each machine thus protecting the other's tail. At this point the "Camel" joined in the action, attacking the rearmost "Blue Bird," diving under her tail and stalling within 50 yards of the enemy and giving him a large volume of fire from both guns. A cloud of smoke came from the machine, which may have been either a smoke screen or escaping steam from a pierced radiator, and the machine dived.

The triplane at the same time circled in behind the other "Blue Bird" and attacked at 100 yards, closing to 50 yards. The machine dived, followed by the triplane, and flattened out 20 feet above the water, the triplane continuing to fire into him, shooting off the extension of the left upper plane and afterwards hitting the pilot in the back.

The "Blue Bird," which was then travelling down wind at 100 knots, hit the water and broke into small pieces, most of the wreckage sinking immediately.

The "Camel," observing the triplane in such a favourable position and fearing that the triplane might be attacked by the other "Blue Bird," came down close behind and above the triplane to protect him.

The triplane then climbed and attacked the enemy two-seater, which was flying at 3,000 feet. The "Camel" meanwhile engaged the remaining "Blue Bird," which he headed off towards Imbros, and got good shooting in until both guns jammed, owing to defective ammunition, cartridges having split in the chamber of each. Accordingly he turned to see what the triplane was doing, and found the latter clearing a jam, while the observer in the two-seater was firing rapidly. The "Camel" thereupon, although he had no guns in action, pretended to attack, and embarrassed the enemy pilot until the triplane's gun jam was cleared, the enemy diving down close to the water.

At this time the remaining "Blue Bird" was observed in the water; his floats had evidently been wiped off in landing, and one wing was already submerged. The "Camel" flew round him and saw the pilot fire a white Very's light. As the "Camel's" engine had a broken inlet valve and was firing erratically it was then flown straight to Imbros Aerodrome and landed.

The triplane continued the action with the enemy two-seater, delivering one attack from in front, where neither the pilot's or observer's guns would bear, when the machine was low under the cliff of Rabbit Island, and closing to within 20 yards.

While getting into position to deliver a second similar attack Flight Sub-Lieut. Fowler arrived from Tenedos on a "Pup" and dived straight on the observer's gun, which was firing at him rapidly. The "Pup" made excellent shooting, the splashes of the bullets being observed from the triplane after they had passed through the machine. Both triplane and "Pup" delivered similar attacks again, and the observer ceased fire, probably having been hit.

By this time the enemy seaplane was almost on the water flying up the Dardanelles close to the forts. The action was accordingly broken off, the "Pup" returning to Tenedos and the triplane proceeding to Imbros. On his return journey he saw the second "Blue Bird" lying low in the water. The pilot of this machine was subsequently picked up by H.M.S. "Acheron," wounded.

The manner in which these three pilots, Flight Lieut. Alcock in the "Camel," Flight Lieut. Mellings in the triplane, and Flight Sub-Lieut. Fowler in the "Pup," worked together, and the dash displayed, reflect the greatest credit on all three pilots. The manner in which Flight Lieut. Alcock sacrificed his own immediate object in order to protect the triplane shows a most praiseworthy balance of judgment and unselfishness.

Earlier in the morning (30th Sept.) a patrol was undertaken over the area to the north of Lemnos, as a submarine had been reported by "Princess Ena" to the west of Lemnos, and it was considered that she might be caught at dawn on the surface proceeding towards the Dardanelles. No submarine was sighted, but in returning from patrol a floating mine was located 8 miles S.E. of Cape Plaka.

Later in the morning a signal was received from R.A.E. requiring occasional submarine patrols to be carried out, and accordingly the area between Lemnos and Mount Athos, the area north of Lemnos and the area to the west of Strati, were examined.

At 2015 L.T. the Handley-Page aeroplane, with Flight Lieuts. J. W. Alcock and H. Aird, and with Mr. S. J. Wise, W.O. (E), left Marsh Aerodrome to carry out a raid on the Constantinople railway stations on the European side and also at Haidar Pasha on the Asiatic side of the Bosphorus.

The machine did not return, and the enemy W/T Press of 4th October reports:—

"In the Ægean Sea.—An English aeroplane of the latest type was forced to land by the anti-aircraft fire from our batteries. The crew, which was composed of three men, fell into our hands."

NOTE.—It is not known whether the machine was shot down on her outward journey or after having delivered her attack. It is probable that the position of her descent was in the water at the head of the Gulf of Xeros, where the isthmus has to be crossed. It is reported that a portion of one strut has been picked up off Imbros, which would indicate that the machine was destroyed and is not in the hands of the enemy.

Search for Handley-Page No. 3124 and Patrol Work.—As the Handley-Page was much overdue at dawn on 1st October, three aeroplanes were sent out from Mudros to search in different directions, taking bombs and looking for submarines at the same time, and, as is reported later, similar patrols were carried out from Imbros.

At 0900 a submarine was sighted first by a trawler and subsequently by H.M.S. "Edgar" south of Pyrgos, Imbros, steering east when first seen at 8 knots. A continuous patrol was carried out by aeroplanes from "G" Flight and by seaplanes from "Ark Royal." One seaplane used hydrophone, but there being so many seaborne craft hunting, the noise made by them was too great for anything to be distinguished from the submarine.

October 7th–15th.

Reconnaissance and Patrol Work.—On the morning of 7th October a patrol was undertaken over the area to the south and east of Lemnos to try and locate submarine reported by patrol launches. No submarine was sighted.

At 1400 and 1450 seaplanes patrolled an area west of Strati.

At 1600 two Henri Farmans patrolled the area Lemnos-Samothraki-Imbros. Nothing was sighted on these patrols.

At dawn on the 8th October one seaplane patrolled the swept channel, and one Henri Farman the area Lemnos-Samothraki-Imbros. At 0915 another Henri Farman carried out a similar patrol.

At 1100 a hostile submarine was sighted in 39° 38′ N., 25° 3′ E. From 1 p.m. to 5 p.m. a continuous patrol was carried out by seaplane from "Ark Royal" and Henri Farmans from Marsh Aerodrome. No submarine was, however, sighted.

At dawn on the 9th, a seaplane and Henri Farman patrolled the Strato area and again in the evening.

The Samothraki-Imbros-Lemnos area was also patrolled by a Henri Farman. No results.

At 0400 on the 10th trawlers sighted a submarine in 40° 6′ N., 24° 40′ E., proceeding south and then north. Practically a continuous patrol was carried out by seaplanes and Henri Farmans from 0720 to 1820 over an area Lemnos-Strati-Piperi-Athos-Lemnos. No submarine was sighted.

At dawn on the 11th a seaplane and Henri Farman patrolled areas, Lemnos-Athos-Samothraki, and another Henri Farman the area Strati-Piperi. Nothing was seen.

At 0958 and 1700 a seaplane patrolled area Lemnos-Athos again without sighting submarine.

Successful experiments were carried out from a seaplane and a portable hydrophone.

A strong southerly gale prevented flying on 12th and 13th October.

KASSANDRA AIRSHIP STATION.

September 30th—October 6th.

Patrol Work.—On 30th September patrols were made which extended from Cape Drepano southwards as far as Psathura, westwards to Skiathos, and searched the whole of the approaches to the Gulf of Salonika between these points and a line west of Kassandra Airship Station.

On 1st October the airship started to patrol the entrances to Gulf of Kassandra and Monte Santo, but had to be recalled owing to increasing wind before the patrol was completed. During the night a patrol to the south of Cape Drepano was also made.

Strong easterly winds accompanied by thunderstorms and rain prevented flying on 2nd and 3rd October, but on 4th October, although the weather was still unsettled, the entrance to the Gulf of Salonika between Cape Pori and Kassandra Point was patrolled.

On 5th October the northern end of Salonika Gulf and the entrance to the Gulf of Kassandra were searched. Weather was unsuitable for flying on 6th October.

October 7th-15th.

Patrol Work.—On 7th October the airship patrolled the Gulf of Salonika. On the 8th the Gulf of Kassandra and Monte Santo and a line Kassandra and Cape Drepano-Pelago. Weather prevented flying on the 9th.

On the 10th patrols were carried out on a line Cape Drepano–Pelago, also the Gulfs of Kassandra, Monte Santo, and the mouth of the Gulf of Salonika.

On the 11th the Gulf of Kassandra and Monte Santo were again patrolled.

SUDA BAY SEAPLANE STATION.

September 30th—October 6th.

Patrol Work.—A patrol was carried out on the morning of 30th September. On the three succeeding days no patrols could be made as there was no seaplane fit for service. Morning patrols were made on 4th, 5th, and 6th October. No detailed reports of these patrols have yet been received, but it is assumed that the ordinary patrol of the approaches to Suda Bay was made on each occasion.

October 7th–15th.

Patrol Work.—Patrols were carried out on the 7th, 10th, and 11th. Wind prevented further work. Details not yet arrived.

H.M.S. "PEONY."

September 30th—October 6th.

Reconnaissance.—On 1st October a reconnaissance was carried out by Schneider seaplane from Port Vathi, of the Turkish coast from Sighajik to Dede Groll Swamps. No shipping was lying either in Sighajik or Scalanuova Harbour, and nothing of any military importance was observed.

On 2nd October a seaplane again left Port Vathi, and reconnoitred the enemy coast of Samos Straits as far as Domathia, again without anything of military importance being seen. No further reports have been received for the current week.

October 7th–15th.

Reconnaissance.—Reconnaissances were carried out on the 9th from Port Vatri by seaplane to Scalanuova, Changli, Cape Kukuaa, Panacia Island, and Daregholl Swamp—nothing of importance was observed. Off Cape Kukuaa enemy fired a few rounds of anti-aircraft at the machines.

ROYAL FLYING CORPS COMMUNIQUÉS.

ROYAL FLYING CORPS COMMUNIQUÉ No. 109.

On the night of the 29th September Flight Commander Munday, Naval Squadron No. 8, left the ground at about 2145, and proceeded to attack a German balloon shed between Brebières and Quiéry-la-Motte, and on finding the objective, he dived down to within 20 feet of the ground and fired 50 rounds from each gun into the shed, which burst into flames. Flight Commander Draper, when over Douai, saw the shed burning furiously, so flew to it and dived down and attacked men who had gathered round in order to extinguish the fire. There is little doubt that the shed contained a balloon.

During the period under review (8th to 15th October, inclusive), the weather has not been good for aerial work. Eighteen enemy aircraft have been brought down, and eighteen driven down out of control. Approximately 10 tons of bombs have been dropped.

October 8th.

The weather was worse that it has been during the last few days.

In spite of this, 10 reconnaissances and three contact patrols by the Second Brigade were carried out, and desired information with regard to enemy movements obtained. No. 20 Squadron went out when the weather was extremely bad. The First Wing fired 650 rounds at ground targets. Two hundred and eighteen photographs were taken during the day.

Artillery Co-operation.—With aeroplane observation, 32 hostile batteries were successfully engaged for destruction; four pits were destroyed, six damaged, nine explosions, and 11 fires caused. Forty-three zone calls were sent down by machines of the Second Brigade.

Enemy Aircraft.—A few enemy machines were encountered, and four were driven down out of control by No. 1 Squadron, one by each of the following pilots:—Captain Fullard, Second Lieuts. Moore, Rogers and Wilson.

Second Lieut. Smith, No. 23 Squadron, engaged and shot down an enemy machine out of control.

Honours and Awards.

The Military Cross.—Second Lieut. C. F. Horsley, Second Lieut. R. Winnicott, Second Lieut. G. W. Ferguson.

The Distinguished Service Cross.—Flight Sub-Lieut. (Acting Flight Lieut.) D. Fitzgibbon, R.N.A.S., Flight Lieut. (Acting Flight Commander) H. J. T. Saint, R.N.A.S.

October 9th.

Owing to a very strong wind and low clouds very little flying was done by Brigades, with the exception of the Second and Fifth.

Eleven reconnaissances were carried out by Army machines, seven of which were carried out by No. 57 Squadron. One trench reconnaissance was carried out by the Fourth Brigade, and 15 contact patrols and 17 counter-attack patrols by machines of the Second and Fifth Brigades.

Artillery Co-operation.—Twenty-one hostile batteries were successfully engaged for destruction and 33 neutralised with aeroplane observation. Four gun-pits were destroyed, 14 damaged, 18 explosions and 16 fires caused. Three hundred and fifty-four zone calls were sent down on active hostile batteries and bodies of infantry. Two hundred and twenty-three of these were sent down by the Second Brigade and 125 by the Fifth Brigade.

Captain Mackay and Lieutenant Rothwell, No. 9 Squadron, carried out a successful shoot on an active hostile battery with the 243rd Siege Battery, destroying two gun-pits and causing two explosions and a fire. They also located and sent down zone calls on 11 active hostile batteries.

Captain Cripps and Dr. West, also of No. 9 Squadron, carried out a successful shoot with the 243rd Siege Battery on a hostile battery, where three pits were damaged, a dump exploded and two fires caused. They then ranged the 21st Siege Battery on to another enemy battery, where two gun-pits were damaged and four fires were caused. Another active hostile battery was then engaged by the 21st Siege Battery with the same observation, which damaged two pits, caused two explosions and a fire.

Enemy Aircraft.—A patrol of Nieuports of No. 1 Squadron engaged about nine enemy aircraft scouts, and one was driven down out of control by Second Lieut. W. Rogers. Second Lieut. G. Moore observed a scout sitting on Second Lieut. Roger's tail, and drove it off. He then saw two others attacking a Nieuport from behind, so drove them off and followed one until it fell out of control and crashed.

Another patrol of this squadron attacked five enemy aircraft which were pursuing two R.E. 8's. Second Lieut. H. Reeves fired a drum into one at close range, and it burst into flames and fell out of control, and the pilot was seen to fall out before it crashed. Second Lieut. R. Birkbeck attacked one of the other machines and shot the pilot, after which the enemy scout went down out of control with the engine full on. Another scout passed in front of him, and after manœuvring for position the German machine was shot in flames, and in this also the pilot was seen to fall out. Second Lieut. F. Baker shot down another German machine, which turned over and over, falling out of control.

Second Lieut. Chattaway and Lieutenant Ward, No. 6 Squadron, were in one of the R.E. 8's which were being pursued, and the observer fired into one of the enemy scouts, and by so doing probably assisted in the destruction of one which fell in flames.

The enemy machines brought down to-day by No. 1 Squadron bring the squadron's total of enemy aircraft shot down and driven down out of control since commencing work as a scout squadron on the 15th February 1917, to 200 machines.

A fight took place between Spads of No. 19 Squadron and an enemy formation, and Captain F. Sowrey shot down a two-seater out of control.

When on offensive patrol Second Lieut. Hobson, No. 70 Squadron, attacked an enemy scout near Staden, and after shooting it down out of control, he watched it crash.

Bombing.—Fifth Brigade.—No. 57 Squadron dropped six 230-lb. and fourteen 112-lb. bombs on Staden. One burst was observed north-east and one on the road south-west of Staden. Several bursts were observed in the village and a large fire was caused, which was afterwards reported by offensive patrol machines.

Miscellaneous.—Lieutenants Warburton and Playford, No. 9 Squadron, carried out an extensive and successful contact patrol giving detailed information as to the progress of four Divisions. This patrol was carried out from 300–1,200 feet. These officers also carried out another extensive contact patrol during the afternoon, locating our troops in 19 places.

Captain Anderson and Lieutenant Ashcroft, No. 9 Squadron, carried out two extensive contact patrols, in the course of which they located our front line on the whole of the front of their Corps and at the junctions with two adjacent Corps.

Second Lieuts. Prosser and Manley, No. 7 Squadron, carried out a successful contact patrol. They examined six points from a height of 300 feet, and also located our troops in five places.

October 10th.

Little flying was possible, except in the early morning and the evening, owing to rain and wind.

Five contact patrols and four counter-attack patrols were carried out by the Second Brigade; three trench reconnaissances by the Fourth Brigade, and three contact patrols and seven counter-attack patrols by the Fifth Brigade.

Lieutenants Warburton and Playford, No. 9 Squadron, carried out a contact patrol and located our troops in 25 places along their Corps front and obtained much information.

Captain Anderson and Lieutenant Ashcroft, of the same squadron, carried out two successful contact patrols, obtaining much information as to the situation of our own troops and the enemy.

Three thousand five hundred rounds were fired at ground targets from low altitudes; 1,650 were by machines of the Fourth Brigade, 800 by No. 101 Squadron, and 400 by No. 102 Squadron, while these two squadrons were bombing at night.

Artillery Co-operation.—Fifty-two hostile batteries were successfully engaged for destruction and eight neutralised with aeroplane observation. Five gun-pits were destroyed, 24 damaged, 29 explosions and 17 fires caused. One hundred and forty-eight active hostile batteries were reported by zone call.

Balloons of the Second Brigade registered 14 targets, five of which were hostile batteries, and located 22 active hostile batteries in addition to reporting on enemy movements. Those of the Fifth Brigade registered one target and located four active hostile batteries.

Enemy Aircraft.—Enemy aircraft were not particularly active, though several formations were encountered round Moorslede.

A patrol of No. 45 Squadron met seven enemy aircraft and attacked them, and Second Lieut. M. Frew shot down two out of control.

Second Lieut. Quigley, No. 70 Squadron, attacked an Albatross Scout and shot it down in flames. He was then attacked by six more, but escaped, and believes one, into which he fired, fell out of control. In the evening a patrol of eight Camels of this squadron engaged five enemy aircraft. Lieutenant Cook shot one down which fell in flames, and around which a number of troops gathered, and Lieutenant Hobson went down and dispersed the enemy from 500 feet with machine gun fire. Captain Jones and Lieutenant Wilson followed one of the enemy machines down until it fell completely out of control.

When returning, after having dropped bombs, Lieutenants Dixie and Rissen, No. 57 Squadron, shot down an Albatross Scout, which attacked them, completely out of control.

Bombing.—First Brigade.—No. 18 Squadron dropped eight 25-lb. bombs on Annoeulin, and No. 25 Squadron nine (112-lb.) bombs on a large gun position north of Brebières.

Fourth Brigade dropped eighteen 25-lb. bombs on various targets.

Fifth Brigade.—No. 57 Squadron dropped four 230-lb. and eight 25-lb. bombs on Oostnieuwkerke.

Ninth Wing.—On the night of the 9th/10th, No. 101 Squadron dropped six 230-lb., two 112-lb. and six 25-lb. bombs on Roulers town and station. On crossing the lines, Lieutenants T. Martyn and H. Steele ran into a bank of mist and completely lost their direction, so flew round trying to discover a target and saw a train which had steamed up and was proceeding in a north-westerly direction. They followed it and dropped a 230-lb. bomb as it was slowing up near a town. The burst was seen quite near the station. The pilot then made a circuit and flew across the train, which was stationary in the station, and dropped two 25-lb. bombs, and one fell on the train and caused a number of explosions.

No. 102 Squadron dropped two 230-lb. bombs on Courtrai, two 230-lb. and four 112-lb. bombs on Menin, and one 230-lb., six 112-lb. and eight 25-lb. bombs on Ledeghem.

Honours and Awards.

The Military Cross.—Captain J. Leacroft, Lieutenant H. G. E. Luchford, Second Lieut. R. F. Hill.

October 11th.

In spite of the bad weather, seven reconnaissances and a contact patrol by the Second Brigade, five counter-attack patrols by the Fifth Brigade and two trench reconnaissances by machines of the Fourth Brigade were carried out, and 408 plates exposed.

Ground targets were attacked by machine-gun fire, and over 2,000 rounds were fired.

Artillery Co-operation.—Considerable artillery work was carried out by the First, Second, and Fifth Brigades. Fifty-eight hostile batteries were successfully engaged for destruction and 15 neutralised with aeroplane observation. Two gun-pits were destroyed, 16 damaged, 36 explosions and 20 fires caused. One hundred and twenty-two active hostile batteries were reported by zone call.

Sixty-three targets were registered by balloons, 11 of which were hostile batteries. Balloons of the Second Brigade located 33 active hostile batteries, and those of the First Brigade, nine.

Enemy Aircraft.—Enemy aircraft were not very active.

A patrol of No. 20 Squadron encountered about 16 enemy aircraft, and in the fighting Lieutenant H. Luchford and Sergeant W. Benger shot down one of the enemy machines and drove down another out of control. Sergeant Johnson and Lieutenant Sanders also shot down one of the German machines out of control.

S.E. 5's of No. 56 Squadron had a certain amount of fighting, and Second Lieut. Rhys Davids shot down an enemy machine out of control.

Lieutenant W. Meggitt and Captain F. Durrad, in a Bristol Fighter of No. 22 Squadron, took part in fighting against six enemy aircraft, and the observer shot down one apparently out of control.

Bombing.—First Brigade.—No. 18 Squadron dropped twenty-four 25-lb. bombs on Haubourdin and twenty-four 25-lb. bombs on Lomme.

A Sopwith Camel of No. 8 (Naval) Squadron dropped two 25-lb. bombs on an enemy strong point.

Fourth Brigade.—Machines dropped fourteen 25-lb. bombs on various targets, and Corps machines of the Fifth Brigade dropped eleven 25-lb. bombs on a rest camp and hutments.

Ninth Wing.—No. 25 Squadron dropped three 112-lb. bombs on Courtrai sidings.

Honours and Awards.

Bar to the Military Cross.—Lieutenant A. E. McKeever, M.C.
The Military Cross.—Captain M. D. G. Scott.

October 12th.

Low clouds and rain made aerial work very difficult. In spite of this a considerable amount was done, especially by the Second and Fifth Brigades, who did their utmost to assist the Second and Fifth Armies in their attack.

Eight reconnaissances were carried out, six of which were by the Second Brigade. Five contact patrols were done by the Second Brigade and seven by the Fifth Brigade, while eight counter attack patrols were done by the Second Brigade and seven by the Fifth Brigade.

Four bomb raids were carried out, and 230 plates were exposed.

Artillery Co-operation.—With aeroplane observation, twenty-six hostile batteries were successfully engaged for destruction and 37 neutralised. Seven gun-pits were destroyed, 11 damaged, 22 explosions and five fires caused. One hundred and twenty-four zone calls were sent down by machines of the Second Brigade and 109 by those of the Fifth Brigade.

Second Lieuts. Dowdall and McCullough, No. 53 Squadron, sent an MQNF call on an active hostile battery, and the 154th Siege Battery obtained eight O.K's and two M.O.K's, causing three explosions.

Captain Carbery and Sergeant Corson, No. 9 Squadron, carried out a successful artillery patrol, and reported 27 active enemy batteries by zone call.

With balloon observation, five hostile batteries were successfully engaged for destruction by artillery of the Second Army which carried out three shoots in which aeroplanes co-operated with balloons, and caused three fires and two explosions. Artillery of this army dealt with 32 other targets.

Two hostile batteries were successfully engaged for destruction by artillery of the Fifth Army.

Enemy Aircraft.—Enemy aircraft were not active except low-flying scouts which were encountered more frequently than usual on ground patrols on the Second Army front.

Second Lieut. R. Birkbeck, No. 1 Squadron, saw a two-seater west of Comines, so attacked and shot it down and saw it crash in a street in the town.

A fight took place between seven Sopwith Camels of No. 45 Squadron and about 20 enemy scouts, and Lieutenant J. Firth shot one down out of control.

Second Lieut. J. Compton, No. 60 Squadron, was fired at from below by a German Scout, so dived at it, and after 20 rounds the enemy machine spun down to the ground and crashed.

Second Lieut. E. Booth, No. 70 Squadron, joined in a fight between our machines and German scouts, and shot one down out of control.

Second Lieut. F. Grant and Second Lieut. H. Attwater, No. 57 Squadron, were attacked by enemy scouts and drove one down, which they believe fell out of control.

Bombing.—Twelve 20 lb. bombs were dropped on trench points by machines of the Fourth Brigade, and No. 57 Squadron of the Fifth Brigade attacked Hooglede and Oostnieuwkerke and dropped one 230-lb. and twenty-four 25-lb. bombs. Corps machines of this Brigade dropped fourteen 20-lb. bombs on Westroosebeke, an enemy rest camp, and other targets.

No. 25 Squadron, Ninth Wing, dropped eight 112-lb. bombs on Ledeghem Station.

Miscellaneous.—Over 10,000 rounds were fired by pilots from low altitudes at German troops, transport, guns, and other targets; 5,600 of these were by the Second Brigade.

Second Brigade.—The pilots who did this work are:—

No. 60 Squadron.—Captain Roberts, Second Lieut. Carter, and Captain Hammersley.

No. 19 Squadron.—Second Lieut. Thompson, Second Lieut. Delamere, Major Carter, Second Lieut. Olivier, and Captain Leacroft.

No. 45 Squadron.—Captain Macmillan, Second Lieut. Brownell, Second Lieut. Crossland, Second Lieut. Frew, Second Lieut. Montgomery, and Second Lieut. Dawes.

Naval Squadron No. 1.—Flight Lieut. Everitt, Flight Sub-Lieuts. Binks, Spence, Kinhead, and Rosevear.

Fifth Brigade.—Three thousand eight hundred and eighty-three rounds were fired by:—

No. 23 Squadron.—Second Lieuts. Fowler, Macrae, Paul, and Fielder, and Lieutenant Trudeau.

No. 32 Squadron.—Captain Fish and Lieutenants Northwood, Jones, and Cuffe.

No. 70 Squadron.—Captain Jones, Lieutenants Cooke, Hobson, and Vinter, Captain Lawrence and Lieutenant Peverell.

No. 7 Squadron.—Captain Williams and Sergeant Morris, Second Lieuts. McClurg and O'Callaghan, and Second Lieuts. Gilbert and Durham.

No. 9 Squadron.—Lieutenants Peace and Gillie, and Lieutenants Yeatman and Miller.

Ninth Wing.—No. 66 Squadron.—Second Lieut. Dore and Second Lieut. Gore fired at several bodies of infantry, mounted troops, and transport. The former brought down a hostile machine from a height of 60 feet on to its aerodrome and then fired into the hangars.

Honours and Awards.

The Military Medal.—No. 540041, Private W. A. Fraser.

October 13th.

Rain and strong wind prevented much aerial work being done.

Four reconnaissances, one contact patrol by the Second Brigade and two by the Fifth Brigade, and four counter attack patrols by the Second Brigade, and two by the Fifth Brigade were carried out. One hundred and seventy-eight photographs were taken.

Artillery Co-operation.—Twenty-three hostile batteries were successfully engaged for destruction and two neutralised with aeroplane observation, four gun-pits were damaged, and five explosions caused.

Thirty-five targets were registered by balloons of the Second Brigade and three by balloons of the First Brigade. Three of the targets were hostile batteries successfully engaged for destruction by the Second Army Artillery.

Enemy Aircraft.—Enemy aircraft activity was slight all day.

When on patrol, Lieutenant W. Sherwood, No. 60 Squadron, attacked a two-seater and drove it down out of control.

Second Lieuts. Dreschfeld and Moore, No. 21 Squadron, were on flash reconnaissance when they encountered an enemy scout which they attacked and destroyed. The R.E. 8 was shot through the petrol tank and landed in "No man's land."

A patrol of six machines of No. 54 Squadron had an engagement with a large number of enemy scouts. French pilots state that they saw several machines of unknown nationality fall out of control. Only two of ours returned, and it is not known if any of the enemy machines were shot down by the four missing pilots.

Bombing.—Twenty-six 25-lb. bombs were dropped on various targets during the day.

October 14th.

The weather improved but visibility was very bad.

Five reconnaissances, two contact patrols by the Second Brigade, and four bomb raids were carried out and 460 plates were exposed.

Artillery Co-operation.—With aeroplane observation 34 hostile batteries were successfully engaged for destruction. One gun-pit was destroyed, 11 damaged, nine explosions, and 10 fires caused. Seventy-two active hostile batteries were reported by zone call.

A machine of No. 4 Squadron fired 200 rounds at a party of the enemy who were trying to salve a wrecked British machine.

Enemy Aircraft.—Enemy aircraft activity was about normal.

Captain P. Fullard, No. 1 Squadron, saw a two seater flying up and down between Wervicq and Houthem, so waited until it was underneath him and then dived at it and shot it down out of control, but was attacked by scouts and unable to watch it crash. Sergeant Olley of the same squadron attacked another two-seater which fell out of control.

Captain J. Leacroft, No. 19 Squadron, attacked an enemy scout which had been engaged by Captain Sowrey and shot it down out of control, and Captain Sowrey followed it and saw it crash.

A patrol of No. 32 Squadron saw about 10 enemy aircraft scouts attacking an R.E. 8, so dived at the enemy machines, and Lieutenant Jones fired 300 rounds into one which broke to pieces in the air and crashed into our lines west of Poel-cappelle.

Bombing.—First Brigade.—No. 18 Squadron dropped six 112-lb. bombs on Wavrin and four 112-lb. bombs on St. Andre. Six 25-lb bombs were dropped by the Third Brigade, 16 by the Fourth Brigade, and eleven 25-lb. bombs on a rest camp by No. 9 Squadron.

Ninth Wing.—No. 27 Squadron attacked Ledeghem Station on which six 230-lb. bombs were dropped. One burst was seen on the line 200 yards south-east of the station.

October 15th.

Weather.—The weather was fine during the morning, clouded over in the afternoon and finally rain came.

Nine reconnaissances were carried out, five of which were by machines of the Fourth Brigade, which included three trench reconnaissances. One counter-attack patrol was carried out by machines of the Second Brigade, and 745 photographs were taken by machines of all Brigades. Four thousand and thirty rounds were fired into the enemy's trenches from low altitudes, 3,186 of these were fired by pilots of the Fourth Brigade.

Artillery Co-operation.—Fifty-three hostile batteries were successfully engaged for destruction and 15 neutralised with aeroplane observation. Nine gun-pits were destroyed, 26 damaged, 24 explosions, and 12 fires caused. One hundred and eighteen active hostile batteries were reported by zone call.

Second Lieut. Mann and Lieutenant Bunt, No. 7 Squadron, observed for 200 rounds on a hostile battery position for the 26th Siege Battery resulting in a gun-pit being damaged and a dump of ammunition catching fire.

Lieutenants Young and Wedgwood, No. 9 Squadron, observed for the 193rd Siege Battery, which succeeded in demolishing one hostile gun-pit and damaging another.

Enemy Aircraft.—On the 14th, whilst on offensive patrol, Lieutenant C. R. J. Thompson, No. 19 Squadron, brought down a hostile machine. This was confirmed by a pilot of No. 84 Squadron who saw the machine crash near Menin.

On the 15th, Captain F. Sowrey, No. 19 Squadron, when leading his patrol against five Albatross Scouts, shot one down which was observed to fall in flames.

Second Lieut. K. B. Montgomery, No. 45 Squadron, shot down an enemy two-seater which he, with four other pilots, saw crash.

Second Lieut. E. O. Krohn, No. 84 Squadron, when on offensive patrol had to leave the formation owing to engine trouble. He was attacked all the way back to the lines by hostile machines, one of which he managed to get several bursts into and which was observed to crash by the infantry of the IX. Corps.

Hostile machines were driven down out of control by Second Lieut. H. G. Reeves, No. 1 Squadron, Lieutenant Kirkpatrick and Second Lieut. Couve, No. 20 Squadron, Captain Macmillan No. 45 Squadron, and Flight Sub-Lieut. Curtis, Naval Squadron No. 10.

Bombing.—First Brigade.—No. 18 Squadron dropped three 112-lb. bombs on Carvin. No. 2 Squadron dropped twenty-two 25-lb. bombs on Auchy, Benifontaine, Haisnes, and Salome.

Fifth Brigade.—No. 57 Squadron dropped two 230-lb., four 112-lb., and twelve 25-lb. bombs on Oostnieuwkerke from 16,000 feet. One burst was observed on the north-east corner of the village.

Ninth Wing.—No. 25 Squadron dropped twelve 112-lb. bombs on the ammunition dump at Harlebeke.

Twenty-three 25-lb. bombs were dropped on various targets by machines of the Third, Fourth, and Fifth Brigades.

Honours and Awards.

Meritorious Service Medal (without Pension).—No. 69380, 2/A.M. A.H. Norris, R.F.C.

S. Wood, Captain,
Staff Officer.

Advanced Headquarters,
Royal Flying Corps,
17th October 1917.

ROYAL FLYING CORPS COMMUNIQUÉ No. 110.

During the period under review (16th to 22nd October inclusive), the weather was unfavourable for aerial work. Activity on the enemy's part was not very marked. In air fighting we have brought down 44 of his machines and have driven 19 down out of control. Two hundred and ninety-three hostile batteries have been engaged for destruction, and 523 zone calls sent. A total of 23,851 rounds were fired at ground targets and 4,530 photographs taken. Approximately $23\frac{1}{2}$ tons of bombs have been dropped with good results.

October 16th.

Weather.—Fine in the morning, clouding over about midday, with rain after 3 p.m.

Five reconnaissances were carried out by Corps squadrons, including one trench reconnaissance by a machine of the Fourth Brigade. A dawn reconnaissance was carried out by four machines of No. 8 Squadron. A total of 823 photographs were taken, 259 being by machines of the Second Brigade and 325 by those of the Third Brigade.

Artillery Co-operation. — Fifty-nine hostile batteries were engaged for destruction and eight neutralised with aeroplane observation; three gun-pits were destroyed, 20 damaged, 29 explosions and 20 fires caused. One hundred and forty-nine active hostile batteries were reported by zone call.

The 319th Siege Battery with observation by Lieutenant Fenton, No. 42 Squadron, destroyed a gun-pit in a hostile battery position, causing two explosions.

From 6 p.m. the 14th to 6 p.m. the 15th, 45 targets were registered by balloons and 25 active hostile batteries located. Of these, balloons of the Second Brigade registered 44 targets and located eight active hostile batteries. Balloons of the First Brigade carried out 15 successful shoots and located 22 active hostile batteries, three of which were engaged and silenced.

October 16th.

Enemy Aircraft.—Enemy aircraft activity varied from slight to about normal.

While on photographic reconnaissance four machines of No. 11 Squadron engaged two two-seater enemy machines escorted by six Albatross Scouts. In the course of the general engagement which ensued Lieutenant McKeever and Second Lieut. Powell shot down two enemy aircraft, which were both observed to crash.

Second Lieuts. Prout and Bird, No. 4 Squadron, whilst doing artillery work were attacked by an Albatross Scout, which they succeeded in driving down out of control.

Anti-aircraft of the Third Army brought down an enemy machine.

Bombing.—First Brigade.—No. 18 Squadron dropped nine 112-lb. bombs on Cuincy. No. 2 Squadron dropped eight 25-lb. bombs on Auchy, six 25-lb. bombs on Benifontaine and nine 25-lb. bombs on trenches.

Third Brigade.—Corps machines dropped eight 25-lb. bombs on villages and trench points.

Fourth Brigade.—Twenty-two 20-lb. bombs were dropped on trench points.

Fifth Brigade. — Corps squadrons dropped eleven 20-lb. bombs on various targets.

Ninth Wing. — On the night of the 15th/16th, No. 101 Squadron dropped one 230-lb. and four 25-lb. bombs on lights, believed to be a railway.

No. 102 Squadron dropped one 230-lb. bomb on Courtrai Railway Station, and twenty-one 25-lb. bombs on searchlights.

Miscellaneous.—Machines of the First Wing fired 1,250 rounds into hostile troops in trenches and on roads.

One thousand three hundred rounds were fired into empty trenches by machines of the Fourth Brigade.

Lieutenants Young and Davy, No. 15 Squadron, silenced an active anti-aircraft battery by firing 200 rounds from 1,200 feet.

October 17th.

Weather.—Fine, with exceptionally good visibility until 2.30 p.m. when it became overcast with some rain.

Reconnaissances.—Nine reconnaissances were carried out, two of which were by Army Squadrons, and one trench reconnaissance by a machine of the Fourth Brigade.

One thousand two hundred and ten photographs were taken and 3,120 rounds fired at the enemy in his trenches and in the open.

Artillery Co-operation.—Ninety-six hostile batteries were engaged for destruction with aeroplane observation and 14 neutralised. Five gun-pits were destroyed, 47 damaged, 47 explosions, and 43 fires caused. One hundred and ninety-four active hostile batteries were reported by zone call.

With observation by Lieutenant Fenton, No. 42 Squadron, the 151st Siege Battery obtained three O.K.'s on a hostile battery position. He then switched on to a high velocity gun firing from a railway. The line was damaged, and trenches, dug-outs, and a house in the vicinity were destroyed. Three fires and two explosions were caused.

Captain Robinson and Lieutenant Borbeck, No. 13 Squadron, during a flight of four hours and 20 minutes ranged the 262nd Siege Battery on to a hostile battery position. Ten O.K.'s were obtained, and all four gun-pits were badly damaged.

Captain Berney and Lieutenant Norton, No. 59 Squadron, gave 69 observations during a flight of 4 hours 15 minutes for the 270th Siege Battery, who obtained six O.K.'s on a hostile battery position, and damaged all four gun-pits.

Successful shoots were carried out with Langley, the 61st Siege Battery, the 94th Siege Battery and the 183rd Siege Battery, with observation by Lieutenant Reeves, Lieutenant Biggar, Captain Rogers, and Lieutenant Simpson, respectively, all of No. 52 Squadron.

Captain Williams and Lieutenant Richards, No. 7 Squadron, observed for the 375th Siege Battery on a hostile gun position, in which a gun-pit was destroyed, and a large explosion and a fire caused. At the conclusion of the shoot the 375th Siege Battery was switched on to another active hostile battery, which was silenced.

Captain Mackay and Lieutenant Rothwell, No. 9 Squadron, observed 114 rounds fired by the 231st Siege Battery on an enemy battery position. Two gun-pits were damaged, two explosions and two fires caused. These observers then reported four active hostile batteries by zone call.

Enemy Aircraft.—Enemy aircraft were particularly active and aggressive during the morning. Several flights were made by single machines over our lines at a great height. The weather was ideal for their machines, the atmosphere being very clear and a high west wind blowing.

Captain P. F. Fullard, No. 1 Squadron, when leading an offensive patrol, brought down one enemy machine and drove two others down out of control.

Flight Commander R. P. Minifie, D.S.C., fired 350 rounds into a hostile two-seater at a height of 16,000 feet over our lines. The machine fell into a dive, turned on its back, and finally crashed within our lines. About the same time Flight Sub-Lieut. Rosevear, Naval Squadron No. 1, fired 200 rounds into a two-seater, which fell completely out of control. He followed it down, but lost sight of it near the ground. The infantry state that this machine crashed in our lines close to the one brought down by Flight Commander Minifie.

A photographic reconnaissance of three machines of No. 20 Squadron, was attacked by eight enemy aircraft. Second Lieut. Jooste and Captain Johnston drove one down in flames, and

Lieuts. Luchford and White shot another down. Both these are confirmed by anti-aircraft.

Second Lieut. Durrand and Second Lieut. Woodbridge, No. 20 Squadron, brought down a hostile machine which was observed to crash by them and by an observer in another machine.

An offensive patrol of No. 20 Squadron, encountered a formation of nine Albatross Scouts. Three of these dived on to the tail of Second Lieut. French and Gunner Veele, who fired at one, which fell out of control and was observed to crash. Second Lieut. Makepeace and Lieutenant Waddington of the same patrol drove another hostile machine down out of control.

Second Lieut. Reeves, No. 2 Squadron, and Flight Lieut. Hinkead, Naval Squadron No. 1, each drove down a hostile machine which fell completely out of control.

An offensive patrol of No. 11 Squadron was attacked by 20 Albatross Scouts, one of which was driven down out of control by Second Lieut. Stanley and Second Lieut. Ross, and two by Lieutenant Mauduit and Second Lieut. McRobert.

Captain Ferreira, No. 29 Squadron, and Second Lieut. Drewitt, No. 23 Squadron, each brought down a hostile two-seater, which was observed to crash by other pilots.

Captain McCudden, No. 56 Squadron, observed our anti-aircraft shells bursting over Bailleul when at a low altitude. He climbed with his patrol to 13,000 feet and found two enemy two-seaters. One of the enemy machines disappeared East, but the other, Captain McCudden managed to surprise from behind and fire a burst into which sent it down in a steep dive. The machine burst into flames; one wing came off, the pieces falling north-west of Dickebusch. This machine is numbered G. 81.

Captain Stuart Wortley and Lieutenant McGrath, No. 22 Squadron, saw a formation of 12 enemy machines over our lines. These were engaged, and the enemy aircraft made off towards their own lines. Lieutenant McGrath opened fire at one of them at close range. It got into a spin and later burst into flames, and was seen to break to pieces and crash near Ypres. This machine is numbered G. 80.

The total for the day was 11 machines brought down (three falling in our own lines and one machine brought down by anti-aircraft gun-fire), and 11 driven out of control.

Bombing—First Brigade.—No. 88 Squadron dropped four 112-lb. bombs on Carbin, four 112-lb. bombs on Seclin, and nine 112-lb bombs on a large gun position North of Brebières, and No. 2 Squadron, dropped twenty-seven 25-lb. bombs on billets east of Lens.

Fifty-five 25-lb. bombs were dropped on various targets.

October 18th.

Weather.—Very fine until 9 a.m.; overcast from then till noon, afterwards ow clouds.

Four reconnaissances were carried out by Corps Squadrons, and one successful photographic reconnaissance by No. 57 Squadron. A total of 408 photographs were taken.

Artillery Co-operation.—Thirty-seven hostile batteries were engaged for destruction and nine were neutralised with aeroplane observation; three gun-pits were destroyed, nine damaged, 19 explosions, and nine fires caused.

One hundred and thirty-eight hostile batteries were reported by zone call, 66 of these were by the Fourth Brigade.

Second Lieut. Brazier and Lieutenant Richards, No. 7 Squadron, observed 200 rounds with the 27th Siege Battery on an active hostile battery. An ammunition store was hit, causing a large explosion.

On the 17th, 18 targets were registered by balloons, 11 of these being hostile batteries. Of the targets registered, 15 were by balloons of the 2nd Brigade, who also located 10 active hostile batteries out of a total of 22.

Enemy Aircraft.—There wes a decided decrease in enemy aircraft activity from the 17th instant, though several large formations were encountered in the vicinity of the Roulers-Menin Railway.

While on offensive patrol Bristol Fighters of No. 20 Squadron engaged several formations of enemy aircraft. Captain Luchford and Lieutenant White attacked three, which were diving on a R.E. 8. Two went east diving steeply, but into the third they managed to fire 200 rounds at a range of 20 yards. The enemy aircraft fell and was observed to crash. Shortly afterwards they saw another, which they attacked, firing 200 rounds into it at point-blank range. The enemy machine fell and was seen to crash. Both these results were confirmed by another formation.

Another Patrol of Bristol Fighters of the same Squadron engaged six or seven enemy aircraft. Second Lieut. Colville Jones and Lieutenant Phelps drove one down completely out of control, which was seen to crash by anti-aircraft battery.

Fifteen Gothas escorted by 10 scouts were encountered by a patrol of Naval Squadron No. 1. Flight Commander Minifie fired 250 rounds into one of the Gothas, which nose-dived vertically for over 2,000 feet into the clouds and was lost to sight.

A two-seater D.F.W. was driven down out of control by Flight Lieut. Kinkead and Flight Sub Lieut. Forman, Naval Squadron No. 1, after it had received 400 rounds from close range.

During a combat between eight machines of No. 41 Squadron, and 10 Albatross Scouts, Lieutenant R. Winnicott and Second Lieut. R. Whitehead each drove down one of the enemy aircraft out of control.

Lieutenant G. Hyde and Second Lieut. M. Gonne, No. 54 Squadron, attacked an enemy aircraft at close range. It went down in a steep dive, and was observed to crash by a Belgian aviator.

Second Lieut. Payne, No. 29 Squadron, fired 60 rounds into a hostile two-seater, which turned on its back and went down completely out of control.

Second Lieut. J. Highman and First Air Mechanic S. Hookway, of the Detached Flight of No. 5 Squadron, whilst on photography were attacked by a hostile machine into which they fired bursts from a range varying from 200 to 400 yards. The hostile machine burst into flames and was seen to crash into the ground.

Lieutenant R. Hoidge, No. 56 Squadron, with his formation attacked four enemy aircraft two-seaters with two Spads. The two-seater escaped and Lieutenant Hoidge returned west and waited for the two-seaters to return. Two came back, one of which he attacked and brought down between the road and river, east of Comines. He then attacked and drove down another two-seater completely out of control.

Bombing.—First Brigade.—Machines of No. 18 Squadron dropped fourteen 20-lb. bombs on Esquerchin, four 112-lb. bombs on Courcelles and eight 25-lb. bombs on Seclin.

Machines of No. 2 Squadron dropped twelve 20-lb. bombs on Benifontaine, Auchy, and on other targets.

Third Brigade.—Machines of No. 59 Squadron dropped thirty-two 25-lb. bombs on a big gun position north of Brebières.

Corps machines dropped five 25-lb. bombs on various trench points.

Fourth Brigade.—Twenty-one 20-lb. bombs were dropped on various targets.

Fifth Brigade.—No. 57 Squadron dropped one 230-lb. bomb, six 112-lb., and twelve 20-lb. bombs on Oostniewuerke, several bursts being observed.

Corps Squadrons dropped fourteen 20-lb. bombs on Spriet and on various targets.

Ninth Wing.—No. 25 Squadron dropped two 112-lb. bombs on Rumbeke and eight on Melle sidings (near Ghent).

Miscellaneous.—A total of 3,300 rounds were fired at the enemy's troops in trenches and in the open by brigades as follows:—

First Brigade, 850; Second Brigade, 100; Fourth Brigade, 1,800; Fifth Brigade, 400.

October 19th.

Clouds and thick mist.

Three reconnaissances were carried out by machines of the Fourth Brigade and one by those of the Second Brigade.

Three photographs were taken during the day.

Artillery Co-operation.—Seven hostile batteries were engaged for destruction and five neutralised with aeroplane observation. One gun-pit was destroyed, six damaged, and four explosions caused. Thirty-eight active hostile batteries were reported by zone call. Twenty-six of these being by machines of the Fourth Brigade.

With observation by Captain Hill, No. 52 Squadron, the 227th Siege Battery destroyed one gun-pit, damaged two, and caused three explosions in a hostile battery position.

With observation by Lieutenant Watson of the same squadron, the 183rd Siege Battery damaged two gun-pits and caused a small explosion.

Lieutenant Pilkington and Driver Green, No. 7 Squadron, observed 80 rounds for the 237th Siege Battery on a hostile battery position. A very large explosion was caused and the position badly damaged.

Captain Mackay and Lieutenant Rothwell, No. 9 Squadron, observed for the 243rd Siege Battery, which damaged two gun-pits in a hostile battery position. They carried out another successful shoot during the same flight with the 145th Siege Battery, and reported six active hostile batteries by zone call, afterwards sending down a GF call on three M.T., one wagon being hit during the shelling.

Enemy Aircraft.—Enemy aircraft activity was practically nil, only a few hostile machines being seen in the afternoon.

Bombing.—On the night of the 18th/19th in spite of the mist and patches of cloud, No. 102 Squadron dropped the following bombs:—

One 230-lb. on Harlebeke Aerodrome, one 230-lb. and two 112-lb. on Marcke Aerodrome, two 112-lb. on Bisseghem Aerodrome, four 112-lb. bombs on Courtrai Station, and two 230-lb. and two 112-lb. bombs on various lighted targets.

One hundred rounds were also fired at transport south of Menin.

On the 19th.—Machines of No. 2 Squadron dropped four 25-lb. bombs on various targets, those of the Third Brigade, twelve 25-lb. bombs on villages; Fourth Brigade, eighteen 25-lb. bombs on trench points from an average height of 2,000 feet; Fifth Brigade, thirteen 25-lb. bombs on enemy headquarters, hutments and rest billets.

Eight machines of No. 27 Squadron started out in the thick mist to bomb Ardoye ammunition dump. Six returned without crossing the lines, owing to unsuitable weather. Lieutenant Bickerton, who was unable to reach the objective, dropped two bombs on Rumbeke Aerodrome, and Lieutenant Stewart dropped his two bombs on the railway line near Vichte.

Miscellaneous.—Three thousand four hundred and fifty rounds were fired at ground targets by brigades as follows:—

First Brigades, 450; Fourth Brigade, 2,480; Fifth Brigade, 400; Attached Flight No. 5 Squadron, 120.

October 20th.

Weather.—The weather was fine, but the thick haze which continued all day prevented observation for the artillery.

Four reconnaissances were carried out by machines of the Fourth Brigades and two successful photographic reconnaissances of hostile aerodromes as far east as Ghent were carried out by two machines of No. 25 Squadron. A total of 661 photographs were taken.

Artillery Co-operation.—Five hostile batteries were engaged for destruction, two gun pits were destroyed, one damaged, one explosion and one fire caused. Six active hostile batteries were reported by zone call. In spite of mist, which rendered observation almost impossible, Captain Mackay and Lieutenant Rothwell, No. 9 Squadron, carried out successful shoots on hostile batteries with the 145th, 231st and 21st Siege Batteries.

Enemy Aircraft.—Enemy aircraft activity varied considerably, but at no time during the day was it above normal.

An offensive patrol of No. 20 Squadron engaged 15 scouts. Second Lieut. Boles and Lieutenant Rowan drove down one out of control.

One hostile machine was driven down out of control by each of the following pilots:—Second-Lieut. Rogers, No. 1 Squadron; Flight Commander Minifie, Naval Squadron No. 1; Captain Macmillan, Lieutenant Clarke, Second Lieut. Davies and Second Lieut. Brownell, all of No. 45 Squadron.

Four Bristol Fighters of No. 11 Squadron engaged seven Albatross Scouts, one of which was shot down in flames by Second Lieut. McKeever and Lieutenant Kent. Two others were driven down out of control by Sergeant Stevenson and Lieutenant Plater.

Nine Albatross Scouts were encountered by a patrol of Naval Squadron No. 10 at a height of 16,000 feet. In the ensuing fight, one of the hostile machines was shot down by Flight Commander Saint, and seen to crash.

During an attack on Rumbeke Aerodrome with bombs by No. 70 Squadron, the escort consisting of machines of Nos. 70 and 28 Squadrons shot down hostile machines as follows:—

Second Lieut. Booth, No. 70 Squadron, fired about 150 rounds into an enemy machine which dived into a field, running into a hedge and being overturned.

Second Lieut. Mickie, No. 70 Squadron, engaged a two-seater taking off the aerodrome; it tried to turn, stalled, and dived straight into the ground.

Second Lieut. Quigley, No. 70 Squadron, attacked a two-seater whose wings folded up in the air.

Second Lieut. Mulholland, Lieutenant Mitchell and Captain Barker, all of No. 28 Squadron, each shot down a hostile machine, which was either seen to crash or break up in the air.

Captain Lawrence, Captain Smith-Grant and Second Lieut. Koch, No. 70 Squadron, drove down hostile machines completely out of control, but none were seen to crash.

Bombing.—During the day almost four tons of bombs were dropped as follows :—

First Brigade.—No. 35 Squadron dropped sixty-four 25-lb. bombs on Pont-à-Vendin; No. 2 Squadron dropped twenty-three 25-lb. bombs on billets east of Lens, and No. 18 Squadron dropped six 112-lb. bomps on Beaumont.

Fifth Brigade.—No. 70 Squadron dropped twenty-two 25-lb. bombs on Rumbeke Aerodrome, and No. 57 Squadron dropped fifty-two 25-lb. bombs on Abeele Aerodrome.

Fifty-nine 25-lb. bombs were dropped on various targets.

Ninth Wing.—Although there were drifting clouds and no moon on the night of the 19th/20th, No. 101 Squadron dropped two 230-lb., one 112-lb., and two 25-lb. bombs on lights in the vicinity of Ingelmunster railway station.

On the 20th, No. 27 Squadron dropped one 230-lb. and seven 112-lb. bombs on Cortemarck railway station, and No. 25 Squadron dropped twelve 112-lb. bombs on Gontrode Aerodrome.

Miscellaneous.—A successful attack was carried out during the day by the 22nd Wing on Rumbeke Aerodrome. A patrol of No. 70 Squadron carrying 25-lb. bombs flew out at a height of 400 feet with a close escort of eight machines of the same squadron. High patrols of Nos. 23 and 28 Squadrons operated in the same neighbourhood at the same time. Twenty-two 25-lb. bombs were dropped from below 400 feet. Second Lieut. Mickie dropped his three bombs on machines lined up on the aerodrome, one of which was blown to pieces. Another bomb was seen to go right through a hangar, and several observed to fall within 20 feet of the sheds. After dropping their bombs the pilots fired at the personnel on the aerodrome and into the hangars from a height of about 20 feet. Two of the pilots' undercarriages actually hit the ground, one sustaining a bent axle. During this attack the patrols brought down seven machines and drove down one out of control in full view of the hostile aerodrome. A total of 4,374 rounds were fired at ground targets, including 3,724 rounds fired by No. 70 Squadron during their attack on Rumbeke Aerodrome. On his way home Second Lieut. Quigley fired into some enemy troops playing football and at horse transport on the roads. Trains were attacked by Lieutenant Primeau and Second Lieut. Hobson, No. 70 Squadron, from a height of 50 feet; the passengers were seen to rush out of the carriages and dive into ditches on each side of the railway.

October 21st.

Weather.—Fine, but fair visibility.

Four reconnaissances were carried out by the Fifth Brigade, one by the Fourth Brigade, and 1,304 photographs taken, 392 of which were by the First Brigade. A total of 3,310 rounds were fired at ground targets, 2,500 being by machines of the Fourth Brigade.

Artillery Co-operation.—Sixty-seven hostile batteries were engaged for destruction and eight neutralised with aeroplane observation, seven gun-pits were destroyed, 21 damaged, 62 explosions and 22 fires caused. Eighty-nine active hostile batteries were reported by zone call, 54 being by the Second Brigade and 27 by the Fifth Brigade.

The 183rd Siege Battery with observation by Captain Rogers, No. 52 Squadron, obtained a direct hit on a hostile battery position; three of the pits were damaged and one explosion caused.

Lieutenant Richards, No. 7 Squadron, carried out a successful shoot on a hostile battery position with the 375th Siege Battery, one gun-pit being destroyed and another damaged.

Captain Mackay and Lieutenant Rothwell, No. 9 Squadron, carried out three successful shoots during one flight. In the first shoot with the 145th Siege Battery, one gun-pit was seen to be demolished, another damaged and an explosion caused; in the second, with the 243rd Siege Battery, one gun-pit was destroyed, one damaged, three explosions and one fire caused; in the third, with the 231st Siege Battery, a fire was caused and a gun-pit damaged. The same pilot and observer later in the day observed for two other successful shoots, one with the 145th Siege Battery on a hostile Battery position, in which one gun-pit was damaged, one explosion and a fire caused; in the second, with the 243rd Siege Battery, one gun-pit was damaged. They also reported the location of 16 hostile batteries by zone call in reply to which four guns were silenced.

Enemy Aircraft.—Enemy aircraft were active and aggressive well east of the lines.

Captain J. Leacroft, No. 19 Squadron, saw two R.E. 8's and four Spads being attacked by 12 hostile machines. He joined in the fight and drove one down out of control, which was seen to crash by an anti-aircraft section.

Captain Luchford and Lieutenant White, No. 20 Squadron, while on patrol with eight others, engaged nine enemy machines consisting of seven scouts and two two-seaters. They poured 250 rounds into one of the two-seaters, which fell out of control, and was seen to crash by the pilot and observer and an anti-aircraft battery.

A patrol of No. 45 Squadron dived on four two-seaters over Lille and were in turn attacked by seven scouts. In the fight that followed Second Lieut. Carpenter shot down one of the scouts in flames, while Second Lieut. Frew pursued one of the scouts, firing 300 rounds into it from a range of about 30 feet. The hostile machine went down out of control with the engine full on.

Lieutenant Rutherford, No. 60 Squadron, attacked several enemy two-seater machines. One of these he drove down, and observed it crash into the ground.

Flight Sub-Lieut. Spence, Naval Squadron No. 1, and Captain Hammersley, No. 60 Squadron, each drove down a hostile machine out of control.

Four Bristol Fighters of No. 11 Squadron engaged two enemy two-seaters escorted by 10 scouts. A fierce engagement took place, in which Lieutenant Mauduit and Corporal Mason drove one of the enemy aircraft down in flames. The same pilot and observer brought down another of the hostile machines, which was seen to crash, and drove down yet another completely out of control.

One of the machines attacked by Second Lieuts. Nixon and Johnson turned over and fell upside down completely out of control.

Lieutenants Davies and Tubbs each fired over 200 rounds into a hostile machine, which went down completely out of control and crashed in the Belgian trenches. Three pilots of Naval Squadron No. 10 attacked three enemy two-seaters, one of which was brought down in flames.

One hostile machine was driven down out of control over Ostende by Captain Baker and Lieutenant Dixon, No. 48 Squadron.

A patrol of eight machines of No. 29 Squadron attacked seven enemy two-seaters, one of which was brought down by Second Lieut. Payne and three driven down out of control by the same pilot assisted by Second Lieuts. J. Leach and C. Hamilton.

Four pilots of No. 32 Squadron attacked three Albatross Scouts which were bothering an R.E. 8. A large number of rounds were fired by all the pilots into the enemy machine, which fell out of control and crashed.

Captain Lawrence, No. 70 Squadron, drove down one hostile machine out of control, and Lieutenants Monkhouse and Lane, No. 32 Squadron, one between them.

On a report that enemy aircraft were flying west of the lines, three pilots of No. 56 Squadron went up in pursuit. Captain McCudden got close up to one of these and fired a good burst from both guns. The hostile machine crashed in our lines.

While leading a patrol of No. 84 Squadron, Captain Leask attacked a two-seater passing over the top. It went down completely out of control. Almost at once a large number of enemy scouts approached from all directions and a big fight ensued lasting for forty minutes. The fighting was so close that it was impossible to say how many of the enemy machines were accounted for, but at the end they were all going east with their noses well down. Captain Child, Captain Leask and Lieutenant Moloney, all claim to have sent down one each completely out of control.

Bombing.—Five and a half tons of bombs were dropped as follows:—

First Brigade.—No. 35 Squadron dropped forty-nine 25-lb. bombs on Annay and 38 on Noyelles.

No. 18 Squadron dropped ten 112-lb. bombs on Fouquieres and six 112-lb. bombs on a big gun north of Brebières.

Third Brigade.—No. 59 Squadron dropped thirty-six 25-lb. bombs on a big gun on a railway mounting.

Fifth Brigade.—No. 57 Squadron dropped one 230-lb., two 112-lb., and thirty-two 25-lb. bombs on Abeele Aerodrome.

9th Wing.—On the night of the 20th/21st, No. 101 Squadron dropped three 230-lb., eight 112-lb., and four 25-lb. bombs on Ingelmunster station and aerodrome.

No. 102 Squadron dropped four 112-lb. bombs on Bisseghem Aerodrome. One hostile machine which was getting off the ground was destroyed by one of the bombs, and a petrol store was hit by another bomb dropped by Captain Duff. One 230-lb. and two 112-lb. bombs were dropped on lighted targets.

On the 21st, No. 25 Squadron dropped ten 112-lb. bombs on Heule Aerodrome.

Eighty-eight 25-lb. bombs were dropped on various targets.

41st Wing.—During the afternoon a second raid into Germany was made by 12 machines of No. 55 Squadron. Two thousand four hundred and sixty-four lbs. of bombs were dropped with excellent results on factories and an important railway junction about 10 miles north-west of Saarbrucken. Bursts were seen in Bous Station and at the glass works at Wadgassen, and a large explosion caused amongst the buildings on the outskirts of this place. Ten enemy aircraft were encountered over the objective, four of which were driven down completely out of control.

October 22nd.

Weather.—Rain and low clouds almost entirely prevented flying till the afternoon, when it cleared up considerably.

Six army reconnaissances were carried out by the Second Brigade and two trench reconnaissances by the Fourth Brigade.

No. 7 Squadron carried out three contact patrols and three counter-attack patrols; No. 9 Squadron three contact patrols and three counter-attack patrols.

Second Lieuts. Prosser and Lillicrap, No. 7 Squadron, in spite of most unfavourable weather, located our infantry by flares and fans.

Lieutenants Walker and Playford, No. 9 Squadron, in the middle of rain, located several small trenches which had been dug and occupied by our troops. The same pilot and observer later in the day carried out a successful contact patrol, locating several scattered groups of our infantry, and enemy strong points.

Captain Anderson and Lieutenant Ashcroft, No. 9 Squadron, carried out a very extensive contact patrol; detailed reports were made as to the disposition of our troops, upwards of 55 locations of our infantry being reported during the period of 2 hours 15 minutes occupied by the patrol.

Artillery Co-operation.—Twenty-four hostile batteries were engaged for destruction and five neutralised with aeroplane observation; one gun pit was destroyed, 15 damaged and five explosions caused.

With observation by balloons of the Second Brigade, nine targets, of which four were hostile batteries, were registered, and the location of 20 active hostile batteries reported.

Second Lieut. Knight, No. 53 Squadron, observing for the 154th Siege Battery, obtained several O.K.'s on a hostile battery position, causing four fires and one explosion.

Lieutenant Biggar and Lieutenant Munden, both of No. 52 Squadron, observing for the 61st and 305th Siege Batteries, respectively, badly damaged the gun positions of two hostile batteries.

The 243rd Siege Battery demolished one gun-pit and damaged another in a hostile battery position with observation by Captain Cripps and Lieutenant Miller, No. 9 Squadron.

Captain Mackay and Lieutenant Rothwell, No. 9 Squadron, reported the location of 11 active hostile batteries by zone call, and carried out a successful shoot on a hostile battery position with the 145th Siege Battery.

Lieutenants Weil and Thornton, No. 9 Squadron, observed for a shoot on a hostile battery position by the 103rd Siege Battery; one gun-pit was seen to be damaged and an explosion caused.

Enemy Aircraft.—Few enemy machines were seen throughout the day.

Machines of No. 57 Squadron, when returning from bombing Hooglede, were attacked from below by three Albatross Scouts. The first zoomed up under the tail of Second Lieut. J. Orrell's machine and opened fire from about 20 yards. Second Lieut. Orrell banked his machine, allowing his observer, First Air Mechanic Spicer, to fire about 60 rounds into the enemy machine, which burst into flames. Another of the scouts opened fire from about 100 feet below the D.H. 4; First Air Mechanic

Spicer fired one drum into this machine, which spun down about 500 feet and burst into flames.

Second Lieut. J. Payne, No. 29 Squadron, saw seven enemy aircraft over Menin. He outclimbed them and dived on one, firing a drum from about 70 yards without effect. After climbing again, he dived at the same enemy aircraft, firing about 50 rounds from 30 yards. The enemy aircraft turned and then dived down vertically out of control.

A patrol of the Fourth Brigade encountered about 12 Albatross Scouts, one of which was driven down out of control.

Bombing.—While the moon was out, the night bombing squadrons concentrated their efforts on hostile aerodromes, and later in the night attacked railway stations. Six tons of bombs were dropped as follows:—

First Brigade.—No. 18 Squadron dropped ten 112-lb. bombs on Courrières, and No. 35 Squadron dropped sixty-two 25-lb. bombs on Harnes.

Fifth Brigade.—No. 57 Squadron dropped one 230-lb., ten 112-lb. and fifty-three 25-lb. bombs on Hooglede.

Machines of the First Brigade dropped 14, Third Brigade two, Fourth Brigade 15, and the Fifth Brigade fifteen 25-lb. bombs on various targets.

9th Wing.—Night 21st/22nd, machines of No. 101 Squadron dropped four 230-lb., twelve 112-lb., and ten 25-lb. bombs on Lichtervelde Station; two 112-lb. bombs on Abeele Aerodrome and two 112-lb. bombs on Ingelmunster Aerodrome. One of the latter exploded in the middle of enemy machines which were just getting off the aerodrome.

Machines of No. 102 Squadron dropped two 230-lb., ten 112-lb., and eight 25-lb. bombs on Roulers Station; two 112-lb. bombs on Courtrai Station; seven 25-lb. bombs on Marcke Aerodrome; two 112-lb. bombs on Bisseghem Aerodrome and two 112-lb. bombs on Moorseele Aerodrome, while four 112-lb. bombs were dropped on various targets.

Five thousand nine hundred and forty-seven rounds were fired at ground targets, including machine gun emplacements, active anti-aircraft batteries, hostile troops in shell-holes, in trenches, on roads, and in villages. The details of some of these rounds are as follows:—

Lieutenant Firth and Second Lieut. Phillips, No. 45 Squadron, fired 650 rounds at a column of transport and guns near Houthulst, which galloped away. Two battalions of infantry on a road were scattered and transport attacked on the Poelcappelle—Westroosebeke Road, which also galloped away.

Captain McAlery, Second Lieut. March, Lieutenant Stringer, Second Lieut. Drewitt and Second Lieut. Fowler, all of No. 23 Squadron, fired 500 rounds at active hostile batteries, a group of 200 infantry resting on a road which were scattered, and into villages.

Lieutenant Northwood and Lieutenant Packs, No. 32 Squadron, fired 220 rounds at a party of 50 men and three stationary lorries.

Lieutenant Wilson, No. 29 Squadron, fired 20 rounds from 40 feet at parties of troops.

Captain Jones and Lieutenants Vinter, Hobson, and Peverell, No. 70 Squadron, fired 1,095 rounds from 300 feet at machine gun emplacements and anti-aircraft batteries.

Captain Anderson and Lieutenant Ashcroft, No. 9 Squadron, fired 1,850 rounds in two flights at the enemy's troops in shell-holes.

(Signed)   R. J. BARTON, Captain,
General Staff.

Advanced Headquarters,
    Royal Flying Corps,
        3rd October 1917.

No. 45.

CONFIDENTIAL.

ROYAL NAVAL AIR SERVICE.

OPERATIONS REPORT

(with Royal Flying Corps Reports attached).

1st to 15th NOVEMBER 1917.

NAVAL STAFF,
OPERATIONS DIVISION.
15th *November* 1917.

ROYAL NAVAL AIR SERVICE.

REPORT OF OPERATIONS

(Completed from Reports during period
1st to 15th November 1917).

CONTENTS.

	PAGE
HOME STATIONS	2
DUNKIRK	5
R.N.A.S. SQUADRONS, WITH ROYAL FLYING CORPS REPORTS ATTACHED	12
EASTERN MEDITERRANEAN	16
EAST INDIES AND EGYPT	24
BRITISH ADRIATIC SQUADRON	26
CAPE STATION	28
ROYAL FLYING CORPS COMMUNIQUÉS	33

HOME STATIONS.

SUBMARINE PATROL WORK.

November 3rd.

Felixstowe.—A patrol in search of hostile submarine was carried out by Large America Seaplane 8694 (Pilot, Flight Lieut. Galpin and F. S. L. Moody), accompanied by two machines of the same type, Nos. 8683 and 8661.

The flight left Felixstowe at 1234 on a course of 95°, and at 1256 the Shipwash Light was on the port beam one mile distant, when course was changed to 98°.

At 0103 both the accompanying machines left to return to the base, Seaplane 8661 reporting to 8694 that she had developed engine trouble.

At 0124 the wireless operator reported that the W/T transmitter was out of order. The patrol was continued, and one minute later (0125) on emerging from a cloud, a hostile submarine was sighted on the port beam approximately 6 miles away. Course was then changed to 360°, and the seaplane dived for the submarine, which was steering west.

After the seaplane had been diving for about one minute the submarine changed course to south, which was head on to the seaplane, and started diving rapidly.

At 0128, and when in position 7 miles W. by N. of the North Hinder Light two 230-lb. bombs were dropped and exploded approximately 30 feet to the left and 20 feet ahead of the swirl of the submarine, which had submerged 10 seconds previously. The seaplane circled round, but nothing was seen except the large dark patch caused by the functioning of the bombs.

The submarine was large, had two masts, and appeared to be camouflaged with a series of fawn or similar coloured stripes. It resembled an "E" boat in general contour, but of a much larger type, with ability to dive very rapidly.

Being unable to repair the wireless to communicate with the base the seaplane returned and rebombed, then proceeded again to the position where the submarine had submerged, but nothing further was observed.

At 1600 the pumps having ceased working and a thick fog arising which made observation difficult, the seaplane returned to the base.

November 8th.

Hornsea.—Whilst returning from a patrol, Hamble Baby Seaplane No. 1469 (Pilot, Flight Sub-Lieut. Lemon), when about $4\frac{1}{2}$ miles east of Scarborough, observed a thin white streak of foam sharp at one end, but gradually fading away at the other and quite distinct from a crest wave. Moreover, the wave crests were running N.W. and S.E., whilst this streak was running about N.N.E., and was certainly caused by a periscope travelling at about 12 knots.

The seaplane at once turned towards it, and came down to within about 500 feet of the surface. When still about 500 yards from the streak, it gradually became smaller as though slackening speed, and finally disappeared altogether.

About 10 seconds afterwards the seaplane arrived as near as could be judged over the spot, and although the pilot was unable to see anything from the machine, owing to this machine having no observation doors in the floor, two 65-lb. bombs were dropped at an interval of about two seconds.

The seaplane then turned and observed two patches of foam where the bombs had dropped, but nothing further was seen although the machine remained in the vicinity for about five minutes.

As there was not a ship within a reasonable distance and petrol was running low, the seaplane returned to the base.

November 11th.

Bembridge.—Whilst on patrol, in seaplane N. 1611 (Pilot, Flight Sub-Lieut. G. Barnes, Observer, A. M. Hooper) the ing conn tower of a submarine was sighted about five miles ahead on the starboard bow steering east at 1445. The seaplane was then at a height of 1,500 feet, and steering a course 20° north by east. The engine was immediately opened out, and the pilot steered a course into the wind, which brought the seaplane over the submarine diagonally. At 1450 one 100-lb. bomb was dropped from 1,200 feet; the submarine by this time was fully blown on the surface. The bomb was observed to burst about 60 feet away, on the starboard side just abreast of the conning tower. The submarine in the meantime continued on an easterly course at about 8 knots, and one minute after the first bomb had been dropped, a second 100-lb. bomb was dropped which exploded 40 feet off on the port side.

The seaplane then descended to 700 feet, and it was observed that the submarine had made a sharp turn to starboard and resumed its former course. The seaplane circled round at heights varying from 700–1,500 feet, and at 1500 a shot was fired from a gun mounted just in front of the conning tower, which however fell short.

The seaplane had in the meantime communicated with Calshot by W/T, then remained in the vicinity until 1535 during which time Calshot was kept informed of the movements and conditions of the submarine which seemed unable to dive.

During this period the submarine pursued a somewhat erratic course, and fired several shots at the seaplane, only one of which, however, came nearer the machine than 100 yards.

At 1525 the seaplane turned N.W. to try and get into communication with surface craft, the submarine still being on the surface steering N.E. at about 8 knots. No patrol boats were encountered until about eight miles S.E. of Dunmore, when communication was made with the destroyer informing her of the submarine's position and course when last seen. Owing to the light failing and visibility becoming poor the seaplane then returned to the base.

November 11th.

Portland.—Whilst on patrol to escort a convoy of 21 merchant ships proceeding up the Channel, Wight Seaplane 9850 (Pilot, Flight Sub-Lieut. Voles) sighted a large submarine in position 49–58 N., 3–22 W., at 1450, and, approximately, 10 miles ahead of the convoy. The seaplane attacked and dropped four 100-lb. bombs, the first being apparently a direct hit on the periscope, which was seen to collapse. The second bomb fell 30 feet ahead of the first and the third fell in the swirl, just by the second; the fourth was not observed to explode. A large upheaval appeared to be taking place after the bombs had dropped.

The seaplane remained in the vicinity for some time, then proceeded to the convoy and reported what had occurred to the leading destroyer; then, owing to the darkness, the seaplane was compelled to return to the base.

November 15th.

Mullion.—Airships C. 5A and C. 9 carried out bomb attacks on hostile submarines (probably two) on the above date.

Airship C. 5A first sighted the periscope of a submarine directly astern and immediately turned to carry out an attack. Good shooting was made, the first bomb dropping directly into the swirl, the remaining three ahead and to the port and starboard of the bubbles, which came to the surface, but not in large quantities. At 1155 the C. 5A returned to the base for more bombs, Airship C. 23A being directed to patrol the vicinity of the attack during C. 5A's absence.

At 1545 C. 5A, when again over the spot, observed bubbles and oil still rising, and directed a trawler to drop depth charges, which was done. It is reported that motor launches working East of the Lizard heard a submarine on the hydrophone at about 1545, and it is probable that the submarine heard by the motor launches was the one giving out oil and bubbles seen by the C. 5A at that time. It was also reported by motor launches that they had seen a submarine at 7 west of the Lizard at about 1600, on which the depth charges were dropped.

It would appear from the above, if the 1630 report is correct, that there must have been two submarines in the vicinity. It is considered that the submarine attacked by C. 5A was undoubtedly damaged.

Airship C. 9 ascended at 0635 and patrolled from the south of Wolff Rock to Hartland Point. A photograph was taken of a natural airship base at Langford, four miles south of Bude, and a course was then set for Land's End and Wolff Rock to search for a submarine, which had been bombed by Airship C. 5A and signalled by the station. It was thought that if the submarine had not been badly damaged he would make Land's End for the northward track, the area south of Land's End was reached with no result, and a course was set for the station.

At 1630 two explosions were seen behind two motor launches, and course was made for these at full speed. The motor launches were unable to give definite information, owing to their lamp failing, but they fired red Very's lights and a signal was received from the station by W/T that the motor launches had dropped depth charges previous to those seen.

C. 9 examined the area, and about 150 yards north of the motor launches a line of light irridescent oil was seen coming up to the surface, and moving W.N.W. A flare was dropped by which it was gauged that the oil forming was due to something moving at about 4 knots, presumably a submarine, with some plates sprung, as a result of the explosion of depth charges dropped by the motor launches.

A line of three bombs ($2\frac{1}{2}$ seconds delay action) were then dropped diagonally along the track, and some 200 feet in front of the head of the line of oil, which then ceased, and the motor launches were informed.

The area was watched till 1710, then, on account of oncoming darkness and difficulty of observation, all airships were recalled.

DUNKIRK.

WEATHER.

In consequence of unfavourable weather conditions generally throughout this period aircraft operations have been greatly impeded, and the number of bombing attacks on enemy objectives has fallen considerably below the average.

OFFENSIVE PATROLS—ENGAGEMENTS WITH ENEMY.

November 4th.

No. 4 Wing (9th Squadron).—Whilst on patrol in the vicinity of Dixmude, a formation of five Sopwith F.I. machines were attacked by a formation of Albatross Scouts.

Flight Sub-Lieut. Narbeth was attacked by two hostile machines at close range, one from behind and one in front.

Flight Commander Fall attacked the rear hostile machine, and fired about 200 rounds into him from 25 yards behind. The hostile machine suddenly turned off and dived towards his own lines, emitting a stream of white smoke. Flight Commander Fall followed this machine down, until attacked by another hostile machine, but was able to watch the former machine, which pulled up suddenly, stalled, then fell over on its back, and spun down for several thousand feet, and was last seen to disappear, still spinning into the clouds. As it was completely overcast south of Pervyse, it was impossible to see whether it was this side of the lines or the other.

Flight Sub-Lieut. Narbeth's machine was badly shot up, but all machines returned safely.

November 9th.

No. 4 Wing (1st Squadron).—A patrol of five Sopwith F.I. machines observed a large two-seater hostile machine about 6,000 feet above Slype. It was too far away to be attacked before it was lost in the clouds. A D.F.W. machine was seen by Flight Sub-Lieut. Tonks over Furnes; it was engaged and driven down apparently out of control.

A later patrol of Sopwith F.I. machines observed a D.F.W. machine S.E. of Pervyse. This was attacked by Acting Flight Commander Estone, and was driven down apparently out of control.

(A subsequent report states that this machine was destroyed.)

November 12th.

No. 4 Wing (1st Squadron).—Whilst on patrol near Dixmude, Flight Lieut. Kinkead and Flight Sub-Lieut. Forman, in Sopwith triplanes, attacked a new type of hostile scout machine at about 9,000 feet. The hostile machine was driven west, looping and side slipping as he went, during which time the Sopwith fired into him, at opportune times.

He then turned east and began to climb; the Sopwiths attacked from above, and when at 4,000 feet the hostile machine appeared to burst into flames, and went into a vertical nose dive which continued until he disappeared from view into a thick mist, which prevented further observation.

November 13th.

No. 4 Wing (1st Squadron).—During a patrol of five Sopwith triplanes, Flight Commander Rowley engaged a two-seater Aviatik, which was gliding back at 10,000 feet south-east of Nieuport, and fired a large number of rounds at close range into his tail. The hostile machine fell out of control, side-slipping from side to side, and eventually diving vertically through the clouds at 4,000 feet. It is considered that this machine was probably destroyed.

November 13th.

No. 4 Wing (4th Squadron).—A flight of Sopwith F.I. machines went up to intercept a formation of Albatross Scouts south-east of Dixmude. Flight Sub-Lieut. Gossip attacked two of the hostile machines, one of which was almost certainly sent down out of control and another probably out of control.

November 15th.

No. 4 Wing (1st Squadron).—A flight of five Sopwith F.I. machines encountered seven hostile scouts, and two two-seaters north-east of Dixmude, and dived on them from 13,000 feet, and a number of combats took place.

Flight Lieut. Kinkead fired a good burst into one, with the result that the hostile machine fell over and over, and crashed near some shattered buildings near Beerst.

The same pilot then attacked another hostile machine, and sent it down out of control just north of Dixmude.

Flight Sub-Lieut. Findlay attacked another hostile machine of this formation, into which he fired 50 rounds at about 20 yards range. The hostile machine fell completely out of control for several thousand feet into the clouds, but the Sopwith pilot did not see whether he crashed or not.

Other combats of an indecisive nature took place, in which one of the Sopwiths was riddled with bullets, two piercing the main tank, but all machines returned safely.

FLEET PROTECTIVE PATROL—ENGAGEMENT WITH ENEMY.

November 4th.

No. 4 Wing (4th Squadron).—A patrol of three Sopwith F.I. machines observed a formation of five Rumpler two-seaters which were spotting for enemy destroyers 15 to 20 miles north-east of Zeebrugge.

The Rumpler machines were escorted by two seaplane Scouts and three Albatross two-seaters at a height of 5,000 feet. Two of the Albatross scouts were attacked from 6,000 feet, one by Flight Sub-Lieut. Gossip who shot the observer dead, and drove the machine down into the sea; the other hostile machine was attacked by Flight Sub-Lieut. Burt, who drove the machine down apparently out of control.

The other hostile machines separated, some going, in the direction of Holland and the others in a southerly direction.

November 9th.

No. 4 Wing (4th Squadron).—Whilst on patrol with the Fleet a flight of three Sopwith F.I. machines attacked an enemy machine near Lombartzyde, which they succeeded in driving down out of control. This was undoubtedly the machine reported to be registering at the time.

Another two-seater was seen to rise from the ground shortly afterwards from near Raversyde, and to proceed in the direction of Lombartzyde.

It was attacked by the patrol and driven away before it could begin to register. Two other two-seaters were seen three miles north-east of Dixmude. On the approach of the patrol they flew away to the north-east.

HOSTILE AIRCRAFT, PURSUIT—ENGAGEMENT WITH ENEMY.

November 13th.

No. 4 Wing (9th Squadron).—A formation of eight Sopwith F.I. machines went up at 1050 and pursued a formation of Gothas back over the lines. During the chase Flight Sub-Lieuts. Mellersh and Redgate attacked one of the Gotha machines, and apparently killed the observer. The attack was given up at Middlekerke, the pilots having exhausted all their ammunition, and the hostile machine was last seen beyond Ostende at 5,000 feet about a mile out to sea.

Flight Lieut. Banbury chased one Gotha as far as Middlekerke firing about 400 rounds, but without apparent result.

Flight Commander Fall chased one Gotha back over the lines firing 550 rounds at 200 yards range; the hostile machine nose dived over his own lines.

During a patrol later in the day, Flight Commander Fall and Flight Sub-Lieut Wood attacked the rear machine of three hostile scouts, this they destroyed and it was seen to crash in the floods east of Pervyse. Flight Commander Fall then attacked a two-seater enemy machine into which he fired 300 rounds at point blank range, and saw it going down on its back and out of control at 500 feet.

Other two-seaters were attacked by this patrol with indecisive results.

SUMMARY.

Hostile Machines driven down out of control - - - 10
    ,,   ,,   destroyed - - - - - - 5

                           Total - - - - - 15

BOMB ATTACKS.

(Carried out during the Period between the dates given.)

*Engel Aerodrome	Nov. 4th	1,301 lbs.	D.H. 4 (A).
Thourout Railway Station and Junction.	Nov. 6th—7th	5,912 lbs.	H.P. (A).
Lichtervelde Railway Station and Junction.	Nov. 6th—7th	7,152 lbs.	H.P. (A).
*St. Denis Westrem Aerodrome	Nov. 9th—10th	1,568 lbs.	H.P. (A).
Bruges Docks	Nov. 9th—10th	8,152 lbs.	H.P. (A).
*Vlisseghem Aerodrome	Nov. 12th	884 lbs.	D.H. 4 (A).
*Houttave Aerodrome	Nov. 13th	1,789 lbs.	D.H. 4 (A).
*North of Handzaeme (sheds).	Nov. 15th	922 lbs.	D.H. 4 (A).
	Total	27,680 lbs.	

* Daylight raid.   (A) Aeroplanes.   (S) Seaplanes.

BOMB ATTACK—ENGAGEMENT WITH ENEMY.

November 4th.

No. 5 Wing (5th Squadron).—A bomb attack was carried out during the afternoon by six D.H. 4 machines on Engel Aerodrome on which three 65-lb., seven 50-lb., forty-six 16-lb., and two 10-lb. bombs were dropped from heights of 14,000 to 15,000 feet.

Visibility was good, but when over the target the formation was heavily attacked by enemy aircraft, rendering observation of results very difficult.

Both the western and eastern group of sheds and hangars were well straddled, and bombs were seen to explode amongst the former.

Most of the D.H.4 machines had engagements with enemy aircraft, several of them were badly shot about, and Acting Gunlayer Burne was wounded in the leg.

Two photographs were taken of the objective.

November 6th–7th.

No. 5 Wing (7th and 7a Squadrons). — A bombing raid was carried out during the night by Handley Page machines on Thourout Railway Station and Junction, and Lichtervelde Railway Station and Junction.

Three machines attacked the former objective with twelve 250-lb., and twenty-six 112-lb. bombs. The North and South Junctions were well straddled, and several direct hits were observed on the lines.

The latter objective was attacked by five machines, and eight 250-lb. and forty-six 112-lb. bombs were dropped, a number of which exploded in close proximity to junctions and the railway track, and a large fire was observed south-west of Lichtervelde.

A train proceeding from Lichtervelde to Roulers was attacked with two bombs.

Poor visibility rendered accurate observation of results difficult; heavy clouds and rain were encountered on the return journey.

November 9th–10th.

No. 5 Wing (7th and 7a Squadrons).—Eight Handley Pages left during the night to carry out a bomb attack on St. Denis Westrem Aerodrome, with Bruges Docks as an alternative target. One of the machines broke a tail skid on getting off; another returned shortly after starting, owing to engine trouble.

Owing to bad weather only one machine reached the original objective, on which fourteen 112-lb. bombs were dropped. With the aid of the searchlights a very good straddle was obtained over the north-west line of sheds.

The alternative target was attacked by the remaining five machines, and twelve 250-lb., and forty-six 112-lb. bombs were dropped. Visibility was very bad, but the searchlights and the usual "flaming onions" aided the observers in locating the target and in noting the direction of their lines of bombs. The East and West Basins and Darses Nos. 1 and 2 appear to have been well straddled and many explosions were seen; one large fire was seen in the docks.

On the return journey, all pilots encountered very low clouds, and heavy rain and hail storms. Notwithstanding these extremely adverse weather conditions, all machines landed safely.

November 12th.

No. 5 Wing (5th Squadron).—A bombing raid was carried out during the morning by eight D.H. 4 machines (four as bombers and four acting as a fighting escort) on Vlesseghem Aerodrome, on which eight 50-lb., twenty-nine 16-lb. and two 10-lb. bombs were dropped at heights of from 15,000 to 16,000 feet.

No direct hits were observed, but some bombs were seen to explode close to the sheds on the south and west sides of the Aerodrome.

Owing to haze, visibility was only fair.

November 13th.

No. 5 Wing (5th Squadron).—A bomb attack was carried out during the afternoon by eight D.H. 4 machines on Houttave Aerodrome, on which three 65-lb., eleven 50-lb., sixty-four 16-lb. and two 10-lb. bombs were dropped at heights of from 14,200 to 16,000 feet.

A number of bombs were observed to explode close to and amongst the sheds on the north side of the road, and on the south side. One direct hit is reported on the former.

Anti-aircraft fire was heavy and accurate, and a considerable number of enemy aircraft were sighted, but did not get near enough to attack the formation.

November 15th.

No. 5 Wing (5th Squadron).—Six D.H. 4 machines were despatched during the forenoon with orders to attack Uytkerke Aerodrome, but owing to a high wind of over 60 miles per hour, the formation was unable to reach this objective, and attacked sheds north of Handzaeme, on which eight 50-lb., thirty-two 16-lb., and one 10-lb. bombs were dropped from heights of 15,400 to 16,400 feet.

Owing to heavy clouds, no results could be observed. Of the six machines despatched, only four dropped their bombs on the above-mentioned target. One machine was obliged to return owing to engine trouble.

News has been received that the sixth machine had landed in the neighbourhood of Herzeale, east of Wormhoudt, and that both pilot and observer are uninjured.

Honours.

Name.	Unit.	Awarded.
Wing Commander C. L. Courtney	No. 4 Wing	D.S.O.
Observer Lieut. R. W. Gow, D.S.C.	No. 2 Squadron	D.S.O.
Flight Commander F. C. Armstrong	No. 3 Squadron	D.S.C.
Flight Lieut. H. F. Beamish	No. 3 Squadron	D.S.C.
Flight Sub-Lieut G. W. Hemming	No. 4 Squadron	D.S.C.
Flight Sub-Lieut. E. T. Hayne	No. 3 Squadron	D.S.C.
Flight Sub-Lieut. J. E. L. Hunter	No. 4 Squadron	D.S.C.

Casualties.

November 1st–15th.

Name.	Squadron.	Date.
Missing.		
Flight Sub-Lieut. H. P. Salter	No. 2.	6.11.17.
Observer Sub-Lieut. H. W. White	No. 2.	6.11.17.
Injured.		
Flight Commander J. Robinson	No. 2.	13.11.17.
Observer Sub-Lieut. W. S. Anderson	No. 2.	13.11.17.

NAVAL SQUADRONS WITH THE ROYAL FLYING CORPS.

(PERIOD, 21ST OCTOBER TO 17TH NOVEMBER 1917 INCLUSIVE.)

NAVAL SQUADRON No. 1.

This squadron has been attached to the Second Brigade, Royal Flying Corps, till the 1st November, when it returned to the R.N.A.S.

From the 21st October to the 1st November 24 offensive patrols were carried out, and 49 special missions in pursuit of enemy aircraft, amounting in all to 310 hours flying.

Hostile Aircraft.—Four enemy machines were crashed and four driven down out of control by pilots of this squadron.

October 21st.

Two hostile machines were driven down out of control by Flight Sub-Lieut. Rosevear and Flight Sub-Lieut. Spence.

October 24th.

Flight Sub-Lieut. Rosevear attacked one of four enemy aircraft at close range without result. He then attacked an enemy aircraft which was diving on the tail of another triplane. He got to within close range and fired all his ammunition. The enemy aircraft fell over, caught fire, and crashed near Comines. Flight Lieut. Kinkead fired 300 rounds into an enemy two-seater, which turned over and dived, the left planes coming off in the air.

October 26th.

A two-seater hostile machine was driven down completely out of control by Flight Sub-Lieut. Spence after 100 rounds had been fired into it.

October 27th.

Flight Commander Minifie sighted a hostile scout coming towards our lines to attack our corps machines. He dived on to it and fired 50 rounds at close range. The enemy aircraft dived vertically and crashed on a house in Westroosebeke.

October 29th.

Flight Lieut. Kinkead drove down a machine completely out of control.

October 31st.

Flight Commander Minifie in the semi-darkness encountered a hostile machine, which he brought down, and was seen to crash near Gheluvelt.

Two thousand eight hundred rounds were fired from low altitudes at ground targets, including parties of hostile troops in shell holes and on the roads, mechanical and horse transport, and machine gun emplacements by the following pilots:—

>Flight Sub-Lieut. Spence.
>Flight Sub-Lieut. Sneath.
>Flight Lieut. Kinkead.
>Flight Sub-Lieut. Forman.
>Flight Sub-Lieut. de Wilde.
>Flight Sub-Lieut. Clapperton.
>Flight Sub-Lieut. Wallace.

Casualties :—

Missing.—Flight Sub-Lieut. J. C. Hough, 20.10.17.

Wounded.—Flight Sub-Lieut. Clapperton, 27.10.17.

Hostile Machines driven down out of control, 4.
      „   „   destroyed, 4.

NAVAL SQUADRON No. 8.

October 21st–November 3rd.

This squadron has been attached to the First Brigade, Royal Flying Corps, and has carried out 15 offensive patrols and 27 special missions in pursuit of enemy aircraft, making a total of 152 hours two minutes flying.

Three combats have taken place, all indecisive.

This squadron has been used to interfere with hostile artillery machines registering their artillery, and although none have been brought down, 13 have had their shoots interrupted and been driven east.

October 22nd.

Flight Commander Munday left the ground just after dark to attack the aerodrome at Moncheaux. He dropped four 20-lb. bombs on to the aerodrome from 1,000 feet and then went down to a height of 50 feet and fired into the hangars. He continued east and attempted to find Bersee aerodrome, but lost his bearings and returned over Cambrai station, into which he fired a burst from his machine gun. He made a successful forced landing in the open country east of Amiens.

Casualties.—*Wounded.*—Flight Sub-Lieut. W. M. Davidson, 27.10.17.

November 4th–17th.

This squadron has been attached to the First Brigade, Royal Flying Corps, and has carried out 57 offensive patrols and 45 special missions in pursuit of enemy aircraft, making a total of 152 hours 28 minutes flying.

Enemy aircraft have not been very active during this period owing to the weather.

On the 7th, Flight Commander R. B. Munday proceeded at dawn to attack an enemy kite balloon, and crossed the lines between Hulluch and Lens, and when over Bauvin shut off his engine and dived at the shed, and then opened fire from 100 yards range. When near the shed he observed a balloon on the ground so swerved round and emptied the last few rounds from his drum into the balloon and then zoomed over it. The balloon burst into flames, and a fire was also seen near the shed. He returned and fired a burst into the shed and on his homeward flight fired into the Metallurgique Works.

On the 8th, Flight Commander R. J. O. Compston, observed an Albatross Scout being engaged by anti-aircraft on this side of the lines, so manœuvred for position, and then attacked and destroyed the enemy scout.

On the same date, six machines of this squadron co-operated with an infantry raid and fired in all 1,600 rounds into the trenches and at guns.

During the period under review a total of 4,500 rounds were fired at various targets from low altitudes.

Casualties.—*Missing.*—Flight Lieut. W. S. Magrath, 9.11.17.

Hostile Machines destroyed - - - - - - - 1

NAVAL SQUADRON No. 10.

October 21st–November 3rd.

This squadron has been attached to the Fourth Brigade, Royal Flying Corps, and has carried out 22 offensive patrols and one special patrol for the protection of artillery machines, making a total of 187 hours 27 minutes flying.

Eight combats have taken place, three of which were decisive.

October 21st.

Flight Sub-Lieuts. Curtis, Emery, and Nelson attacked a hostile two-seater, which went down in flames, the débris falling behind our front line. Shortly afterwards, Flight Sub-Lieut. Curtis engaged an Albatross Scout, which went down out of control and was seen to crash.

October 27th.

In a general engagement between a patrol of this squadron and six Albatross Scouts, Flight Sub-Lieut. Curtis drove one down completely out of control.

One thousand five hundred rounds were fired into the enemy's trenches from heights ranging between 200 and 600 feet by—

Flight Lieut. Trapp.
Flight Sub-Lieut. Bowyer.
Flight Sub-Lieut. Nelson.
Flight Sub-Lieut. Manuel.
Flight Sub-Lieut. Carroll.
Flight Sub-Lieut. Hall.

Casualties.

Missing.—Flight Sub-Lieut. G. H. Morang, 27.10.17.
Wounded.—Flight Sub-Lieut. W. N. Fox, 21.10.17.

Hostile Machines driven down out of control - 1
,, ,, destroyed - - - - 2

November 4th–17th.

This squadron has been attached to the Fourth Brigade, Royal Flying Corps, and carried out 30 offensive patrols, comprising a total of 169 flights and a total flying time of 266 hours.

Hostile activity, on account of the weather, was not very pronounced.

On the 4th, Flight Lieut. Curtis attacked one of a formation of Albatross Scouts and shot it down out of control. He then attacked a second, which he shot down out of control, and on flying round, saw the first one crashed on the ground.

On the 5th, Flight Sub-Lieut. Cameron shot down an enemy Scout out of control, and on the 12th, Flight Lieut. Trapp, and Flight Sub-Lieut. Beattie attacked an enemy two-seater in which the observer was shot, and the machine eventually fell out of control.

On the 15th, an enemy formation of Scouts was attacked and Flight Lieut. Curtis drove one down which appeared to be out of control, while Flight Sub-Lieut. Manuel drove down another which he followed until he saw it crash.

On the same day, Flight Sub-Lieuts. Alexander and Maund attacked a two-seater and drove it down out of control, while Flight Sub-Lieut. Hall attacked a Scout which had been driven down by a D.H. 5 and shot it down out of control.

Casualties.—*Killed.*—Acting Flight Lieut. G. L. Trapp, 12.11.17.

Hostile Machines driven down out of control - - - 6
,, ,, destroyed - - - - - - 2

SUMMARY.

Hostile Machines driven down out of control - - - 11
,, ,, destroyed - - - - - - 9

Total - - - - 20

EASTERN MEDITERRANEAN STATION.

(Compiled from Weekly Reports Nos. 83 and 84, dating from 15th-29th October inclusive.)

Remarks.—The interesting feature of the operations carried out during this period is the bombing of Chanak during the time as indicated by intercepted W/T messages, that the German Emperor was present there. It was considered that although the chances of doing any harm to the Kaiser or his staff were remote, bombs dropped on the town during the night would result in his instant departure, which under such circumstances might considerably increase the already reported bad feeling between the Germans and the Turks, and much of the glamour of his visit would be obliterated by a bomb attack immediately on his arrival. (*See* following report of attack.)

Another feature of particular interest is the success obtained by the regular minefield reconnaisance from Stavros mentioned in this and the two preceding operation reports, which resulted in an entire minefield having been swept. It is believed that this is the first instance of aircraft leading sweepers to the exact position of each remaining mine, and indicating to them by W/T the precise spot where indicator buoys should be placed.

New Aerodromes.—"B" Squadron evacuated Thermi Air Station, and moved to the new Air Station at Kalloni. A separate report dealing with the removal is being prepared, but has not yet come to hand (*see* Kalloni Air Station, Mitylene).

"C" Squadron has removed to the new Imbros Aerodrome at Gliki, which is on the N.E. side of the island, and is now being used instead of Kephalo.

Weather.—Broken weather with frequent rain storms, strong winds and low clouds have been experienced through the Aegean during the latter half of the period under review, and has interfered with flying at all stations.

BOMB ATTACKS ON CHANAK.

October 17th-18th.

The German Emperor who had been at Sofia, was reported in the enemy W/T press as having arrived at Constantinople on 15th October. W/T messages subsequently intercepted at R.N.A.S. Headquarters, Mudros, indicated that the Kaiser had proceeded to Chanak on 17th October. Abnormal activity on the part of the enemy in the Dardanelles and elaborate precautions for reporting movements of British aircraft all tended to confirm the genuineness of the report.

Accordingly bomb attacks on Chanak were arranged to be undertaken on the night of 17th and morning of 18th October.

The weather was most unfavourable for a 70 mile night flight over the sea. The force of the wind was "6," *i.e.*, about 25 m.p.h. on the ground. The night very dark, and a few low fast scudding clouds and no moon. It was realised that the operation was attended with considerable risk.

Accordingly two Henry Farmans left Marsh Aerodrome, one piloted by Flight Sub-Lieut. Wild, with Observer Sub-Lieut. Piper as observer, the other with Flight Sub-Lieut. Parker, with Leading Mechanic Goodwillie as gunlayer.

After three-quarters of an hour the first Henry Farman returned to Marsh, the pilot having been quite unable to fix himself in the existing weather conditions.

The pilot of the second Henri Farman was also unable to find his way to the Peninsula in the wind, low clouds, and the darkness, and having dropped his bombs, landed in 5 feet of water off Cape Omanez at Thasos after a two hours flight, both pilot and observer being unhurt. This machine has been salved.

Meanwhile two B.E. 2 E's, piloted by Flight Lieut. Waistell and Flight Sub-Lieut. Grigson, had left Imbros at 0045.

Flight Sub-Lieut. Grigson was also unable to find Chanak owing to darkness, so dropped his bombs on the peninsula and returned to Imbros at 0150.

Flight Lieut. Waistell, having been at Imbros for some time and having done a considerable amount of night flying over the peninsula, including successful night raids on Chanak, was able to reach his objective. He dropped 128 lbs. of bombs on the town.

On returning to Imbros, however, he hit the side of a mountain when 2,000 feet up on his glide to the aerodrome, being unable to see it on account of the darkness, and the machine caught fire on crashing. The pilot, although severely injured about the face and knee, was able to climb out of the machine, and was eventually found next morning and brought back to the aerodrome by a Greek shepherd, arriving there at 1000, having ridden 10 miles over extremely rough country on a donkey, with a badly lacerated knee.

As no information had been received by dawn of the Henri Farman, which had not returned to Mudros, or the B.E., which had not landed at Imbros Aerodrome, two seaplanes were sent out from "Ark Royal" at dawn to search triangle Imbros–Mudros–Tenedos.

At dawn on 18th the attack on Chanak was resumed, the following machines participating in the raid :—

Three Sopwith bombers, piloted by Lieut.-Commander Moraitinis, Flight Lieut. Wincott, and Flight Sub-Lieut. Hosking, and two De Haviland 4's, piloted by Flight Lieuts. Mellings and Marlowe, being escorted by two "Camels," piloted by Flight Lieut. Donald and Flight Sub-Lieut. Mackenzie.

Sixteen 65-lb. bombs were dropped by these machines, eight of which were observed to burst in the town, one large building was destroyed, and considerable damage was inflicted on small houses in the south part of the town; the remaining bombs were not observed owing to intervening clouds obscuring the view.

Heavy anti-aircraft fire was encountered especially over Chanak, but all machines returned safely to Mudros, three machines landing at Imbros *en route*.

MUDROS AIR STATION.

October 15th–21st.

Anti-Submarine and Mine Patrols.—On the morning of the 15th, one aeroplane patrolled to the south of Lemnos and searched for mines in the swept channel. On the 16th a seaplane searched for mines in the swept channel and two aeroplanes patrolled—one an area north and north-west of Lemnos as far as Athos, and one an area east of Lemnos and Strati.

On the night of the 17th, two Henri Farmans left to bomb Chanak, and on the morning of the 18th two De Haviland 4's, three Sopwith Bombers and two "Camels" dropped bombs on Chanak. (*See* Attack on Chanak.)

At dawn on the 18th, two seaplanes searched the triangle, Lemnos–Imbros–Tenedos, for the missing Henri Farman, the report of whose landing at Thasos was not received till after the seaplanes had started.

At dawn on the 19th a seaplane patrolled to Cape Drepano, and on return, landed three times and worked hydrophone, but without hearing anything on each occasion. In the afternoon, hydrophone machine carried out practice to the west of Lemnos.

On the 20th one aeroplane patrolled round the north side of Lemnos to a point midway between Athos and Thasos, another aeroplane patrolled to a point between Strati and Skyros, a seaplane patrolled to Piperi, then north to Cape Drepano and back to Lemnos. Machine landed between Cape Drepano and Mudros, and worked hydrophone.

No submarines or mines were sighted by aircraft during the week.

October 22nd–29th.

Anti-Submarine Patrols.—On receipt of the information that a submarine had been sighted off Suvla and that Gliki Air Station was unfit for use, two seaplanes, a Short and Hamble Baby as escort, were sent from Mudros to Kusu Bay to report on S.O. Second D.S. for orders.

The Short in landing burst her tail float, and a second Short seaplane was despatched from Mudros with another tail float.

This second Short returned later in the day, carrying out a submarine reconnaissance *en route.*

The Hamble Baby was also sent back, starting at 1740 L.T., 10 minutes after sunset, a stiff southerly breeze blowing at the time. It was clear that she could not arrive in daylight, and accordingly "Ark Royal" was directed to show her searchlights vertically in order to direct the seaplane.

As the seaplane did not arrive, but Very's lights were reported off Cape Plaka at 2125, a Henri Farman was despatched from Marsh Aerodrome, which located the seaplane close inshore near Petza Point. A party was then sent from Marsh, which succeeded in beaching and securing the seaplane before dawn.

The other Short Seaplane endeavoured to carry out a reconnaissance from Kusu Bay, but failed to rise in time, and was damaged through fouling Kusu Nets. She was subsequently taken on board H.M.S. "Edgar," where she remains awaiting the arrival of a repair party from Mudros.

No further operations have been carried out during the week.

THASOS AIR STATION.

"A" Squadron and "Z" (Greek) Squadron.

October 15th–21st.

Anti-Submarine Patrols.—On 15th October two submarine patrols of line Plati–Cape Nikita (Athos Peninsula) were carried out, and on 16th a local submarine patrol off Thasos Island and a submarine patrol of line Thasos Island—Mount Athos.

On the 17th a hostile machine was chased by Sopwith Fighter, our machine landed in the sea close to aerodrome, but damage was slight. No detailed report has yet been received.

On the 18th, at 0140, H. Farman No. 9148, Pilot Flight Sub.-Lieut. Parker, Gunlayer L. M. Goodwillie, which had taken part in the operations at Chanak from Mudros, landed in the sea in one fathom of water off Cape Omanez (the northernmost point of Thasos). Occupants were unhurt, and parts of the machine were salved. A submarine patrol to Mount Athos was also undertaken.

On the 19th a local submarine patrol was made, also one to Mount Athos, a large patch of oil was observed near Limanaria (south-west of Thasos Island). Two bombs were dropped on this patch, but no bubbles were observed.

On the 20th a submarine patrol round Thasos Island and a submarine patrol to Mount Athos were carried out.

Beyond the oil patch seen on the 19th, nothing of importance was observed on the submarine patrols during the week.

October 22nd–29th.

Anti-Submarine Patrols and Mine Reconnaissances.—No flying took place until 26th October, when "Z" Squadron made patrols in the vicinity of Thasos.

On the 27th October two submarine and mine reconnaissances were made over the area between Thasos and the Akte Peninsula, no submarine was sighted, but five mines were located 10 miles east of Eleuthera Island.

Bomb Attack on Drama.—On the same day a machine from "Z" Squadron delivered a bomb attack on Drama. Details of these operations have not yet been received, but will be incorporated in next week's report.

STAVROS AIR STATION.

"D" SQUADRON.

October 15th–21st.

Mine Patrols and Reconnaissance.—On the morning of the 14th October, a patrol of the minefield reported in W.O.R's., Nos. 81 and 82 was attempted, but abandoned, due to weather. A machine again proceeded in the afternoon, but did not observe any further mines. A reconnaissance of the Neohori front was carried out, a new communication trench between redoubts at 60 C 5 and 60 D S being reported. Clouds obscured the greater part of the front line.

On the 15th a mine patrol on a line Isle of Kafkanas-Cape Deuthero was carried out, no mines being observed. A reconnaissance machine escorted by two Sopwith "Pups" carried out a thorough reconnaissance of Angista Valley. A new camp one mile north of the camp $2\frac{1}{2}$ miles W.N.W. of Razolivos was discovered, consisting of dug outs capable of holding about 200 men. Rolling stock on the railway and movements appeared normal on the return; 25 photographs of front line area were taken. Anti-aircraft fire was observed over Stavros, but the hostile machine was not sighted.

On the 16th the remaining mine of the minefield was discovered by the morning mine patrol machine, and a motor launch was directed to its position by W/T. The motor launch on being informed it was over the mine was ordered to stop by W/T from the machine, and the position was buoyed.

One machine carried out hostile aircraft patrol; the enemy was not, however, seen.

Photographic Reconnaissance.—A front line photographic reconnaissance was carried out on the 18th, and an enemy battery, N. 32, was reported to be severely damaged.

Weather conditions prevented further work on the 19th and 20th October.

October 22nd–29th.

Mine Patrol.—A reconnaissance of the Gulf of Ruphini for mines was made during a lull in the bad weather on 24th October.

On 26th October a photographic reconnaissance of the enemy front line was attempted, but proved abortive owing to low cloud and rain.

This was again attempted on 27th, but met with no better success.

Reconnaissance.—On the same day an escorted reconnaissance of the enemy lines of communication up the Angista Valley showed no important change or movement.

Mine Patrol.—One machine also reconnoitred the Gulf of Ruphini for mines and observed objects, probably mines, but which could with absolute certainty be identified as a minefield. This was reported, and later in the day motor launches were guided to the position.

KALLONI AIR STATION (MITYLENE).

"B" SQUADRON.

October 15th–21st.

Enemy 4·1-inch gun attack on Thermi Aerodrome.—As was briefly reported in W.O.R. No. 82, while Thermi Air Station was being evacuated on 9th October, the enemy opened fire from Tuz Burnu on Thermi Aerodrome. Some 250 to 300 shells were fired, and, so far as has been ascertained at present, all were from 4·1-inch guns; at least 90 per cent. of the shell being armour piercing, which had an angle of descent of rather over 30°, and buried themselves so deeply in the ground that those which detonated did little more than break the surface. Short bursts of impact fused H.E. were also fired, the firing lasting until 11th inst., after which attention was directed to Gymno Island.

A matter of considerable interest was the accuracy of guns of this calibre firing at 16,000 yards and the fact that those objectives which were in close proximity to residential property were not shelled while those which stood apart received severe and accurate attention. A number of successive shells pierced one Bessoneau, and a Dorling hut were also hit.

A separate report on the evacuation of Thermi is being prepared. All that is necessary to say here is that working parties from H.M.S. "Forward" energetically assisted during the evacuation, while H.M.S. "Lowestoft" hurried on the preparation of Kalloni Air Station so that within a week it was ready for occupation, and all air service gear and personnel were transferred there by 16th October.

Reconnaissance.—One machine was sent up from Kalloni on 14th October to reconnoitre the area around Tuz Burnu and Aivalik as look outs on Gymno Island reported a concentration of troops there, the inference being that a raid was contemplated either on Gymno or on Thermi. No unusual enemy activity was seen on the reconnaissance and no raid has as yet materialised.

October 22nd–29th.

No service flying has been undertaken, but the opportunity has been taken of pressing on the completion of the Air Station with all despatch.

GLIKI AIR STATION (IMBROS).

"C" SQUADRON.

October 15th–21st.

Reconnaissance and Photography. — Weather prevented flying on the 14th October. A photographic reconnaissance of the coast from Cape Baba (S. of Tenedos) northwards to Kum Kale was carried out on the 15th. The photographic machine was escorted by the Sopwith "Pup" stationed at Tenedos. A reconnaissance of the Straits reported a 800-ton ship in the Ak Bashi Limen.

Photography.—Another flight was made to photograph the new Imbros Aerodrome at Gliki, which is on the N.E. side of the Island and is now being used in lieu of Kephalo.

Anti-Submarine Patrol.—On the 16th two machines patrolled at dawn from Gliki to the N.E. of Samothraki in search of submarines. On report of approach of hostile machines, a machine went up and proceeded as far as Gaba Teke, but the enemy was not sighted. A reconnaissance of the Straits reported that the 800-ton ship seen on previous day had left the Straits. In the evening a submarine patrol from N.E. of Imbros to Mudros and back was carried out.

Reconnaissance and Photography.—On the 17th afternoon reconnaissance of Straits reported one T.B. off N.E. of Galata steering south; photographs were again taken of Gliki Aerodrome. Two B.E. 2 E.'s from Imbros took part in the night operations against Chanak. (*See* attack on Chanak.)

A submarine patrol was attempted at dawn on the 18th, but had to be abandoned owing to very strong N.E. wind.

On the 19th a photographic reconnaissance was carried out, intense anti-aircraft fire being encountered over Chanak.

Anti-Submarine Patrol and Photography.—On the 20th two machines patrolled to the north and east of Samothraki for submarines. A reconnaissance reported buildings resembling a new aerodrome near Damler—50 photographs taken of this area —and photographs of Chanak were taken by another machine. A hostile machine was pursued, but no details have as yet been received.

October 22nd–29th.

At 0800 on 24th October a submarine was reported off Suvla, but in a later amplifying report this was considered third class information. H.M.S. "Fury," however, struck something with her Paravanes subsequently six miles west of the reported position. Two machines attempted to get off from Gliki Aerodrome, but the ground was sodden and they failed to rise.

As is detailed later, seaplanes from Mudros were accordingly sent to Kusu Bay to undertake any reconnaissance and offensive action required.

Reconnaissance.—No flying was possible during the remainder of the week until 27th when during a bright interval a reconnaissance of the Dardanelles was made which disclosed the presence of only the usual small shipping.

KASSANDRA AIRSHIP STATION.

October 15th–21st.

The envelope of the airship was in such a dangerous state that it required to be deflated at the end of last week, and until another is received from England no airship work can be undertaken from this station.

October 22nd–29th.

No airship is yet available for duty.

SUDA BAY SEAPLANE STATION.

October 15th–21st.

Anti-Submarine Patrols.—Submarine patrols were carried out on the 15th, 16th, 17th 0000 and 1200 again on the 18th

0000 and 1200 and the morning of the 19th and 20th. Nothing of importance is reported except on 15th October, when a hostile submarine having been reported in position 20 miles N. by E. of Suda Bay, Short 9764 was sent out on an offensive patrol. In the vicinity of position indicated the Greek s.s. "Peleponnesus," which had been unsuccessfully attacked by submarine, was observed being escorted by H.M.S. "Reindeer" and H.M.S. "Renard." The seaplane circled round, and after having called the attention of the destroyer, by means of Very's lights, to rafts carrying passengers, landed near the waterlogged boat, about which some 12 bodies were floating, in order to assist in rescue work and to obtain orders from the destroyer by visual. Upon receipt of orders the seaplane patrolled to westward of "Reindeer" for nearly two hours, when owing to shortage of petrol the pilot was forced to return to the base.

October 22nd–29th.

Anti-Submarine Patrols.—Only on the mornings of the 21st and 25th October were patrols carried out. During the remainder of the week bad weather prevented the routine patrols of the approaches to Suda Bay.

PHALERUM SEAPLANE STATION.

October 15th–21st.

Work in training Greek pilots have been carried out regularly during the last fortnight. It is now possible to estimate which of the pilots are likely to make useful pilots, and those who do not show sufficient promise will be discarded.

EAST INDIES AND EGYPT.

H.M.S. "EMPRESS."

October 8th–12th.

Bomb Attack on Chikaldere Bridge.—H.M.S. "Empress" left Port Said at 0500 on October 8th, arriving about 10 miles south of Karatash Burnu at 0600 on October 9th.

To face page 24.

Bomb Attack on Chikaldere Bridge.
Direct hits with Four 16-lb. bombs (see page 24).

Seaplanes were then hoisted out in the following order :—

Short 8018, Pilot, Flight Sub-Lieut. M. C. Wood.
Short 1091, Pilot, Flight Sub-Lieut. H. de V. Leigh, Observer, Second Lieut. E. A. Newton.
Short 8021, Pilot, Flight Lieut. G. Stephens, Observer Captain W. R. Kempson.
Short 8091, Pilot, Flight Lieut. A. E. Popham.

A slight swell made it difficult for the machines to leave the water, and in two cases bombs had to be dropped in order to enable the machines to rise.

Short 8018, after some difficulty in getting off the water and being apparently unable to climb above 700–800 feet, was observed to drop some of his bombs, and then return and alight near the ship, when the remaining bombs exploded, blowing the machine to pieces, instantly killing the pilot, Flight Lieut. M. C. Wood. The body was recovered and buried in Lat. 36° 12", 35° 8", the burial service being read, and all available officers and members of the crew being present. In consequence of this accident, Short machine 1091, which had been detailed to accompany 8018, returned to the ship, and after patrolling for submarines, while the wreckage of 8018 was being examined, was hoisted in at 0830.

The remaining two machines reached Chikaldere Bridge at 0741 and 0748 respectively, and proceeded to bomb the bridge, on which direct hits were made with two 65-lb. and nine 16-lb. bombs. The damage, however, was slight, and it is thought that most of the bombs fell through the bridge, which is open metal work and open sleepers, and exploded in the water. The railway line at the south end of the bridge was damaged. Considerable and accurate rifle fire was experienced, also shrapnel fire, the majority of the latter being very inaccurate, apparently from field guns, one of which was located and bombed.

It is probable that one anti-aircraft gun was in action, as some good shooting was made against 8019 when flying at about 4,000 feet and west of the bridge, but this gun was not located.

Short 8021 was followed by shrapnel fire from the village of Kurt Kalak on the return journey.

Enemy troops and a company of Camel Corps were engaged with Lewis gun fire and dispersed. Short 8019 returned to the ship at 0848, followed by 8021 at 0920, both being hit in several places by rifle fire.

The machines having been hoisted in, H.M.S. "Empress" proceeded to Famagusta to coal and re-fit, the machines arriving there at 1800.

On October 10th a satisfactory test was carried out with 8021, but 8019 was found unfit for further use, several sections of the radiators being wrecked.

At 1730 H.M.S. "Empress" left Famagusta and proceeded to rendezvous 10 miles south-west of Karatash Burnu, arriving there at 0600 on October 11th.

At 0629 "8021" was hoisted out (Pilot, Flight Commander Clemson, Observer, Second Lieut. E. A. Newton, A.S.C.) and after some difficulty, rose from the water and flew inland.

At 0638 "1091" was hoisted out (Pilot, Flight Lieut. H. de V. Leigh, Observer, Captain W. R. Kempson, R.F.A.).

The order for both machines was to proceed in company to Adana and bomb the locomotive shed.

It was found impossible at first to start up 1091; this was finally done at 0703, and the seaplane rose to 1,000 feet, but was forced to descend owing to engine trouble, and was hoisted in.

The engine trouble was located and repaired, and as 8021 did not return, 1091 was again hoisted out at 0918 to fly inland in the direction of Adana to search for the missing seaplane, Leading Mechanic Prince taking the place of Captain Kempson, as observer. After rising to 1,000 feet, 1091 was again forced to descend, with engine trouble; as this was impossible to repair immediately, no further flight could be made.

H.M.S. "Empress" and escort patrolled along the line of coast until 1200, but 8021 was not sighted, and no news has been received of it.

Further operations being impossible, H.M.S. "Empress" proceeded to Port Said, arriving there at 1200 on 12th October.

The French destroyers "Arbalete" and "Hache" provided a very efficient escort and rendered every assistance.

BRITISH ADRIATIC SQUADRON.

No. 6 WING, R.N.A.S., OTRANTO.

(*Period 1st to 15th November*)

ANTI-SUBMARINE OPERATIONS.

Remarks.—The weather during the early part of the week was too bad for flying, but during the latter part of the week, a regular patrol has been carried out morning and evening to the northward, to search for possible raiding ships or submarines.

November 3rd.

At 1145 a submarine was reported by the Italian and R.N.A.S. look-out station at Palascia 18 miles, 120 degrees from Cape Otranto, on the surface, steering north.

An aeroplane left and flew straight to the spot where the submarine had been reported.

The submarine was sighted when six miles distant from the aeroplane and dived when the aeroplane was about 1½ miles away. From the wash it appears that the submarine altered course to N.N.W. on submerging. The aeroplane then warned some drifters, which were operating six miles south of where the submarine had submerged, of its presence.

A British seaplane and some Italian seaplanes were sent out and patrolled the area where the submarine had submerged from 1230 to 1530, but nothing further was seen of the submarine.

November 7th.

On the report from Saseno look-out station that a submarine had been sighted, an aeroplane was immediately despatched, and found the submarine on the surface steering south-east.

As the aeroplane approached, the submarine prepared to dive, and two 65-lb. bombs were dropped, one of which fell 50 feet, and the other 30 feet from the submarine on the port quarter.

The aeroplane then circled round the submarine, the conning tower of which was still visible, and two trays of ammunition were fired with the Lewis gun, many of the tracer shots being seen to hit the conning tower before the submarine completely disappeared.

Seaplanes were sent out from both the British and Italian seaplane bases, and a constant watch was kept of the area until dark.

At 1510 a patch of oil, and then a periscope were seen by an Italian pilot.

The submarine was about 200 feet long; no gun or other details were observed.

It is interesting to note that a well-known submarine commander has stated that in his opinion machine-gun fire can be used very effectively against submarines, as, if the lenses of the periscopes were broken, the submarine would be blind.

There was no flying on the 8th, 12th and 13th of November owing to stormy weather. On the other days routine patrols were carried out.

There has been considerably less activity of surface craft working in the Lower Adriatic this week compared with last week, which was exceptional.

CAPE STATION.

R.N.A.S. SUB-STATION, LINDI.

(*August 23rd to September 27th*, 1917).

Remarks.—During this period, flights for the purposes of bombing, spotting, reconnaissance, and photography, have been carried out almost daily by R.N.A.S. aeroplanes co-operating with the military.

In all, a total of 34 flights have been made.

August 23rd.

A bombing and reconnaissance flight was carried out by Aeroplane 8703 over the enemy positions at Nurunyu during which one 65-lb. and one 16-lb. (H.E.) bombs were dropped on trees in the north-east part of the position. While lining up to drop bombs from 1,400 feet the aeroplane was hit by machine gun fire, one bullet going through both planes about two feet from the nacelle. At the same time aeroplane 8522 attacked the enemy force encamped at Kilosa about one mile west of Nurunyu and dropped one 65-lb. and one 16-lb. H.E. bombs, and after the pilot had climbed to 2,000 feet 500 darts were also dropped. All bombs were seen to reach the objectives, but no movement was observed.

Photos were taken of the camp by aeroplane 8703, during which time the machine was hit by rifle fire.

August 25th.

Aeroplane 8703 carried out a spotting flight over Nurunyu for the howitzer and 13-pounder gun. Owing to the military W/T station failing to receive the W/T signals from the aeroplane, only one shot was fired, which fell 200 yards over the target. The machine then returned to the aerodrome.

August 27th.

Aeroplane 8522 proceeded to Nurunyu to spot for the howitzer and 13-pounder gun. The first shell burst 100 yards over Z target, and the next one hit. After reporting this by W/T the aeroplane headed for Kilosa giving "open fire" en route, and a direct hit was made with the fourth shot. The 13-pounder was then spotted for and obtained a hit on Z target with her second shot, and with a first on Kilosa.

August 29th

Aeroplane 8703 carried out a spotting flight over Kilosa for the howitzer, and a direct hit was scored with the second shot.

The "ready to observe for Z target" was then sent, and here also only one correction was needed.

Owing to low clouds, observation was difficult.

August 31st.

A spotting flight was carried out over Nurunyu for the 4-inch gun fire, and after two corrections a direct hit scored on the Red House at Mtua. Great difficulty was experienced in seeing the target owing to low clouds, and the aeroplane was fired on while making a circuit.

September 3rd.

A spotting flight was carried out over Mtua for the 4-inch gun by Aeroplane 8703. All the shots fell short, the last one bursting near some trenches in the porters camp, but no movement was observed.

September 4th.

Aeroplane 8703 carried out a spotting flight over Mtua for the 4-inch gun, and observed the first and second shots to fall in entrenched positions. The third shot scored a direct hit on the porters camp.

After this only one other shell was observed; this fell 700 yards over the trenches situated on the bank of the Nongo stream.

September 8th.

A spotting flight was carried out over the enemy gun position at Mtua by Aeroplane 8701.

The first shell exploded 1,000 yards short of the presumed gun position, but the next shot was a direct hit.

While spotting operations were being carried out the aeroplane was heavily fired on by machine-gun fire from two positions in the vicinity of the target.

This was signalled by W/T, and after the shell following this signal had exploded no further hostile fire was experienced.

September 8th.

A bombing and reconnaissance flight was carried out over the Mtua area by Aeroplane 8522, during which one 16-lb. bomb was released on the porters' camp, and a 65-lb. bomb on the enemy position north-west of the junction of Old Mandawa road and Massassi road. Darts were dropped on the porters' camp on recrossing it with the wind, but no movement was seen.

September 9th.

A spotting flight was carried out for the 4-inch gun on to the enemy 4·1-inch gun position by Aeroplane 8703. The first shell exploded near the trenches between Longa and Nongo streams. All shells following this fell near the target until a hit was obtained.

A bombing flight was carried out by Aeroplane 8522 on the enemy gun positions south-west of Mtua. Clouds were low, and the air was bumpy, rendering accurate bombing uncertain. Two bombs were dropped at the target, then the aeroplane turned and released darts over the position. A machine gun opened fire on the aeroplane when it was passing over the junction of the path from Mtua buildings and old Mandawa road, but the position of it was not observed.

Aeroplane 8701 also carried out a bomb attack on the same objective, and dropped four bombs in a line, which were observed to explode in the vicinity of the target; 500 darts were also dropped here, but no enemy movement was observed.

September 10th.

Aeroplane 8701 carried out a bomb attack on buildings at Mtua, on which two 16-lb. bombs were dropped, both scoring direct hits; 500 darts were also dropped, but no enemy movements were observed.

September 11th.

Aeroplane 8522 carried out a photographic reconnaissance over Mtua, and succeeded in taking several photographs for mapping purposes, despite unfavourable weather conditions.

September 12th.

A spotting and photographic flight was carried out by aeroplane 8701, and several photographs were obtained of the Lower Mossassi Road and around Kilosa Camp.

When approaching Nurunyu on the return journey a shell burst was observed in a large clump of trees near road A about 1,000 yards from the junction of road A and the trolley line. A W/T signal was sent reporting this, and after three minutes a second burst was observed in the same place.

As the wind was becoming very gusty, the machine was headed for the aerodrome, and was fired on by an anti-aircraft gun and machine gun when over F. 15 A. No movement of enemy was observed.

September 13th.

Aeroplane 8522 carried out a spotting flight for the howitzer over Nurunyu, and only small corrections were needed before a hit was obtained.

The firing at the second target was then commenced, all shells falling right until the O.K. was given; the last two shells fired exploded in the one man trenches near the bend in the road.

One 65-lb. bomb was dropped in a clump of trees near the trolley near the S.W. of the Kilosa position.

The aeroplane was fired on by anti-aircraft fire before returning to the base.

September 14th.

Aeroplane 8701 carried out a bombing and reconnaissance flight over the Nurunyu and Mtua area, and bombs and darts were released over the trenches by Nongo Stream, both bombs bursting in an effective area.

September 15th.

A spotting flight for the 4-inch gun on the enemy camp and new 4·1 gun position at Mtua was carried out by aeroplane 8703. Owing to low clouds spotting was very difficult, but a hit was obtained with the sixth shot. Before returning to the Base, the aeroplane dropped one 65-lb. bomb on the enemy camp scoring a direct hit.

September 17th.

Aeroplane 8703 carried out a spotting flight on the enemy camp and supposed new position of the 4·1 gun at Mtua.

A hit was obtained with the sixth shell and "O.K." was given; after this all firing was effective.

The aeroplane was fired on by machine guns at the gun position.

Aeroplane 8522 made a flight with Captain Boileau, O.C. (Topographical) as observer for the purpose of observing the country between Mtua and Mtama for map making.

A satisfactory flight was made and all the information required was obtained.

September 19th.

Aeroplane 8703 carried out a flight over Mtua-Likanga with General O'Grady as observer.

A successful flight was made and the General obtained all the information he required.

Aeroplane 8522 carried out a spotting flight tor the 4-inch gun on the enemy 4·1 gun position as given by Captain Dooner, I.D. The first shot fell about 300 yards short of the position, but all firing after then fell in an effective area, causing movement. Two parties of men were seen to make for cover.

Towards the end of the flight difficulty was experienced in spotting owing to low clouds and the pilot was forced to descend to 1,500 feet to carry on.

September 20th.

Aeroplane 8703 carried out a spotting flight for the 4-inch gun on to the enemy 4·1 gun position. A hit was scored with the third shot, the preceding shots falling very close. All shots after these fell in an effective area.

While over the target the aeroplane was fired on by anti-aircraft with H.E. shell, but no damage was sustained.

September 24th–27th.

On and between the above dates flights were carried out daily for the purpose of reconnaissance to locate and report on the position of our attacking troops, and to obtain information required by Headquarters.

Weather conditions made observation difficult, but a good deal of useful information was obtained.

ROYAL FLYING CORPS COMMUNIQUÉS.

ROYAL FLYING CORPS COMMUNIQUÉ—No. 111.

During the period under review (23rd to 29th October, inclusive) the weather for the most part was unfavourable for much aerial work owing to mist, thick haze, and clouds. In spite of this, large enemy formations were occasionally encountered well east of the lines. We have brought down 24 enemy machines, and have driven down 13 out of control. Two hundred and fifty-two hostile batteries have been engaged for destruction, and 779 zone calls sent. A total of 38,834 rounds were fired at ground targets, and 1,600 photographs taken. Approximately $32\frac{1}{4}$ tons of bombs have been dropped, with good results.

Correction.—In Royal Flying Corps Communiqué No. 110, paragraph 9 on page 5 should be deleted, and the following substituted :—A patrol of eight machines of No. 29 Squadron attacked seven enemy two-seaters, one of which was brought down and another driven down out of control by Second Lieut. Payne, and one each driven down out of control by Second Lieuts. J. Leach and C. Hamilton.

October 3rd.

Rain and mist prevented much flying being done.

One contact patrol and one counter-attack patrol were carried out by No. 7 Squadron, and one contact patrol by No. 9 Squadron. Eighteen photographs were taken and 150 rounds fired into the enemy's trenches.

Artillery Co-operation.—Fifteen hostile batteries were engaged for destruction, and three neutralised with aeroplane observation; five gun-pits were damaged, five explosions and two fires caused. Thirty-four active hostile batteries were reported by zone call.

The 342nd Siege Battery, with observation by Lieutenant Higham, of the detached flight of No. 5 Squadron, badly damaged two pits of a hostile battery position.

The 79th Siege Battery, with observation by Lieutenant Morris of the same flight, damaged one pit of a hostile battery position and caused two large explosions.

On the 22nd 16 targets were registered by balloons and 22 hostile batteries located; of these, balloons of the Fifth Brigade registered seven targets and located 20 hostile batteries.

Bombing.—During the night of the 22nd/23rd $2\frac{1}{2}$ tons of bombs were dropped as follows :—

Ninth Wing.—No. 101 Squadron dropped four 112-lb. and eight 25-lb. bombs on Lichtervelde Aerodrome, four 112-lb. bombs on Moorsele Aerodrome, four 112-lb. bombs on Rumbeke Aerodrome, two 112-lb. bombs on Ingelmunster Aerodrome (one bomb hit the aerodrome, the other just missed a train on the railway line in the vicinity), one 230-lb. bomb on Roulers.

No. 102 Squadron dropped one 230-lb. bomb and two 112-lb. bombs on Marcke Aerodrome, two 112-lbs. bombs on Bissighem Aerodrome, two 112-lb. bombs on Cuerne Aerodrome, two 112-lb. bombs on Ingelmunster Aerodrome, eight 25-lb. bombs on an aerodrome near Tourcoing, two 112-lb. bombs on Ledeghem, three 230-lb., eight 112-lb., and eight 25-lb. bombs on Courtrai Railway Station (one of the 230-lb. bombs hit the rear portion of a moving train, which burst into flames).

During the day twelve 25-lb. bombs were dropped on various targets.

Flight Commander Munday, Naval Squadron No. 8, flew out to Moncheaux Aerodrome just after it was dark, and dropped four 25-lb. bombs on the sheds, which were lit up. He then fired several bursts from a height of 50 feet into the hangars, which were by this time in darkness. On his way back he fired a burst into the Cambrai Railway Station.

Honours and Awards.

Bar to the Military Cross.—Captain H. G. E. Luchford, M.C. Lieutenant V. R. S. White, M.C.

Military Medal.—No. 78563 First Air Mechanic A. G. Whitehouse.

October 24th.

Weather.—Fine early, afterwards thick clouds with bright intervals.

Two reconnaissances were carried out by the corps squadrons of the Second Brigade, one trench reconnaissance by the Fourth Brigade, and one counter-attack patrol by the Fifth Brigade.

A total of 374 photographs were taken, and 2,100 rounds fired at ground targets, including a party of 200 infantry, which were engaged by Second Lieut. E. Peverell, No. 70 Squadron, and scattered in all directions.

Artillery Co-operation.—Sixty-seven hostile batteries were successfully engaged for destruction and nine neutralised with aeroplane observation; six gun-pits were destroyed, 29 damaged, 27 explosions and 23 fires caused.

One hundred and ninety-eight hostile active batteries were reported by zone call, 49 of which were sent down by pilots of the Fifth Brigade.

On the 23rd balloons of the Second Army registered three targets.

All four gun-pits in a hostile battery position were damaged and five explosions caused by the 333rd Siege Battery, with observation by Lieutenant Barrinton, No. 4 Squadron.

Four pits in another hostile battery were damaged by the 301st Siege Battery, with observation by Lieutenants Croft and Settle, No. 12 Squadron.

Captain Stevenson and Lieutenant Randall, No. 12 Squadron, during a patrol which lasted 3 hours and 15 minutes, sent down the GF call on some stationary mechanical transport. Although the M.T. when engaged moved on, direct hits were obtained, causing a dense column of smoke lasting several minutes.

Enemy Aircraft.— Enemy aircraft activity varied throughout the day, although it was never above normal.

Lieutenant J. Womersley, No. 43 Squadron, attacked a two-seater Aviatik over Lens. He continued firing at it till within 800 feet of the ground, when it went down completely out of control. This wrs confirmed by anti-aircraft observers.

Captain P. Fullard, No. 1 Squadron, drove an enemy two-seater down out of control from 2,000 feet after firing 100 rounds into it at a range of 10 yards.

Second Lieut. T. Williams, No. 45 Squadron, whilst on patrol with four others, was attacked from behind by one of seven Albatross Scouts. He made a sharp turn, placing himself behind the enemy machine, and fired 150 rounds into the cockpit at close range. The enemy machine went down in a slow spin and crashed.

Flight Sub-Lieut. S. Rosevear, Naval Squadron No. 1, fired 100 rounds into an enemy machine which was attacking one of our triplanes. The enemy aircraft turned over, caught fire, and crashed near Comines.

Flight Lieut. S. Kinkhead, Naval Squadron No. 1, fired 300 rounds at point-blank range into an enemy two-seater, which dived vertically for 2,000 feet and crashed after the left-hand planes had broken off.

A patrol of No. 19 Squadron encountered nine Albatross Scouts over Menin. Three of these were driven down out of control by Captain J. Leacroft, Captain Huskinson, and Lieutenant Bryson.

Six enemy machines were encountered by a patrol of No. 48 Squadron. One of these, which dived on the tail of the machine of Second Lieut. H. Jenkins and First Air Mechanic E. Dunford, was shot down in flames.

Second Lieut. J. Payne, No. 29 Squadron, fired 50 rounds into one of five Albatross Scouts which he attacked over Roulers. The enemy scout got into a spin, turned over, and went down completely out of control.

Bombing.—During the day $3\frac{1}{2}$ tons of bombs were dropped as follows :—

First Brigade.—No. 18 Squadron dropped ten 112-lb. bombs on Carvin.

No. 35 Squadron dropped fifty-six 25-lb. bombs on Wingles and fifty-six 25-lb. bombs on Billy Montigny.

Ninth Wing.—No. 25 Squadron dropped twelve 112-lb. bombs on Abeelhoek Aerodrome.

Machines of the First Brigade dropped 26, Third Brigade 25, Fourth Brigade 10, and Fifth Brigade fourteen 25-lb. bombs on various targets.

Honours and Awards.

The Military Cross.—Captain H. C. W. Hill, Royal Flying (S.R.).

Military Medal.—7443 First Air Mechanic F. A. Biscoe, Royal Flying Corps. 8009 First Air Mechanic R. Johnson, Royal Flying Corps.

October 25th.

Weather.—Rain, with a violent gale. No service flying was done, except by the First and Second Brigades.

Four reconnaissances were carried out by army machines of the Second Brigade, and 650 rounds rounds were fired at ground targets by corps machines of the First and Second Brigades.

Artillery Co-operation.—Ten hostile batteries were engaged for destruction and four neutralised with aeroplane observation. One gun-pit was damaged, 10 explosions and seven fires caused. Machines of the First Brigade reported 23 active hostile batteries by zone call, and those of the Second Brigade 47. Four O.K.'s were obtained on a hostile battery position, and one explosion caused by the 176th Siege Battery with observation by Second-Lieut. G. McCoo, No. 53 Squadron.

From 1800 23rd to 1800 24th 79 targets were registered by balloons and 52 active hostile batteries located. Five of the shoots by balloons of the Second Brigade were in conjunction with aeroplanes. Second Lieuts. Daly and Pell, No. 23 Squadron, observed for four destructive shoots and two registrations.

Bombing.—The first night raid into Germany was carried out on the night of the 24th/25th by machines of the Naval Squadron "A" and No. 100 Squadron. Four and a half tons of bombs were dropped on the town and works at Burbach, north-west of Saarbrucken. Many fires were started and explosions caused. Over 50 bombs fell on the works and 20 in the town. A further $1\frac{1}{2}$ tons were dropped on the railway communications south-west of Saarbrucken, good results being obtained. One train was hit by a 230-lb. bomb and completely demolished.

October 26th.

In spite of the heavy rain which continued most of the day a good deal of low flying and artillery work was carried out.

Ten hostile batteries were engaged for destruction and nine neutralised with aeroplane observation; three gun-pits were destroyed, eight damaged, two explosions and four fires caused. One hundred and eighteen zone calls were sent down, 65 by machines of the Second Brigade, and 44 by those of the Fifth Brigade.

Three contact and four coumter-attack patrols were carried out by the Second Brigade, and five contact and four counter-attack patrols by the Fifth Brigade.

Captain Youdale and Second Lieut. Mott, No. 21 Squadron, while on contact patrol, were unable to get any reply to a call for flares, so went down to 200 feet and made a detailed report on the position of our troops. Their machine was shot down by rifle fire, but the report was handed in at Divisional Headquarters.

Captain Holmes and Lieutenant Tyler, No. 6 Squadron, flying at 1,000 feet, sent 25 N.F. calls in a flight of 2 hours 40 minutes. Four replies were observed and two fires caused in battery positions.

The following are descriptions of attacks on ground targets, during which a total of 8,780 rounds were fired:—

Second Lieut. Olivier, No. 19 Squadron, fired 300 rounds from 150 feet at troops marching along the Ypres–Gheluwe road, and afterwards attacked a two-seater enemy machine, which he shot down out of control.

Lieutenant Jennings, also of No. 19 Squadron, fired 70 rounds from 600 feet at machine guns, which were silenced.

Second Lieuts. Montgomery and Frew, No. 45 Squadron, fired 700 rounds from 500 feet at troops who were loading wagons from railway trucks, and the horses of the wagons bolted. They also fired at troops and transport on roads. The same two pilots subsequently saw two enemy aircraft, dived at the rear one, and after firing about 15 rounds each saw it fall out of control and crash. The other enemy machine succeeded in escaping.

Flight Lieut. Kinkead, Naval Squadron No. 1, fired 300 rounds from 500 feet at groups of men on roads, while Flight Sub-Lieut. Clapperton, of the same squadron, fired 250 rounds from 400 feet at men behind a house.

Flight Sub-Lieut. de Wilde, also of Naval Squadron No. 1, fired 50 rounds from 600 feet at troops in trenches.

Captain Roberts, No. 60 Squadron, fired 250 rounds from 200 feet at 12 pack mules, one of which fell, the remainder galloping away; 70 rounds were fired by Captain Hammersley, of the same squadron, from a height of 50 feet, at men who were repairing wire.

Lieut. Hewitt and Second Lieut. Drewitt, No. 23 Squadron, fired 1,150 rounds from 100 feet at parties of men on roads, while stationary mechanical transport were engaged by Lieutenant Trudeau and Second Lieut. Allen, of the same squadron, who fired 150 rounds from 300 feet. Captain McAlery, No. 23 Squadron, fired 30 rounds at transport from 500 feet.

Second Lieut. Payne, No. 29 Squadron, fired 50 rounds at two lorries and 15 men from 1,000 feet, while Second Lieut.

Hilton fired 40 rounds into an occupied trench, and then silenced two active hostile batteries.

One hundred rounds were fired from 100 feet by Second Lieut. Fenton, No. 98 Squadron, at transport on roads, as the result of which two lorries were set on fire.

Active hostile batteries were attacked by Second Lieut. Tyrrel, No. 32 Squadron, who fired 100 rounds from 1,000 feet.

Parties of hostile troops and various ground targets were attacked with good effect by Captain Mackay and Lieutenant Rothwell, Lieutenants Pearce and Gillie, and Captain Anderson and Lieut. Ashcroft, by whom a total of 1,700 rounds were fired from altitudes varying between 150 and 800 feet.

Lieutenants Hewat and de Pencier, No. 19 Squadron, attacked about 20 men on a road south of Moorslede, and then went to Moorslede. Seeing troops in the main street, they flew down it practically between the house-tops at a height not greater than 50 feet. Lieutenant de Pencier stated that he himself was lower than the church spire, and Lieutenant Hewat was below him. Lieutenant Hewat fired 200 rounds at these troops, and Lieutenant de Pencier 80 rounds, when he had a stoppage. Both pilots then flew to Gheluwe, and when just north of the town Lieutenant Hewat saw an enemy two-seater at 800 feet; he attacked it at very close range, and despite very heavy fire from the ground followed it down to 400 feet; while correcting a stoppage he was hit in the face by a bullet, and was badly cut over the eye and mouth and had his glasses broken, but returned safely to the aerodrome. The enemy aircraft was seen to be going down completely out of control when not more than 200 feet up.

Flight Sub-Lieut. Spence, Naval Squadron No. 1, attacked a two-seater enemy aircraft, which he shot down out of control.

Captain Barker, No. 28 Squadron, attacked a German scout west of Roulers, and after fighting for 15 minutes he secured a favourable position, from which he shot down the enemy machine in flames, and saw it crash. He was then attacked by another scout, and succeeded in destroying this one also.

Second Lieut. Williams, of No. 29 Squadron, and Second Lieut. Malik, No. 28 Squadron, each shot down an enemy machine out of control.

Bombing.—Nineteen 25-lb. bombs were dropped by machines of the Fourth Brigade, and six 25-lb. bombs by those of the Fifth Brigade, on various targets.

On the night of the 25th/26th No. 101 Squadron attacked Rumbeke and Abeele Aerodromes, thirteen 112-lb. bombs being dropped on the former place, where a direct hit was obtained on a group of hangars.

During the same night No. 102 Squadron attacked Bisseghem Aerodrome, on which one 230-lb., four 112-lb., and eight 25-lb. bombs were dropped. Machines of the same squadron also dropped five 112-lb. bombs on Marcke Aerodrome and two 230-lb. bombs on Menin.

On the 24th "A." Naval Squadron dropped fifty-four 112-lb. bombs on the Burbach Works, on the western side of Saarbrucken; all the bombs were observed to hit the objective. Sixteen 112-lb. bombs were also dropped on the town of Saarbrucken, where all the bombs again hit the objective.

On the night 24th/25th, No. 100 Squadron dropped twelve 230-lb. and twenty-three 25-lb. bombs on trains, railway junctions and stations and goods sidings on the railway line between Falkenberg and Saarbrucken. Bombs were seen to burst on buildings around Saarbrucken Station, others were observed to burst on the railway line, while one of the 230-lb. bombs dropped from 400 feet fell on a train near Wallersberg Junction. A parachute flare showed the front portion of the train to be considerably damaged as a result. The railway stations at St. Avold and Homberg are both believed to have been hit.

During this raid 1,200 rounds were fired at various targets.

October 27th.

Weather.—Fine all day.

Twelve reconnaissances were carried out, six of which were by machines of the Second Brigade. One contact patrol and one counter-attack patrol were carried out by the Second Brigade and two contact patrols by the Fifth Brigade.

A total of 848 photographs were taken, 254 of which were by machines of the Second Brigade.

Artillery Co-operation.—Ninety-five hostile batteries were engaged for destruction and 21 neutralised. Seven gun-pits were destroyed, 55 damaged, 35 explosions and 21 fires caused. A total of 218 zone calls were sent down, 83 of which were by machines of the Fifth Brigade.

Lieut. Reeder, No. 53 Squadron, observing for the 266th Siege Battery, remained in the air for 4 hours and 10 minutes, giving 115 observations on a hostile battery position.

Lieutenant Scaramanga and Lieutenant Ferrier, No. 12 Squadron, during two flights for the 126th Siege Battery, gave 110 observations, obtaining seven O.K.'s, destroying one gun-pit, damaging one other, and causing an explosion.

The 227th Siege Battery, with observation by Sergeant Smith, No. 52 Squadron, badly damaged a hostile battery position.

Lieutenant Lines and Lieutenant Biggar and Lieutenant Reeves, all of No. 52 Squadron, carried out successful shoots with the 91st Siege Battery and a 7·5 gun on hostile batteries, destroying a total of five gun-pits and damaging two others.

The 346th Siege Battery, with observation by Lieutenant Higham, Detached Flight of No. 5 Squadron, destroyed one gun-pit and damaged four in a hostile battery position.

The 243rd Siege Battery carried out a very successful shoot on a hostile battery position, with observation by Captain Mackay and Lieutenant Rothwell, No. 9 Squadron, causing two explosions and damaging two pits with 28 rounds. During the same flight the pilot observed a shoot by the 21st Siege Battery on a bridge, which was completely demolished.

Captain Williams and Sergeant Morris, No. 7 Squadron, sent down a zone call on a train, the rear portion of which was hit by the guns answering the call. The position of another train was sent down by Lieutenant Darneley and Lieutenant Wilmott, No. 7 Squadron, in response to which a large explosion and fire were caused and 15 carriages destroyed.

Enemy Aircraft. — Captain Fellowes, No. 43 Squadron, attacked a D.F.W., which he drove down out of control. He then attacked an Albatross Scout, fired several bursts into it, and drove it down in flames.

Captain Fullard, No. 1 Squadron, fired 35 rounds into a D.F.W. two-seater doing artillery work, which he saw crash into some trees. He then attacked with his patrol a formation of 14 enemy aircraft composed of Gothas and D.F.W.'s. Into one of the latter he fired 70 rounds at close range and drove it down out of control. This machine was observed to crash by the personnel of an anti-aircraft battery.

Flight Commander Minifie, Naval Squadron No. 1, brought down a hostile machine which was attacking one of our artillery machines.

A patrol of No. 45 Squadron saw an enemy formation attacking three of our R.E.8's. Second Lieut. Frew engaged the rear enemy machine, which broke to pieces in the air. Lieutenant Firth also shot one down in flames. Second Lieut. Frew then noticed a Camel 3,000 to 4,000 feet below him going down smoking, pursued by three enemy scouts. One of these he singled out and fired 20 rounds into it at about 15 feet range. It burst into flames, and was seen to crash east of Moorslede.

Captain Huskinson, No. 19 Squadron, fired three bursts into a hostile two-seater, which went down completely out of control.

A reconnaissance of No. 20 Squadron engaged 10 enemy aircraft over Comines. Second Lieut. Durrand and Second Lieut Woodbridge shot down one of these, which was seen to crash by our anti-aircraft, and Second Lieuts. McGouan and Couve drove down one out of control. Another enemy machine was driven down out of control by Second Lieut. Babbage and Gunner McMechan, No. 20 Squadron, whilst on offensive patrol.

Four Bristol Fighters of No. 11 Squadron engaged five enemy aircraft Albatross Scouts from a range of 500 yards. One of these was driven down completely out of control by Lieutenant Coath and Second Lieut. Jones.

One of six Albatross Scouts attacked by Flight Sub-Lieut. Curtis and Flight Sub.-Lieut. Stratton, Naval Squadron No. 10, was driven down out of control, and one other was driven down by a patrol of No. 24 Squadron.

A patrol of 13 machines of No. 28 Squadron engaged a formation of 14 Albatross Scouts. One of these was shot down in flames by Lieutenant Mitchell, and another shot down and seen to crash by the same pilot. Second Lieut. Cooper of the same patrol drove one of the Albatross Scouts down completely out of control. A patrol of No. 70 Squadron then joined in the fight and drove another of the enemy aircraft down out of control.

In other combats Second Lieut. Drewitt, No. 23 Squadron, and Captain Laurence, No. 70 Squadron, each drove down a hostile machine out of control.

Five other hostile machines were driven down out of control by the following pilots :—

Captain Bowman, No. 56 Squadron, Lieutenant Boby, No. 22 Squadron, Second Lieut. Oades, No. 22 Squadron, Second Lieut. Pfeiffer and First Air Mechanic Harris, No. 25 Squadron.

Bombing.—First Brigade.—No. 35 Squadron dropped forty-eight 25-lb. bombs on Douvrin, and fifty-six 20-lb. bombs on Drocourt.

Third Brigade.—No. 59 Squadron dropped twenty-seven 25-lb. bombs on a gun on railway mounting north of Brebieres.

Fifth Brigade.—No. 57 Squadron dropped eight 112-lb. and twelve 25-lb. bombs on Roulers.

Ninth Wing. — No. 25 Squadron dropped six 112-lb. bombs on Abeele Aerodrome and nine 112-lb. bombs on Roulers.

One hundred and fourteen 25-lb. bombs were dropped on various targets.

Miscellaneous.—A total of 6,290 rounds were fired at ground targets as follows :—

First Brigade.—Eight hundred and fifty rounds into enemy's trenches.

Second Brigade.—Four thousand three hundred and twenty rounds at various targets, including machine guns and active batteries.

Third Brigade.—Two hundred rounds at a motor car.

Fourth Brigade.—Six hundred and forty-five rounds into enemy trenches.

Fifth Brigade.—Two hundred and seventy-five rounds at machine-gun emplacements.

Honours and Awards.

The Distinguished Service Order.—Captain P. F. Fullard, M.C., General List, Royal Flying Corps.

The Distinguished Service Cross.—Flight Sub-Lieut. S. W. Rosevear, R.N.A.S.

The Military Cross.—Captain F. Sowrey, D.S.O., Royal Fusiliers and Royal Flying Corps.

October 28th.

Weather.—Fine, but work in the air was largely hindered by a thick haze which hung over the lines.

Four reconnaissances and three contact patrols were carried out by machines of the Second and Fifth Brigades.

Artillery Co-operation.—Twenty-five hostile batteries were engaged for destruction, and 13 neutralised; five gun-pits were destroyed, 14 damaged, 10 explosions and five fires caused. Eighty-nine active hostile batteries were reported by zone call.

Lieutenants Hilton and Diespecker, No. 9 Squadron, with the Siege Battery, observed for 120 rounds on an active hostile battery, causing three explosions and a fire; one gun-pit was damaged, and one believed to be destroyed.

Captain Mackay and Lieutenant Rothwell of the same squadron, working with the 145th, the 232nd, and the 231st Siege Batteries, successfully ranged on three hostile battery positions during one flight, three pits being damaged.

On the 27th excellent work was done by balloons, 78 targets being registered and 75 active hostile batteries located. Of these, balloons of the First Brigade registered 15 targets and located 23 hostile batteries, and those of the Second Brigade registered targets and located 22 hostile batteries.

Enemy Aircraft.—Enemy aircraft activity was slight all day.

An offensive patrol of No. 60 Squadron engaged nine Albatross Scouts, one of which was driven down out of control by Lieutenant Rutherford.

Second Lieutenants Jones and Watson, No. 4 Squadron, engaged a formation of two Gothas and 11 Albatross Scouts, one of the former being driven down under control.

Four Sopwith Scouts of No. 46 Squadron encountered four Albatross Scouts. A stiff engagement followed in which one enemy aircraft was shot down completely out of control, and another driven down vertically by Lieutenants Ferrie and Cooper; the third was damaged by Lieutenant Robinson and retired, and the fourth fled east

Captain Hall and Lieutenant Hartigan, No. 57 Squadron, while on photography, dived on an enemy scout and fired 70 rounds at close range, after which the enemy aircraft nose-dived and fell out of control.

Lieutenant R. Maybery and Captain Bowman, both of No. 56 Squadron, while engaging two Albatross Scouts, were attacked by another enemy aircraft scout, which was above, with 14 others, in the clouds. Lieutenant Maybery manœuvred and attacked this enemy aircraft, which he drove down out of control; this machine was seen to crash by pilots of the Second Brigade. The enemy aircraft attacked by Captain Bowman went down steeply, but the result could not be observed.

Bombing.—First Brigade.—On the night of the 27th/28th, No. 2 Squadron dropped thirty-two 25-lb. bombs on Meurchin, sixteen 25-lb. on Estevillers, thirty-one 25-lb. bombs on Carvin, and sixteen 25-lb. bombs on Courrieres; No. 5 Squadron dropped sixteen 25-lb. bombs on Beaumont and six on Vitry, and No. 10 Squadron dropped sixty-six 25-lb. and six 40-lb. phosphorous bombs on various billets and on Chateau du Sart Aerodrome.

On the 23rd, No. 35 Squadron dropped nine 112-lb. bombs on Quiéry la Motte.

Second Brigade.—Thirty-six 20-lb. bombs were dropped on advanced enemy positions.

Third Brigade.—Corps machines dropped eight 25-lb. bombs on various targets.

Fourth Brigade.—Fourteen 20-lb. bombs were dropped into enemy trenches.

Fifth Brigade.—Corps machines dropped twenty-three 20-lb. bombs on enemy hutments and other objectives.

Ninth Wing.—On the night of the 27th/28th, No. 101 Squadron dropped one 230-lb. bomb on Gontrode Aerodrome, four 230-lb., thirty-eight 112-lb., and eight 25-lb. bombs on Rumbeke, Moorseele, Abeele and Bisseghem Aerodromes and on Ingelmunster and Iseghem Railway Stations.

No. 102 Squadron dropped nine 230-lb., twenty 112-lb., and two 25-lb. bombs on Harlebeke, Bisseghem, and Marcke Aerodromes, on Courtrai Railway Station and on trains. One direct hit was obtained on a train, starting a fire.

On the 28th, No. 25 Squadron dropped seven 112-lb. bombs on Harlebeke Aerodrome.

October 29th.

Weather.—Fine, with low clouds at intervals.

Three reconnaissances were carried out, one each by the Third, Fourth, and Fifth Brigades. Eighty-eight artillery and two contact patrols were also carried out by Corps Squadrons.

A total of 245 photographs were taken—127 being by the Second Brigade, and 13,414 rounds were fired at ground targets, chiefly by the Second Brigade and Ninth Wing.

Artillery Co-operation.—During the day 36 active hostile batteries were engaged for destruction and two neutralised;

one gun-pit was destroyed, twelve damaged, sixteen explosions and three fires caused. Thirty-nine zone calls were sent down, twenty-one by the Second Brigade.

Second Lieutenant Watts, No. 53 Squadron, observed for the 374th Siege Battery (12-in. howitzer) on a hostile battery position, which was completely destroyed.

Second Lieutenant Whitehead, No. 5 Detached Flight, with the Fifth R.M.A. (15-inch howitzer) destroyed a strong point.

With balloon observation, two targets were engaged by the Fourth Brigade and two by the Fifth Brigade.

Enemy Aircraft.—Enemy aircraft activity was not great. Several large formations, however, were encountered in the afternoon over the Roulers-Menin road.

Flight Lieutenant Kinkead, Naval Squadron No. 1, attacked an enemy scout in the semi-darkness at 15 yards range. The enemy aircraft was hit and went down out of control.

Second Lieutenants Williams and Croft, No. 48 Squadron, when on offensive patrol encountered a large formation of enemy aircraft at 16,500 feet. One was attacked at 150 yards range, burst into flames and crashed.

Second Lieutenants Hartley and Birch, of the same patrol, attacked one of the other enemy machines, which went down and crashed.

Second Lieutenants W. Ives and A. Cooper, No. 24 Squadron, while on offensive patrol observed an Albatross Scout attacking a Camel. They attacked the enemy aircraft and drove it down apparently out of control.

An offensive patrol of No. 23 Squadron engaged 12 enemy aircraft, which appeared unwilling to close with them. Captain McAlery, who was leading, attacked one of the enemy machines which was manœuvring for position, and it turned on its back and went down out of control.

Lieutenant Baker, of the same squadron, singled out one of four enemy aircraft, and, during a short encounter, fired a burst from 25 yards range. The enemy aircraft went down out of control, crashed and burst into flames.

Captain Bowman, No. 56 Squadron, while on offensive patrol, attacked an enemy aircraft, Nieuport type, which went down in a steep spiral and crashed badly. Later on during the same patrol he had a close encounter with another enemy machine and drove it down, but was unable to follow, as his ammunition was exhausted.

An offensive patrol of the same squadron encountered a formation of seven enemy aircraft at 14,000 feet. A brisk fight ensued, during which Lieutenant Muspratt singled out the leader, which he attacked at close range and drove down entirely out of control.

During the same encounter Lieutenant Coote also attacked one enemy machine at close range and drove it down out of control. The two machines driven down by this patrol were obviously out of control, but were not observed to crash owing to the thick clouds which were underneath the formation.

Bombing.—First Brigade.—On the night of the 28th/29th, No. 5 Squadron dropped seven 40-lb. phosphorous bombs on Meurchin.

On the 29th, No. 18 Squadron dropped nine 112-lb. and four 112-lb. bombs on Cuincy and Quiéry la Motte respectively, while Nos. 2, 5 and 35 Squadrons dropped two 112-lb. and eight 25-lb. bombs on various billets.

Second Brigade.—Thirty-two 20-lb. bombs were dropped on enemy billets in villages close behind the line.

Third Brigade.—Corps machines dropped five 25-lb. bombs on various targets.

Fourth Brigade.—Four 20-lb. bombs were dropped on enemy trenches from low altitudes.

Fifth Brigade.—No. 57 Squadron dropped one 230-lb., eight 112-lb., and eight 25-lb. bombs on Roulers, and six bursts were seen in the town. Corps machines dropped nineteen 20-lb. bombs on hutments and other targets.

Ninth Wing.—On the night of the 28th/29th, No. 101 Squadron dropped three 230-lb., four 112-lb. and eleven 25-lb. bombs on Oostnieuwkerke, where a large fire was caused; two 230-lb. and seven 25-lb. bombs on Most; twenty-one 25-lb. bombs on Vierkaventhoek, a fire being caused among huts in a wood; one 230-lb. and four 25-lb. bombs on Westroosebeke; one 230-lb. and four 25-lb. bombs on Ledeghem Station, and four 112-bombs on Ingelmunster Station, where a large fire was caused which was seen by several pilots.

No. 102 Squadron dropped two 112-lb. bombs on Gontrode Aerodrome; two 230-lb. and two 112-lb. bombs on Courtrai Railway Station; one 230-lb. bomb on Bisseghem sidings, and one 230-lb. and three 112-lb. bombs on trains.

On the 29th, No. 25 Squadron dropped one 230-lb. on Westkerke Aerodrome.

R. J. BARTON, Captain,
Advanced Headquarters, General Staff.
Royal Flying Corps,
31st *October* 1917.

ROYAL FLYING CORPS COMMUNIQUÉ No. 112.

During the month of October 149 bomb raids were carried out and 113 tons of explosives dropped. Many of the objectives have been in Germany and the results have often been most satisfactory. One hundred and eight enemy aircraft were brought down and 60 driven down out of control. Over 11,000 photographs were taken and 1,189 hostile batteries successfully engaged for destruction with aeroplane observation, and 491 targets dealt with by balloon observation.

October 30th.

The weather was unfavourable for aerial work.

One reconnaissance, 119 offensive, 52 artillery and 10 contact patrols were carried out and 113 photographs were taken.

Artillery Co-operation.—Eighteen hostile batteries were successfully engaged for destruction, 44 were neutralised and seven other targets dealt with.

Lieutenant Reeder, No. 53 Squadron, in a flight of $4\frac{1}{4}$ hours, obtained five O.K.'s and caused one fire on a hostile battery position as the result of an A.N.F. call.

During a flight of 3 hours and 20 minutes, Second Lieuts. Mann and Bunt, No. 7 Squadron, reported by zone call 18 active hostile batteries, four of which were silenced by our artillery.

Lieutenant Moor and Sergeant Corson, No. 9 Squadron, during a flight of 3 hours and 45 minutes, located and reported 19 active hostile batteries.

A very successful shoot with the 21st Siege Battery (9·2 inch) on an active hostile battery was carried out by Lieutenants Turner and Fuller, No. 9 Squadron. Observations were sent for 40 rounds, two pits were destroyed, one damaged and a large explosion caused. During the same flight they located and reported by zone call seven active hostile batteries.

With balloon observation, three hostile batteries were successfully engaged for destruction, five neutralised and 18 other targets dealt with, most of this work being done by balloons of the Second Brigade.

Enemy Aircraft.—Enemy aircraft activity was very slight.

Captain Fullard, No. 1 Squadron, shot down one enemy aircraft, which was destroyed.

Machines of the Fifth Brigade took part in 19 combats, and Lieutenants D. Robertson and D. Hilton, No. 29 Squadron, each drove down one enemy machine out of control.

Bombing.—First Brigade.—On the night of the 29th/30th, No. 5 Squadron dropped twenty-four 25-lb. bombs on Quiery-la-Motte; No. 2 Squadron dropped thirty-two 40-lb. phosphorous bombs on Meurchin, thirty-four 25-lb. and eight 40-lb. phosphorous bombs on Courrieres, and thirty-two 25-lb. bombs on Carvin; No. 10 Squadron dropped seventy-five 25-lb. bombs on Hantay, two on Sainghin, and four on Berclau.

Ninth Wing.—On the night of the 29th/30th, No. 101 Squadron dropped two 112-lb. bombs on Ledeghem sidings; four 112-lb. and eight 25-lb. bombs on Oostnieuwkerke-Vierkaventhoek area, and two 112-lb. bombs on a train south of Staden, on which a direct hit was obtained.

Forty-first Wing.—On the night of the 29th/30th, No. 100 Squadron dropped one 230-lb. and three 25-lb. bombs on Saarbrucken; one 230-lb. and three 25-lb. bombs on St. Avold Station, and one 230-lb. and three 25-lb. bombs on Falkenberg.

During this raid 400 rounds were fired into searchlights and at trains and sheds along the railway.

On the 30th, 12 machines of No. 55 Squadron dropped 2,712 lbs. of bombs on the munition factories and town of Pirmasens, 80 miles distant from their aerodrome. A number of bombs were seen to burst on the factories. One pilot obtained a direct hit on the gas works.

October 31st.

Seven reconnaissances were carried out, three of which were by the Fourth Brigade, and seven contact patrols—three by the Second Brigade and four by the Fifth Brigade.

Artillery Co-operation.—Thirty-eight hostile batteries were successfully engaged for destruction and 12 neutralised. Forty-four other targets were dealt with and 21 points registered. Many flashes were located, and 143 targets were reported by zone call.

As the result of an M.Q.N.F. by Second Lieut. McCullough, No. 53 Squadron, the 154th Siege Battery (9·2 inch howitzer), obtained six O.K.'s and eight Y.'s on a hostile battery position, causing two fires. The same observer then sent an A.N.F. call, to which successful response was made.

Three observers of No. 52 Squadron, Lieutenants Reeves, Lines, and Simpson, carried out successful counter-battery shoots, in which two gun-pits were entirely destroyed and three damaged.

The 342nd Siege Battery, with observation by Lieutenant Williams, No. 5 Squadron, also dealt successfully with another hostile battery.

A considerable amount of work was done by the Fifth Brigade. The 231st Siege Battery, with observation by Lieutenants Hilton and Diespecker, No. 9 Squadron, successfully dealt with a hostile battery position. One hundred and twenty-one rounds were observed, one gun-pit being damaged and two explosions caused.

During the day no work was possible with balloons owing mist.

Enemy Aircraft.—During the day 389 offensive patrols were done, during which seven enemy aircraft were brought down and 16 driven down out of control.

Second Lieuts. Bate and Broadhurst, No. 18 Squadron, when on photography, encountered a hostile formation of four machines. They turned on one, a two-seater, and fired 200 rounds at close range, and drove the enemy aircraft down completely out of control.

In response to a wireless call Lieutenant Womersley, No. 43 Squadron, went up in pursuit of an enemy aircraft, which he attacked at close range and sent down out of control.

An offensive patrol of No. 19 Squadron engaged six Albatross Scouts, which were dispersed, one being driven down out of control by Lieutenant Bryson. The next encountered a formation of four enemy aircraft; one, a two-seater, was driven down by Lieutenant Oliver. Major Carter attacked an Albatross at 10,000 feet, and fired two short bursts at close range. It dived steeply, but was followed closely by Major Carter, who succeeded in getting several more bursts into it. Finally the enemy aircraft turned over several times, nose-dived to earth and crashed near the lines.

An offensive patrol of No. 1 Squadron engaged two enemy aircraft, one of which was brought down by Second Lieutenant Birkbeck and observed to crash.

Flight Commander R. P. Minifie, Naval Squadron No. 1, met an enemy aircraft firing into our trenches in the semi-darkness and attacked it at point-blank range. The enemy aircraft was brought down and crashed.

On various offensive patrols four other machines piloted respectively by Lieutenant Firth, No. 45 Squadron; Lieutenant Gartside-Tippinge, No. 19 Squadron; Major Carter, No. 19 Squadron; and Lieutenant Warnum, No. 20 Squadron, each drove down out of control an enemy aircraft.

While on offensive patrol, eight machines of No. 11 Squadron encountered 11 enemy aircraft scouts. A general engagement at close range ensued, during which one enemy aircraft, attacked by Lieutenant McKeever and Second Lieut. Powell, after a burst of 50 rounds at 50 yards range, was driven down completely out of control. The observer then attacked another enemy aircraft at 75 yards range. This one nose-dived, burst into flames, and fell to the ground. A third he attacked at 50 yards range; this one turned over, and also fell out of control, but could not be observed to crash owing to clouds.

An R.E. 8 of No. 5 Squadron, when taking photographs, was attacked by two two-seater enemy aircraft. The first was driven down apparently out of control, the second was driven away east, and the photographs were then taken. The pilot and observer were Lieutenant Griffen and A. M. Hookway respectively.

Captain Leask, when leading an offensive patrol of No. 84 Squadron, was attacked from above by a formation of nine enemy aircraft. A fight lasting 10 minutes ensued, during which one enemy aircraft was sent down out of control by Lieutenant Ralston. A fight with another formation during the same patrol resulted in another Albatross being sent down out of control by Captain Leask.

Lieutenant Maybery, No. 56 Squadron, drove down an enemy aircraft out of control, and Lieutenant Muspratt, of the same squadron, destroyed one.

Bombing.—First Brigade.—On the night of the 30th/31st No. 2 Squadron dropped thirty-nine 25-lb. bombs on Henin-Liétard.

On the 31st No. 18 Squadron dropped eight 112-lb. bombs on Esquerchin, six 112-lb. bombs on Pont-a-Vendin, and six 112-lb. bombs on Wingles. No. 35 Squadron dropped ninety-eight 25-lb. bombs on billets. No. 2 Squadron dropped seventeen 25-lb. bombs on Benifontaine, and three 112-lb., twenty 40-lb., and sixty-three 25-lb. bombs on other targets.

Fifth Brigade.—On the 31st No. 57 Squadron dropped two 230-lb., six 112-lb., and eight 25-lb. bombs on Roulers.

9th Wing.—On the night of the 30th/31st No. 101 Squadron dropped eight 112-lb. bombs on Roulers Station, four 112-lb. bombs on Ingelmunster Station, four 112-lb. and fourteen 25-lb. bombs on billets and hutments in the Roulers area. One thousand three hundred rounds were also fired at ground targets.

No. 102 Squadron dropped one 112-lb. bomb on Bisseghem Aerodrome, twelve 112-lb. and six 25-lb. bombs on moving trains, and fired 500 rounds at trains with machine guns.

On the 31st No. 25 Squadron dropped ten 112-lb. bombs on Carvin and five 230-lb. bombs on Roulers.

41st Wing.—On the night of the 30th/31st No. 100 Squadron carried out another raid into Germany in spite of very bad weather. Seven 230-lb. and twenty-two 25-lb. bombs were dropped on Volklingen Steel Works, which are situated a few miles west of Saarbrucken. The works were so brilliantly illuminated that the pilots had no difficulty in placing their bombs on main gas boiler range, central power house, and blowing engines. A direct hit was obtained on a train in the Saar Valley. One thousand one hundred and fifty rounds were also fired into the works, at the station, and at trains and searchlights.

Seventy-six 25-lb. bombs were also dropped on various targets by machines of the Royal Flying Corps.

November 1st.

Work was considerably hampered by low clouds throughout the day, but successful co-operation with the artillery was carried out in the short bright intervals.

Artillery Co-operation.—Eight hostile batteries were engaged for destruction and one neutralised and 18 other targets dealt with. Thirty targets were sent down by zone call.

During the day exceptionally good work was done by balloons, especially by those of the Second Brigade. In all 11 hostile batteries were engaged for destruction, six neutralised, and ·33 registrations carried out by this brigade.

Enemy Aircraft.—Enemy aircraft activity was slight, but several combats took place at low altitudes; two enemy machines were driven down out of control, one by Lieutenant

Young, of No. 60 Squadron, and the other by Lieutenant Rutherford, of the same squadron, while on offensive patrol. In the latter case Lieutenant Soden, also of No. 60 Squadron, contributed in bringing down the enemy machine.

Bombing. — First Brigade. — On the night 31st October/1st November machines of No. 10 Squadron dropped sixty-seven 25-lb. bombs on Chateau de la Vallee.

Ninth Wing.—Machines of No. 101 Squadron dropped six 112-lb. bombs on Roulers Station, two 112-lb. on Thourout Station, two 112-lb. on Beythem Station, and two 112-lb. on Staden; 1,550 rounds were also fired at trains, lights on roads, and active anti-aircraft batteries doing this work.

Machines of No. 102 Squadron dropped one 112-lb. bomb on Gontrode Aerodrome, one 230-lb. on Heule Aerodrome, seven 112-lb. and ten 25-lb. bombs on Courtrai Station, two 112-lb. and one 25-lb. bombs on Marcke Aerodrome, while eight 112-lb. and six 25-lb. bombs were dropped on trains, with the result that one was hit and derailed near Ghent, and another hit and wrecked at Iseghem.

At 1400 on the 1st, when the clouds were at a height of about 200 feet, four Martinsydes, of No. 27 Squadron, left the ground to bomb Gontrode Aerodrome. Sergeant S. Clinch, who was one of the pilots, climbed through the clouds and flew for 40 minutes, and, on diving down through the clouds, found himself over Ghent. He followed the canal at a low height and dropped his bombs on the aerodrome, but was unable to see results owing to drizzle and strong anti-aircraft fire. He landed again at 1625. The three other pilots became completely lost and returned with their bombs after a flight of two hours.

Forty-first Wing.—On the 1st instant twelve machines of No. 55 Squadron set out in two formations of six machines each to bomb the works at Kaiserslautern, a distance of 100 miles from their aerodrome. One formation reached the objective and dropped three 230-lb. and six 112-lb. bombs from 15,000 feet. Results were not observed, as the sky was very cloudy with only a few gaps. The other formation encountered seven enemy aircraft, so dropped their bombs behind the German lines to enable them to fight. One hostile machine was shot to bits and fell in pieces. All our machines returned.

November 2nd.

During the night of the 1st/2nd November and the following day, low clouds and heavy ground mist almost entirely prevented aerial work.

A successful reconnaissance of enemy wire was carried out by Major Tyson and Captain Owen, of No. 5 Squadron, from a height of 100 feet. They also fired 200 rounds into enemy trenches.

November 3rd.

Owing to low clouds and mist there were few flying operations during the day.

The Fifth Brigade was able to do a little artillery work. Two hostile batteries were successfully engaged for destruction, two pits damaged, one explosion and one fire caused by the 145th Siege Battery (8-inch) and 231st Siege Battery (6-inch) with observation by Captain Mackay and Lieutenant Rothwell, No. 9 Squadron, who also located and reported by zone call 10 active hostile batteries.

Two reconnaissances were carried out at a low height of enemy trenches and works by the Fourth Brigade.

Honours and Awards.

Bar to the Military Cross.—Second Lieut. M. B. Frew, M.C.

November 4th.

The weather generally was overcast, with thick mist, except on the fronts of the Fourth and Fifth Brigades.

Four reconnaissances, 121 offensive, nine artillery and two contact patrols were carried out during the day. In addition, 100 plates were exposed by a photographic machine. The balloons were unable to work owing to the mist.

Artillery Co-operation.—Fifteen hostile batteries were successfully engaged for destruction and two neutralised. Six gun-pits were destroyed and two damaged, two explosions and two fires caused. Fourteen hostile batteries were located and reported by zone call.

The Fourth Brigade carried out 14 successful counter-battery shoots. The 203rd Siege Battery (9·2-inch howitzers), with observation by Lieutenant Canning, No. 5 Squadron Detached Flight, destroyed one pit and damaged a second of a hostile battery position. Another hostile battery position appeared completely obliterated by the 125th Siege Battery (6-inch howitzer), observed for by Lieutenant Higham, No. 5 Squadron Detached Flight.

Enemy Aircraft.—Offensive patrols were only possible in the Fourth and Fifth Army areas. Several large formations of enemy aircraft were encountered by patrols of the Fourth Brigade. A patrol of No. 54 Squadron attacked a formation of five enemy aircraft scouts, one of which was out-manœuvred by Second Lieuts. Schooley and Maddocks, and it fell and was seen to crash.

Flight Sub-Lieuts. Curtis, Naval Squadron No. 10, when on offensive patrol, engaged two enemy aircraft. Into the first he fired 150 rounds at close range, and drove it down quite out of control. The second one went down in a spin but was not seen to crash.

An R.E. 8, of No. 5 Squadron Detached Flight, while on photography with an escort of two scouts, was attacked by six enemy aircraft. Captain Douglas and Lieutenant Whitehead, in the R.E. 8, with the help of the two scouts, drove off the enemy aircraft, one of which went down in a nose-dive. The observer of the R.E. 8 was wounded in the foot and the machine riddled with bullets.

Bombing. — Thirty-three 25-lb. bombs were dropped on enemy works and strong points behind his lines.

November 5th.

There was a slight improvement in the weather, but mist still prevented counter-battery work.

During the night of the 3rd/4th, Lieutenants Russel and Collier, No. 3 Balloon Section, went up at 2120 owing to the activity of the enemy's artillery, and took a compass bearing on the hostile flashes, which were reported to the French, who put five batteries on to the suspected area and silenced the hostile guns.

Six contact patrols were carried out by the First Brigade, and one contact patrol, one counter attack patrol, and two reconnaissances were carried out by the Second Brigade.

Thirty-six photographs were taken and eight 25-lb. bombs were dropped, while 4,400 rounds were fired at ground targets.

The following is a *résumé* of this work in the Fifth Brigade :—

Captain Turner and Lieutenant Fuller, No. 9 Squadron, fired 250 rounds at an enemy strong point from 1,000 feet.

A patrol of No. 32 Squadron, consisting of Captain Fish, Lieutenant Claydon, and Second Lieuts. Blane, Bateman, Tyrrell, and Cuffe, fired in all 1,870 rounds into trenches in the vicinity of Poelcappelle, Houthulst Forest (at a body of troops), into Westroosebeke, Vyfwegen, and buildings in Houthulst Forest from a height of 700 to 1,000 feet.

Captain Faure and Second Lieuts. Cross, Evans, and Wood, of the same squadron, fired 1,400 rounds into Houlthulst Wood, Vyfwegen, and Westroosebeke from a height of about 1,000 feet.

Enemy Aircraft.—Enemy aircraft activity was above normal on the front of the Second Army up till 1300.

Captain H. Hammersley, No. 60 Squadron, attacked one of six enemy aircraft with a yellow fuselage, and drove it down out of control, and saw it crash. Lieutenant F. Soden, of the same squadron, attacked another, which he drove down, and which crashed in a forest.

A patrol of No. 45 Squadron encountered seven enemy scouts, and in the fighting Captain Firth shot down one enemy aircraft, which fell completely out of control.

Infantry of the Second Army shot down a German machine, which fell in our lines.

Honours and Awards.

Under authority granted by His Majesty the King, the Field-Marshal Commanding-in Chief awards the *Military Cross* to Lieutenant E. D. Clarke, Royal Flying Corps (S.R.).

S. WOOD, Captain,
Staff Officer.

Advanced Headquarters,
   Royal Flying Corps,
      7th November 1917.

ROYAL FLYING CORPS COMMUNIQUÉ.—No. 113.

During the period under review (6th to 12th, inclusive), the weather has been persistently bad for aerial work. Six enemy aircraft have been brought down and 17 driven down out of control, and approximately 13 tons of bombs have been dropped and over 55,000 rounds fired from low altitudes at ground targets.

November 6th.

Weather.—Weather conditions were bad for aerial work.

Two reconnaissances were carried out by the Fourth Brigade.

Four hostile batteries were successfully engaged for destruction, and 17 neutralised with aeroplane observation. One hundred and ninety-eight zone calls were sent down, of which 159 were by the Second Brigade.

Fifty-two plates were exposed by machines of the Third Brigade. Eleven thousand one hundred and forty-two rounds were fired at German troops and other ground targets from low altitudes. One thousand seven hundred and twenty of these were by the Second Brigade and 8,400 by the Fifth Brigade.

The following narrative by Second Lieut. E. Oliver, No. 19 Squadron, is of interest. The town near which he landed was probably Ghent :—

> "I left the aerodrome with Lieutenant Jennings on a ground patrol. As we approached Moorslede, I noticed three enemy aircraft above us and slightly to the north-east. After calling the other pilot's attention to their presence, I climbed into the overhanging mist to attack unseen. I did not see Lieutenant Jennings after this.
>
> "I remained in the clouds and flew westwards according to my compass; evidently this was completely at fault, as when at times I came below the mist, I was unable to locate my position.
>
> "At length, I reached a big town with a large common on its north or north-east side; a river ran south-west through the town. I saw a party of Germans working on the railway, and assuming that they were prisoners,

decided to come down. After making two circuits of the town, I made a landing on the common. Remaining in my seat and keeping the engine running, I beckoned to a peasant who was standing near by, and hurriedly asked whether the French or English were in possession of the country. He answered that it was occupied by German troops, and indicated in which direction lay the French lines. Hastily I opened out my engine, and "took off" again. As I passed over the town once more, I was subjected to intense machine gun and anti-aircraft fire. I flew steadily in the direction I had been told, half hidden in the mist.

"I saw two two-seater enemy aircraft just below the clouds. I remained unseen between them in the mist, and saw them descend towards an aerodrome near a town (probably Audenarde).

"From time to time I came down very low to find out my position; but the grey-green uniforms on the roads told me that I was still over the enemy's lines. Knowing which way the wind was blowing, I was able to decide my direction by the smoke from the chimneys.

"I finally passed Tournai and Lille, and at length crossed the lines north-east of Armentières. I could hardly identify these towns, as I had passed so many places of similar appearance; but I could see khaki-clad troops below. As my petrol was now practically exhausted, I landed on the first good landing ground.

"I noticed the enemy territory was well marked with ground signals, the apex pointing to the east."

Enemy Aircraft. — Enemy aircraft were not particularly active and only a little fighting took place. A two-seater was driven down out of control by Lieutenants F. Soden and W. Rutherford, No. 60 Squadron, while Lieutenant W. Duncan, of the same squadron, destroyed a two-seater near Polygon Wood.

Lieutenant. R. Holt, No. 19 Squadron, attacked and drove down an enemy scout out of control.

Flight Sub-Lieut. Cameron, Naval Squadron No. 10, drove down a single-seater scout, which he followed, firing from close range until it fell into the clouds completely out of control.

Bombing. — Ten 25-lb. bombs were dropped on various targets by machines of the First Brigade; 24 by the Second Brigade; four by the Fourth, and four by the Fifth Brigade.

November 7th.

The weather was not good.

A reconnaissance was carried out by the Fourth Brigade and four contact patrols were done by the Second Brigade. 114 plates were exposed.

Fifteen hostile batteries were successfully engaged for destruction with aeroplane observation, three gun-pits were destroyed, six damaged, five explosions and one fire caused.

Forty-four zone calls were sent down.

Lieutenant Woollard and First Air Mechanic Wilkes, No. 15 Squadron, sent a zone call on a train entering Bourlon Station. The engine of the train appeared to be hit.

Lieutenant Entwistle, No. 5 Squadron Detached Flight, ranged the 125th Siege Battery on to a hostile battery where two pits were destroyed, two damaged and two fires caused.

Over 11,000 rounds were fired at ground targets; 1,275 of these were by No. 40 Squadron, 2,850 by No. 101 Squadron during a bomb raid, and 2,700 by No. 32 Squadron.

Enemy aircraft were not active, and only one, which was attacked by Second Lieut. F. Gorringe, No. 70 Squadron, was driven down out of control.

Flight Commander Munday, Naval Squadron No. 8, crossed the lines at dawn and attacked a balloon north of Meurchin. He opened fire at about 100 yards range and the balloons burst into flames. He then returned and attacked the shed, but machine-gun fire was too active so he left and on his return flight fired into the Metallurgique Works.

Bombing.—Fifty-two 25-lb. bombs were dropped on various targets by the First, Second, Fourth, and Fifth Brigades.

Fifth Brigade.—No. 57 Squadron dropped one 230-lb. and four 112-lb. bombs on five trains in Iseghem Railway Sidings.

Ninth Wing.—On the night of the 6th/7th, No. 101 Squadron dropped one 230-lb., twenty-six 112-lb., and eight 25-lb. bombs on Roulers Station. The station was hit and the explosion of the 230-lb. bomb was followed by a second explosion. Four 112-lb. bombs were dropped on Roulers town; one 230-lb., eleven 112-lb., and four 25-lb. bombs on and about Rumbeke Aerodrome. In addition, nine 112-lb. bombs were dropped on other targets.

During this raid 2,850 rounds were fired at ground targets.

No. 102 Squadron dropped sixteen 112-lb. and ten 25-lb. bombs on various targets, including a railway and billets near Menin, billets at Moorslede and Halluin, and on trains in railway sidings.

Honours and Awards.

Bar to the Distinguished Service Cross.—Acting Flight Commander R. P. Minifie, D.S.C., Royal Navy.

Bar to the Military Cross.—Lieutenant R. A. Maybery, M.C., Lancers and Royal Flying Corps.

The Military Cross.—Second Lieut. W. Durrand, Royal Flying Corps General List.

November 8th.

More work was possible than on the previous few days.

Eleven reconnaissances and two contact patrols were carried out, and 723 plates were exposed during the day.

With aeroplane observation, 56 hostile batteries were successfully engaged for destruction and 33 neutralised; one gun-pit was destroyed, 23 damaged, 38 explosions and 15 fires caused. One hundred and eighty-nine zone calls were sent down and 39 were seen to be answered. Twenty-seven of the batteries engaged for destruction were by artillery of the Second Army and 12 by artillery of the First Army.

Lieutenant Baldwin, No. 53 Squadron, ranged the 276th Siege Battery on to a hostile battery position, where six O.K.'s were obtained, which caused two explosions.

Very successful results were obtained by the 199th Siege Battery, with observation by Lieutenants Owles and Carden, No. 12 Squadron, during a flight of four hours and five minutes.

Ground targets were again attacked from low altitudes by aeroplanes, and 18,340 rounds were fired, 1,700 of these being by No. 101 Squadron during a night bombing raid.

Flight Commander Munday, Naval Squadron No. 8, and Lieutenant Higham, No. 52 Squadron, each silenced a machine gun, which was firing at them from the ground.

Enemy Aircraft.—A considerable amount of fighting took place during the day.

Flight Commander Compston, Naval Squadron No. 8, observed some of our anti-aircraft bursts in the vicinity of Oppy, so flew in that direction and encountered an enemy scout, which he shot down and which was seen to crash.

While engaged on photographic work, Second Lieut. Jackson and Private J. Reid, No. 4 Squadron, were attacked by seven scout, but they returned after having driven down one enemy machine apparently out of control.

Second Lieut. B. Starfield and Lieutenant A. Hutchinson, No. 20 Squadron, in a fight between a formation of that squadron and enemy aircraft, shot down one of the German machines out of control, and it was seen by ground observers to crash. Two other German scouts were driven down out of control, one by Lieutenants J. Kirkpatrick and G. Brooke, and the other by Captain W. Durrand and Second Lieut. A. Woodbridge, No. 20 Squadron.

Major A. Carter, No. 19 Squadron, dived at an enemy aircraft two-seater and after several bursts of fire the enemy machine went down out of control and was seen to crash.

A fight took place between nine enemy aircraft and a patrol of No. 45 Squadron, and Second Lieut. Child destroyed one of the enemy machines, while a second—a two-seater—was driven down out of control by Second Lieut. Carpenter. In another patrol, pilots of this Squadron dived at an Albatross Scout which Second Lieut. Williams shot down in flames, and after this he and Captain Firth attacked another which went down out of control.

A patrol of No. 60 Squadron found a two-seater enemy aircraft near Zillebeke and Captain Selous shot it down in our lines. A second patrol of this squadron engaged a two-seater near Houthem and it was destroyed by Second Lieut. Pope, who shortly afterwards attacked and destroyed a second two-seater. Captain Hammersley, of the same squadron, destroyed an Albatross Scout, and Lieutenant Rutherford drove one down out of control.

Captain Molesworth, No. 29 Squadron, when leading his patrol, attacked the rear machine of a formation of 15 enemy aircraft and shot it down in flames. Shortly after this he attacked one of two reconnaissance machines and also shot this machine down in flames. Lieutenant Coombe attacked the other two-seater and drove it down out of control.

Second Lieutenant Koch, No. 70 Squadron, shot down a machine out of control, and Captain Cook and Lieutenant Drudge, No. 57 Squadron, shot down an Albatross Scout, which attacked them, out of control.

A formation of No. 22 Squadron encountered and fought eight enemy scouts, and Lieutenants H. McKenzie and S. McClenaghan dived at one which was attacking another Bristol Fighter and shot it down in flames. Another was shot down out of control by Captain J. Butler and Second Lieut. H. Johnstone.

In other fighting by the Ninth Wing, Captain Child and Lieutenant F. Brown, No. 84 Squadron, shot down an enemy machine out of control, while another fell out of control after being engaged by Captain T. Hunter, No. 66 Squadron.

Anti-aircraft of the Second Army shot down an enemy machine, which fell in our lines.

Bombing.—First Brigade.—No. 2 Squadron dropped twenty-seven 25-lb. bombs on Pont-à-Vendin, Auchy, Benifontaine, and on trenches. No. 18 Squadron dropped ten 112-lb. bombs on Cuincy.

No. 5 Squadron dropped eight phosphorus bombs on Chez-Bontemps.

No. 69 Squadron dropped eight 112-lb. bombs on Oppy, nineteen 20-lb. bombs on Neuvireuil, and six phosphorus bombs on Chez-Bontemps.

The bombing by Nos. 18 and 69 Squadrons was carried out in conjunction with a raid by the 31st Division. Six pilots of Naval Squadron No. 8 also assisted in this raid by engaging enemy troops and guns with machine-gun fire.

Fifth Brigade. — No. 57 Squadron dropped nine 112-lb. bombs on Roulers.

In addition, sixty-four 25-lb. bombs were dropped by the brigades on various targets.

No. 9 Wing.—On the night of the 7th/8th, No. 101 Squadron dropped thirty-four 112-lb. bombs on Gontrone Aerodrome, Roulers and Ingelmunster Railway Stations. A bomb burst in front of a train entering Ingelmunster, and another burst on the line behind the train. During this raid 1,700 rounds were fired at ground targets from the air.

No. 102 Squadron dropped seven 112-lb. and forty-six 25-lb. bombs on Gontrode, St. Denis Westrem, Bisseghem, Moorseele, and Marcke Aerodromes, Courtrai Dump and sidings, and lights at Wervicq. Bombs were seen to burst among hangars on the aerodromes.

November 9th.

On the 9th, quite a lot of work was done, in spite of unfavourable weather.

Seven reconnaissances were carried out, and the Second Brigade did two contact patrols.

Two bomb raids were successfully concluded and 409 photographs taken.

Over 14,004 rounds were fired at ground targets, 6,200 being by the Second Brigade, and 6,814 by the Fifth Brigade.

Artillery Co-operation.—Fifty hostile batteries were successfully engaged for destruction, with aeroplane observation, 22 being by the Second Brigade; and 12 others were neutralised. Three gun-pits were destroyed, 18 damaged, 30 explosions and 10 fires caused. One hundred and eleven zone calls were sent down, and 19 were seen to be answered.

Captain Cherry, No. 42 Squadron, carried out two successful shoots, one with the 82nd Siege Battery and one with the 255th Siege Battery. In the former shoot two pits were damaged and an explosion caused, and in the latter two explosions were caused.

With balloon observation of the Second Brigade, five hostile batteries were successfully engaged for destruction, and 20 other targets were dealt with.

Bombing.—No. 18 Squadron dropped two 112-lb. bombs on Pont-à-Vendin, and No. 57 Squadron dropped one 230-lb. and eight 112-lb. bombs on Hooglede.

During the day, one hundred and ten 25-lb. bombs were dropped by the brigades on various other targets.

Enemy Aircraft.—Enemy aircraft were not particularly active.

A patrol of No. 19 Squadron engaged five enemy aircraft scouts near Zuidhoek, and Lieutenant C. R. J. Thompson destroyed one which was attacking another Spad from behind. The patrol then engaged a scout which was interfering with two R.E.8's, and Lieutenant Thompson drove this machine down out of control. Shortly after this the patrol attacked a two-seater enemy aircraft, and it fell out of control after Major Carter had fired into it from close range.

Second Lieut. K. B. Montgomery, No. 45 Squadron, Second Lieut. P. Kelsey and Second Lieut. Birkbeck, both of No. 1 Squadron, each drove down an enemy machine out of control.

Four other enemy machines are believed to have been driven down out of control, one by Second Lieut. J. Payne, No. 29 Squadron, one by Second Lieut. C. Runnels-Moss, one by Second Lieut. E. Booth, and the fourth by Lieutenant J. Aldred, all of No. 70 Squadron.

Second Lieutenants J. Macaulay and G. Bliss, No. 25 Squadron, were on an instructional flight when they were attacked by three enemy aircraft scouts, and in the fighting they shot down one of the enemy machines completely out of control.

Honours and Awards.

Bar to the Military Cross.—Second Lieut. L. A. Powell, M.C., Gloucester Regiment and Royal Flying Corps.

November 10th.

Rain fell all day on the 10th and very little work was accomplished.

Thirty-four zone calls were sent down by No. 2 Squadron, and six were seen to be answered. In all fifty-one zone calls were sent down during the day.

Six hostile batteries were neutralised by artillery of the Second Army and a certain amount of successful work was done by Corps Squadrons of the Fifth Brigade.

With balloon observation, ten hostile batteries were successfully engaged for destruction by artillery of the Second Army, two by artillery of the Fourth Army, and one by the Fifth, and 27 other targets were dealt with by artillery of the Second Army.

One thousand three hundred rounds were fired into enemy trenches by Nos. 2 and 5 Squadrons, and 36 plates were exposed by the Third Brigade.

On the night of the 9th/10th, No. 101 Squadron dropped nineteen 112-lb. and twelve 25-lb. bombs on Rumbeke Aerodrome, on transport (which was hit), and on other targets, and fired 1,870 rounds at billets and transport on roads.

November 11th.

Low clouds and rain still interfered with work.

Three reconnaissances were carried out, and seven contact patrols by the Second Brigade.

Two hundred and forty-four photographs were taken, and sixty-six 25-lb. bombs were dropped by the brigades on various targets.

With aeroplane observation, 15 hostile batteries were succcessfully engaged for destruction and six neutralised; one gun-pit was damaged, five explosions and two fires caused.

One hundred and four zone calls were sent down and nine were seen to be answered.

Ten thousand nine hundred and thirty rounds were fired at ground targets, 6,700 being by the Second Brigade.

Captain McKay, No. 23 Squadron, attacked a machine gun, which he silenced.

Lieutenant Hewett, of the same squadron, fired 100 rounds into a body of infantry and scattered them.

Enemy Aircraft.—Enemy aircraft activity was below normal.

Second Lieut. S. Pope, No. 60 Squadron, saw an enemy aircraft scout through a gap in the clouds, so dived at it and opened fire and the enemy machine went down and crashed.

Lieutenants T. Candy and G. Rice, No. 19 Squadron, drove down another machine apparently out of control.

Lieutenants A. McKeever and L. Pogson, No. 11 Squadron, attacked one of two enemy two-seaters and drove one down completely out of control.

A patrol of No. 48 Squadron encountered a formation of four large bombing machines, escorted by about 30 scouts. During a fight with 15 of these machines, Captain B. Baker and Second Air Mechanic B. Jackman drove down two of the scouts completely out of control, both of which are believed to have crashed.

In another fight with six enemy aircraft scouts, Lieutenant N. Millman and Second Lieut. T. Tuffield drove down one of the hostile scouts out of control.

November 12th.

The weather was fine, but a thick ground mist made work in the morning difficult.

With aeroplane observation 30 hostile batteries were successfully engaged for destruction; two gun-pits were destroyed, eight damaged, eight explosions and six fires caused; 33 zone calls were sent down and eight were seen to be answered.

With balloon observation eight hostile batteries were successfully engaged for destruction, of which five were by the Second Army, and 38 other targets were dealt with.

Three contact patrols were carried out by the Second Brigade and five reconnaissances, one by the Second, two by the Fourth, and two by the Fifth Brigade, and 1,283 photographs were taken.

Nearly 12,000 rounds were fired at ground targets, 6,700 being by the 5th Brigade.

Enemy Aircraft.—Enemy aircraft activity was normal, but a large number of combats took place.

A patrol of Sopwith Camels of No. 43 Squadron observed four Albatross Scouts about to attack some of our Corps machines, so immediately engaged the enemy aircraft. Major Dore shot one down out of control. The same patrol attacked another scout shortly afterwards and Second Lieutenant C. King, who was assisted by Lieutenant MacLanachan, No. 40 Squadron, shot it down out of control.

A patrol of five machines of No. 20 Squadron attacked seven enemy aircraft scouts. In the fighting, two were driven down out of control by Captains Knight and Wornum. Later, a third fell out of control after having been engaged by Second Lieutenants Boles and Wallis.

Another enemy aircraft was driven down out of control by Lieutenant Bryson, No. 19 Squadron, who attacked it when it was interfering with R.E.8's.

Lieutenant Balmford and Corporal Elliot, No. 6 Squadron, were taking photographs when they were attacked by a formation of enemy aircraft scouts. The observer, who was wounded, shot down one of the enemy machines out of control.

A patrol of Naval Squadron No. 10 attacked a two-seater enemy aircraft, and Flight Lieut. Trapp and Flight Sub-Lieut. Beattie shot it down out of control and it was seen by the French to crash.

Another machine was shot down out of control by Captain Beanlands, No. 24 Squadron.

Second Lieutenant Quigley, No. 70 Squadron, and Second Lieutenant P. de Fontenay, No. 29 Squadron, each drove down a machine, which appeared to be out of control.

A reconnaissance of No. 57 Squadron encountered about 10 enemy aircraft over Staden, and in the fighting Second Lieutenants O. McOustra and A. Flavell shot one down out of control. Second Lieutenant Drinkwater and Lieutenant Menendez, of the same squadron, fought three enemy aircraft, and one went down apparently out of control, while shortly afterwards they shot down another, which fell out of control.

Bombing.—First Brigade.—No. 18 Squadron dropped six 112-lb. bombs on Libercourt, two on Beaumont, four on Pont-à-Vendin, and two on Henin Liètard.

5th Brigade.—No. 57 Squadron dropped one 230-lb., eight 112-lb, and twenty-four 25-lb. bombs on Roulers. Bursts were observed in the town and on the petrol dump, and a large fire was caused. They also dropped one 230-lb. bomb on enemy hutments.

Brigades dropped eighty 25-lb. bombs on various targets.

S. WOOD, Captain,
Staff Officer.

Advanced Headquarters,
 Royal Flying Corps,
  14th November 1917.

No. 46.

CONFIDENTIAL.

ROYAL NAVAL AIR SERVICE.

OPERATIONS REPORT

(with Royal Flying Corps Reports attached).

16th to 30th NOVEMBER 1917.

NAVAL STAFF,
OPERATIONS DIVISION.
30th November 1917.

ROYAL NAVAL AIR SERVICE.

REPORT OF OPERATIONS

(Completed from Reports during period
16th to 30th November 1917.)

CONTENTS.

	PAGE
HOME STATIONS - - - - -	2
DUNKIRK - - - - - -	5
R.N.A.S. SQUADRONS WITH ROYAL FLYING CORPS REPORTS ATTACHED - - - - - -	8
EASTERN MEDITERRANEAN - - -	9
BRITISH ADRIATIC SQUADRON - - - -	16
ROYAL FLYING CORPS COMMUNIQUÉS - -	19

HOME STATIONS.

SUBMARINE PATROL WORK.

November 17*th.*

Cattewater.—Whilst on a Series 4 patrol, in Short Seaplane N. 1257 (Pilot Flight-Lieut. Woolner, Observer W. G. Farley), a paravane towed by H.M.S. "Lance" was observed to explode at 1252 in position 50° 03 N. 03° 30 W., after which two depth charges were dropped by the destroyer.

The seaplane, however, was unable to see any trace of a submarine and after a search of 20 minutes in the vicinity, proceeded on patrol.

At 1340 when in position approximately 50° 03 N. 03° 05 W. one bomb was dropped on a suspicious looking object sighted beneath the surface, and 20 minutes later a second bomb was dropped on a swirl on the surface in the same position. The pilot states that the object seen when the first bomb was dropped appeared to be a dark shadow, either stationary or moving very slowly, and had what he thought to be the appearance of a periscope submerged.

No further indication of a submarine appeared, but in view of the reports received later from Guernsey of the sighting of a submarine by a seaplane at 1100 in approximately 49° 58 N., 02° 58 W., and from Cherbourg *via* Portsmouth of a sighting at 1117 near to this position (both of which may possibly refer to the same incident), it seems quite probable that the attack was made on a submerged submarine, but there is no evidence of any damage having been caused.

While on a scout patrol from 1425 to 1625 a big disturbance was observed on the surface at 1450. Two bombs were dropped but nothing further was observed.

During a routine patrol from 1500 to 1645 a long patch of disturbed water was observed at 1530, and one bomb was dropped but nothing further was seen.

November 18*th.*

Calshot.—Large America Seaplane 8670 (Pilot Flight Sub-Lieut. A. G. B. Ellis, Observer Flight Lieutenant Shaw) left on a special patrol to lat. 49° 47′ N., long. 2° 47′ W., in search of a reported submarine. When returning, a submarine was sighted submerged with the periscope just showing. The seaplane dropped two 230-lb. bombs from 600 feet, the first one exploding about five yards, and the second about 15 yards, astern of the submarine, which dived and was not seen again. The seaplane searched the vicinity until forced to return owing to lack of petrol.

November 18th.

Westgate.—During an anti-submarine patrol carried out by a seaplane, a large patch of fairly thick oil about 100 yards long and 20 yards wide was observed when half a mile due west of South Knock Buoy. One bomb was dropped but no details of results are given.

November 18th.

Hornsea.—Sopwith Baby Seaplane N. 1446 (Pilot Flight Sub-Lieut. E. J. Addis) left on a patrol to Filey at 0750, and at 0810 an enemy submarine with the periscope showing was sighted steering north-west in lat. 54° 20′ N., long. 0° 17′ W.

By the time the seaplane had got into position the periscope had submerged, but the outline of the submarine was visible, and one 65-lb. delay action bomb was dropped from about 800 feet, which appeared to explode three or four yards short. No other explosion occurred, but about two minutes afterwards several large bubbles appeared to westward of where the bomb struck, and the water appeared smooth as if oil were on the surface. The pilot then fired a red Very's light to warn the convoy, which was steering north by west, bearing about two miles to the south.

The seaplane then proceeded to the south and circled round the leading trawler of the convoy, firing another red Very's light, then returning to the oil patch circled round it, and went back to the convoy, repeating this operation three times. The leading trawler observed the signal and started to follow the direction of the seaplane to the oil patch, but at that moment the seaplane's engine gave out, and a forced landing was made at 0845. The armed trawler "Ninus" came alongside and towed the seaplane into Scarborough, where it arrived undamaged and was dismantled.

November 23rd.

Fishguard.—Hamble Bay Seaplane N. 1199 (Pilot Flight Sub-Lieut. de la Rue) left at 1443, steering N.W. to carry out a patrol.

At 1457 a white V-shaped wake, with a disturbance of water on the surface about 20 to 30 feet ahead of the wake was observed 3 miles distant on the starboard bow, and steering a course West, at about 6 to 10 knots. The height of the seaplane at the time of sighting the object was 1,000 feet, and the seaplane immediately proceeded at full speed to close and attack. When in a favourable position for bombing, the pilot shut off the engine, putting the machine into almost a vertical dive over the subject, and flattened out at 500 feet, releasing two 65-lb. bombs.

A turn was then made to observe the effect, and it was seen that the first bomb had hit the water astern to the left and clear of all the wash. This bomb did not explode owing, as it was afterwards found, to the fusing lever jumping its contact slot and returning to the "safe" position, in all probability caused by vibration.

The second bomb hit the water about 10 feet ahead and 10 to 15 feet to starboard of the forward water disturbance and, shortly after exploding, a large white patch was seen, followed by one large bubble.

The seaplane then circled round and observed a large black patch of sediment due to the explosion of the bomb, but the periscope, with its attendant wake, and all water disturbance, had disappeared.

AIRSHIP ATTACKS ON HOSTILE SUBMARINES.

November 16th.

Longside.—Airship C. 14 carried out No. 3 patrol for five hours and 37 minutes, during which bombs were dropped on the wash of a submarine off Kinnaird Head. (No further details to hand.)

November 17th.

Mullion.—Airship C. 23 A. gave up a special patrol as ordered at 1240, in order to carry out a normal patrol, and at 1315, in 59 F. observed a large amount of wreckage in 59 A. with the trawler "Flintshire" and S.S. "Trevisa" standing by, from which vessels it was communicated to the airship that S.S. "Victoria" was sunk at 1310, the survivors stating that she had been torpedoed. C. 23 A. cruised round the wreckage, and at 1330 observed what appeared to be a submarine about 20 feet under the water, making apparently 3—4 knots, one mile east of the wreckage on the port bow. The airship altered course towards it, rose to 800 feet, and dropped one 100-lb. bomb which fell 20 yards ahead, and turning through 16 points eased both engines and dropped a second 100-lb. bomb, which fell about 5 feet ahead, after which bubbles were seen to rise to the surface.

The trawler "Flintshire" then came up, and at 1045 dropped one depth charge fairly over the patch of air bubbles, and what looked like a small piece of wood came to the surface. At 1420 the airship dropped a calcium flare on the patch, and at 1430 the trawler dropped two depth charges 20 yards on either side of the patch. At 1440 a second calcium flare was dropped from the airship, the first one having floated with the tide west of the patch.

The trawler dropped two more depth charges, and large quantities of bubbles, and some oil, were observed rising. At 1440 the airship having no flares left, indicated the patch by

Lewis gun-fire, and directed the trawler to drop two more depth charges and buoy the position, which was carried out, and a slight increase in the oil coming up was observed. At 1545 motor launch 331 joined the trawler, and at 1555 the motor launch straddled the patch with two depth charges and a small air bubble patch appeared near the original one, which was also buoyed by the trawler.

At 1620 air bubbles ceased to rise, although small patches of oil still rose intermittently. C. 23 A. then returned to the base and made a night landing at 1830 after a flight of 9 hours 45 minutes.

November 17th.

Mullion.—Whilst on patrol airship S.S.Z. 15 sighted a thin line of oil about 200 yards in length, on which bombs were dropped, after which a quantity of oil rose to the surface. A trawler was called up, which dropped a depth charge; and further bombs were dropped by the airship, after which more oil and large swirls came to the surface. Another depth charge was dropped by the destroyer and the swirls stopped. The line of oil now extended for about two miles, but nothing further was seen.

DUNKIRK.

WEATHER.

During this period the weather conditions have been extremely unfavourable for aircraft operations, strong gales and low clouds being almost continuous, considerably impeding patrol work and rendering bombing raids impossible.

OFFENSIVE PATROL—ENGAGEMENTS WITH ENEMY.

November 18th.

Seaplane Defence Squadron (No. 1 Wing).—A patrol of five Sopwith Camels sighted a formation of four hostile seaplanes five miles north of La Panne, and engaged them in running combats. During the engagement tracers were seen to enter the rearmost enemy machine, which appeared to be in difficulties.

Gun jambs greatly hampered the Sopwith pilots, who nevertheless engaged the hostile seaplanes at a height of 200 feet to within one mile of Ostende.

November 23rd.

No. 4 Wing (9th Squadron).—A patrol of three Sopwith Camels encountered a formation of nine hostile scout machines at 14,000 feet between Dixmude and Houthulst Forest. Flight Commander Banbury and Flight Sub-Lieut. Hales engaged an Albatross machine, and fired 350 rounds into it; the hostile machine was probably destroyed.

The flight was also engaged in several other combats, all of which, however, were indecisive.

November 23rd.

No. 4 Wing (4th Squadron).—A patrol of six Sopwith Camels encountered a formation of six Albatross Scouts at 2,000 feet, with two others hovering about them, to the east of Keyem. The Albatross Scouts attacked the Camels, and Flight Sub-Lieut. Tonks brought one down completely out of control.

Flight Sub-Lieut. Hickey shot down another, probably out of control, and Flight Sub-Lieut. Gossip engaged a third machine, into which he fired several shorts at short range, but did not observe the result. A D.F.W. fired on Flight Sub-Lieut. Gossip at a point about four miles to the east of the position of the combat.

November 26th.

No. 4 Wing (1st Squadron).—A formation of four Sopwiths F.I. machines encountered two hostile two-seaters south of Dixmude at 8,000 feet. Upon being attacked they dived down east. One hostile Scout was also encountered over Westende, and was driven east.

November 29th.

No. 4 Wing (1st Squadron).—Whilst on patrol Flight-Commander Minifie dived on four hostile scouts near Middelkerke and fired 400 rounds into one, which turned over and fell completely out of control from 12,000 feet.

Flight Sub-Lieut. Forman attacked two of the hostile scouts and fired into one, which, however, got away. The same pilot then attacked the other hostile scout which went down out of control after 200 rounds had been fired into him.

HOSTILE AIRCRAFT PURSUIT, ENGAGEMENT WITH ENEMY, AND ATTACK ON ENEMY INFANTRY.

November 20th.

No. 4 Wing (9th Squadron).—Observing that anti-aircraft guns were firing on enemy aircraft south of Nieuport, a flight of six Sopwith Camels started out in pursuit, but a patrol of Bristol Fighters and D. H. 5 machines, which were already up, drove the hostile machines back before the Camels could get near enough to engage.

Flight Sub-Lieut. Knott saw a company of enemy infantry crossing a bridge N.E. of Dixmude, and coming down to about 500 feet, fired about 300 rounds into them, killing some, and scattering the rest.

Flight Sub-Lieut. Redgate engaged two Albatross Scouts at a height of 10,000 feet south of Pervyse, diving on the tail of one, and firing into him at 100 yards range. He followed the enemy machine down to 100 feet, when it was seen to crash about 3 miles behind the enemy lines.

FLEET PROTECTIVE PATROL—ENGAGEMENT WITH ENEMY.

November 23rd.

Seaplane Defence Squadron, No. 1 Wing.—Whilst returning from patrol work, Flight Sub-Lieut. Pinder, in Sopwith Camel B. 6357, sighted three hostile aircraft, flying in close formation from the west, towards Ostende.

The Sopwith tried to intercept the hostile formation by steering a course for Ostende, but only managed to overtake them within 1½ miles of the coast, and fired 150 rounds at the nearmost machine at ranges from 200 to 100 yards, the enemy observer replying with his rear gun. The Sopwith pilot was then compelled to break off the engagement owing to a gun jamb, and the presence of two Albatross Scouts, which were diving on him from above.

FIGHTER ESCORT PATROL—ENGAGEMENT WITH ENEMY.

November 23rd.

Seaplane Defence Squadron, No. 1 Wing.—Whilst on patrol, Squadron Commander Graham, in Sopwith Camel B. 6300, was attacked by eight hostile machines. The Sopwith pilot fired two short bursts at one, then spun to get away. The Sopwith was not hit, although under continuous fire from the hostile machines.

ESCORT TO PHOTOGRAPHIC RECONNAISSANCE— ENGAGEMENT WITH ENEMY.

November 23rd.

No. 1 Wing (2nd Squadron).—Whilst gliding down from escort duty just off Nieuport, Flight Commander F. E. Sandford in D.H. 4, N. 5985, observed a hostile machine following at about 10,000 feet. The D.H. 4 climbed to the same level, and the hostile machine closed up and fired a few rounds.

The D.H. 4 observer, Sub-Lieut. Russell, replied with about 10 rounds, and the hostile machine turned away.

The D.H. 4 pilot then fired about 20 rounds into the hostile machine, but owing to his sight being badly fogged, he had to break off the engagement. When turning, the observer fired about 15 more rounds, after which the hostile machine got out of range.

NAVAL SQUADRON WITH THE ROYAL FLYING CORPS.

FROM 18TH NOVEMBER TO 1ST DECEMBER 1917 (INCLUSIVE).

NOTE.—Naval Squadron No. 8 is now the only squadron operating with the Royal Flying Corps, No. 9 Squadron having ceased operations with the Royal Flying Corps on 29th September, No. 1 Squadron on 1st November, and No. 10 Squadron on 20th November 1917.

NAVAL SQUADRON No. 8.

This squadron has been attached to the 1st Brigade, Royal Flying Corps, and has carried out eight offensive patrols, and 45 special missions in pursuit of enemy aircraft, and low reconnaissances, making a total of 129 hours 35 minutes flying.

The squadron took part in the aerial operations in connection with the advance of the Third Army west of Cambrai. At times, when the bad weather almost made flying impossible, pilots of this squadron carried out low reconnaissance flights, obtaining valuable information of the enemy's movements, and engaged the hostile troops and transport with machine guns from a low altitude.

Only two combats took place during the period, both of which were indecisive.

Casualties :—*Accidentally killed*—Flight Sub-Lieut. A. S. Smith, 23.11.17.

EASTERN MEDITERRANEAN STATION.

(Compiled from Weekly Reports, No. 86 and 87, dating from November 5th–18th, 1917.)

NOTE.—Weekly Operations Report No. 85 has not yet come to hand and will be included in the next number of the Operations Report, if received.

THASOS AIR STATION.

"A" SQUADRON AND "Z" (GREEK) SQUADRON.

November 5th–10th.

Anti-Submarine and Mine Reconnaissances.—On 6th November a submarine and mine reconnaissance was made to the north and west of Thasos and a submarine patrol to the west of the island towards the Akte Peninsula.

On 7th November a seaplane reconnoitred the area to the south and west of Kavalla and on the following day two seaplanes searched to the south of Thasos for an enemy submarine which was last reported proceeding north from Cape Murtzephlos, Lemnos. These patrols were again made on the morning of 9th November, the area selected being the approaches to Stavros, in case the submarine was proceeding there to lay mines.

On 10th November extended submarine patrols were made by three machines and practically all the area between Athos and Samothraki to the north was covered during the day without result.

November 11th–17th.

Anti-Submarine Patrols.—Submarine patrols were made over a large area to the south, south-east, south-west and west of Thasos on 11th November, machines from both squadrons participating.

On the following day the area to the north-west of a line joining Cape St. Georgios, Thasos, with Cape Santo, Akte Peninsula was exhaustively searched, the same patrol being undertaken on 13th November and again on 15th November.

Rain fell heavily accompanied by strong winds on the remaining days of the week and prevented flying.

STAVROS AIR STATION.

"D" SQUADRON.

November 5th–10th.

Reconnaissances.—An exhaustive mine reconnaissance of the approaches to Stavros was made on 6th November by a Farman preparatory to return to "Endymion." During the day enemy aircraft were reported approaching and fighting patrols with six aeroplanes were made but no enemy aircraft were sighted. A reconnaissance of the enemy front lines was made by a machine with two escorts and a new battery position was located.

Similar work was undertaken on the following day, two fighter patrols for enemy aircraft, one reconnaissance of the front line and a patrol of the approaches to Stavros being made.

On 9th November, a reconnaissance was made of Drama, which disclosed that the aerodrome had been increased, and that there were now seven sheds. One 65-lb. and one 112-lb. bomb were dropped at these. An enemy aeroplane was engaged but the result proved indecisive. A reconnaissance of the Angista valley and enemy lines of communication was made in the course of the flight.

Bomb Attack on Zdravik.—On 10th November, the Gulf of Ruphini was patrolled for enemy submarines on two occasions by Farman aeroplanes. A patrol was also made for enemy aircraft and the D.H. 4 dropped two 65-lb. bombs on Zdravik.

Only signalled reports of this week's operations have as yet been received.

November 11th–17th.

Anti-Submarine Patrols.—On 11th November three submarine patrols extending to nearly six hours were made over the Gulf of Ruphini and down the coast of the Akte Peninsula to Mount Athos.

During one of these patrols a landing was made near Stratone on Erisos Bay, in order to see whether the ground was suitable for use as an emergency landing ground. It was found to be satisfactory.

Mine Patrol.—On 12th November a patrol was made by a Farman over the swept channel for mines, and then from Cape Deuthero to Mount Athos for enemy submarines.

Engagement with Enemy.—A "D. 3" type Albatross Scout was engaged by a Sopwith 2-seater. No details of the action have yet been received, but the signalled report states that the Albatross was damaged.

Mine Patrol.—On 13th November the Gulf of Ruphini was searched for mines and submarines.

On 14th November two offensive patrols were made for hostile aircraft. One enemy machine was sighted and pursued, but could not be overtaken.

Bomb Attack on Enemy Camp.—The De Haviland 4 on patrol observed a camp $2\frac{1}{2}$ miles W.N.W. of Razilivos, on which she dropped two 112-lb. bombs, which made direct hits.

Anti-Submarine and Mine Reconnaissances.—On 15th November the Gulf of Ruphini and the area eastwards to Thasos were reconnoitred for mines and submarines, and a reconnaissance of the enemy front line was made.

Difficulty having been experienced with the disintegrating belts for Vickers gun in a "Camel," a machine of that type was flown to Salonika in order to obtain the most recent experience from Royal Flying Corps.

On the return journey an enemy machine was encountered and pursued to Drama, the engagement being indecisive. Only a signalled report of this engagement has as yet been received.

During the remainder of the week unfavourable weather conditions have prevailed, and no flying has taken place.

KALLONI AIR STATION (MITYLENE).

"B" SQUADRON.

November 5th–10th.

No operations have been undertaken during the week. Work has progressed rapidly on the new aerodrome, which is now quite fit for service, and buildings for accommodation of the personnel during the winter are nearing completion.

The enemy have not fired at the old aerodrome at Thermi since 1st November 1917.

November 11th–17th.

No service flying has been undertaken during the current week.

GLIKI AIR STATION (IMBROS).

"C" SQUADRON.

November 5th–10th.

On the early morning of 6th November enemy aircraft were reported over Kephalo and Tenedos and a Sopwith two-seater and a "Pup" were sent in search of them but without result.

Later in the day two D.H. 4 aeroplanes arrived from Mudros, having been detailed for special duty.

Reconnaissance.—On 7th November a reconnaissance of the Straits for shipping was made and also a search for enemy aircraft.

Reconnaissance and Bomb Attacks.—The two D.H. 4 aeroplanes left Imbros with orders to reconnoitre, photograph, and bomb suitable objectives on the section of the Berlin–Constantinople Railway, which lies between Uzun Keupru and Muradli, and along which all the through traffic from Austria and Germany to the Caucasus, the Palestine and the Mesopotamia fronts is obliged to go, besides the produce of Turkey being sent westwards for consumption in Germany. Along this railway approximately 45 divisions are supplied.

Flight-Lieut. R. Sorley and Observer Sub-Lieut. F. Smith in De Haviland 4, No. N 5976, left Imbros at 11 a.m. on 7th

November, with orders to proceed to Uzun Keupru and reconnoitre the railway to the eastward until the second D.H. 4 was sent, when both machines were to return in company.

Heavy clouds were encountered until nearing Uzun Keupru, but the air was found clear along a good length of the railway, which runs along the bank of the Ergere Su.

There are numerous bridges on this section, but these are all narrow, and therefore difficult targets (the line being single track), with the exception of the first bridge to the eastward of Lule Burgas, which consists of three iron spans, and the first two bridges east of Pavlo Station, all of which are good objectives for daylight or night bombing.

Sidings with rolling stock were observed at Uzun Keupru, Pavlo, Alapie and Lule Burgas Stations, but, being accommodation sidings only, do not present good targets. Pavlo Station was attacked with two 65-lb. bombs, the first of which hit a large building alongside the railway (probably a warehouse) and the second exploding on the permanent way a little to the west of the town. The damage was not ascertained owing to the cloud of smoke which hung over the line.

No anti-aircraft fire was experienced during the whole journey, nor were any enemy aircraft seen.

Not having encountered the second D.H. 4, this machine turned when 2 miles E. of Lule Burgas, and proceeded direct to Imbros, completing her journey in 3 hours 2 minutes.

The second D.H. 4 was ordered to proceed to Muradli and reconnoitre the railway to the north and westward. After crossing the coast at Cape Gremen heavy and continuous clouds were encountered, and after 25 minutes flight without being able to see anything, abandoned the reconnaissance somewhere near Keshan, altering course and proceeding to Ferejik Station on the Adrianople–Dedeagatch Railway.

Two 65-lb. bombs were dropped at the Kal Derkoz Road bridge over the Maritza, one of which fell 25 yards to the south of the bridge head in a small military camp, while the other fell 100 yards beyond. Two hundred rounds were fired from low altitude at a train in Ferejik Station, heavy anti-aircraft and machine-gun fire being experienced in reply.

The machine returned direct to Imbros from Ferejik, having been 1 hour 45 minutes *en route*.

Photography.—On the morning of 8th November, a B.E. was sent to Mudros with reports and photographs of the railway reconnaissance and undertook a submarine patrol *en route*. Two enemy aircraft came over Imbros and were pursued by two Sopwith two-seaters and one "Pup," which, however, could not catch the enemy before they landed at Nagara.

On 9th November the B.E., which had flown to Mudros on the preceding day, returned carrying out a submarine patrol on the way.

November 11th–17th.

Reconnaissance and Bomb Attack.—On the morning of 11th November, Flight Lieut. R. Sorley with Observer Sub-Lieut. F. Smith made a further reconnaissance of the Constantinople-Berlin Railway between Lule Burgas and Alapie in D.H. 4, No. N. 5976.

It was noticed when the machine started that smoke signals were started at Chanak-Keshan and other places on the mainland. Course was steered over Keshan to Lule Burgas Bridge, where the machine descended to 2,000 feet, both machine-gun and rifle fire being experienced on this occasion. One 45-lb. bomb was dropped, which fell 20 yards beyond the bridge and just to the N. of the rails. A 100-lb. bomb which was released at the same time hung up in the bomb gear and eventually dropped off in a field after many attempts to get rid of it.

The machine proceeded westward along the railway, bursts of machine-gun and rifle fire being experienced at stations, bridges, and other important points.

At Alapie the large forage store located during the previous reconnaissance was attacked with one Carcass bomb and one small petrol bomb. A fire was started on the windward side of one large area of stacks, and this when last seen was burning fiercely. A subsequent reconnaissance showed that this area of stacks was completely destroyed.

The machine returned *viâ* Hairobolu and Ipsala, making a reconnaissance en route, and arrived at Imbros after a three-hour trip.

Reconnaissance of Mine Field.—An escorted reconnaissance of the British minefields at the entrance to the Dardanelles was undertaken during the morning, and showed that a considerable number of mines in each line were "watching" on the surface.

Colour Filter Goggle (No. 61) were used and proved a great help in picking up the submerged lines of mines.

Two offensive patrols for enemy aircraft were also made, without, however, encountering an enemy machine, and a reconnaissance of the Straits for shipping was effected.

Reconnaissance and Bomb Dropping.—On the morning of the 12th November, Flight Lieut. A. Woodward with Observer Lieut. O. Palmer in D.H. 4, No. N 5975, reconnoitred the Constantinople-Berlin Railway from Muradli to Mandra. On approaching the railway at Muradli a train of 12 large trucks was observed steaming towards Constantinople. One 100-lb. and one 16-lb. bomb were first dropped at it, but these fell about 200 yards wide of the objective. On a second attempt from 1,800 feet a 65-lb. bomb fell on the track immediately behind the train.

Machine gun fire was experienced from the train.

Two other trains also proceeding towards Constantinople were seen, into the second of which 50 rounds of machine-gun were put. The D.H. 4 flew west as far as Alapie, where the destruction of the hay stacks on the previous day was confirmed.

From this point the machine returned direct to Imbros, having been absent 2 hours 50 minutes.

Offensive Patrol.—During the day three machines carried out an offensive patrol for enemy aircraft, and later endeavoured to intercept enemy aircraft which were reported to be bombing Mavro Island, on both occasions without success.

The Dardanelles were also reconnoitred for enemy shipping.

Reconnaissance.—On 13th November a D.H. 4 again attempted to reconnoitre the Constantinople–Berlin Railway, but was obliged to return with magneto trouble.

Anti-Submarine Patrol.—A submarine reconnaissance was also made to the north of Imbros and east of Samothraki as far north as Dedeagatch.

On 15th November a machine was sent to locate guns which were firing at Mavro Island.

During the remainder of the week bad weather has prevented operations.

MUDROS AIR STATION.

November 5th–10th.

Anti-Submarine Patrols.—At dawn on 7th November two Farman aeroplanes carried out submarine patrols, one searching to the north of the island and in the vicinity of Samothraki, while the other searched in the direction of Mount Athos.

At patrol was again made to the west and north of Lemnos at dawn on the 8th November, nothing being sighted. Subsequently it transpired that M.L. 204, on guard duty at Kondia, had heard a submarine on hydrophone on the preceding evening, had fired at her on the surface, and afterwards had hunted her by hydrophone until midnight west of Cape Murtzephlos. Submarine patrols were accordingly carried out at intervals by Farman aeroplanes to the west and north of Imbros, and a seaplane was also sent to work hydrophones west of Lemnos. After her first descent for hydrophone work she was obliged to alight with engine trouble, and was eventually towed back to Mudros.

November 11th–17th.

Anti-Submarine Patrols.—In view of an enemy submarine having been sighted off the entrance to the Gulf of Salonika, a continuous patrol by aircraft to the W. and S.W. of Lemnos was carried out by two seaplanes from "Ark Royal," and two aeroplanes from "G" Flight, Marsh Aerodrome.

On the following day the continuous patrol was maintained until dark, three seaplanes and two aeroplanes participating.

The last machine away had not returned by dark, and it subsequently transpired that her engine failed when she was N.W. of Kastro. Her distress signals by W/T were jammed by ships in harbour, and she was obliged to come down in the water.

The Pilot, Flight Sub-Lieut. Harben, and Observer, First Air Mechanic White, swam for 1½ hours, until they reached a rock, which they located by its phosphorescence. From this they were eventually rescued by a Greek fishing boat.

On 13th November two B.E.'s with Greek pilots searched for the missing machine, which had by this time sunk. Later in the morning in accordance with R.A.E.'s orders continuous escorting patrols were made by seaplanes and aeroplanes while "Lord Nelson" was out of port for the purpose of carrying out target practice.

On 15th November a Greek officer under instruction, carrying out a solo flight to the north of the island, reported having seen what he believed to be an enemy submarine 5 miles north of Cape Plako. The report was considered doubtful, but three machines were sent successively over that area, none, however, added any confirmation to the report.

KASSANDRA AIRSHIP STATION.

November 5th–10th.

No airship is yet in action.

November 11th–17th.

The rigging of the airship and inflation of the envelope were completed on 13th November, when, however, the weather was too bad to undertake trials.

Patrol Work.—On the morning of the 14th November trials were carried out, and as these proved satisfactory a patrol of the entrance to the Gulf of Salonika as far south as Psathura was made.

On the following day a similar patrol, but extending further to the westward, was made in a wind which freshened up to 25 miles per hour, and caused difficulty in housing the airship on her return.

On the succeeding days weather prevented flying.

SUDA BAY SEAPLANE STATION.

November 5th–10th.

Patrol Work.—Owing to heavy winds, accompanied by rain, no patrols were carried out on 5th, 6th, 7th, and 9th November. On the remaining days of the week patrols of the approaches to Suda Bay were made both in the morning and evening.

November 11th-17th.

Anti-Submarine Patrol.—A patrol was made on the afternoon of 11th November, after which the weather prevented any patrol until 15th, when three reconnaissances were made in search of a reported submarine.

Since then the weather has been persistently bad.

H.M.S. "PEONY."

November 2nd-6th.

In the morning of 2nd November an enemy machine was sighted approaching Port Vathi at about 10,000 feet. A Schneider seaplane left in pursuit and flew straight to Scalanouva to gain sufficient height and attempt to cut the enemy off from his base. The enemy, however, returned inland over Samsun Dagh at 12,000 feet, and could not be engaged by the Schneider.

Submarine patrols were made from Port Vathi on 5th and 6th November, without anything being sighted.

BRITISH ADRIATIC SQUADRON.

No. 6 WING, R.N.A.S., OTRANTO.

ANTI-SUBMARINE OPERATIONS.

November 19th.

On the report from Saseno at 0700 that a submarine had been sighted steering south, two aeroplanes were immediately despatched, the sea being too rough for seaplanes. Owing to the strong gale that was blowing at the time it was extremely difficult to distinguish the wash of a submarine from the waves themselves.

However, just as one of the aeroplanes had turned to go home, the observer noticed a more persistent wave on the starboard quarter and soon distinguished that it was caused by a submarine on the surface proceeding south. The submarine was preparing to dive, and the aeroplane attacked at once, dropping two 65-lb. bombs, one of which fell 20 feet and the other 40 feet on the port quarter of the submarine.

As the machine turned to observe the effect of the bombs, the conning tower was seen to submerge and no oil or other traces were visible afterwards.

The bombs were dropped at 0749, and nothing more was heard of the submarine until 1400 when S. Maria di Leuca hydrophones reported a submarine coming from a northerly direction.

The submarine had therefore accomplished the distance from where she had been bombed to S. Maria di Leuca at an average speed of between six and seven knots.

During the last six weeks, seven submarines have been sighted by either Saseno or Palascia look-out stations passing through the Straits on the surface. On each occasion aircraft have been sent out from Otranto with the following results:—

> On two occasions the submarines have been bombed.
>
> On one occasion submarine was sighted but dived before it could be attacked.
>
> On one occasion Italian seaplanes only went out, as the news was not received by the British station until just before dark, and for this reason the search was only a short one.
>
> On three occasions the submarines have dived before being sighted; either they themselves saw or heard aircraft or destroyers coming towards them.

MALTA.

INTELLIGENCE REPORT (week ending 17.11.17).

H.M. Seaplane Base.—There have been no reports during the week of either enemy submarines or mines, and it would appear that the submarines must have been withdrawn from this area.

Ships sunk	Nil.
Ships attacked	Nil.
Mines found	Nil.
"Allos" received	Nil.

Weather.—On the whole rough weather and high winds have been experienced this week.

On three days flying was impossible; on the remaining days there were strong westerly winds and a considerable swell at sea.

ROYAL FLYING CORPS COMMUNIQUÉS.

ROYAL FLYING CORPS COMMUNIQUÉ.—No. 114.

During the period under review, 13th to 19th inclusive, the weather has been very unfavourable for aerial work. Ten enemy aircraft have been brought down by aeroplanes and six driven down out of control. Over 33,000 rounds were fired from low altitudes at ground targets.

November 13th.

The weather was fine, but heavy ground mist prevented much work being done.

One reconnaissance was carried out by the Fifth Brigade, two contact patrols by the Second Brigade, and 189 photographs were taken.

Eleven hostile batteries were successfully engaged for destruction with aeroplane observation, 10 of which were by the Fourth Army, which damaged eight gun-pits and caused four explosions and two fires.

Low flying aeroplanes fired over 8,000 rounds at ground targets; 3,500 of these were fired by pilots of No. 32 Squadron.

Enemy Aircraft.—Enemy aircraft activity varied considerably, but on the whole was about normal.

Captain P. Huskinson, No. 19 Squadron, saw a formation of 12 enemy aircraft bombing machines coming west, so dived at one, and after 150 rounds had been fired, the enemy aircraft went down in a slow glide to about 3,000 feet, then got into a spin and crashed. Two other enemy aircraft were driven down out of control, one by Major A. Carter, and the other by Second Lieut. T. Candy, of the same squadron.

Lieutenant Trudeau, No. 23 Squadron, and Second Lieuts. Williams and Moody, both of No. 45 Squadron, also drove down an enemy machine each out of control.

Second Lieuts. Beaver and Agelaste, No. 20 Squadron, destroyed an Albatross Scout near Houthulst, and another was driven down out of control by Lieutenant Kirkman and Captain Burbage, of the same squadron, east of Passchendaele.

A patrol of No 24 Squadron attacked eight enemy scouts, and Captain Beanlands shot one down out of control, and in another fight drove one down, which fell into a cloud and was seen by ground observers to crash.

Lieutenant E. Williams and Second Air Mechanic T. Jones, No. 48 Squadron, attacked an enemy scout, which went into a spin, and then fell apparently out of control.

Aeroplanes of No. 52 Squadron had very hard fighting, and three enemy machines are believed to have fallen out of control as the result of different combats, and one of these appeared to fall into the sea.

Second Lieut. D. Hilton, No. 29 Squadron, shot down an enemy scout, which fell apparently out of control.

One enemy machine was brought down by aeroplanes in the Fourth Brigade area, and another was forced to land within our lines, after having been hit by anti-aircraft of the Second Army. The machine was slightly damaged and the pilot unhurt.

Bombing.—First Brigade.—No. 18 Squadron dropped four 112-lb. bombs on Libercourt, two on Henin-Liétard and four on Pont-à-Vendin. No. 2 Squadron dropped six 25-lb. bombs on Benifontane.

Fifth Brigade.—No. 57 Squadron dropped one 230-lb., three 112-lb. and eight 25-lb. bombs on Roulers.

Ninth Wing.—On the night of the 11th/12th, No. 102 Squadron dropped two 112-lb. bombs on Menin.

Brigades also dropped forty-three 25-lb. bombs on various targets during the day.

November 14th.

A thick ground mist prevented work.

November 15th.

Although the weather was fine, visibility was bad owing to ground mist and low clouds.

Nine reconnaissances were carried out, two by the Second Brigade, one by the Third Brigade and six by the Fourteenth Wing, and two contact patrols in which much information was obtained, were done by the Second Brigade.

With aeroplane observation five hostile batteries were successfully engaged for destruction, two were neutralised and one pit was damaged; 5,100 rounds were fired from low altitudes at ground targets.

Flight Commander Mundy, Naval Squadron No. 8, fired 500 of these at an active hostile battery.

Three hundred and four photographs were taken and thirty-two 25-lb. bombs were dropped on various targets.

Enemy Aircraft.—Enemy aircraft were active in the morning and endeavoured to stop our artillery machines working, while 15 of theirs attempted to work on the Second Army front.

A fight took place between enemy aircraft scouts and No. 65 Squadron over Dadizeele, and Lieutenant F. Symons shot one down out of control. Lieutenant G. Cox shot down another, which was badly damaged.

Second Lieut. J. Leach, No. 29 Squadron, dived at four enemy scouts which were attacking Camels, and after firing 30 rounds at close range into one of the machines, it went down in flames and crashed.

A patrol of No. 45 Squadron attacked a German two-seater, which was destroyed by Second Lieut. P. Carpenter. Shortly afterwards this patrol engaged another formation of enemy aircraft scouts, and Second Lieut. K. Montgomery shot one down in flames which broke to pieces before reaching the ground;

another was shot down in flames by Second Lieut. E. Hand, while Captain J. Firth shot one down out of control.

Major A. Carter and Second Lieut. E. Oliver, No. 19 Squadron, were pursuing an enemy machine when they saw a two-seater near Zandvoorde, so attacked and destroyed it.

Captain P. Fullard, No. 1 Squadron, dived at an enemy scout, which had obtained a favourable position on a Nieuport's tail, and destroyed it. Meanwhile another scout was getting into a favourable position on his tail, but he out-manœuvred this machine, and after firing three-quarters of a drum into it, the enemy aircraft fell out of control, and was seen to break up before reaching the ground. Second Lieut. L. Cummings, of the same squadron, shot down a German scout out of control during the same fight.

Second Lieuts. Makepeace and Harmer, No. 60 Squadron, shot down a hostile scout out of control, near Moorslede.

A fight took place south-east of Dixmude between an offensive patrol of No. 24 Squadron and enemy aircraft scouts. Lieutenant J. Jephson and Second Lieuts. E. Macdonald and P. MacDougall each drove down one of the enemy scouts out of control, while another was driven down damaged by Second Lieut. J. Jackson.

Flight Sub-Lieut. Maund, Naval Squadron No. 10, attacked a German two-seater which had been driven down by another naval pilot, and after following this machine for some time, and firing, it fell out of control. Flight Sub-Lieut. Manuel attacked an Albatross Scout, which he drove down and followed until he saw it fall out of control and crash, while Flight Lieut. Curtis shot one down out of control. Flight Sub-Lieut. Hall attacked an Albatross Scout which had been driven down by a D.H. 5 and followed it through a cloud, firing until the enemy aircraft went down in an erratic dive and appeared to be out of control.

A German aeroplane was hit and brought down by anti-aircraft gunners of the Second Army.

November 16th.

Very little flying was possible owing to low clouds and a mist.

Two trench reconnaissances were done by the Third Brigade and four by the Fourteenth Wing.

One hostile battery was successfully engaged for destruction by artillery of the First Army, which caused two large explosions of ammunition and started large fires.

Another hostile battery was successfully engaged for destruction by artillery of the XV. Corps, with balloon observation.

Forty 25-lb. bombs were dropped on various objectives, and 4,500 rounds were fired from low altitudes at ground targets.

Enemy aircraft were inactive, and only a few indecisive combats took place.

November 17th.

Low clouds and mist prevented much flying being done.

One hostile battery was successfully engaged for destruction by artillery of the Third Army, and 37 photographs were taken by the Third Brigade.

Six 25-lb. bombs were dropped on various targets, and 1,200 rounds were fired by machines of the First Wing into enemy trenches.

On the night of the 16th/17th, No. 59 Squadron carried out a reconnaissance of their Corps area.

November 18th.

Low clouds and mist again interfered with aerial work.

Five reconnaissances were carried out and 22 counter-attack patrols by the Second Brigade. Twenty-five plates were exposed by the Third Brigade, and thirty-one 25-lb. bombs and one 112-lb. bomb were dropped on various targets.

With aeroplane observation five hostile batteries were successfully engaged for destruction, and 14 neutralised. One pit was destroyed, three damaged, one explosion and two fires caused. Ninety-three zone-calls were sent down, of which 20 were seen to be answered. Nine thousand and fourteen rounds were fired at ground targets from low altitudes, of which 6,614 were by the Second Brigade.

Enemy Aircraft.—Enemy aircraft were not very active.

While on offensive patrol, Major Carter and Second Lieut. E. Oliver, No. 19 Squadron, attacked a two-seater which they drove down out of control, while two other two-seaters were driven down out of control, one by Captain H. Reeves, No. 1 Squadron, and the other by Second Lieut. J. Macrae, No. 23 Squadron.

Captains R. Chidlaw-Roberts and H. Hammersley, No. 60 Squadron, saw two enemy two-seaters at work, so attacked them and destroyed one.

When on line patrol, S.E. 5's of No. 56 Squadron observed a two-seater flying west, and Captain J. McCudden dived on its tail, and after a burst from both guns, the enemy gunner was seen to collapse. The machine went down and was completely wrecked in a trench in the enemy's lines.

A patrol of No. 48 Squadron engaged six enemy scouts, and in the fighting Lieutenant J. Cordes and First Air Mechanic E. Dunford shot down one which crashed and burst into flames. Two others were driven down apparently out of control—one by Captain A. Field and Second Lieut. G. Horsfall, and the other by Captain B. Beanlands and Second Lieut. D. Sutherland.

Infantry of the Second Army shot down a German machine which was destroyed.

November 19th.

Not much work was possible on account of low clouds and **mist.**

Two successful reconnaissances were carried out—one by Captain Duncan and Lieutenant Henderson, No. 5 Squadron, and the other by Captain Youdale and Lieutenant Worthington, No. 21 Squadron.

Six hostile batteries were successfully engaged for destruction with aeroplane observation, and seven neutralised. Five pits were damaged, five explosions and three fires caused. Five thousand six hundred rounds were fired from low altitudes at infantry, which were dispersed, and at other targets.

Forty-four 25-lb. bombs were dropped on various objectives.

Enemy Aircraft.—Captain A. E. Mackay, No. 23 Squadron, saw two enemy two-seaters patrolling south-west of Moorslede, so attacked the lower one, which he shot down apparently out of control. He was not able to watch its ultimate fate owing to the other machine, which attacked him and forced him to turn round and engage it, which he did, and after a while destroyed it.

Lieutenant W. Jenkins, No. 60 Squadron, and Second Lieut. J. Allen, No. 23 Squadron, each drove down an enemy machine, which was hit and went down possibly out of control.

S. WOOD, Captain,
Staff Officer.

Advanced Headquarters,
    Royal Flying Corps,
        22nd November 1917.

No. 47.

CONFIDENTIAL.

ROYAL NAVAL AIR SERVICE.

OPERATIONS REPORT

(with Royal Flying Corps Reports attached).

1st to 16th DECEMBER 1917.

NAVAL STAFF,
  OPERATIONS DIVISION.
  16th December 1917.

ROYAL NAVAL AIR SERVICE.

REPORT OF OPERATIONS

(Completed from Reports during period
1st to 16th December 1917).

CONTENTS.

	PAGE
HOME STATIONS	2
DUNKIRK	9
R.N.A.S. SQUADRONS, WITH ROYAL FLYING CORPS REPORTS ATTACHED	19
EASTERN MEDITERRANEAN	20
EAST INDIES AND EGYPT	25
BRITISH ADRIATIC SQUADRON	34
CAPE STATION	35
ROYAL FLYING CORPS COMMUNIQUÉS	37

HOME STATIONS.

SUBMARINE PATROL WORK.

December 3rd.

Newlyn.—Short Seaplane, N. 1604 (Pilot, Flight Lieut. J. W. Hobbs; Observer R. L. Hobson, A.M.), left on patrol at 0835 in response to signals reporting the presence of an enemy submarine the previous evening. After patrolling the area in concentric triangles for 2½ hours the seaplane sighted large patches and circular tracks of oil on the starboard bow about 5 miles distant. The seaplane altered course to investigate the oil patches, shortly after which a small object, having the appearance of a mine, was observed directly underneath, and the seaplane descended to 800 feet for closer observation. Whilst flying round the mine, a long dark object came to the surface suddenly in the midst of the oil patches 2 miles to the westward. The seaplane was immediately turned towards it, and the object, which was then clearly seen to be a submarine, began to submerge, and from the appearance of its wake it had just increased speed. The observer was unable to get his sights on as the target was under afloat; the seaplane accordingly doubled back and passed over the target again. One 100-lb. H.E. bomb (2·5 sec. delay) was then dropped on the position at 1105, the submarine being clearly visible deep down in the water just before the bomb exploded. Nothing further was observed, and a W/T report was sent and calcium flares dropped on the spot. The seaplane continued to patrol the area for three-quarters of an hour, then returned to the base. Details are not given as to the size or build of the submarine, but its deck appeared to be camouflaged.

December 3rd.

H.M.S. "Riviera."—A patrol in search of hostile submarine was carried out at 1325 by Sub-Lieut. Larter with Observer Sub-Lieut. Sivil in Short Seaplane N. 1678.

The patrol was carried out at 4,000 feet, owing to the visibility being good, and there being less chance of submarines sighting or hearing the seaplane. At 1525 a submarine was sighted, steering south, at an estimated speed of 10 knots. It was cream-coloured, no guns or masts were observed, and its length was estimated at 250 feet.

The seaplane altered course immediately to intercept it, and the submarine at once submerged. Owing to the rapid submerging, which took place in 30 to 45 seconds, no recognition signal was fired.

Two 100-lb. bombs were dropped at 1530, the first from 3,000 feet, and the second two minutes later from 1,000 feet. They were observed to burst about 30 feet from the track of the submarine. The seaplane circled over the spot for ten minutes. but nothing was observed and the patrol was resumed.

December 4th.

Felixstowe.—Large America Seaplane 8689 left on patrol at 0955, in company with machines N. 64 and 8677. When near Shipwash Light Vessel, 8677 sent a signal and returned. followed a few minutes later by N. 64.

Seaplane 8689 continued on its course, and at 1050 sighted the North Hinder Light Vessel on the port bow; at the same time a small object, which turned out to be a Dutch sailing vessel, was sighted. The seaplane passed the vessel on the starboard beam, and was on the point of returning to carry out its original patrol when a submarine, half submerged, was sighted about 50 feet on the further side of the sailing vessel and a dinghy with one man on board, which seemed to be returning from the submarine. Two recognition signals were fired, after which the seaplane turned to bomb the submarine, but found it had fully submerged, leaving no disturbance on the water whatever. The seaplane then circled round the ship, and after taking a photograph of it came down to within a few feet of the water, and observed the name "Holland" on the stern of the vessel and the number "K.W. 16" on the bow.

The seaplane then climbed to 1,000 feet, and endeavoured to send a signal, but found that the aerial had been lost in going close to the water. This was repaired as quickly as possible, but by this time the seaplane had reached the shipping channel, and it was decided not to send a signal, but to return to the base and report direct, and a landing was made at 1234. After refilling, the seaplane left again at 1335 for North Hinder in company with machine 8661, and at 1433 North Hinder was sighted, also the Dutch vessel a few miles further south. After taking another photograph of the ship the machines did a large circle (10 miles area) around it, and returned to the base.

December 5th.

Westgate.—Whilst returning from a patrol, Seaplane N. 1275 (Pilot Flight Sub-Lieut. Hodgson, Observer A.M. (2) Worthington W/T) observed a thin oil patch, approximately 30 feet long, 11 miles N.E. of North Foreland, heading north and south. Three 100-lb. bombs were dropped at 1003; the first dropped 300 yards to the starboard of the patch slightly to port; the second dropped 200 yards in front slightly to starboard, southward end, and the third bomb dropped 100 yards in front to the southward.

The machine circled round the spot for some time, but nothing further was observed.

December 6th.

Cherbourg.—Seaplane 9860 (Pilot Flight Sub-Lieut. Mossop, D.S.C.) left on a patrol at 1045 and at 1215 sighted a hostile submarine. The seaplane proceeded to attack and the submarine immediately submerged and disappeared before the seaplane could get into position to drop bombs. Two bombs were dropped, however, both of which were seen to explode just ahead of the wake made by the submarine diving.

The seaplane remained in the vicinity for about 30 minutes, but nothing further of the submarine was seen; the seaplane was then forced to land owing to engine trouble. An attempt was made to get the engine working, but sufficient revolutions to get the machine off the water could not be obtained, so the pilot decided to attempt to " taxi " to the Isle of Wight.

Owing to the westerly wind, however, it was found impossible to keep the machine on to a northerly course while " taxiing," so the pilot turned south in the hope of being picked up.

At about 2115 H.M.S. " P " 32 was sighted and communicated with by using the distress signal and Aldis lamp; the seaplane was then picked up in a very damaged condition and sinking. As it was necessary for H.M.S. " P " 32 to proceed on escort duty the Commanding Officer decided to abandon the seaplane, which was done after all confidential codes and maps had been salved, but owing to the rough sea and damaged condition of the seaplane it was impossible to salve any of the fittings, wireless, or Lewis gun.

Both pilot and passenger were taken on board the " P " boat and conveyed to Bembridge.

Note.—It is considered improbable that the submarine was hit or damaged, but in view of the fact that it would appear possible the submarine was waiting for a convoy which was approaching the position, and was at the time a short distance away, also that H.M.S. " Revenge " was shortly expected, the presence of the seaplane, which undoubtedly caused the submarine to dive, prevented an attack on these vessels being made by the submarine.

December 8th.

Cattewater.—Between 1335 and 1700 a special patrol was carried out by Short Seaplane N. 1624, and at 1412 the periscope of a submarine was sighted and a bomb dropped three minutes later, which fell three feet ahead of the periscope. At 1455 the submarine was again sighted on the surface, and at 1458 another bomb was dropped on the swirl after the submarine had submerged. The vicinity was searched and at 1535 a large stretch of oil 200 or 300 yards long was observed with two blobs of thick oil to the south-west of the long streak. One of five destroyers, five miles south-west, escorting a convoy steering E.N.E., was warned of the presence of the submarine in the vicinity.

December 8th.

Great Yarmouth.—Short Seaplane N. 1675 (Pilot Flight Lieut. Cross, Second Air Mechanic Raymond W/T) left at 0800 on a patrol to Cross Sands, Smith's Knoll, Jim Howe, Haisboro' and War Channels. After passing Smith's Knoll Pillar Buoy at 0303, course was altered to the N.E., the seaplane then being at a height of 1,500 feet. At 0837 the V-shaped wake of the periscope of a submarine was observed, approximately two miles away on the port bow. The wake disappeared as the submarine submerged, then started again about 1½ minutes later a short distance south of the first position and continued for about 50 yards, then again disappeared. This occurred a third time, after which the submarine was not sighted again. The seaplane was turned into a north and south line, descending to 800 feet and dropped a bomb at 0840, where the submarine's last wake had been seen, and a second and third bomb at intervals of 50 yards south of the spot. All the bombs exploded under the surface but no oil or bubbles were observed. A W/T signal was immediately sent reporting the position of the submarine, and after spending 15 minutes in the vicinity the seaplane made for Cross Sands. At 0905 six trawlers were sighted steering east and signalled to by Aldis lamp, but as the trawlers had no means of replying to this signal a landing was made beside the leading trawler, which was informed by semaphore giving the position of the submarine, after which the seaplane returned to the base.

AIRSHIP ATTACKS ON HOSTILE SUBMARINES.

December 7th.

Pembroke.—Whilst returning from patrol, Airship S.S.Z. 16 sighted and attacked a submarine from a height of about 1,000 feet. The weather was misty and visibility bad. The submarine, on being sighted, turned towards the airship, fired one round and then submerged rapidly, but not before her decks had been swept by machine-gun fire from the airship.

Two bombs were dropped one minute after the submarine had submerged, the first exploding about 25 feet on the port bow, the second one failing to explode. The position was marked by a calcium flare, and 25 minutes later communication was effected with two destroyers in the vicinity.

H.M.S. "Badger" and "Foxhound" en route to the Skerries were diverted in order to hunt the neighbourhood, but in view of the fact that British submarines were known to be working in this area they were instructed to resume their previous duties at 2340.

The submarine in question was about 240 feet long, painted light grey, one gun forward of the conning tower, double hatches, and had the appearance of a minelayer.

December 8th.

Mullion.—Whilst on patrol Airship C. 9 observed a thin moving oil track at 1150. The airship followed the track, which was seen to make right angle turns, and dropped one 230-lb. bomb about 100 feet ahead of the track, after which large air bubbles rose to the surface and the forward movement of the track stopped. Oil then came up but not in large quantities, but nothing further was observed. The airship was then recalled owing to the weather.

December 8th.

Pembroke.—Whilst on patrol off Hartland Point, Airship S.S.Z. 16 sighted a line of oil bubbles moving south-west at about 4 knots. Two bombs were dropped, 150 and 250 feet respectively, ahead of the oil track, which caused it to increase and move slower.

Airship C. 2 from Mullion, and an armed trawler No. 2657 "Ben Strome" co-operated in the attack, and at 1330 the trawler dropped three depth charges on the position indicated by the airships. The position was buoyed and airship was forced to return at 1406.

Trawlers and drifters were despatched but nothing further was seen of the submarine, but at 1100 the following day oil was observed still rising from the buoyed position, and two depth charges were dropped without any visible result.

December 8th.

Pembroke.—While acting as escort to a convoy, Airship C. 5A (Pilot Lieutenant J. F. Hart, R.N.) sighted the periscope of a submarine in a position 7 miles to the south-west, steering north-west. Course was altered in that direction, and the submarine was seen to submerge. Three 100-lb. (2½-second delay) bombs were dropped, one on the swirl, one 200 feet ahead of the swirl, and one 400 feet ahead of it.

At 1525 the periscope was again sighted 400 yards south-west of the first position, and a fourth bomb was dropped about 200 feet ahead of the swirl. A group of minesweepers in charge of H M. Drifter "Comily Bank" co-operated with the airship in this engagement, and dropped a total of 10 depth charges on the position. Oil and bubbles were reported rising to the surface by both the airship and drifters.

December 12th.

Pembroke.—Airship C. 3 carried out a patrol to Coningbeg between 0915 and 1715, during which an oil patch was sighted and bombed 5 miles south-west of St. Ann's Head at 1545. Oil rose to the surface after the first bomb had been dropped; this was observed to increase after the second bomb had exploded.

December 15th.

Mullion.—Whilst on patrol from 0720 to 1820 Airship C. 23A dropped a bomb at 0910 on what, on closer examination, appeared to be a whale. At 1210 a torpedo was observed to explode on the beach half a mile east of Bolt Head, and three minutes later a vessel south of Bolt Head was torpedoed. At 1215 the periscope of a submarine was observed between one and two miles south 10° east of Bolt Head. The airship, being to leeward, although at full speed, took some time to close, and the periscope was lost sight of some 10 minutes before the airship could get over the spot. The approximate position was marked, and T.B. 81 was instructed to drop a depth charge. Nothing was observed until 1435, when a small oil patch appeared south-east of Bolt Head. One 100-lb. bomb was dropped on the oil patch by the airship, and slightly more oil came to the surface. A trawler was then instructed to drop a depth charge, which she did, but nothing further was observed, and C. 23A left at 1540.

NIGHT ATTACK BY HOSTILE AIRCRAFT.

December 5th–6th.

A bombing attack was carried out during the night of approximately five hours' duration by hostile aeroplanes over the area Thames Estuary, Essex, Kent, and London. It is impossible to estimate accurately the number of machines, but probably about 25 enemy aeroplanes took part in the raid, of which number only five or six reached Central London. The hostile machines crossed the Kentish Coast near the North Foreland at about 0130. One machine penetrated as far as Sheerness and dropped two bombs. The remainder attacked various places in Thanet and on the Kentish coast. This attack was preliminary to a succession of more serious attempts on the part of the hostile machines, and may have been made with light machines with the object of drawing gunfire. Between 0308 and 0315 further attacks developed over Sandwich and Broadstairs. One group of machines bombed Deal and Dover. The movements of the remainder are somewhat uncertain, with the exception of one, which penetrated to near Maidstone, and a second, which passed *via* Canterbury to Whitstable, and thence to sea. Of the others, none appear to have come far inland.

Between 0400 and 0440 two groups of machines crossed the Essex coast and three groups came over the North Foreland, then all five, which may be designated (A, B, C, D, E) steered a course for London.

Group A, which crossed at the mouth of the Crouch at 0415, steered a course Danbury, Billericay, Brentwood, and Wanstead. Some machines of this group appear to have been turned, but one or more passed into London from the north-east at about 0450.

Group B, which passed Foulness at about 0412, steered a course *via* Wakering and Southend, thence up the river, passing into East London at about the same time as Group A.

Group C, which passed Barton's Point at 0410, joined up with Group B.

Group D, which passed the North Foreland at about 0420, entered the mouth of the Swale at about 0450, and some of the machines proceeded towards London *viâ* Chatham. South of Dartford they were turned by gunfire at about 0505. The others followed a more southerly course, passing Maidstone, and appear to have been turned by gunfire from the outer defences near Ide Hill.

Group E., which was off the south of the Swale at about 0400, steered a course *viâ* Chatham, Rochester, Meopham, and Eynesford. Here some machines turned back, but one proceeded to London *viâ* Chislehurst, Sidcup, and Eltham at about 0445, while another came in over Beckenham and Streatham at 0500.

A number of incendiary bombs were dropped in London, but the damage and casualties were slight. Four large fires were caused at Shoreditch, Whitechapel, and South Lambeth Road. In addition to these, a number of small fires were started, one of these being at Somerset House.

Outside London bombs were dropped at Chislehurst, Ramsgate, Margate, Deal, Chatham, Dover, Herne Bay, and Sheerness, causing a few casualties and slight damage.

The tactical plan seems to have been to exhaust the defences by preliminary attacks, and then to deliver four simultaneous attacks from the north-east, east, and south-west.

Two of the enemy machines crashed, one near Rochford and the other near Canterbury. The crews consisted of three to each machine, one member of each crew was wounded; all were made prisoners.

ACCIDENTS TO AIRSHIPS.

December 11th.

H.M. Coastal Airship "C. 27" left from Pulham at 0740 on patrol, and was in wireless communication until 0920, but at 0940 there was no response to further signals. The skipper of the sailing trawler "Pet" reports that about 0930 on the 11th December, and when about one mile south of Smiths Knoll Spar Buoy, an airship (presumably "C. 27") was seen practically in the water, in flames. The skipper hauled the trawl and sailed in the direction of the airship, which was about six miles south of Spar Buoy, but no trace of the airship was left. Shortly after first sighting the airship the skipper noticed a square object on the water with two poles attached to it, which was in sight for only a few minutes, and then disappeared. This was thought to be either a submarine or part of the airship.

Names of crew :—
 Pilot, Flight Lieut. J. F. Dixon, D.S.O.
 Second Officer, Flight Lieut. H. Hall.
 Coxswain, Acting Air Mechanic J. E. Martin.
 Engineer Air Mechanic 1. E. R. White.
 W/T Air Mechanic 2.—Collett.

December 12th.

H.M. Coastal Airship "C. 26" left on patrol at 0636, with the following crew :—

    Pilot, Flight Lieut. G. C. C. Kilburn.
    Second Officer, Flight Lieut. H. E. C. Plowden.
    Coxswain, J. 17056, Petty Officer A. C. Townsend.
    Engineer, F. 6632, L.M. (E) F. D. Johncock.
    W/T Operator, F. 14604, Air Mechanic 2. F. W. Warman.

Signals were exchanged, the last complete signal being received from "C. 26" to Pulham at 1715, saying, "Both engines broken down, drifting out to sea, three miles south of Lowestoft."

On December 13th an incomplete signal was received at 0123, after which nothing further was heard of the airship. On receipt of the signal at 1715 that "C. 26" was in difficulties, instructions were immediately issued from the Naval Base, Lowestoft, to search, and render assistance if possible, but nothing further of the airship was seen.

News has been received that the "C. 26" landed in Holland on December 13th, and the crew were interned. Further details will be given when the pilot's report comes to hand.

DUNKIRK.

PHOTOGRAPHIC RECONNAISSANCE.

December 6th.

No. 1 Wing (2nd Squadron).—A photographic reconnaissance was carried out over Zeebrugge and Ostende, and interesting photographs were taken of the Mole and the coast between Blankenberghe and De Haan.

December 10th.

Photographs were taken of Varssenaere and Houttave Aerodromes. A certain amount of alteration has taken place at the Varssenaere Aerodrome, and photographs show that there are now a total of 11 large sheds, 12 small sheds, and one Bessoneaux on this aerodrome. Eight machines can also be seen.

OFFENSIVE PATROLS—ENGAGEMENTS WITH ENEMY.

December 4th.

No. 4 Wing (1st Squadron).—Flight Sub-Lieut. Findlay, when on patrol with three other Sopwith Camels, attacked an

Albatross Scout over the Forest D'Houthulst from about 28 yards range, and fired about 350 rounds into him. The hostile machine fell over, side-slipped for several thousand feet, and then dropped into the clouds. It is considered that this machine was probably destroyed.

Flight Lieut. Kinkead sighted a two-seater D.F.W. and attacked him south-east of Dixmude, firing 800 rounds from point blank range. The hostile machine went into a tail slide, then side-slipped, finally nose-diving vertically, and completely out of control, until lost to sight.

December 5th.

No. 4 Wing (1st Squadron).—Whilst returning from a special patrol, Flight Sub-Lieut. Rosevear, D.S.C., met an Albatross Scout in the locality east of Dixmude. The Sopwith pilot fired 150 rounds into him from close range, after which the hostile machine spun on its back, then fell completely out of control for 12,000 feet, and was last seen close to the ground still out of control. It is considered that this machine probably crashed.

December 5th.

No. 4 Wing (10th Squadron).—Whilst on patrol between Keyem and Leke, at 12,000 feet, a formation of five Sopwith Camels was attacked from behind by one of a formation of four Albatross Scouts. This machine was engaged, and after Flight Lieut. Curtis had fired 150 rounds into it from 15 yards range, the hostile machine went down vertically, smoking profusely, and was seen to crash on the ground. This machine was also attacked by Flight Sub-Lieut. Hall, who fired 150 rounds and observed it going down out of control.

December 6th.

No. 4 Wing (1st Squadron).—Whilst on patrol, in company with four other Sopwith Camels, Flight Commander Ridley attacked an enemy scout south-east of Passchendale, firing 50 rounds at close range. The enemy machine plunged down vertically for 12,000 feet, and was lost to sight just near the ground; it is considered probable that this machine was destroyed.

Flight Sub-Lieut. Rosevear, D.S.C., attacked a two-seater enemy machine in the locality of Ostende, and fired 200 rounds into him at point blank range. The hostile machine fell over and plunged downwards vertically until he disappeared from view. It is considered that this machine was probably destroyed.

Squadron Commander Dallas, D.S.C., attacked a two-seater enemy machine near Ostende from close range and fired about 100 rounds. The enemy machine spun for 1,000 feet and then fell over, but the Sopwith pilot could not watch the result owing to his being attacked by six hostile scouts and forced back.

Flight Lieut. Kinkhead attacked a two-seater enemy machine, which he approached unobserved until within very close range, and fired 200 rounds. The enemy machine stalled and dived vertically, but was lost sight of owing to the light being bad.

The same pilot also attacked an Albatross Scout, and after firing a long burst into him from point blank range the hostile machine toppled over and went into a flat spin for over 7,000 feet. This was witnessed by another pilot, who states he watched the machine almost to the ground.

Flight Sub-Lieut. Forman attacked a Gotha with lights on, returning from a raid over Dunkerque, two miles out to sea off Westende. He got right on its tail and fired 200 rounds from about 70 yards; coming up under its tail he got into the eddy caused by the retreating hostile machine, and the Sopwith Camel turned over. When the pilot had righted his machine the Gotha had disappeared from view.

December 6th.

No. 4 Wing (9th Squadron).—Whilst on patrol a formation of five Sopwith Camels dived on an Albatross two-seater about 4 miles west of Courtrai, at about 13,000 feet. The hostile machine dived away and was followed down to 2,000 feet when it went into a vertical dive, and was observed to crash on the ground.

December 6th.

No. 4 Wing (9th Squadron).—Whilst on patrol Flight Commander Fall observed a hostile machine south-east of Ypres, and dived on him from the sun. The Sopwith attacked at close range, at one time within 20 yards, and fired about 150 rounds, followed by a further 100 rounds from behind. The hostile machine dived and spun down, part of the time on its back, and was finally seen to crash.

On a later patrol Flight Commander Fall, when about 8 miles west of Staden, attacked a hostile machine from behind and above, and approaching from the sun, in consequence of which he had got to within 50 yards range, and had fired about 100 rounds before the hostile pilot was aware of his presence. The hostile aircraft attempted to dive away, but the Sopwith pilot dived after him, and fired 250 rounds at less than 50 yards range, after which the hostile machine dived steeper and steeper, eventually going down on its back into the haze. It is considered certain that this machine was destroyed. Flight Commander Fall was then pursued by four other hostile machines on his return journey, as far as the lines.

December 8th.

No. 4 Wing (9th Squadron).—Whilst on patrol a flight of six Sopwith Camels dived on two Albatross Scouts and one Albatross two-seater, about 5 miles west of Courtrai, and Flight Sub-Lieut. Knott got on the tail of the two-seater and opened fire at very close range. The observer was probably shot almost immediately as he soon ceased firing, and after the Sopwith pilot had fired 300 rounds the hostile machine got into a vertical nose dive and went down several thousand feet, then on to its back, and it is considered almost certain that this machine crashed. Flight Sub-Lieut. Winter fired 200 rounds into a hostile machine without any apparent result, and the rest of the formation were compelled to discontinue the attack, the guns refusing to fire owing to the cold.

On a later patrol to the N.E. of Houthoulst Forest, Flight Commander Fall saw two hostile scouts at about 13,000 feet, when about 3,000 feet above them. He attacked the nearer one, and fired about 250 rounds at very close range. After a brisk engagement, the two machines exchanging shots whenever possible, the hostile machine's left wing folded up, and it spun down very fast. The other hostile machine pursued the Sopwith Camel part of the way back to the lines; heavy shell fire was also experienced at about 3,000 feet.

December 8th.

No. 4 Wing (1st Squadron).—While returning from a patrol inland beyond Ostende, Flight Commander Minifie, D.S.C., in Sopwith Camel C. 6420, encountered a two-seater D.F.W., which he attacked from close quarters, firing 150 rounds. The hostile machine went into a vertical nose dive, and was observed to crash east of Dixmude.

December 10th.

No. 4 Wing (9th Squadron).—Whilst on patrol a formation of seven Sopwith Camels drove four hostile machines down in the neighbourhood of Ostende at 2040. Later, Flight Sub-Lieuts. Redgate, Wood, and Knott attacked a D.F.W. at 1,000 feet, four miles east of Pervyse, into which about 1,000 rounds were fired. The observer was evidently hit in the first burst of fire, as he did not reply, and the hostile machine was then seen to catch fire, turn on its back, and go down still in flames.

December 10th.

No. 4 Wing (10th Squadron).—Whilst on patrol west of Roulers, at 9,000 feet, a formation of eight Sopwith Camels observed one Albatross Scout, which was attacked by Flight Sub-Lieut. Clark, and afterwards by Flight Commander Macgregor, who fired about 100 rounds altogether at close range. The hostile machine was seen to burst into flames and go down entirely out of control. Four hostile aircraft were observed later over Thourout at 6,000 feet, but were beyond range.

December 12th.

No. 4 Wing (10th Squadron).—A patrol of nine Sopwith Camels passed Nieuport 5 miles out to sea at 1515, and swept round by Ghistelles and Dixmude. When 6 miles east of

Dixmude the patrol encountered six Albatross Scouts at 14,000 feet, and a general engagement took place. Acting Flight Commander Macgregor fired about 70 rounds at one hostile machine which had been firing at Flight Sub-Lieut. Clark in Sopwith Camel 6330, but was unable to follow it down for more than 3,000 feet, but it appeared to go down out of control. Flight Sub-Lieut. Clark also appeared to go down out of control, and confirmation has been received from the Belgians that both a British and a hostile machine were seen to go down about this time. In this locality Flight Sub-Lieut. Maund attacked two hostile machines indecisively, one of which had been attacking Flight Commander Macgregor. Flight Sub-Lieuts. Stratton and Hall followed a two-seater Aviatik from north of Dixmude to Gravelines at 14,000 feet and attacked it at long range, but eventually this machine disappeared into the mist.

ATTACKS ON ENEMY TRENCHES, KITE BALLOONS, BATTERIES, AND OTHER OBJECTIVES.

December 5th.

No. 4 Wing (9th Squadron).—Flight Commander Fall, in Sopwith Camel B. 6570, fired into enemy trenches E. of Nieuport piers and along the canal S.E. of Nieuport, also at a machine gun between Westende bains and Nieuport piers. The latter target was attacked with 150 rounds, finishing at a range of 25 yards, compelling the machine gun to cease firing.

December 6th.

No. 4 Wing (1st Squadron).—Whilst on a special patrol, Flight Commander Minifie descended to 200 feet and fired all his ammunition into enemy trenches at Nieuport and Dixmude.

Flight Sub-Lieut. Findlay fired 500 rounds into the hangars at Ghistelles Aerodrome, at a train coming out of St. Pierre Capelle, and into enemy trenches.

Flight Sub-Lieut. Rosevear fired 100 rounds at a "flaming onion" battery from 1,000 feet, east of Nieuport.

December 10th.

No. 4 Wing (4th Squadron).—Whilst on a low patrol a flight of five Sopwith Camels attacked a kite balloon near Ghistelles, and another at Conckdaere, with no apparent result.

About 2,000 rounds were fired into trenches and the road behind Lombartzyde on the return journey.

On a later patrol about 1,000 rounds were fired into trenches and on an active anti-aircraft battery in the neighbourhood of Lombartzyde.

GROUND PATROL ATTACK ON TROOPS.

December 11th.

No. 4 Wing (10th Squadron).—A patrol was carried out, keeping the coast line in view, by Flight Sub-Lieuts. Stratton and Hall in Sopwith Camels until off Ostende, when the machine flew landward. Flight Sub-Lieut. Hall then dived through the clouds at a party of soldiers, which he observed on the beach near Mariakerke, and fired 150 to 200 rounds, completely scattering them. He then proceeded inland along a road, and then along the Nieuport-Plasschendaele Canal, but observed no target. Later he fired 200 rounds from 300 feet into a trench at Nieuwendamme Old Fort, but was forced to climb into the clouds owing to heavy machine-gun fire. Flight Sub-Lieut. Stratton fired 220 rounds at various targets, mostly personnel, between Ostende and Houthoulst Wood at a height of under 1,000 feet.

FIGHTER PATROL—ATTACK ON HOSTILE BALLOON.

December 4th.

Seaplane Defence Squadron (No. 1 Wing).—Flight Sub-Lieut. Greene, in Sopwith Camel B. 6358, attacked a hostile balloon from 1,000 feet above in the vicinity of Zarren. He fired about 100 rounds, and saw a parachute leave the balloon and open out. The Sopwith pilot then made for home, but lost his way in the fog, and owing to lack of petrol made a forced landing in a marsh at Pitgam. The machine crashed and the pilot sustained slight injuries.

FIGHTER PATROL—ENGAGEMENT WITH ENEMY.

December 5th.

Seaplane Defence Squadron (No. 1 Wing).—Whilst on patrol at 16,000 feet, about 4 miles N.W. of Wenduyne, a formation of four Sopwith Camels sighted two Albatross two-seaters flying on a course W.N.W. at 11,000 feet. Flight Sub-Lieut. Pinder dived, and opened fire at ranges of from 100 to 20 yards on one of the hostile machines. Flight Sub-Lieut. Mackay dived and fired 100 rounds at the same machine. At the same time Flight Sub-Lieut. Paynter, whose guns were frozen, was attacked by the second hostile machine.

Flight Sub-Lieuts. Mackay and Cooper attacked the first machine again, and fired 200 rounds at close range ; the hostile machine made for the shore, and was again attacked by Flight Sub-Lieut. Pinder, and was seen to make a sharp turn to the right and crash into the sea. Flight Sub-Lieut. Pinder descended to 50 feet, and observed the pilot in the partly submerged machine, and the observer swimming about 20 yards away. Meanwhile, Flight Sub-Lieut. Paynter's guns had thawed, and he attacked the other hostile machine, into which he fired 80 rounds, and was compelled to break off the engagement owing to his close proximity to the shore.

Later two Albatross Scouts attacked Flight Sub-Lieut. Cooper off Nieuport, hitting the machine in five places. Flight Sub-Lieut. Cooper was unable to fight, as his guns were giving trouble from the previous combat.

FIGHTER PATROL OVER THE FLEET—ENGAGEMENT WITH ENEMY.

December 10th.

Seaplane Defence Squadron (No. 1 Wing). — Flight Sub-Lieuts. Pinder and Moyle observed five Albatross Scouts at 15,000 feet, 10 miles to sea north-east of Ostende. Flight Sub-Lieut. Pinder dived at one, and fired 150 rounds at ranges of from 150 to 75 yards. The hostile machine did a cart-wheel, and tried to get under the Sopwith's tail. In the meantime Flight Sub-Lieut. Moyle had attacked another hostile machine, and fired two bursts, without apparent result. The combat was broken off owing to the close proximity of the shore, and seven enemy seaplanes being sighted making for the Fleet at 12,000 feet. Upon turning to engage the latter they made for Ostende, diving. Flight Sub-Lieut. Moyle attacked one and fired a short burst without any result.

Flight Sub-Lieut. Pinder engaged another and fired about 200 rounds at very close range. The action was broken off owing to gun jamming, and immediately afterwards the enemy machine was observed to do a sharp right-hand turn, and went down in a nose dive, but was not observed to crash.

Both pilots returned to the Fleet, where they remained for 30 minutes, but no hostile aircraft returned.

BOMB ATTACKS.

(Carried out during the period between the dates given.)

*Sparappelhoek Aerodrome	Dec. 5th	1,044 lbs.	D.H. 4. (A.)
St. Denis Westrem Aerodrome.	,, 5th–6th	3,576 ,,	H.P. (A.)
St. Engel Aerodrome	,, ,,	336 ,,	,,
Bruges Docks	,, ,,	1,336 ,,	,,
Train	,, ,,	336 ,,	,,
North of Ghent (Sidings)	,, ,,	1,568 ,,	,,
Bruges-Ghent (Railway)	,, ,,	448 ,,	,,
Ghent S.W. (Railway)	,, ,,	224 ,,	,,
Ghent (South) (Railway)	,, ,,	224 ,,	,,
*Uytkerke Aerodrome	,, 6th	1,140 ,,	D.H. 4. (A.)
*Aertrycke Aerodrome	,, 8th	1,495 ,,	,,
*Varssenaere Aerodrome	,, 10th	1,560 ,,	,,
Oostacker Aerodrome	,, 10th–11th	5,136 ,,	H.P. (A.)
Bruges Docks	,, ,,	8,148 ,,	,,
Bruges Docks	,, 11th–12th	4,584 ,,	,,
	Total	31,156 lbs.	

* Daylight raid. (A) Aeroplanes. (S) Seaplanes.

December 5th.

No. 5 Wing (5th Squadron).—A bombing raid was carried out during the day on Sparappelhoek Aerodrome by five D.H. 4 machines. The formation were dispatched at 1105, accompanied by three escorting machines. Of these one was obliged to return with engine trouble, and another because the pilot could not keep up with the formation. The other six machines reached the objective, on which ten 50-lb. and thirty-four 16-lb. bombs were dropped at 1215 at heights of from 12,500 to 16,500 feet.

Bombs were seen to explode close to the hangars in the S.W. corner, but no direct hits were observed. Other bombs were seen to burst among the living-quarters on the eastern side of the aerodrome. Four 16-lb. bombs were dropped on, and burst close to, a train leaving Engel Dump, going towards the lines, at 1225.

Several hostile aircraft were seen but did not attack, and all machines returned safely.

December 5th–6th.

No. 5 Wing (7 and 7a Squadron). — Seven Handley-Page machines left at 1900 to carry out a bombing attack on the following objectives :—St. Denis Westrem Aerodrome, Engel Aerodrome, Bruges Docks, and railway tracks and trains in the vicinity of Bruges and Ghent. Two of the machines were obliged to return owing to engine trouble.

Four 250-lb. and twenty-three 112-lb. bombs were dropped on the aerodrome of St. Denis Westrem, and were seen to fall on the western side and in the north-east corner. The target was intermittently obscured by detached clouds and no observations could be made.

At Engel Aerodrome landing lights were on at 2110, and three 112-lb. bombs were dropped which fell close to the Ostende-Thourout road. The pilot of this machine did not consider the visibility good enough to attack St. Denis, and proceeded to Bruges Docks, on which four 250-lb. and three 112-lb. bombs were dropped. These were seen to explode on the western side of the West Basin, and also on the spit of land between the East and West Basins. Three 112-lb. bombs were dropped on a train on the main line between Bruges and Ghent, two of which fell very close to the track.

Fourteen 112-lb. bombs were dropped on sidings north of Ghent (east of Basin du Commerce) on which railway traffic was seen. All the bombs were seen to fall on and in close proximity to the sidings.

Four 112-lb. bombs, which fell very close to the lines, were dropped on the railway track between Bruges and Ghent.

The railway track S.W. of Ghent near St. Denis was attacked with two 112-lb. bombs, and two more 112-lb. bombs were dropped on the railway track south of Ghent. Visibility was only fair, and searchlights and anti-aircraft fire was very active at Bruges.

One machine was slightly damaged owing to striking a ditch after landing.

December 6th.

No. 5 Wing (5th Squadron).—A bombing raid was carried out during the day on Uytkerke Aerodrome by eight D.H. 4 machines at 1145, during which ten 50-lb. and forty 16-lb. bombs were dropped from heights of 13,000 to 15,000 feet. Bombs were observed to explode among the living-quarters and huts, on the west side of the road, one of which appeared to be a direct hit.

Bombs were also seen to burst close to sheds on the east side of the road, and Shed No. 3 was observed to be on fire. Three machines were observed lined up outside this shed and five outside shed No. 1.

BOMB ATTACK—ENGAGEMENT WITH ENEMY.

December 8th.

No. 5 Wing (5th Squadron).—A bombing attack was carried out during the day on Aertrycke Aerodrome by 10 D.H. 4 machines (four acting as escort), during which twelve 50-lb. and fifty-six 16-lb. bombs were dropped at 1130 at heights of from 14,000 to 16,000 feet. The visibility was only fair, as the target was partially obscured by clouds and observations were therefore difficult to make. Nevertheless, a number of bombs were seen to explode close to the south-east group of sheds, and one appeared to make a direct hit. Anti-aircraft fire was intense and accurate, nine out of the ten machines being hit. Several of the D.H. 4's were attacked by enemy aircraft, and two of these are claimed as having been driven down out of control.

Flight Sub-Lieut. C. R. Lupton, D.S.C., in D.H. 4, N. 6000, was followed from the target by five hostile machines, and when about two miles from the lines they got into position under the D.H. 4's tail, which swung round, and was attacked by two of the hostile machines, the other three keeping out of range. The attack was carried out one from above and one from below. Flight Sub-Lieut. Gamon, in D.H. 4, then joined in the attack and drove off the lower enemy machine, whilst the first D.H. 4 attacked the upper one. The fight lasted for about five minutes, when the lower machine held off, and all the guns of both D.H. 4 machines fired at the remaining enemy machine, which happened to come into the zone of fire of both the D.H. 4's. This machine was then seen to go down in a spin, and when last seen was near the ground still spinning.

Flight Sub-Lieut. E. Dickson, D.S.C., with Observer A. G. L. Saw, in D.H. 4, N. 5962, observed three hostile machines following them after leaving the target, and these were joined by two others a little later. The Observer got his guns on the nearest machine and gave him a burst of 60 or 70 rounds.

By this time the D.H. 4 had closed in considerably and had to turn back to the lines to avoid being surrounded by the enemy aircraft, of which there were eight in number. The Observer attacked the same machine as the D.H. 4 turned, firing about 40 rounds, and the enemy machine went down in a steep dive, which turned into a spin, and was still seen spinning when he disappeared through the clouds, which were at about 2,000 feet.

December 10th.

No. 5 Wing (5th Squadron).—A bombing attack was carried out during the day by 10 D.H. 4 machines (four acting as escort) on Varssenaere Aerodrome, and twelve 50-lb. and sixty 16-lb. bombs were dropped at 1220 at heights varying from 13,000 to 15,000 feet. Two direct hits were observed, one on a shed in the north-east corner, and one on a small shed on the west side of the aerodrome. Bombs were also seen to drop close to, and among, sheds on both west and east sides, also on the northern corner of the aerodrome. The last machine to drop bombs reports that on the return, when over Ostende, a large explosion was observed to take place in the direction of Varssenaere.

Three photographs were taken, one each of Varssenaere, Houttave, and Wenduyne. Anti-aircraft fire was heavy and accurate, several machines being hit.

December 10th–11th.

No. 5 Wing (7th and 14th Squadrons). — At 1800 five Handley-Page machines from No. 7 Squadron, carrying four 250-lb. and sixty-two 112-lb. bombs, followed at 1830 by five Handley-Pages from No. 14 Squadron, carrying sixteen 250-lb. and thirty-eight 112-lb. bombs, left to attack Oostacker Aerodrome and Bruges Docks.

The visibility at the beginning was generally good, but deteriorated considerably, and the last machine from No. 14 Squadron returned with bombs intact owing to the pilot being unable to see the ground.

Two machines from each squadron attacked Oostacker Aerodrome with twenty-eight 112-lb. bombs in the first attack and eight 250-lb. bombs in the second attack.

The machines of No. 7 Squadron were able to pick up the Chateau, which is the leading mark according to the map for this objective, and bombs were released in a good line although observations were difficult owing to the visibility. Four 250-lb. and thirty-four 112-lb. bombs were dropped on Bruges Docks in the first attack, and four 250-lb. and twenty 112-lb. bombs in the second attack. Good shooting appears to have been made in both cases, although in the second attack the visibility made accurate observation difficult. A number of bombs were seen to explode amongst the sheds just north of East Basin, while one bomb was seen to burst close to the anti-aircraft battery on the land west of West Basin. The Docks were well straddled, and a fire was started.

December 11th–12th.

No. 5 Wing (7th and 14th Squadrons). — A bombing raid was carried out during the night by Handley-Page machines on Bruges Docks, on which four 250-lb. and thirty-two 112-lb. bombs were dropped. Visibility was very bad owing to low-lying clouds, which caused two of the machines to return with bombs intact, being unable to find the objective. One machine is missing and another crashed near the aerodrome, the pilot and passenger sustaining slight injuries.

NAVAL SQUADRON WITH THE ROYAL FLYING CORPS

(From 2nd to 15th December 1917 inclusive.)

NAVAL SQUADRON No. 8.

During the period under review the squadron has been attached to the First Brigade, Royal Flying Corps. Flying has been possible on 10 days during this period, and a total of 213 hours 35 minutes flying has been done. Seventy-four offensive patrols and 138 special missions were carried out.

Enemy aircraft scouts were not often encountered, but hostile artillery machines were abnormally active, and 13 combats took place.

On nine days, on receipt of wireless messages, machines went up in search of enemy aircraft artillery machines.

On the 5th instant, Flight Commander Price and Flight Sub-Lieut. Sneath drove an Albatross scout east, and then observed an enemy two-seater, which Flight Sub-Lieut. Sneath dived at and drove down apparently out of control, and this machine appeared to be on fire. Flight Commander Price, while on special mission, attacked a two-seater enemy aircraft, which he drove down in a steep nose-dive. Flight Commander Compston and Flight Sub-Lieut. Dixon observed a Rumpler two-seater, which they attacked and drove down apparently out of control.

On the 6th instant, Flight Commander Compston and Flight Sub-Lieuts. Dennett and Johnstone attacked a D.F.W. which went down steeply, and the pilots are of opinion that it crashed. Flight Commander Compston and Flight Sub-Lieuts. Jordon and Reid encountered a two-seater, which they drove down apparently out of control. Flight Commander Price drove away another machine which he found interfering with two R.E. 8's. In another patrol he and Flight Sub-Lieut. Day attacked a D.F.W., which they shot down apparently out of control.

Hostile Machines.—Driven down out of control - - 5
„ „ Destroyed - - - - 1
Total - - - 6

SUMMARY.

Hostile Machines.—Driven down out of control - 16
„ „ Destroyed - - - - 5
Total - - 21

EASTERN MEDITERRANEAN STATION.

(Compiled from Report No. 88, dating from 16th–25th November 1917 inclusive.)

THASOS AIR STATION.

"A" Squadron and "Z" (Greek) Squadron.

The weather throughout the week has been unfavourable for flying, but advantage has been taken of such fair intervals as occurred to carry out submarine patrols.

Reconnaissance.—On 19th November a Baby Seaplane made a reconnaissance in the vicinity of Thasos.

On 21st November a Short Seaplane examined the area between Thasos and the Akte Peninsula.

Anti-Submarine Patrols.—On 24th November a submarine patrol was made between Thasos and the Akte Peninsula, and another to the south of Thasos.

STAVROS AIR STATION.

"D" Squadron.

Fighter Patrols and Reconnaissance.—On 16th November two fighter patrols were made with a view to getting into touch with enemy aircraft patrolling over their lines, but no hostile aircraft were discovered. A photographic reconnaissance of the ground surrounding the White House at Deuthbro was also made. A front line reconnaissance was also made and a possible new gun position observed near N. 35 battery.

Fighter Patrols—Engagement with Enemy.—On the following day four patrols for enemy aircraft were made. One of these patrols was made by a D.H. 4 accompanied by a "Camel," and was successful in inducing a "D. 3" type Albatross Scout to come up to engage the D.H. 4. Apparently he did not observe the "Camel," which was piloted by Flight Lieut. H. T. Mellings, D.S.C. The Albatross eventually got into position not more than 80 yards behind and under the tail of the D.H. 4, when the "Camel" dived on him and opened fire from 30 to 40 yards. The first burst of fire was seen to pass through the Albatross fuselage a few inches behind the pilot.

The Albatross dived to avoid the "Camel," and was followed by the latter, which riddled him from distances varying from 10 to 50 yards. After 60 to 80 rounds were fired the Albatross turned on its back, and then got into a vertical nose dive, which continued from 12,000 feet to within 100 feet of the ground. Both the "Camel" and D.H. 4 followed him down at 130 to 150 knots, but the Albatross dived much faster. When about 100 feet from the ground the Albatross suddenly shot upwards, stalled, and crashed on to its nose into the marsh near Dzanos, turning upside down, a complete wreck.

The end of the Albatross was observed from both the D.H. 4 and the "Camel." The latter, after landing at Monhui to make adjustments, returned to the spot at 3,000 feet, and observed three soldiers standing beside the wreck. On the following day a machine was sent to photograph the wreck, but it had been removed during the night.

On 21st November a fruitless patrol for enemy aircraft was made, and subsequently enemy aircraft were sighted and pursued, but could not be closed.

Reconnaissance.—On 23rd November a reconnaissance was carried out to search for a gun, which was reported firing, but it was not located.

Fighter Patrol and Reconnaissance.—On 24th November a fighting patrol and reconnaissance of the enemy lines of communication up the Angista Valley were made.

Photography.—A Sopwith two-seater was also sent to Thasos with immediate letters from S.O. 6th D.S., and the opportunity was taken to photograph more of the area surrounding Deuthero White House.

Details have now been received of actions on 12th and 15th November, which were reported briefly in W.O.R. No. 87.

On the first occasion a Sopwith two-seater, No. N. 5086, piloted by Flight Lieut. H. T. Mellings, with Sergeant Lizieri as observer, had been sent to Mouuhi to make arrangements about Kukos landing ground, and was about to return when an enemy aeroplane was seen approaching from Serres.

Engagement with Enemy.—The Sopwith rose to meet him and found him to be a " D. 3 " type Albatross aeroplane flying throttled down to 70 m.p.h., at 6,000 feet. Both pilot's and observer's guns were brought into action alternately, the observer obtaining one excellent opportunity from directly underneath the enemy. Only on one occasion did the enemy machine get into position for her guns to bear and this was obviated by side-slipping the Sopwith. After the first burst from Sopwith's observer it was seen that the front cylinder of enemy's engine was pierced and fire emerged continuously ; it was also apparent that she was otherwise damaged, as she could only manoeuvre to the left very slowly. The enemy glided off towards Drama, and it was unfortunate that lack of ammunition prevented the Sopwith pushing home her advantage.

Engagement with Enemy.—On 15th November Flight Lieut. Mellings, returning from Salonika on " Camel " No. N. 6367, observed an enemy aeroplane shoot down a kite balloon near the lines N.W. of Marian. He attempted to close the enemy, but the enemy retreated first towards the Rupel Pass, afterwards altering course for Drama. The " Camel " made direct for Drama to intercept the enemy, but the H.A. with his engine full on and nose down was too fast for the " Camel " to get close range and all firing was done from 500 to 600 yards. The action was not abandoned until the enemy was at 5,000 feet over his own aerodrome.

KALLONI AIR STATION (MITYLENE).

"B" Squadron.

The only operations reported during the current week were photographic reconnaissances made on 24th November of the coastal area between Cape Baba and Sivriji Bay.

GLIKI AIR STATION (IMBROS).

"C" Squadron.

No operations were undertaken during the week until 21st November as strong winds accompanied by low clouds and rain prevailed.

Bomb Attack on Constantinople-Berlin Railway.—On 21st November a further offensive reconnaissance of the Constantinople-Berlin Railway was made by Flight Lieut. R. Sorley and Observer Sub-Lieut. F. C. Smith in D.H. 4, No. N. 5976.

Course was shaped over Hairobolu to the railway line where the machine turned and followed the line at 2,000 feet. No traffic was seen on the railway and accordingly the three stone pillar bridges lying on a straight mile of railway a little to the westward of Alapie were selected as targets. One 65-lb. bomb fell five yards N. of the first bridge, in the dry river bed, and a second 65-lb. fell about 20 yards from the second bridge. Accurate bomb dropping was difficult on account of a strong drift across the railway.

The D.H. 4 thereafter turned, descended to 1,000 feet and dropped one Carcass bomb in an attempt to set fire to the remainder of the forage store, but the bomb failed to ignite.

One 16-lb. bomb remained and the railway to the east was searched for a suitable target, but no trains were seen. Accordingly the D.H. 4 followed the Alapie-Hairobolu road where ten transport wagons were observed proceeding south. These were attacked with machine-gun. Six more transport wagons were seen packed in a small village to the east of the road and the 16-lb. bomb was dropped at them, the result, however, could not be ascertained on account of the tail intervening. Transport and small camps were observed along the road between Hairobolu and Malgara and these were attacked in passing with machine gun.

The D.H. 4 returned to Imbros after a flight of 2 hours 40 minutes.

Photography.—On the same day a reconnaissance was made to photograph the coast north of Suvla Point and to observe the results of blasting which had been seen from a ship on the previous day.

Bomb Attack on Nagara Seaplane Base.—In the afternoon a raid on Nagara Seaplane Base was made by Flight Lieut.

Browne in B.E. 2, E.A. 1385, carrying one 65-lb. and eight 16-lb. bombs.

Flight Lieut. Donald and Observer Lieut. Abbott in Sopwith No. N. 5213, carrying four 16-lb. bombs.

Flight Lieut. Woodward and Observer Lieut. Palmer in Sopwith N. 5083, carrying three 16-lb. bombs.

Flight Sub-Lieut. Grigson and Observer Sub-Lieut. Gayford in Sopwith N. 5163, carrying three 16-lb. bombs.

Flight Commander Feeny as escort in "Pup" N. 6471.

On account of the number of bombs exploding at the same time it was impossible to distinguish individual shooting, but all was fairly accurate, all bombs falling around the sheds and slipway without, however, scoring a direct hit. The 65-lb. bomb fell 10 yards from the slipway, causing a heavy explosion.

On the return journey two 16-lb. bombs, which had previously failed to release, were dropped on a camp in the Kurija Valley.

Heavy anti-aircraft fire with H.E. was experienced by all machines in the vicinity of Nagara.

Reconnaissance.—On 22nd November nothing further was done than an examination of the Straits for shipping.

Photography.—On the following day four machines pursued enemy aircraft which reconnoitred Imbros, without, however, being able to catch them, and later in the day a photographic reconnaissance of the Enos area was made.

Bomb Attack on Nagara Seaplane Base.—On the 24th November two D.H. 4 and three Sopwith two-seaters again bombed Nagara Seaplane Base. No details are yet available, but it is stated that two enemy aircraft were sighted but not engaged. A "Camel" also went in pursuit of an enemy machine, but could not catch it.

MUDROS AIR STATION.

No operations were attempted owing to coarse weather until 22nd November, when "Lord Nelson" was escorted by seaplanes and aeroplanes continuously during target practice, 11 flights totalling over 18 hours being made.

Anti-Submarine Patrol.—At 1000 L.T. on 24th November a submarine was reported on the surface two miles south of Kombi Lighthouse, Mudros, and from the time the signal was received until dark, seaplanes, one of which was fitted with and worked her hydrophone, and aeroplanes maintained a continuous patrol over the area.

KASSANDRA AIRSHIP STATION.

Anti-Submarine Patrols.—On 19th November the airship examined the entrances to the Gulfs of Salonika and Kassandra.

She was unable to carry out patrols on the two succeeding days on account of high winds. On 22nd November in view of a submarine having been reported off the coast of Euboea in the early hours of the morning, a patrol was made to the south of the entrance to the Gulf of Salonika.

On 24th November when a submarine was reported off Kombi (Lemnos), patrols were made between Cape Drepano and Psathura and the eastern approaches to the Gulf of Salonika.

French seaplanes from Kassandra were asked to patrol the Gulfs of Kassandra and Monte Santo. Their report has not yet been received.

SUDA BAY SEAPLANE STATION.

It rained steadily during the first three days of the current week and consequently no patrol were made. On 22nd November two patrols were undertaken of the approaches to Suda Bay and on 23rd and 24th an afternoon patrol was made on each day, the mornings having been unfavourable for flying.

EAST INDIES AND EGYPT.

(Dating from October 28th to November 9th 1917.)

H.M.S. "CITY OF OXFORD" AND "RAGLAN."

October 28th.

Spotting Operations. — At 1000, Seaplane No. 8019 was hoisted on board H.M.S. "Raglan."

Flight Lieut. E. J. Burling and Captain W. R. Kempson, together with six mechanics, embarked at noon. H.M.S. "Raglan" left Port Said at 1800 and arrived off Gaza at 0500, 30th October.

H.M.S. "Raglan" then proceeded to the firing position off Wady el Hesy, 9 miles north of Gaza.

At 0630 hostile aeroplanes bombed the escorting trawlers, the same trawlers being subjected to gun-fire from shore batteries situated north of Sheikh Hasan.

H.M.S. "City of Oxford" arrived off Wady El Hesy and closed H.M.S. "Raglan" at 0830.

October 15th.

Spotting Operations.—Engagement with Enemy.—Seaplane No. 8019, Pilot, Flight Lieutenant E. J. Burling, Observer, Captain W. R. Kempson, was hoisted out from H.M.S. "Raglan" at 1000, to spot the 6-inch and 14-inch guns on to the railway station south of Deir Sineid and about 5 miles inland.

H.M.S. "Raglan" opened fire with the 6-inch gun and obtained several direct hits on the railway station.

A large ammunition dump was then observed near the station and the 6-inch gun was switched on to it. At about the eighth round a direct hit exploded the dump which continued exploding for 35 minutes, demolishing the railway station and tearing up many yards of line.

The 6-inch gun was then ranged on to the railway bridge crossing Wady El Hesy at Deir Sineid, and having got "OK" with the 6-inch and the 14-inch turret-fire was directed on to the bridge.

The second round blew up the bridge leaving only the pillars standing.

So important was this bridge to the enemy at Gaza that two days later a sand embankment was built alongside the demolished bridge and the rails relaid.

The 14-inch fire continued on the bridge embankment and caused heavy damage to the line and junction near by.

At 1230, the seaplane was hoisted on board H.M.S. "City of Oxford" with leaking floats. At 1445, Seaplane No. 1262, Pilot, Flight Lieut. E. J. Burling, Observer, Captain W. R. Kempson, was hoisted out from H.M.S. "City of Oxford" and continued spotting on to the railway junction south of Deir Sineid and road leading over Wady El Hesy. Several direct hits with the 6-inch and 14-inch guns caused great damage to the junction and road bridge across Wady. Towards the end of the flight the seaplane was attacked by a single-seater Halberstadt Scout, and heading towards the ship, was followed down by the scout to within 800 feet of the water, firing at the seaplane from a gun firing straight ahead. The Observer, Captain W. R. Kempson, opened fire on the pursuing scout at close range and let him have two trays from Lewis gun. The scout still followed; the seaplane was then turned sharply to the right, enabling anti-aircraft guns from H.M.S. "Raglan" to drive off the scout which had until then been too near the seaplane for anti-aircraft from ships.

Estimated speed of the scout was well over 100 knots.

Seaplane was hit in about 36 places in the fuselage and top centre section; one elevator control was shot away and Captain Kempson sustained a slight splinter wound in the thigh. The floats of the seaplane were so badly holed by machine gun fire that, after landing, it became waterlogged and turned over alongside H.M.S. "Raglan" before it could be hoisted inboard.

The wrecked machine was eventually got on board H.M.S. "Raglan," and the subsequent concussion, caused by gun-fire of the 14-inch turret blew the machine to pieces.

The same evening the captain of H.M.S. "Raglan" received congratulations from General Bulfin, of Twenty-first Army Corps, on the destruction of Deir Sineid Bridge and ammunition dump.

Photographs taken bear out "Raglan" statement that this bridge and ammunition dump were destroyed.

October 31st.

Spotting operations.—At 0900 H.M.S. "City of Oxford" closed with H.M.S. "Raglan."

At 1020, Seaplane No. 1090, pilot, Flight Lieut. G. D. Smith, D.S.C.; observer, Captain W. R. Kempson; was hoisted out from H.M.S. "City of Oxford" to spot H.M.S. "Raglan's" 14-inch turret on the roads and bridge up Wady-El-Hesy. The shooting was good, but later on, threw off to the left into the village of Deir Sineid; the machine returned at 1204.

At 1400, H.M.S. "Raglan" left Wady-El-Hesy for Deir El Belah.

November 1st.

At 1000, Flight Lieut. Burling and Captain Kempson went ashore to obtain information from the Royal Flying Corps regarding the country around Deir Sineid.

H.M.S. "Raglan" left Deir El Belah at 1800 and arrived at her original firing position off Wady-El-Hesy at 0900 on the 2nd November.

November 2nd.

Spotting operations.—At 1000, H.M.S. "Raven II." closed with H.M.S. "Raglan," and hoisted out Seaplane No. 8022 at 1115; pilot, Flight Lieut. E. J. Burling; observer, Captain W. R. Kempson, to spot H.M.S. "Raglan" on to the new railway embankment which had been constructed across Wady-El-Hesy.

The machine returned at 1145 owing to poor visibility.

Between 1445 and 1545, the weather cleared, and seaplane No. 8022 was hoisted out from H.M.S. "Raven II.", pilot, Flight Lieut. E. J. Burling; observer, Captain W. R. Kempson.

H.M.S. "Raglan" was ranged on to the embankment with the 6-inch gun, and then carried on with the 14-inch; several direct hits were made causing considerable damage.

Seaplane No. 1263 was hoisted on board H.M.S. "Raglan" after dark, and H.M.S. "Raven II." proceeded to Port Said at 1900.

November 3rd.

Spotting operations.—Seaplane No. 1263; pilot, Flight Lieut. E. J. Burling; observer, Captain W. R. Kempson; was hoisted out from H.M.S. "Raglan" at 0610 with orders to spot H.M.S. "Grafton" on to trenches south-east of El Nuzle.

On arriving down the coast over H.M.S. "Grafton," the seaplane was ordered by searchlight from H.M.S. "Grafton" to return to H.M.S. "Raglan," owing to the sun coming up over the land and obscuring the point of aim.

The seaplane was hoisted on board H.M.S. "Raglan" at 0643. At 1000, seaplane No. 1263, pilot, Flight Lieut. E. J. Burling; observer, Captain W. R. Kempson; was hoisted out from H.M.S. "Raglan" to spot the 14-inch turret up Wady-El-Hesy on to the embankment and road bridge.

Several direct hits were obtained and visibility from the air was good, but a sand storm came up and obscured the point of aim on shore; the machine returned at 1130.

November 4th.

Spotting Operations --At this time Beersheba had fallen, and our cavalry had advanced some 10 to 12 miles north. The main defences of Gaza were taken and Sheikh Hasan was in our possession, and our troops were endeavouring to advance along the coast towards Wady El Hesy, but were prevented from doing so by strong batteries around El Nuzle; so that during the next day or so seaplanes were required to spot various monitors on to these positions around El Nuzle.

At 0900, November 4th, H.M.S. "City of Oxford" arrived off Wady El Hesey and closed with H.M.S. "Raglan."

At 1000, Seaplane No. 1263, pilot, Flight Lieut. E. J. Burling; observer, Captain W. R. Kempson; was hoisted out from H.M.S. "Raglan" to spot H.M.S. "Raglan" on to batteries near El Nuzle.

A very effective rapid fire was kept up by 6-inch gun. The seaplane was attacked by two hostile machines, which were eventually driven off by anti-aircraft gun-fire from the ships.

At 1106, the machine was hoisted on board H.M.S. "City of Oxford" in preference to H.M.S. "Raglan," as the weather was unsettled, and the handling seaplanes from H.M.S. "Raglan" was a risky operation at the best of times.

Four seaplanes were now on board H.M.S. "City of Oxford."

From 1145 till 1345, Seaplane No. 1091, pilot, Flight Lieut. E. M. King; observer, Second Lieut. A. D. Ferguson, carried on spotting for H.M.S. "Raglan" and obtained three direct hits on the new railway embankment with 14-inch turret. Other shots tore up rails to the north and south of the bridge over the Wady.

Rapid fire from the 6-inch gun caused much damage in the vicinity.

The Captain of H.M.S. "Raglan" the same evening received congratulations from the Admiral on destroying the new railway embankment.

November 5th.

Spotting Operations.—At midnight of 4th/5th November, the Captain of H.M.S. "Raglan" received urgent signal from the flagship to destroy troublesome batteries at El Nuzle. (Square M. 25) which were threatening the advance of our troops along the coast, and at 0300 H.M.S. "City of Oxford" closed with H.M.S. "Raglan."

Seaplane No. 1090 was ready for flight at 0415, but a thick fog came up and obscured everything : rain also fell.

At about 0600, the fog lifted a bit, but the shore was still obscured.

At 0800, Seaplane No. 1090, pilot, Flight Lieut. A. E. Popham ; observer, Captain W. R. Kempson ; was hoisted out, but was unable to spot for H.M.S. "Raglan" on account of low clouds, and as conditions were getting worse, the machine returned to the ship at 0900.

Towards mid-day, the weather cleared a little, and at 1330 Seaplane No. 1091, pilot, Flight Lieut. A. E. Popham ; observer Captain V. Millard ; spotted for H.M. Monitor 29 on to the trenches west of El Nuzle, and although the machine was kept off the coast by anti-aircraft gun fire several good hits were obtained on the objectives.

From 1430 till 1530, Seaplane No. 1091, pilot, Flight Lieut. E. M. King ; observer, Second Lieut. A. D. Ferguson ; carried on spotting for H.M. Monitor 29, and H.M.S. "Raglan" on to emplacements and trenches west of El Nuzle with very good results.

Rain clouds came up and put a stop to further spotting at 1530.

November 6th.

Spotting Operations.—Early morning spotting was impossible owing to low clouds over the coast.

At 0900 H.M.S. "Raglan" was relieved off Wady-El-Hesy by "Requin," and Flight Lieut. E. J. Burling, Captain W. R. Kempson, and six mechanics transferred permanently to H.M.S. "City of Oxford."

Information was received from the army that the Turks were retreating northwards along the road leading through Deir Sineid, and that large convoys were situated at Deir Sineid Junction up Wady-El-Hesy.

At 0930 "Requin" took up firing position off Wady El Hesy, and was spotted for by seaplanes for the best part of the day.

The following spotting flights for "Requin" were made :—

From 1000 till 1150 Seaplane No. 1091, pilot, Flight Lieut. G. D. Smith, D.S.C. ; observer, Second Lieut. B. H. Pakenham-Walsh. During this flight the seaplane was disturbed by two hostile machines, and later by a single seater scout, which were kept off by observer's fire and eventually driven off by anti-aircraft gunfire from the ships.

From 1330 till 1500 Seaplane No. 1091, pilot, Flight Lieut. A. E. Popham; observer, Second Lieut. Ferguson; carried on spotting for "Requin," and although attacked by hostile machine, succeeded in getting guns on to the railway embankment and road bridge.

From 1527 till 1627 Seaplane No. 1091, pilot, Flight Lieut. E. M. King; observer, Second Lieut. A. D. Ferguson; continued spotting for "Requin" on to Deir Sineid Junction up Wady El Hesy. Several direct hits were obtained, other shots going to the left destroyed the line leading into Deir Sineid.

November 7th.

Spotting Operations.—The Turks were apparently now trying to check our advance northwards along the coast by placing field guns north of Deir Sineid, and by occupying trenches previously made, south of Askalan, and "Requin" was subsequently spotted for on to these targets.

At 0650 Seaplane No. 1091, pilot, Flight Lieut. E. J. Burling; observer, Captain W. R. Kempson; was hoisted from H.M.S. "City of Oxford," but reported visibility impossible for spotting owing to low clouds over the target. The machine returned to ship at 0727.

At 0810 Seaplane No. 8019, pilot, Flight Lieut. E. M. King; observer, Captain V. Millard, spotted for "Requin" on to trenches and the outskirts of the village. A very consistent fire was directed against these in Sq. J.I. S.E. of Askalan. The machine returned at 0930, visibility still being very poor.

At 0900 Flight Lieut. Burling and Captain Kempson went to the flagship to arrange spotting for H.M. Monitor 159, 12-in. turret on to the railway junction at Julis, north-east of Askalan, as large convoys were reported to be collected here, and this would be the last junction within reach of the guns from the sea.

Hostile Bomb Attack.—At 0915 a hostile machine dropped four bombs near H.M.S. "City of Oxford."

From 1138 till 1421, Seaplane No. 1263, pilot, Flight Lieutenant E. J. Burling; observer, Captain W. R. Kempson; spotted H.M. "Monitor 15" on to Julis Junction. Spotting was very difficult owing to clouds at 1,200 feet, and spotting had to be carried out below this height. Hits were obtained all round the village and on the junction.

From 1400 to 1640, Seaplane No. 1091, pilot, Flight Lieut. A. E. Popham; observer, Second Lieut. A. D. Ferguson; carried on spotting for H.M. "Monitor 15" on to Julis with good results.

H.M.S. "Raglan," taking up position off Askalan was also given the range and did good work with the 14-inch turret.

At 1430 H.M.S. "City of Oxford" was ordered north to the coast off Ramleh and Jaffa, but ordered to return to H.M.S. "Raglan" at 1700, owing to operations being abandoned.

Seaplane No. 1091 flew back to the ship, and was hoisted in off Ramleh. Hostile machines appeared high up, but no bombs were dropped.

At 1713 H.M S " City of Oxford " was ordered to cruise off during the night with escort and close with H.M.S. " Raglan " at daybreak.

Meanwhile Flight Lieut. Burling and Captain Kempson were sent by trawler to H.M.S " Raglan " at 1900 to arrange spotting for the bombardment of Ramleh.

This was abandoned owing to the weather, and H.M.S. " Raglan " was ordered to Port Said.

November 8th.

At 0600 Captain of H.M.S. " Raglan " sent Flight Lieut. Burling and Captain Kempson to H.M.S. " City of Oxford " by trawler, and they were on board H.M.S. " City of Oxford " at 1030 off Askalan.

At 1045 it was reported to the flagship that all machines were available, and closed the flagship for orders.

The previous evening at 1700 our guns and some cavalry had advanced along the coast as far north as Wady el Hesey, although the Wady was occupied by Turks about 5 miles inland.

Our troops continued advancing northwards along the coast in strength, and were being threatened by shrapnel from the Turks, who were just over the sandhills a few miles inland. All ships then took up firing positions along the coast from Wady el Hesy to a few miles north of Askalan, with a view to shifting the Turks further inland.

At 1130 four flights were made to spot ships on to their positions.

Seaplanes were allocated as follows :—

Seaplane 1091, Pilot, Flight Lieut. E. M. King ; Observer, Captain V. Millard, to spot H.M. Monitor 15 on to high ground north-east of Wady el Hesy.

Seaplane No. 1263, pilot, Flight Lieut. G. D. Smith, D.S.C. ; observer, Second Lieut. L. H. Pakenham-Walsh, to spot H.M. Monitors 31 and " Aphis " on to L. 9, L. 15 and L. 20.

Seaplane No. 8019, pilot, Flight Lieut. A. F. Popham ; observer, Second Lieut. A. D. Ferguson ; to spot for " Requin " on to the trenches north-east of Askalan.

Seaplane No. 1263, pilot, Flight Lieut. G. D. Smith, D.S.C. ; observer, Second Lieut. L. H. Pakenham Walsh ; to spot H.M. Monitors 31 and " Ladybird " on to the line running east and west through Burberah.

At 1400, our troops had advanced well on towards Askalan, and Seaplane 1263 landed alongside H.M.M. " Ladybird " for further orders and, in attempting to get off again, smashed her undercarriage in a heavy sea, and would have sunk but for the prompt assistance of H.M.M. L. 31, who towed her safely to H.M.S. " City of Oxford,"

The machine was hoisted inboard at 1422.

Seaplane No. 8012 was badly hit in the floats by shrapnel.

At 1500 H.M.S. " City of Oxford " was ordered to hoist in all machines and proceed with escort to Port Said.

H.M.S. " City of Oxford " arrived in Port Said at 0900 on November 9th.

H.M.S. "RAVEN."

October 31st.

Spotting Operations. — H.M.S. " Raven " left Port Said during the afternoon at 5 p.m. escorted by H.M.S. " Managan " and H.M. Trawler " Verises," and proceeded to an arranged rendezvous off the Wadi-El-Hesy to meet the French Cruiser " Requin."

The rendezvous was reached at 9 a.m., and H.M.S. " Raven II " steamed about awaiting orders from the French Cruiser " Requin." During this period a hostile aeroplane was sighted reconnoitring our positions, but disappeared flying in a north-easterly direction.

At 0930 a signal was received from the " Requin " to hoist out seaplanes.

At 0915 Seaplane N 1263 (Flight Lieutenant Bronson, Pilot, and Second Lieutenant Pakenham-Walsh, observer) was hoisted out and proceeded to spot for the French Cruiser " Requin."

Firing commenced at 0958 and continued until " Requin " sent C1 at 1125.

Seaplane N 1263 was hoisted in at 1130, and signal received from " Requin " that she would be ready to fire again at 1400.

The damage observed during the morning's shooting was :—

Several direct hits on railway, south and north of railway station, also at Junction for Huj.

One direct hit from 4 inch gun on stone bridge, but no material damage was observed.

Severe hostile machine-gun fire was experienced from camps south of railway station, and hostile machines were observed in the vicinity, but no encounter took place.

Signal received from " Requin " to hoist out seaplane at 1412.

Seaplane No. 8022 (pilot, Flight Lieutenant H. V. Worral, observer, Second Lieutenant Pakenham-Walsh), was hoisted out and proceeded to spot for " Requin."

Apparently " Requin's " wireless was not working, and at 1518 she sent signal to seaplane to that effect by means of searchlight.

No, 8022 was hoisted inboard at 1555.

A hostile gun fired and hit " Requin," who replied to her fire ; this gun was located in the afternoon.

At 1615 the following signal was received from "Requin." "Many thanks to pilot and observer for spotting."

H.M.S. "EMPRESS."

November 1st.

H.M.S. "Empress" left Port Said at 1030, arriving at the rendezvous with H.M.S. "City of Oxford" at 0600 on 2nd inst. The necessary pilots were then transferred to "Empress," who then proceeded to the rendezvous (according to sailing orders) off El Haram, arriving about 0900.

Machines were then hoisted out as follows:—

Hamble Baby,	No. 1209.	Flight Lieut.	King.
Hamble Baby,	No. 1210.	,,	Popham.
Schneider Baby,	No. 1129.	,,	Leigh.
Schneider Baby,	No. 1038.	,,	Smith.

The last machine (No. 1038), immediately began to sink by the tail, slowly turned over and became completely waterlogged. Immediate efforts were made to salve the machine, but these had to be abandoned owing to the wind vanes on the 65-lb. bombs becoming unwound, thus making the bombs dangerous and salvage impossible.

The machine had therefore to be sunk by gun-fire from "Empress."

Bomb Attack on Jiljulie Bridge.—The three other seaplanes were then given the pre-arranged signal to proceed. They returned at 1055 and reported that the weather, from a flying point of view, was exceedingly "bumpy," especially over the land, and that when they reached their objective (Jiljulie Bridge), the wind was directly across the target. Six 65-lb. bombs were dropped on this target, but, although the bridge itself was not actually hit, the line on both N. and S. sides of the bridge was hit in several places.

Bomb Attack on Haifa.—After the seaplanes had been hoisted inboard "Empress" proceeded to her rendezvous off Haifa, arriving at about 1345. Seaplanes were then hoisted out as follows:—

Schneider Baby		No. 1036.	Flight Lieut.	Stephens.
Hamble Baby		No. 1209.	,, ,,	King.
Schneider Baby	-	No. 1129.	,, ,,	Leigh.
Hamble Baby	-	No. 1210.	,, ,,	Popham.
Schneider Baby	-	No. 1028.	,, ,,	Smith.

The first machine had orders to proceed and drop two 16-lb. bombs *in the vicinity* of the Oil Factory at Haifa, in order to give the Christian employees time to evacuate the factory and take cover.

When the first machine returned to "Empress," the pilot reported that two of the seaplanes had been seen on the water in Haifa Bay. It was eventually discovered that the missing pilots were Flight Lieuts. Stephens and Popham.

A signal was made to the French destroyer "Coutelas," who immediately proceeded towards Haifa." She returned about 1830, making the signal "All saved," machines lost. It appears that Flight Lieut. Popham's engine suddenly "cut out" and that he made a safe landing in the bay, Flight Lieut. Stephens saw that this had occurred, and after dropping his warning bombs near the factory, he returned and landed alongside Flight Lieut. Popham. The latter, after having vainly tried to set fire to his machine, swam to and boarded the other machine. Flight Lieut. Stephens then tried to proceed, but owing to extra weight on the floats, they were more deeply immersed, and the spray thrown up was sufficient to break the propeller.

One of the machines was eventually destroyed by gun-fire from "Coutelas."

Flight Lieut. Stephens was slightly injured in the leg by a splinter of wood from a broken strut, and Flight Lieut. Leigh was also slightly injured in hands, head and body, as the result of a landing in a confused sea.

Four direct hits by 65-lb. bombs were obtained on this factory at Haifa, and it is considered that great damage was caused.

On completion of this second operation "Empress" proceeded to Port Said, it being too late to carry out the third part of the programme.

BRITISH ADRIATIC SQUADRON.

(*Week ending November 27th, 1917*).

Anti-Submarine Patrols.—Routine patrols were carried out throughout the week except on the 23rd and 24th.

November 22nd.

At 0650 a submarine was reported by "Saseno," steering south. Two Baby Seaplanes and one aeroplane were immediately sent out to search the area, but nothing was seen.

November 25th.

At 0848 Palascia reported on Allo message received from an Italian destroyer reporting a submarine in position 40° 40′ N., 16° 23 E.

An aeroplane was immediately sent out and searched the area, but nothing was seen. Just after the aeroplane left at 0918, an Allo message was sent out by the drifter "Floandi" that a submarine had been sighted in position 40° N., 19° 10′ E., steering north. This was probably the submarine with call sign L.K., which called earlier in the morning. A seaplane was sent out at once and patrolled near the drifter line, but nothing was sighted.

A French seaplane sent out a message to say she had attacked a submarine in position 30° 50′ N., 19° 10′ E. at 0947.

In the afternoon another seaplane patrolled near the drifter line, and the drifters still appeared to be in touch with the submarine. Nothing, however, was seen except a patch of oil 6 miles north of the drifter line.

From reports received subsequently it appears that "Floandi" sighted a large submarine, with one gun forward, which dived $2\frac{1}{2}$ miles away from her at 0913. Three drifters kept in touch with this submarine until 1640, when the rising sea prevented further use of the hydrophones.

At 1037 H.M.S. "Huon" reported a submarine in position 40° 19′ N., 18° 58′ E., and seaplane was sent out to search this area, but no submarine was seen.

CAPE STATION.

No. 8 SQUADRON, R.N.A.S., ZANZIBAR.

(Period 1st September to 18th October, 1917.)

They flying carried out during this period has been chiefly for spotting and reconnaissance work, in addition to which a number of flights for the purpose of taking photographs and making maps for the military have been made. With regard to the spotting, reports have been received that the shooting of the 4-inch gun, controlled by W/T from aeroplane, has been very good, as indicated by the shell holes on the gun positions which have been captured.

On September 19th a flight was made with General O'Grady as observer for the purpose of affording him a view of the country he was about to advance over, and a lot of useful information was gained. In connection with flights carried out for the purpose of dropping messages to troops, General Bevis has on two occasions signalled his thanks for the excellent work done by R.N.A.S. machines.

Bomb attacks have been carried out on enemy camps, trenches and gun positions, and a number of direct hits scored. In all a total of seven 65-lb. and eight 16-lb. bombs have been dropped, as well as 2,000 darts. During these operations heavy machine gun fire was experienced on several occasions, and anti-aircraft fire once.

At the request of the general officer commanding the military forces, this squadron has now moved its headquarters to Mtua, and continues to do valuable work.

Accident.—On September 24th, Voisin Aeroplane, No. 8705, (Pilot, Flight Sub-Lieut. E. E. Deans), while on a reconnaissance flight in the Mtua area, was forced to land through engine trouble, on broken ground covered with numerous tree stumps, and the machine was wrecked. Neither the pilot or observer were injured, and the machine, although having been under shell fire from the enemy, was rescued after dark, and is now under repair.

ROYAL FLYING CORPS COMMUNIQUÉS.

ROYAL FLYING CORPS COMMUNIQUÉ.—No. 115.

During the period under review, 20th to 26th November inclusive, the weather has been very bad for flying. In air fighting 10 enemy machines have been brought down and six driven down out of control, and an enemy balloon shot down in flames. Fifty-two thousand six hundred and seventy-three rounds have been fired at ground targets.

November 20th.

On the 20th low clouds and mist again made aerial work very difficult, but quite a considerable amount was carried out on account of the attack by the First and Third Armies south and south-west of Cambrai.

Twenty reconnaissances were carried out by the First Brigade, one by the Second Brigade, and eight by the Third Brigade.

With aeroplane observation six hostile batteries were successfully engaged for destruction.

The chief work throughout the day was the attack by our scouts of enemy troops from low altitudes with machine gun-fire and dropping bombs on all suitable targets.

Machines of the Third Brigade dropped seventy-eight 25-lb. bombs and fired 5,500 rounds. In all 10,600 rounds were fired during the day.

No. 3 Squadron.—Lieutenant R. Brown dropped four 25-lb. bombs on Caudry Aerodrome from 150 feet. A hangar was hit and wrecked, and the pilot then fired 200 rounds at five machines and several mechanics on the ground. He then attacked three wagons carrying road material; the first bolted, three horses were shot in the team of the second, and the third overturned into a ditch.

Second Lieut. D. Chamberlain also dropped four bombs on the above aerodrome and destroyed a small hut. Another bomb damaged an enemy aeroplane on the ground which was also riddled with machine-gun fire.

Lieutenant H. Brokensha dropped four bombs on Carnieres Aerodrome and destroyed a hangar.

Lieutenant J. McCash dropped four 25-lb. bombs from 150 feet on Estourmel Aerodrome where three chairs were hit and one bomb exploded on an Albatross two-seater on the ground.

No. 46 Squadron.—Second Lieut. J. Cooper, after firing 200 rounds into transport, dropped a bomb on a wagon which blew up. He then scattered infantry, but had his machine badly hit and the spar of the bottom plane collapsed, but he managed to return safely by putting on full aileron control.

He also dropped a bomb from 100 feet on a small factory at Noyelles which appeared to be wrecked.

Second Lieuts. R. Ferrie, E. Macleod and J. Cooper dropped bombs from 150 feet on a shed at Awoingt Aerodrome which was wrecked, and also damaged another shed and billets.

Second Lieut. W. Robinson dropped two bombs from 50 feet on a battery and obtained a direct hit which damaged a gun.

Second Lieut. A. Lee dropped four bombs on a battery at which he also fired a burst, but was then driven away by three enemy aircraft. Subsequently he attacked a party of German cavalry and other bodies of troops. In one instance a number took cover in a thicket, but he attacked frequently and drove them out.

No. 64 Squadron.—Captain R. St. C. McClintock, when flying at 100 feet, saw a gun team galloping along the road, so dropped three 25-lb. bombs, one of which killed four horses. He fired 200 rounds at other targets and scattered several parties of infantry.

Captain J. Slater obtained a direct hit on a gun with a bomb and dispersed troops.

Lieutenant I. Harris silenced a battery on which he dropped bombs and then attacked a train with machine-gun fire, after which he dropped a bomb on a large dump at Marcoing.

Lieutenant A. Duffus dropped two bombs on fortified shell holes in which there were many Germans, and one bomb burst directly in the hole. He then fired 350 rounds at the enemy in trenches.

Second Lieut. E. Ashton dropped bombs and then attacked troops.

Second Lieut. L. Williams also attacked troops, but his machine was hit and he had to land in "No-man's-land."

Captain E. Tempest obtained direct hits on two gun emplacements with bombs and then attacked troops with machine-gun fire, after which he returned to his aerodrome for more bombs and ammunition and went out again.

Captain St. C. Morford and Lieutenant J. McRae also dropped bombs and engaged ground targets.

No. 68 Squadron.—Lieutenant H. Taylor, while engaging troops at 30 feet, had his machine hit, so landed in "No-man's-land." On crawling out of his machine he was fired at by German snipers, so he took up a German rifle with which he fired at the enemy and then crawled back. On the way he picked up a wounded man and carried him until reaching one of our patrols. He then found another British machine which had landed owing to the pilot being wounded, so he got into it and endeavoured to fly off but could not start it.

Second Lieut. F. Huxley dropped bombs an a gun and horses and obtained a direct hit. He also obtained a direct hit on a G.S. wagon which was destroyed, and two of the personnel were killed. He then attacked 300 troops marching in fours and shot about 14 of them.

Other pilots of this squadron also attacked various troops.

Second Lieut. M. Clark and Lieutenant V. Westerby, No. 15 Squadron, and Second Lieutenants R. Bentley and C. Nathan, No. 59 Squadron, and Captain Soloman and Lieutenant B. Morgan, No. 15 Squadron, carried out contact patrols from 50 to 300 feet and obtained very valuable information.

Four reconnaissances were done by Bristol Fighters of No. 11 Squadron, and information of considerable value was brought back.

Eighteen scouts of the First Brigade left the ground under the most unfavourable weather conditions in order to reconnoitre certain areas, and Captain E. Mannock, No. 40 Squadron, returned first with valuable information, while many other machines brought back information that was of considerable use.

Four 25-lb. bombs were dropped on Oppy by No. 5 Squadron and two on Auchy by No. 2 Squadron.

One machine of No. 57 Squadron dropped two 112-lb. bombs on Courtrai sidings from 300 feet.

Two other machines of this squadron attacked Menin, on which one 230-lb. and two 112-lb. bombs were dropped, and one was seen to burst on the railway.

Eighteen 25-lb. bombs were dropped by Nos. 7, 9, and 69 Squadrons on various targets.

Fifteen 25-lb. bombs were dropped by Corps machines of the Third Brigade, six by the Fourteenth Wing, and two 112-lb. bombs by machines of No. 27 Squadron.

Enemy Aircraft.—Only a few were encountered during the day, and two were driven down apparently out of control, one by Second Lieut. Cuffe, No. 32 Squadron, and the other by Captain Fry, No. 23 Squadron.

Honours and Awards.

The Distinguished Service Cross.—Flight Sub-Lieut. W. A. Curtis, R.N.A.S.

The Military Cross.—Lieutenant A. Mann, Army Service Corps and Royal Flying Corps.

November 21st.

Practically no work was done owing to rain and low clouds.

Lieutenant G. Lloyd, No. 40 Squadron, carried out a very low reconnaissance of the area south of Douai and north of the Sensee River and reported on the position of the enemy.

Nine successful reconnaissances were carried out by the Third Brigade, one being by a Bristol Fighter of No. 11 Squadron and the others by Nos. 15 and 59 Squadrons, while four successful contact patrols were also carried out.

Corps machines dropped two 230-lb. bombs on Buissy and then fired at troops in the village from 200 feet.

Second Lieut. C. Brown, No. 27 Squadron, dropped two 112-lb. bombs from 200 feet on Brebieres Station, and two bursts were seen among the trucks in the station.

November 22nd.

Low clouds and thick ground mist again considerably hindered aerial work. In spite of the weather conditions, however, machines went out in very bad weather in order to interfere with the enemy's movements as much as possible and to gain information,

Ten reconnaissances were carried out by the First Brigade, and scouts fired 950 rounds at troops and transports, one pilot scattering parties of troops. Three reconnaissances were carried out by the Second Brigade, when Captain Youdale and Lieutenant Wilson, No. 21 Squadron, obtained very valuable information, and 16 were carried out by the Third Brigade, and given areas were successfully reconnoitred by Major Walker and Lieutenant Trotman, Lieutenants Jeffrey and Desborough, No. 15 Squadron, and Lieutenants Owen and Hegan, No. 59 Squadron.

Six hostile batteries were successfully engaged for destruction with aeroplane observation and nine neutralised.

Six 112-lb. and eighty-four 25-lb. bombs were dropped and 5,200 rounds were fired at ground targets. No. 18 Squadron dropped four 112-lb. bombs on Dechy Railway Station, and No. 2 Squadron dropped six 25-lb. bombs on Benifontaine and trenches.

No. 3 Squadron.—Lieutenant L. Nixon saw a train, so dropped a bomb, which hit and wrecked a house beside the track.

Lieutenant R. Brown dropped three 25-lb. bombs on two guns and 12 limbers on a road, and one bomb burst on one of the limbers and two others close by. He then fired 300 rounds and disorganised traffic and brought back valuable information.

Second Lieutenant D. Chamberlain engaged the same convoy with machine-gun fire and obtained a direct hit with one bomb.

No. 11 Squadron.—Lieutenant R. Mauduit and Corporal Mason carried out a valuable reconnaissance of the area between Denain and Cambrai.

No. 64 Squadron.—Captain E. Tempest obtained a direct hit on enemy troops in trenches with a 25-lb. bomb and dropped another which exploded in a machine-gun pit.

Captains St. Clair Morford and Fox-Russell, Lieutenant Barrett, Second Lieuts. Burge and Thompson all fired at various targets from low altitudes and dropped bombs.

No. 46 Squadron.—Captain Robeson fired at troops in Bourlon Wood, dropped four 25-lb. bombs and brought back valuable information.

Lieutenants Bulman and Wilcox also dropped bombs on troops and other targets and used their machine guns against the enemy on the ground.

No. 68 Squadron.—Lieutenant Huxley dropped two 25-lb. bombs on enemy in close formation and obtained direct hits. He saw many bodies round the holes which the bombs had made.

Captain R. Phillips fired 300 rounds at gun crews and then dropped some bombs, one of which fell in the middle of a machine gun crew. After this he attacked transport and the horses bolted and a wagon was overturned.

Lieutenants Howard and Griggs also dropped bombs and fired at enemy troops.

Corps machines of the Third Brigade dropped twenty-two 25-lb. bombs on various targets and fired 4,000 rounds.

Captain H. Smith, No. 27 Squadron, dropped two 112-lb. bombs from 200 feet which burst on the line south of Douai Station.

Enemy Aircraft.—A number of low flying enemy machines were encountered chiefly by the Third Brigade.

Flight Commander Compston, Naval Squadron No. 8, and Second Lieut. L. Herbert, No. 40 Squadron, each drove down a German machine apparently out of control.

Captain J. Child, No. 84 Squadron, met a German machine east of Bourlon Wood and engaged it at close range and shot it down completely out of control. This machine was seen by other pilots to crash. He then saw two enemy two-seaters approaching the lines from the east, so climbed into the clouds and waited until they had crossed the lines and then attacked one of them and hit the engine which stopped. The enemy pilot tried to fly east but was prevented from doing so by Captain Child, so he went down and landed within our lines. Both pilot and observer were unhurt and were captured.

Lieutenant F. Huxley, No. 68 Squadron, engaged a single-seater enemy scout which he destroyed.

November 23rd.

There was a slight improvement in the weather and machines were out during the day co-operating with the successful attack on Bourlon Wood and Village.

With aeroplane observation 26 hostile batteries were successfully engaged for destruction; three gun-pits were destroyed, 13 damaged, 12 explosions, and three fires caused.

Fourteen reconnaissances were carried out by machines of the First Brigade, 11 by the second, 11 by the third, three by the Fourteenth Wing, and two by the Ninth Wing.

Bristol Fighters of No. 11 Squadron obtained valuable information during five different reconnaissances. No. 8, 15, and 35 Squadrons also obtained valuable information.

Scouts were employed in dropping bombs and firing machine guns at enemy troops, transport batteries, and other targets, and a total of 24,175 rounds were fired during this work; 1,400 were by scouts of the First Brigade, 3,920 by the Second Brigade, and 14,600 by scouts of the Third Brigade, who also dropped one hundred and twenty 25-lb. bombs.

Captains Slater, McClintock, Tempest, St. Clair Morford, and Second Lieuts. Burge, Ashton, Barrett, and Thompson, of No. 64 Squadron, all fired at enemy troops and dropped bombs.

Lieutenants Wilcox, Bulman, Robertson, Cooper, Fernie, Odell, and Captains Robeson and Courtneidge, No. 46 Squadron, did the same work.

Captain Wilson, No. 68 Squadron, when engaged on similar duties, dropped a bomb on a gun which was being man-handled towards the line and knocked out two gunners, after which he fired 100 rounds at the men, who deserted the gun. He then dropped two bombs and fired 250 rounds at troops in a wood, after which he returned to the aerodrome for more ammunition and bombs and went out again.

Lieutenant F. Huxley, also of No. 68 Squadron, saw three tanks held up in Bourlon Wood, so dropped four bombs from 100 feet one by one upon the two anti-tank guns, which were holding them up. The guns were silenced, and the tanks then advanced into the wood. He then saw a strong point, which was preventing the advance of our infantry, so he dived on a number of occasions and fired 500 rounds. This caused great confusion, and so assisted in the taking of the strong point, which soon occurred.

These are just two instances of the work performed by scout pilots during the day.

Captain Phillipps and Lieutenants Sands, Holden, Griggs, and Clark, of No. 68 Squadron, also took part in this work.

Pilots of the Fourteenth Wing fired over 1,000 rounds.

In all three hundred and twenty-five 25-lb., forty-six 112-lb., and one 230-lb. bombs were dropped during the course of the day.

Thirty-six 112-lb. bombs were dropped on Dechy Railway Station by No. 18 Squadron, direct hits being obtained on the station and railway lines.

No. 2 Squadron dropped eighteen 25-lb. bombs on Benifontaine.

No. 8 Squadron dropped sixteen 25-lb. bombs on an enemy camp, which was hit, and No. 13 Squadron dropped thirty-two 25-lb. bombs on a Divisional Headquarters at Escadœuvres, while No. 15 Squadron dropped fifteen 25-lb. bombs on transport along roads.

No. 27 Squadron dropped six 112-lb. bombs on Douai Station, and No. 25 Squadron dropped twenty-two 112-lb. bombs on Dechy, Somain, Douai, Denain, and Bugnicourt. A direct hit was obtained on a crossing at Douai, and another on a dump near the station.

The remaining bombs were dropped on various targets by the brigades.

Enemy aircraft were more active than on previous days, and attacked our bombing and low flying machines.

When returning from a bomb raid to Dechy, Second Lieut. C. Evans and First Airman K. Gellan, of No. 18 Squadron, were attacked by four Albatross Scouts, but the D.H.4 succeeded in shooting down one of the scouts, which crashed on a house south of Douai.

Captain R. Chidlaw Roberts, No. 60 Squadron, fought an enemy scout east of Passchendaele and destroyed it.

Major Carter, No. 19 Squadron, Captain McKay, No. 23 Squadron, and Second Lieut. Hobson, No. 70 Squadron, each drove down an enemy machine out of control.

Captain J. McCudden, No. 56 Squadron, saw two Albatross Scouts attacking a Bristol Fighter, so joined in the fight and destroyed one of the German machines. Two other enemy aeroplanes were destroyed by pilots of the same squadron; one by Captain G. Bowman and the other by Lieutenant B.. Harmon.

Second Lieut. Rivers and Podgson, No. 11 Squadron, shot down an enemy machine completely out of control. This makes the 100th machine accounted for by the squadron since changing F.E. 2 b's for Bristol Fighters in June 1917.

Second Lieut. J. Mc. F. Stewart and Lieutenant W. Borthistle, No. 25 Squadron, were attacked by four enemy scouts just after having dropped bombs, and the observer, Lieut. Borthistle, fired 80 rounds into one of the machines, which burst into flames and fell out of control.

Honours and Awards.

The Military Cross.—Lieutenant J. H. G. Womersley, R.G.A. (T.F.) and Royal Flying Corps.

November 24th.

A little flying was done up to 11 a.m., after which it was impossible, owing to a gale.

Six reconnaissances were carried out, one by the Second Brigade, and five by the Third Brigade, and six counter-attack patrols were also done; 1,488 rounds were fired at ground targets, 1,050 being by machines of the Second Brigade.

Eighty-two 25-lb. and fourteen 112-lb. bombs were dropped. No. 2 Squadron dropped thirty 20-lb. bombs on billets east of Henin-Liétard, 16 on Douai Station and 16 on Pont-à-Vendin. The Second Brigade dropped twenty-two 25-lb. bombs on various targets, and the Third Brigade two 25-lb. bombs on Cherisy. On the night of the 23rd-24th, No. 102 Squadron dropped five 112-lb. bombs on Douai Station and sidings (four bombs were seen to hit the railway track, and one hit a shed alongside the sidings, and three 112-lb. bombs on Dechy Sidings and all were seen to explode on the objective. No. 101 Squadron dropped two 112-lb. bombs on a train north of Menin, where a large fire was caused.

Practically no enemy aircraft were encountered, and no decisive combats took place.

November 25th.

A strong west wind and low clouds made work almost impossible.

With aeroplane observation four hostile batteries were successfully engaged for destruction.

Three reconnaissances and a contact patrol were carried out by machines of the Third Brigade, two of the reconnaissances being by No. 11 Squadron.

The following additional work, which took place on the 23rd instant, is interesting :—

Lieutenant Duffus, No. 64 Squadron, engaged enemy infantry in the open north of Bourlon Wood by machine-gun fire. He dropped four bombs on dug-outs and the R.R. embankments, and fired 100 rounds at long range at four enemy aircraft, which retired. Being then hit in the engine and petrol tanks, Lieutenant Duffus just managed to clear Bourlon Wood, landing in some barbed wire. He fired in all 400 rounds at enemy infantry from about 200 feet.

Captain Fox-Russell, No. 64 Squadron, dropped three bombs from 100 feet on enemy trenches north-east of Bourlon Wood. He could not observe the results. He attacked groups of infantry returning from the wood. He was then hit by a shell and was forced to land in front of our line.

Captain Lee, No. 46 Squadron, assisted in driving down an enemy two-seater north of Bourlon Wood. He dropped four bombs into the wood, but the bursts were difficult to observe owing to shell fire. He then fired at hostile troops on Fontaine. While retiring temporarily to correct jams in his guns a shell burst underneath him, and brought his machine down so close to the Germans that he had to run 100 yards under machine-gun fire, and was consequently unable to destroy the machine. While walking back to Cantaing with a guide a shell burst in a house he was passing and blew him across the road. On the way back to get into communication with the squadron he assisted stretcher bearers to bring in wounded.

Honours and Awards.

The Military Cross.—Lieutenant F. H. Holmes, Second Lieut. C. G. Fenton, Lieutenant G. R. Hunter, Second Lieut. D. H. Sessions, Second Lieut. A. J. Tyler, Captain J. L. Vachell.

November 26th.

A little more work was possible, although low clouds and a strong wind made flying difficult.

Three reconnaissances were carried out by the Second Brigade, four by the third, and one by the Ninth Wing. Three contact patrols were also done by machines of the Third Brigade.

With aeroplane observation, six hostile batteries were successfully engaged for destruction by artillery of the First Army and three by artillery of the Third Army.

A total of 5,660 rounds were fired from low altitudes at ground targets. Nos. 68, 56, 46, and 84 Squadrons, in addition to dropping forty-five 25-lb. bombs, fired 3,190 of these rounds.

Seventy-seven 25-lb. and forty-three 112-lb. bombs were dropped. Of these eight 112-lb. bombs were dropped on Moisnil Station by No. 18 Squadron; five 112-lb. bombs on Sailly, where store sheds were hit, eight 112-lb. bombs on Rieux, and one 112-lb. bomb on an anti-aircraft battery by No. 49 Squadron.

Scouts of the Third Brigade dropped forty-five 25-lb. bombs from low altitudes on various targets. No. 25 Squadron dropped eighteen 112-lb. bombs on Aubigny and Neuville, and No. 27 Squadron dropped eight 112-lb. bombs on bridges between Tortequenne and Lecluse. The remaining bombs were dropped on various targets.

November 26th.

Enemy Aircraft.—Enemy aircraft were not very active. Four were shot down out of control by pilots of the Second Brigade; two of these were by Captain J. Payne, another by Lieutenant J. Coombe, and the fourth by Captain Molesworth, all of No. 29 Squadron, who fought and dispersed 12 enemy aircraft scouts.

Lieutenant Taylor, No. 68 Squadron (Third Brigade) shot down a two-seater machine, which crashed into the ground, and Second Lieut. W. Brown and Lieutenant J. Larson, flying S.E.'s of No. 84 Squadron, each shot down a German scout out of control.

S. WOOD, Captain,
Staff Captain.

Advanced Headquarters,
   Royal Flying Corps,
      29th November 1917.

ROYAL FLYING CORPS COMMUNIQUÉ No. 116.

During the month of November 49 enemy aircraft were brought down and 37 were driven down out of control. Fifty-five and a half tons of bombs were dropped and 5,000 photographs taken, while 177,000 rounds were fired from low altitudes at ground targets. The weather throughout the month was bad for flying, and most of the work was done at extraordinarily low altitudes.

November 27th.

Very high wind and rain during the greater part of the day made flying difficult.

On the Second Army front there were one or two fair intervals after 11.30 a.m., when a certain amount of flying was done.

Two reconnaissances were carried out by machines of the Second Brigade, and one reconnaissance and two contact patrols by the Third Brigade.

Two hostile batteries were successfully engaged for destruction, and six neutralised with aeroplane observation.

During the day twenty-five 25-lb. bombs were dropped on various targets by machines of the First and Second Brigades and Fourteenth Wing.

During the night of the 26th/27th, in spite of the very stormy weather, 11 machines of No. 102 Squadron dropped bombs as follows:—

Ten 112-lb. on Douai Railway Station. Six bombs hit the track and three hit sheds at the side of the railway. Three 112-lb. bombs on Vitry Railway Station and six 112-lb. bombs on Somain Railway Station.

Lieutenant Hammond was wounded while dropping his bombs on Douai station from a height of 500 feet. On recrossing the lines he fainted and fell forward on his control lever. His observer, Lieutenant Howard, managed to pull the lever back and landed the machine near Bethune.

One thousand four hundred rounds were fired into the enemy's trenches by machines of the First and Second Brigades and Fourteenth Wing, and 34 plates were exposed by the Second Brigade.

Machines of the Second Brigade had seven combats, in one of which Second-Lieut. Colville-Jones and Captain Speakman, No. 20 Squadron, drove a hostile machine down out of control near Westroosebeke.

On the 22nd Second Lieut. Moloney, No. 84 Squadron, became separated from his patrol and was attacked by six enemy aircraft. He was hit almost at once in the thigh, but continued to fight for 10 minutes, during which his machine was very badly shot about. One of the hostile machines was driven down in a spin completely out of control, and the others, into which the pilot had poured several bursts, all disappeared. As his compass had been hit he steered back to our lines by the sun, and made a good landing, in spite of feeling very weak from loss of blood and the damaged condition of his machine, close to an anti-aircraft battery.

November 28th.

Low clouds and a strong west wind during the greater part of the day hindered aerial work.

Two successful reconnaissances were carried out by Army machines of the Second Brigade, and five reconnaissances and two contact patrols by those of the Third Brigade.

A total of 420 photographs were taken, 237 of which were by the Second Brigade, and 110 by the First Brigade, and 2,772 rounds were fired into enemy trenches from low heights.

Twenty-two hostile batteries were successfully engaged for destruction, and seven neutralised with aeroplane observation. Four gun pits were destroyed, 11 damaged, 15 explosions, and 8 fires caused. One hundred and seventy-three active hostile batteries were reported by zone call. Eleven of the hostile batteries engaged for destruction were by the First Army artillery.

Lieutenant Robinson and Lieutenant Ferrier, No. 12 Squadron, sent down a G.F. call on two anti-aircraft guns on lorries and gave four corrections. Lieutenants Owles and Carden, No. 12 Squadron, during a flight of 3 hours 35 minutes, reported the position of 17 active hostile batteries by zone call, giving corrections in one case. During the same flight a G.F. call was sent down on an engine, and three 25-lb. bombs were dropped from this machine.

Eleven hostile batteries were successfully engaged for destruction with observation by machines of the Fourteenth Wing. The 227th Siege Battery, with observation by Second Lieut. Theak, No. 52 Squadron, obtained seven direct hits on a gun-pit of a hostile battery. Two gun-pits in a hostile battery position were very badly damaged by the 94th Siege Battery with observation by Sergeant Smith, No. 52 Squadron. The 61st Siege Battery, with observation by Lieutenant Dean, No. 52 Squadron, damaged a hostile battery position and caused a large fire. A fire was caused in a hostile battery position by the 19th Siege Battery, with observation by Lieutenant Bussey and Lieutenant Entwistle, Detached Flight of No. 5 Squadron. Captain Douglas and Lieutenant Whittaker, Detached Flight of No. 5 Squadron, observing for the 79th Siege Battery, destroyed one hostile gun-pit and damaged three others, causing a fire. Other successful shoots on hostile batteries were done by the 267 Siege Battery, the 169th Siege Battery, the 183rd Siege Battery, 125th Siege Battery, the 78th Siege Battery, and the 342nd Siege Battery, with observation by Lieutenants Worthing,

Munden, and Lieutenant Simpson, No. 52 Squadron; Lieutenants Hamel and Cooke, Detached Flight of No. 5 Squadron; Lieutenant Phillips, Detached Flight of No. 5 Squadron; and Lieutenant Ellis and Captain Yarde, Detached Flight of No. 5 Squadron.

Bombing.—Over four tons of bombs were dropped as follows :—

Ninth Wing.—One 230-lb., two 212-lb., and two 25-lb. bombs on Menin Railway Station on the night of the 27th/28th. One of the 112-lb. bombs dropped on a train entering the station. One thousand three hundred rounds were fired on searchlights, active machine, and anti-aircraft guns and billets during this raid by No. 101 Squadron.

On the 28th No. 25 Squadron dropped twelve 112-lb. bombs on Courtrai Railway Station, and No. 27 Squadron dropped ten 112-lb. bombs on Roulers Railway Station.

First Brigade.—No. 18 Squadron dropped eight 112-lb. bombs on Grand Moisnil, two 112-lb. bombs on Annoeulin, and eight 25-lb. bombs on various targets.

Second Brigade.—No. 57 Squadron dropped one 230-lb. and two 112-lb. bombs on Menin, one 230-lb. bomb on Thourout, and seventy 25-lb. bombs on other targets.

Third Brigade.—Dropped twelve 25-lb. and the Fourteenth Wing four 25-lb. bombs on various targets.

Enemy Aircraft.—Enemy aircraft activity was slight, except on the battle front, where it was above normal most of the day.

While on offensive patrol over Gheluvelt, Captain Dalton, No. 70 Squadron, fired 50 rounds into a hostile two-seater from 100 feet, driving it down completely out of control. Captain Smith and Second Lieut. Hill, No. 27 Squadron, drove down one of four enemy aircraft which attacked their bombing formation just after their bombs had been dropped.

November 29th.

On the 29th there was a distinct improvement in the weather, and a large amount of flying was done.

Five reconnaissances were carried out, two by the Second Brigade and two by the Third Brigade, and a photographic reconnaissance was done by the Ninth Wing.

With aeroplane observation 39 hostile batteries were successfully engaged for destruction, 13 being by machines of the First Brigade. Six gun-pits were destroyed, nine damaged, 26 explosions, and 12 fires caused. One hundred and fifty-five active hostile batteries were reported by zone call, of which 80 were by machines of the Third Brigade.

Low flying machines fired 4,748 rounds at ground targets, and 746 photographs were taken during the day.

The following pilots of No. 68 Squadron dropped sixteen 25-lb. bombs on enemy's infantry, at which they also fired with their machine guns:—Captain Phillips, Lieutenant Holden, Lieutenant R. W. Howard, Captain G. C. Wilson, Lieutenant H. Taylor, Lieutenant F. G. Huxley, Lieutenant G. C. Sands.

Enemy Aircraft.—Enemy aircraft were especially active on the Third Army front.

Second Lieuts. J. Pattern and P. Leycester, No. 10 Squadron, were taking photographs when they were attacked by three enemy scouts. The pilot opened fire with his forward gun, and then manœuvred in order to give his observer a free field of fire, and after a short burst the enemy scout burst into flames and crashed.

Captain W. W. Rogers, No. 1 Squadron, dived at an enemy two-seater which he shot down and out of control, while another was driven down out of control by Second Lieut. French and Lieutenant Keith, No. 20 Squadron.

Three enemy aircraft two-seaters were destroyed and two scouts shot down out of control by pilots of the Third Brigade. Captain McCudden, when leading a patrol of No. 56 Squadron, got on the tail of an enemy two-seater which he shot to pieces in the air. Another patrol of the same squadron observed three enemy two-seaters through a gap in the clouds, so dived at them, and Captain McCudden followed one down to 500 feet, when all its wings folded up. Captain McCudden was almost forced to land owing to loss of air pressure, and he was only a few feet from the ground when he was able to get his engine to work satisfactorily again. Second Lieut. H. Walkerdine drove down one of the other two-seaters out of control and it was seen by anti-aircraft to crash.

Lieutenant Turnbull, No. 56 Squadron, and Lieutenant Macgregor, No. 41 Squadron, each drove down an enemy machine completely out of control.

A patrol of No. 48 Squadron engaged nine scouts, and one was forced to land after having been engaged by Captain B. E. Baker and Second Air Mechanic Jackman, who drove down another out of control.

Second Lieuts. W. Pudney and G. Hayward, No. 22 Squadron, left their patrol owing to engine trouble, and were attacked by five enemy aircraft. The observer, Second Lieut. Hayward, shot one down, and it was seen to crash.

Bombing.—On the night of the 28th/29th and on the 29th over $4\frac{1}{2}$ tons of bombs were dropped.

First Brigade.—No. 18 Squadron dropped eight 112-lb. bombs on Grand Moisnil, two 112-lb. bombs on Wavrin, two 112-lb. bombs on Annoeulin, and six 112-lb. bombs on gun positions at Maugre.

No. 2 Squadron dropped fifteen 25-lb. bombs on Auchy, Benifontaine, Vendin-le-Vieil and Pont-à-Vendin.

Second Brigade.—Ninety-one 25-lb. bombs were dropped on various targets.

Third Brigade.—Eight 112-lb. bombs were dropped on Iwuy dump. Corps machines dropped twenty-two 25-lb. bombs, while scouts of No. 68 Squadron dropped sixteen 25-lb. bombs on various targets.

Fourteenth Wing.—Eight 25-lb. bombs were dropped on various targets.

Ninth Wing.—No. 25 Squadron attacked Roulers Railway Station on which twelve 112-lb. bombs were dropped.

On the night of the 28th/29th, although the clouds were at 2,500 feet, 12 machines of No. 101 Squadron went out to bomb Roulers Railway Station, and eight of the machines reached their objective and dropped one 230-lb., fourteen 112-lb. and two 25-lb. bombs, and fired 1,400 rounds into the station and at huts beside the station.

November 30th.

Very hard fighting took place on the ground all day. Machines of the Third Brigade co-operated with our troops by carrying out reconnaissances, contact patrols, bombing and firing at ground targets all day, although clouds were very low.

Machines of the Third Brigade carried out 19 contact patrols, and the Second Brigade one counter-attack patrol.

In all 20,000 rounds were fired from the air, 4,000 being by corps machines of the Third Brigade, and over 11,000 by Scout Squadrons, which dropped eight-eight 25-lb. bombs, while corps machines dropped twenty-three 25-lb. bombs.

No. 3 Squadron.—Captain E. Brokensha dropped four 25-lb. bombs with the following results:—One bomb exploded on four limbers, killing several horses and causing considerable damage to the limbers; one exploded on a railway culvert under which the enemy were assembling, partly destroying the culvert and causing several casualties among the enemy, one exploded on a large body of the enemy who had assembled in a large trench, and one exploded on three limbers. He then attacked and dispersed with machine-gun fire a party of about 50 enemy infantry.

Captain C. E. Barrington dropped four 25-lb. bombs on a convoy of six limbers on a road from 800 feet. He returned home on the gravity tank, owing to the pressure pipe of his machine breaking.

Lieutenant W. R. Haggas dropped four 25-lb. bombs—two on a company of enemy troops on a road, and the other two on an active hostile battery.

Twenty-fourth Squadron.—The following pilots fired at ground targets:—Lieutenant Johnston, Lieutenant McDonald,

Captain Ives, Captain Davies, Lieutenant Crosbee, Lieutenant Sutherland, and Lieutenant Hepburn.

Forty-sixth Squadron.—Lieutenant Lee was in the neighbourhood of Gouzeaucourt when he saw that the enemy were attacking in force. He was then at about 2,000 feet, so dived and fired 600 rounds from about 500 feet, and afterwards attacked an enemy two-seater with two other machines at which he fired about 150 rounds at close range. He came back to the advanced landing ground, filled up with ammunition, returned and expended all of it (about 700 rounds).

Lieutenants Bulman, Cooper and Blakely, and Captain Robeson also dropped bombs and fired with good results.

Sixty-fourth Squadron.—Captains Slater, Fox-Russell, and Tempest, Lieutenants Duffus and Hardie, and Second Lieutenants Thompson, Ashton, Barrett and Burge all fired at ground targets and a number of the pilots dropped bombs.

Sixty-eighth Squadron.—The following pilots fired at ground targets and most of them dropped bombs also:—Captains Phillips and G. C. Wilson, Lieutenants H. G. Forrest, C. L. Johnson, Robertson, Holden, R. L. Clark, G. C. Sands, F. G. Huxley, H. Taylor, and Howard, and Second Lieutenants Benjamin and Cornell.

In many instances, the pilots fired all the ammunition they had and dropped their bombs and then returned to the advanced landing ground for more bombs and ammunition and went out again and continued doing the same work.

With aeroplane observation, seven hostile batteries were successfully engaged for destruction and four were neutralised, three gun-pits were destroyed, two damaged, six explosions and a fire caused. Two hundred and seventy-six active hostile batteries were reported by zone call, 203 of these being by the Third Brigade.

Twenty targets were registered by balloons, 18 being by the Second Brigade, while balloons of the Fourteenth Wing located three active hostile batteries and reported ten trains opposite their front.

In addition to the bombs dropped by the Third Brigade, No. 2 Squadron dropped four 25-lb. bombs on billets; the Second Brigade dropped thirty-nine 25-lb. bombs on various targets; No. 48 Squadron dropped four 25-lb. bombs on various targets, and No. 25 Squadren attacked Oisy-le-Verger on which ten 112-lb. bombs were dropped from 2,000 feet, while one pilot went down to 500 feet before releasing his bombs. No. 27 Squadron dropped seven 112-lb. bombs on Marquion from about 6,000 feet. The raids by Nos. 25 and 27 Squadrons were carried out by machines flying singly or in pairs through the clouds.

Enemy Aircraft.—Enemy aircraft were active on the battle front and a great deal of fighting took place. The result was that 16 hostile machines were brought down, two falling within our lines, and six were driven down out of control, all by machines of the Third Brigade. Pilots of No. 56 Squadron accounted for five of the enemy machines that were destroyed. Captain J. B. McCudden with other pilots drove away enemy machines from over Bourlon and then attacked two two-seater machines. He secured a good position behind one which he hit in the engine with the first burst and forced it to glide west and land in our lines.

Captain R. A. Maybery attacked a large formation of enemy aircraft with his patrol and singled out one which turned to fight, but on turning offered a good target and was shot down and destroyed. After this he saw another scout dive out of the clouds, so flew to within very close range without being seen, and then opened fire with both guns and the enemy machine completely crumpled up and the pieces fell to earth.

Lieutenant M. Mealing shot one enemy machine down out of control near Lesdain and then turned and drove another away, after which he watched the first one crash to earth.

Captain G. H. Bowman saw an enemy aircraft Scout flying west so got on its tail; and as the enemy aircraft was diving past he opened fire from long range with both guns and the enemy aircraft continued straight down and crashed.

Captain A. E. McKeever and Second Lieutenant L. A. Powell, No. 11 Squadron, were on line patrol in the morning when they encountered nine enemy machines which they attacked. The pilot and observer each destroyed two of the enemy machines. The first one, engaged by the pilot at 15 yards range, crashed and burst into flames; the next two were shot down by the observer, and crashed, and the fourth, which overshot the Bristol Fighter, was destroyed by the pilot. During the fighting the observer's gun had a stoppage and the pilot fought the enemy machines to within 20 feet of the ground, and then as the enemy aircraft were still attacking, he pretended to land. This deception enabled him to suddenly put on his engine, zoom up and get away before the remaining enemy aircraft, which had climbed to a considerable height, realised his intention.

Captain G. C. Wilson, No. 68 Squadron (A.F.C.), was engaging one enemy machine when he was attacked by another, so he did a sharp turn, got underneath his opponent and shot him down out of control and saw the machine crash on landing, so then dropped a bomb which he was carrying and it exploded right on the enemy machine. He had expended all his ammunition in firing at ground targets and at this enemy aircraft and when flying towards the lines was cut off by two German machines, so he manœuvred and pretended to attack the enemy aircraft, who flew away and allowed him to return safely.

Captain M. Thomas and Lieutenant R. Winnicott, No. 41 Squadron, each destroyed an enemy machine, while a third was destroyed by Captain L. J. MacLean and Lieutenant D. McGregor. Another was driven down out of control by Captains Thomas and MacLean and Lieutenants Winnicott and F. H. Taylor.

Lieutenant G. Thompson, No. 46 Squadron, observed three enemy aircraft flying west so attacked and shot one down which fell within our lines. He drove down another out of control after it had recrossed the lines.

Captain J. M. Child, No. 84 Squadron, pursued two enemy aircraft across the lines, but saw a large formation, so climbed within the clouds and on coming out again saw six enemy aircraft underneath him. He dived at the rear machine and destroyed it. He noticed that the enemy aircraft always watched their anti-aircraft bursts which appeared to be also used for purposes of signalling.

A German machine was driven down and fell in a field after being engaged by Captain Leask, of the same squadron.

Captain E. R. Pennell, No. 84 Squadron, Captains J. Slater and E. Tempest, both of No. 64 Squadron, and Second Lieut. L. Nixon, No. 3 Squadron, drove down an enemy machine each out of control, while another was driven down, possibly out of control, by Second Lieut. C. T. Travers, No. 84 Squadron.

The following was received from General Plumer, dated 30th November 1917 :—

"Our airmen commenced flying yesterday and shot down one hostile machine."

December 1st.

Little flying was done by the Brigades, except the Third Brigade, whose pilots carried out 13 reconnaissances and many patrols in spite of low clouds and mist.

Over 4,000 rounds were fired at infantry in the trenches and in the open, and sixty-three 25-lb. bombs were dropped at the same targets. Forty-eight of the bombs dropped and over 2,500 of the rounds fired were by the Third Brigade.

Lieutenant Huxley, No. 68 Squadron (A.F.C.), during two flights, dropped three bombs, and one, from a height of 50 feet, burst among troops, and another burst among a crowd of the enemy who had gathered round a German two-seater machine which had been brought down. Lieutenant Sands also went out twice and secured direct hits with bombs from 300 feet and fired 300 rounds. Both these pilots made very valuable reports on the enemy's dispositions. Lieutenant Taylor hit Beet Factory with two bombs, fired at infantry, and drove away two enemy two-seaters. Lieutenants Forrest and Benjamin also hit troops with bombs and gun-fire and brought back valuable information.

Captain McClintock and Lieutenants Duffus, Hardy and Ashton, No. 64 Squadron, all went out twice, dropping bombs and using their machine guns, and Lieutenants Brown and Johnston fired 400 rounds at enemy troops.

Other bombs were dropped as follows:—Four 112-lb. bombs on Libercourt, by No. 18 Squadron; two 25-lb. bombs on Benifontaine, by No. 2 Squadron; eight 25-lb. bombs by the Second Brigade and twelve 25-lb. bombs by Corps machines of the Third Brigade. The latter also fired approximately 1,400 rounds.

During the night of the 30th November/1st December Nos. 101 and 102 Squadrons went out all through the night, although the clouds were at a height of 2,000 feet, and dropped approximately five tons of bombs.

No. 101 Squadron dropped four 230-lb., thirty-eight 112-lb. and eight 25-lb. bombs. Fifteen direct hits were obtained on Douai Station, four trains were hit and eight explosions and one fire caused. Twelve 112-lb bombs were dropped on Dechy and two direct hits were obtained on the station, two on the junction, three on the sidings and two near a train. Two 112-lb. bombs were also dropped on a train at Lambres. During this raid, 2,670 rounds were fired at Douai, 650 at Dechy, 150 at Lambres, and 600 at troops on roads and at searchlights.

No. 102 Squadron dropped one hundred and ninety-two 25-lb. bombs on Marquion, five on Barelle, eight on Sauchy-Lestree, four on half a battalion of troops, 14 on other targets, and fired 900 rounds at German infantry.

Captain H. A. Duff and Second Lieut. W. E. Davis went out four times and Second Lieut. B. C. Windle and Lieut. A. L. Shaw, Second Lieut. R. M. Loudon and Second Lieut. E. H. Lawrence, Second Lieut. D. R. Wilson and Lieut. J. T. Richardson, Second Lieut. A. B. Whiteside, and Second Lieut. C. T. Marshall went out three times and bombed Marquion.

Enemy Aircraft.—Enemy aircraft activity was very slight and only five combats took place between enemy aircraft and pilots of the Third Brigade.

Lieutenant F. G. Huxley, No. 68 Squadron (A.F.C.), dived at an enemy machine and by careful manœuvring avoided the hostile fire while he succeeded in shooting down the German machine which crashed.

Lieutenant E. Hughes, No. 46 Squadron, had completely lost his bearings in a thick mist, when he met an Albatross Scout, so at once opened fire and the enemy machine crashed.

Lieutenant R. W. McKenzie, No. 68 Squadron (A.F.C.), drove down a German machine which attempted to land but ran into a shell-hole.

Honours and Awards.

The Distinguished Service Cross.—Flight Sub-Lieut. J. G. Manuel, R.N.A.S.

The Military Cross.—Captain B. P. G. Beanlands, Captain R. M. Charley and Captain C. T. Lally.

December 2nd.

Squalls and very strong wind prevented much flying being done

Machines of the Third Brigade carried out 14 reconnaissances in order to ascertain the position and movements of enemy troops and obtain other information. This Brigade also carried out 12 contact patrols.

Machines of the Second Brigade worked in conjunction with our infantry who were attacking north-west of Passchendaele and carried out two reconnaissances.

A machine of No. 25 Squadron reconnoitred the line Cambrai—Busigny—Bohain.

With aeroplane observation 16 hostile batteries were successfully engaged for destruction; one gun-pit was destroyed, six damaged, two explosions and five fires caused.

Three hundred and sixty-three photographs were taken, and approximately 2,200 rounds were fired at ground targets from low altitudes and over two tons of bombs were dropped.

First Brigade. — Machines dropped six 25-lb. bombs on billets.

Second Brigade.—Pilots of No. 70 Squadron flying Sopwith Camels dropped twenty-eight 25-lb. bombs on active hostile batteries. Seventy-two 25-lb. bombs were also dropped on active hostile batteries by No 57 Squadron and ten 25-lb. bombs on various targets by Corps machines.

Third Brigade.—D.H. 5's, of No. 68 Squadron (A.F.C.), dropped fourteen 25-lb. bombs on trenches. No. 64 Squadron, also D.H. 5's, dropped six bombs on the same targets, while Corps machines dropped twelve 25-lb. bombs on various targets.

Ninth Wing.—No. 27 Squadron attacked Tortequenne and Lecluse and dropped four 112-lb. bombs on the former and six 112-lb. bombs on the latter target.

No. 25 Squadron dropped twelve 112-lb. bombs on Ecourt St. Quentin.

Enemy aircraft activity was very slight, except on the Second Brigade front where it was about normal. Three Bristol fighters of No. 20 Squadron saw a two-seater near Passchendaele, so dived at it, and Second Lieut. W. Beever and First Air Mechanic M. Mather shot it down out of control, and it was seen to crash.

December 3rd.

The weather was fine and visibility good and a large amount of reconnoitring, photographic, and artillery work was done.

Thirteen reconnaissances were carried out, two by the Second Brigade and nine by the Third, while five contact patrols were done by the Second Brigade and 12 by the Third Brigade. Machines of the Ninth Wing carried out two successful reconnaisances of aerodromes in the neighbourhood of Courtrai and Phalempin.

With aeroplane observation, 29 hostile batteries were successfully engaged for destruction and 15 neutralized; one gun-pit was destroyed, 12 damaged, 14 explosions, and 12 fires caused.

One hundred and thirty-nine zone calls were sent down of which 115 were by the Second Brigade.

Over 3,000 rounds were fired from low altitudes at ground targets and 887 plates were exposed.

Bombing.—**First Brigade.**—No. 2 Squadron dropped thirteen 25-lb. bombs on various targets.

Second Brigade.—No. 57 Squadron dropped fifty-one 25-lb. bombs on various targets, including Gheluwe and hostile batteries, and camels of No. 70 Squadron dropped thirty-four 25-lb. bombs on Gheluwe, hostile batteries, and moving targets on the Ypres–Menin Road, in order to assist the infantry in their attack on Polderhoek Chateau.

Twenty-two 25-lb. bombs were dropped on various targets by Corps Squadrons.

Third Brigade.—Six 25-lb. bombs were dropped on various targets.

No. 9 Wing.—No. 27 Squadron attacked Honnecourt on which seven 112-lb. bombs were dropped. Thirty 25-lb. bombs were also dropped on Crevecoeur by machines of the same squadron.

No. 25 Squadron dropped eight 112-lb. bombs on Menin Railway Station and four 112-lb. bombs on Crevecoeur.

Observation of results was very difficult owing to ground haze.

Enemy Aircraft.—Enemy aircraft activity was below normal, except on the Third Army front, where it was great.

Sergeant F. Johnson and Second Lieut. S. Masding, No. 20 Squadron, encountered eight enemy machines over Wervicq when with the rest of their patrol. This pilot and observer shot down one of their opponents completely out of control.

Captain P. Huskinson, No. 19 Squadron, fought an Albatross scout and shot it down out of control.

Honours and Awards.

The Military Cross.—Captain J. B. Solomon.

S. WOOD, Captain,
Staff Officer.

Advanced Headquarters,
  Royal Flying Corps,
    5th December 1917.

ROYAL FLYING CORPS COMMUNIQUÉ, No 117.

During the period under review, 4th to 11th December inclusive, we have claimed officially 13 enemy aircraft brought down, 10 driven out of control, and one enemy balloon destroyed.

Approximately 36,000 rounds have been fired at ground targets and nearly 20 tons of bombs dropped.

December 4th.

The weather was fine but thick ground mist, and in the Second Brigade area snow prevented our machines from working freely.

Machines of the Second and Third Brigades each carried out three successful reconnaissances, when valuable information was obtained.

Captain Youdale and Lieutenant Wilson, No. 21 Squadron, completed a detailed contact patrol of the Eighth Corps front, while two other contact patrols were done, one by No. 10 Squadron and the other by No. 21 Squadron.

With aeroplane observation, nine hostile batteries were successfully engaged for destruction, four pits were damaged, one explosion and one fire caused.

Low flying aeroplanes fired approximately 6,000 rounds at ground targets, 2,200 being by pilots of Naval Squadron No. 8.

Nearly six tons of bombs were dropped by day and night, as follows :—

First Brigade.—No. 2 Squadron dropped eighty-eight 25-lb. bombs on Estevelles, Provin, Pont-à-Vendin, Annay, and other targets, and on the night of the 3rd/4th this squadron dropped eight 25-lb. bombs on various objectives. No. 18 Squadron dropped four 112-lb. bombs on Moncheaux Aerodrome.

Second Brigade.—Nos. 7, 9, 10, 21, and 69 Squadrons dropped fifty-four 25-lb. bombs on Comines and other targets.

Third Brigade—No. 49 Squadron dropped ten 112-lb. bombs on Marquion. Scouts dropped thirty-two 25-lb. and Corps machines six 25-lb. bombs on various targets.

Ninth Wing.—On the night of the 3rd/4th, No. 101 Squadron dropped one hundred and twenty-six 25-lb. bombs on Sains-lez-Marquion, and No. 102 Squadron one hundred and forty 25-lb. bombs on Honnecourt, four on Malincourt, and four on a train north of Malincourt, which was hit, and fired 300 rounds at ground targets.

The majority of the pilots of these two squadrons made two trips, and some three, during the night.

Enemy Aircraft.—Enemy aircraft activity was slight all day and only nine combats took place.

One hostile machine was driven done out of control by Captain Pearson and Second Lieut. Howsam, No. 22 Squadron.

December 5th.

There was heavy mist in the afternoon, but it was clear during the rest of the day.

A reconnaissance of enemy wire from a height of 200 feet was carried out by Lieutenant Crawford and Captain Broadbent, No. 2 Squadron, and two enemy aerodromes were observed and photographed by other members of the First Brigade.

Bristol Fighters of the Third Brigade carried out three reconnaissances and took photographs, including some of hostile aerodromes.

A successful reconnaissance was carried out by a Corps machine of the Corps front, and six counter attack patrols were done by the Third Brigade.

Captain Jardine and Second Lieut. Bliss, No. 25 Squadron, took photographs of stations filled with rolling stock, and reconnoitred the country round Douai, Denain, Valenciennes, Lens, Bavai and Busigny.

With aeroplane observation, 44 hostile batteries were successfully engaged for destruction, eight gun-pits were destroyed, 21 damaged, 30 explosions and 17 fires caused.

Thirteen of the batteries engaged for destruction were by artillery of the First Army which destroyed four pits, damaged nine, caused six explosions and one fire.

Twenty-one were by artillery of the Second Army which destroyed four pits, damaged five, caused 20 explosions and 13 fires, and machines of this Army reported 50 active hostile batteries by zone call.

The 194 Siege Battery, with observation by Captain Hilton and Lieutenant Clayton, No. 9 Squadron, obtained four O.K's on a hostile battery position, demolishing one pit and damaging another, while three fires and an explosion were also caused. Second Lieut. Jarrett and Lieutenant Hughes, No. 53 Squadron, ranged the 218th Siege Battery on to another hostile battery; four O.K's were obtained which caused an explosion and fire which burned for half an hour.

Ten of the hostile batteries were successfully engaged for destruction by artillery of the Third Army which damaged seven pits, caused four explosions and three fires. During a flight of three hours 55 minutes Lieutenant Robinson and Corporal Triese, No. 12 Squadron, ranged the 86th Siege Battery on to three hostile batteries and three O.K's were obtained. This pilot and observer reported three active hostile batteries by zone call and took 16 photographs. The First R.M.A. obtained a direct hit on a bridge on to which they had been ranged by Lieutenant Martin-Smith and Lieutenant Smith, No. 59 Squadron.

Balloons of the Second Brigade engaged seven targets, of which two were active hostile batteries successfully engaged for destruction.

During the day, 1,229 photographs were taken and 7,932 rounds were fired—1,940 by the First, 4,612 by the Second, and 1,380 by the Third Brigade.

Enemy Aircraft.—Enemy aircraft activity was very marked on the Third Army front all day, but normal on other fronts.

Flight Commander Price and Flight Sub-Lieut. Sneath, Naval Squadron No. 8, attacked an Albatross Scout and drove it down out of control.

Lieutenant Kirkpatrick and Second Lieut. Hamer, No. 20 Squadron, destroyed an Albatross Scout near Dadizelle, and three others were driven down out of control by machines of this squadron—a two-seater by Sergeant Johnson and Captain Hedley, another by Second Lieut. Beaver and First Air Mechanic Mather, and the third by Lieutenant Kirkman and Captain Burbidge.

Second Lieutenant Quigley, No. 70 Squadron, attacked two German Scouts and destroyed one.

Captain Pearson and Second Lieut. Tyrrell, No 32 Squadron, attacked a two-seater, shot the observer and then shot the machine down out of control.

Lieutenants Paul and Macrae, No. 23 Squadron, and Captain Hamilton, No. 29 Squadron, each drove down an enemy machine out of control.

Captain J. B. McCudden, No. 56 Squadron, was testing a new engine at a height of 19,000 feet over Havrincourt Wood when he saw a two-seater enemy aircraft flying west over Bourlon. He waited until the German machine was well over the lines, and then secured a good position and attacked, and after firing with both guns the enemy machine went into a vertical dive, broke to pieces at 16,000 feet over Hermies and crashed within our lines.

Sergeants J. Bainbridge and J. Johnston, No. 22 Squadron, went up after a German two-seater machine seen from the ground and attacked and destroyed it.

Second Lieut. S. Oades and Second Aircraft Mechanic Jones, of the same squadron, dived at several enemy aircraft and shot one down which appeared to fall in flames.

Second Lieuts. J. Macaulay and M. St. Clair-Fowles, No. 25 Squadron, were on a practice patrol, and were attacked by three enemy aircraft, and in the fighting they shot one down, which fell apparently out of control.

An enemy machine was shot down by anti-aircraft of the Third Army and fell in our lines, and another was shot down in flames by a French pilot, and fell in the Second Army area.

Bombing.—First Brigade.—No. 2 Squadron dropped twelve 35-lb. bombs on Benifontaine, Auchy, Vendin-le-Vieil and on trenches. No. 18 Squadron dropped eight 112-lb. bombs on Moncheaux Aerodrome.

Second Brigade.—One hundred and twenty-three 25-lb. bombs were dropped on various targets.

Third Brigade.—No. 49 Squadron attacked Marquion, on which eight 25 lb. bombs were dropped. Corps machines dropped eight 25-lb., while scouts dropped eight 25-lb. bombs on various targets.

Forty-first Wing.—Two raids were carried out into Germany in the afternoon, the first that have been possible for over a month owing to incessant bad weather. In one raid twelve 112-lb. bombs were dropped on the railway sidings at Zweibrucken by No. 55 Squadron, 80 miles from their aerodrome, and in the second raid eight 112-lb. and eight 25-lb. bombs were dropped by the same squadron on the Burbach works at Saarbrucken, and many direct hits were seen and two fires started. Anti-aircraft fire was heavy and accurate, but the machines were not troubled by enemy aircraft. Although one or two were seen in the vicinity of Saarbrucken they did not attack our machines, all of which returned safely.

Honours and Awards.

The Military Cross.—Lieutenant E. T. Owles, Second Lieut. R. R. Bentley, Second Lieut. P. T. Carden, Second Lieut. C. F. Nathan, Lieutenant S. L. Quine.

December 6th.

The weather was fine, but there was ground mist in the afternoon.

Eighteen reconnaissances were carried out, one by the First Brigade, eight by the Second Brigade, in which Nos. 9, 21, 69, 10, and 57 Squadrons obtained valuable information. Four successful reconnaissances were carried out by Bristol Fighters of No. 11 Squadron (Third Brigade) who took photographs, and Corps machines carried out two successful reconnaissances. Two long reconnaissances, during which photographs were taken, were done by No. 25 Squadron.

Eight hundred and twenty-nine photographs were taken, during the day and 5,502 rounds fired at ground targets—3,444 being by the Second Brigade.

With aeroplane observation, 38 hostile batteries were successfully engaged for destruction; one gun-pit was destroyed, 12 damaged, 16 explosions, and nine fires caused. Ten of these batteries engaged were by the First Army, 16 by the Second Army, and 13 by the Third Army. The 40th Siege Battery obtained six direct hits on a hostile battery, causing two explosions and a fire after being ranged by Second Lieuts. Remington and Wilby, No. 9 Squadron. Three direct hits were obtained on another hostile battery where two pits were damaged by the 103rd Siege Battery, with observation by Captain Balmain and

Lieutenant Swales, No. 12 Squadron. Captain J. Solomon and Lieutenant Rowbotham, No. 15 Squadron, ranged the 277th Siege battery on to a hostile battery, where a fire was caused and two pits damaged.

Balloons of the Second Brigade ranged on 54 targets which were engaged—17 being hostile batteries. Eight of the shoots were done in conjunction with aeroplanes.

Enemy Aircraft.—Enemy aircraft activity was not great considering the fine weather and most of the activity took place in the morning on the First Army front.

Sopwith Camels of Naval Squadron No. 8 had several different engagements, and Flight Commander Compston assisted by other pilots drove one enemy machine down out of control, and in another fight he and other pilots shot down a two-seater, which fell hopelessly out of control into the mist, whilst Flight Commander Price and Flight Sub-Lieut. Day shot down another out of control.

Second Lieut. B. Bate and Lieutenant C. Ffolliott, No. 18 Squadron, were taking photographs and were approaching Valenciennes when they were attacked by a large formation of enemy aircraft. After a short combat with the leading machine at close range the tail of the German machine snapped as though shot through the longerons and crashed to earth. This pilot and observer finished the photography although they had several more encounters, and fired nearly 1,000 rounds at enemy machines and had 40 bullet holes through their aeroplane.

While on offensive patrol Lieutenant J. Kirkpatrick and Second Lieut. W. Harmer, No. 20 Squadron, met an enemy aircraft which flew directly at them out of the sun. The observer (Second Lieut. Harmer), fired a drum into the enemy aircraft at close range and it turned over, fell out of control and crashed.

Lieutenants A. Pitman and C. Pearson, No. 57 Squadron, were engaged on photography when they saw two enemy scouts which they attacked and shot one machine down, from off which a wing was seen to fall.

Several enemy aircraft were driven down by pilots of No. 19 Squadron; and Second Lieut. E. Meek, No. 29 Squadron, shot one down which he lost sight of but it was seen by other pilots to be burning on the ground afterwards.

Captain J. B. McCudden, No. 56 Squadron, saw a two-seater apparently engaged on photography over Vendelles, so manœuvred for position and opened fire and after a short burst from both guns a lot of material, resembling maps and such like, fell from the machine which fell out of control with the observer hanging over the side of the fuselage. When about 8,000 feet from the ground the right-hand wings fell off and the wreckage fell in our lines.

Lieutenant F. Huxley, No. 68 Squadron (A.F.C.), was flying at about 2,000 feet when he saw two two-seater German machines below him, so dived at one and opened fire and the enemy aeroplane went down, burst into flames and crashed.

A patrol of No. 84 Squadron shot down an enemy machine completely out of control, while another was driven down out of control by Captain Thomas, No. 41 Squadron.

Second Lieutenant S. Oades and Second Air Mechanic J. Jones, No. 22 Squadron, engaged an enemy aircraft which they destroyed, while Second Lieutenants W. Pudney and G. Hayward, of the same Squadron, drove one down out of control.

Bombing.—First Brigade.—No. 18 Squadron dropped eight 112-lb. bombs on Moncheaux Aerodrome and two 112-lb. bombs on Billy Montigny. No. 2 Squadron dropped sixteen 25-lb. bombs on various targets.

Second Brigade.—One hundred and fifteen 25-lb. bombs were dropped on various objectives. One bomb dropped by a pilot of No. 21 Squadron was seen to burst on a hostile battery position.

Third Brigade.—No. 49 Squadron attacked Marquion on which eight 112-lb. bombs were dropped with good results. Low flying aeroplanes dropped thirty-three 25-lb. bombs and corps machines two 25-lb. bombs on trench and other targets.

Ninth Wing.—No. 25 Squadron dropped twelve 112-lb. bombs on Valenciennes Railway Station and obtained many direct hits on the line causing fires in the station, while a direct hit was also obtained on the railway bridge.

On the night of the 5th/6th, No. 101 Squadron attacked Gontrode Aerodrome on which ten 112-lb. bombs were dropped. Two direct hits were obtained on a large shed, while other bombs dropped amongst building round the aerodrome. No. 102 Squadron attacked Douai Station with four 112-lb. bombs, and Dechy Railway Station with two 112-lb. bombs, causing a fire and hitting the railway track at the latter place.

Forty-First Wing.—Eleven machines of No. 55 Squadron carried out a raid into Germany and dropped bombs on the Burbach Works, Saarbrucken. One 230-lb., eighteen 112-lb., and eight 25-lb. bombs were dropped from 13,000 feet, and fires were started in two of the factories and in the railway station, while large columns of smoke were seen to rise from the station and other buildings. After leaving the aerodrome the pilots ran into heavy clouds, but succeeded in finding their objective and a large clear gap over Saarbrucken enabled them to drop their bombs with accuracy. Anti-aircraft gun-fire was heavy and accurate, and although eight enemy aircraft were seen they did not attack, and all our machines returned safely.

December 7th.

Low clouds prevented much flying being done during the day.

A low-flying reconnaissance was carried out by Lieutenant Crawford and Second Lieut. Abraham, No. 2 Squadron. Four reconnaissances were carried out by machines of the Second Brigade, and useful information was obtained by No. 69 Squadron, and two were done by the Third Brigade, both by machines of No. 11 Squadron. Machines of the latter brigade also carried out seven successful contact patrols.

On the night of the 6th-7th, Lieutenant Windsor, No. 100 Squadron, carried out a reconnaissance.

Five thousand one hundred and forty rounds were fired at ground targets.

Artillery Co-operation.—With aeroplane observation twenty-six hostile batteries were successfully engaged for destruction; one gun-pit was destroyed, 11 damaged, seven explosions, and four fires caused.

During a flight of three and half hours Lieutenants Hayter and Scott, No. 12 Squadron, ranged the 262nd Siege Battery on a hostile battery and observed for 52 rounds, reporting two O.K.'s and three pits damaged. Lieutenants Clarke and Westerby, No 15 Squadron, ranged the 112th Siege Battery on to another hostile battery and observed for 53 rounds. The position was damaged and a house set on fire, while three direct hits were obtained and an explosion caused in a third hostile battery position by the 173rd Siege Battery which was ranged by Lieutenants Ashton and Thomas, No. 12 Squadron.

With balloon observation of the Second Brigade four hostile batteries were successfully engaged for destruction and 31 other targets dealt with. One shoot was done in conjunction with an aeroplane.

Enemy Aircraft.—Enemy aircraft activity was slight all day. One enemy scout landed in our lines near Vermelles under control. The machine was little damaged, but appeared to have been hit by both anti-aircraft and machine-gun fire.

Captain W. Anderson and Lieutenant J. Bell, No. 69 Squadron (A.F.C.), were engaged on artillery observation when they encountered a German two-seater and drove it down out of control, and it was seen by ground observers to crash.

Bombing.—First Brigade.—No. 4 Squadron dropped eight 25-lb. bombs on hostile trenches and No. 3 Squadron dropped three 25-lb. bombs on Benifontaine.

Second Brigade.—Machines of this Brigade dropped fifty-one 25-lb. bombs on various targets, and the Third Brigade dropped thirty-nine 25-lb. bombs on various targets.

A photographic reconnaissance was attempted by a machine of the Forty-first Wing, but although the objective was reached, clouds prevented photographs being taken.

Honours and Awards.

Under authority granted by His Majesty the King, the Field Marshal Commanding-in-Chief has made the following awards:—

The Military Cross.—Lieutenant H. Hammond, Dorset Regiment and Royal Flying Corps. Second Lieut. H. Howard, Northumberland Fusiliers and Royal Flying Corps.

December 8th.

Little flying was possible owing to the unfavourable weather until the afternoon when there were occasional bright intervals. Lieutenant Crawford and Second Lieutenant Abraham, No. 2 Squadron, carried out a successful reconnaissance of wire from a height of 200 feet.

Two reconnaissances were carried out by the Second Brigade, three by the Third Brigade, and one by the Ninth Wing, when 18 plates were exposed in the neighbourhood of Bruges by Captain Lalley and Lieutenant Cole, No. 25 Squadron.

With aeroplane observation 21 hostile batteries were successfully engaged for destruction; one gun-pit was destroyed, 13 damaged, four explosions, and seven fires caused. Fifty-two zone calls were sent down, 31 of which were by machines of the Second Brigade.

Three hundred and fifteen photographs were taken during the day and 6,178 rounds fired at ground targets, of which 4,510 were by the Second Brigade.

Bombing.—First Brigade.—No. 2 Squadron dropped six 25-lb. bombs and No. 4 Squadron seven 25-lb. bombs on various targets.

Second Brigade. — Ninety-five 25-lb. bombs on various targets.

Third Brigade.—Fourteen 25-lb. bombs on various targets.

Enemy Aircraft.—Captain A. Bryson and Lieutenant A. Fairclough, No. 19 Squadron, went up after a German wireless machine and found a two-seater which they engaged and shot down out of control. They could not, however, see it crash owing to the presence of six enemy aircraft scouts.

December 9th.

On the 9th instant practically no work in the air was done owing to the weather.

One successful shoot was carried out by artillery of the Third Army with aeroplane observation, and four artillery patrols were done by the Third Brigade when four hostile batteries were reported by zone call and two were seen to be engaged. Corps machines of the same Brigade dropped six 25-lb. bombs on various targets and fired 100 from the air.

Two hostile batteries were successfully engaged for destruction by artillery of the Second Army with balloon observation. Two were neutralised and 11 other targets dealt with. One shoot was carried out in conjunction with an aeroplane and two fires were caused.

Honours and Awards.

Under authority granted by His Majesty the King, the Field Marshal Commanding-in-Chief has made the following awards :—

The Military Cross.—Lieutenant J. B. Williams, General List and Royal Flying Corps and Second Lieut. P. J. Moloney, Royal Flying Corps (S.R.).

December 10th.

The weather was fine but with low clouds and mist.

Lieutenant Crawford and Second Lieut. Abraham, No. 2 Squadron, carried out a reconnaisance of wire at a height of 50 feet. Nos. 7 and 20 Squadrons of the Second Brigade carried out successful reconnaissances, and No. 21 Squadron of the same Brigade a counter attack patrol. Bristol fighters of the Third Brigade, No. 11 Squadron carried out five reconnaissances on two of which photographs were taken, while two reconnaissances and four counter-attack patrols were carried out by Corps machines.

Five hundred and fifty-six photographs were taken during the day and 4,277 rounds fired, of which 1,150 were by Naval Squadron No. 8.

Artillery Co-operation.—With aeroplane observation 24 hostile batteries were successfully engaged for destruction; nine gun-pits were damaged, 15 explosions and nine fires caused and 65 zone calls were sent down. Thirteen of the counter battery shoots were carried out by the Second Brigade.

The 231st Siege Battery obtained direct hits on a hostile battery, damaging two pits and causing a fire and an explosion, with observation by Second Lieutenant Harris and Lieutenant Hibbs, No. 9 Squadron, and Lieutenants Young and Clayton of the same Squadron, ranged the 152nd Siege Battery on to another hostile battery where two pits were damaged and a large fire caused.

The 199th Siege Battery, with observation by Lieutenants Turnbull and Marriott, No. 12 Squadron, caused two explosions and a large fire which lasted for 20 minutes in a hostile battery position.

Captain Owles and Air Mechanic Calvert of the same Squadron, during a flight of $3\frac{1}{2}$ hours, reported six active hostile batteries, giving corrections in one case and sent GF calls on three separate convoys of M.T., and on two occasions the fire in reply appeared to be accurate.

Bombing.—First Brigade.—No. 2 Squadron dropped thirteen 25-lb. and No. 4 Squadron twelve 25-lb. bombs on billets.

Second Brigade.—One hundred and eight 25-lb. bombs were dropped on villages, hutments, and other targets.

Third Brigade.—No. 49 Squadron attacked Marquion on which ten 112-lb. bombs were dropped, while forty-four 25-lb. bombs were dropped on various targets by Corps machines.

Enemy Aircraft.—Enemy aircraft were active, especially on the Third Army front, where they endeavoured to stop our artillery machines from working.

Four Bristol Fighters of No. 20 Squadron attacked seven enemy aircraft, and Sergeant F. Johnson, who had as observer Captain J. Hedley, shot down one which crashed.

Lieutenants A. Pitman and C. Pearson, No. 57 Squadron, were taking photographs when they observed a two-seater German machine climbing upwards. They continued with their photography until the enemy machine had reached the same height as themselves when they engaged and shot it down out of control.

Lieutenant MacDonald, No. 24 Squadron, observed a formation of enemy aircraft attacking an aeroplane of his patrol below him, so dived and opened fire at close range at one of the machines which fell out of control. Another D H.5 pilot, of the same squadron, Lieutenant A. Brown, also succeeded in hitting one of the hostile formation and it went down in a vertical dive.

Lieutenant L. Franklin, No. 56 Squadron, shot down a German scout out of control and Lieutenant G. Thompson, of No. 46 Squadron, also shot down one which appeared to be out of control.

Lieutenant M. Mealing, No. 56 Squadron, with other S.E.'s, drove away a formation of five enemy aircraft, and when diving after them he saw an enemy balloon which he attacked and shot down in flames.

December 11th.

Low clouds and a slight drizzle prevented much work being done.

Lieutenant Crawford and Second Lieut. Barford, No. 2 Squadron, carried out a reconnaissance of enemy wire from a height of 200 feet.

No. 59 Squadron reconnoitred the area in front of their Corps, and a machine of No. 12 Squadron went out on the night of the 10th/11th and reported on the lighting of certain towns and other points of interest.

A total of 1,052 rounds were fired at ground targets, 550 being by two machines of No. 5 Squadron.

Eight 25-lb. bombs were dropped by the Second Brigade, and eighteen 25-lb. bombs by the Third Brigade on various targets.

With aeroplane observation, five hostile batteries were successfully engaged for destruction by artillery of the Third

Army, which destroyed one pit and caused an explosion. Machines of this brigade sent down 10 zone calls.

With observation by balloons, two hostile batteries were successfully engaged for destruction, six neutralised, and 21 other targets were successfully dealt with by artillery of the Second Army. Two of the shoots were carried out in conjunction with aeroplanes, and one fire and three explosions were caused.

Artillery of the Third Army dealt with three targets.

Enemy aircraft were inactive and no combats took place.

No. 41 Wing.—Seven machines of No. 55 Squadron left the ground in fine weather to bomb the boot factory at Pirmasens, but found the target obscured by clouds, so flew to a gap farther north from which point they saw the large railway junction north-east of Pirmasens, and dropped twelve 112-lb. and ten 25-lb. bombs from 13,000 feet. The results were not observed owing to the drifting clouds.

On the return flight the machines kept together, but became split up after recrossing the lines owing to the heavy banks of clouds at 600 feet. All machines, however, landed safely in different places, with one exception, when a machine was damaged, but the occupants were uninjured.

S. WOOD, Captain,
General Staff.

Advanced Headquarters,
 Royal Flying Corps,
  12th December 1917.

No. 48.

CONFIDENTIAL.

ROYAL NAVAL AIR SERVICE.

OPERATIONS REPORT

(with Royal Flying Corps Reports attached)

16th to 31st DECEMBER 1917.

NAVAL STAFF,
OPERATIONS DIVISION.
31st December 1917.

ROYAL NAVAL AIR SERVICE.

REPORT OF OPERATIONS

(Completed from Reports during period
16th to 31st December 1917.)

CONTENTS.

	PAGE
HOME STATIONS - - - - -	2
DUNKIRK - - - - - -	9
R.N.A.S. SQUADRONS WITH ROYAL FLYING CORPS REPORTS ATTACHED - - - - -	17
EASTERN MEDITERRANEAN - - -	18
CAPE STATION - - - -	28
ROYAL FLYING CORPS COMMUNIQUÉS -	29

HOME STATIONS.

SUBMARINE PATROL WORK.

SEAPLANES.

December 19th.

Newlyn.—Short Seaplane N. 1606 (pilot, Flight Sub-Lieut. J. S. Hughes, observer, Sub-Lieut. G. S. Speight) left on patrol at 1515 to escort the Penzance Mercantile Convoy. At 1559, when flying at 1,500 feet, a large disturbance was observed on the water about 200 yards south of a merchant vessel (the s.s. Prince Charles de Belgique) of about 3,500 tons, steaming east at 10 knots.

Following this, the wake of a torpedo was seen, which missed the vessel, passing just a few yards astern. The seaplane immediately planed down to 1,000 feet, and within a minute of first sighting the disturbance in the water dropped two 100-lb. H.E. bombs (2·5 sec. delay action), which fell directly on the disturbance, the bombs exploding on either edge, there being about 8 yards between them. W/T signals were then sent to T.S. 3 and to all ships, giving the position of the attack, after which the area was searched for 20 minutes and large quantities of oil and bubbles were observed rising to the surface. Two calcium flares were dropped, and as darkness was approaching it was decided to return to the base, which was done, after giving the position of the submarine to motor launches escorting the convoy by Aldis lamp. The submarine may have been seriously damaged, and the merchant vessel was undoubtedly saved from further attack.

December 22nd.

Felixstowe.—Large America Seaplane, No. 8676 (pilots Flight Lieut. Galpin and Flight Sub-Lieut. Moody) left at 0952 to carry out a patrol, and at 1116 two hostile submarines were sighted in position lat. 52° N., long. 3° 3' E.

One submarine seen ahead on the surface was of a large type, light in colour, and submerged rapidly. It being obvious that the seaplane could not reach it in time to attack, course was altered to starboard, to attack the second submarine, the periscope of which was showing above the surface, but this submarine was lost sight of in a thick bank of mist. The seaplane climbed to 2,000 feet and circled round, and at 1135 a periscope was sighted on the port bow, 4–5 miles off, steering the same course as the seaplane, which dived down to 500 feet to attack. Just as the sights were coming on the submarine started to turn to starboard and the periscope disappeared. Four seconds later one 230-lb. bomb was dropped, followed three seconds later by another.

The first bomb fell 100 feet ahead and 30 feet to the side of the track of the periscope, and the second bomb 250 to 300 feet from where the first bomb fell. Neither of the bombs exploded and both fuse wires were found on the bomb frames, thus leaving no apparent cause for the bombs failing to explode.

The visibility in parts was exceptionally good, but frequent rain and hail storms were encountered, also large thick banks of mist and fog extending right down to the water.

December 19th.

Felixstowe.—When returning from a patrol at 1435, Large America Seaplane 8661 (pilots, Flight Sub-Lieut. Cutler and Flight Sub-Lieut. Rees, Engineer Dowdal, W/T Operator Strathern) was attacked by four hostile seaplanes about 15–20 miles east of Shipwash. The Large America was at 3,500 feet; the engine was opened full out, and the machine dived down towards the water. The hostile machines pursued and gained on 8661 rapidly, and when they came within range machine-gun fire was exchanged, and the aerial of Large America 8661 was shot away. Tracers fired by Engineer Dowdal were observed to strike the wings of one of the hostile seaplanes. The shipping channel was reached and ships being near, all the hostile seaplanes drew off. Large America Seaplane then made for the base at full speed to report, and to ask that help might be sent to Large America Seaplane 8676, which had come down with engine trouble before the arrival of the hostile seaplanes.

AIRSHIPS.

December 26th.

Mullion.—H.M. Airship C. 23a left at 1105 on patrol, and when off Falmouth at 1130, observed a convoy of 23 ships at anchor inside the boom defence. C. 23a proceeded to patrol and at 1420 observed the leading ship of the convoy turning south-east, the remainder in single-line ahead, the rear ship of the line just leaving Falmouth.

A destroyer was ahead of the leading ship, and one trawler on the port side, with nine trawlers at various intervals on the starboard side.

C. 23a proceeded to escort the convoy on the port side and at 1500, one of the leading ships of the line was seen to be torpedoed. The airship proceeded at full speed to close the torpedoed ship and about three minutes later a second ship was torpedoed. At 1510 C. 23a had closed the torpedoed ships, which were the s.s. "Treganna" and s.s. "Benito"; having informed the base and sent the general signal, "Submarine in vicinity."

At 1513 one of the torpedoed ships sank, by the bow, the other ship was abandoned with two trawlers standing by, and a destroyer patrolling round her. C. 23a patrolled the immediate vicinity of the position where the ships had been attacked on the leeward side, it being considered that the submarine would naturally have, if possible, placed herself thus for attack. Meanwhile the ships ahead of the torpedoed ships had continued south-east and eventually turned south-west. The ships astern, at first continued east in zig-zag courses and did not turn south-west for nearly fifteen minutes.

At 1535 the ships astern in a group were proceeding south-west, and were about two to four miles from the scene of the attack, when at 1540 a torpedo was observed to break surface just astern of the last ship of the group about a quarter of a mile to leeward of C. 23a.

The torpedo ran for about 600 yards on the surface, but its track, owing to oil, was observed before it broke surface. C. 23a immediately closed the commencement of the track which was about a mile and a half on the starboard beam of the target, and in less than one minute, after the torpedo broke surface, two 100-lb. bombs (2½ seconds delay) were dropped, one on either side of the track, about 40–50 feet from where it commenced.

The wind was N.E., 40–50 m.p.h., at 500 feet, and consequently the airship was flying low, *i.e.*, about 500 feet and had no time to reach the recognised altitude for bombing. This, however, combined with the airship being almost stationary when brought into the wind, permitted of very good bomb dropping results being obtained. Owing to the very rough seas running at the time and the whole surface being flecked with scud it was quite impossible to observe if the bombs had taken effect or not; the disturbance due to the bombs themselves was hard to find a very few seconds later.

The torpedo track was just discernible over a length of about 2½ miles crossing its target's course at right angles, about half a mile up.

C. 23a then informed the destroyer of the third attack made, and indicated the position bombed by two calcium flares, after which the airship continued to patrol the vicinity, guarding the rear of the group of ships proceeding south-west and eventually landed at the base at 1715.

December 27th.

Mullion.—H.M. Airship S.S. Z. 25 (pilot, Flight Lieut. A. S. Elliot, R.N.) having ascended at 1145 for a patrol over the Lizard, observed a suspicious oil patch on the surface. Speed was increased towards the oil patch, and at 1350 oil and air bubbles were observed rising to the north-east of the patch. At 1327 two bombs were dropped, and about one minute after the bombs had detonated two swirls were observed just to the north-east of the bubbles, apparently caused by twin propellers. These disappeared shortly afterwards, and the oil also decreased in quantity. A flare was dropped to mark the spot, and at 1450, when the airship was still over the position, a trawler was observed to drop depth charges about 3 miles northward of the position of the airship. At about 1555 two trawlers to the eastward were observed to fire approximately seven shots, and at 1600 the airship received orders from the base to land, which was done at 1625.

ACCIDENTS TO AIRSHIPS.

December 20th.

Polegate.—H.M. Airship S.S. Z. 10 after carrying out a patrol from 1110 until 1630 was forced to land at Jevington, and moored there owing to the fog.

At 1405 S.S. Z. 7 left on patrol and was forced to land on Beachy Head at 1730 owing to fog. At 2145 the airship left, and on landing at Jevington collided S.S. Z. 10 and caught fire. The pilot, Flight Sub-Lieut. Swallow, was killed, and Air Mechanic W/T Dodd and Air Mechanic (E.) Hughes were seriously injured. Before the flames could be extinguished a bomb on S.S. Z. 7 exploded, causing serious injuries to Flight Lieut. Watson, who had to have an arm amputated. This pilot had been sent from Polegate to render assistance.

LOSS OF H.M. AIRSHIP "C. 26."

Remarks.—Reports of the loss of airships "C. 26" and "C. 27" were published in Operations Report No. 47, since when a detailed report of the loss of "C. 26," and the internment of the crew in Holland, has come to hand and is given below, as received from the pilot, Flight Lieut. G. C. C. Kilburn.

December 12th.

Airship "C. 26" left for patrol at 0645 on the 12th, crossing the coast at Yarmouth, and patrolled between Smiths Knoll and a point 50 miles east of this, keeping a look out for any signs of H.M.A. "C. 27."

Names of the crew:—
- Flight Lieut. H. E. C. Plowden.
- Flight Lieut. G. C. Kilburn.
- Petty Officer Townsend.
- Leading Mechanic Johncock.
- Second Air Mechanic Warman.

About 1200 the forward engine broke down, apparently due to magneto trouble.

The airship turned for the base at 1230, reaching the coast just south of Lowestoft instead of Yarmouth at about 1600.

The visibility was very bad, and apparently the wind was stronger than had been reckoned. The coast was followed up towards Lowestoft to make sure of the airship's position, and Beccles was reached a little before 1700.

The after engine then suddenly stopped, for some cause unknown, there being just over 30 gallons of petrol left. The airship was slightly light and rose to 800 feet. The opinion of the pilot and the engineer was that the engine would start again, and every effort was made to do so. As she did not start immediately, efforts were made to bring the airship down, so as to make the land, but it was not possible to valve sufficient gas to come down in time owing to the lack of a top valve, and to the fact that the auxiliary blower would not start, and so enable pressure to be obtained for using the bottom valves. The airship crossed the coast at 400 feet and hit the sea at about half a mile out, but without submerging the car.

A quantity of ballast was thrown out, and the airship ascended sufficiently high to send a W/T message to the base, and then descended and put the drogue in the water, reducing the speed a little. As there was only five bags of ballast on board at the start the airship could not afford to ascend again to send any more W/T signals.

About 2300 the drogue suddenly opened (it had got caught up in some way) and reduced the speed to about 8 knots.

Very's lights and the rifle were fired periodically, and the Aldis lamp flashed. The code books were not thrown overboard, as it was intended to go up again when reaching the Dutch coast, and to send another W/T signal. At 0100 on December 13th the wind rose a little, and the airship started to kite, hitting the sea several times and necessitating the use of the remaining ballast and a bomb.

Shortly after, the drogue lifted out of the water, and the airship ascended to 3,700 feet, where she was kept in equilibrium for two hours. Directly "C. 26" rose, efforts were made to send a W/T message. This took some time owing to slight damage to W/T instruments when hitting the sea. The operator heard the base asking for information, but he was unable to get anything through.

At 0230 (earlier than expected) it was discovered that the airship was over land by the cessation of the sound of the waves, thus unfortunately losing the chance of throwing the codes overboard. It was intended on landing to rip and then burn the codes and ship, and to send the pigeons off. Everything was prepared to do this. Again, owing to the lack of a top valve it was impossible to start descending, and a small hole had to be cut in the bottom of the envelope. Since the blower was useless, the airship got into a very bad shape, and the car turned practically upside down, necessitating everyone sitting on the port rail. The rips and top patch were got ready, and remaining petrol were used as ballast. No lights were seen at the coast or on the land, and owing to the fog the land was never seen at all.

The grapnel caught in something and brought the airship up with a jerk that nearly threw everyone off, but "C. 26" did not touch the ground, and before the crew could rip she broke loose. The ground could not be seen (although it must have been fairly close) even with the aid of the Aldis lamp.

At 0315 the grapnel caught again. This time the order to jump was given, the crew holding on to the rip lines, thinking the airship was only 10 feet up, but she was at least 30 feet up, and in the drop the rips were jerked from the hands of the crew. Lieutenant Plowden was saved by falling into a canal, but Petty Officer Townsend unfortunately dislocated his leg. Leading Mechanic Johncock was shaken, but escaped unhurt. Second Air Mechanic Warman was caught up somehow, and was taken off in the ship before anything could be done. Apparently the ship came down some way off, when Air Mechanic Warman jumped out, the ship continuing and being taken by the Dutch authorities.

The pilot highly commends the behaviour of the crew, who showed no signs of panic, and carried out all orders with energy and precision.

It is reported that Petty Officer Townsend is doing well.

Second Air Mechanic W. Warman, W/T, 30659, R.N.A.S., who was caught up and carried away by the airship, states that when the order was given to jump out his feet caught in the skid of the airship, and he was unable to free himself. He managed to hang on, upside down, underneath the skid, which was covered with oil and petrol. The airship was at an angle of about 25 degrees, down by the tail, and he could not get back into the boat, but remained on the skid. He estimates that he was there about an hour, and having cleared his foot, when the ship came low again he dropped off the skid, falling on his back in a ditch, where he fell asleep, the ship having immediately risen again. Warman landed at Sliedrecht, near Dordrecht, and the Dutch newspapers report that the airship landed at Eemnes.

RAID BY HOSTILE AIRCRAFT.

December 18th.

A night bombing raid of approximately four hours was carried out by hostile aeroplanes over the area Thames Estuary, Essex, Kent and London.

The total number of machines that crossed the coast was probably between 16 and 20. The first attack developed over East Kent, three groups of hostile machines making the North Foreland, Broadstairs, and Sandwich between 1815 and 1825. The machines then made for the mouth of the Thames and were engaged by the guns of the Chatham Defences on their way west.

Simultaneously with these attacks three other groups of machines made the estuaries of the rivers Blackwater and Crouch and the neighbourhood of Shoeburyness respectively between 1810 and 1845.

A number of the hostile machines were turned back by gun-fire before reaching the outer London defences, and went out to sea over the North Foreland at various times between 1956 and 2055.

The first and main attack on London developed shortly after 1900, a total of five or six machines passing over the Capital from the north-east and dropping bombs at various places between 1900 and 2000. After the main attack on London had terminated a single aeroplane, supposed to be of a very large type, passed over the Metropolis about 2100. It crossed the north of London towards Regent's Park, and then passed over Mayfair and Belgravia, finally turning north-east and crossing the dock area on its way out. After completing their attack on London, the majority of the raiding machines seemed to have turned south-east and made their way out along the line Sevenoaks, Maidstone, Ashford and Folkestone. One Gotha came down as the result of injury by gun-fire, and fell in the sea off Folkestone, and was being towed in by a trawler when the machine blew up and sank. The explosion was possibly caused by a timed bomb on the Gotha; one of the crew of the trawler was seriously injured and one of the crew of the Gotha killed by the explosion. Two other occupants of the machine were taken prisoners, subsequently landed at Folkestone and handed over to the military.

Bombs are reported in London as follows:—

        Buckingham Palace Road.
        Chelsea.
        Eaton Square.
        Borough Market, Southwark
        Cleopatra's Needle.
        Farringdon Road.
        Chancery Lane.
        King's Cross.
        Aldersgate Street.
        Pentonville Road.
        Great Perry Street.
        Bermondsey.

The majority of bombs dropped were incendiary, causing several fires and some casualties.

Westgate, Bokesbourne and Margate were also attacked; some casualties and damage were caused at the latter place.

Hostile machines were engaged by R.F.C. machines, two over London and one in the vicinity.

ATTEMPTED RAID BY HOSTILE AIRCRAFT.

December 22nd.

Enemy aircraft were reported off the North Foreland shortly after 1800, and a few minutes later a Gotha biplane landed in a field near Margate, and was set on fire by the crew, all three of whom were captured. It appears that this machine was one of a large squadron which set out to attack England, but snow, rain and clouds were encountered off the English coast, with the result that all turned back with the exception of this single machine which was forced to land owing to engine trouble.

A second attack was attempted about 2130, when two or three machines approached the North Foreland and Deal. After dropping a few bombs in the sea near Broadstairs, these machines turned back again. Snow was falling at several places in Kent; this and adverse weather conditions probably caused the second detachment of raiders to abandon the attack.

No damage or casualties were caused.

DUNKIRK.

WEATHER.

The weather conditions during this period have been generally unfavourable owing to low clouds, mist and sleet.

PHOTOGRAPHIC RECONNAISSANCE.

December 18th.

No. 1 Wing (2nd Squadron).—A reconnaissance was carried out and photographs taken of the Westcappelle–Ramscappelle area. The Zeebrugge–Bruges Canal and the new railway sidings on the Blankenberghe–Bruges railway were also taken.

December 19th.

A photographic reconnaissance was carried out and photographs taken of Oostacker, Mariakerke and Ghent, including the docks and railway centres. Thirty-two plates were exposed with good results.

SPOTTING OPERATIONS.

December 19th.

No. 1 Wing (2nd Squadron.)—Spotting operations were carried out by D.H. 4 machines for ships firing on Ostend, and the shooting appears to have been good.

Spotting machines and escort were attacked by hostile aircraft on the way home. (*See* Seaplane Defence Squadron.)

December 19th.

Seaplane Defence Squadron.—Whilst acting as escort to D.H. 4 spotting machines, three Sopwith Camels encountered two Albatross two-seaters between Ostend and Zeebrugge. Flight Sub-Lieut. Mackay attacked one driving towards Zeebrugge, and fired two bursts. The observer then stood up, holding up his hands, and was shortly afterwards seen to fall out of the machine, which went down out of control.

Later Flight Commander Collishaw carried out a surprise attack on four Albatross scouts, shooting down one out of control.

OFFENSIVE PATROLS—ENGAGEMENTS WITH ENEMY.

December 18th.

No. 4 Wing (9th Squadron).—Whilst on patrol a formation of five Sopwith Camels dived on hostile machines about 5 miles south-east of Nieuport. Flight Sub-Lieut. Taylor got on the tail of one and followed it down from 5,000 feet to below the level of the trees. The two machines circled round, sometimes nearly hitting the ground, until the Sopwith got about 600 rounds into the hostile machine at very close range and observed several tracers enter his fuselage and wings, ultimately forcing this machine to land.

December 22nd.

No. 4 Wing (10th Squadron).—A patrol of five Sopwith Camels crossed the lines near Ypres at 14,000 feet, and owing to heavy clouds to the northward, the patrol operated to the south where the visibility was good with considerable detached clouds. At 1050 four Albatross Scouts were observed at 6,000 feet, about 8 miles west of Lille, and pursued by the Sopwith formation. About 2 miles west of Lille Flight Commander MacGregor got into position on the tail of one of the hostile machines and got to within 28 yards range, but his gun refused to fire. He pulled the toggle on the right gun and fired about 20 rounds into the hostile machine's fuselage and observed a cloud of steam coming from the machine as it went down in a vertical nose dive into the clouds below.

The Sopwith pilot then attacked another machine and fired 50 rounds into it from fairly close range. This machine went down immediately in a long gentle glide, and was observed still going down to within 1,000 feet of the ground.

Flight Sub-Lieut. Wilmot attacked one of the hostile machines but his guns jammed, and the pilot pulled off to clear. While trying to rejoin the formation he saw another hostile machine at about 4,000 feet and a Camel diving on it, then pulling off, so attacked this machine firing a number of rounds into him from a good position. The hostile machine stalled, then went down into a steep side-slipping dive, and appeared to be out of control.

Flight Sub-Lieut. Wright attacked a Kite Balloon from 300–100 yards, firing about 80 rounds, and the balloon was immediately hauled down.

December 22nd.

No. 4 Wing (9th Squadron).—Whilst on a solo patrol Flight Commander Fall attacked a two-seater Albatross in the vicinity south-east of Quesnoy. The Sopwith pilot attacked from the front, and to one side and above, firing about 100 rounds at very close range, then turning suddenly attacked from behind and above firing another burst of about 100 rounds.

The enemy observer replied with about 10 to 12 rounds, after which the Albatross seemed completely out of control, alternately spinning on its back and just gliding for a short time.

The Sopwith pilot followed him down to about 2,000 feet, firing another 200 rounds, and observed the hostile machine go right down and crash in a field. When under 2,000 feet the Sopwith was heavily shelled by hostile gunfire, but returned safely.

BOMB ATTACKS.

(Carried out during the Period between the dates given.)

*Engel Aerodrome and Dump.	Dec. 18th	912 lbs.	D.H. 4 (A).
Brugeoise Works	18th—19th	11,288 lbs.	H.P. (A).
*Vlisseghem Aerodrome	19th	1,400 lbs.	D.H. 4 (A).
Mariakerke Aerodrome	22nd—23rd	3,136 lbs.	H.P. (A).
St. Denis Westrem Aerodrome.	,, ,,	3,464 lbs.	,,
Oostacker Aerodrome	,, ,, ,,	6,584 lbs.	
St. Denis Westrem	,, 23rd—24th	1,568 lbs.	
Bruges Docks	,, ,, ,,	6,480 lbs.	
Ghistelles Aerodrome	,, ,, ,,	1,566 lbs.	
	Total -	36,400 lbs.	

* Daylight raid.   (A) Aeroplanes.

BOMB ATTACKS.

December 18th.

No. 5 Wing (5th Squadron).—A bombing raid was carried out during the day on Engel Aerodrome and dump. Nine D.H. 4 machines (three acting as escort) left at 1344, one returning with engine trouble.

Eight 50-lb. and thirty-two 16-lb. bombs were dropped at 1435 at heights of from 14,000 to 14,700 feet.

Two 50-lb. bombs were observed to explode close to the south-west sheds of the aerodrome, from which all Bessonneaux sheds have been removed.

The dump was well straddled, and a number of bombs were seen to burst on the railway and railway sidings and sheds.

Direct hits are reported on the sheds; this is confirmed by pilots and observers.

Visibility was good, and heavy and accurate anti-aircraft fire was experienced.

Several combats with enemy aircraft took place, and two Albatross Scouts are claimed as being shot down by Acting Flight Commander Sproatt, D.S.C., and Acting Gunlayer Naylor in D.H. 4 6001. One of the hostile machines went down in flames, which is confirmed by another pilot, and the other was seen still nose diving when near the ground.

Three photographs of Engel Aerodrome and dump were taken.

December 18th–19th.

No. 5 Wing (7th and 14th Squadrons).—A formation of eight Handley-Pages (four from each squadron) left at 1735 to carry out a bombing attack on Brugeoise Works. One machine was obliged to return with engine trouble.

Twelve 250-lb. and seventy-four 112-lb. bombs were dropped with apparently considerable success. The visibility was good, enabling good observations to be made of the shooting. The northern end of the works is claimed as having been hit several times, and a large fire was started, which was still burning when the machines re-crossed the lines.

The remainder of the works were also straddled several times, and some bombs were seen to fall among large buildings to the south of the docks.

December 19th.

No. 5 Wing (5th Squadron).—A formation of 10 D.H. 4 machines (three acting as escort) left at 1134 to carry out a bombing attack on Vlisseghen Aerodrome, and twelve 50-lb. and fifty 16-lb. bombs were dropped at heights of from 13,000 to 14,000 feet. A number of bombs were observed to explode amongst the group of sheds on the west side, and a direct hit was scored on one of the smaller sheds. Bombs were also seen to burst close to the large sheds on the south side, and near the sheds in the north-east corner of the aerodrome.

Visibility was good, and anti-aircraft fire was heavy and accurate, several of the D.H. 4's being hit.

Flight Sub-Lieut Richardson and Acting Gunlayer Furby on D.H. 4 N. 6008 failed to return, and no news has been received of them. Flight Sub-Lieut. Willis reports that two anti-aircraft shells were seen to burst directly underneath the fore part of one of the D.H. 4's, and that the machine was then seen to descend in a spiral.

An attack was made on an Albatross Scout, one of four, which attacked the formation in the rear, by Acting Flight Commander Sproatt, D.S.C., and Acting Gunlayer Naylor in D.H. 4 N. 6001, and the enemy machine was totally destroyed.

Six photographs were taken of Vlisseghem, Handzaeme, and Houttave.

December 22nd–23rd.

No. 5 Wing (7th and 14th Squadrons).—A bombing attack was carried out during the evening by eight Handley-Page machines, four from each squadron, on Mariakerke, St. Denis Westrem, and Oostacker Aerodromes.

At 1742 four machines of No. 7 Squadron left the Mariakerke Aerodrome, on which twenty-eight 112-lb. bombs were dropped.

Clear visibility allowed an excellent sight of this new target, the whole aerodrome being clearly defined, and bombs were seen to burst close to, and amongst the sheds and buildings in the north-west and north-east portions of the aerodrome.

St. Denis Westrem Aerodrome was then attacked, over which the visibility was also good, and twenty-two 112-lb. and four 250-lb. bombs were dropped on the south and south-east sheds.

Four machines from No. 14 Squadron left at 1720, two of which were detailed to attack Oostacker Aerodrome, and two to reconnoitre and attack enemy aerodromes, showing signs of night activity.

Oostacker Aerodrome was found to be very active, and was attacked by all machines, twelve 250-lb. and thirty-two 112-lb. bombs were dropped. Good shooting appears to have been made, and during the course of many runs which were made over this target bombs were seen to burst with great accuracy on and amongst the principal groups of sheds on the aerodrome.

Two direct hits are claimed, and it is considered that credence may be given to this claim as the visibility was excellent.

In all, close on six tons of bombs were dropped on these objectives.

December 23rd–24th.

No. 5 Wing (7th and 14th Squadrons).—Eight Handley-Page machines left during the night to carry out a bombing raid on St. Denis Westrem, Mariakerke, Oostacker, and active enemy aerodromes in the Naval area with Bruges Docks as an alternative target.

Four machines from Squadron 7 left at midnight for St. Denis Westrem and Mariakerke, but the visibility became poor after the machines started, and only one of the four reached the vicinity of Ghent and attacked the aerodrome at St. Denis Westrem with fourteen 112-lb. bombs. Two bombs fell near a train in the north-west corner of the aerodrome, and the remainder were seen to explode in close proximity to the buildings and amongst the huts and trees on the south-west side. Owing to the unfavourable weather conditions the remaining three machines attacked Bruges Docks,. on which four 250-lb. and thirty-four 112-lb. bombs were dropped; the dock area was well straddled.

At 0100 four machines of 14th Squadron left to attack Oostacker and active enemy aerodromes in the naval area. The visibility was extremely poor, and shortly after the last machine had left banks of mist appeared, making it necessary to recall two of the machines. The other two machines got away, but owing to the adverse weather conditions the alternative target, Bruges Docks, was attacked by one machine with four 250-lb. and six 112-lb. bombs. A good straddle was made, but the searchlights playing on the mist prevented actual results being observed. The other pilot when passing over Ghistelles observed lights on the aerodrome, and dropped fourteen 112-lb. bombs, but no results could be seen.

BOMB ATTACK ON DUNKERQUE SEAPLANE STATION.

December 18th.

At about 1830 hostile aircraft attacked the French Seaplane Base, dropping bombs, causing a large fire, which spread rapidly.

Immediately afterwards bombs were dropped across the Chantier de France, the first exploding on the stern of the ship on the stock, the second and third in front of the seaplane sheds, and the fourth on the Bastions. The second and third bombs also caused slight material damage to the station. The petty officers and men's wash-houses and the end of No. 2 Hut were blown in; the windows of the shed were broken and the doors punctured.

Short Seaplane N. 9065 was slightly damaged by splinters, and is now repaired.

Two bombs appeared to have hit the French sheds, one Bessonneaux, and the main sheds were damaged. Several French machines were saved; a number of these were being stowed in these sheds.

The undermentioned men did exceptionally good work at the French sheds, and had it not been for the prompt manner in which these men extinguished the fire in the Main French Shed and pulled out burning machines the fire would have been very much bigger.

F. Moore,	C.P.O. 3 (E.)	F. 1,637
G. H. White,	P.O. (A.)	15,912
G. H. Pritchard,	P.O. (A.C.)	F. 14,791
G. D. Fraser,	P.O. (E.)	F. 2,255.

The Casualties consisted of two ratings, wounded, and one slightly hurt.

Honours during period 16th to 31st December.

Name.	Unit.	Awarded.
Flight Sub-Lieut. W. L. Jordan	No. 10 Squadron	D.S.C.

Casualties.

Name.	Unit.	Date.
Missing.		
Flight Sub-Lieut. S. S. Richardson	No. 5 Squadron	19.12.17.
A.C. 1 (G/L) R. A. Furby, 0. No. F.13925	No. 5 Squadron	19.12.17.
Killed.		
Flight Sub-Lieut. D. R. C. Wright	No. 10 Squadron	23.12.17.
Flight Sub-Lieut. T. M. Greeves	No. 10 Squadron	23.12.17.

SUMMARY OF WORK CARRIED OUT BY R.N.A.S. SQUADRONS AT DUNKIRK, FROM JULY TO DECEMBER, 1917.

Total weight of bombs dropped, 646, 128 lbs. (approximately $228\frac{1}{2}$ tons).

Hostile machines destroyed and driven down out of control (approximate), including those accounted for by R.N.A.S. squadrons attached to the Royal Flying Corps :—

Hostile machines destroyed	84
Driven down out of control	252
Total	336
*Machines lost from Dunkirk squadrons	21
*Casualties. Killed and missing	28
Casualties (R.N.A.S. attached to Royal Flying Corps), killed and missing	45

* Including bombing machines.

NAVAL SQUADRON WITH THE ROYAL FLYING CORPS.

NAVAL SQUADRON No. 8.

(Period from 16th *December to* 29th *December* 1917 *inclusive.)*

This squadron has been attached to the First Brigade, Royal Flying Corps, and has carried out 29 offensive patrols, 12 escorts to Corps photographic machines, and 55 flights in pursuit of hostile artillery machines, making a total of 152 hours 17 minutes flying. A total of 15 combats took place, four of which were decisive.

On the 27th Flight Commander Price and Flight Sub-Lieut. Day while patrolling for enemy artillery machines observed a D.F.W. which, when dived on, immediately went east. They got him within range, however, and, after firing 450 rounds, the hostile machine went down out of control. This is confirmed by an anti-aircraft battery. On the 28th the same two pilots again encountered a D.F.W., which they drove down out of control after firing 550 rounds at an average range of 30 yards.

On the 28th Flight Sub-Lieut. Jordon, while leading an offensive patrol of four machines, fired 20 rounds into an Albatross Scout at very close range from behind. A large cloud of brownish black smoke came from the enemy aircraft's cockpit, and it fell over on one side and went down completely out of control.

Flight Sub-Lieut. Crundall, when flying in the rear of a formation of four machines, was attacked from the right by an Albatross Scout. After the pilot of the hostile machine had fired a burst from a range of 50 yards, Flight Sub-Lieut. Crundall dived and came up behind him and fired 500 rounds into the Albatross Scout, which went down completely out of control.

Pilots of this squadron have effectively hindered the work of hostile artillery machines, and the percentage of interferences has risen from 41 per cent. to 71 per cent. during this period. Altogether 21 warnings were received and machines sent up, of which only five were unsuccessful in locating a hostile machine.

Honours.

Flight Sub-Lieut. W. L. Jordon awarded D.S.C.

Hostile Machines driven down out of control - - - 4

EASTERN MEDITERRANEAN STATION.

(*Compiled from Weekly Reports, No. 89, dating from
November 25th to December 2nd, 1917.*)

THASOS AIR STATION.

"A" SQUADRON AND "Z" (GREEK) SQUADRON.

Weather.—The weather throughout the week has been unfavourable for flying and active service operations have been considerably curtailed.

Anti-Submarine Patrols.—On the 25th November two anti-submarine patrols were carried out by Short seaplane over the area Thasos—Cape Deuthero—Mount Athos. Large patches of oil were observed about 10 miles south of Thasos at about 0730 (L T.). These may have some connection with the submarine which was sighted to the north of Lemnos at 0600, and to the east of Lemnos during the afternoon of the same day.

Photography.—On 26th November a Sopwith Fighter from "D" Squadron was flown from Stavros and a photographic reconnaissance of Deuthero Cove and defences was subsequently carried out, 36 exposures being made over this area.

During the remainder of the week no service flights were made except on the 1st December, when a Short seaplane was flown to Stavros, carrying out a submarine patrol *en route*.

STAVROS AIR STATION.

"D" SQUADRON.

Patrol Work.—Engagement with Enemy.—On the morning of 25th November two patrols for hostile aircraft were carried out, no enemy machines, however, being encountered. Early in the afternoon a two-seater Rumpler, evidently returning from a Salonica reconnaissance, passed over Stavros Aerodrome at 9,000 feet, proceeding in a N.E. direction. Two machines gave chase, one of which (Sopwith F. 1, No. N. 6367, Flight Lieut. H. T. Mellings) pursued the enemy, gradually gaining height, until a position behind the hostile aircraft's tail was obtained at about 16,000 feet, when a few miles south of Drama. Fire was opened at 400 to 500 yards range and the "Camel" had some difficulty in getting closer, the hostile machine being at that height almost as fast as the "Camel." Attempts on the part of the enemy to get head on with his front gun were frustrated and eventually "Camel" closed in on hostile aircraft's tail from the sun, firing obliquely from the rear. The enemy machine was observed to be hit by tracers passing through his top plane, centre-section, and down the fuselage through the seat of the gunner, who was seen to drop down in the cockpit, being either killed or badly wounded. The attack was then pressed as the gunner did not fire again, and the enemy machine was repeatedly hit, although the pilot made himself a difficult target by turning while making a steep nose-dive. The enemy's gravity tank was eventually hit, however. This caught fire and burned for a few minutes, emitting a dense cloud of smoke, while the machine dived almost vertically till the fire was apparently extinguished. The "Camel" followed down to 7,000 feet, but being gradually outdived could not engage again at close range. Pursuit was abandoned at this point and the enemy machine descended to Drama Aerodrome, decreasing his dive from about 3,000 feet.

Photography.—On tha same day a photographic reconnaissance was made in the Struma Valley in order to locate the guns which had been firing at Tasli on 23rd. Three emplacements were located and photographs of all positions were obtained.

Spotting.—On the morning of 26th November an escorted spotting flight was made for Monitor 18 firing on an enemy battery position. The monitor did not reply to any W/T signals sent (which were received by aerodrome W/T station) and flight was therefore abandoned. In the afternoon the spotting flight was repeated, the spotting machine (Sopwith Fighter) being escorted by a D.H. 4. No acknowledgment of signals was observed, though seven spotting corrections were sent.

On this same day two "Camels" were sent to Thasos in order to escort the machine carrying out a photographic reconnaissance of Deuthero Cove area (*see under* Thasos Air Station). While at Thasos one "Camel" started in pursuit of a hostile machine sighted at 1,400 feet, but decided that it was impossible to overtake it after climbing to 5,000 feet, so abandoned the pursuit.

Bomb Attack on Drama Aerodrome.—On 27th November a bomb attack was carried out on Drama Aerodrome. Eight 16-lb. and two 65-lb. bombs were dropped and one hangar was destroyed. One enemy machine was observed during the attack, but no engagement took place. A flight was made to Salonica on the same day in order to obtain tracer ammunition.

On 28th November three patrols were made for hostile aircraft, no enemy machines, however, being encountered.

Bomb Attack on Drama Aerodrome.—Engagement with Enemy.—On the following day the attack on Drama Aerodrome was resumed, four 16-lb. and two 65-lb. bombs being dropped. One enemy machine was encountered and forced to land. Two patrols for hostile aircraft were also carried out.

Patrol Work.—On 30th November a submarine and mine patrol was carried out by Henri Farman in the Gulf of Ruphini, and two patrols for hostile aircraft were made.

Bomb Attack on Provista.—One spotting flight was made for H.M. ships on 1st December, and an escorted bomb attack on Provista was made on the same day, eight 16-lb. and two 65-lb. bombs being dropped and direct hits being made.

Except for those of the 25th and 26th November, only signalled reports of these operations have been received. Details will follow.

KALLONI AIR STATION (MITYLENE).

"B" Squadron.

Photography.—Except on 29th November, when a photographic survey was made of the entrance to Port Kalloni, no operations have been carried out during the current week.

GLIKI AIR STATION (IMBROS).

"C" Squadron.

Anti-Submarine Patrols.—On 25th November, a submarine having been reported to the west of Imbros at 0600, submarine patrols were carried out from dawn till 0930, and throughout the afternoon from noon till dusk; patrols extending over the area Kephalo-Lemnos-Tenedos-Imbros-Suvla-Enos-Samothraki. Machines kept in touch with the aerodrome by W/T throughout the patrols. Sopwith Fighter No. N. 5168 was forced to land, owing to engine trouble, on the beach at Samothraki, the observer returning to Imbros in a caique in order to fetch spares.

Two patrols were made for hostile aircraft on the same day.

On 26th November a B.E. proceeded to Samothraki with a mechanic, and spares and repairs were carried out on the Sopwith Fighter, which had been forced to land there on the preceding day. Both machines returned to Gliki in the afternoon.

Bomb Attack on Gallipoli Mills and Warehouses.—On 27th November, as a reprisal for the recent bombardment of Mavro Island, a raid was made by two D.H. 4's on Gallipoli flour mills and warehouses. One 100-lb. bomb fell on some buildings close to the harbour, and one 16-lb. and one 100-lb. bomb exploded amongst buildings about 100 yards from the quayside.

Another 16-lb. and 100-lb. bomb fell on the warehouses close to the harbour, but the results were not observed owing to clouds. Several buildings were demolished and considerable damage must have been done.

Pilots, Flight Lieut. A. Woodward with Observation Lieutenant C. Palmer in D.H. 4, No. N. 5975, and

Flight Lieut. R. Sorley, with Observation Sub-Lieut. F. C. Smith in D.H. 4, No. N. 5976.

Photography.—On the return journey the aerodrome at Galata, which had not been in use for some months, was seen to be again occupied, three large hangars being observed as well as a new landing "T."

Two photographs were accordingly taken of the aerodrome, with a view to future bombing operations.

Reconnaissance.—A reconnaissance of the Dardanelles shipping was carried out in the afternoon, two ships of about 200 tons being sighted at Chanak, and proceeding from Chanak to Nagara. During this flight the machine, Sopwith Fighter No. N. 5083 attained a height of 15,000 feet without undue effort. This is considered a good performance, as she is a year old, and has flown over 130 hours.

Spotting.—On 28th November a spotting exercise was carried out with H.M.S. "Edgar." No service flights were made.

Special Reconnaissance and Bomb Attack on Adrianople.—On 29th, in continuation of the recent attacks on the Uzun-Keupru-Muradli sector of the Berlin-Constantinople Railway, a special reconnaissance and bomb attack on Adrianople was carried out by two D.H. 4's. The first machine, No. N. 5976, pilot Flight Lieut. R. Sorley and observer Sub-Lieut. F. C. Smith, left Imbros at 0826, and reached the mainland at Cape Gremea at 0850. Here it was seen that the whole of the area between the coast line and Kuleli Burgas was obscured by clouds, so that reconnaissance of the Neshan region was impossible. A few breaks in the clouds at Demotika enabled the observer to locate a number of long sheds and camps to the S.W. and to the N. of that town, though owing to the clouds no photographs could be taken.

Adrianople was reached at 0955, clouds obscuring a large part of the town and the railway bridge over the Arda, previously designated as one of the principal targets for bomb attack. A large number of buildings, apparently warehouses, were observed at Karagatch Station (Adrianople), and these were accordingly attacked with one petrol and two 100-lb. bombs, but the results could not be definitely observed owing to clouds, except that large clouds of smoke were seen to proceed from near the target. A large number of camps were seen close to the town, and eight photographs of these were obtained. Adrianople was left at 1003, and the machine landed at Imbros at 1110.

The second machine, D.H. 4, No. N. 5975, pilot Flight Lieut. Woodward, observer Lieutenant Palmer, left Imbros at 0830, and proceeded straight to Adrianople, which was reached at 1000, course being entirely steered by compass owing to the clouds. Two 100-lb. bombs were released on the workshops and warehouses alongside the railway at Karagatch Station, and direct hits were made, considerable damage being done. Two photographs of the station were taken, and a considerable amount of information regarding sidings, rolling-stock, and camps was obtained. Owing to the clouds only slight and inaccurate anti-aircraft fire was experienced. This machine landed at Imbros at 1115.

While the De H. 4's were away a hostile machine was reported making towards Imbros. Two "Camels" went up to attack, one of which sighted a hostile scout over the peninsula near the Narrows at between 2,000 and 3,000 feet. The "Camel" dived steeply from 10,000 feet, but was evidently sighted by the enemy, who dived into the shelter of anti-aircraft barrage which was put up from Nagara. Fifty rounds were fired at the enemy, who eventually made off and was lost to sight near the village of Karajeuren, E. of Chanak. The "Camel" remained in the vicinity for 15 minutes, but the hostile machine was not sighted again.

On 30th November an escorted photographic reconnaissance of Galata Aerodrome was carried out, and on the following day this aerodrome was attacked by one D.H. 4, escorted by two Sopwith Fighters. Only a signalled report of the operation has been received, which states, however, that one hangar was hit and that one enemy machine was engaged.

Three patrols for hostile aircraft were also carried out on 1st December.

MUDROS.

December 1st.

Anti-Submarine Patrols.—A submarine having been sighted off the entrance to Mudros Harbour on 24th November dawn patrols were carried out by seaplanes and aeroplanes and on the receipt of a signal reporting another sighting of submarine to the north-west of Cape Plako on 25th, continuous patrols were carried out by seaplanes and aeroplanes until dusk. During one of these patrols a mine was sighted two miles north-east of Cape Plako and a warning signal was sent by Aldis lamp to two destroyers which were in the vicinity.

On the following day the patrol was resumed at dawn, aeroplanes and seaplanes searching to north-east and west of Lemnos.

On 29th November, at the request of S.N.O. Mudros, a patrol of Mudros swept channel was carried out by one seaplane and one aeroplane, prior to "Republique" leaving the harbour.

KASSANDRA AIRSHIP STATION.

Anti-Submarine Patrols.—On 25th November, on the occasion of a submarine being sighted to the north of Lemnos, the airship patrolled the whole of the area Kassandra, Skiathos, Psathura, Cape Drepano, Mt. Athos, over 13 hours flying being done during the day.

On the remaining days of the week patrols have been carried out over the Gulfs of Kassandra, Monte Santo, and Volo, and over the entire area Kassandra, Skopelos, Athos, as well as a daily patrol over the approaches to the Gulf of Salonica.

Over 47 hours flying has been done during the week.

SUDA BAY SEAPLANE STATION.

Anti-Submarine Patrols.—Except on 27th November, when flying was prevented by thunderstorms, seaplane patrols have been carried out daily. Only signalled reports have been received, and it is presumed that all patrols were to the north and east of Suda Bay except on 28th November, when a patrol was made to Grabusa, an unreliable report having been received of a submarine in Kissamo Bay.

On 25th a patrol by moonlight was attempted but was abandoned owing to engine trouble.

Remarks.—Weekly Operations Report No. 85 was omitted from **Operations Report No. 46** owing to a delay in transmission; details of the work carried out are therefore included in this number (**30th October to 4th November 1917**).

Weather.—The broken weather experienced during the preceding week has continued, and has curtailed the amount of flying from all stations.

Owing to the paucity of the ferry services written reports of the various operations are in most cases lacking, signals being available.

THASOS AIR STATION.

"A" Squadron and "Z" Squadron (Greek).

Attack on Gerevtz Seaplane Station.—During the night of 27th/28th October an attack was made on Gereviz seaplane station by a Henri Farman aeroplane. Two submarine patrol flights were also made, one to the eastward of Thasos and the other between the island and the Akte Peninsula.

Anti-Submarine Patrol.—On the following day a Farman again reconnoitred for submarines along the coast of the Akte Peninsula as far as Mount Athos, and subsequently examined the area between there and Cape Kephalo, Thasos.

A Baby Seaplane accompanied by a Sopwith bomber searched the area for 25 miles to the southward of Thasos on 31st October.

Bomb Attack on Works at Cape Koyan, Nakla.—A Farman aeroplane bombed enemy works at Cape Coyan, Nakla, on 1st November. During the remainder of the week weather conditions prevented further flying.

STAVROS AIR STATION.

"D" Squadron.

Offensive Patrols.—An offensive patrol for enemy aircraft was undertaken by four machines on 28th October, but the coverts were drawn blank.

On the following day a patrol was carried out along the enemy coast to Thasos, the machine returning in company with a Sopwith Bomber, which was flown to Stavros for the purpose of undertaking bombing operations at night.

Bomb Attack on Drama Air Station.—Shortly after midnight on 29/30th October a Sopwith Bomber, accompanied by a Henri Farman, left Stavros for the purpose of bombing Drama Air Station, which had recently been reported to have increased in size, there now being seven hangars there. Weather conditions were bad, but the Sopwith Bomber, piloted by Flight Lieut. J. L. A. Sinclair, succeeded in reaching the objective, and dropped four 65-lb. bombs at the hangars from 2,000 feet. Owing to the very restricted view obtained from this type of machine the results could not be observed.

Bomb Attack on Spider Redoubt.—The Henri Farman's engine began to give trouble when going up the Pravi Valley, and the machine therefore was unable to climb over the hill tops, accordingly she turned for home, passing over Spider Redoubt, and dropping one 112-lb. bomb, which made a direct hit on the redoubt. Another 112-lb. bomb and a 65-lb. bomb were dropped on enemy emplacements in square 48, P. 2/3.

Bomb Attack on Enemy Observation Posts.—On the afternoon of 30th October the Sopwith Bomber returned to Thasos, dropping two 65-lb. bombs on observation posts, which had previously been located on the coast near Cape Deuthero, and two more bombs on the castle further to the eastward.

Three other machines were flown to Thasos, carrying out submarine reconnaissance on the way.

Reconnaissance.—On 31st October an escorted reconnaissance of Angista Valley was made, which disclosed a new camp at Provista and an increase in the size of the two dumps at Angista Station.

The anti-aircraft fire along the route was much better than before, that put up from Provista being particularly good at 11,000 feet.

Anti-Submarine Patrol.—In the afternoon a patrol of the swept channel and Gulf of Orfano for mines was undertaken.

Reconnaissance.—Enemy Bomb Attack on Aerodrome.—A mine reconnaissance of the Gulf of Ruphini was made on the morning of 1st November, and also a reconnaissance of the area around Provista, for enemy gun positions. An enemy aeroplane dropped three bombs at the aerodrome, without, however, doing any damage.

During the morning two "Camels" and one De Havilland 4 which had been sent from Mudros by air arrived safely.

Offensive Patrols.—On 2nd and 3rd November offensive patrols by the "Camels" and "Pups" were made, but no enemy aircraft appeared.

KALLONI AIR STATION.

"B" Squadron.

About 0800, L.T., on 1st November the sound of firing was heard to N.E. of the aerodrome, so a Sopwith Fighter was sent to investigate. A gun, Tuz Burnu, was seen to fire three times in 10 minutes, but the fall of shot could not be observed. The French authorities, however, reported that Eleos Island and Thermi had again been bombarded. Probably the shell were the same armour-piercing shell as previously used, and going straight into the ground without bursting could not be observed. It was noticeable that as soon as the aeroplane got close enough to Tuz Burnu to be observed the firing ceased.

Bomb Attack on Enemy Gun Emplacement.—Later in the day a Sopwith Bomber was sent over and dropped two 65-lb. bombs at the emplacement.

No further flying could be undertaken during the week on account of unfavourable weather.

IMBROS AIR STATION.

"C" Squadron.

Reconnaissance.—On 28th and 29th October reconnaissances of shipping in the Dardanelles were made, but no unusual shipping and no activity at the enemy seaplane base were observed.

Photographic Reconnaissance.—On the latter day a photographic reconnaissance of the Nagara Seaplane Base was attempted, but proved abortive on account of low clouds. This was again attempted on 31st October, but again frustrated by low clouds, and was only accomplished at the third attempt on 1st November, when two flights were made also to intercept enemy aircraft whose spotting signals were picked up at the W/T station. The enemy machines could not, however, be found.

Enemy Bomb Attack, and Reprisal Attack on Chanak.—On 3rd November an enemy machine appeared over Tenedos, and eventually dropped her two bombs in the sea near Mavro. As a reprisal nine bombs were dropped by one Sopwith and one B.E. 2E on Chanak, the machines being escorted on their attack.

MUDROS.

On 30th October a seaplane was sent to the S.S.W. of Starti to meet and escort two colliers and their escorting trawlers to Mudros. The weather, however, was hazy, and in a flight lasting over two hours the ships were not located. The rising wind and threatening weather prevented any subsequent flights being made for this purpose.

Apart from the above no operations have been undertaken during the week, but all opportunities have been taken during lulls of carrying out tests and practice flights.

KASSANDRA AIRSHIP STATION.

No airship is yet available for duty.

SUDA BAY SEAPLANE STATION.

Anti-Submarine Patrols.—Patrols of the approaches to Suda Bay were carried out on 29th, 30th (twice), 31st October, 1st November (twice), and 3rd November. A night reconnaissance was also made on 1st November in search of a submarine which had been sighted between Suda Bay and Cape Stavros.

H.M.S. "PEONY."

Anti-Submarine Patrols.—On 30th October a submarine patrol was made from Port Vathi along the north coast of Samos and searched the Furni Pass.

Hostile Aircraft Pursuit.—On the following morning an enemy aeroplane was observed approaching Port Vathi from the direction of Scalanouva at about 10,000 feet. A Schneider seaplane was sent in pursuit. She flew eastward to endeavour to get between the enemy and her base, but when the Schneider had reached 4,000 feet serious engine trouble set in and, the machine losing height the whole way, was only just able to make Port Vathi.

ENEMY AIRSHIP ACTIVITY.

A Zeppelin has been operating in the Aegean since about the 18th November. The first record of any sightings of this Zeppelin was on the 21st November, when it was observed from Lero Island at 0018 G.M.T. flying from the direction of the Anatolian Coast, over Lero and Patmos, and then returning to the mainland. On November 22nd and 23rd the airship was sighted from Dakhla Oasis (Soudan) on both occasions at 0017 G.M.T.. having apparently travelled on a southerly course for approximately 24 hours. This seems to have been the most southern point reached, as the Zeppelin was next sighted from 0900 to 1100 on the 24th by S.S. "Ovid" in position 35° 22′ N., 28° 52′ E. The Zeppelin at this time was steering east by south, and at 1100 altered course to north-east. At noon on the same day it was sighted by the French trawler "Alexondria" over Phineka Bay, and at 1350 it was again sighted from Castellorizo proceeding in the direction of Adalia. At 1730 it was located by wireless bearings, position approximately 40 miles south of Lemnos at 1745 a few miles west of Cape Tigani, Lemnos, and at 2010 somewhere on the line Stavros to Dedeagatch.

At 2245 its approximate position was about 16 miles east by south of Burgas, and at 2300 about 37 miles E. by N. of this place. The last location was at 0306 on the 25th in the immediate vicinity of Yamboli.

The Zeppelin had evidently lost its way on the 24th, but there is no evidence from intercepts of any bearings having been passed to it. It was communicating chiefly with Yamboli, Constantinople, and Damascus.

It is thought possible that this Zeppelin was working in conjunction with the submarine which sank the British S.S. "Ovid" 1150 on November 25th.

CAPE STATION.

No. 8 SQUADRON, R.N.A.S., MTUA.

(Period, October 19th to 30th, 1917.)

A total of 12 reconnaissance flights have been carried out by aeroplanes during this period, and on two occasions General O'Grady went up as observer for the purpose of examining the enemy country round Nangoo. On four occasions Captain Dooner, I.D., has been taken up as observer in connection with intelligence work.

During these flights a number of bombs and darts were dropped on enemy positions in the area of Mahiwa, and with the exception of one instance no enemy movement was observed during these operations. One spotting flight was carried out during this period for guns firing on the enemy positions at Mremba.

ROYAL FLYING CORPS COMMUNIQUÉS.

ROYAL FLYING CORPS COMMUNIQUÉ No. 118.

During the period under review, 12th to 17th December (inclusive), we have claimed officially seven enemy aircraft brought down by aeroplanes, and seven driven down out of control. Approximately nine tons of bombs were dropped, and 37,000 rounds fired at German troops and other targets.

December 12th.

The weather was fine in the morning, but clouds interfered with work in the afternoon.

Three reconnaissances were carried out by the Second Brigade and 11 by the Third, who also did eight contact patrols.

Captain Owles and Lieutenant Black, No. 12 Squadron, made five flights during the day. In the first they reconnoitred the whole Corps front from a height of 300 feet, and then did four contact patrols, during which they fired 2,200 rounds and dropped ten bombs. In one instance they observed enemy troops penetrating into one of our trenches, so dived down and drove them back with machine-gun fire, and by dropping bombs on them from a height of 40 feet.

Artillery Co-operation.—With aeroplane observation, five hostile batteries were successfully engaged for destruction by the First Army artillery. One was neutralised, five gun-pits were destroyed and three explosions and four fires caused.

Seventy-two zone calls were sent down, 63 of which were by the Third Brigade.

Twelve thousand three hundred and thirty-four rounds were fired at ground targets, 1,100 were by pilots of Naval Squadron No. 8 and 1,150 by No. 24 Squadron.

Bombing.—First Brigade.—No. 2 Squadron dropped four 25-lb. bombs, and No. 4 Squadron seven 25 lb. bombs on various targets.

Second Brigade.—Seventy-five 25-lb. bombs were dropped by Corps machines.

Third Brigade.—Fifty-four 25-lb. bombs were dropped by machines of the Corps Wing, which also fired 2,177 rounds. Low-flying scouts dropped twenty-five 25-lb. bombs on troops and other targets.

Enemy Aircraft.—Enemy aircraft activity was slight on all fronts except the Second Brigade, where a number of combats took place, and a Gotha machine was destroyed.

Captain W. Rogers, No. 1 Squadron, flying a Nieuport, saw two formations of eight or nine Gothas flying west, so climbed up with his patrol. Observing one of the enemy machines turn back, he attacked it, and after firing three-quarters of a drum at from 20 to 30 yards range, the machine burst into flames, fell to pieces and crashed just north of Frelinghien. This is confirmed by infantry and anti-aircraft.

Another hostile machine was brought down in our lines by Lieutenant V. Wigg, No. 65 Squadron, who, with the assistance of Lieutenant C. Matthews, drove one down out of control and then attacked the second, with which he nearly collided owing to the closeness of the fighting, and finally shot it down in flames in our lines.

The following pilots each drove down an enemy machine out of control :—

    Lieutenant K. Seth Smith and Second Lieut. F. Quigley, No. 70 Squadron ; Captains A. McKay and W. Fry, No. 23 Squadron ; and Captain E. Hughes, No. 3 Squadron, who drove down another in a damaged condition.

Anti-aircraft of the Second Army shot down a German machine, which fell in our lines.

None of our machines were missing or brought down during the day.

December 13th.

Low clouds and ground mist made work in the air practically impossible.

One reconnaissance was carried out by the First Brigade and five by the Third Brigade.

Nine contact and counter-attack patrols were carried out by machines of No. 12 Squadron, during one of which Lieutenants Hayter and Scott remained at a low height for three hours, and observed 17 active hostile batteries and dropped six 25-lb. bombs.

Eight thousand seven hundred and two rounds were fired at ground targets, and seventy 25-lb. bombs dropped during the course of the day. Machines of the First Brigade dropped six, the Second Brigade four, and the Third Brigade sixty 25-lb. bombs, while pilots of No. 12 Squadron fired 7,011 rounds from heights varying from 100 to 2,000 feet.

Enemy aircraft were inactive and no combats took place. One hostile machine was shot down by infantry of the Third Army.

December 14th.

Practically no work was possible owing to low clouds, mist, and rain. One reconnaissance was carried out by the First Brigade, and a machine of this brigade fired 60 rounds into Fosse 8.

Twelve 25-lb. bombs were dropped by Nos. 7 and 53 Squadrons, and 700 rounds fired at enemy in Houthulst Forest.

Honours and Awards.

    Distinguished Service Order.—Captain A. E. McKeever, M.C. ; Captain J. B. McCudden, M.C.

Bar to the Military Cross.—Captain L. J. McLean, M.C.

The Military Cross.—Captain V. A. H. Robeson ; Captain C. E. Barrington ; Captain A. S. Lee ; Captain H. T. F. Russell ; Captain J. A. Slater ; Lieutenant R. S. S. Brown ; Second Lieut. P. W. S. Bulman ; Second Lieut. J. H. Cooper ; Second Lieut. R. M. L. Forrie ; Second Lieut. A. M. Kinnear ; Captain J. M. Child ; Captain J. C. L. Barnett ; Captain G. C. Wilson ; Captain R. C. Phillips ; Lieutenant F. G. Huxley ; Lieutenant R. W. Howard ; Lieutenant L. H. Holden ; Lieutenant H. Taylor ; Lieutenant R. F. S. Manduit.

December 15th.

The weather was fine, but ground mist interfered with artillery work.

Eight reconnaissances were carried out by the Second Brigade, during one of which useful information was obtained by No. 20 Squadron in the early morning, and three reconnaissances were done by the Third Brigade.

Four thousand six hundred and twenty-seven rounds were fired at ground targets and 1,287 plates exposed.

With aeroplane observation 29 hostile batteries were successfully engaged for destruction, and 30 were neutralised ; nine gun-pits were damaged, 12 explosions, and four fires caused.

Lieutenants Young and Bernstein, No. 9 Squadron, observed for the 214th Siege Battery, which destroyed a pit and caused an explosion in a hostile battery.

Major Garrod and Lieutenant Lilley, No. 13 Squadron, worked for three hours with the 179th Siege Battery, which damaged a hostile battery position.

The 112th Siege Battery was ranged on to a hostile battery by Lieutenants Corsan and Scott, No. 15 Squadron, who also worked for three hours, and two gun-pits were badly damaged.

Bombing.—Nearly three tons of bombs were dropped during the day.

First Brigade.—No. 18 Squadron droppd ten 112-lb. bombs on a large gun position at Maugre and four 112-lb. bombs on another large gun position at Bauvin, while Corps machines dropped nineteen 25-lb. bombs on various targets.

Corps machines of the Second Brigade dropped eighty-three 25-lb. bombs, and those of the Third Brigade dropped eighty-one 25-lb. bombs.

Enemy Aircraft.—Enemy aircraft activity was considerable on all Army fronts, and his machines dropped bombs in the neighbourhood of Bapaume in the morning.

A patrol of Sopwith Camels of No. 43 Squadron fought five enemy aircraft Scouts, and Second Lieut. A. H. Raynor shot one down out of control.

S.E. 5's of No. 40 Squadron attacked four hostile scouts near Douai and Captain J. H. Tudhope hit one, which appeared to fall out of control, while in another patrol Second Lieut. R. C. Wade attacked a two-seater, which also appeared to fall out of control.

Nieuport Scouts of No. 29 Squadron met five enemy scouts and a two-seater and Second Lieut. P. de Fontenay shot one down, which fell vertically, after which Second Lieut. E. S. Meek dived and fired at it and it was seen to fall out of control.

Major A. D. Carter, No. 19 Squadron, attacked a two-seater from behind at about 25 yards range and shot it down in flames, while Lieutenants E. Blyth and M. Jennings of the same Squadron shot down a two-seater, which was seen by ground observers to crash.

The following account is given by Captain J. B. McCudden, No. 56 Squadron, who has just been awarded the D.S.O., of his encounters with two different two-seater enemy aircraft:—

"While looking for enemy aircraft I thought would probably be about over our lines, I saw one two-seater going N.N.W. at 18,500 feet over Gouzeaucourt at 10.30. I stayed in the sun at 19,800 and dived on enemy aircraft over Metz. Owing to miscalculation of enemy aircraft's speed, I was only able to fire a few shots at it, as I was closing on it too fast. Enemy aircraft continued to glide down with me pursuing him, but he got off too far east, as the wind was very strong and we were going at 160 miles per hour. I returned west climbing and at 11.0 a.m. saw an enemy aircraft two-seater going northwest over Villers at 16,000 feet. I pursued enemy aircraft, who turned east and secured a firing position at 200 yards range, just north of Gonnelieu at 11.5, and after firing about 30 shots from both guns, enemy aircraft half spun to the right and then went into a spiral dive for about 5,000 feet, then went down in an almost vertical dive and hit the ground half a mile east of Bois de Vancelles and nothing was left of it."

Lieutenant A. Blenkiron, No. 56 Squadron, shot down an enemy aircraft scout out of control during a fight between eight enemy machines and S.E.'s.

In these combats none of our machines were shot down.

December 16th.

The weather was fine in the morning, but in the afternoon snow fell and completely stopped work. Up till then two reconnaissances were carried out by the First Brigade, and on the night of the 15th/16th a machine of No. 2 Squadron went out and reconnoitred certain areas. Four reconnaissances were carried out by Bristol Fighters and D.H. 5's of the Third Brigade, whose Corps machines did three contact patrols.

With aeroplane observation 19 hostile batteries were successfully engaged for destruction; one gun-pit was destroyed, seven damaged, 13 explosions and six fires caused. Fifty-nine hostile batteries were reported by zone call.

The 231st Siege Battery were ranged on to a hostile battery, where a pit was damaged by Lieutenant Madden and Sergeant Corson, No. 9 Squadron, who worked for four hours.

A total of 7,499 rounds were fired at ground targets and 120 photographs taken during the day.

Enemy Aircraft.—Enemy aircraft activity was about normal during the fine period.

An offensive patrol of No. 29 Squadron attacked 13 enemy aircraft scouts over Roulers, and four were shot down probably out of control—one by each of the following pilots:—Lieutenants J. Coombe and A. Wingate-Grey, Captain R. Rusby and Second Lieut. E. Meek. All our machines returned safely.

Bombing.—Corps machines dropped bombs as follows:—

First Brigade.—Thirteen 25-lb. bombs.

Second Brigade.—Sixty-three 25-lb. bombs; and the

Third Brigade. — Sixty-one 25-lb. bombs on various targets.

Ninth Wing.—In spite of bad visibility and darkness on the night of the 15th/16th, machines of No. 101 Squadron dropped two 230-lb., eight 112-lb. and six 25-lb. bombs on the large gun at Maugre, which had been firing into Hazebrouck the previous day. During this raid 700 rounds were fired into Maugre village and at trench points.

Honours and Awards.

The Military Cross.—Captain W. H. N. Shakespeare.

December 17th.

Snow fell heavily on the whole front except on the Second Army.

With aeroplane observation by the Second Brigade, eight hostile batteries were successfully engaged for destruction; seven explosions and one fire were caused, and 16 zone calls sent down.

Lieutenants Garrett and Barrow, No. 69 Squadron, ranged the 242nd Siege Battery on to a hostile battery, on which seven O.K.'s were obtained, causing a small fire and three explosions.

Three thousand one hundred and sixty-five rounds were fired at ground targets by the Second Brigade, and nearly a ton of bombs were dropped—fourteen 25-lb. by machines of the First Wing; thirty-one 25-lb. by Corps machines of the Second

Brigade, and eleven 25-lb. by 11 pilots flying Sopwith Camels of No. 70 Squadron. During this raid by No. 70 Squadron, fire of all description was put up in an enormous quantity, yet in spite of this the pilots dropped their bombs from a height of 1,500 feet and returned safely.

Enemy Aircraft.—Enemy aircraft were fairly active on the front of the Second Army. Six hostile scouts attacked Lieutenant Sandy and Sergeant Hughes, No. 69 Squadron, flying an R.E. 8. This pilot and observer refused to dive away from the enemy machines, but fought and shot one down within our lines. Lieutenants Jones and Hodgson of the same squadron went to their assistance and fired away all their ammunition, so returned for more, but did not find the enemy. Lieutenant Sandy and Sergeant Hughes were unfortunately shot down and killed.

An offensive patrol of No. 1 Squadron engaged scouts and two-seaters near Gheluvelt, and Captain Rogers and Second Lieut. G. Moore shot down one each out of control, while Second Lieut. B. Kelsey, of the same squadron, engaged a scout over Passchendaele, which went down in flames, broke to pieces, and crashed in our lines north of Ypres.

S. WOOD, Captain,
Staff Officer.

Headquarters,
Royal Flying Corps,
18th December 1917.

ROYAL FLYING CORPS COMMUNIQUÉ No. 119.

During the period under review, 18th to 24th December (inclusive), we have claimed officially 19 enemy aircraft brought down by aeroplanes and five driven down out of control. During this period we have lost only five machines missing and three shot down. Approximately 25,300 rounds were fired at ground targets and $13\frac{1}{2}$ tons of bombs dropped.

December 18th.

Although fine, the dense haze greatly interfered with artillery work and photography, with the exception of on the front of the Second Army where 26 hostile batteries were successfully engaged for destruction, two gunpits were destroyed, eight damaged, 19 explosions and five fires caused.

Artillery of the First Army successfully engaged three hostile batteries for destruction.

Second Lieut. Simpson and Sergeant Millington, No. 69 Squadron, with the 82nd Siege Battery obtained three O.K.'s, causing two explosions and a fire in a hostile battery position.

Three reconnaissances were carried out by the First Brigade, one by the Second, two by the Third, and a long-distance photographic reconnaissance by No. 27 Squadron.

One thousand and fifty-seven plates were exposed, 583 being by the Second Brigade, and 6,541 rounds were fired at ground targets.

Enemy Aircraft.—Enemy aircraft activity was slight on all fronts except on the Second Army, where 40 combats took place.

Pilots of No. 19 Squadron took part in a number of different fights with considerable success. A two-seater enemy aircraft was attacked by Captain A. Bryson and Lieutenant A. Fairclough, and was shot down out of control. Later in the day Lieutenant Fairclough saw six enemy aircraft and with his formation attacked them from above. He got good bursts into two of the machines, both of which he saw going down steeply. In the same combat, Captain G. Taylor engaged another scout, which went down apparently out of control. An anti-aircraft battery witnessed the fight and saw two German machines crash.

Captain P. Huskinson of the same squadron drove down another enemy aircraft, which was obviously hit, and Major A. D. Carter drove one down out of control and shortly afterwards engaged another, which he also drove down out of control.

Second Lieut. F. Gorringe, No. 70 Squadron, observed an enemy machine approaching the lines, so got into the sun and then dived at it, and shot it down, and it was seen to crash and burn on the ground.

Captain A. McKay, No. 23 Squadron, was patrolling in the vicinity of Becelaere when he saw two two-seaters, so led his patrol to attack them. He got on the tail of one which did not see him and opened fire at close range and the enemy aircraft spun straight to the ground and was completely wrecked. Shortly afterwards he attacked another, and after firing 100 rounds from close range the enemy machine, which was a two-seater, went down completely out of control. He then had a stoppage, and in rectifying this lost sight of the falling aeroplane.

Second Lieutenant G. Bremridge, No. 65 Squadron, was flying with other pilots of his squadron when a scout dived on his tail, but this was driven off by Lieutenant Knocker. Second Lieutenant Bremridge then followed it and shot it down out of control.

Captain J. Gilmour, also of No. 65 Squadron, took part in a large fight between a number of Camels and a large enemy formation, and he dived at a single-seater, which he shot down in flames. He then attacked another two-seater and shot it down out of control. Major J. Cunningham in the same fight got to within 20 yards of a scout which was on another pilot's tail and shot it to pieces. He then attacked another scout, with which he nearly collided, and last saw this machine falling completely out of control as he turned round to engage others.

Five Nieuports of No. 1 Squadron attacked seven enemy aircraft scouts and Captain W. Rogers shot one down out of control, while Second Lieut. W. Patrick fired 50 rounds into one from about 10 yards range just when it was firing at a Nieuport, and it fell down vertically with its engine full on and was seen by anti-aircraft to crash.

In all this fighting only three of our aeroplanes were missing or brought down. These were three of No. 65 Squadron and were the only ones missing during the day.

One enemy aircraft was brought down near Gavrelle by machine-gun fire from the ground (First Army), and another was shot down by anti-aircraft of the Second Army and fell in our lines near St. Julien.

Bombing.—First Brigade.—Corps machines dropped thirty-two 25-lb. bombs.

Second Brigade.—Corps machines dropped one hundred and fourteen 25-lb. bombs on various targets, and No. 70 Squadron dropped five 25-lb. bombs from 2,800 feet on a railway siding.

Third Brigade.—Sixteen 25-lb. bombs were dropped on various targets.

Ninth Wing.—On the night of the 17th/18th December, No. 101 Squadron dropped fourteen 112-lb. and eight 25-lb. bombs on Roulers and Ledeghem Stations and Rumbeke Aerodrome.

One machine was hit by anti-aircraft fire on the outward journey, carrying away portions of the lower plane and breaking the main spar and aileron. The pilot, however, proceeded and dropped his bombs on Rumbeke Aerodrome.

No. 102 Squadron dropped ten 112-lb. and five 25-lb. bombs on Menin.

On the 18th, No. 27 Squadron dropped seven 112-lb. bombs on Menin.

Honours and Awards.

The Distinguished Service Cross.—Flight Sub-Lieut. W. L. Jordan, R.N.A.S.

Second Bar to the Military Cross.—Captain A. C. Youdale, M.C.

The Military Cross.—Second Lieutenant B. D. Bate, Second Lieutenant L. E. Shaw-Lawrence.

December 19th.

Dense haze greatly interfered with work.

With aeroplane observation 11 hostile batteries were successfully engaged for destruction; two gun-pits were damaged, five explosions and two fires caused.

Three reconnaissances were carried out by the First Brigade, five by the Third Brigade, and eight by the Ninth Wing, when valuable photographs were taken of new enemy aerodromes. In all 683 photographs were taken during the day and 6,520 rounds fired at ground targets, 3,800 being by pilots of Naval Squadron No. 8.

Nearly three tons of bombs were dropped as follows :—

First Brigade.—Two 112-lb. bombs were dropped on a big gun position at Maugre and two 112-lb. bombs on Bauvin by No. 18 Squadron.

Machines of the First Wing dropped seventeen 25-lb. bombs on various targets.

Corps machines of the Second Brigade dropped thirty-nine 25-lb. and those of the Third Brigade eight 25-lb. bombs on various targets.

Ninth Wing.—No. 27 Squadron attacked Ledeghem Station, on which eight 112-lb. bombs were dropped.

On the night of the 18/19th No. 101 Squadron dropped six 112-lb., two 230-lb. and four 25-lb. bombs on Rumbeke Aerodrome, one 230-lb. and two 25-lb. on Thourout, where a direct hit was obtained on a train, two 112-lb. on Lichtervelde Aerodrome and eight 25-lb. on Ledeghem Station, and 1,220 rounds were fired at lights and other targets during this raid. No. 102 Squadron dropped four 112-lb. on St. Denis Westrem Aerodrome, where three bombs were seen to fall on sheds in the south-east corner of the aerodrome, two 112-lb. on Courtrai, and four 112-lb. and eight 25-lb. on Menin. Lieutenant A. B. Whiteside and Second Lieut. J. T. Richardson in one machine and Second Lieuts. R. W. Loudon and Lawrence in another machine, flew over Gontrode Aerodrome, but it appeared to be deserted, so they flew back to St. Denis Westrem, which was lit up, and dropped their bombs.

Enemy Aircraft.—Enemy aircraft activity was not great, although on several occasions formations were encountered in the Second Army front.

A patrol of No. 40 Squadron met four enemy aircraft scouts, and Captain Lewis and Captain Tudhope each shot down one out of control.

Pilots of No. 19 Squadron again had a considerable amount of fighting, with successful results. Captain O. Bryson and Lieutenant A. Fairclough attacked a two-seater, which they destroyed. In another patrol Lieutenant Fairclough shot a two-seater down out of control, and then attacked another, which went down vertically. Major A. Carter drove down one which appeared to be hit, and Second Lieut. H. Galer drove one down, which he followed near the ground, when he broke off the combat owing to a stoppage. The enemy machine appeared to be completely out of control.

Second Lieut. F. Hobson, No. 70 Squadron, was leading a patrol of Camels when he saw three enemy aircraft two-seaters below, so dived at them and attacked one, which he destroyed. He then attacked a second, but swerved round as he was attacked from behind, so lost sight of the one he had just fired at, but another pilot saw it fall in flames. Second Lieut. F. Gorringe and Second Lieut. F. Quigley attacked a scout which was manœuvred extraordinarlly well by a man who appeared to be a very experienced pilot. The enemy machine, however, was eventually driven down, and was last seen falling near the ground into the mist. There is little doubt that it was destroyed.

Second Lieut. F. Lewis and Corporal G. Holmes, No. 53 Squadron, were taking photographs when they were attacked by a formation of enemy aircraft. They succeeded in escaping, and one of the enemy machines was hit and fell out of control.

An S.E. 5 formation of No. 56 Squadron saw eight enemy aircraft scouts south of Masnières, so dived at them. Captain R. A. Maybery failed to return from this combat, and he was last seen behind a German machine which he had shot down in flames. This pilot has accounted for 20 enemy aircraft, and his is the only machine missing during the day.

December 20th.

Very little work was possible, owing to thick fog and mist.

Second Lieut. Douglas and Second Air Mechanic Coulson, No. 15 Squadron, flew for 2 hours 20 minutes and ranged the 36th Siege Battery on to a hostile battery, which was hit, while four direct hits were obtained on another target.

Major A. D. Carter, No. 19 Squadron, was flying in the vicinity of Hollebeke when he saw an enemy scout attacking one of our artillery machines, so dived at it and drove it down. Unfortunately his engine cut out and he was unable to follow it down, but ground observers report that it fell completely out of control.

On the night of the 19th/20th five machines of No. 101 Squadron went out, but had to return owing to unfavourable weather.

Honours and Awards.

The Military Cross.—Captain O. C. Bryson.

The Distinguished Conduct Medal.—No. 2015, Sergeant F. Hopper.

December 21st.

A thick ground mist and fog made aerial work practically impossible.

Three hostile batteries were successfully engaged for destruction by artillery of the First Army, and machines of the First Brigade took 32 photographs, and fired 1,130 rounds at ground targets. One hundred and twenty-six photographs were taken by machines of the Third Brigade.

December 22nd.

Thick ground mist prevented flying early, but visibility improved at about 11 a.m. and a large amount of work was done.

Twelve reconnaissances were carried out, one by the First Brigade, four by the Second, five by the Third, and two by the Ninth Wing.

A total of 582 photographs were taken during the day, and 5,595 rounds fired at ground targets.

With aeroplane observation, 55 hostile batteries were successfully engaged for destruction, five gun-pits were destroyed, 16 damaged, 19 explosions and 16 fires caused, and 51 active hostile batteries were reported by zone call. Thirteen of the hostile batteries engaged for destruction were by artillery of the First Army, 28 by the Second, 13 by the Third and one by the Fifth.

Captain Watts and Lieutenant Richards, No. 7 Squadron, ranged the 375th Siege Battery (12-in. howitzers) on a hostile battery, obtaining six O.K.'s and causing three explosions, two fires, and considerably damaging the position.

Lieutenant Maden and Sergeant Corson, No. 9 Squadron, worked for four hours and carried out a successful destructive shoot.

The 239th Siege Battery damaged a pit and caused a large explosion in a hostile battery with observation by Lieutenants Cook and Love, No. 13 Squadron, who worked for $3\frac{1}{2}$ hours.

Lieutenants Corsan and FitzHerbert, No. 15 Squadron, worked for three hours and 40 minutes with the 333rd Siege Battery, which badly damaged the whole position of a hostile battery, destroying one pit and damaging two.

Enemy Aircraft.—Enemy aircraft activity was not great.

Captain J. B. Paine was leading an offensive patrol of No. 29 Squadron which attacked four enemy aircraft, and he got on the tail of one and shot it down out of control.

Captain O. Bryson and Lieutenants E. Olivier and A. Fairclough, No. 19 Squadron, fought a formation of eight enemy aircraft, and one was seen to fall completely out of control.

Second Lieut. F. Hobson was leading a patrol of No. 70 Squadron which engaged six enemy aircraft scouts, so he picked one out and shot it down out of control.

Second Lieut. G. Elliott, of the same squadron, engaged a two-seater enemy aircraft, which he shot down out of control, and which was seen to burn after crashing.

A patrol of No. 20 Squadron engaged seven enemy aircraft over Moorslede. Sergeant Johnson and Captain Hedley shot one down completely out of control, and then engaged two others, and Captain Hedley fired 80 rounds from close range into one, which burst into flames and crashed. One enemy scout secured a favourable position under his machine, so Second Lieut. Makepiece and Lieutenant Brooke dived, and after a burst of fire the German scout went down in a vertical dive, and was followed until it was seen to crash.

Second Lieut. Bacon and First Air Mechanic Connor, No. 10 Squadron, were attacked by five enemy aircraft scouts, but returned safely after having shot one down out of control.

Captain J. B. McCudden, No. 56 Squadron, when looking for enemy aircraft, saw two machines flying west, so attacked one of them. He shot the gunner and hit the engine, and the enemy aircraft glided west partially under control, so he left this machine and attacked the other, but saw that the pilot of the first machine had turned and was gliding east. He therefore swerved round, fired a burst at 50 yards range, and the German aeroplane went into a spiral glide and crashed in our lines south-west of St Quentin.

Bombing.—First Brigade.—No. 18 Squadron dropped four 112-lb. bombs on a large gun position at Bauvin, and Corps machines dropped thirty-seven 20-lb. bombs on various targets.

Third Brigade.—Thirty-seven 25-lb. bombs were dropped on various targets.

Honours and Awards.

The Military Cross.—Captain W. W. Rogers.

The Military Medal.—No. 87595, First Air Mechanic H. Else.

December 23rd.

The weather was fine, but a thick haze allowed only a little artillery work to be done.

Six hostile batteries were successfully engaged for destruction with aeroplane observation. Three gun-pits were damaged and two fires caused.

With balloon observation, two hostile batteries were successfully engaged for destruction by artillery of the First Army, and two neutralised, while artillery of the Second Army engaged eight for destruction, neutralised one and dealt with 22 other targets.

During an artillery patrol, Lieutenants Horton and Harris, No. 8 Squadron, and Lieutenants Buchanan and Matthews, No. 35 Squadron, obtained valuable information.

Three reconnaissances were carried out by machines of the Third Brigade, during which 320 photographs were taken. A total of 631 photographs were taken by brigades during the day and 5,861 rounds fired at ground targets. Of the latter, 1,100 were fired by pilots of Naval Squadron No. 8.

Enemy Aircraft.—Enemy aircraft were not particularly active and nearly all the machines encountered were two-seaters.

Seven enemy machines were brought down; five within our lines. Three of these were by Captain McCudden, No. 56 Squadron, who shot down a fourth on the enemy's side; and two were by anti-aircraft, one of which was a Gotha.

This is the first occasion on which one pilot has shot down four enemy aircraft in a day, and Captain McCudden's accounts are as follows :—

"Left ground at 10.50 to look for enemy aircraft west of our lines, and at 11.15 a.m. saw three enemy aircraft two-seaters together over Vendelles, north-west of St. Quentin, at 13,000 feet. As they were above I could not engage them decisively, but drove them all east of the lines. At about 11.10 an L.V.G. came west just north of St. Quentin at 17,000. Chased him and caught him up over Etreillers. He then turned south. I secured a firing position and fired a burst from both guns, when enemy aircraft's engine stopped and water came pouring from the radiator in the centre section. Enemy aircraft turned south, and I tried to turn him west because the observer was waving his right arm, apparently in token of surrender, but the machine was still going south-east very fast. However, I fired another burst at close range, whereupon he went down in steep dive and crashed completely between the canal and the road at Anguilcourt, which is north-east of La Fere, at 11.25. I returned north climbing, and at 11.50 saw a Rumpler at 17,500 just south of Peronne. I climbed for 20 minutes and attacked enemy aircraft over Beauvois at 18,200 feet at 12.15. Going south-east, enemy aircraft fought extraordinarily well and we got down to 8,000 feet over Roupy, when after a burst from both guns at close range enemy aircraft's right-hand wings fell off and the wreckage fell in our lines near Gontescourt at 12.20. Returned north climbing and at 12.50 attacked two L.V.G.'s over Gouzeaucourt at 16,000. However, both machines co-operated very well, using their front guns as well as the rear, and I fought them east of the lines and then left them, as I had no more petrol."

"Leading my formation east over Ypres towards the lines at 14,000 feet, at 2.30 I saw a Rumpler coming west over Metz at 14,000. Enemy aircraft saw my formation and then turned east, nose down. I caught up to enemy aircraft at 13,000 feet over Bois de Gouzeaucourt, and engaged him down to 6,000 feet, when enemy aircraft went into spiral dive and crashed in our lines north-west of Gouzeaucourt at 2.40 p.m. Re-formed my patrol and crossed lines at 13,000 over Masnières. At about 3.5 engaged six Albatross Scouts over Fontaine at 13,000. My patrol fought these enemy aircraft down to 8,000 feet over Bourlon Wood and then left enemy aircraft, who dived east. The fight was indecisive except that Lieutenant Galley, in fighting one enemy aircraft end on, got hit in the oil tank and had to land at advanced landing ground, and apparently he hit the enemy aircraft's engine, and he went off down east as if to land. The enemy aircraft scouts (red-nosed Albatross) kept rolling and spinning down. After the fight, whilst re-forming the patrol over Flesquieres, I saw an L.V.G. coming west over Trescault at 12,000 feet. I got into position at close range, fired about 20 shots, when enemy aircraft went down absolutely out of control, alternately stalling, turning upside down, and then spinning for a short distance before stalling again, &c. Enemy aircraft took five minutes to reach the ground and in a vertical dive landed on a train in our lines a few hundred yards west of Metz at 3.30. Returned at 3.50."

Second Lieut. F. Gorringe, No. 70 Squadron, observed a large amount of anti-aircraft fire over Ypres, so flew in that direction and found a German machine, which he attacked and shot down.

Lieutenant J. Ralston, No. 84 Squadron, drove down one enemy machine out of control, while another fell out of control after having been engaged by Captain E. Pennell and Second Lieut. W. Brown.

None of our machines were missing during the day, but one was shot down in "No Man's Land."

The Gotha machine, which was hit by anti-aircraft of the Third Army, landed near Achiet le Grand, and the three occupants were taken prisoners.

Bombing.—First Brigade.—On the night of the 22nd/23rd, No. 2 Squadron dropped fifty-four 25-lb. bombs on Meurchin, and on the 23rd No. 4 Squadron dropped two 25-lb. bombs on Benifontaine.

Third Brigade.—Twenty-nine 25-lb. bombs were dropped by Corps machines on various targets.

Fifth Brigade.—Corps machines dropped thirty-three 25-lb. bombs on various targets.

Ninth Wing.—On the night of the 22nd/23rd No. 101 Squadron dropped eight 25-lb. bombs on Rumbeke Aerodrome, where a direct hit was obtained on a hangar; eight 25-lb. and two 40-lb. phosphorus bombs on Scheldewendeke Aerodrome; two 230-lb. and eighty-four 25-lb. bombs on Maria Aalter Aerodrome, where five direct hits were obtained.

Captain Vickers and Lieutenant Wardrill made two trips to Maria Aalter, and besides obtaining direct hits with bombs, they fired 500 rounds into the sheds.

Lieutenants Middleton and Walker also made two successful trips, obtaining direct hits and firing 300 rounds into sheds, while Lieutenant Holdsworth and Second Air Mechanic Rennie obtained direct hits on two hangars and fired 300 rounds into sheds.

Three thousand and fourteen rounds were fired altogether during this raid, and some pilots carried extra 25-lb. and incendiary bombs in the nacelles of their machines.

During the same night No. 102 Squadron dropped eight 112-lb. and eighty 25-lb. bombs on Sotteghem, Audenarde, Courtrai, Menin, and Comines Railway Stations, and Scheldewendeke, St. Denis Westrem, and Cuerne Aerodromes.

December 24th.

Very little flying was done owing to dense fog.

A reconnaissance was carried out on the night of the 23rd instant by No. 2 Squadron, of the area bounded by Douai, Valenciennes, Tournai, Lille, to discover, if possible, from which aerodrome the enemy aircraft which had bombed Bethune and Bruay had come. The result was that no active enemy aerodrome with landing lights was discovered.

A reconnaissance was carried out by the Third Brigade, and 744 rounds were fired at ground targets.

With aeroplane observation two hostile batteries were successfully engaged for destruction by artillery of the Third Army and two targets were dealt with by balloons.

Eight 25-lb. bombs were dropped by machines of the Third Brigade.

On the night of the 23rd/24th, No. 2 Squadron dropped sixty 25-lb. bombs on Noyelle-Godault, Don, and Carvin. No. 101 Squadron dropped forty 25-lb. bombs on Maria Aalter Aerodrome, and eight 25-lb. bombs on Thielt Aerodrome. No. 102 Squadron dropped forty-five 25-lb. bombs on Cruyshautem, Gontrode, Oyghem, and Waereghem Aerodromes, and on Deynze, Menin, and Comines Stations.

Forty-first Wing.—Ten machines of No. 55 Squadron dropped sixteen 112-lb. and two 230-lb. bombs on the factory at Ludwigshafen west of Mannheim, on the Rhine. Direct hits were obtained in the sidings of Badische and Heinrichlanz Works and in the Gas Works and a fire was started in the town. The station was full of rolling stock and a great number of dumps were also seen.

Anti-aircraft fire was very heavy over Mannheim. One machine was evidently hit, as it went down under control near Speyer. Eleven enemy aircraft attempted to attack the formation, but were kept at a distance of 300 yards. All our machines returned except the one mentioned above.

A photographic reconnaissance was also carried out by Second Lieut. Thaskrah and Lieutenant D. Fluke, No. 55

Squadron, who photographed Puzieux and Mars-le-Tour. The machine was attacked by two enemy aircraft who followed it from Chambley on the outward journey until it recrossed the lines.

Honours and Awards.

The Military Cross.—Captain R. L. Chidlaw-Roberts; Captain I. A. J. Duff; Second-Lieut. W. E. Davie.

S. WOOD, Captain,
Staff Officer.

Headquarters,
    Royal Flying Corps,
        26th December 1917.

No. 49.

CONFIDENTIAL.

ROYAL NAVAL AIR SERVICE.

OPERATIONS REPORT

(with Royal Flying Corps Reports attached).

1st to 16th JANUARY 1918.

NAVAL STAFF,
　OPERATIONS DIVISION.
　　16th January 1918.

ROYAL NAVAL AIR SERVICE.

REPORT OF OPERATIONS

(Completed from Reports during period
1st to 16th January 1918).

CONTENTS.

	PAGE
DUNKIRK	2
R.N.A.S. SQUADRON, WITH ROYAL FLYING CORPS REPORTS ATTACHED	5
EASTERN MEDITERRANEAN	7
BRITISH ADRIATIC SQUADRON	20
ROYAL FLYING CORPS COMMUNIQUÉS	21

DUNKIRK.

WEATHER.

During this period the weather conditions have been generally bad, and flying operations have been greatly curtailed by high winds, low clouds and snow storms.

PHOTOGRAPHIC RECONNAISSANCE.

January 4th.

No 1 Wing (2nd Squadron).—A photographic reconnaissance was carried out during the morning over Bruges Docks and La Brugeoise Works. Haze prevented a certain amount of visual observations.

ATTACK ON HOSTILE MACHINE.

January 3rd.

No. 1 Wing (Seaplane Defence Squadron).—Sopwith Camel, N. 6340 (Pilot, Flight Lieut. Day) engaged a two-seater Albatross photographic machine in the vicinity of Bruges at 17,500 feet. The Albatross, apparently unaware of the presence of the Sopwith, glided down close in front of the Sopwith, which enabled the Sopwith pilot to get in 300 rounds under his tail from about 30 yards range, and tracers were observed entering his fuselage. The hostile machine dived steeply; owing to intense anti-aircraft fire the Sopwith pilot was prevented from observing the result, but it is estimated that the hostile machine was badly hit.

ATTACK ON ENEMY GUN POSITION.

January 6th.

No. 4 Wing (9th Squadron).—A patrol of three Sopwiths when returning in the vicinity of Nieuport were attacked by large quantities of "flammenwerfer," which was fired at the Sopwiths from various points behind Nieuport. One of these points was located half way between Lombartzyde Bains and the road running parallel with the coast, and was attacked with several hundred rounds by the Sopwith's machine guns.

ATTACK ON ENEMY TRENCHES.

January 13th.

No. 4 Wing (9th Squadron).—Whilst on an offensive patrol, a formation of five Sopwiths, failing to observe any hostile aircraft, attacked enemy trenches at Nieuport, into which 750 rounds were fired.

OFFENSIVE PATROLS—ENGAGEMENTS WITH ENEMY.

January 14th.

No. 4 Wing (10th Squadron).—During an offensive patrol by five Sopwith Camels, a formation of six Albatross Scouts and two two-seaters were observed east of Houthulst Forest at 9,000 feet.

A number of indecisive engagements took place, but one hostile machine was driven down out of control by Flight Commander Curtis.

OFFENSIVE PATROL, ATTACK ON HOSTILE MACHINE AND ENEMY TRENCHES.

January 14th.

No. 4 Wing (9th Squadron).—Whilst returning from an offensive patrol, Flight Lieut. A. W. Wood in a Sopwith F. 1 dived on an enemy spotting machine over Nieuport and drove him east. The hostile machine returned later, and the Sopwith again attacked at long range, and drove the hostile machine back to Middlekerke, getting in several long bursts, but could not get nearer than 100 yards. The Sopwith's guns then jambed, and by the time they had been got into working order the hostile machine had disappeared from view.

The Sopwith then came under anti-aircraft and pom-pom gunfire, several of the anti-aircraft shells coming very close. The Sopwith's pilot used the remainder of his ammunition firing into enemy trenches, also at an anti-aircraft battery at Spermalie from a low altitude.

BOMB ATTACKS.

Ghistelles Aerodrome	January 4th	1,548 lbs.	D.H. 4. (A.)
Engel Dump - - -	,, 13th	684 ,,	,,
	Total - -	2,232 lbs.	

January 4th.

No. 5 Wing (5th Squadron).—A bombing attack was carried out during the day on Ghistelles Aerodrome by seven D.H. 4 machines, with three others acting as escort, and fourteen 50-lb. and fifty-three 16-lb. bombs were dropped at 1120 at heights of from 15,000 to 16,000 feet.

Visibility was good, and many bombs were observed to explode close to and among the sheds on the south-west, south and east sides of the aerodrome, and a direct hit with one 50-lb. bomb on a small shed on the south side is reported, and is confirmed by the pilot and observer of another machine.

Anti-aircraft fire was heavy, and in some cases very accurate, and several enemy aircraft were seen but did not engage the bombing formation. No observations of importance were made, but four photographs of the aerodrome were taken.

January 13th.

No. 5 Wing (5th Squadron).—Six D.H. 4 bombing machines, accompanied by three escorting machines, were despatched at 1108 to carry out a bombing raid on Varssenaere Aerodrome, with Engel Dump as an alternative target.

D.H. 4, N. 5968, crashed when leaving the aerodrome; the machine caught fire and was completely destroyed.

D.H. 4, N. 5967, was obliged to return before crossing the lines owing to engine trouble. The remaining machines reached Engel Dump, which was attacked instead of the original objective, owing to the high wind. Six 50-lb. and twenty-four 16-lb. bombs were dropped at 1220 from heights of 14,000 to 17,000 feet.

Several bombs were observed to burst among the sheds and on the railway sidings. A direct hit with a 50-lb. bomb on one of the sheds is reported, and a large cloud of smoke was seen to rise. One machine did not drop its bombs owing to the gunlayer not picking up the target, and after having dropped the heavy bombs in the sea brought back the smaller ones. Visibility was good, and anti-aircraft fire light. One photograph of the vicinity of the dump was secured. On the return journey Acting Flight Commander Lupton, D.S.C., was obliged to land on the beach in shallow water at Malo owing to engine trouble.

Honours during Period 1st to 15th January.

Name.	Unit.	Awarded.
Flt. Comdr. G. W. Price	No. 8 Squadron	D.S.C.
Flt. Lieut. S. M. Kinkhead	No. 1 Squadron	D.S.C.

Casualties.

Name.	Unit.	Date.
Accidentally Killed.		
Flt. Sub-Lieut. C. R. Barber	No. 2 Squadron	7.1.18
Observer Sub-Lieut. H. R. Easby	No. 2 Squadron	7.1.18
Died of Wounds.		
Flt. Sub-Lieut. H. Willis	No. 5 Squadron	15.1.18
Died of Injuries.		
A. L. Jefferies, Act. A.M. 1 (A), O. No. F. 27501.	No. 5 Squadron	13.1.18
Wounded.		
A. Foster, A.M. 2 (Act. G.L.), O. No. F. 11691.	No. 5 Squadron	13.1.18
Injured.		
E. Whittaker, A.M. 8 (A), O. No. F. 2192	No. 5 Squadron	13.1.18
Missing.		
Flight Sub-Lieut. A. G. Beattie	No. 10 Squadron	3.1.18
Flight Sub-Lieut. F. Booth	No. 10 Squadron	3.1.18
Flight Sub-Lieut. A. J. Dixon	No. 8 Squadron	3.1.18

NAVAL SQUADRON WITH THE ROYAL FLYING CORPS

(PERIOD 30TH DECEMBER 1917 TO 12TH JANUARY 1918.)

NAVAL SQUADRON No. 8.

This squadron has been attached to the First Brigade, R.F.C., and has carried out 30 offensive patrols, 59 flights in pursuit of hostile artillery machines, and seven special missions, making a total of 154 hours 15 minutes flying.

A total of 21 combats took place, 10 of these being decisive.

January 1st.

Flight Commander Compston and Flight Lieut. Cooper brought down a wireless machine in our lines at Fampoux.

Flight Commander Compston and Flight Sub-Lieut. Dixon, after firing 400 rounds into one of 10 Albatross Scouts, drove it down completely out of control, with spurts of smoke coming out of the pilot's cockpit.

Flight Lieut. Jordan and Flight Sub-Lieuts. Johnstone and Reid fired 450 rounds into a single seater hostile machine. The machine stalled, fell on its side, and went down completely out of control.

January 2nd.

Flight Commander Price, whilst on a special mission, attacked a patrol of seven Albatross Scouts, and fired 300 rounds into the rear machine, which burst into flames and fell to the ground.

January 3rd.

Flight Commander Compston fired 100 rounds into a hostile two-seater, which went down out of control, with smoke coming out of the fuselage.

Flight Commander Compston, Flight Lieut. Jordan and Flight Sub-Lieut. Dennett attacked a twin-tailed two-seater, which was being engaged by our anti-aircraft on our side of the lines. They tried to prevent it crossing the lines, but failed although they managed to fire over 400 rounds into it and saw it crash in the enemy's lines.

January 4th.

Flight Commander Munday dived down to within 50 feet of the ground and fired 200 rounds into a shed containing a hostile balloon. No results were observed.

Flight Sub-Lieut. Day shot a twin tail two-seater down out of control.

Flight Commanders Compston and Munday, Flight Lieut. Cooper and Flight Sub-Lieut. Fowler observed a two-seater escorted by an Albatross Scout coming towards our lines. They attacked the Scout and drove it down completely out of control.

Flight Lieut. Jordan and Flight Sub-Lieuts. Johnstone, Dixon, and Dennett had six different engagements with two-seater enemy aircraft doing wireless. In five cases the hostile machine was forced to dive away steeply East and in the sixth the machine was driven down out of control.

January 6th.

Flight Commander Compston and Flight Lieut. Jordan picked out one of a formation of 10 Albatross Scouts and drove it down out of control.

Flight Sub-Lieut. Day fired 200 rounds from a range of 50 yards into a hostile two-seater, which crashed in the enemy's lines.

Flight Commander Price, whilst out in pursuit of enemy machines doing wireless, encountered a two-seater, which he brought down in the enemy's lines.

The results of attempts to interfere with hostile wireless machines have again been most successful. The percentage of interferences during the week rose from 71 per cent. to 81 per cent.

Honours.—Flight Commander G. W. Price awarded D.S.C.
Flight Sub-Lieut. H. Day awarded D.S.C.

SUMMARY.

Hostile Machines driven down out of control - - - 7
" " destroyed - - - - - 3

Total - - - - 10

Casualties.—*Missing.*—Flight Sub-Lieut. A. J. Dixon, 4th January 1918.

EASTERN MEDITERRANEAN STATION.

(Compiled from Weekly Reports Nos. 90, 91, 92 and 93, dating from December 2nd to 30th 1917.)

December 2nd–9th.

NOTE.—Only signalled reports of this week's operations have been received. Details of the more important events will be forwarded when written reports are received from stations.

THASOS AIR STATION.

"A" SQUADRON AND "Z" SQUADRON (GREEK).

Anti-Submarine Patrols.—Except on 8th December, when bad weather prevented flying, anti-submarine patrols have been carried out daily during the week by "A" and "Z" Squadrons, the Gulfs of Ruphani and Kavalla being kept under close observation.

Hostile Aircraft Pursuit.—On 5th December a hostile aeroplane, which was sighted from Thasos Aerodrome, was pursued by a Sopwith Fighter, but no engagement took place owing to the superior speed of the enemy.

December 10th–16th.

Anti-Submarine Patrols.—Submarine patrols in the vicinity of Thasos were carried out on 9th and 11th December. On 10th a more extended patrol was carried out by Henri Farman and Short seaplane over the area to the S. and S.W. of Thasos, extending as far as Mount Athos.

Bomb Attack on Kavalla.—On 14th December a raid on Kavalla was attempted by "Z" Squadron, but owing to low clouds all machines—two Sopwith Bombers, escorted by one Fighter and the Triplane, returned without having dropped their bombs. The attack was repeated on the following day, but owing to low clouds results were not observed. A look out for submarines in the Gulf of Kavalla was kept on both days.

Accident.—On returning from the attack of the 15th, Sopwith Bomber, No. N. 5200, and Sopwith Fighter, No. N. 5648, flying at 3,000 feet, collided in the air when 1½ miles from the aerodrome. No details of the accident have been received, but a signalled report states that both machines fell into the sea, Flight Sub-Lieut. Logiardis, Chief Petty Officer Economou, and Gunlayer Saketopoulos being killed.

December 17th–23rd.

NOTE.—Owing to the bad weather, which has been prevalent throughout the Ægean during the past week, all flying has been considerably curtailed. No flying reports have been received of such operations as have been carried out, so that the report is compiled from signals only. Details will follow when received.

Anti-submarine patrols were carried out by Short seaplane on 18th and 19th December over the area between Thasos and the Akte Peninsula. On 21st the area within a radius of 30 miles to S. and S E. of Thasos was patrolled by a Henri Farman and Sopwith Bomber from "Z" Squadron. No further service flights were carried out.

December 24th–30th.

NOTE.—Strong winds accompanied by low clouds and rain have been prevalent throughout the Ægean during the week under review. Aerodromes have consequently been too soft to allow of machines getting off on such days, as flying was not actually prevented by weather conditions.

No service flights have been carried out during the current week.

STAVROS AIR STATION.
"D" Squadron.

December 2nd–9th.

Reconnaissance.—Reconnaissances of the enemy's front line from Orfano to the Angista Valley were carried out on 3rd and 4th December. No important changes were observed.

Patrol Work.—On the 2nd four patrols for hostile aircraft were made, and on the 5th one enemy aeroplane was pursued, but not engaged.

Mine Patrol.—On 7th December a mine patrol was carried out by a Sopwith Fighter over Stavros swept channel and the Gulf of Ruphani, and on the 8th a reconnaissance of the Angista Valley and Drama was attempted, but was abandoned owing to engine trouble.

Note.—Details have now been received of the bomb attacks on Drama Aerodrome, carried out on 27th and 29th November, which were briefly reported in W.O.R. No. 89.

Bomb Attacks on Drama Aerodrome.—Both attacks were carried out by Flight Lieut. Marlowe and W. M. Sherlock, Petty Officer (Gunlayer) in De H. 4, No. N. 5984, escorted by Sopwith F. 1, Nos. N. 6367 and B. 3769, and eight 16-lb. and two 65-lb. bombs were carried on each occasion.

On the occasion of the first attack two direct hits were made from 8,000 feet with the 65-lb. bombs on one of the eight Bessoneau on the aerodrome. Half the hangar was wrecked, and a fire was started, dense clouds of smoke being emitted. A new hangar was also observed under construction. On the return journey an enemy aeroplane was observed flying low and climbing up after our machines. It was unable to overtake them, however, and was not seen for long.

In the second attack (on 29th) the bombs were dropped at a line of three sheds on the northern side of the aerodrome. A perfect line was obtained, and all bombs exploded parallel to the target, one of the 65-lb. bombs falling only a few feet from one of the hangars. The Bessoneau, which had been wrecked during the raid of 27th, was observed to have been removed.

On the return journey a hostile aeroplane was again sighted, approaching from Angista and making for the D.H. 4, which was then at 11,000 feet. Flight Lieut. Mellings, having signalled to the other machines, dived steeply and made a surprise attack on the enemy from behind, opening fire at 300 yards, and obtaining several hits with tracers on the enemy's wings and fuselage. The hostile machine attempted to avoid attack by side-slipping, and a chase for several miles along the Drama road ensued, the enemy being again hit at 80–100 yards range, and tracers being observed to pass through his front cylinders. Owing to gun jambs the "Camel" was unable to press the attack, and rejoined the D.H. 4 and the other "Camel" at about 3,000 feet half a mile behind, rifle and machine-gun fire being avoided as much as possible. Heavy and accurate anti-aircraft fire was experienced throughout the return journey. The enemy machine engaged by Flight Lieut. Mellings was a modern type Albatross Scout, and was slightly faster than the "Camel" at a low altitude.

December 10th-16th.

Owing to unfavourable weather conditions no service flying has been carried out during the week under review, except on 14th December, when a flight was made to Thasos, carrying a pilot to bring back a Sopwith Fighter to Stavros. A submarine patrol over the area Stavros-Thasos was carried out en route.

Accident.—On 10th December Sopwith Fighter, No. N. 5618, was flown to Salonika by Flight Commander P. C. Douglas, with Observer Sub-Lieut. W. Hinsley as passenger. The machine side-slipped when about to land, and was wrecked. Flight Commander Douglas being killed and Observer Sub-Lieut. Hinsley being slightly injured. No details of the accident have been received.

December 17th-23rd.

Reconnaissance.—An escorted tactical reconnaissance of the Angista Valley was carried out on 15th December. Forty to fifty transport wagons were observed at Angista, and a train was sighted near Fotolivo proceeding towards Drama; otherwise no unusual movements were observed.

Anti-Submarine Patrols.—Submarine and mine patrols were carried out over Stavros swept channel and the Gulf of Ruphani by Henri Farman and Sopwith fighter on 17th, 18th, 19th, and 20th December.

Hostile Aircraft Pursuit.—On 18th a hostile machine was reported, and two "Camels" started in pursuit, but no engagement took place, the enemy disappearing into clouds before he could be overtaken. Two patrols for hostile aircraft were carried out on 19th, and an escorted reconnaissance of the enemy's front line was also made.

December 24th-30th.

Mine Patrols and Reconnaissances.—Escorted mine patrols over Stavros swept channel and the Gulf of Ruphani were carried out by Henri Farmans on 23rd, 25th, and 27th December. On 25th an escorted tactical reconnaissance of the Angista Valley and Drama area was also made, no important changes being observed, however. During the remainder of the week flying has been prevented by weather conditions.

GLIKI AIR STATION (IMBROS).

"C" SQUADRON.

December 2nd–9th.

Fighter Patrol—Engagement with Enemy.—On the morning of 2nd December two "Camels" and a "Pup" carried out a fighting patrol over Galata Aerodrome. Two machines were encountered and driven down, but no details of the engagements have been received.

Attempted Bomb Raid on Gliki Aerodrome.—During the afternoon of the same day seven enemy machines attempted a raid on Gliki Aerodrome. No casualties or damage were suffered. Four machines went up in pursuit of the enemy and four engagements took place, one enemy aeroplane being driven down.

Reconnaissance.—Owing to bad weather no flying was carried out on 3rd, 4th, 6th, and 7th December, but an escorted reconnaissance of the Dardanelles was carried out on 5th and 9th, none but the usual small shipping being observed.

December 10th–16th.

Engagement with Enemy.—On the morning of 9th December an enemy aeroplane flew over Imbros. Three machines went in pursuit, and an engagement was carried out by Flight Lieut. P. Fowler in "Camel," No. B. 6254, who fired 270 rounds at 150 yards range at the hostile machine—a two-seater about the size of a D.H. 4. Tracers were seen to enter the fuselage and no reply was made by the enemy, the observer being probably killed or injured.

Owing to the guns jambing the attack could not be pressed and while the jams were being cleared the hostile machine made off and disappeared flying low towards Galata Aerodrome.

Reconnaissance.—On 11th December an escorted reconnaissance of the Dardanelles was carried out, none but the usual small shipping being observed. During this flight the escorting "Camel" carried out a fighting patrol over Galata Aerodrome at 8,000–9,000 feet. No hostile machine came up, however.

Bomb attack on Berlin–Bagdad Railway, and Photography.—On the morning of 12th December a further attack was made on the Uzum Keupru–Lule Burgas sector of the Berlin–Bagdad Railway by D.H. 4's, Nos. N. 5975 and N. 5976.

The first machine, piloted by Flight Lieut. R. Sorley with Observer Sub-Lieut. F. Smith, left at 0805 and proceeded to Alapie Railway Station. Descending to 2,000 feet two 100-lb. bombs were dropped, one falling on the permanent way just in rear of one of two trains which were standing in the station, while the second made a direct hit on one of the three large warehouses on the north side of the line. Four trays of ammunition were poured into the trains and at the men seen scattering about the station buildings. Rifle and machine-gun fire was also silenced by the fire from Lewis gun. One photograph of the station was taken.

After dropping the bombs the machine proceeded eastwards along the railway in search of other trains. None were observed, however, and the machine returned to Imbros *via* Hairobolu and Keshan, carrying out a photograph reconnaissance en route.

The second D.H. 4, piloted by Flight Lieut. A. Woodward, with Observer Lieutenant C. O. Palmer, left at 0820 and also proceeded to Alapie where two 100-lb. bombs were dropped from 2,000 feet. One of these secured a direct hit on the rear end of one of the trains in the station and apparently set fire to one of the trucks, as considerably more smoke was observed than was caused by the bomb explosion. Photographs of Alapie Station were taken after the bombs had been dropped, and an exposure was made over Keshan on the return journey.

Bombing attack on Suvla Point.—During the afternoon of the same day an attack on Galata Aerodrome was attempted with two Sopwith Fighters escorted by two "Camels." One Sopwith Fighter was obliged to return owing to the propellers splitting through the muzzle attachment of the Vickers gun coming adrift and falling into it.

The remaining machines ran into heavy clouds and rain when north of Suvla, so abandoned the first objective and dropped three 16-lb. bombs on military huts and a gun emplacement in the vicinity of Suvla Point. One of the bombs apparently hit an ammunition store, as a violent secondary explosion was observed.

Bomb attack on Galata Aerodrome.—Later in the afternoon the raid upon Galata Aerodrome was resumed, being carried out on this occasion by the two D.H. 4's, with the same pilots and observers who made the morning attack on Alapie. Two 112-lb. bombs exploded within 30 yards of the hangars.

Bomb attack on Nagara.—No flying was carried out on 13th and 14th owing to unfavourable weather, but on 15th the seaplane sheds at Nagara were bombed by two Sopwith Fighters escorted by two "Camels." No details of the attack have been received, except that one enemy machine was encountered and driven off.

Engagement with Enemy.—Details have now been received of the operations carried out on 2nd December which were briefly reported in W.O.R. No. 90.

During the morning a fighting patrol was carried out over Galata Aerodrome by two "Camels" and a "Pup." One hostile aeroplane scout was seen to leave the aerodrome and start to gain height over the Asiatic Coast. When at about 5,000 feet an attack was made by one of the "Camels," the enemy being driven across the Straits and forced to land again on his aerodrome.

A second enemy machine (a captured Bristol Scout), which came up from the vicinity of Chanak was engaged by the "Pup." The hostile machine made a "nose-on" attack firing a short burst. The "Pup" side-slipped to avoid the fire and, turning on the enemy, fired on him as he continued his nose dive away; the enemy did not attack again.

Hostile Raid on Gliki Aerodrome.—Engagement with Enemy.—In the afternoon a raid was made by the enemy on Gliki Aerodrome, one large two-seater aeroplane, three two-seater seaplanes, one seaplane scout and one aeroplane scout participating in the attack. Two "Camels," one "Pup," and a Sopwith Fighter went up in pursuit of these machines and a series of engagements took place, all of which were indecisive. It is possible, however, that the observer of the two-seater was either killed or badly injured as he suddenly ceased fire while being attacked by the Sopwith Fighter and made no further effort to carry on the action, the machine diving steeply towards the Peninsula, where it was last seen only a few feet off the water and under cover of machine guns.

December 17th–23rd.

Reconnaissance.—In view of unusual W/T activity in the Dardanelles on the night of 15th/16th December, a special reconnaissance of the Straits was carried out at dawn on 16th December by Sopwith Fighter escorted by a "Camel." Low clouds and heavy rain were encountered the whole way, making observation almost impossible. A ship, about the size of a destroyer, was seen, however, to the north of Nagara, and five vessels of about 400–500 tons were observed in Chanak Harbour. No details could be observed.

Reconnaissance and Bomb Attack on Sofia–Constantinople Railway.—On 17th December a special reconnaissance and bombing flight was again carried out over the Sofia–Constantinople Railway by Flight Lieut. A. Woodward and Observer Lieutenant C. O. Palmer in D.H. 4, No. N.5975, the section in vicinity of Muradli being chosen on this occasion as the objective.

December 24th–30th.

Bomb Attack on Galata Aerodrome.—Owing to the bad weather and subsequent condition of the aerodrome, no flying was carried out until 29th December, when a bomb attack was made by Sopwith Fighter, escorted by two Camels, on Galata Aerodrome. No details of the attack are yet available, but a signalled report states that three bombs were dropped at the sheds, which were also attacked with machine-gun fire from a low altitude.

Note.—Details have now been received of the special reconnaissance on 17th December of the Muradli section of the Oriental Railway, which was briefly reported in W.O.R. No. 92.

Reconnaissance and Bomb Attack on Muradli Station.—The reconnaissance was carried out by Flight Lieut. A. Woodward and Observer Lieutenant C. O. Palmer in D.H. 4, No. N. 5975. After leaving Imbros the machine proceeded direct to Muradli, the weather being cloudy and the atmosphere hazy during the journey. On approaching Muradli a goods train consisting of about 20 trucks, which appeared to be empty, was observed to the east of the station, travelling westwards. Descending to 1,000 feet two 100-lb. bombs were released at the train which fell 20 yards and 30 yards respectively. At Muradli Station itself a second train of about 30 trucks was observed under way, the engine of which was also attacked from a low altitude with machine-gun fire. Detailed information about the station, warehouses, sidings, and the general topography of the country in this region was obtained, and two photographs were taken of an iron bridge to the east of Muradli with a view to further bomb attack. Whilst gaining height on the return journey an additional tray of ammunition was fired on flocks of sheep, these being numerous in this area. A reconnaissance of the area between Muradli and the coast revealed nothing, but a military encampment of 25 tents and five huts at Malgara. No hostile aircraft were encountered, and the machine was not hit by machine-gun fire.

No details of the reconnaissances have been received, but a signalled report states that a goods train under way to east of Muradli was bombed, two 100-lb. bombs falling within 30 yards of the permanent way. A second train observed under way to north of Muradli was attacked with 200 rounds machine-gun fire. A considerable amount of rolling stock was observed at Muradli Station and photographs were taken.

Bomb Attack on Nagara Seaplane Base.—On the same day a submarine patrol was carried out by Sopwith Fighter of the area Imbros–Lemnos–Melles, and a bomb attack was carried out by two Sopwith Fighters escorted by two Camels on Nagara Seaplane Base. No details of the attack are available.

An enemy machine which approached Imbros during the day was pursued by a Camel, but no engagement took place.

Bomb Attack on Galata Aerodrome.—On 20th December a bomb attack was carried out by a Sopwith Fighter escorted by two Camels on Galata Aerodrome, and on 22nd three Camels pursued an enemy machine, which approached Imbros, but no engagement took place, the enemy disappearing in clouds.

MUDROS AIR STATION.

December 2nd–9th.

Weather.—Strong N.E. winds, accompanied by rain and low clouds have considerable curtailed flying during the week.

Anti-Submarine Patrol, Loss of Short Seaplane N. 1234.—

At noon on 2nd December 1917, a submarine was reported in the vicinity of Mount Athos, and accordingly patrols were sent out from Mudros, Thasos, and Kassandra, all converging towards Mount Athos.

From Mudros a Short seaplane was ordered to patrol to the west of Lemnos. A Henri Farman aeroplane was also directed to patrol XY and Z, to the W.N.W. of Lemnos.

Machines on patrol are ordered to communicate their positions by W/T every 10 minutes, and this is of particular importance in relation to over-sea patrols by aeroplane, as in the event of engine failure it gives the only chance of rescuing the crew.

No wireless signals were received from either of these machines, owing in the case of the Short seaplane to breakage of the main lead from the alternator, and in the case of the Farman aeroplane through jambing by "Europa" on Poulsen Harmonic Wave.

The Farman aeroplane being overdue at 1550, local time, a second seaplane, N. 1234, with Flight Sub-Lieut. L. H. G. Gillespie and Observer Sub-Lieut. H. Odle, was sent out to patrol the same area as the Henri Farman, to look for her and to render any assistance. Shortly after the Henry Farman returned, but N. 1234 was not fitted with W/T receiving gear and could not be recalled. Soon after she left on patrol a strong southerly wind sprang up, accompanied by low clouds. Between 1625, local time, and 1723, nine signals in all were received from N. 1234, but his Morse was bad and the positions, so far as they could be made out, were obviously wrong. Thus at 1655, the position given was 103 D. 3, which is to the north of Thasos; at 1755, 103 B. 4, which is in the neighbourhood of Deuthero Cove. At 1713 the position was given of 103 G. 5, and a last signal was received at 1723, of which the only thing that could be made out were the figures "16." Assuming that the last signal was meant to be "716," which means "Am experiencing engine trouble," and that the former signal giving position as 103 G. 5 was a defect in Morse, and really meant 103 Z 5, a difference of one "short" by Morse, and which would place the machine on her proper patrol, it was reported to S.N.O. that "the seaplane was believed to be down with "engine trouble north-west of Cape Murtzephlos, or on a line "between that and Athos," and it was requested that patrol craft should be detailed to search.

Nothing further was heard of the missing seaplane during that night, a strong southerly wind blowing throughout the night. On the following morning, 3rd December 1917, a seaplane was sent to search the western and northern coast of Lemnos, but without result. A search party was also organised, starting from Kastro, and at noon on 3rd December this party discovered the wreckage of the Short seaplane being washed ashore at Cape Murtzephlos. The Civil Guard at Cape Murtzephlos stated that between 1900 and 2150, on the preceding night, red and white Very's lights were observed to the south-west of Cape Murtzephlos at intervals, these coming from six miles seaward. The Civil Guard had no boat with which to attempt a rescue, nor had they a telephone or other appliance by which they could communicate the fact that these lights had been observed.

Nothing has been seen or heard of either the pilot or the observer, and they are presumed to be drowned.

The machine, when recovered, was very much broken up, and a considerable part of it, including the engine, is missing. Officers from the Royal Naval Air Service examined the wreckage and were satisfied that this was the wreckage of seaplane N. 1234.

As regards the defective signalling from seaplane N. 1234, it is believed that this was due to the new model W/T key installed in this machine, which has a full ¼-inch " make and break," and is much heavier to operate than the older type of transmission keys. The observer having had his experience with keys of a small gap, and not being able to see the spark or hear his messages as transmitted, and accordingly failing at times to press the key completely home, made unreadable Morse.

As the lives of pilots and observers may always depend on accurate W/T transmission, and as the utility of patrols also to a large extent depends upon this, steps have been taken to give practice to all observers on the station on the new type of key.

December 10th–16th.

Anti-Submarine and Mine Patrol.—On 12th December a continuous anti-submarine, mine and escort flight was maintained by Henri Farman's from the Marsh Aerodrome from 0110 to 1500, while " Republique " carried out battle practice to the south-west of Lemnos.

No other service flights have been made during the week.

December 17th–23rd.

Anti-Submarine Patrols. — Submarine patrols were carried out on 17th December by Henri Farman's and Short seaplane over the area Lemnos–Strati, and to west and north of Lemnos. Preparatory to " Sentinel's " target practice on 20th December a reconnaissance of her projected course was made by seaplane, and weather conditions were found to be so bad that no further escorting flights were made. No other service flights have been made during the week owing to bad weather.

December 24th–30th.

Escort to H.M.S. "Foresight."—On 26th December, H.M.S. "Foresight" was escorted during firing practice by a Short, a Schneider and two Blackburn Baby Seaplanes. No service flights have been carried out during the remainder of the week, but test and practice flights on seaplanes and aeroplanes have been carried out whenever the weather and conditions of aerodrome have permitted.

NOTE.—With reference to the loss of the Handley Page aeroplane, which left Mudros on 30th September 1917 to bomb Constantinople (*vide* W.O.R. No. 81) information has now been received from Flight Lieut. J. W. Alcock, D.S.C., at Constantinople, that after having flown for $1\frac{1}{2}$ hours, either a propeller burst or the reduction gear of one engine broke. An attempt was made to return to Mudros on one engine, but eventually the Handley Page was obliged to alight on the sea. The crew remained in the machine firing Very's lights at intervals of two hours, but apparently they were too far up the Gulf of Xeros for these to be seen from the destroyer which had been stationed 8 miles north of Suvla Point. After two hours on the sea, the Handley Page was sinking, and the crew were obliged to swim ashore, being an hour in the water before landing. On the following morning the crew, consisting of Flight Lieut. Alcock, Flight Lieut. H. Aird and Mr. Wise, W.O., were discovered and made prisoners of war, being subsequently taken to Constantinople.

This story flatly contradicts the version given in the Ottoman W/T Press that the machine was shot down.

KALLONI AIR STATION.

"B" SQUADRON.

December 2nd–9th.

No service flying has been carried out during the week under review.

December 10th–16th.

Reconnaissance.—A reconnaissance of the coast line from Cape Suna to Port Ajanos was carried out on 11th December with a view to locating gun positions. A possible emplacement was observed on the hill overlooking the Mitylene Channel, and photographs were taken. Owing to a slight ground mist these were not successful. During the remainder of the week no service flights have been made.

December 17th–23rd.

Hostile Aircraft Pursuit.—On 17th December at 1100 a hostile machine appeared from south-east, and circled round the aerodrome at about 7,000 feet, making off to north-east. Two Sopwith Fighters were sent in pursuit, but had insufficient speed to overtake the enemy, which from descriptions received was possibly a twin-engined machine.

December 24th–30th.

No service flights have been carried out during the current week.

KASSANDRA AIRSHIP STATION.

December 2nd–9th.

Anti-Submarine Patrols.—Patrols of the entrance to the Gulf of Salonika and the Gulfs of Kassandra and Monte Santo were carried out by S.S. Airship on 2nd, 3rd, 7th, and 8th December. On the remaining days of the week flying was prevented by bad weather. The French seaplanes were also requested to search the Gulfs of Kassandra and Monte Santo on the 2nd December, but no reports have been received of the areas they actually covered.

December 10th–16th.

Patrol Work.—Patrols over the entrance to the Gulf of Salonika and the Gulf of Kassandra were carried out on 9th, 10th, 14th, and 15th December, a daily average of over seven hours flying being made. On the remaining days of the week flying was prevented by bad weather.

December 17th–23rd.

Anti-Submarine Patrol—Loss of Airship. — On the 17th December a patrol of nine hours was made over the Gulf of Kassandra and Monte Santo and the entrance to the Gulf of Salonika. On 18th, while out on patrol, the airship developed engine trouble, when about six miles south-west of Kassandra Point, came down on the water, and commenced to drift to south-east. The crew were rescued, and the airship was taken in tow by torpedo boat 30, with the object of towing her to Skopelos. At the first attempt at towing the tow parted, and at the second the envelope was torn, the remainder being sunk by gun-fire. No further details of the accident have been received. Rear-Admiral Commanding British Ægean Squadron has ordered a Court of Enquiry to be held regarding the loss of the airship.

December 24th–30th.

An inquiry into the loss of the airship at Kassandra on 18th December was held at Salonika on 27th.

A new envelope has been received from England, and an old fuselage is being renovated in order to provide a complete airship until a new fuselage arrives from England.

SUDA BAY SEAPLANE STATION.

December 2nd–9th.

Anti-Submarine Patrols.—Two patrols to north and east of Suda Bay were carried out by Short seaplane on 2nd December. Since that date all flying has been prevented by high wind and rain.

December 10th–16th.

Bad weather has considerably interfered with patrol work during the current week.

Patrol Work.—Patrols to the east, north and north-west of Suda Bay were carried out on 12th, 13th and 15th December.

While carrying out the evening patrol on the 12th, Short, No. N. 1222, developed engine trouble and made a forced landing about 18 miles north-east of Suda Bay at 1718 the last position of the machine not being ascertained at the base owing to W/T being jammed. The missing machine was found by Short 9764 on the following morning and was taken in tow at 1100 by H.M.S. "Gazelle."

December 17th–23rd.

Anti-Submarine Patrols.—Patrols of the entrance to Suda Bay and to the northwards were carried out by Short seaplane on 16th, 17th, 19th and 21st December..

December 24th–30th.

Anti-Submarine Patrols.—Patrols of the approaches to Suda Bay, the Anti-Kithera Channel and the area to the north of Suda Bay were carried out by Short seaplanes on 25th, 27th, and 29th December. Bad weather prevented flying during the remainder of the week.

SYRA SEAPLANE STATION.

December 10th–16th.

A suitable site was chosen at Syra for a seaplane station and the work in building a slipway and erecting a Bessoneau, camp, &c., is now completed. Machines and personnel have been despatched to Syra, and the station will be in a position to start regular submarine patrols in the vicinity of Doro, Mykoni, Zea, Thermia, and Serpho Channels, where a considerable amount of submarine activity has existed.

December 17th–23rd.

The station is now ready to start regular seaplane patrols. No flights have been made during the past week, however, owing to the bad weather conditions.

December 24th-30th.

Anti-Submarine Patrols.—Patrols by a Short seaplane were carried out on 25th December in the vicinity of Syra. No other flights have been made owing to persistent gales.

BRITISH ADRIATIC SQUADRON.

January 3rd.

Attack on Submarine.—Short seaplane N. 1096 left the station at 1115 for escort duties. At 1225 the pilot observed what appeared to be the conning tower of a submarine in the act of submerging. The seaplane got into position, and the observer endeavoured to drop two 65-lb. bombs (delay action), one of which, however, failed to release, and the other fell about 30 feet to the left of the target. The machine then circled round for some considerable time, but nothing further was observed.

January 13th.

Anti-Submarine Operation.—At 0550 a two-seater seaplane left on patrol. Less than half an hour later, at 0615, the observer sighted a submarine awash, moving N.W., nine miles to starboard of the machine, which was at the time 22 miles W. of Saseno. The conning-tower was just visible through glasses. The submarine dived two minutes after it was first seen. An Allo signal was sent out by W/T, giving the position as 40° 30′ N., 18° 55′ E., and the seaplane circled round the area where the submerged, although, owing to bad weather conditions, the position could not be accurately located. A further signal was made at 0644, giving course, and bearing from Saseno, of the submarine; and shortly afterwards, by reason of very adverse weather and engine trouble, the seaplane was forced to return.

In the meantime, as soon as the Allo signal was received, two Baby seaplanes were sent to search the area stated, but both returned without having seen anything further of the submarine.

ROYAL FLYING CORPS COMMUNIQUÉS.

ROYAL FLYING CORPS COMMUNIQUÉ.—No. 120.

During the month of December 1917, we have claimed officially 57 enemy aircraft brought down by aeroplanes (of which 17 fell in our lines) and 28 driven down out of control (nine others were brought down in our lines by anti-aircraft, infantry and machine gunfire). Sixty-six tons of bombs were dropped and 122,836 rounds fired at ground targets. We had 30 machines missing.

December 25th.

Very little work was possible owing to snow and mist.

Four reconnaissances were carried out by the First Brigade, three by the Second, and two by the Fifth.

With aeroplane observation, one hostile battery was successfully engaged for destruction by artillery of the First Army, and one zone call was sent down.

One hundred and sixteen plates were exposed and 2,300 rounds fired at ground targets. One thousand one hundred and fifty of these were by No. 4 Squadron, which also dropped twelve 25-lb. bombs. Machines of the Third Brigade dropped nine 25-lb. bombs and fired 200 rounds, and Corps Squadrons of the Fifth Brigade dropped thirty-four 25-lb. bombs and fired 950 rounds at various targets.

December 26th.

Snow storms interfered with aerial work.

One reconnaissance was carried out by the First Brigade, one by the Second, and one by the Fifth.

Six hostile batteries were successfully engaged for destruction with aeroplane observation, four of which were by artillery of the First Army; one gun-pit was destroyed, two damaged, six explosions and one fire caused, and 35 zone calls were sent down.

Lieutenants Francis and Neilson, No. 69 Squadron, with the 161st Siege Battery (nine 2-in. howitzers) destroyed one pit and caused one large and four minor explosions in a hostile battery.

Four hundred and fifty-nine photographs were taken, 70 25-lb. bombs dropped and 5,443 rounds fired at ground targets, as follows:—

First Brigade.—No. 2. Squadron dropped five 25-lb. bombs and fired fifty rounds; No. 4 Squadron dropped seven 25-lb. bombs; Corps Squadrons fired 1,250 rounds, and Naval Squadron No. 8 fired 1,250 rounds.

Second Brigade.—Seven hundred and forty-three rounds were fired.

Third Brigade.—Ten 25-lb. bombs were dropped and 900 rounds fired.

Fifth Brigade.—Forty-eight 25-lb. bombs were dropped and 1,250 rounds fired.

Enemy Aircraft.—There was very little enemy aircraft activity in the morning, but at times in the afternoon enemy aircraft were quite active.

Second Lieut. F. Quigley, No. 70 Squadron, attacked a two-seater, which dived vertically after a burst of fire, but was followed and more shots fired into it, then, when it had gone down to 1,500 feet, Second Lieut. Quigley circled round and watched the pilot attempting to flatten out. This he did not succeed in doing, and the machine crashed into the ground and burst into flames.

December 27th.

Very little flying was possible owing to snow storms and high wind. Two reconnaissances were done by the First Brigade, two by the Second Brigade, four by the Third Brigade, and one by the Fifth Brigade, when Lieutenants Mackensen and Hurr, No. 35 Squadron, obtained useful information.

On the night of the 26th Major Portal and Lieutenant Nicholls, No. 16 Squadron, ranged one of our batteries on to a hostile battery by moonlight, and bursts were clearly visible and an explosion caused in the battery position.

Five thousand two hundred and seventy rounds were fired at ground targets, 63 photographs taken, and 136 bombs dropped, as follows:—

Night, December 26th–27th.

First Brigade.—No. 2 Squadron dropped thirty-six 25-lb. bombs on Carvin, twenty-three 25-lb. on Estevillers and ten 25-lb. on Avelin. No. 16 Squadron dropped twelve 25-lb. on billets.

Day, December 27th.

First Brigade.—No. 4 Squadron dropped twelve 25-lb. bombs on various targets. Corps Squadrons fired 750 rounds and Naval Squadron No. 8, 300 rounds at various targets.

Second Brigade.—Machines of this Brigade fired 2,750 rounds.

Third Brigade.—Nine 25-lb. bombs were dropped by Scout Squadrons and fourteen 25-lb. by Corps Squadrons. Five hundred and fifty rounds were fired at various targets.

Fifth Brigade.—Corps Squadrons of the Fifth Brigade fired 1,100 rounds at various ground targets.

Enemy Aircraft.—Enemy aircraft activity was slight all day. Flight Commander G. Price and Flight Sub-Lieut. H. Day, Naval Squadron No. 8, shot down one machine which appeared to fall out of control.

Second Lieuts. Hanna and Burnand, No. 35 Squadron, observed an enemy scout on our side of the line in the vicinity of Vermand, so they attacked it and forced it to land in our lines north of Vermand.

Miscellaneous.—With reference to the raid on Mannheim by the 41st Wing on the 24th instant, the "Daily Express," Geneva, states:—

> "The Kaiser and his Staff had a narrow escape during the British raid on Mannheim, the Kaiser's train passing through the station only one hour before the structure was partially wrecked by bombs. The line was destroyed some distance beyond the station. Bombs fell on the palace of the Palatinate and on the suspension bridge which crosses the Neckar. Both were badly damaged. A munition factory was blown up and a number of persons killed and injured. Heavy damage was done."

December 28th.

The weather was fine with the exception of on the front of the Fifth Brigade where snow fell, but in the afternoon a very strong north-easterly wind blew.

Two reconnaissances were carried out by the Second Brigade, five by the Third, and one by the Ninth Wing.

Artillery Co-operation.—With aeroplane observation 29 hostile batteries were successfully engaged for destruction, one gun-pit was destroyed, 12 damaged, 13 explosions, and two fires caused. Forty-eight active hostile batteries were reported by zone call.

Lieutenants Weil and Burnstein, No. 21 Squadron, worked with the 124th Siege Battery, which obtained two O.K.'s on a hostile battery, damaging two pits and causing three explosions.

One thousand two hundred and forty-five were taken, 5,200 rounds fired at ground targets and approximately five tons of bombs dropped, as follows:—

First Brigade.—On the night of the 27th/28th, No. 16 Squadron fired 640 rounds at searchlights and other targets. No. 2 Squadron dropped fifty-six 25-lb. bombs on Meurchin and 50 on Carvin. No. 5 Squadron dropped one 112-lb. on Carvin, and one 112-lb. and one 25-lb. on Vitry, also twelve 25-lb. bombs on Meurchin. No. 16 Squadron dropped fourteen 25-lb. bombs on Meurchin, four 25-lb. on Carvin, and three 25-lb. on Pont-à-Vendin.

On the 28th, No. 2 Squadron dropped sixteen 25-lb. bombs on various targets. No. 18 Squadron dropped eight 112-lb. bombs on Moncheaux Aerodrome and two 112-lb. on Annay.

Machines of the First Wing fired 1,400 rounds at ground targets and Naval No. 8 Squadron fired 950 rounds.

Second Brigade. — No. 57 Squadron dropped twenty-four 25-lb. bombs on Rumbeke Aerodrome, and machines of this Brigade fired 940 rounds.

Third Brigade. — Machines dropped thirty-eight 25-lb. bombs on various targets and fired 100 rounds.

Fifth Brigade. — Machines dropped twenty 25-lb. bombs and fired 270 rounds.

Ninth Wing. — No. 27 Squadron dropped six 112-bombs on Menin.

On the night of the 27/28th No. 101 Squadron dropped seventy-six 25-lb. bombs and fired 850 rounds. Twenty of the bombs were dropped on Rumbeke Aerodrome, 18 on Staden Aerodrome and sidings, and direct hits were obtained on buildings, railway and billets. Twelve bombs were dropped on Ledeghem, eight on hutments on either side of the Roulers-Menin railway line, which were hit; four on Moorslede; twelve on Roulers, where the railway and station were hit; one 25-lb. and one incendiary bomb on huts at Hooglede.

On the same night, No. 102 Squadron dropped forty 25-lb. bombs on Gheluwe, Comines, Wervicq and other targets, and one observer fired 50 rounds at an enemy machine.

Enemy Aircraft. — Enemy scouts were not particularly active, but a number of two-seaters crossed our lines.

Thirteen of his machines were brought down during the day, seven of which fell in our lines. Three of these were by anti-aircraft, which shot down one on the other side also, and five were driven down out of control. We had only three machines missing.

Lieutenant G. McElroy, No. 40 Squadron, observed a two-seater approaching the lines, so attacked and destroyed it.

A patrol of Naval No. 8 Squadron attacked a hostile scout, and Flight Sub-Lieut. W. Jordan shot it down out of control. Two more were shot down out of control; Flight Commander Price and Flight Sub-Lieut. Day accounting for one and Flight Sub-Lieut. W. Crundall for the other.

Pilots of No. 70 Squadron took part in a number of fights and destroyed three enemy aircraft. Second Lieut. F. Gorringe destroyed one of these, a second was destroyed by Second Lieut. G. Howsam and a third by Second Lieut. F. Hobson, who dived at one which Lieut. Seth-Smith had driven down. This machine, which was a two-seater, landed on its nose, when Second Lieut. Hobson fired another burst at it, after which it burst into flames and was seen to burn up.

Major A. D. Carter, No. 19 Squadron, secured a favourable position on an enemy aircraft's tail, which he followed down until he saw it fall out of control and crash.

Lieutenant J. Green and W. McMillan, No. 13 Squadron, saw a German aeroplane apparently doing photography and attacked it. This machine eventually landed in our lines west of Monchy-le-Preux, and on examination was found to have been hit by an anti-aircraft shell.

Second Lieuts. Robinson and Lamburn, No. 46 Squadron, attacked a two-seater which they shot down in flames and which broke to pieces before reaching the ground near Gouzeaucourt in our lines.

Captain J. B. McCudden, No. 56 Squadron, during one flight engaged four enemy aircraft and shot three of them down in our lines. The following is his report:—

"Left aerodrome at 1015 to look for enemy aircraft west of the lines. At 1110 I saw a Rumpler coming west over Boursies. I got into position at 75 yards, fired a short burst from both guns, when enemy aircraft at once went into a right-hand spiral dive and its right-hand wings fell off at about 17,000, and the wreckage fell in our lines north of Velu Wood at 1115. At 1130 saw a Rumpler going north over Haplincourt at 17,000. I secured a firing position and fired a good burst from both guns, when flames at once came from enemy aircraft's fuselage, and he went down in a right-hand flat spin and crashed in our lines near Flers (as near as I could judge), as I remained at 17,000 feet so as not to lose time by going down and having to climb up again. Enemy aircraft crashed about 1135. I now saw an L.V.G. being shelled by our anti-aircraft over Havrincourt at 16,000. Anti-aircraft fire did not stop until I was within range of enemy aircraft. I obtained a good position at fairly long range, fired a burst with the object of making him dive, which he did. Enemy aircraft dived very steeply (about 200 miles per hour) starting at about 16,000 feet, and at about 9,000 feet I fired another burst into enemy aircraft at 100 yards range, when flames issued from enemy aircraft's fuselage and then he broke up over Havrincourt Wood, the wreckage falling in our lines. The enemy aircraft had been diving so fast that the hostile observer could not fire, even if I gave him the chance. I climbed again at 1215, at 18,000 I saw an L.V.G. being shelled by our anti-aircraft over Lagnicourt. Enemy aircraft dived down east, and I caught up to him just east of the lines and fired a good burst from Lewis at 100 yards, when a small burst of flame came from enemy aircraft but at once went out again. Enemy aircraft dived steeply, kicking his rudder from side to side, and I last saw him gliding north-east over Marquion at 1220 at 9,000 feet, under control. Returned at 1225 as I had no more petrol."

Anti-aircraft of the First Army shot down an enemy machine which crashed near Auchy, and anti-aircraft of the Third Army shot one down at Saillisel, one at Tranlow and one at Monchy which a machine of No. 13 Squadron also attacked.

December 29th.

Low clouds and mist prevented much work being done.

Three reconnaissances were carried out by the Third Brigade, and two by the Fifth Brigade.

Nine long photographic reconnaissances were attempted by the Ninth Wing, but all proved unsuccessful owing to the weather. Eight hundred and one photographs were taken during the day (442 by the Third Brigade). One hundred and eighty-eight bombs dropped and 4,960 rounds fired at ground targets, as follows:—

First Brigade.—Eighteen 25-lb. bombs on various targets. (No. 4 Squadron). Thirteen 25-lb. bombs on various targets. (Corps Squadron). One thousand one hundred rounds fired by Corps Squadron. One thousand one hundred rounds fired by Naval Squadron No. 8.

Second Brigade. — Forty-eight 25-lb. bombs on Staden. (No. 57 Squadron). Five hundred rounds at various targets. Three hundred rounds on an active machine-gun, which was silenced. (No. 70 Squadron.)

Third Brigade.—Fifty-one 25-lb. bombs. Four hundred and sixty rounds.

Fifth Brigade.—Fifty-eight 25-lb. bombs. (Corps Squadrons.) Four hundred rounds. (No. 8 Squadron.) One thousand one hundred rounds. (No. 35 Squadron.)

With aeroplane observation, seven hostile batteries were successfully engaged for destruction, one gun-pit was destroyed and one fire caused.

Enemy aircraft activity was slight all day. Second Lieut. F. Westfield and Lieutenant Fenelon, No. 10 Squadron, were attacked by three enemy aircraft scouts. After considerable fighting, one of the enemy's machines was shot down completely out of control, and the R.E. 8 returned safely.

Pilots of No. 19 Squadron had considerable successful fighting, but had one machine missing. Major Carter shot one enemy aircraft down out of control, while Lieutenant Candy attacked another which was diving on Major Carter from behind, and shot it down out of control. Lieutenant Fairclough destroyed one and shot down a second out of control, and Lieutenant De Pencier hit one which fell out of control, while Captain Huskinson shot down two out of control.

Captain J. B. McCudden, No. 56 Squadron, brought down two enemy aircraft in our lines. The following are his reports:—

"Left aerodrome at 0900 and crossed the lines east of Gouzeaucourt at 0945 at 14,000. Saw three enemy aircraft two-seaters coming west. I dived on these, followed by my patrol, and drove an L.V.G. down from

13,500 to the ground, when enemy aircraft made a pretence of landing in our lines, but put his engine on again and made north-east at about 10 feet. I headed him west again, but he again turned east, so I fired another burst into him, and then he got into a flat spin, and crashed near Havrincourt at 0955. Climbed and only found two members of my patrol. I then approached four Albatross Scouts over Bois de Vancelles, who went down east. Several enemy aircraft two-seaters patrolling east of the Canal at Vendhuille at about 3,000, too low to engage. Returned 1050.

Second Report.—Left ground at 1125 to look for enemy aircraft west of the lines. At 1155, attacked an L.V.G. over Lagnicourt at 16,000. I fired a short burst into enemy aircraft at 100 yards, when water and steam came from enemy aircraft's centre section. Enemy aircraft dived very steeply, and by the time I caught up to enemy aircraft again he was to far east of the line to re-engage. Last saw him gliding down north over Haucourt at 4,000 at 1200 under control, but certainly damaged. At 1350 I dived on an L.V.G. over Gouzeau-court at 15,000. Enemy aircraft saw me and started a left-hand circle, the enemy aircraft gunner firing at long range. After half a dozen turns, aircraft pushed his nose down as we were drifting west. I now fired a drum of Lewis and 100 rounds of Vickers into him at 100 yards range, and then his right-hand wings fell off, and the wreckage fell in our lines north-east of Epéhy at 1355. Returned at 1405 as I had no more petrol. Enemy aircraft not very active west of the lines."

Honours and Awards.

The Distinguished Service Order.—Major A. D. Carter.

Bar to the Military Cross.—Captain C. T. Lally, M.C.

The Distinguished Conduct Medal.—No. 7756, First Air Mechanic A. Leyland.

December 30th.

No service flying was possible on account of unfavourable weather.

December 31st.

Low clouds and mist interfered with work.

Two reconnaissances were done by the First Brigade, one by the Second Brigade—Captain Martin and Second Lieut. Lomax, No. 53 Squadron—and five by the Third Brigade. A pilot of No. 53 Squadron fired 100 rounds at ground targets.

Sixteen 25-lb. bombs were dropped on various targets, and 200 rounds fired by the Third Brigade. Two of the bombs were seen to burst among massed infantry near Cambrai and caused many casualties.

S. WOOD, Captain,
Staff Officer.

Advanced Headquarters,
Royal Flying Corps,
2nd January 1918.

ROYAL FLYING CORPS COMMUNIQUÉ No. 121.

During the period under review, 1st to 7th January, we have claimed officially 24 enemy aircraft brought down and eight driven down out of control. Approximately 23 tons of bombs were dropped and 42,154 rounds fired at grounds targets. Eleven of our machines are missing.

January 1st, 1918.

The weather was fairly good for flying and four reconnaissances were carried out by the Third Brigade, one by the Fifth Brigade, and four long distance reconnaissances by Nos. 27 and 25 Squadrons.

With aeroplane observation 14 hostile batteries were successfully engaged for destruction, four gun-pits were destroyed, six damaged, one explosion and two fires caused, and 23 active hostile batteries were reported by zone call.

A total of 1,585 photographs were taken during the day, 4,750 rounds fired at ground targets, and approximately four tons of bombs dropped, as follows :—

Night, December 31st–1st January.

No. 9 Wing.—No. 101 Squadron dropped ninety-six 25-lb. bombs on billets at Stadenberg, Vyfwegen, Westroosebeke, Roulers, Menin, Staden, and Hooglede.

Captain Payne and Lieutenant Wardill bombed Staden with excellent results, obtaining four direct hits on the railway and completely demolishing one hut and a small house. The hut, before being demolished, had a light burning in it, thus giving away its position. 1,350 rounds were fired at lights on the roads and other targets.

No. 102 Squadron dropped eight 25-lb. bombs on hutments near La Bassée, and eight 25-lb. on a train, the rear portion of which was hit.

January 1st.

First Brigade.—No. 5 Squadron dropped twenty 25-lb. bombs and fired 150 rounds. Army Squadrons fired 1,200 rounds.

Second Brigade.—No. 57 Squadron dropped forty-four 25-lb. bombs on the ammunition dump at Bisseghem, and No. 69 Squadron fired 100 rounds.

Third Brigade.—Sixty-five 25-lb. bombs were dropped and 900 rounds fired.

Fifth Brigade.—No. 35 Squadron dropped twenty-two 25-lb. bombs and fired 500 rounds, and No. 8 Squadron dropped thirty-two 25-lb. bombs, and fired 450 rounds at various targets.

Ninth Wing.—No. 25 Squadron dropped six 112-lb. and thirty 25-lb. bombs on Ingelmunster Aerodrome.

Enemy Aircraft.—Enemy two-seaters were active.

Flight Commander Compston and Flight Sub-Lieut. Dixon, Naval Squadron No. 8, drove down an enemy scout apparently out of control, and in another patrol Commander Compston fought one, which he drove down. It was then attacked by Captain E. Mannock, No. 40 Squadron, and crashed in our lines at Fampoux. Three other pilots of Naval Squadron No. 8 fought a formation of scouts and drove one down apparently out of control.

Second Lieut. F. Gorringe, No. 70 Squadron, saw two enemy machines approaching the lines, so got into the sun and attacked one. Lieutenant C. Smith, of the same Squadron, also fired at this machine, and it eventually went down apparently on fire.

Another machine was driven down and appeared to be out of control by pilots of No. 23 and No. 60 Squadrons.

Second Lieut. Chick and Lieutenant Kincaird, No. 11 Squadron, were taking photographs when they saw an enemy scout, which they attacked and shot down out of control.

Captain A. M. Swyny and Second Lieut. A. Lyons, No. 8 Squadron, were flying towards the lines when they saw anti-aircraft shells bursting and then saw an enemy machine, which they attacked and shot down out of control.

D.H. 4's of No. 25 Squadron, when bombing, were attacked by seven enemy aircraft scouts. In the fighting three of the latter went down steeply, possibly out of control; one of these had been engaged by Captain Pearce and Second Lieut. Walsh, one by Second Lieuts. Pfeiffer and Thornhill, and the third by Lieutenant Green and Second Lieut. Gibson.

Anti-aircraft of the Fifth Army shot down a German machine, which fell in our lines.

Only one of our aeroplanes failed to return during the day.

January 2nd.

Thick mist and low clouds prevented much flying being done.

Three reconnaissances were carried out, one by the First, one by the Second, and one by the Third Brigade. Several long distance photographic reconnaissances were attempted by the Ninth Wing, but the weather was too bad to enable them to successfully accomplish anything. One hundred and twenty-five photographs were taken during the day, 2,500 rounds fired and forty-four 25-lb. bombs dropped, as follows:—

First Brigade.—No. 5 Squadron dropped twelve 25-lb. bombs and fired 130 rounds, and No. 43 Squadron fired 1,100 rounds.

Second Brigade.—No. 21 Squadron fired 400 rounds.

Third Brigade.—Dropped twenty-two 25-lb. bombs and fired 100 rounds.

Fifth Brigade.—No. 8 Squadron dropped ten 25-lb. bombs and fired 220 rounds, and No. 35 Squadron fired 450 rounds.

Enemy Aircraft.—Enemy aircraft were not active.

Flight Commander Price, Naval Squadron No. 8, picked out one of seven Albatross Scouts which his patrol encountered, and after manœuvring for position got in a good burst from about 50 yards range from behind the tail of the enemy machine, and it immediately burst into flames and crashed.

January 3rd.

A considerable amount of work was done.

Thirteen successful reconnaissances were carried out; three by the Second Brigade, three by the Third Brigade, two by the Fifth, and five by the Ninth Wing.

Lieutenants Williams and Jeffrey, No. 69 Squadron, Captain Gardner and Second Lieut. Durham, No. 7 Squadron, obtained valuable information. Pilots of Nos. 7, 9, and 69 Squadrons also made useful reports. Lieutenants Hill and Balfour, No. 8 Squadron, did very good work, and the information they obtained and the 72 photographs which they took proved of considerable value.

The following photographic reconnaissances were carried out by No. 25 Squadron:—

Captain C. T. Lalley and Second Lieut. Campbell-Martin, No. 25 Squadron, photographed Scheldewendeke Aerodrome and other areas. The machine, when over Brussels, was pursued by enemy aircraft, but they were unable to overtake it.

Second Lieutenants Wright and Hobbs, of the same squadron, took 54 photographs of the Audenarde–Brussels–Ath area.

Lieutenant Wensley and Second Lieut. Matson, No. 25 Squadron, took 24 photographs of the area: Ath–Mons–Maubeuge–Le Cateau and of Grandglise Aerodrome.

Captains Jardine and Graham exposed 54 plates of Iwuy–Quesnoy–Foret de Mormal.

Artillery Co-operation.—With aeroplane observation 45 hostile batteries were successfully engaged for destruction and five were neutralised. Five gun-pits were destroyed, 19 damaged, 17 explosions and 11 fires caused, and 76 active hostile batteries were reported by zone call.

Captain Martin and Lieutenant Lomax, No. 53 Squadron, with the 218th Siege Battery, obtained three O.K.'s on a hostile battery, causing a fire and a large explosion. After this work they attacked an enemy balloon.

Lieutenants Jeffrey and Vernon, No. 15 Squadron, ranged the 48th Siege Battery on to a hostile battery, where one gun-pit was destroyed and two damaged.

Lieutenants McPherson and Briggs, No. 35 Squadron, ranged the 228th Siege Battery on a hostile battery, where two pits were destroyed and a third damaged.

One thousand eight hundred and sixty photographs were taken during the day, 5,087 rounds fired at ground targets and approximately three tons of bombs dropped, as follows :—

First Brigade.—No. 18 Squadron dropped twenty-four 25-lb. bombs on various billets, and twenty-nine 25-lb. bombs were dropped by Corps Squadrons.

One thousand and fifty rounds were fired and 315 photographs taken.

Second Brigade.—No. 57 Squadron dropped forty-eight 25-lb. bombs on Ledeghem Railway Junction, and twelve 25-lb. bombs on hutments north of Houthulst Forest and on Staden.

Five hundred and fifty four photographs were taken.

Third Brigade.—Seventy-nine 25-lb. bombs were dropped by low-flying scouts and corps machines on various targets.

Two thousand two hundred and ten rounds were fired and 619 photographs taken.

Fifth Brigade.—No. 8 Squadron dropped forty-two 25-lb. bombs and fired 1,027 rounds.

No. 35 Squadron dropped sixteen 25-lb. bombs, fired 700 rounds and took 174 photographs.

Ninth Wing.—On the night, 2nd–3rd, machines of No. 102 Squadron dropped two 230-lb. and two 25-lb. bombs on Carvin.

During the day No. 25 Squadron dropped six 112-lb. and ten 25-lb. bombs on Scheldewendeke Aerodrome, while No. 27 Squadron attacked Maria Aalter Aerodrome, on which they dropped three 112-lb. and eight 25-lb. bombs.

Enemy Aircraft.—Enemy aircraft activity was not very pronounced, though more single-seaters were encountered than during the last few days.

A patrol of Naval Squadron No. 8, consisting of Flight Commander Compston, Flight Lieut. Jordan, and Flight Sub-Lieut. Dennett, attacked an enemy two-seater, which they drove down out of control and which was seen to crash. Flight Commander Compston attacked another two-seater, which he shot down out of control.

Captain R. Chidlaw-Roberts and Lieutenant Cunningham, No. 60 Squadron, attacked a two-seater, which was seen by anti-aircraft to fall in flames.

Second Lieut. F. Gorringe, No. 70 Squadron, engaged a hostile machine, which he drove down until it fell out of control and crashed, and Second Lieut. F. Quigley, of the same squadron, shot down a two-seater out of control.

A formation of Nieuport Scouts of No. 29 Squadron attacked a scout which Captain W. Molesworth shot down out of control, and another was engaged and driven down out of control by Second Lieuts. L. Tims and F. Williams. Captain H. Rusby attacked an enemy balloon which was pulled down smoking.

While on photographic work Second Lieuts. W. Beaver and H. Easton, No. 20 Squadron, attacked a scout, which they shot down out of control and which crashed and burst into flames.

Lieutenant H. M. Beck, No. 3 Squadron, attacked a two-seater and shot it down out of control.

Captain H. Maddocks, No. 54 Squadron, engaged an enemy two-seater, which he shot down in flames, and Second Lieut. A. Beauchamp-Proctor, No. 84 Squadron, shot down a two-seater out of control, while a third was shot down in flames by Lieutenant J. Larson of the same Squadron, who picked it off the tail of another pilot.

Bombing machines of No. 27 Squadron had hard fighting and drove down two enemy machines, one was hit by Second Lieut. W. Henney and Lieutenant P. Driver, the other by Second Lieut. C. Gannaway and Lieutenant J. Proger, while a third was shot down out of control by Lieutenant E. Green and Corporal R. Allan, No. 25 Squadron, who were returning alone when four scouts attacked them.

Captain K. Park and Lieutenant J. Robertson, No. 48 Squadron, were taking photographs when six enemy aircraft attacked them. After hard fighting they shot down one scout out of control and evaded the rest, although the Bristol's engine was hit.

January 4th.

The mist interfered with artillery work.

Two reconnaissances were carried out by the First Brigade, two by the Second, four by the Third, and two long distance reconnaissances by the Ninth Wing.

Lieutenants Phillips and Helsby, No. 35 Squadron, fired 400 rounds at an active hostile machine gun, silencing it. They also fired 400 rounds into Bellicourt and 100 rounds into enemy trenches from 1,000 feet.

With aeroplane observation 31 hostile batteries were successfully engaged for destruction, five gun-pits were destroyed, 16 damaged, 17 explosions and six fires caused, and 61 active hostile batteries were reported by zone call.

Major Garrod and Lieutenant Carswell, No. 13 Squadron, carried out an experimental night shoot with the 123rd Siege Battery.

With balloon observation five hostile batteries were successfully engaged for destruction and 21 other targets dealt with.

A total of 1,594 photographs were taken, 547 bombs dropped and 9,500 rounds fired, as follows:—

First Brigade.—On the night of the 3rd/4th, No. 2 Squadron, dropped forty-four 25-lb. bombs on Oignies and forty-four 25-lb. bombs on Courriéres.

On the 4th, No. 2 Squadron dropped twenty-four 25-lb. bombs on various targets; No. 4 Squadron dropped 18 and No. 5 Squadron dropped 17 on various targets. No. 18 Squadron dropped eight 25-lb. on Billy Montigny and Douai Railway Stations. Five hundred rounds were fired by the First Wing and 1,900 rounds by the Tenth Wing.

Second Brigade.—No. 57 Squadron dropped twelve 25-lb. bombs on Ledeghem, 12 on Roulers, 12 on Menin, 12 on Rumbeke Aerodrome, and fired 1,290 rounds.

Third Brigade dropped ninety-six 25-lb. bombs and fired 2,170 rounds.

Fifth Brigade.—No. 8 Squadron dropped fourteen 25-lb. bombs and fired 240 rounds, and No. 35 Squadron dropped four 25-lb. bombs and fired 1,050 rounds.

Ninth Wing.—On the night of the 3rd/4th, No. 101 Squadron dropped twelve 25-lb. bombs on Gontrode, 72 on Ramegnies Chin, obtaining two direct hits on sheds, 24 on Ingelmunster, 24 on the railway line at Eschem and Blandian, and fired 2,350 rounds into the hangars of the aerodromes. No. 102 Squadron dropped seventy-four 25-lb. bombs on hostile batteries, railway junctions and aerodromes, including Maria Aalter, Scheldewendeke and Ennetieres.

On the 4th, No. 27 Squadron dropped four 112-lb. and twenty-four 25-lb. bombs on Douai Railway Junction.

Forty-first Wing.—On the night of the 3rd/4th, 10 machines of No. 100 Squadron left the ground at 5.30 p.m. to attack the factories and railways in the neighbourhood of Mazieres. The temperature on the ground was minus 27 degrees centigrade, and consequently a considerable amount of trouble was experienced with engines. Eventually five of the machines crossed the lines, but only two reached the chief objective—a factory—which was brilliantly lit up. Two 230 lb. and eight 25-lb. bombs were dropped, and good bursts were observed, a very large explosion taking place close to the blast furnaces. One 230-lb. and six 25-lb. bombs were dropped on a railway station just north of Metz, probably Woippy, and one 230-lb. and six 25-lb. bombs on a railway junction south of Metz, probably Saint Privat. All machines returned.

Enemy Aircraft.—Enemy aircraft were not so active as on the previous day, with the exception of in the neighbourhood of Lens, where activity was very pronounced.

Four machines of Naval Squadron No. 8 had several combats, and in one of these Flight Sub-Lieuts. Jordan, Johnstone and Dennett shot down a two-seater out of control. A second patrol shot down another two-seater out of control, while a third patrol shot down a scout out of control.

Second Lieut. F. Gorringe, No. 70 Squadron, fought a German pilot, who manœuvred his machine skilfully, but was beaten and his machine fell in flames. In another patrol Second Lieut. Gorringe and Lieutenant H. Soulby attacked two two-seater enemy aircraft, one of which they drove down and saw crashed on the ground. After this Second Lieut. Gorringe attacked two more enemy aircraft and drove them east.

A patrol of No. 65 Squadron engaged four enemy two-seaters and several scouts and the fight lasted for half-an-hour. Captain J. Gilmour shot down a two-seater in flames and a scout out of control. He was then attacked from behind, but succeeded in out-manœuvring the scout which attacked, and destroyed it. Second Lieut. G. Knocker, of the same squadron, shot down a scout out of control, and Lieutenant E. Eaton drove one down out of control and another down damaged.

A formation of Spads of No. 23 Squadron dived to the assistance of R.E.8's which were being attacked, and Captain W. Fry shot down a scout, which crashed, while Second Lieut. C. Fowler shot one down, which fell in flames and broke to pieces before reaching the ground.

Second Lieut. G. Moore, No. 1 Squadron, fought a scout, which he eventually destroyed.

No. 20 Squadron also had a number of combats. In one, Second Lieuts. G. Jooste and S. Masding shot down a Scout, which crashed. While on a photographic reconnaissance, Second Lieut. R. Makepeace and Captain J. Hedley were attacked by five Scouts and shot one down completely out of control.

Two other enemy machines were driven down out of control, one by Second Lieuts. R. Pohlmann and O. Hinson, No. 25 Squadron, who were attacked by seven enemy aircraft Scouts while doing a photographic reconnaissance, and the other by Second Lieuts. G. Walker and W. Jones, No. 35 Squadron, who were also attacked while engaged on similar work.

Honours and Awards.

Bar to Distinguished Service Order. — Captain J. B. McCudden, D.S.O., M.C.

The Military Cross.—Second Lieut. F. G. Quigley.

January 5th.

Very little work was possible owing to low clouds and mist.

Two successful reconnaissances were carried out by Bristol Fighters of No. 11 Squadron, and one by a Corps machine.

One hostile battery was successfully engaged for destruction by artillery of the First Army, with aeroplane observation, and eight active hostile batteries were reported by zone call.

Thirty-eight photographs were taken by the Fifth Brigade, fifty-seven 25-lb. bombs dropped and 4,583 rounds fired, as follows:—

> First Brigade.—Eight bombs and 650 rounds.
> Second Brigade.—347 rounds.
> Third Brigade.—Forty-five bombs and 2,547 rounds.
> Fifth Brigade.—Four bombs and 1,044 rounds.

On the night of the 4th/5th, a machine of No. 101 Squadron dropped eight 25-lb. bombs in the vicinity of Wavrin. Four were seen to hit hutments and four fell on the railway line.

Forty-first Wing. — On the night of the 4th/5th, nine machines of No. 100 Squadron again left to bomb the factories at Maizieres, but owing to the low clouds and heavy mist some of the machines failed to find the target and dropped their bombs, as follows:—

> One 230-lb. and six 25-lb. bombs on the railway station at Marly.
> Three 230-lb., sixteen 25-lb. bombs and one phosphorous bomb of Maizieres.
> One 230-lb. and six 25-lb. bombs on a railway junction between Woippy and Devant-les-Ponts.
> One 230 lb. and six 25-lb. on Courcelles Railway Junction.
> One 230-lb. and six 25-lb. on a railway bridge 4 miles south of Maizieres.
> One 230-lb., four 25-lb., and one phosphorous bomb on a train at Wurtemberg Junction.

All machines returned.

Enemy Aircraft.—Enemy aircraft were inactive. One scout was shot down out of control by Second Lieut. M. Gonne, No. 54 Squadron.

January 6th.

Although misty, the weather was fine and a considerable amount of work was done.

Fifteen reconnaissances were carried out—one by the First Brigade, six by the Second, when Lieutenants Walker and Playford, No. 9 Squadron, Lieutenants Jones and Johnson, No. 21 Squadron, and pilots of No. 10 and 69 Squadrons made valuable reports.

Two reconnaissances were carried out by Bristol Fighters of No. 11 Squadron, 3rd Brigade, one by No. 8 Squadron and another by No. 35 Squadron of the Fifth Brigade, and four by No. 25 Squadron of the Ninth Wing.

On the night of the 3rd/4th, Captain L. Payne and Lieutenant H. Wardill, No. 101 Squadron, carried out a special long reconnaissance, while another was done by Captain G. Talbot-Willcox and Second Lieut. F. Lyll of the same squadron.

With aeroplane observation 39 hostile batteries were successfully engaged for destruction. Six gun-pits were destroyed, 15 damaged, 14 explosions and six fires caused, and 39 active hostile batteries were reported by zone call.

Lieutenants Philcox and Fenton, No. 8 Squadron, worked with 110th Siege Battery, which damaged a pit and caused two explosions in a hostile battery where a large fire and an explosion occurred shortly afterwards.

Nine hundred and twenty-six photographs were taken, 12,594 rounds fired at ground targets from low altitudes, and 318 bombs dropped, as follows:—

First Brigade.—No. 18 Squadron dropped four 25-lb. bombs on Perenchies. Forty-four 25-lb. bombs were also dropped on and 4,459 rounds fired at various ground targets.

Second Brigade.—No. 57 Squadron dropped forty 25-lb. bombs. Two thousand five hundred and seventeen rounds were fired at various ground targets.

Third Brigade.—Eighty-five 25-lb. bombs were dropped on and 2,910 rounds fired at various targets.

Fifth Brigade.—Fifty-one 25-lb. bombs were dropped on various targets and 2,177 rounds fired, of which 2,370 were by No. 35 Squadron.

Ninth Wing.—No. 27 Squadron dropped four 112-lb. bombs on Cambrai.

On the night of the 5th/6th No. 101 Squadron dropped forty-five 25-lb. bombs, two phosphorus and three incendiary bombs on Ramegnies Chin Aerodrome and St. Andre engine shops and fired 1,000 rounds at ground targets. No. 102 Squadron dropped forty 25-lb. bombs on Roulers, Courtrai, billets at Menin and Comines and on Gontrode, where eight bombs were seen to hit the objective.

Forty-first Wing.—On the night of the 5th/6th Naval "A" Squadron dropped twelve 112-bombs on Courcelles, and No. 100 Squadron dropped six 230-lb., thirty-two 25-lb. and two phosphorus bombs on Conflans and on a railway station near there. A large explosion and fire were caused.

Enemy Aircraft.—Enemy aircraft were fairly active. While engaged on photography over Valenciennes Second Lieut. Stewart and Lieutenant Mackay, No. 18 Squadron, were attacked by five enemy scouts. One scout was shot down completely out of control, but unfortunately the camera and plates of the De Haviland 4 were completely destroyed by bullets. Another De Haviland 4 of the same squadron, in which were Second Lieuts. Fenn and Priestman, was attacked by seven scouts, and this pilot and observer fought for 20 minutes before the scouts were evaded and one shot down out of control.

Pilots of Naval Squadron No. 8 fought 10 scouts and Flight Commander Compston shot one down out of control. While in another patrol Flight Commander Price destroyed a two-seater, and later in the day Flight Sub-Lieut. Day shot down a two-seater, which also crashed.

Second Lieuts. Green and Wilson, No. 57 Squadron, shot down a scout apparently out of control, and Sergeant Clayton and Second Lieut. Slcot, of the same squadron, who were attacked by eight scouts, also shot one down out of control.

Second Lieuts. Beaver and Easton, No. 20 Squadron, shot down one enemy machine out of control, while a second was shot down out of control by Captain Huskinson, No. 19 Squadron.

Captain J. Payne, No. 29 Squadron, Captain W. Fry, No. 23 Squadron, and Second Lieut. Quigley, No. 70 Squadron, each destroyed an enemy machine. The machine shot down by Captain Fry fell in our lines. In one of the fights Second Lieut. F. Gorringe, No. 70 Squadron, assisted in the destruction of a machine.

Lieuts. F. McCall and F. Farrington, No. 13 Squadron, were engaged on artillery work when they were attacked by an Albatross scout. The observer opened fire at close range, and the German scout crashed into the wire on the enemy's side near Noyelles.

January 7th.

Very little flying was done owing to bad weather.

Four reconnaissances were carried out by Nos. 7, 10, 21 and 69 Squadrons and much valuable information was obtained.

With aeroplane observation nine hostile batteries were successfully engaged for destruction, five gun-pits were damaged, four explosions and two fires caused.

Captain Duigan and Lieutenant Biddle, No. 69 Squadron, with the 155th Siege Battery obtained direct hits on three enemy gun-pits and caused an explosion in one of them.

In the evening of the 6th inst., Lieutenant Corsan and Lieutenant Munro, No. 15 Squadron, worked with the 48th Siege Battery, which destroyed two gun-pits, damaged a third, and exploded ammunition of a hostile battery. Lieutenants Douglas and Haddow of the same squadron, worked for $3\frac{3}{4}$ hours with the 56th Siege Battery, which destroyed a pit and badly damaged the whole of an enemy battery position.

Twenty-eight plates were exposed during the day and 3,140 rounds fired at ground targets.

Enemy Aircraft.—Enemy aircraft were not active. A two-seater was shot down out of control by Lieut. F. Hobson, No. 70 Squadron. Second Lieuts. R. Nixon and E. Church, No. 11

Squadron, were attacked by seven hostile scouts and they shot one down completely out of control.

Honours and Awards.

Bar to Military Cross.—Captain C. A. Stevens, M.C.

Headquarters,
Royal Flying Corps,
9th January 1918.

S. WOOD, Captain,
Staff Officer.

ROYAL FLYING CORPS COMMUNIQUÉ.—No. 122.

During the period under review, 8th to 14th January (inclusive), we have claimed officially 13 enemy aircraft brought down and six driven down out of control. Approximately 13 tons of bombs were dropped, and 33,098 rounds fired at ground targets. Nine of our machines are missing.

January 8th.

Very little work was possible owing to snow-storms.

One reconnaissance was carried out by the Second Brigade (No. 57 Squadron), two by the Third Brigade (No. 11 Squadron), and two by the Fifth Brigade (Nos. 8 and 35 Squadrons).

One thousand three hundred and forty-two rounds were fired at ground targets and 92 bombs dropped, as follows:—

First Brigade.—No. 5 Squadron dropped four 25-lb. bombs.

Third Brigade.—Twenty-two 25-lb. bombs were dropped and 97 rounds fired.

Fifth Brigade.—Nos. 8 and 34 Squadrons dropped sixteen 25-lb. bombs: No. 8 Squadron fired 445 rounds, No. 35 Squadron, 150, and No. 84 Squadron, 50.

There were no combats.

January 9th.

On the 9th the weather was fine during the morning, but in the afternoon snow stopped flying.

Five reconnaissances were carried out by the First Brigade, two by the Second Brigade, when Lieutenants Walker and Playford, No. 9 Squadron, and Lieutenant Abell and Captain Eyden, No. 21 Squadron, obtained useful information, and two were done by Nos. 8 and 52 Squadrons of Fifth Brigade.

With aeroplane observation, 39 hostile batteries were successfully engaged for destruction, and 17 were neutralised. Four gun pits were destroyed, 11 damaged, 10 explosions and six fires caused, and 15 hostile batteries were reported by zone call.

Eight hundred and sixty-eight photographs were taken, 3,050 rounds fired at ground targets, and 136 bombs dropped, as follows:—

First Brigade.—No. 40 Squadron dropped forty-four 25-lb. bombs and fired 250 rounds at various ground targets. Corps squadrons fired 620 rounds.

Second Brigade.—Six hundred and ninety rounds were fired at various targets, 60 of which were by No. 10 Squadron.

Third Brigade.—Sixty 25-lb. bombs were dropped and 420 rounds fired at ground targets.

Fifth Brigade.—No. 8 Squadron dropped twelve 25-lb. bombs, No. 35 Squadron twenty 25-lb. bombs and fired 500 rounds. No. 84 Squadron fired 180 and No. 8 Squadron 390 rounds.

Enemy Aircraft.—Activity was not as pronounced as usual during the fine period; only a few combats took place. Lieutenant E. Peverell, No. 70 Squadron, saw a two-seater, at which he dived and opened fire. The German pilot at once dived, and in attempting to land, his machine turned over on its nose and crashed.

Second Lieuts. Kingsbury and Dorey, No. 21 Squadron, while on photography, were attacked by enemy aircraft scouts, and they shot one down apparently out of control. Another machine of this squadron was engaged in the same work when it was attacked by seven enemy aircraft. Captain G. Zimmer enabled his observer, Second Lieut. H. Somerville, to fire at close range into one of the scouts, and it immediately fell out of control and in flames.

Captain W. Patrick, No. 1 Squadron, shot down a two-seater out of control, and Captain J. Payne, No. 29 Squadron, fought a two-seater, which he drove down apparently out of control, but could not follow it down owing to three scouts attacking him.

Captain McCudden, No. 56 Squadron, attacked two enemy aircraft, and the following is his account:—

"Crossed lines at 1040 over Flesquieres at 14,000 feet. At about 1105 attacked two two-seaters over Bourlon Wood at 12,000 feet. I engaged a new type enemy aircraft at 50 yards range, but could not see enemy aircraft through my Aldis sight owing to water freezing on the lens, so had to sight by tracer. Enemy aircraft then went down in a spiral with petrol or water issuing from him, and I last saw him gliding down under control north of Raillencourt at about 500 feet at 1110.

"At 1120 drove an Albatross Scout away from over Ribecourt. At 1130 attacked an L.V.G. over Graincourt at 9,000 feet, and after a short burst from both guns, enemy aircraft's engine stopped and he started coming west, after which he did a flat spiral glide. I got under his tail again and fired at close range, but Vickers now got a No. 4 and Lewis finished drum, but enemy aircraft continued to go down steeply east, and finally hit the ground in a fast glide down wind."

A patrol of No. 41 Squadron met five scouts and a two-seater which they attacked, but the scouts immediately dived away east. The pilot, however, succeeded in catching up the two-seater and shot it down completely out of control.

Lieutenant R. Dodds and Second Lieutenant W. Hart, No. 48 Squadron, were taking photographs when three enemy air craft attacked. One two-seater was shot down out of control. Shortly afterwards they engaged three scouts and shot down another out of control.

January 10th.

A good deal of flying was done in spite of low clouds and a strong wind.

Two reconnaissances were carried out by the First Brigade, two by the Second, three by the Third, and two by the Fifth Brigade.

With aeroplane observation, 29 hostile batteries were successfully engaged for destruction, 17 being by the Second Brigade; two gun-pits were destroyed, seven damaged, 11 explosions and five fires caused, and 86 active hostile batteries were reported by zone call.

Second Lieut. Nutt and Lieutenant Baker, No. 10 Squadron, carried out a successful shoot on Dadizeele Church, on which two direct hits were obtained by the 148th Siege Battery, which afterwards made a direct hit on a hostile battery with the same observation.

Three hundred and twenty-three photographs were taken, 6,416 rounds fired at ground targets, and 166 bombs dropped, as follows :—

First Brigade.—(No. 40 Squadron)—Twenty-nine 25-lb. bombs, 36 photographs, 600 rounds. (Corps Squadrons)—One hundred and sixty rounds.

Second Brigade.—(No. 57 Squadron)—Fifty-six 25-lb. bombs on Deerlyck Ammunition Dump. (Nos. 21 and 69 Squadrons)—Eighteen 25-lb. bombs, 251 photographs, 1,676 rounds.

Third Brigade.—Thirty-two 25-lb. bombs, 36 photographs, 2,200 rounds.

Fifth Brigade.—(No. 8 Squadron)—Eighteen 25-lb. bombs. (No. 35 Squadron)—Thirteen 25-lb. bombs. (No. 8 Squadron)—730 rounds. (No. 35 Squadron)—1,050 rounds.

Enemy Aircraft.—Captain Stevenson and Lieutenant Rosborough, No. 16 Squadron, were on artillery work when they were attacked by five enemy aircraft scouts, but returned safely after shooting one down apparently out of control.

Lieutenant H. Symons, No. 65 Squadron, was testing his engine when he saw two enemy aircraft diving at an R.E. 8, so he dived at one and shot it down completely out of control and drove the other away.

January 11th.

Very little flying was done owing to low clouds and the high wind.

A reconnaissance was carried out by Second Lieut. Skinner and Lieutenant Johnson, No. 21 Squadron, and a dawn reconnaissance was carried out by No. 8 Squadron.

Twelve photographs were taken and sixteen 25-lb. bombs dropped.

Five active hostile batteries were reported by zone call.

On the night of the 9th–10th, Captain E. Wilcox, and 2nd Air Mechanic Rennie, No. 101 Squadron, left the ground at 1720 to test the weather. Having reached a 1,000 feet the pilot decided to cross the lines, although the weather was getting worse and the wind stronger. He flew to Menin, on which place he dropped eight 25-lb. bombs, and then turned in order to re-cross the lines.

"He had a dead head-wind against which it was practically impossible to make any way, the wind having a velocity of about 50 miles per hour. The hostile anti-aircraft soon realised the difficulties with which the machine had to contend and were not slow to take advantage of it. Owing to the very high wind the machine drifted by Lille in spite of efforts to prevent it, and immediately a heavy barrage of machine guns and anti-aircraft guns, firing tracer and burning shells ('flaming onions') was opened up at it. This lasted for some considerable time as the machine was unable to get away. The machine having been fitted with wireless, the aerodrome from time to time received messages from it and these proved to be of the greatest assistance . . By this means intimation was received that bombs had been dropped and the whereabouts and condition of the machine. The aeroplane still continued to drift south, and Captain Wilcox was unable to do anything to prevent it. For a short time he was lost, and a message was received asking for rockets. These were fired, and the assistance of the searchlight section (anti-aircraft) was asked for. They put on their lights, which proved to be very useful to the pilot. By this time another message was received, stating that the machine was near Bethune and being shelled heavily by our own anti-aircraft guns in spite of it having fired the colour of the night. Eventually No. 23 Lighthouse was reached and the pilot shortly after saw the aerodrome."

The Squadron Commander says: "This flight is in
" my opinion the finest that any night-flying pilot has
" yet put up. It was impossible for Captain Wilcox to
" go higher than 2,000 feet as the wind above was

" 90 miles per hour (viz., 30 miles per hour faster than
" the speed of the machine). Captain Wilcox's machine
" was very badly hit, both while on this and the other
" side of the lines."

Honours and Awards.

The Military Cross.—Second Lieut. (T/Captain) H. A. Smith.

January 12th.

Low clouds and wind greatly interfered with work.

Two successful reconnaissances were carried out by the First Brigade, two by the Second, when Captain Burgess and Lieutenant Durham, No. 7 Squadron, and Lieutenants Herbert and Taylor, No. 69 Squadron, made valuable reports.

No. 11 Squadron (Third Brigade) carried out two successful reconnaissances, and Nos. 8, 35, and 48 Squadrons (Fifth Brigade) carried out one each.

With aeroplane observation, 19 hostile batteries were successfully engaged for destruction and 24 neutralised. Of the former, 11 were by the First Brigade and seven by the Fifth.

The 223rd Siege Battery, with observation by Lieutenants George and Kniveton, No. 35 Squadron, obtained four O.K.'s on a hostile battery. Two explosions were caused and a pit damaged in another hostile battery by the 294th Siege Battery which had been ranged by Lieutenants Monk and Channing, No. 8 Squadron.

Fifty-nine photographs were taken during the day, 8,014 rounds fired at ground targets and 165 bombs dropped, as follows:—

First Brigade.—(1st Wing)—Thirty-two 25-lb. bombs, 44 photographs. (10th Wing)—3,450 rounds.

Second Brigade.—(No. 69 Squadron)—Eight 25-lb. bombs. (No. 53 Squadron)—Two 25-lb. bombs. (No. 69 Squadron)—650 rounds.

Third Brigade.—Fifty-eight 25-lb. bombs, 10 photographs, 1,097 rounds.

Fifth Brigade.—(No. 8 Squadron)—Thirty-one 25-lb. bombs, 915 rounds, five photographs. (No. 35 Squadron)—Thirty-four 25-lb. bombs, 1,900 rounds.

Enemy Aircraft.—Enemy aircraft was not active and his scouts kept well east of the lines.

Honours and Awards.

Distinguished Service Cross.—Flight Commander G. W. Price, R.N.A.S.

Military Cross.—Second Lieut. A. C. B. Harrison, Captain L. G. S. Payne, Lieutenant (temporary Captain) G. Talbot-Willcox.

January 13*th.*

The weather was mainly fine, and a large amount of flying was done by all brigades.

Ten successful reconnaissances were carried out, one by the First Brigade, two by the Second Brigade, two by the Fifth Brigade, four by the Third Brigade, and one by the Ninth Wing.

Ten long-distance photographic reconnaissances were attempted by the 9th Wing, but all except one proved unsuccessful owing to clouds.

With aeroplane observation, 239 hostile batteries were successfully engaged for destruction, 15 neutralized, two gun-pits were destroyed and 12 damaged, 11 explosions and five fires were caused, and 54 hostile batteries reported by zone call.

One thousand six hundred and sixty-seven plates were exposed, 421 bombs dropped, and 10,889 rounds fired, as follows :—

First Brigade.—No. 18 Squadron dropped four 25 lb. bombs on Pont-à-Vendin ; First Wing dropped sixty-nine 25-lb. bombs and fired 135 rounds, and Tenth Wing fired 1,850 rounds.

Second Brigade.—No. 57 Squadron dropped sixty-four 25-lb. bombs on Ledeghem ammunition dump ; No. 65 Squadron dropped forty-four 25-lb. bombs on Ledeghem ammunition dump ; Second Wing dropped sixty-two 25-lb. bombs ; No. 32 Squadron fired 50 rounds at a hostile balloon, which was hauled down ; No. 70 Squadron fired 650 rounds at German infantry trying to extinguish a fire, and Second Wing fired 2,608 rounds.

Third Brigade.—No. 49 Squadron dropped six 112-lb. bombs on Marquion. One hundred and four 25-lb. bombs were dropped, and 2,725 rounds at various targets.

Fifth Brigade.—No. 8 Squadron dropped forty-one 25-lb. bombs and fired 2,321 rounds, and No. 35 Squadron dropped twenty-two 25-lb. bombs and fired 550 rounds.

Ninth Wing.—No. 27 Squadron dropped five 25-lb. bombs on Deynze Railway Junction.

Enemy aircraft were extremely active. Lieutenant McElroy, No. 40 Squadron, shot down out of control an enemy two-seater near Pont-à-Vendin. Captain Tudhope of the same squadron attacked a D.F.W. in the vicinity of Hulloch. He fired about 120 rounds into him, and the enemy aircraft went down steeply out of control.

Captain Robinson and Second Lieut. Venmore, No. 57 Squadron (Second Brigade), while on photography were attacked by 10 Albatross Scouts. The observer fired at one under its tail, and it went down rolling and spinning. He then fired at another enemy aircraft, which burst into flames and fell to pieces. The observer then took 12 more photographs, but the pilot was forced to return, as his machine was becoming unmanageable, two flying wires, rudder control and petrol pipe having been shot away.

Second Lieuts. Colville-Jones and Crowe, No. 20 Squadron, while on O.P. dived on an enemy aircraft two-seater; they fired 150 rounds, and the enemy aircraft went down emitting smoke and crashed.

Captain McCudden, No. 56 Squadron, reports as follows:—

"Left aerodrome at 0840 to pursue enemy aircraft. At 0935 I saw a L.V.G. going north over Belinglise at 8,000. I glided from in the sun and secured a firing position at 50 yards without being seen, fired a short burst from both guns, when enemy aircraft went into a right hand spiral glide, which got steeper, and he then crashed just north of Lehancourt at 62B, H31B at 0940. Went north and saw two D.F.W.'s being shelled at about 5,000 feet north-east of Ronnsoy at 0950. Engaged one at close range and fired a long burst from both guns. Enemy aircraft went down steeply, emitting smoke and water, and hit the ground in a vertical dive just east of Vendhuille at 57B, S27a as far as I could judge, as I could not pay too much attention to it as I was being engaged by remaining D.F.W. This enemy aircraft continued to circle round and got well east of the line like this, so I left him. Went north and saw two L.V.G.'s going west over Epehy at 1000. I engaged one at 200 yards range at 9,000 feet and fired 200 rounds of Vickers into him. Enemy aircraft stalled, went down in a vertical dive, left-hand wings fell off, and enemy aircraft then burst into flames and crashed into our lines just east of Lampire at 62B, F16b at 1015. At 1030 had an indecisive engagement with a D.F.W. over Gonnelieu, but enemy aircraft got away. Returned 1105."

Second Lieuts. Rough and Dreschfield, No. 49 Squadron, attacked a two-seater and fired a burst of 20 rounds; the enemy aircraft turned away climbing. A triplane then fired on them, but Second Lieutenant Dreschfield fired a burst, and the triplane turned over and went down in a spin completely out of control.

An offensive patrol of machines of No. 84 Squadron (Fifth Brigade) encountered several two-seater enemy machines, two of which were destroyed and two more driven down out of control.

Second Lieut. Sorsoleil attacked one two-seater over Graincourt, opening fire from 200 yards range. He closed with the enemy machine and got under its tail, firing a second burst. The enemy aircraft then went down vertically, and was seen to crash south-west of Graincourt.

Lieutenant Ralston dived on an enemy two-seater machine near Forenville. He got on to its tail and fired two bursts with both guns at very close range. It fell out of control and crashed in the vicinity of the enemy's reserve trenches.

Second Lieut. Payne attacked an Albatross two-seater, getting on to its tail and firing a good burst with both guns. The enemy aircraft turned over steeply and fell out of control.

Captain Penell attacked a large two-seater near Bantouzelle, diving on to it and firing with both guns from close. The enemy aircraft stalled and fell vertically out of control.

No. 41 section's balloon was destroyed by an enemy triplane; the observers both made safe parachute descents. The triplane was brought down in our lines by anti-aircraft fire.

January 14th.

The weather was mainly overcast, except on the Second Brigade front, where it was fair.

Three reconnaissances were carried out by the Second Brigade and two by the Fifth Brigade.

Ten hostile batteries were successfully engaged for destruction, with observation by machines of the Second Brigade; five gun-pits were damaged, eight explosions and four fires caused. Ten active hostile batteries were reported by zone call.

On the 13th instant balloons of the Third Brigade engaged three targets and located two active hostile batteries.

Two hundred and thirty-two photographs were taken, 131 bombs dropped, and 3,387 rounds fired, as follows:—

Second Brigade.—Thirty-four 25-lb. bombs were dropped, and 1,427 rounds fired on various targets.

Third Brigade dropped six 25-lb. bombs.

Fifth Brigade.—No. 8 Squadron dropped eight 25-lb. bombs and fired 150 rounds, and No. 35 Squadron dropped eight 25-lb. bombs and fired 1,060 rounds.

Ninth Wing.—On the night of the 13th/14th, machines of No. 101 Squadron dropped six 112-lb. and forty-two 25-lb. bombs on Roulers and Monscron Railway Stations. One direct hit was obtained on the railway at Roulers. Second Lieut. Montgomery and Second Lieut. Strang being unable to see the ground descended to 500 feet and dropped their bombs, and became the target of a great many anti-aircraft guns and machine-gun fire. Machines of No. 102 Squadron dropped thirteen 25-lb. bombs on Menin.

Forty-first Wing.—At noon on the 14th instant 12 machines of No. 55 Squadron carried out a successful raid on the munition factories and railway centre at Karlsruhe in Germany. One and a quarter tons of bombs were dropped, four bursts being observed on the buildings and sidings of the main railway junction in the centre of the town; two on the railway workshops and two on the smaller junction in the town.

Fifty-two photographs were taken, which confirm the bursts and show a very large fire indeed in one of the workshops by the railway.

Anti-aircraft fire was very heavy and accurate over the objective. The formation was attacked by seven enemy aircraft, but only three were able to attain the height of our machines, and these were kept at a distance by the observers. All machines returned safely.

Enemy Aircraft.—Very few combats took place. Captain Cox, No. 65 Squadron (Second Brigade), shot down a two-seater in flames at Westroosebeke, which was confirmed by the Second Corps, who saw it crash.

Miscellaneous.—Second Lieut. McLeod and Lieutenant Thomson, No. 2 Squadron, observed a hostile balloon over Bauvin. They flew through the clouds towards it and dived, the pilot firing 100 rounds into the balloon, which folded up and fell quickly.

Honours and Awards.

The* Distinguished Service Order.—Captain B. E. Baker, M.C.

Distinguished Service Cross.—Flight Sub-Lieut. H. Day.

L. A. K. BUTT, Captain,
Staff Captain.

Headquarters,
    Royal Flying Corps,
        16th January 1918.

No. 50.

CONFIDENTIAL.

ROYAL NAVAL AIR SERVICE.

OPERATIONS REPORT

(with Royal Flying Corps Reports attached)

17th to 31st JANUARY 1918.

NAVAL STAFF,
OPERATIONS DIVISION
31st January 1918.

ROYAL NAVAL AIR SERVICE.

REPORT OF OPERATIONS

(Completed from Reports during period
17th to 31st January 1918.)

CONTENTS.

	PAGE
HOME STATIONS	2
DUNKIRK	4
EASTERN MEDITERRANEAN	12
ROYAL FLYING CORPS COMMUNIQUÉS	23

HOME STATIONS.

January 28th and 29th.

A bombing raid of approximately five hours' duration was carried out by hostile aircraft (number unknown) over the area Thames Estuary, Essex, Kent and London.

At about 2000 hostile aircraft made the coast almost simultaneously at the mouth of the Rivers Blackwater and Crouch and at Foreness, followed at short intervals by other machines.

The machines which crossed the Essex coast proceeded towards London across Essex on roughly parallel courses, the most northerly via Maldon, Ingatestone, Brentwood, and the most southerly along the north bank of the Thames, being engaged by the Chatham defences between 2045 and 2151. London was approached from the east and north-east about 2045, the first bombs being dropped at Cannon Street and Vauxhall about 2100.

Of the machines which crossed the coast of the Isle of Thanet, one dropped six bombs on Ramsgate at 2020 and a second dropped a few bombs in Sheerness Dockyard at about the same time.

The remaining machines, probably two in number, crossed the Thames Estuary and also approached London from the east via Ilford and Romford. Of the total number of machines which crossed the coast probably four or five reached London between 2100 and 2200, and dropped bombs in the vicinity of Cannon Street, Vauxhall, Wandsworth Road, Poplar, Stepney, Somers Town, and Eastcheap, causing extensive damage to property and a few casualties.

Meanwhile, at 2236 a single machine made the coast near Orfordness. It circled round Ipswich and Woodbridge for some time, as if unable to locate its position, dropping a few bombs two or three miles south of the latter place. At 2323 it was reported from Castle Hedingham, whence it steered south to Coggeshall. Ten minutes later it passed over Chelmsford and was next reported from Sawbridgeworth at 2355, whence it turned south and proceeded into north-east London, along the River Leigh. Between 0015 and 0030 bombs were dropped at Meath Gardens, High Holborn, Strand, Long Acre, Spitalfields, and Aldersgate Street Station. A large fire was caused in Long Acre, where a bomb struck an air raid shelter, resulting in many deaths, and a large number of persons being injured. The hostile machine subsequently proceeded to sea across Essex.

In the vicinity of Sheerness a W.D. vessel and an R.G.A. cutter were badly damaged, and a Customs boat sunk; an ordnance store containing grenades was blown out, and damage was also caused at the Garrison Point Fort, and the Ordnance Office.

One enemy machine was brought down by R.F.C. pilots at South Benfleet, Essex. The machine fell in flames and the crew perished.

R.N.A.S. machines ascended from Eastchurch and Dover, and one of the hostile machines was attacked, but without result.

January 29th and 30th.

Night Attacks by Hostile Aircraft.— A bombing raid of approximately $4\frac{1}{2}$ hours' duration was carried out during the night by hostile aeroplanes (number unknown) over the area Thames Estuary, Essex, Kent and London.

Hostile machines approached the Kentish coast at the North Foreland at about 2130 and proceeded up the Thames Estuary towards London. None of these machines penetrated further than the neighbourhood of Chatham, where they were turned by gunfire. Practically at the same time three or four other machines made the land betwen the Rivers Blackwater and Crouch, and proceeded across Essex towards London. At Brentwood they were engaged by guns of the outer defences, and altered course to the north-west. One of them appears to have reached the neighbourhood of Waltham Cross, while the others turned back and proceeded to sea. Meanwhile, a giant aeroplane, which crossed the coast at the mouth of the Blackwater about 2230, proceeded due west across Essex and Hertfordshire to the neighbourhood of St. Albans; thence it turned south to Kew, where bombs were dropped at 2340. It then proceeded seaward along the south side of the river, and thence via Maidstone, Ashford and Folkestone to the coast.

Another giant aeroplane crossed the coast south of Harwich at 2225, proceeded across Essex on a south-westerly course, being over St. Margarets, Herts, at 2300, and dropped bombs at Wanstead at 2335; then went eastward via Ockenden, Canvey Island, and Southend to the sea.

Other enemy machines which crossed the Kent and Essex coasts between 2225 and 2250 were all turned back by the outer defences.

Bombs were dropped at Rayleigh, Whitstable and Rochford.

A final attack was delivered between the Blackwater and the Thames about 2330 by three or four machines.

Some damage was caused to houses and property, and a few casualties are reported.

R.N.A.S. machines went up from Walmer and Dover, but no engagements took place.

DUNKIRK.

PHOTOGRAPHIC RECONNAISSANCE.

January 22nd.

No. 1 Wing (2nd Squadron).—A photographic reconnaissance was carried out to Zeebrugge and Ostend. The only clear patch in the sky, however, was at Zeebrugge, and two plates were exposed over the Solway Works.

January 23rd.

No. 1 Wing (2nd Squadron).—A photographic reconnaissance was carried out, and plates were exposed over the Mole at Zeebrugge and Donkerlok battery; all other objectives were hidden by clouds.

January 25th.

A photographic reconnaissance was carried out, and 40 plates were exposed between Selzaete, Bruges, and Westcappelle.

A later reconnaissance took photographs of the Jacobinessen Battery, Turkyen Battery, and the Ateliers de la Marine.

Photographs show that a direct hit was made on the floating dry dock of the Ateliers de la Marine, and one on the principal sheds of the Atelier buildings by the monitor bombardment of January 19th.

January 30th.

A photographic reconnaissance was carried out, and 40 plates were exposed between Selzaete, Bruges, and Westcappelle.

January 31st.

No. 1 Wing (2nd Squadron).—A photographic reconnaissance was carried out, and plates were exposed over Breedene, but on account of the mist no accurate observations of Ostend could be made.

A later reconnaissance was made to the east of Bruges, and plates were exposed between Selzaete, Bruges, and Knocke.

RECONNAISSANCE.

January 18th.

No. 1 Wing (2nd Squadron).—A special coastal reconnaissance was carried out over Zeebrugge, and to a point 15 miles north of the Mole at a height of 7,000 feet. No hostile shipping was seen to seaward or in Zeebrugge Harbour.

Visibility was poor, and observations could only be made through gaps in the clouds.

January 23rd.

No. 1 Wing (2nd Squadron).—Two special reconnaissances were carried out to search for reported enemy shipping off Schouwen Bank. Owing to low clouds the patrols were carried out at heights ranging from 200 to 6,000 feet. No enemy activity was seen, and the Belgian coast appeared clear of enemy shipping. Visibility was very poor.

January 24th.

No. 1 Wing (2nd Squadron).—A special reconnaissance to Zeebrugge and Ostend was carried out in search of enemy shipping, during which 250 rounds were fired with machine guns at the coast and trenches from heights varying between 1,500 and 2,000 feet.

One of the D.H. 4 machines was hit by shrapnel when over Ostend at 2,000 feet, and was compelled to make a forced landing on the beach at La Panne.

SPOTTING.

January 19th.

No. 1 Wing (2nd Squadron).—Spotting was carried out for the monitor firing on Ostend, and good shooting appears to have been made. After the third shot the enemy put up their usual dense smoke screens; nevertheless, spotting was able to be continued. Batteries at Tirpitz, Deutschland, and Blankenberghe were observed in action against the Fleet.

FLEET PROTECTIVE PATROLS—ENGAGEMENTS WITH ENEMY.

January 22nd.

No. 4 Wing (3rd Squadron).—A patrol of three Sopwith machines picked up the Fleet off Nieuport and escorted it to Dunkirk. A formation of six hostile machines was observed to the north of Blankenberghe, and an engagement took place, but without any decisive results.

An enemy destroyer about 5 miles off the coast opened fire on the Sopwiths with anti-aircraft fire, but there were no hits.

January 29th.

No. 1 Wing (13th Squadron).—A patrol of five Sopwith Camels, when about 16 miles north of a point half-way between Zeebrugge and Blankenberghe, sighted two hostile seaplanes proceeding towards Zeebrugge. The Sopwiths dived and engaged them immediately, and one of the hostile machines, after bursting into flames, fell into the sea 100 yards from Blankenberghe Pier.

The other seaplane, although 200 rounds were fired into it, got away and reached Zeebrugge.

One of the Sopwiths was hit through the cowl, one plug being damaged.

January 30th.

No. 1 Wing (13th Squadron).—Whilst on patrol a formation of five Sopwith Camels sighted three hostile aircraft west of Wenduyne, steering west and climbing. A general engagement ensued, during which one of the hostile machines was suddenly observed to explode and fall into small pieces. It is presumed that a bomb was hit.

OFFENSIVE PATROLS.

January 19th.

No. 4 Wing (9th Squadron).—Attack on Enemy Trenches.—Whilst on patrol a formation of five Sopwith machines observed two formations of four and five hostile machines, respectively, behind Houthulst Forest, but were unable to attack them owing to a thick layer of clouds at 12,000 feet. The Sopwith pilots fired into enemy trenches east of the Floods.

On a later patrol Flight Lieut. Wood also attacked enemy trenches with machine-gun fire.

January 23rd.

No. 4 Wing (10th Squadron).—Engagement with Enemy.—Whilst on patrol a formation of Sopwith Camels encountered three enemy two-seaters and one Albatross Scout over Staden. The hostile machines dived through the clouds, and were followed by some of the Sopwiths. Below the clouds the hostile machines were joined by five more Albatross Scouts, and a general engagement took place, in which one enemy two-seater was driven down out of control by Flight Commander Curtis, and was observed to break up in the air by another pilot. An Albatross Scout was driven down entirely out of control by Flight Commander Alexander, who had become separated to some extent from the formation.

Flight Sub-Lieut. Blyth's machine (B. 5663) was observed going down out of control together with an enemy scout machine, and both machines were seen to crash simultaneously on the ground. It is considered that these two machines must have collided during the engagement.

January 23rd.

No. 4 Wing (3rd Squadron).—Engagement with Enemy.—A formation of eight Sopwith machines carried out an offensive patrol south of Ostend–Thourout–Roulers, and when over Houthulst Wood met a formation of seven hostile machines (four D.F.W.'s and three scouts, new type). Flight Lieut. Anderson attacked and drove one D.F.W. down out of control. A general engagement took place, and a number of indecisive combats ensued.

Flight Sub-Lieut. Youens, in Sopwith Camel B. 7184, failed to return, and has not been heard of since.

January 24th.

No. 4 Wing (9th Squadron). —Attack on Enemy Trenches.— A special patrol was carried out by Flight Commander Winter and Flight Lieut. Wood, in Sopwith machines, during which they fired 1,200 rounds into enemy trenches behind Nieuport. "Flammenwerfer" anti-aircraft and machine-gun fire was experienced, and one of the machines was hit in several places.

On a later patrol Flight Lieut. Wood fired 300 rounds at an enemy anti-aircraft battery.

January 25th.

No. 1 Wing (13th Squadron).—Attack on Enemy Trenches.— Whilst on patrol Flight Lieut. Poynter, in Sopwith Camel B. 3782, crossed the enemy lines at Pervyse at about 15 feet and fired about 100 rounds into a communication trench. No fire was returned until well over 100 yards east of the front line. About 1½ miles further the pilot fired at a corrugated iron hut; several men ran out and made for a dug-out. Turning north-east the pilot attacked two lorries and observed tracers to enter one of them. He then fired into a working party of men from an altitude of about eight feet and 50 yards range. Fire was returned from a machine-gun emplacement on the coast between Middlekerke Bains and Baversyde Bains, but this ceased after about 20 rounds. Altogether the Sopwith pilot fired about 480 rounds.

January 26th.

No. 4 Wing (10th Squadron).—Attack on Enemy Hangars.— Whilst returning from a flight in search of an enemy spotting machine, Flight Commander MacGregor, in Sopwith Camel B. 6449, attacked the two southern hangars on Vlisseghem Aerodrome with 250 rounds from an average height of 300 feet. The enemy replied with machine-gun fire from a point west of the southern shed.

January 28th.

No. 4 Wing (3rd Squadron).—Engagement with Enemy.— A formation of eight Sopwith Camels encountered a number of hostile machines in the vicinity of Roulers and several combats ensued.

Flight Commander Rochford observed two D.F.W. two-seaters near Houthulst Forest at about 10,000 feet. He dived on the rearmost machine, and fired until within 15 yards, when his guns jammed. The same machine was attacked by two other Sopwiths at the same time, and the observer was either killed or wounded, and the engine hit, as the propeller ceased to work.

The hostile machine was last seen by Flight Lieut. Hayne going down in a spin.

Flight Sub-Lieut. Macleod attacked another of the hostile machines behind the enemy lines south-east of Dixmude. The Sopwith pilot attacked from the side, and after firing about 100 rounds the hostile machine turned up on one wing and slipped into a slow spin and was still spinning at approximately 2,000 feet. The Sopwith pilot was unable to see the final result, but when last seen the hostile machine was falling out of control.

January 29th.

. No. 4 Wing (9th Squadron).—Engagement with Enemy.— Whilst on patrol, a formation of five Sopwith machines attacked fourteen hostile aircraft of various types in the Dixmude-Ypres sector, and fired about 1,100 rounds into them at ranges varying from 60 to 100 yards.

Two of the hostile machines went down spinning, but the final results were not observed.

January 29th.

No. 4 Wing (3rd Squadron).—Engagement with Enemy.— During a patrol by five Sopwith Camels, Flight Commander Armstrong saw five hostile machines above his formation over Roulers.

The Sopwith machines climbed above the hostile machines, and Flight Commander Armstrong fired about 200 rounds into one which finally turned on its back and fell in a spin. While trying to watch it going down, the Sopwith pilot was attacked by a hostile machine, which prevented him observing the final result, but up to the time of leaving the vicinity, which was ten minutes afterwards, this machine was not observed to rejoin the enemy formation. A few shots were fired into the other hostile machine, but without any results.

January 30th.

No. 4 Wing (3rd Squadron).—Engagement with Enemy.— A patrol was carried out by five Sopwith Camels over the Ypres–Roulers–Dixmude line, during which a formation of six Albatross single-seaters were encountered near Gheluvelt at about 15,000 feet. Flight Commander Rochford and Flight Lieuts. Glen and Ellwood got behind them and dived, opening fire at about 50 yards range, and carried on until within about 15 yards, when one hostile machine fell sideways to the right and went into a spin. The same pilots then attacked a second hostile machine at about the same ranges until he fell sideways and went down out of control. The remainder of the hostile machines flew down low and disappeared from view.

January 22nd.

No. 4 Wing (9th Squadron).—Flight Sub-Lieut. Beveridge in Sopwith N. 6370 failed to return from a patrol during which accurate anti-aircraft fire was experienced. He has since been reported wounded by No. 29 Squadron, R.F.C.

BOMB ATTACKS.

Varssenaere Aerodrome -	Jan. 25th	1,120 lbs.	D.H. 4.
Aertrycke Aerodrome -	,, 27th	684 ,,	,,
Engel Dump - -	,, ,,	300 ,,	,,
Aertrycke Aerodrome	,, 28th	992 ,,	,,
Engel Aerodrome -	,, ,,	196 ,,	,,
Engel Dump - -	,, ,,	64 ,,	,,
Coolkerke Aerodrome	,, ,,	1,468 ,,	,,
Oostcamp Aerodrome	,, 30th	1,660 ,,	,,
Engel Aerodrome -	,, 31st	856 ,,	,,
Engel Dump - -	,, ,,	278 ,,	,,
	Total -	7,618 lbs.	

January 25th.

No. 5 Wing (5th Squadron).—A bombing attack was carried out on Varssenaere aerodrome by five D.H. 4 machines (with two escorting machines), during which eight 50-lb., eight 20-lb. (Cooper) and thirty-five 16-lb. bombs were dropped on the objective at 1340 from heights of 15,400 to 17,000 feet. The visibility was good and anti-aircraft fire very heavy and accurate. A line from south to north was taken over the target and all the sheds and hangars on the east side appear to have been well straddled. A direct hit is reported on the small shed at the north-east corner of the aerodrome.

Other hits are reported on the group of small square sheds forming the three sides of the square on the eastern side of the aerodrome.

Two 50-lb. bombs dropped close in front of sheds, while in addition a line of four 20-lb. bombs were dropped close to and along the front of other sheds.

Two photographs were secured, one of the Ostend-Thourout railway north-west of Engel, and one of the objective. The latter was taken when only three of the bombing machines had dropped their bombs, after which the camera jammed.

January 27th.

No. 5 Wing (5th Squadron).—Seven D.H. 4 machines, one of which was detailed to attack Engel Dump and the others Aertrycke aerodrome, accompanied by three escorting machines, were despatched at 1045.

Visibility was fair, but both targets were almost completely obscured by clouds which made observation of results impossible.

Six 50-lb. and twenty-four 16-lb. bombs were dropped on Aertrycke aerodrome at 1155 from heights of 15,000 to 16,000 feet.

Two 50-lb. and eight 25-lb. (Cooper) bombs were dropped on Engel Dump from 16,000 feet.

One machine, which was late in leaving, was unable to catch up the formation, and therefore did not cross the lines. Another machine was forced to land on the return journey owing to engine trouble between Oost Dunkerque and Nieuport and crashed; neither pilot nor gunlayer were injured.

January 28th.

No. 5 Wing (5th Squadron).—Seven D.H. 4 bombing machines, accompanied by three escorting machines, were despatched at 1131, but of these, three were obliged to return, before crossing the lines, from engine troubles. The other machines reached the objectives on which bombs were dropped with the following results.

Eight 50-lb., eight 20-lb. (Cooper) and twenty-seven 16-lb. bombs were dropped on Aertrycke aerodrome at heights varying from 16,000 to 17,000 feet. A line south to north was taken over the objective, and bombs were seen to explode among two groups of hangars and sheds and also among new hangars to the north of these. Smoke was seen to rise from the latter, and a direct hit is reported on a Hervieux hangar opposite the hospital.

Two 50-lb. and six 16-lb. bombs were dropped on Engel aerodrome from 16,500 feet. The sheds and hangars were straddled, but no direct hits were observed.

One pilot was unable to cover Aertrycke aerodrome and dropped his four 16-lb. bombs on Engel Dump. Visibility was good, and the bombs were observed to burst on the sheds on the siding.

Four hostile aircraft were engaged at long range on the return journey between Ostend and Nieuport, but without any decisive result.

January 29th.

No. 5 Wing (5th Squadron).—Six D.H. 4 machines, accompanied by two escorting machines, were despatched at 1204 to carry out a bombing attack on Coolkerke Aerodrome.

Twelve 50-lb. four 25-lb. (Cooper) and forty-eight 16-lb. bombs were dropped from heights of 15,000 to 17,000 feet.

A line from north-east to south-west was taken over the objective, and both groups of sheds were straddled. Bombs were seen to explode amongst the sheds and a fire was started; a dense column of smoke was also seen to rise from close to another shed. Some bombs were dropped on Bruges Docks, and two fires were seen to break out, one on the Quay on the west side of West Basin, and the other on the Quay on the west side of the East Basin.

Visibility was good, and anti-aircraft fire heavy, but all machines returned safely.

January 30th.

No. 5 Wing (5th Squadron). — Seven D.H. 4 bombing machines, accompanied by three escorting machines, were dispatched at 1149 to carry out a bomb attack on Oostcamp Aerodrome. Of these, nine machines reached the objective, on which fourteen 50-lb. and sixty 16-lb. bombs were dropped from heights of 16,000 to 17,000 feet. The three groups of sheds and hangars of the Southerly Aerodrome were straddled and a direct hit is reported on a hangar in the most southerly group, from which fire and a dense cloud of smoke arose. Two direct hits, causing a fire in each case, are reported on the sheds to the north-west of Oostcamp Village. The D.H. 4 formation was attacked by a number of hostile aircraft after leaving the target, and several combats took place; two enemy machines are claimed as having been driven down out of control.

All the D.H. 4 machines returned safely with the exception of N. 5982 (Flight Sub-Lieut. Williams and Acting Gunlayer Leitch). This machine was seen over the objective, and Acting Flight Commander Bartlett states that he observed it crossing the Floods on the return journey, but nothing further has been heard of this machine or its crew.

Visibility was good, and anti-aircraft fire fairly heavy.

Four photographs were obtained, two of the objective, one of Conckelaere and one of Sparappelhoek Aerodrome.

January 31st.

No. 5 Wing (5th Squadron). — A bombing raid by six D.H. 4 bombing machines, accompanied by two escorting machines, was carried out at 1205 on Engel Aerodrome, during which four 50-lb. and forty-one 16-lb. bombs were dropped from heights of 15,000 to 17,000 feet.

Good runs were made over the group of sheds and hangars on the western side of the Aerodrome, and two direct hits are reported, one on a group of small huts, and the other on the easternmost hangar; a fire was started in each case. Several other bombs were seen to burst on the Aerodrome close to the sheds.

Three 50-lb. and eight 16-lb. bombs were dropped on Engel Dump from heights of 15,500 to 16,000 feet. Two hits are reported, and a fire was observed to break out in the south-east corner of the Dump.

Visibility was good vertically and anti-aircraft fire very light; four hostile machines were seen close to the objective, but they did not attack.

Photographs were taken of Engel Aerodrome and Dump.

HONOURS DURING PERIOD 16th to 31st JANUARY.

Name.	Unit.	Awarded.
Acting Flight Commander N. M. Macgregor.	No. 10 Squadron -	D.S.C.

Casualties.

Name.	Unit.	Date.
Missing.		
Flight Sub-Lieut. H. S. J. E. Youens -	No. 3 Squadron -	23.1.18.
Flight Sub-Lieut. R. A. Blyth -	No. 10 ,, -	23.1.18.
Flight Sub-Lieut. J. H. T. Carr -	No. 12 ,, -	25.1.18.
Flight Sub-Lieut. F. T. P. Williams -	No. 5 ,, -	30.1.18.
F. 23539, A.C. 1 (G.L.) C. A. Leitch -	No. 5 ,, -	30.1.18
Wounded.		
Flight Sub-Lieut. A. A. Cameron -	No. 10 Squadron -	18.1.18.
Flight Sub-Lieut. J. E. Beveridge -	No. 9 ,, -	22.1.18.

Details of the work carried out by Squadron No. 8, R.N.A.S., attached to the R.F.C. have not yet come to hand, and will be included in Operations Report No. 51.

EASTERN MEDITERRANEAN STATION.

(Compiled from Weekly Reports, Nos. 94, 95, and 96, dating from December 30th, 1917, to January 20th, 1918.)

December 30th–January 6th.

Note.—The week has been one of high winds and gales accompanied by low clouds, rain, and snow storms. All flying from Ægean stations has consequently been considerably curtailed.

THASOS AIR STATION.

"A" SQUADRON AND "Z" (GREEK) SQUADRON.

December 30th–January 6th.

Anti-Submarine Patrols. — Submarine patrols of Thasos Strait and of the area to W. and S.W. of Thasos were carried out by Short seaplane on 1st and 3rd January 1918. Further flying was prevented by the bad weather conditions.

January 7th–13th.

Note.—The week again has been one of high winds, a gale from the south-west being followed by a stiff breeze from the north-west, and rain rendered aerodromes unfit for work.

January 7th–13th.

Anti-Submarine Patrols.—"A" Squadron carried out a submarine patrol on January 7th between Thasos and Akte peninsula. Nothing of importance reported.

"Z" Squadron did no flying during the week.

January 13th–20th.

Note.—Every day has been fine during the week, so that practically all pilots and machines have been employed, and in consequence a considerable strain was placed on machines and personnel. Included in this work is 120 hours' submarine patrol, covering approximately 8,250 miles. Test and practice flights are not included.

January 13th–20th.

Attacks on Hostile Submarines.—On Sunday the 13th instant, at 9.25 a.m., about 15 miles east of Cape Santo, Flight Lieut. Burton observed a submarine's periscope heading N. by E. about 6 to 8 knots. He glided down from about 800 feet, getting a line on the submarine, and at 150 feet dropped a bomb, which fell 8 yards off on the starboard bow. As the periscope disappeared below the surface, a second bomb was dropped about 10 yards ahead of the first. Nothing more was seen of the submarine. A general warning was given.

Later on in the day, a Greek pilot of "Z" Squadron (Flight Lieut. Hambas) saw the periscope of a submarine, and dropped two 65-lb. bombs, one each side, but no damage was observed. Written report of these operations has not yet been received.

Hostile Aircraft Pursuit.—During the same day, 13th, hostile seaplanes came over Limena, but were chased away by other flights.

Hostile aircraft were also chased on the 14th and 18th, and long patrols were carried out on the 14th, 18th, and 19th instant, but nothing of importance has been reported.

STAVROS AIR STATION.

"D" Squadron.

December 30th–January 6th.

Mine Patrols.—Escorted mine patrols over Stavros swept channel and the Gulf of Ruphani were carried out by Henri Farmans on 30th December and 2nd January.

Reconnaissance and Photography.—On 1st January a reconnaissance of the enemy's front line on the Neohori–Orfano sector was made, and new emplacements were located on the foothills between Orfano and Dranli. On 3rd January an escorted photographic reconnaissance of the gun position of the same sector was carried out.

January 7th–13th.

Reconnaissance and Photography.—On Monday the 7th two reconnaissances were made, and photographs were taken of a gun position at Dodsambos. There was a hostile aircraft over the aerodrome, but this was not engaged. Again on the 11th and 12th a photographic reconnaissance was made over the front line. No important changes reported. On the 12th a reconnaissance of the enemy's lines of communication up the Angista Valley was made, but nothing of importance reported.

Machines were sent to the front line for spotting work on the 6th and 8th January, but no firing was carried out owing to unsuitable conditions.

On the 12th January a mine patrol was attempted, but the weather also rendered this impracticable.

January 13th–20th.

* **Photography.**—Photographic flights were made along the coast, and to the front on the 13th, 17th, and 18th, on the 13th of the coast near Orfano, on the 17th of four new gun positions on the side of Hill 350, and on the 18th of a new small camp.

Spotting.—Spotting was carried out for the Navy on the 14th.

On the 17th a hostile aeroplane of the Rumpler type was engaged by a Sopwith Scout, but with no decisive result, and again on the 18th a similar machine was driven off.

Bomb Attack on Drama Aerodrome.—On the 18th Drama Aerodrome was bombed, and one hangar is reported as being wrecked. It was observed that one new shed is being constructed, and the Drama Aerodrome has now 11 small hangars instead of seven.

GLIKI AIR STATION (IMBROS).

"C" SQUADRON.

December 30th–January 6th.

Owing to bad weather all flying has been prevented during the week.

January 7th–13th.

Reconnaissance.—On the 6th and 12th January reconnaissances of the Straits were made. On both occasions only the usual small shipping were reported. Both reconnaissances were escorted, but no hostile aircraft was seen.

January 13th–20th.

Reconnaissance and Bomb Attack on Nagara.—On the 13th a reconnaissance of the Straits was made, and only the ordinary craft were observed. On the 14th, at dawn, a raid was carried out on the seaplane sheds at Nagara, and 11 bombs burst just behind the sheds and near the anti-aircraft battery, and one near the slipway. A ship of from 800 to 1,000 tons was seen lying alongside the jetty in Ak Bashi Liman, but otherwise the Straits were clear of shipping. Fairly accurate anti-aircraft fire was experienced, one of our machines being hit, but no serious damage was done to it. Later on in the day a raid was made on the ship just mentioned. No direct hits were registered, but three bombs burst among the adjacent store sheds. During this raid an engagement took place with a machine of the Albatross D III. type, and numerous tracers were seen to enter the enemy machine, which came from the direction of Chanak, and which was camouflaged with dark green and red paint; the identification crosses being scarcely noticeable until at very close quarters.

In the early reconnaissance it was noted that the nets at Nagara appeared very irregular, inasmuch as the Northern Line was not straight as it usually is, and that the net floats were not evenly spaced ; moreover, no "net vessel" was there.

Seven craft of about 200 tons were moored in Chanak Harbour. The military camp just behind Suvla Salt Lake, was composed of six large huts and six large tents.

On the 16th a hostile machine was seen over Kusv and pursued, but was lost to sight in the hills behind Eren Keui: and on the return journey a seaplane was seen south of Helles, and took shelter under Killid Bahr. On the same day a special reconnaissance was carried out to bomb Lule Burgas Bridge, and during the flight the following notes were made :—

Bomb Attack on Galata Aerodrome.—"The clouds were too low for the main object to be carried out, and so at Varnitza two trays of ammunition were fired into a camp. At Galata two machines were seen on the aerodrome, one just landing, and a small scout in the centre. The former appeared to be a two-seater, with light coloured fabric and very conspicuous black crosses. The Scout was well camouflaged. One 65-lb. bomb was dropped on the aerodrome, but its effect was not observed, as in the meanwhile the two-seater got off, and followed our machine down the Straits for a few minutes. Very hot anti-aircraft fire was directed on our machine."

Here it may be observed that W.A.R. 92, paragraph 11, ordered the deletion of Galata from the map of enemy aerodromes, but Imbros reports (as seen above) and from other and verbal reports, that it is certainly occupied at present. There are two Bessoneaux, but the number of machines is doubtful. Anti-aircraft guns appear to have been taken from Bulair and Gallipoli and taken to Galata.

Bomb Attack on Nagara.—In the above reconnaissance, the remaining bomb (100-lb.) was dropped at Nagara on the sheds and burst about 50 yards behind them.

Mine Reconnaissance, Destruction of Hostile Seaplane.—On the 17th January a special mine reconnaissance, ordered by R.A.E., was carried out, and during this Flight Commander Donald shot down a two-seater seaplane when nearing Suvla. The machine crashed into the water from 1,000 feet. The pilot had apparently been killed. The wreck of the machine was salved by a monitor, which proceeded to within 700 ft. of the wreck. The machine was of the Friedrichshaven type. The body of the observer was picked up, and the engine and gun were brought to Mudros.

Bomb Attack on Lule Burgas Bridge and Troop Train.—Another attempt to bomb Lule Burgas Bridge was made on the same day by Flight Commander Sorley and Observer Lieutenant Smith. A train of about 30 coaches was observed approaching the bridge, but pulled up about 20 yards short, while a large number of troops climbed out and ran into the fields. A 100-lb. bomb was released, which fell over the bridge and a few yards to the left of the engine. A second bomb was released and a direct hit was observed about two feet from one of the stone pillars, wrecking the permanent way and making a hole in the bridge. Our machine attacked the train and fired seven trays of ammunition, scattering the troops in all directions. At Seidler a photograph was taken of the five-span iron girder bridge, about 300 feet long, adjoining (only 50 feet of embankment between) a stone bridge of three arches, 100 feet long. The bridge is situated midway between Seidler Station and Seidler Town.

The train attacked was the only one between Lule Burgas and Seidler, but considerable traffic was observed on the roads, mainly going east, a little north.

Bomb Attack on Galata Aerodrome.—On the 18th January an attack was made on Galata Aerodrome, and many bombs were dropped—no direct hits being registered—and some damage was done to the Aerodrome. Only the usual small shipping was observed in the Straits. Hostile aircraft were driven off.

Reconnaissance, and Bomb Attack on Arda Bridge.—A special mine reconnaissance was made in the vicinity of Mavro, and a special reconnaissance was made to the railway. Several trains were observed, and Arda Bridge was attacked, a 100-lb. bomb being dropped alongside the western support, which probably severely damaged the foundations; and another bomb damaged the station buildings. This reconnaissance reported that the barracks to the north of Adrianople have been much increased. Machine-gun fire was used against trains.

Reconnaissance, and Bomb Attack on Seidler Bridge.—On the 19th January enemy aircraft were driven off; a Straits reconnaissance was made and the usual small shipping reported, but a special reconnaissance dropped four heavy bombs on Seidler Bridge and twisted the framework. This reconnaissance reported that the bridge at Lule Burgas was temporarily repaired, and that a considerable amount of traffic was passing over the line.

MUDROS.

December 30th–January 6th.

No flying has taken place during the week owing to adverse weather conditions.

January 7th–13th.

On the 6th January, at 1107 L.T., Mavro reported a hostile machine and fighting machines were got ready to engage. No hostile aircraft was sighted here.

The Marsh aerodrome being flooded has not been available for work, and the machines from there have been brought into the repair base.

Weather rendered work impossible on other days.

January 13th–20th.

Anti-Submarine Patrols.—During the whole week constant patrols were carried out at dawn, and at other times during the day, but no submarine was positively observed, although it was thought on two occasions that a "U" boat had been seen.

On the 18th patrols were maintained all the morning, escorting H.M.S. "Skirmisher" at target practice, land machines and seaplanes acting in concert.

In the afternoon of that day a hostile seaplane flew over Mudros at a great height—over 10,000 feet. Machines were sent up to engage, but could not get into touch.

Anti-Submarine Patrols.—Very strenuous work in submarine hunting was carried out on Saturday 19th, when seaplanes were sent as far south as Piperi, Skyros, Mitylene, in consequence of an "Allo" in that direction, and the patrol was maintained during the whole of that day. One seaplane was sent out with hydrophone, but nothing was observed A machine was sent out from Syra towards Mitylene to work in conjunction with this patrol.

Advantage was taken of the fine weather to make considerable transfers of new machines by air to out stations; flying back old ones, and effecting at the same time an exchange of flying personnel.

KALLONI AIR STATION (MITYLENE).

"B" SQUADRON.

December 30th–January 6th.

No service flights have been carried out during the week.

January 7th–13th.

No service flights have been carried out during the week.

January 13th–20th.

Reconnaissance.—The only work carried out by this station during the week was a reconnaissance of the enemy's aerodrome on Kromylo Island, and its neighbourhood. Nothing of importance was observed.

SUDA BAY.

December 30th–January 6th.

Anti-Submarine Patrols.— Anti-submarine patrols of the approaches to Suda Bay and of the area 30 miles to north and eastward were carried out by Short seaplane on 30th December 1917 and 2nd January 1918.

January 7th–13th.

A patrol to the approaches of this bay was carried out on the 9th January. Nothing of importance was seen. There was no flying during the remainder of the week.

January 13th–20th.

Anti-Submarine Patrols.—Submarine patrols were carried out outside the harbour on the 13th, 15th, 16th, 18th and 19th, the weather being unsuitable on the other days. Nothing of importance was sighted.

SYRA SEAPLANE STATION.

December 30th–January 6th.

Anti-Submarine Patrols.—Anti-submarine patrols were carried out by Short seaplane on 30th and 31st December 1917 and on

2nd and 4th January 1918, the areas patrolled including the Siphano, Serpho, Thermia, Zea and Doro Channels.

January 7th-13th.

Anti-Submarine Patrol.—A submarine patrol of the Doro Channel was made on the 7th. Nothing of importance was seen. The machine was completely destroyed on landing. The pilot was unhurt. The remains of the machine were successfully salved.

On the 8th the slipway was carried away by the sea, and no work could be carried out during the rest of the week.

January 13th-20th.

Anti-Submarine Patrol.—The damaged slipway, reported last week, not yet being in working order, very little work could be carried out, but an anti-submarine patrol was made on the 14th inst., to co-operate with the search being made from Mudros.

H.M.S. "PEONY."

January 7th-13th.

On the 7th January an attempt was made at reconnaissance, but the machine was wrecked beyond repair. The pilot was saved. (Only signal reports have been received as yet.)

BRITISH ADRIATIC SQUADRON.

OTRANTO.

January 16th.

Attack on Submarine.—During the early morning at 0610, the Palascia (Italian) and R.N.A.S. look-out station sighted a submarine steering south on the surface at an estimated speed of 16 knots, about 15 miles east-south-east of the station. Two aeroplanes followed by two Baby seaplanes left to attack the submarine, which was sighted by one of the Baby seaplanes (Pilot Flight Lieut. Maxton). The submarine dived before the seaplane could reach the position, but one 65-lb. (delay action) bomb was dropped on the swirl caused by the submersion about 80 yards ahead of the last bubbles seen, as the submarine was observed to alter course sharply to starboard. Two large patches of oil appeared on the surface about one minute later, just ahead of where the bomb exploded. The seaplane continued flying round the position and fired two red Very's lights to attract the attention of a trawler five miles to the westward. Later a message was dropped to the boat, saying that the submarine had dived, and altered course to the west under the surface. A continuous patrol was maintained until dusk by both British and Italian aircraft. In all nine R.N.A.S. machines were despatched, but none had anything further to report.

MALTA.

(Extract from Intelligence Report, week ending 19th January 1918).

Remarks. — Considerable submarine activity has been reported in this area (covering within 2° east of Malta) during the week although few ships appear to have been attacked.
On 13th January the British S.S. "Rapallo" was torpedoed in the Straits of Messina and beached. On the 16th a submarine was sighted at Cape Passaro at 1400. On the 18th H.M.S. "Campanula" was missed by two torpedoes.

Weather.—Favourable weather has enabled flying to be carried out every day this week. The days have been bright and warm, but the clouds, though considerable compared with the summer weather, have not been low enough to restrict observations. Mistiness over the land has rendered the island difficult to see, but the improved wireless receiving work points to this difficulty being diminished, if not removed.

Photography. — Thirty-two negatives have been exposed during the week, four of British submarines on and under the surface, one of an oil patch after bombing an enemy submarine, three technical photographs, and the remainder for experimental purposes.

Anti-Submarine Operations.—On January 17th at 1730, a message was received from the Chief of Staff calling for an investigation of an intercepted W/T signal from an enemy submarine on a bearing 170 and probably about 40 miles away.
Short seaplane No. N.1823, being already on patrol, was picked up by wireless and diverted to this position, but was unable to observe anything unusual. After 2 hours 40 minutes' search the pilot was compelled to return owing to faulty engine, and was forced to land just before reaching the harbour.
At 0740 Short seaplane No. 9053 (Pilot Flight Lieut. Nunn, Observer L. A. C. Chapman) left to investigate. Oil streaks were observed in this position. Both the pilot and observer were confident that these were submarine tracks, but no

submarine was actually seen. The machine, therefore, returned after three hours' flying.

At 1005 Short seaplane No. N. 1097 (Pilot F. S. L. Bentley, Observer A.M. Clarke, left to relieve machine No. 9053, and to continue investigation. The pilot flew direct to the position reported, and the observer saw a long thin oily patch, under which was observed what appeared to be a submarine at a considerable depth. The observer dropped two 65-lb. bombs, one with ·25 second delay, the other with 2·5 seconds delay. Two photographs of patch on the water were taken after the explosions. Nothing further was seen, and having expended his bombs the pilot decided to return.

A continuous patrol was maintained throughout the remainder of the day until dusk.

On the 18th January at 1130 a request for assistance of an aerial escort was received from H.M.S. "Campanula," which had been attacked by an enemy submarine.

At 1220 Short seaplane No. N. 1096 (Pilot Flight Lieut. Nunn, and Observer L. A. C. Chapman) left, and picking up the sloop with convoy, signalled to her by Aldis lamp, asking for the position of the submarine when last seen. An answer "Submarine two miles south" was received. The pilot flew to this position, and finding oil track and patch, dropped two 65-lb. bombs with delay action. A search was continued between this point and the convoy until the latter reached the swept channel. The machine then returned to base.

CAPE STATION.

R.N.A.S. SUB-STATION, MTUA.

(Period November 15th to 22nd, 1917.)

Reconnaissance flights have been carried out on four occasions for the purpose of examining the enemy positions, but owing to heavy clouds, rain and bad weather generally, few observations could be made.

ROYAL FLYING CORPS COMMUNIQUES.

ROYAL FLYING CORPS COMMUNIQUÉ No. 123.

During the period under review, 15th to 21st January (inclusive), we have claimed officially nine enemy aircraft brought down and four driven down out of control. Six of our machines are missing. Approximately 11 tons of bombs were dropped, and 34,112 rounds fired at ground targets.

The weather generally throughout the week was adverse to flying.

January 15th.

Heavy rain during the day prevented any flying, except two test and practice flights, taking place.

41st Wing.—On the 14th one machine of No. 55 Squadron attempted photography, but was forced to return owing to heavy banks of clouds and thick mist. No plates were exposed.

On the night of the 14th–15th instant, 11 machines of No. 100 Squadron left to bomb the steel works at Diedenhofen (Thionville) in Germany. Six 230-lb., twenty-nine 25-lb., and two phosphorus bombs were dropped on the objective with good results; two 112-lb. and twelve 25-lb. bombs were dropped on the railway junction two miles south-east of Metz, and one 230-lb., two 25-lb., and one phosphorus bombs were dropped on Ebingen Railway Junction, while 1,680 rounds were fired at searchlights and trains in the railway stations. Anti-aircraft fire was heavy, but very inaccurate, and the searchlight barrages were considerable. All machines returned.

January 16th.

High wind and rain all day made flying practically impossible.

Second Lieut. McLeod and Lieutenant Hammond, No. 2 Squadron (First Brigade), attempted an artillery patrol. They fired 225 rounds at an anti-aircraft gun and a group of men near La Bassée, and dropped two 20-lb. bombs on La Bassée.

A machine of the Second Brigade fired 300 rounds at a party of the enemy.

January 17th.

Low clouds, rain, and mist made operations impossible.

41st Wing.—On the night of the 16th–17th, six machines of No. 100 Squadron left the ground to attack the railway and factory at Diedenhofen. Owing to a thick mist, four machines were forced to return; the remaining two crossed the lines. The weather conditions rapidly deteriorated. One machine dropped one 230-lb. and two 25-lb. bombs on the large railway sidings at Bernsdorf: the other machine dropped one 230-lb.

and one 25-lb. bombs on lights at Orny, and one 25-lb. bomb on a searchlight near Vigny. All results were obscured.

January 18th.

In spite of mist and rain-storms, a certain amount of flying was done.

A total number of 13 successful reconnaissances were carried out—nine by the Fifth Brigade. Forty-two hostile batteries were successfully engaged for destruction, and one neutralised: three gun-pits were destroyed, 22 damaged, 35 explosions, and 16 fires caused. Fifty-five zone calls were sent down. Out of the total batteries successfully engaged for destruction 22 were by the Second Brigade.

Sixty-nine photographs were taken, 115 bombs dropped, and 7,791 rounds fired as follows:—

First Brigade.—Corps Wing dropped forty-eight 25-lb. bombs; 10th Wing fired 1,370 rounds; No. 40 Squadron fired 100 rounds, and No. 43 Squadron fired 400 rounds into a procession, where many casualties were caused.

Second Brigade.—Took 40 photographs, dropped twenty-nine 25-lb. bombs, and fired 1,910 rounds.

Third Brigade.—Took 11 photographs, dropped twenty-six 25-lb. bombs, and fired 1,890 rounds.

Fifth Brigade.—Eighteen photographs were taken; No. 8 Squadron dropped four 25-lb. bombs and fired 721 rounds; No. 35 Squadron dropped eight 25-lb. bombs and fired 900 rounds, and No. 52 Squadron fired 500 rounds.

Enemy Aircraft.—Second Lieutenant A. E. Wylie, No. 65 Squadron, shot down one enemy aircraft near Westroosebeke.

Major R. Maxwell, No. 54 Squadron, fired a burst at 70 yards at an enemy scout, which turned over, the right bottom wing came partly away, and the enemy aircraft went down in a steep spiral.

Second Lieut. G. Clapham, of the same Squadron, attacked an Albatross Scout and fired a burst at point blank range. The enemy aircraft went down in flames.

One enemy aircraft was brought down near Lens by infantry.

Miscellaneous.—Captain J. Medcalf, No. 43 Squadron, whilst on patrol, lost his way in the clouds, and coming down found himself in the vicinity of Douai. He saw a party of infantry 500 strong marching through a village, and fired at them from a low altitude. They all scattered and left several casualties on the road. Captain Medcalf reports that he glided down to 500 feet and intended to land on an aerodrome, because he saw there an R.E. 8 and two A.W.'s standing on the ground. Hostile machine-gun fire was opened on him.

He noticed that the R.E.8 and the A.W.'s were camouflaged blue and green and had no national markings of any kind.

Lieutenant McCall and Lieutenant Farrington, No. 13 Squadron, ranged the 78th Siege Battery on hostile batteries. Seventy-nine observations were given, and two direct hits were obtained on gun-pits, in one case a large explosion being caused.

Captain Solomon and Lieutenant Morgan, No. 15 Squadron, gave 53 observations for the 48th Siege Battery on hostile batteries, and three gun-pits were badly damaged and one set on fire.

January 19th.

The weather was fine all day and the sky was covered with high clouds. The visibility was good.

Nineteen reconnaissances were carried out; 10 of these were by machines of the Fifth Brigade, including eight by No. 52 Squadron.

Ninety hostile batteries were successfully engaged for destruction, and six were neutralised; 16 gun-pits were destroyed, 44 damaged, 52 explosions, and 26 fires caused. One hundred and forty-seven zone calls were sent down.

Eight hundred and seventy photographs were taken, 317 bombs dropped, and 14,458 rounds fired at ground targets as follows:—

First Brigade.—One hundred and eighty-seven photographs. 1st Wing dropped sixty-nine 25-lb. bombs and fired 380 rounds, and 10th Wing fired 2,450 rounds.

Second Brigade.—Two hundred and sixty-three photographs. 2nd Wing dropped sixty-one 25-lb. bombs; No. 57 Squadron dropped sixty-eight 25-lb. bombs on Heule Ammunition Dump, and 3rd Squadron A.F.C. fired 2,400 rounds. Two thousand one hundred and ten rounds were fired by other squadrons.

Third Brigade.—Two hundred and twenty-one photographs were taken, seventy-three 25-lb. bombs dropped, and 2,826 rounds fired.

Fifth Brigade.—One hundred and ninety-five photographs. No. 8 Squadron dropped twenty-two 25-lb. bombs and fired 1,652 rounds; No. 35 Squadron dropped twenty-four 25-lb. bombs and fired 1,140 rounds, and No. 52 Squadron fired 1,500 rounds.

Enemy Aircraft.—Enemy aircraft were active, especially in the neighbourhood of Lens.

Captain J. L. Trollope, No. 43 Squadron, while on offensive patrol over Vitry, shot down one D.F.W., which was seen to crash.

Lieutenant G. McElroy, No. 40 Squadron, shot down out of control an Albatross Scout, and Second Lieut. W. Harrison, of the same squadron, shot down a D.F.W. out of control.

Flight Commander Price, Naval Squadron No. 8, observed three Albatross Scouts near Vitry. He dived and attacked one of these and fired 300 rounds The enemy aircraft fell over sideways and fell vertically.

In a general engagement between Naval Squadron No. 8 and 14 Albatross Scouts, Flight Sub-Lieut. Johnstone attacked one enemy aircraft and followed it down to 8,000 feet, firing all the while. The enemy aircraft was observed to fall completely out of control. Flight Sub.-Lieut. Dennett fired a good burst at another enemy aircraft at very close range, and it went down completely out of control. Flight Lieut. Jordan fired a burst of 50 rounds into an enemy aircraft, which turned on its side and spun. Flight Sub-Lieuts. Dennett and Johnstone followed this machine down, each firing 250 rounds, and the enemy aircraft went down out of control.

Second Lieut. F. Hobson, No. 70 Squadron, dived at an enemy aircraft two-seater, which went down out of control and then burst into flames. Second Lieut. G. Howsam, of the same squadron, attacked an enemy two-seater which had been pointed out to him by anti-aircraft fire. He fired a burst, and the enemy aircraft went down out of control.

Second Lieut. Jones and Lieutenant Phelps, No. 20 Squadron, dived at an Albatross Scout, and after firing 50 rounds brought it down out of control.

Captain Harrison and Lieutenant Noel, No. 20 Squadron, saw four enemy aircraft and dived on one and fired 20 rounds, after which the enemy aircraft went down out of control.

Sergeant E. Clayton and Second Lieut. L. Sloot, No. 57 Squadron, when returning from a bomb raid were attacked over Roulers by six Albatross Scouts. The observer fired 200 rounds, and one enemy aircraft went down in a vertical dive for 8,000 feet.

Captain R. Hilton and Lieutenant A. Clayton, No. 9 Squadron, were attacked by six enemy aircraft, two of which dived on the R.E. 8. The observer opened fire at 100 yards, and the leading enemy aircraft was seen to lose a wing and crash; the other enemy aircraft was driven off after 150 rounds were fired.

A patrol of four machines of No. 54 Squadron engaged seven Albatross Scouts, and Captain K. Shelton dived on two of them and followed them down to 500 feet. One of these fell out of control, and was later seen to be crashed on the ground by two other pilots of the same patrol.

January 20th.

Although the sky was covered with clouds, the visibility was good, and a lot of artillery work was carried out.

Seventeen reconnaissances were carried out, 12 of which were by machines of the 5th Brigade.

Seventy-two hostile batteries were successfully engaged for destruction and 12 neutralised with aeroplane observation; five gun-pits were destroyed, 30 damaged, 18 explosions, and 18 fires caused. One hundred and fifty-four zone calls were sent down.

Three hundred and twenty-three photographs were taken, 222 bombs dropped, and 10,572 rounds fired at ground targets as follows:—

First Brigade.—Fifty-six photographs. First Wing dropped fifty-five 25-lb. bombs and fired 1,150 rounds, and Tenth Wing fired 2,050 rounds.

Second Brigade.—Nine photographs were taken, thirty-six 25-lb. bombs dropped, and 1,040 rounds fired.

Third Brigade.—Sixty photographs were taken, seventy-six 25-lb. bombs dropped, and 2,682 rounds fired.

Fifth Brigade.—One hundred and ninety-eight photographs. Fifteenth Wing dropped fifty-five 25-lb. bombs; No. 8 Squadron fired 830 rounds; No. 35 Squadron 250 rounds; No. 52 Squadron 870 rounds; and No. 84 Squadron 700 rounds.

Enemy aircraft activity was slight all day.

Captain J. B. McCudden, No. 56 Squadron, brought down one enemy machine.

On the 19th, eight targets were registered by balloons of the Second Brigade, four of the targets being hostile batteries.

January 21st.

Low clouds and rain prevented much flying being done.

Six reconnaissances were carried out, one by the Second Brigade, two by the Third Brigade, and three by the Fifth Brigade.

Twenty-two hostile batteries were successfully engaged for destruction with aeroplane observation, and five neutralised; 15 gun-pits were damaged, 26 explosions, and seven fires caused. Seventy-five zone calls were sent down.

One hundred and forty bombs were dropped, and 9,086 rounds fired at ground targets as follows:—

First Brigade.—Forty-three 25-lb. bombs were dropped. First Wing fired 3,600 rounds, and No. 4a Squadron 100 rounds.

Second Brigade.—Second Wing dropped thirty-nine 25-lb. bombs; 2,455 rounds were fired.

Third Brigade.—Dropped twenty-nine 25-lb. bombs, and fired 1,150 rounds.

Fifth Brigade.—No. 8 Squadron dropped sixteen 25-lb. bombs and fired 591 rounds; No. 35 Squadron dropped four 25-lb. bombs and fired 500 rounds; No. 48 Squadron dropped nine

25-lb. bombs; No. 52 Squadron fired 500 rounds, and No. 54 Squadron 100 rounds.

Enemy aircraft activity was slight all day, a few indecisive combats taking place.

Second Lieut Churchman and Lieutenant Lewis, No. 10 Squadron, obtained many O.K.'s on a hostile battery. During this shoot, a hostile battery was seen firing, and a switch was given on to it and the hostile battery was silenced.

Lieutenant Douglas and Lieutenant Senior, No. 15 Squadron, made many observations and three O.K.'s were obtained. Direct hits were obtained on two pits, and the whole position badly damaged. During the same flight, seven active hostile batteries were reported by zone call.

Forty-first Wing.—On the night of the 21st–22nd, 17 machines of No. 100 Squadron started to bomb the steel works at Thionville and Bernsdorf railway sidings. Twelve machines crossed the line and dropped bombs as follows:—

Four 230-lb., twelve 25-lb. and one phosphorus bombs on Thionville; five 230-lb., sixteen 25-lb., and two phosphorus bombs on Bernsdorf, and two 230-lb. and eight 25-lb. bombs on various targets. One thousand five hundred and twenty rounds were fired at searchlights, trains, and factory lights.

One machine of Naval Squadron No. 16 dropped twelve 112-lb. bombs on the railway junction at Arnaville, south of Metz.

L. A. K. BUTT, Captain,
Headquarters,   Staff Officer.
    Royal Flying Corps.
        23rd January 1918.

ROYAL FLYING CORPS COMMUNIQUÉ No. 124.

During the period under review, January 22nd–28th, inclusive, we have claimed officially 26 enemy aircraft crashed and 19 driven down out of control. Approximately 37 tons of bombs were dropped and 77,911 rounds fired at ground targets.

January 22nd.

In spite of occasional rain storms, a considerable amount of flying was done, especially by the Second Brigade, who, considering the time of the year, did a record day's work.

Seventy-nine hostile batteries were successfully engaged for destruction, 11 neutralised, seven gun-pits destroyed, 37 damaged, 37 explosions, and 31 fires caused. One hundred and ninety-six active hostile batteries were reported by zone call.

A total of 1,258 photographs were taken, 576 bombs dropped, and 18,670 rounds fired at ground targets as follows:—

First Brigade.—One hundred and eighty-seven photographs were taken, sixty-five 25-lb. bombs dropped, and 475 rounds fired by the First Wing, and 5,800 rounds fired by the Tenth Wing.

Second Brigade.—Six hundred and forty-one photographs were taken, seventy-five 25-lb. bombs dropped, and 3,785 rounds fired. No. 57 Squadron dropped fifty-two 25-lb. bombs on Bisseghem ammunition dump. Eleven machines of No. 70 Squadron, carrying 20-lb. bombs, carried out a very successful raid on the Canal Wharf at Menin. Nine hits were observed on the objective, one on the wharf and six on the town.

Third Brigade.—Two hundred and five photographs were taken, forty-nine 25-lb. bombs dropped, and 2,380 rounds fired.

Fifth Brigade.—One hundred and eighty-two photographs were taken. Twenty-second Wing fired 2,530 rounds and dropped sixteen 25-lb. bombs; No. 8 Squadron dropped twenty-eight 25-lb. bombs and fired 2,145 rounds; No. 35 Squadron dropped twenty 25-lb. bombs and fired 1,450 rounds; No. 48 Squadron dropped sixteen 25-lb. bombs; and No. 52 Squadron fired 1,050 rounds.

Ninth Wing.—No. 25 Squadron, while on a bomb raid over Roulers, caused two fires—one in buildings beside the railway and one in buildings on the road.

On the night of the 21st–22nd January, No. 101 Squadron dropped sixteen 25-lb. bombs on Bisseghem Aerodrome, obtaining one direct hit on hangars; forty-eight 25-lb. and eight incendiary bombs on Heule Aerodrome; thirty-six 25-lb. bombs on Rumbeke Aerodrome; twenty-eight 25-lb. bombs on Moorslede Aerodrome; sixteen 25-lb. bombs on Harlebeke Aerodrome, obtaining three direct hits on hangars, and fired 1,850 rounds.

Artillery Co-operation.—Machines of the Second Brigade carried out 35 counter-battery shoots.

Captain Reeve and Lieutenant Rees, No. 15 Squadron (Third Brigade), working with the 303rd Siege Battery, made 29 observations and destroyed two pits. Lieutenants Sayers and Dewey, No. 59 Squadron, working with the 194th Siege Battery, obtained nine O.K.'s; two pits were badly damaged and a fire caused.

With observation by machines of the Fifth Brigade, four direct hits on gun positions were obtained, two gun-pits were demolished, three damaged, four fires and an explosion caused. Captain Wolton and Lieutenant Hurr, No. 35 Squadron, working with the 354th Siege Battery, destroyed two pits and caused two fires. Captain Milton and Lieutenant Channing, No. 8 Squadron, working with the 245th Siege Battery, damaged two pits and caused one explosion.

Enemy Aircraft.—Enemy aircraft were unusually active on the First Brigade front until noon.

A patrol of Naval Squadron No. 8 attacked seven Albatross Scouts in the vicinity of Vitry. Flight Commander Price and Flight Sub-Lieut. Day each shot down an enemy aircraft out of control. Several indecisive combats took place.

A patrol of No. 70 Squadron were attacked by seven enemy aircraft scouts. In the fighting Lieutenant Seth-Smith dived on one which was about 500 feet below him; he fired a good burst, and the enemy aircraft half rolled over and went down completely out of control.

Second Lieut. G. Howsam, of the same squadron, destroyed one enemy aircraft. Captain F. Quigley attacked one enemy aircraft from the side, and Lieutenant Howsam attacked from beneath its tail. The enemy aircraft started to spin, and then burst into flames. An Albatross Scout attacked Captain Quigley from above. He turned and fired at it nose on. The enemy aircraft then dived, and Lieutenant J. Todd followed it down, firing at it, and it was observed to fall and crash north-east of Houthulst Forest. Captain Quigley and Lieutenant Howsam engaged another Albatross Scout, and followed it down until it became enveloped in a cloud of black smoke. Lieutenant Howsam, while on a bomb raid, attacked an enemy two-seater over Houthulst Forest. After 400 rounds had been fired the enemy aircraft burst into flames and crashed north-east of the Forest.

Captain W. Molesworth, No. 29 Squadron, engaged an enemy aircraft at about 100 yards range, and the enemy machine went down out of control emitting a long string of smoke.

A patrol of 11 Bristol Fighters of No. 20 Squadron were attacked by about 20 Albatross Scouts. Second Lieuts. D. Cooke and H. Crowe shot down one of the enemy machines completely out of control, and dived on another, which was seen to fall, issuing smoke, and crash in flames south of Moorslede. Captain R. Kirkman and Second Air Mechanic J. McMechan shot down one Albatross Scout out of control. Sergeant H. Smith and Second Lieut. Agelasto engaged an Albatross Scout and were able to get in a good burst at close quarters. The enemy aircraft fell out of control and crashed.

Lieutenant J. McCone, No. 41 Squadron, dived on an enemy aircraft, firing two bursts, and observed tracers entering the cockpit. The enemy aircraft turned to the right, and Lieutenant McCone got off another burst of 40 rounds. The enemy aircraft immediately went down completely out of control, sideslipping and spinning, and was followed down to within 2,000 feet of the ground.

Miscellaneous. — Flight Commander R. Munday, Naval Squadron No. 8, made a night attack on an enemy balloon. He crossed the lines at 3,000 feet, dived down to 1,000 feet, making for a point where he judged the position to be. He twice dived to within 100 feet, firing two bursts of 100 rounds each. When passing the balloon the second time at about 30 feet it burst into flames.

Captain Quigley, No. 70 Squadron, went up at 2220 on receipt of warning that an enemy aircraft was doing wireless over Passchendaele. He did not see the enemy aircraft, but it immediately broke off the shoot. Captain Quigley returned to his aerodrome, and made a good landing at 2310.

January 23rd.

The weather was mainly fine, but cloudy all day.

Five reconnaissances were carried out, one by the First Brigade, three by the Second Brigade, and one by the Fifth Brigade. Lieutenant Gilbert and Second Lieut. Wilson, No. 7 Squadron, whilst reconnoitring for wire, were heavily fired upon, and had their controls shot away. A successful reconnaissance was carried out by Lieutenants Biggar and Toplis, No. 52 Squadron, during which they fired 500 rounds into the enemy trenches from heights between 50 and 500 feet.

On the 22nd January balloons of the Second Brigade registered 21 targets; four hostile batteries were successfully engaged for destruction and three were neutralised. Twenty-three active hostile batteries were located.

Enemy aircraft activity was very slight; no combats took place.

Sixty-nine photographs were taken, 59 bombs dropped, and 5,015 rounds fired at ground targets as follows: —

First Brigade.—First Wing dropped twelve 25-lb. bombs; Tenth Wing fired 500 rounds; and No. 4 Squadron fired 100 rounds.

Second Brigade.—Sixteen photographs were taken, twenty-seven 25-lb. bombs dropped, and 3,735 rounds fired.

Third Brigade.—Fifty-three photographs were taken, twelve 25-lb. bombs dropped, and 180 rounds fired.

Fifth Brigade.—Eight 25-lb. bombs were dropped, and No. 52 Squadron fired 500 rounds.

Eighth Brigade.—On the night of the 21st/22nd:—

Two machines of Naval Squadron No. 16, in spite of a very strong south-west wind, set out to bomb Diedenhofen. Twelve 112-lb. bombs were dropped, several of which fell near the village of Arnaville, and two direct hits were observed on the railway bridge just north of Arnaville. One machine was forced to return owing to low clouds and a strong wind.

Seventeen machines of No. 100 Squadron set out to bomb the steel works at Diedenhofen and Bensdorf railway sidings. Twelve machines crossed the lines.

Four 230-lb., one 40-lb. phosphorus, and twelve 25-lb. bombs were dropped on the factory at Diedenhofen from an average height of 800 feet. Several explosions were caused, and a series of flashes continued for some time.

Seven 230-lb., two 40-lb. phosphorous, and twenty-four 25-lb. bombs were dropped on Bensdorf Railway Station and sidings, and on the railway junction at Falkenburg. Large explosions were caused and a fire started at Bensdorf. Bombs were observed to burst on the rails, and a train was seen to be derailed.

Captain Windsor and Second Lieut. Edwardes-Evans, who started the fire at Bensdorf railway sidings, dropped their bombs from 400 feet.

One machine failed to return.

January 24th.

The weather was fine in the north; in the south there were low clouds, and visibility was bad.

Six reconnaissances were carried out, 42 hostile batteries were successfully engaged for destruction (30 of these were by the Second Brigade) and three neutralised; one gun-pit was destroyed, 12 damaged, 30 explosions and 35 fires caused. Forty-four zone calls were sent down.

A total of 1,309 photographs were taken, 446 bombs dropped, and 14,812 rounds fired at ground targets as follows:—

First Brigade.—Four hundred and two photographs were taken. No. 18 Squadron dropped eighteen 25-lb. bombs; First Wing dropped fifty-seven 25-lb. bombs; No. 4A Squadron fired 137 rounds; Tenth Wing fired 3,200 rounds; and No. 43 Squadron fired 500 rounds into the hangars on Douai Aerodrome.

Second Brigade.—Five hundred and sixty-eight photographs were taken, sixty-eight 25-lb. bombs dropped, and 4,895 rounds fired. No. 57 Squadron dropped sixty 25-lb. bombs on Harlebeke Aerodrome.

Third Brigade.—Three hundred photographs were taken, forty-three 25-lb. bombs dropped on Quèant, and 530 rounds fired.

Fifth Brigade.—No. 35 Squadron dropped four 25-lb. bombs and fired 500 rounds; No. 8 Squadron fired 1,000 rounds; and No. 52 Squadron fired 1,000 rounds.

Ninth Wing.—Thirty-nine photographs were taken. No. 25 Squadron dropped nine 112-lb. bombs on Courtrai Railway Station; No. 27 Squadron dropped two 112-lb. and fourteen 25-lb. bombs on Ledeghem, and two 112-lb. and twenty-four 25-lb. bombs on Douai.

On the night of the 23rd/24th, in spite of low clouds which blew up after machines of No. 101 Squadron had left the ground, all machines crossed the lines, and dropped six 112-lb., seventy-four 25-lb., four phosphorus, and seven incendiary bombs on Heule, Oostacker, Abeelhoek, Abeele, Moorseele, Beveren, and Rumbeke Aerodromes, and on Thourout, Lichtervelde, and Roopebeke. Two thousand one hundred rounds were fired at hangars, lights on roads, searchlights and billets.

Second Lieutenants Paull and Golding successfully bombed the station and a train at Roopebeke with phosphorus bombs; one of these exploded and caused a large fire which burned for a considerable time and could be seen from the lines.

No. 102 Squadron also went out on the night of the 23rd/24th and dropped thirty-four 25-lb. bombs on Roulers, and twenty-nine 25-lb. bombs on Rumbeke. Forty-nine 2-lb shells and 1,850 rounds were fired at Rumbeke and other ground targets.

Enemy Aircraft.—Captain A. O'Hara Wood, Fourth Squadron, A.F.C., shot down a D.F.W., which fell straight into the ground north of La Bassée.

Lieutenant McElroy, No. 40 Squadron, fired two bursts at about 75 yards range at a D.F.W., and the enemy aircraft went down completely out of control.

Naval Squadron No. 8, while on offensive patrol encountered a formation of Albatross Scouts, and a general engagement ensued. Flight Commander Munday fired 250 rounds at one of the enemy aircraft at close range, and it fell on its back and went down in a nose dive. Flight Sub-Lieut. J. B. White attacked one enemy aircraft which was attacking one of our machines. He fired 150 rounds at point blank range, and tracers were observed going into the pilot's cockpit. The enemy aircraft turned over sideways and fell out of control.

Another patrol of this squadron encountered several Albatross Scouts, and Flight Sub-Lieuts. Jordan and Johnstone both fired bursts at one enemy aircraft, which went down apparently quite out of control. Later, Flight Sub-Lieuts. Johnstone and Johns attacked a single Albatross Scout close to the lines. They fired between them about 200 rounds, and the enemy aircraft was last seen at 1,500 feet still descending quite out of control.

When on wireless patrol, Flight Commander Price, of the same squadron, dived on an Albatross Scout over La Bassée. He fired 300 rounds into the enemy aircraft, which fell vertically, and was confirmed as having crashed by anti-aircraft observers.

Flight Sub-Lieut. Sneath got in a good burst at one enemy aircraft scout, which he encountered east of Lens, and the enemy aircraft dived for a short distance and finally went down completely out of control slipping from side to side, and was confirmed as crashed by anti-aircraft observers.

While on offensive patrol Captain Quigley, No. 70 Squadron, attacked an enemy two-seater, firing many rounds. Captain Quigley turned west, the two-seater turning after him, so he again attacked the enemy aircraft, which dived and crashed into a hedge. Second Lieut. G. Howsam fired 400 rounds into an Albatross two-seater which went down and crashed in a field. Second Lieut A. Koch attacked an enemy two-seater, into which he fired 150 rounds from close range, and the enemy aircraft went down in a spin completely out of control, and was observed to be still spinning at 1,000 feet.

Whilst on photography Second Lieuts. W. Green and H. Gros, No. 57 Squadron, were attacked by 10 enemy aircraft, five from below and five from above. The observer (Second Lieut. Gros) fired a burst at a triplane below him, and the enemy aircraft burst into flames. Another drum was fired at an Albatross Scout, which fell into a steep side-slip, and was last seen falling out of control.

Captain H. Drewitt, No. 23 Squadron, while on offensive patrol, attacked one of six Albatross Scouts and fired several bursts at very close quarters, the enemy aircraft diving straight east, making an excellent target, as he did not endeavour to manœuvre at all. Captain Drewitt continued to fire until the enemy aircraft eventually fell over, got into a spin, and was lost sight of as it entered the clouds.

Captain W. Molesworth, No. 29 Squadron, while leading a patrol, attacked an enemy two-seater from behind and fired a drum at 150 yards range. The enemy aircraft went down completely out of control, and this is confirmed by another pilot. Captain Molesworth then attacked another enemy aircraft at about 100 yards range. A burst of smoke appeared, and the enemy aircraft dived east out of control and crashed. Second Lieut. J. Coombe, of the same patrol, fired 80 rounds at 150 yards range at an enemy aircraft, which went down out of control.

Whilst on offensive patrol Second Lieut. F. Clark, No. 60 Squadron, was attacked by an Albatross Scout. Lieutenant Morey, of the same squadron, did a left-hand bank towards the enemy machine and collided with it. Both machines crashed.

Second Lieut. P. de Fontenay, No. 29 Squadron, dived on an enemy aircraft and fired a burst of 20 rounds into it at about 40 yards range, the enemy aircraft immediately going down in a spin. This is confirmed as having crashed by another pilot.

Lieutenant E. Comber-Taylor and Sergeant J. Morris, No. 7 Squadron, whilst on photography were attacked by about 12 enemy aircraft. The observer fired 170 rounds as each enemy aircraft attacked. One enemy machine went down out of control, and another appeared to have a piece of the machine shot off, as something was seen to fall from it. Second Lieut. Taylor's machine was badly shot about by bullets.

Captain J. B. McCudden, No. 56 Squadron, left the ground to look for enemy aircraft. He attacked a D.F.W. when at 30 yards range, and apparently hit the pilot, as the gunner was seen to be leaning into the pilot's cockpit as if taking control, so Captain McCudden fired another burst, and the enemy aircraft went down alternately diving and stalling and eventually got into a spin. It was last seen at 2,000 feet still spinning.

Miscellaneous.—At Aix-la-Chapelle a telegram was put up by the Germans on the 29th December 1917 saying that Mannheim had been bombarded. It is reported that the Central railway station, the electric power station, the chemical factory, and a locomotive repair works were seriously damaged. The Mannheim fire brigade did not succeed in extinguishing the flames, and the brigades of Ludwigshaven, Schwetsingen, and Karlsruhe were called in to help. Several hundred thousand marks' damage was done. Five children, one woman, and two men were killed. (Agent.)

Mannheim was bombed on 24th December 1917.

January 25th.

After the mist had cleared, at about 1000, the weather was mainly fine on the whole front.

Seventeen reconnaissances were carried out, two by the First Brigade, three by the Second Brigade, four by the Third Brigade, and three by the Fifth Brigade, and five long-distance photographic reconnaissances, on which 189 photographs were taken by No. 25 Squadron (Ninth Wing).

Sixty-five hostile batteries were successfully engaged for destruction, and eight neutralised; eight gun-pits were destroyed, 23 damaged, 27 explosions, and 18 fires caused; 41 active hostile batteries were reported by zone call.

On the 24th balloons of the Second Brigade engaged two targets, and located one active hostile battery.

One thousand seven hundred and ninety-one photographs were taken, two hundred and sixty-one 25-lb. and fourteen 112-lb. bombs were dropped, and 9,672 rounds fired at ground targets as follows :—

First Brigade.—Three hundred and fifty-eight photographs. First Wing dropped fifty-eight 25-lb. bombs and fired 560 rounds, and Tenth Wing dropped eight 25-lb. bombs and fired 1,340 rounds.

Second Brigade.—Five hundred and thirty-seven photographs. No. 10 Squadron, on a night bombing raid, dropped thirty-five 25-lb. bombs on a cinema at Bousbecque, and some of the bombs were seen to burst on the objective.

During the day No. 57 Squadron dropped eight 112-lb. bombs on Courtrai railway sidings, and four bursts on the objective were observed. Two thousand four hundred and sixty-five rounds were fired.

Third Brigade.—Three hundred and ninety-four photographs were taken, twelve 25-lb. bombs dropped, and 560 rounds fired.

Fifth Brigade.—Three hundred and thirteen photographs. Twenty-second Wing dropped sixteen 25-lb. bombs and fired 200 rounds, and Fifteenth Wing dropped thirty-six 25-lb. bombs and fired 3,047 rounds.

Ninth Wing.—One hundred and eighty-nine photographs. No. 27 Squadron dropped two 112-lb. and sixteen 20-lb. bombs on Roulers.

On the night of the 24th/25th No. 101 Squadron dropped four 112-lb., forty-nine 25-lb., three phosphorus and eight incendiary bombs on Oostacker, Rumbeke, Abeele, Bisseghem, and Heule Aerodromes, and Lendelede Station, Beveren and Roulers. Direct hits were obtained on the hangars at Oostacker and Rumbeke. One thousand five hundred rounds were fired at ground targets.

No. 102 Squadron dropped ten 25-lb. bombs on Roulers.

Eighth Brigade.—On the night of the 24th/25th January 16 machines of No. 100 Squadron set out to bomb Trier barracks and railway station. Five returned with engine trouble and 11 crossed the lines. Bombs were dropped as under from an average height of 1,500 feet :—

Eight 230-lb., two 112-lb., seventeen 25-lb., and two 40-lb. phosphorus bombs, making a total of 2,569 lbs. One thousand nine hundred and fifty rounds were fired at ground targets.

Two 230-lb., two 112-lb., five 25-lb., and two 40-lb. phosphorus bombs were dropped on Trier. Very good bursts were observed in the northern portion and centre of the town, and a very large fire was started in the north-east portion of the town, and was later observed by other pilots.

Four 230-lb. and eight 25-lb. bombs were dropped on Thionville steel works, bombs bursting and large explosions being observed. Seven hundred rounds were fired at searchlights, trains, and moving lights on the roads.

One 230-lb. and two 25-lb. bombs were dropped on the railway at Oberbillig, 6 miles south-west of Trier.

One 230-lb. and two 25-lb. bombs were dropped on the railway station and junction at Saarburg, 10 miles south of Trier, causing large explosions in the town.

Captain Windsor and Captain Scudamore obtained good hits on the north-east portion of the town of Trier and caused a fire which was observed by other pilots and helped to guide them to their objective.

Captain Albu and Captain Lindsay were attacked by an enemy machine near Homburg. Enemy aircraft used tracer ammunition. Captain Albu, although handicapped by load of bombs, managed to elude the enemy machine. On his return his machine was found to be shot about.

Owing to the very heavy banks of clouds from the north, only those machines that left the aerodrome early were able to reach Trier. One pilot, Lieutenant Martin, made four attempts and only reached Thionville on his fourth attempt.

Two machines of Naval Squadron No. 16 left for Mannheim, and a third for Thionville. One machine succeeded in reaching Mannheim, where six 112-lb. bombs were dropped on the Badische Aniline and Soda Fabrik, three on the docks, and three on the town itself. As a result of the bomb bursts on the factory dense clouds of smoke were seen to rise after the explosion. The second machine for Mannheim did not reach its objective owing to bad weather, and returned with its bombs. The third machine reached Thionville, dropped three bombs on the town and nine in and around the railway junction and factories.

During the day Second Lieut. J. B. Fox and Lieutenant S. S. Jones, No. 55 Squadron, in spite of the sky being completely covered with clouds, managed to expose nine plates, photographs being taken of Puxieux and Mars-le-Tour through gaps in the clouds.

Enemy Aircraft.— A patrol of Naval Squadron No. 8, on special mission, observed five Albatross Scouts near Beaumont. Flight Lieut. Jordan dived on two of these and fired into one of them at about 50 yards range. The enemy aircraft fell over on its side and went down slipping from side to side. Flight Lieut. Jordan and Flight Sub-Lieut. Johnstone followed the enemy aircraft down and fired between them another 250 rounds. The enemy aircraft was observed by both pilots to crash.

An offensive patrol of No. 40 Squadron observed a two-seater enemy aircraft below, and Second Lieut. J. Hambley dived at it and opened fire. Tracers were seen to enter the fuselage and engine of the enemy aircraft, which stalled and fell over sideways and eventually got into an almost vertical nose-dive. The enemy aircraft was last seen at about 3,000 feet still falling out of control.

Second Lieut. D. Richardson, No. 18 Squadron, whilst on photography, observed five enemy aircraft. He fired a burst at about 50 yards at one of them, and it went down in a spin completely out of control emitting a cloud of smoke.

Captain R. Boby and Lieutenant W. Wells, No. 22 Squadron, whilst on offensive patrol, observed 14 Albatross Scouts in three groups below them. They dived and attacked one of the enemy aircraft, which spiralled, turned upside down, and eventually fell completely out of control.

Captain H. Hamersley, No. 60 Squadron, whilst on offensive patrol, attacked an Albatross Scout. After firing two bursts at the enemy aircraft it fell down out of control.

Second Lieut. G. Bremridge, No. 65 Squadron, attacked one of two enemy aircraft two-seaters doing artillery work. He dived at it and opened fire at 200 yards. The enemy aircraft finally burst into flames and crashed.

Second Lieut. G. Howsam, No. 70 Squadron, dived at an Albatross Scout which was attacking an R.E. 8. He followed the enemy aircraft down to 1,000 feet, firing all the way. The enemy aircraft eventually fell over on its back and went down completely out of control.

Second Lieuts. J. Allen and F. Wakeford, No. 57 Squadron, whilst on photography were attacked by an Albatross Scout, into which the observer fired 60 rounds. The combat was then broken off, the enemy aircraft suddenly falling out of control.

Sergeant Gay and Second Lieut. A. Flavell, of the same squadron, were attacked by nine Albatross Scouts. After a burst of 120 rounds out of the observer's gun at one of the enemy aircraft it fell out of control.

An offensive patrol of No. 20 Squadron engaged 12 Albatross Scouts. In the combat that ensued Captain R. Kirkman and Second Lieut. A. Keith drove down one, which was observed by No. 60 Squadron to be falling with the wings folded back. Second Lieuts. McGoun and A. Agelasto fired at one enemy aircraft, which went down out of control, and was confirmed as crashed on the ground by another pilot. They then engaged another enemy aircraft, which they shot down out of control. Lieutenant Leigh-Pemberton and Captain N. Taylor attacked another enemy aircraft, which they shot down out of control. Sergeant F. Johnson and Second Lieut. D. Prosser attacked an enemy aircraft, which eventually broke up, the wings folding back. This machine was observed to be crashed on the ground. Second Lieuts. D. Weston and W. Noble fired at one enemy aircraft, whose wing fell off. They then attacked another enemy aircraft, which they shot down out of control.

Second Lieuts. C. Matheson and C. Brown, Third Squadron, A.F.C., whilst on flash reconnaissance, were attacked by two two-seater enemy aircraft. They fired 100 rounds at one of the enemy aircraft, which went down in flames.

A patrol of No. 56 Squadron, led by Captain J. B. McCudden, attacked a D.F.W. Several pilots fired at it, and after Lieutenant Durrant had fired a final burst the enemy aircraft went down out of control. Captain McCudden attacked an enemy aircraft and fired about 200 rounds at ranges varying from 30 to 100 yards. The enemy aircraft was last seen at about 6,000 feet diving vertically and completely out of control, and has since been confirmed by infantry in the trenches to have crashed. Captain G. Bowman attacked one enemy aircraft from under its tail. The enemy observer disappeared into the cockpit, leaving his gun pointing up. Lieutenant Blenkiron then dived on it and drove it down completely out of control. Captain Bowman then got behind another enemy aircraft, which went into a steep dive and eventually crashed. Lieutenant Mealing attacked a two-seater enemy machine at close range. A large piece of this enemy aircraft was seen to fall off; the machine then turned over on its back and went down in a spin out of control. At the same time Second Lieut. D. Woodman dived on another enemy aircraft, which turned over and went down completely out of control. Owing to the intensity of the fighting it was impossible to watch this machine crash.

Lieutenant Taylor, No. 41 Squadron, dived on one of eight Albatross Scouts. After Lieutenant Taylor had fired 50 rounds at 40 yards range the hostile scout turned completely over and nose-dived. Anti-aircraft confirm this as having crashed.

Second Lieut. D. Lawson, Lieutenant W. Kelleg, and Captain M. Gonne, No. 54 Squadron, all attacked an enemy aircraft, which was last seen diving vertically in flames. Captain Gonne got directly behind another enemy aircraft, which was evidently unaware of his presence. After a short burst at point blank range had been fired the enemy aircraft went down completely out of control and was watched down for 10,000 feet, when it was lost in the haze.

Second Lieut. E. Krohn, No. 84 Squadron, opened fire on an enemy aircraft two-seater at about 300 yards, and enemy aircraft was last seen diving in flames.

Second Lieuts. H. Elliottt and R. S. Herring, No. 48 Squadron, whilst on photography were attacked by an Albatross Scout, Second Lieut. Herring fired two bursts and the enemy aircraft turned over on its back and dropped in a spin, but owing to the haze it was not seen to crash.

Miscellaneous.—Second Lieut. Paull, No. 101 Squadron, received a direct hit by a "flaming onion," which fortunately only went straight through the plane, doing no further damage. His machine was also badly hit by machine gun fire.

Second Lieut. Wilson and Lieutenant Richardson, No. 102 Squadron, in spite of very thick mist, managed to reach their objective, and were guided back to their aerodrome by means of one lighthouse and rockets. Nothing else could be seen.

Honours and Awards.

Military Cross.—Captain P. D. Robinson.
Military Medal.—First Air Mechanic H. Doran.

January 26th.

The visibility was bad on the whole front all day, and in some places fog prevailed.

Ten hostile batteries were successfully engaged for destruction, two explosions caused and five zone calls sent down; 272 photographs taken, 731 bombs dropped (over eight tons on the night of the 25th/26th), and 6,400 rounds fired at ground targets as follows:—

First Brigade.—On the night of the 25th/26th, No. 2 Squadron dropped sixty-four 25-lb. bombs on Oignies and fifty-four 25-lb. bombs on Courrières; No. 4 Squadron dropped twenty-one 25-lb. bombs on Fournes; No. 5 Squadron dropped forty-five 25-lb. bombs on Quiéry-la-Motte, Vitry, Esquerchin, and Izel, and No. 16 Squadron dropped twenty-six 25-lb. bombs on Billy-Montigny, Noyelles, and Henin-Liétard.

During the day 236 photographs were taken. First Wing dropped sixteen 25-lb. bombs and fired 650 rounds; No. 18 Squadron dropped sixteen 25-lb. bombs; No. 40 Squadron fired 200 rounds and No. 2 Squadron fired 50 rounds.

Second Brigade.—No. 57 Squadron dropped fifty-six 25-lb. bombs on Mouscron.

Third Brigade.—Thirty-six photographs were taken, sixteen 25-lb. bombs dropped, and 600 rounds fired.

9th Wing.—On the night of the 25th/26th:—

No. 101 Squadron dropped forty-eight 25-lb. and five incendiary bombs on Gontrode, obtaining two direct hits on hangars; forty-eight 25-lb. bombs on Oostacker, five direct hits being obtained on hangars; eight 25-lb., two 40-lb., and three incendiary bombs on St. Denis Westrem; eight 25-lb. and two 40-lb. bombs on Maria Aalter; twelve 25-lb. bombs on Scheldewindeke, obtaining one direct hit on a large shed, and forty-four 25-lb. and two incendiary bombs on various targets. Three thousand six hundred rounds were fired at hangars, lights on roads, &c. Several of the pilots made two trips.

No. 102 Squadron dropped one hundred and sixty-six 25-lb. bombs on Marquain Aerodrome, and one hundred and five 2-lb. shells were fired from a Vickers quick-firing gun into the hangars on the aerodrome and at a train from a height of 20 feet. During the bombing the above aerodrome was being used by the enemy's night-flying machines. Thirty-four 25-lb. bombs were also dropped on various targets. The majority of the pilots carried out two raids.

Captain Vickers and Lieutenant R. E. Smith, No. 101 Squadron, whilst on night bombing, obtained no less than three direct hits on the hangars at Gontrode Aerodrome. They also obtained a direct hit on a hut on the aerodrome, which blew up.

Lieutenant J. A. Middleton and Second Lieut. McConville obtained two direct hits on hangars at Oostacker.

Captain Martyn and Lieutenant Harvey obtained several direct hits on sheds at Marquain and fired over 30 rounds of H.E. shells into the sheds. On the way back they came down to about 20 feet above a train moving from Annappes to Lille. Twenty 2-lb. H.E. shells were fired into the train, which stopped; several hits on the train were observed.

Second Lieut. A. B. Whiteside and Second Lieut. E. F. Howard, No. 102 Squadron, by the light of a parachute flare saw three enemy aircraft at Marquain Aerodrome. They came down to 300 feet and dropped six bombs on the sheds and one on enemy aircraft in front of the sheds, which they believe was hit. The petrol tank of Second Lieut. Whiteside's machine was hit and he came back on the service tank and was obliged to make a forced landing before reaching the aerodrome.

During the later part of the evening, while several pilots were in the air, a sudden mist came up which made flying practically impossible. In spite of this, several pilots reached their objective, and by determination managed to get back safely.

Enemy aircraft activity was practically nil all day (no combats took place).

One hostile machine was brought down by anti-aircraft of the Fourth Army.

Honours and Awards.

Distinguished Conduct Medal.—No. 11,559 Corporal C. J. French.

January 27th.

Very little flying was done owing to thick mist.

Thirty-nine photographs were taken, 28 of which were by the First Brigade.

Machines of No. 43 Squadron dropped four 25-lb. bombs on Henin-Liètard, and four 25-lb. bombs on a working party near La Bassée. Ten 25-lb. bombs were dropped by machines of the First Wing.

No combats took place all day.

Eighth Brigade.—Two formations of six machines each of No. 55 Squadron left the ground to bomb the barracks and station at Treves. The outline of the objective could just be seen through the mist, and five pilots of the first formation dropped their bombs on the town. The second formation, owing to the thick mist, were unable to see the town and returned with their bombs with the exception of one pilot who could just see the bend in the river at the town and dropped one 230-lb. bomb. All the results were obscured. Second Lieut. J. Fox and Lieutenant S. Jones took photographs of an aerodrome east of Mars-le-Tours and of Les Baraques, 45 plates being exposed. All surrounding ground was covered by thick fog.

January 28th.

The weather was fine all day, but there was a certain amount of ground mist in some places.

During the day a record number of photographs were taken, 2,404 plates being exposed in all.

Seventy hostile batteries were successfully engaged for destruction and eight neutralized ; three gun-pits were destroyed, 23 damaged, 16 explosions, and 19 fires caused. Forty-two zone calls were sent down.

A total of three hundred and eighty-one 25-lb., two 230-lb., and nineteen 112-lb. bombs were dropped, and 13,007 rounds fired at ground targets, as follows :—

First Brigade.—First Wing dropped eighty 25-lb. bombs and fired 800 rounds; No. 18 Squadron dropped twenty-four 25-lb. bombs and Tenth Wing fired 2,250 rounds.

Second Brigade.—No. 57 Squadron dropped sixty-seven 25-lb. bombs on Roulers ammunition dump ; Second Wing dropped seventy-one 25-lb. bombs ; Third Squadron A.F.C. fired 1,737 rounds and 1,400 rounds were fired on various targets.

Third Brigade.—Forty-seven 25-lb. bombs were dropped and 2,020 rounds fired.

Fifth Brigade.—Fifteenth Wing dropped seventy 25-lb. bombs and fired 4,400 rounds ; twenty-second Wing dropped nine 25-lb. bombs and No. 84 Squadron fired 600 rounds.

Eighth Brigade.—Eight 112-lb. and two 230-lb. bombs on Treves.

Ninth Wing.—No. 25 Squadron dropped nine 112-lb. bombs on Marquain Aerodrome, and No. 27 Squadron dropped three 112-lb. and thirteen 25-lb. bombs on Menin.

Enemy Aircraft.—Enemy aircraft were very active and a considerable amount of fighting took place, in which two enemy machines were brought down and 13 driven down out of control.

Flight Commander Price, Naval Squadron No. 8, dived on an enemy aircraft two-seater and fired 200 rounds at 20 to 50 yards range. The enemy aircraft nose-dived and burst into flames at about 4,000 feet and crashed near La Bassée.

An offensive patrol of the same squadron had a general engagement with seven Albatross Scouts. Flight Lieut. Jordan fired at about 50 yards range at one of the enemy airmen until his ammunition was exhausted. The enemy aircraft pullled up and stalled, then proceeded to dive vertically apparently out of control.

A patrol of No. 40 Squadron observed a formation of enemy scouts about six strong. Second Lieut. H. M. Hutton attacked one enemy aircraft and shots were seen to enter the fuselage. The enemy aircraft stall turned and went down in a vertical nose-dive, emitting smoke, and apparently out of control. Second Lieut. Wolff attacked an enemy aircraft two-seater, firing several bursts at point blank range—tracers being seen to enter the enemy aircraft fuselage. The enemy aircraft was eventually seen to turn completely over and dive very steeply out of control, followed by Second Lieut. Wolff, who was forced to break off the combat owing to being attacked by two enemy aircraft scouts.

An offensive patrol of No. 29 Squadron engaged eight enemy aircraft scouts and one two-seater. During the fight four enemy aircraft were driven down out of control, the following officers accounting for one each :—Captain Meek, Lieutenant Wingate-Grey, Lieutenant de Fontenay, and Lieutenant Coombe.

Whilst on photography, Sergeant Noel and Second Lieut. Stennett, No. 57 Squadron, were attacked by three Albatross Scouts, one of which was driven down out of control.

Second Lieut. Hegarty, No. 60 Squadron, attacked one of eight Albatross Scouts and drove one down out of control.

Second Lieut. Colville-Jones and Lieutenant Phelps, No. 20 Squadron, attacked the rear machine of four Albatross Scouts. After 150 rounds had been fired the enemy aircraft went down out of control.

Second Lieut. Todd, No. 70 Squadron, while on special mission attacked four Albatross Scouts and two triplanes who were helping a German two-seater against some Belgian Nieuports. He dived at one of the enemy aircraft scouts and kept firing till within 40 yards. The enemy aircraft went down out of control, falling from side to side and finally getting into a spin.

Second Lieut. Chick and Captain Makepeace, No. 11 Squadron, attacked a D.F.W., and the pilot and observer each fired 50 rounds, after which the enemy aircraft went down out of control and was lost to sight in the mist.

Second Lieut. Clapham, No. 54 Squadron, dived on one of three enemy scouts. The enemy aircraft went down out of control and was later seen to crash.

Second Lieuts. F. Ransley and R. Herring, No. 48 Squadron, whilst on photography, attacked four enemy aircraft two-seaters. One enemy aircraft was shot down completely out of control and the remaining enemy aircraft broke off the combat.

Five successful long distance photographic reconnaissances were carried out by No. 25 Squadron, during which 188 photographs were taken as follows:—Second Lieuts. A. Wright and P. Campbell-Martin carried out a reconnaissance of Ghent-Mons and exposed 44 plates; Second Lieuts. R. Pohlmann and F. Creek carried out a photographic reconnaissance of five hostile aerodromes and exposed 18 plates; Second Lieut. W. Milnes and Lieutenant H. E. Pohlmann exposed 54 plates in the Bruges area; Lieutenant J. Pugh and Second Lieut. W. Walsh took 36 photographs of six hostile aerodromes, and Second Lieuts. G. Pike and O. Hinson took 36 photographs while on a long distance reconnaissance in the neighbourhood of Namur.

Note.—Reference Royal Flying Corps Communique No. 122, January 11th, regarding a message received by wireless from Captain Willcox and Second Air Mechanic Reynolds, No. 101 Squadron, that their machine was near Bethune and being shelled by our anti-aircraft guns, it has since been ascertained that no guns of the First Army fired at all that night, and that the machine was over the German lines, but owing to the weather conditions it was impossible for the pilot to accurately locate his position.

L. A. K. BUTT, Captain,
Staff Officer.

Headquarters,
Royal Flying Corps,
1st February 1918.

No. 51.

CONFIDENTIAL.

ROYAL NAVAL AIR SERVICE.

OPERATIONS REPOR

(with Royal Flying Corps Reports attached)

1st to 14th **FEBRUARY** 1918.

NAVAL STAFF,
OPERATIONS DIVISION.
14th February 1918.

ROYAL NAVAL AIR SERVICE.

REPORT OF OPERATIONS

(Completed from Reports during period
1st to 14th February 1918).

CONTENTS.

	PAGE
HOME STATIONS	2
DUNKIRK	2
R.N.A.S. SQUADRON, WITH ROYAL FLYING CORPS REPORTS ATTACHED	6
EASTERN MEDITERRANEAN	9
BRITISH ADRIATIC SQUADRON	28
ROYAL FLYING CORPS COMMUNIQUÉS	31

HOME STATIONS.

ENGAGEMENT WITH HOSTILE AIRCRAFT.

February 5th.

Felixstowe.—Large America Seaplanes 8661 and 8677 left on an anti-submarine patrol at 0855 and at 1110, when approximately 17 south-west of the late position of the North Hinder, five enemy seaplanes, three single-seaters and two two-seaters were sighted, which dived on the large America machines.

Seaplane 8677, which was some distance behind 8661, put up a running fight, but without any decisive result. Seaplane 8661 was attacked by three single-seaters, which closed in behind its tail and fired at a range of from 200 to 300 yards, hitting the machine repeatedly. By steering a slightly zig-zag course the engineer and W/T operator at the rear guns were able to bring their guns to bear alternately.

At 1130, when approximately 16 miles south of Outer Gabard, Engineer G. H. Robinson (A.M. 2 E.) hit one of the single-seaters, which turned off to port, side-slipped, and crashed into the water.

The two-seaters circled around the crashed machine, while the remaining two single-seaters followed on for another five minutes, then turned back.

Both the engineer and W/T operator of Seaplane 8661 are mentioned for their coolness during the attack.

Names of crew of 8661 :—

Flight Lieut. C. J. Clayton.
Flight Lieut. A. Adamson.
Engineer G. H. Robinson (A.M. 2 E.), O.N.F. 26789.
W/T operator F. C. Callen (A.M. 2 W/T), O.N.F. 6066.

Both machines eventually returned safely to their base.

DUNKIRK.

WEATHER.

Owing to high winds, cloudy weather, and unfavourable weather conditions generally, aircraft operations have been greatly hindered during this period.

PHOTOGRAPHIC RECONNAISSANCE.

February 2nd.

No. 1 Wing, 2nd Squadron.—A photographic reconnaissance was carried out over Zeebrugge Harbour and the new Knocke Battery, during which 16 plates were exposed.

During a second reconnaissance photographs were obtained of the Mole at Zeebrugge, and the new battery at Het Zoute. The regions of Salzeate, Bruges, and Knocke were also photographed.

February 3rd.

A photographic reconnaissance was carried out, and plates exposed, over the coast line from the Dutch frontier to Westende.

OFFENSIVE PATROL WORK—ENGAGEMENT WITH ENEMY.

February 2nd.

No. 1 Wing, 13th Squadron.—Whilst on patrol in the locality of Oostkerke, Acting Flight Commander Day, in a Sopwith Camel, sighted a Rumpler two-seater photographic machine crossing the lines at about 18,000 feet over Dixmude. The Sopwith pilot attacked from the sun, firing about 50 rounds, after which the hostile machine dived very steeply, smoking a great deal. Finally one of the wings came off, and the machine fell in the region of Oostkerke.

February 3rd.

No. 4 Wing, 9th Squadron.—Whilst on patrol a formation of five Sopwith machines encountered two Albatross two-seaters over Staden. The Sopwith formation dived on the enemy machines and fired several hundred rounds into one of the machines at close range. The enemy machine dived steeply, but flattened out near the ground and appeared to land near Hooglade.

Flight Commander Redgate attacked the other machines from about 50 yards range, and one was seen to go down in a slow glide, then dropped vertically, and eventually fell over, completely out of control. It is considered that this machine was destroyed.

On a later patrol a formation of seven Sopwith machines attacked three hostile machines about 2 miles S.W. of Roulers. The Sopwith formation dived on them, splitting up their formation, and one of them afterwards seemed to be out of control. Another was driven down, and eventually landed safely in a field.

February 3rd.

No. 4 Wing, 10th Squadron.—Whilst on patrol a formation of five Sopwiths encountered four Albatross Scouts and one two-seater at 12,000 feet over Rumbeke. One of the enemy machines was driven down out of control by Flight Lieut. Hinchcliffe, and observed to crash into a tree.

Other combats took place, but with no decisive results. Flight Sub-Lieut. Wilmot in Sopwith Camel B. 6370 failed to return from this patrol.

SUMMARY.

Hostile machines driven down out of control - 2
   „   „   destroyed - - - - - 3
                                  Total - - 5

BOMB ATTACKS.

Varssenaere Aerodrome	February 2nd	1,120 lbs.	D.H. 4's.
Houttave Dump -	„ 3rd	923 „	„
	Total - -	2,043 lbs.	

February 2nd.

No. 5 Wing, 5th Squadron.—A bombing attack was carried out during the day on Varssenaere Aerodrome by six D.H. 4 bombers, accompanied by two escorting machines, during which thirty-two 25-lb. and twenty 16-lb. bombs were dropped from heights of 15,600 to 17,000 feet. The sheds on the eastern side were principally attacked, and a direct hit, causing a fire, is reported on a shed in the south-east corner. Bombs were also seen to burst on the western group of sheds and among those situated in the north-east corner, but no other direct hits are reported.

Visibility was good, and anti-aircraft fire heavy and accurate; four enemy aircraft were seen, but did not attack the bombing formation.

Three photographs were taken, one each of Engel and Varssenaere Aerodromes and one at St. Pierre Cappelle.

No. 5 Wing, 5th Squadron.—A bombing attack was carried out on Houttave Aerodrome by six D.H. 4 bombers, accompanied by two escorting machines, during which two 50 lb., fifteen 25 lb., and twenty-eight 16-lb. bombs were dropped from heights of 15,200 to 17,000 feet.

A number of bombs were observed to burst among the sheds and hangars, and a direct hit is reported on the large sheds.

Three hostile aircraft were seen, of which one attacked D.H. 4 A. 7664, and after firing about 300 rounds it was apparently driven down out of control by the fire of the after guns of the D.H. 4, which fired about 250 rounds. Visibility was good, and anti-aircraft fire moderate; only one photograph was secured in the vicinity of the objective.

Honours and Awards.

Name.	Unit.	Awarded.
Flight Commander R. G. O. Compston	No. 8 Squadron	2nd Bar to D.S.C.
Flight Commander G. W. Price	No. 8 Squadron	Bar to D.S.C.
Flight Lieut. W. L. Jordan	No. 8 Squadron	Bar to D.S.C.
Flight Sub-Lieut. E. G. Johnstone	No. 8 Squadron	D.S.C.

French Honours.

Ldg. Mechanic H. Simpson, D.S.M., O. No. F. 2647.	No. 17 Squadron	Croix de Guerre.
S. B. A. G. Rothwell, D.S.M., O. No. M. 15814.	No. 17 Squadron	Croix de Guerre.

Belgian Honours.

Flight Commander R. B. Munday	No. 8 Squadron	Belgian Croix de Guerre.
Flight Lieut. G. W. Hemming	No. 4 Squadron	Chevalier de la Couronne.
Do. do.	No. 4 Squadron	Croix de Guerre.

Casualties.

Name.	Unit.	Date.
Missing.		
Flight Commander R. R. Winter	No. 9 Squadron	3.2.18
Flight Sub-Lieut. W. H. Wilmot	No. 10 Squadron	3.2.18
Flight Sub-Lieut. H. Day	No. 8 Squadron	5.2.18
Wounded.		
Flight Sub-Lieut. G. O. Smith	No. 10 Squadron	16.2.18

NAVAL SQUADRON WITH THE ROYAL FLYING CORPS.

(PERIOD JANUARY 13TH TO FEBRUARY 9TH, 1918.)]

NAVAL SQUADRON No. 8.

This squadron has been attached to the 1st Brigade R.F.C., and has carried out 78 offensive patrols, 46 flights in pursuit of hostile artillery machines, and 20 special missions, making a total of 188 hours 20 minutes flying.

A total of 21 combats took place, 12 of these being decisive.

January 19th.

Flight Lieut. Jordan, Flight Sub-Lieut. Johnstone, and Flight Sub-Lieut. Dennett attacked a hostile machine which they drove down completely out of control.

Flight Commander Price while on special mission attacked one of three Albatross Scouts, which fell over sideways, and, after side-slipping for a while, went down vertically out of control.

Flight Lieut. Jordan and Flight Sub-Lieuts. Johnstone, Dennett, Walworth, and Johns, observed 14 Albatross Scouts in two groups. One group of three was attacked and they dived away east. Flight Sub-Lieut. Johnstone followed one machine down to 8,000 feet, firing at it all the time, and enemy aircraft was then seen to go down out of control. Flight Sub-Lieut. Dennett got in a good burst at one enemy aircraft of the other group at very close range, and this machine was seen to go down completely out of control, falling from side to side, and then diving vertically.

January 21st.

Flight Commander Munday made a night flight for the purpose of attacking a hostile balloon. He came down to 1,000 feet and found his objective. He dived twice at it, and after the second dive balloon burst into flames.

Flight Commander Price attacked the rear machine of a formation of seven Albatross Scouts. Enemy aircraft was very cleverly handled, and Flight Commander Price had great difficulty in bringing his gun to bear on it. He fired about 300 rounds at enemy aircraft, which was eventually seen to stall, turn completely over, and disappear through a thick bank of clouds completely out of control.

January 22nd.

Flight Sub-Lieut. Day on the same patrol dived at a machine which was preparing to attack Flight Commander Price. Tracers were seen to enter the enemy machine, which turned on its back and fell out of control.

January 24th.

Flight Commander Munday and Flight Lieut. Cooper, whilst on offensive patrol, observed two formations of 4–5 Albatross Scouts. Flight Commander Munday shot down one completely out of control, and Flight Commander Cooper shot down another one completely out of control. This enemy aircraft was last seen at 5,000 feet still descending in a very steep nose dive. In the same engagement Flight Sub-Lieut. White dived on an Albatross Scout which was attacking a Camel. Tracers were seen to enter the pilot's cockpit, and enemy aircraft stalled and fell over sideways. Flight Sub-Lieut. White is convinced that enemy pilot must have been shot. Anti-aircraft report one Albatross Scout shot down in this engagement.

Flight Commander Price on wireless patrol attacked an Albatross Scout. Enemy aircraft went down in an almost vertical dive, and the Camel followed it for some way, but was not able to keep up with enemy aircraft. This combat is confirmed by anti-aircraft battery.

Flight Sub-Lieut. Sneath shot down out of control one of four Albatross Scouts.

Flight Lieut. Jordan and Flight Sub-Lieuts. Johnstone, Walworth, and Johns attacked a single Albatross Scout which had come very close to the lines. This machine was shot down quite out of control.

Flight Lieut. Jordan and Flight Sub-Lieut. Johnstone attacked two or three Albatross Scouts. One enemy aircraft was shot down out of control.

Activity of hostile wireless machines has been below normal during this period.

January 27th to February 9th, 1918, inclusive.

This squadron has been attached to the 1st Brigade, R.F.C., and has carried out 119 offensive patrols, 41 flights in pursuit of hostile artillery machines, and six special missions, making a total of 223 hours 50 minutes flying. A total of 28 combats took place, 12 of these being decisive.

January 28th.

Flight Commander Price attacked an enemy two-seater which nose-dived and burst into flames at about 4,000 feet, and was eventually seen to crash.

Flight Lieut. Jordan, whilst on offensive patrol, attacked a formation of seven Albatross Scouts, attacked one enemy aircraft which became detached, and shot it down out of control.

January 29th.

Flight Sub-Lieut. Day attacked an Albatross Scout at very close range. Tracers were seen to enter the enemy aircraft, which fell completely out of control.

Flight Commander Munday, whilst leading an offensive patrol, attacked one of the five enemy aircraft, which he shot down out of control.

Flight Sub-Lieut. Dennett attacked an enemy aircraft which had become slightly separated from its formation. Enemy aircraft after a series of stalls and side-slips, eventually went down vertically out of control.

February 2nd.

Flight Commander Compston attacked an enemy aircraft two-seater at point-blank range. Enemy aircraft went down completely out of control, and was watched until quite near the ground, and was seen to crash.

Flight Commander Compston and Flight Sub-Lieuts. Crundall, Day, and Johns attacked one enemy aircraft, which they shot down completely out of control.

February 3rd.

Flight Commander Compston attacked one of two enemy aircraft, which fell over on its left side and went down completely out of control, so fast that Flight Commander Compston was unable to keep up with it. On the same patrol he attacked another machine at very close range. Enemy aircraft elevators were seen to be moving violently backwards and forwards as he fell, but without any effect. Other pilots also fired 400 rounds at this machine, which was observed to fall completely out of control and crash.

February 3rd.

Flight Commander Munday attacked an enemy aircraft which had become cut off from the formation, and getting to within close range apparently unobserved, he shot the enemy aircraft down vertically and completely out of control.

Flight Sub-Lieut. White also shot one down out of control; enemy aircraft turning over on one wing and falling vertically.

Flight Lieut. McDonald and Flight Sub-Lieuts. Day and Fowler fired at an Albatross Scout, which they shot down out of control.

Hostile wireless activity has again been much below normal, and weather conditions on the whole not favourable for observation work.

SUMMARY.

Hostile machines driven down out of control - 21
    ,,   ,,   destroyed - - - - 3

Total - - 24

Casualties.—Flight Sub-Lieut Day, D.S.C., missing.

EASTERN MEDITERRANEAN STATION.

OPERATIONS AGAINST "BRESLAU" AND "GOEBEN."

(Period January 20th to 29th, 1918.)

At Mudros dawn patrols had been arranged and were carried out as follows:—

(a) Seaplane to Mount Athos and returned—one hour 30 minutes. Owing to misty weather, pilot made northern route both ways. Nothing to report.

(b) Seaplane searching area between Skyros and Strati, as well as of the eastern and southern coasts of Skyros. A quantity of wreckage of s.s. Trocas was seen, including two capsized boats, 28 miles south of Strati. Nothing else of importance. A patrol of 4 hours 55 minutes.

(c) At 0507, G.M.T., Henri Farman machine patrolled south-west of Strati, returning at 0650. Nothing to report.

(A) Bombing of "Breslau" and "Goeben" at Sea.—While these machines were out, at 0546 a signal was intercepted that the "Goeben" and "Breslau" were out. Immediately all available machines and pilots were ordered to stand by, and out-stations were told to carry out previous orders. At this time there was a thick mist over Lemnos. "G" flight was directed to send patrols towards Mitylene, and smaller machines were sent on short patrols in every direction with orders to return in half an hour if nothing had been seen. The general effect of the previous orders was to concentrate machines from out-stations on Mudros and Imbros.

At 0610 a telephone message was received from Imbros that Kusu and Kephalo were being shelled, and at 0540 that Scout machines had been sent away. Imbros at 0530, through the mist, had heard firing in the direction of Kusu, and machines were got out and the pilots stood by. With the first clear light for observation, the "Raglan" was seen to be sunk at anchor and that Monitor 28 was on fire amidships. The "Goeben" and "Breslau" were then about five miles out to sea off Kusu and steering south. They were followed by the W/T planes, who reported their movements, but could not be heard owing to the continual jamming by the enemy ships. Shortly after 0600 the magazine of Monitor 28 blew up, and she sank.

At 0635 a general signal was received, "Take all necessary steps to engage the enemy." For the time being no further orders could be sent.

At 0645 Imbros had 8 to 10 machines in the air continuously harrying the enemy ships. This action of our aircraft was causing the "Breslau" to steer a zigzag course which brought her into one of our minefields, to the north-west of Rabbit Island, where she struck a mine. Very shortly afterwards she was hit by an aircraft bomb. She hauled out a line, and the "Goeben," after searching round her, proceeded in a southerly direction. Shortly afterwards the "Breslau" sank. This was probably about 0700. Five Turkish destroyers endeavoured to reach the spot, but were driven off by two British destroyers. At 0745 the Air Service was told that the "Lowestoft," "Agamemnon," and "Skirmisher" were about to proceed out of Mudros Harbour, and were ordered to provide machines to escort them. All seaplanes and aeroplanes not otherwise engaged were ordered on this duty, and carried out a continuous patrol from 0755 till 0930, when the ships returned to harbour. The "Goeben" continued on her southerly course for about 20 minutes, after the sinking of the "Breslau," but on being attacked again with bombs, altered her course and headed for the Dardanelles. Soon after this she struck one of our mines, and developed a list to port of 15 degrees. She thereupon altered course to port, and steered for the entrance to the Straits, at not more than 10 knots. Aircraft continued to bomb her while she entered the Straits; her speed declined to "dead slow" and she ultimately ran aground at the point at Nagara Burnu.

Further details of the air work carried out during this period are :—

1. Flight Lieut. Moore in a Sopwith Camel, escorting machines dropping bombs on the "Goeben" and "Breslau," saw two seaplanes coming up from Helles, dived on one, which turned and dived. He opened fire at about 200 yards and drove the enemy down till he landed off Helles. He then turned and climbed towards Imbros at 8,000 feet and continued patrol over "Goeben" and "Breslau," when a second seaplane approached at about 5,000 feet. He dived into it but could not get close enough to fire until it had nearly landed. He

finished his ammunition into her on the water. He then flew back to Imbros and observed the "Breslau" sinking.

2. Anti-aircraft fire was being experienced from "Goeben," a portion of W/T aerial wire being shot away from our reconnaissance machine (pilot Flight Lieut. Grigson, observer Sub-Lieut. Gayford) who had reported all the previous movements, but as already explained the W/T was jammed by enemy ships. This machine, however, was able to make a semaphore signal to the destroyers to the effect that the "Breslau" had hit a mine.

3. Flight Sub-Lieut. Murray in a Sopwith Bomber dropped four 65-lb. bombs on the "Goeben" and "Breslau." Good shooting was made, but no direct hits were registered. The enemy ships were seen to be firing at two of our destroyers.

4. After the "Breslau" had sunk, Flight Lieut. Grigson and observer Sub-Lieut. Gayford went up again to report on the enemy's movements, and reported on the shooting of our destroyers at the Turkish destroyers, numerous hits being registered, and a fire was caused on one of the enemy craft. They observed also that our destroyers were under the fire of the land batteries during this engagement. The "Goeben" now was in position Lat. 39.52, Long. 25.52, and still steering south, not so much anti-aircraft fire as previously being experienced from her. She was attacked for a second time with bombs, a hit being registered. Shortly afterwards she hit a mine amidships on the port side and developed a list to port, also settling by the stern a good deal. She altered course to port and steered for the entrance to the Dardanelles. Her anti-aircraft fire now became very feeble and she was more down by the stern.

5. Flight Commander Hackman and observer Lieutenant Piper, and Flight Commander Sorley and observer Sub-Lieut. Smith, in two D.H. 4's, dropped four 112-lb. bombs on the "Goeben" and "Breslau" while they were about four miles south-east of Kephalo Point.

Observer Sub-Lieut. Smith states:—

During this flight the enemy ships, about 2 miles south of Kephalo, were going west at full speed, zigzagging. The "Breslau" was seen to strike a mine aft, and reduced speed. Our machine proceeded to attack "Breslau" from astern at 5,000 feet, and as the ship went astern a 112-lb. bomb was released, which appeared to fall on the stern of the "Breslau." A cloud of smoke and spray obscured the quarter-deck, and the disturbance in the water enveloped the whole of her stern. Both ships circled round, making a dense smoke screen. We then attacked the "Goeben" at 6,000 feet, a 112-lb. bomb falling 30 yards off the starboard quarter. The "Goeben" was then seen to go completely round the "Breslau," and then go almost alongside and stop. The anti-aircraft fire from both ships was good and in quantity, the "Goeben's" being high explosive. Leaving both ships close together and neither having way on, our machine returned for more bombs.

A D.H. 4 (Flight Commander Hackman, observer Lieut. Piper) at 0700 left for a *second flight*, and arrived over "Goeben" at 0720, dropped two 65-lb. bombs from 4,000 feet, both dropping on the port side, 15 yards from bow and from stern. Observed three enemy destroyers in action with two of our destroyers and one of the enemy's destroyers afire, steaming towards Kumkale. "Goeben" altered course towards destroyer with a slight list to port.

A D.H. 4 (Flight Commander Sorley and observer Lieutenant Smith), *second flight*, at 0735 left with two more 112-lb. bombs. The "Goeben" was turning from south course to north-east, and two destroyers were making away from the sunken "Breslau" towards Cape Helles, our destroyers going towards "Breslau," and being shelled by "Goeben" and Cape Helles batteries. When in position about latitude 40 N., longitude 26·07 E., the "Goeben" was seen to strike a mine amidships on the starboard side and stopped engines; then carried on at half speed. This machine at 0750 released one 112-lb. bomb at 5,500 feet, which fell 50 yards out from the port beam. A second 112-lb. bomb fell on the port quarter, and appeared to hit the side, covering the whole of the quarter-deck with water. The Turkish ensign was conspicuous at the gaff. "Goeben" continued towards the Straits at half speed, putting in some accurate anti-aircraft fire. Returned for more bombs.

Another attack was made by Flight Sub-Lieut. Murray in Sopwith Bomber, escorted by Flight Lieut. Wincott and Flight Lieut. Fowler in "Camels." About 0752 dropped four 65-lb. bombs at the "Goeben." She was then about 1 mile up the Straits, and was observed to have a very heavy list to port and was down at the stern. No anti-aircraft fire was experienced from the "Goeben" and very little from the Helles batteries. Ten machines were observed flying round the "Goeben" at an estimated height of 1,000 feet, and two seaplanes were seen on the water.

Flight Commander Sorley and observer Sub-Lieut. Smith and Flight Commander Hackman and observer Lieutenant Piper carried out a *third attack* on the "Goeben" at 0938, and found her passing Chanak, going slowly up the Straits, followed by two torpedo boats and two destroyers. When just S. of Nagaru Burnu she went "dead slow" and steered straight for the point, ultimately going aground about a ship's length off the water line on the point. The destroyers and torpedo boats hurried towards her, as well as a number of small ships from Chanak, one destroyer going alongside, the other destroyer taking up position two lengths ahead. Both machines dropped both their bombs, these falling quite close to the "Goeben," one direct hit being registered. These machines returned at 1010, having experienced anti-aircraft fire from Nagara and ships and destroyers, the "Goeben" firing a few rounds from heavy guns. On looking back, the "Goeben's" stern appeared to be swinging slightly towards mid-channel, bows remaining fast, as though the tide up Straits was the cause.

At 0730 a raid was carried out from Mudros, with orders to look for and bomb the enemy's ship. The machines were two Blackburn Baby (Flight Sub-Lieut W. Johnston and Flight Sub-Lieut. R. W. Peel), escorted by Commander A. Moraitinis in a "Camel." At 0750 the Camel pilot observed the "Goeben" with two T.B.D.'s to starboard and two more T.B.D.'s astern. At the same time hostile aircraft came in sight; 10 hostile seaplanes were seen in all, three of which were two-seaters. The British machines immediately engaged. Commander Moraitinis drove down two enemy machines, then fought away a two-seater attacking one of our seaplanes. At this time Flight Sub-Lieut. Johnston's machine was observed to fall in flames. Flight Sub-Lieut. Peel passed over the "Goeben," but his bomb failed to release. In spite of the superior hostile aircraft which he was encountering, he returned to make another attack, fighting two enemy two-seaters, forced his way back, got over the "Goeben" (now about half a mile up the Straits), and being still engaged by the two hostile machines, dropped his 65-lb. bomb. His engine being damaged, Sub-Lieut. Peel was forced to descend and land about a quarter of a mile up the Straits near Cape Helles, landing between a Turkish torpedo boat and the shore. There his engine picked up a little, and half taxying and half flying, he managed to round the Cape, and eventually reached the coast of Imbros, beaching the machine at Pyrgos at 0900. He remained there for two days, awaiting new parts for the engine, and arrived back at Mudros at 1100 on the 22nd January.

There are two very gallant points about Flight Sub-Lieut. Peel's action. First in returning to the attack to carry out his orders to bomb the "Goeben" in spite of the superior force threatening him, and secondly in his work in returning to Imbros with his damaged machine. Commander Moraitinis in his report speaks of the very gallant fight which both Sub-Lieut. Johnston and Sub-Lieut. Peel put up against this superior force.

Flight Sub-Lieut. Peel mentions in his report that there appeared to be four enemy machines on the water, evidently out of control, at 0830, at which time he managed to restart his engine. While Sub-Lieut. Peel was returning to the attack, Commander Moraitinis proceeded to attack a two-seater, and then followed Sub-Lieut. Peel and attacked another hostile machine. While busy with this machine, he (Moraitinis) was attacked from behind by a single-seater, and this attack riddled his petrol tank and he was forced to return to Imbros, where he landed at 0900. Very gallant work on the part of the three officers concerned.

Commander Moraitinis adds that the torpedo boat destroyers escorting "Goeben" were "Penleok-i-Derla" and "Peik-i-Shevket" class, and two smaller.

Commander Moraitinis made another flight in the afternoon as escort for a bombing raid, leaving 1200 from Mudros, and reported the position of "Goeben," encountering anti-aircraft fire and seeing two hostile aircraft, which made away. He returned to Mudros at 1340.

"B" Squadron at Kalloni, Mitylene, had a patrol of three Sopwith ½-Strutter Fighters out at dawn on the 20th January, as S.O. 4th D.S. had requested a reconnaissance of the Chesme Peninsula, as 2,000 troops and 40 sailing vessels had been reported to be preparing for a raid on Khios. At 0715 this patrol returned, having seen absolutely nothing. Interesting, as pointing to hostile camouflage.

Immediately on receiving the "G.B." signal at 0550, steps were taken to maintain a patrol from Cape Baba to Johnston's Bank, which was kept up till 1410, when orders were received to discontinue.

This practically ends reports of R.N.A.S. work from dawn on the 20th January 1918, till "Goeben" was reported grounded.

(B) Bombing operations against the "Goeben" when ashore at Nagara Burnu.—After the "Goeben" had been definitely located at 1030 on the 20th January 1918, orders were sent to Imbros for the machines to be collected for a bombing raid at 1300 from Imbros, and a special reconnaissance was ordered to report on the "Goeben's" position. This reconnaissance was carried out by Flight Lieut. Grigson and Observer Lieut. Abbott. They started at 0920 and returned with their report at 1030. The report states :—

"Goeben" is lying a ship's length from Nagara Burnu and seems in difficulties. She looks as though aground, as she is slightly tilted up forward and a large amount of disturbed mud was seen around her. Five destroyers were steering about in the Narrows at this time—they did not attempt to tow the "Goeben."

This reconnaissance was escorted by a "Camel" (Flight Lieut. Moore), who reported that no hostile aircraft were sighted.

Photographs of the "Goeben" were taken and her position was placed on an Admiralty Chart, and photographs taken of the sketch. The soundings are taken from Admiralty Chart 2429, and it is fairly certain that she could not be so far on the sandbank as would appear from that chart. The position of the bank has possibly shifted since 1880.

It was a great misfortune that the weather had now become misty and the clouds low, and this state of the weather continued throughout the afternoon and the night of the 20th–21st January.

At 1330 two D.H.4's (Flight Commander Sorley and observer Sub-Lieut. Smith, and Flight Commander Hackman, observer Lieutenant Piper) accompanied by seven "Camels" (Flight Commander Donald, Flight Lieuts. Wincott, Moore, and Fowler, Flight Sub-Lieuts. Mackie, Girling, and Cantrill), left with four 112-lb. bombs to attack "Goeben." The bombs fell close around her, but no direct hits were observed. She was still in the same position. Her high explosive fire was heavy and fairly accurate and she also appeared to be firing her 11-inch gun when the bombers were approaching. Nagara Battery and Chanak were also firing. There were two destroyers cruising up and down in the Straits and 11 Caiques hovering astern. A small tug was alongside "Goeben," but she left when the bombing commenced; the Caiques scattering at the same time. The escort did not observe any enemy aircraft. Heavy clouds of brown smoke were coming from the "Goeben's" funnels.

At about 1400 on the 20th January, Imbros reported that an enemy minelayer laid mines across the entrance to the Straits from Kum Kale to Sedd-el-Bahr. She then proceeded back up the Straits and was lost to sight.

Meanwhile, at Mudros information was received from the rescued "Breslau's" crew that submarines had been laying mines off Mudros Harbour. As H.M.S. "Lord Nelson" might be expected back to harbour at any moment, all available seaplanes and land machines were sent on mine patrol over the mouth of the harbour and the swept channel. No mines or submarines were observed.

During this afternoon, bombing and fighting machines were being concentrated at Imbros and Mudros ready to renew the attack at dawn on the 21st January.

Four machines were sent over from Mudros to Imbros taking a renewal of the M/G ammunition supply, and the "Elpiniki" was stocked with petrol, bombs and extra personnel required for continued work and she sailed during the afternoon.

At 1830 Flight Lieut. Gaskell left Imbros to bomb the "Goeben," but owing to the heavy low fog bank covering the whole of the Straits, was unable to pick up his position, so dropped bombs in the locality, but was unable to observe any results.

At 2130 Flight Sub-Lieut. Harben also made a raid and dropped his bombs, but, for the same reason, was unable to make any observation.

In all 65 flights were made during the day, and as will have been observed a great many pilots and observers made two or three attacks on the enemy's ships, as well as carrying out other flights.

At dawn on the 21st January 1918 a raid was made on the "Goeben" by five bombers escorted by six "Camels." It was commenced in semi-darkness and the Narrows were obscured by clouds, so that the 10 heavy bombs were dropped in the estimated position of the "Goeben," and no observation could be made. No hostile machines were sighted and the anti-aircraft fire was well below our machines.

A further reconnaissance was made by one machine at 0930. Clouds were reported at about 500 feet over land, both sides, and over the Nagara Narrows. The "Goeben" was in position.

At 1120 another reconnaissance was made, which observed that the "Goeben" was in view and that the Straits were clear of clouds. Immediate preparations were made for another raid.

At 1200 a bombing raid commenced from Imbros in which 14 machines took part, leaving at intervals of 10 minutes. The visibility over the enemy's country was excellent and some good bomb-dropping was made, but no direct hits were registered. One bomber, owing to engine trouble, did not reach the target and dropped bombs on a camp at Baghali, one shed being completely destroyed.

A 4,000-ton vessel was observed alongside "Goeben" and a smaller vessel was approaching her from the other side; this sheered off, however, when bombs commenced to drop. Smoke was issuing from both the "Goeben's" funnels and she was surrounded by numerous small craft. The Nagara nets were broken in the middle and a destroyer was anchored just north of the gap. Owing to increasing fog and cloud over the Imbros Aerodrome, only five machines made a landing there; four landed safely at Kephalo and five at Mudros.

One of the D.H. 4's in this raid (Flight Commander Sorley and Observer Sub-Lieut. Smith) made the following interesting Report :—

"The 'Goeben' was in the same position as yesterday, her bows being close to nets, which appeared to have been drawn in towards her. Two 'Blue Birds' were seen climbing towards us, about 3,000 feet below. We continued towards 'Goeben' and dropped both bombs in quick succession. We turned as the two enemy machines were preparing to attack under our right wing. One promptly dived—we dived on the other, firing Vickers gun and got in about 100 rounds. She cart-wheeled, passing the wing-tip at about 30 yards. The observer opened fire when she passed our wing and fired one pan into her while passing.

The tracers were seen to enter her fuselage and floats. She turned some way astern, and followed at a safe distance for a few minutes, when she was engaged by another machine."

This was a Sopwith "Camel" (Pilot Flight Commander Donald), who dived at the machine, which swung off to the left and began to dive away. Flight Commander Donald got in a short burst, but the hostile scout got away at very high speed, under shelter of heavy anti-aircraft fire.

During the morning of the 21st January four seaplanes and four land machines were employed in submarine and mine patrol over the swept channel and in escorting H.M.S. "Lord Nelson" back to Mudros Harbour. No hostile submarines or mines were observed.

During this afternoon, a D.H. 4 (Flight Lieut. Woodward, observer Lieutenant Palmer) made another attack on "Goeben," and dropped two 112-lb. bombs, one of which hit the "Goeben," and the other fell about 15 to 20 yards over her. The cloud and mist again came down and hindered operations.

In addition to the actual bombing attacks made during the day and night, very heavy work was undertaken by the whole of the R.N.A.S. in preparing to continue the operations during the succeeding days. Petrol and bombs were obtained from Salonika and reinforcements were offered from Otranto and Egypt, and preparations were made to fit seaplanes for carrying torpedoes.

During the afternoon of the 21st January, at 1600, a flight of Royal Flying Corps arrived at Mudros from Salonika, three B.E. 12's, with the promise that three more bombers would follow on the morning of the 22nd. These machines duly arrived.

Shortly after 1800 on the 21st January, nine machines made a night raid from Mudros. Four searchlights were observed, two coming from the "Goeben," which were immediately extinguished when the attack commenced. Continuous but inaccurate anti-aircraft fire was directed on the machines from shore batteries and also from the "Goeben." Six heavy bombs were dropped on the "Goeben" from heights of 2,500 to 3,000 feet. The target was difficult to define and no claim to a direct hit can be made, but certainly one explosion took place in close proximity to the two searchlights on the "Goeben," which seemed to be the reason for their immediate extinction. All the machines returned safely.

There were 51 flights made during the 24 hours, and some two tons of bombs were dropped.

On the morning of the 22nd January, operations were again hindered by the dense mist; but about 1000 the atmosphere cleared sufficiently for a machine to leave on a special reconnaissance at 1040, and at 0900 four D.H.4's were sent on a raid from Mudros which was most successful, the machines returning without damage. One machine (Flight Lieut. Woodward and observer Lieut. Palmer) made a direct hit amidships, and a volume of steam and smoke appeared directly afterwards from the ship. This observation was confirmed by the other machines, each of which had also released two 112-lb. bombs, which, although not making direct hits, fell very close on different sides of the ship. Three plates were exposed and satisfactory results obtained. From these photographs plans were prepared for observers, showing the exact position of the "Goeben." All the machines reported having seen a Turkish cruiser in the vicinity of the "Goeben."

The R.F.C. flight which had come from Salonika left Mudros at 1300 on the 22nd January to attack "Goeben," escorted by "Camels."

All the above machines returned safely.

A special reconnaissance was made from Imbros at 0840 with captain of E. 12 as passenger. A bombing raid at 1345 dropped eight 112-lb. bombs, which all fell close to "Goeben," but no direct hit was claimed. The machines encountered considerable anti-aircraft fire from her and from the shore batteries.

All daylight raids by bombers were escorted by flights of fighting machines, but there was no interference from hostile aircraft, with the exception of the fights individually reported.

There was a night raid at 2220 from "Ark Royal" by three small seaplanes which all dropped bombs on the "Goeben." One of these (pilot Flight Sub-Lieut. Barnard Smith) had a strange adventure. He reached the objective after some difficulty owing to poor visibility and dropped his bombs on or near the ship from a height of 4,000 feet, the results not being clearly visible. The anti-aircraft fire was intermittent and poor, the majority of the shells bursting beneath him. No searchlights were seen. On the return flight he landed midway between Lemnos and Imbros at 2015 owing to engine trouble on changing petrol supply to rear tank. On gliding to the surface six shots were fired at his machine, apparently by a submarine, when at a height of approximately 600 feet; he was not molested, however, when on the water, and although Very's lights were fired from the seaplane and calcium flares dropped, he received no assistance during the night of the 22nd January. At 0530 on the 23rd January, Short Seaplane N. 1668 (Flight Lieut. Silk and observer Lieutenant Sole)—sent out in search—found the seaplane and towed her to the mouth of Mudros Harbour, where she was taken in tow by a destroyer and brought alongside "Ark Royal," undamaged, at 0900.

At midnight another raid was made from Imbros on the "Goeben," and four direct hits were registered. A Turkish cruiser was seen leaving her and proceeding up the Straits.

From 0800 on the 22nd to 0800 on the 23rd January 1918 48 flights were made and the total weight of bombs dropped was $56\frac{1}{2}$ cwts.

On the morning of the 23rd January, at 0922, four D.H. 4's left Mudros for a bombing raid on "Goeben." Each machine dropped two 112-lb. bombs. No direct hits claimed, but all bombs dropped close and two small boats pulling towards the ship were not seen again after the bombs dropped. The stern of the "Goeben" appeared lower. A large steamer of about 6,000 tons was anchored about ¼ mile astern of her, and appeared to be engaged in lightening her. One of the machines claims to have sunk a tug alongside her.

A raid in the afternoon of the 23rd January reported bombs dropped close around "Goeben," that a small vessel was alongside her, and a large vessel (about 2,000 tons) anchored about two cables astern. Five torpedo boat destroyers were patrolling the Narrows between Chanak and Kelid Bahr. Very little anti-aircraft fire was experienced from "Goeben" and no hostile aircraft were encountered. A Greek officer (Flight Sub-Lieut. Hambas) was shot down by a direct hit from anti-aircraft guns during this raid, the fire from which was heavy.

A further raid during the evening from about 1800 to 2300 claims three direct hits on the "Goeben." The anti-aircraft batteries at Nagara Point, eight in number, were very active, several shots bursting very close to our machines. No ship was observed in the vicinity of the "Goeben." One of the machines in this raid was driven out of her course by a strong wind and made a good landing at Samothraki. She returned safely on the 24th January.

A further special flight was made by a D.H. 4, leaving Mudros at 1830, to spot for monitor. The machine went to the position arranged, and waited for 1¼ hours, constantly calling up the monitor to open fire, but no reply was received. There was no indication that the W/T was jammed. It had been arranged that if W/T failed, the monitor should fire one round to indicate her position, and that the spotting should be carried out by Aldis lamp. The monitor was never seen to fire, and was not located. This machine in returning was blown nearly to Thasos by the strong wind, and eventually landed at Mudros at 2200.

Forty-nine flights were carried out between 0800 on the 23rd and 0800 on the 24th January 1918, and 72 cwts. of bombs were dropped on the "Goeben," ships and boats round her, and on Galata Aerodrome. This rate of expenditure becoming rather serious, energetic steps were taken to obtain reinforcements of bombs from Salonica, Otranto, Alexandria, Malta, and home, and requests were also made for more pilots and more machines. The pilots of the B.A.S. were getting flown out by their constant work in the air since Sunday morning the 20th January.

It should be mentioned that during the night of the 21st–22nd January a hostile raid was made by two machines on Imbros Aerodrome. Several bombs were dropped without effecting any damage.

The following intercepted hostile wireless is of interest :—

"The armoured cruiser 'Goeben' and the small cruiser 'Breslau,' and torpedo boats at Dardanelles, pushed forward against enemy forces which had been announced near the island of Imbros by aeroplane observation. A large and a small English monitor were destroyed—a transport of 2,000 tons sunk—several hulks severely damaged, and the English Signal Station at Raphalo Bay destroyed. On returning to the Dardanelles the small cruiser 'Breslau' was sunk by several underwater blows from mines or a submarine. The 'Goeben' ran slightly aground at entrance within Dardanelles Narrows, near Nagara. She has not been run aground on account of severe damage, as asserted in the English official report."

An air raid was carried out at 0807 on the 24th January from Imbros. One direct hit was made on the "Goeben," and one sank a small ship alongside her. The "Goeben" did not seem to have so much list. There was a 1,000-ton ship and two smaller vessels in Chanak Harbour.

A raid from Imbros during the afternoon of the 24th January, about 1400, dropped ten 112-lb. bombs; no direct hits reported. The anti-aircraft fire was very accurate, but all our machines returned safely. There was no sign whatever of repair ship or any craft around "Goeben," which was in the same position. There was less smoke from her funnels, and there appeared to be a net about 40 yards long across the Straits about 600 yards from the "Goeben" on Cape Helles side. No hostile machines were sighted, but the usual torpedo boat patrols were observed in the Narrows.

Two special escorted reconnaissances ordered by H.A.E. were carried out during the day. No large shipping was observed in the Straits, but three small steam vessels were seen 3 or 4 miles south of Chanak on the opposite side.

A Hamble Baby seaplane on submarine patrol reported having bombed an enemy submarine below the surface at 1415 on 24th January 20 miles west of Cape Tigani. The machine did not wait to observe results, and was sent out again immediately with another seaplane, returning again before dark, having failed to locate the submarine.

A machine was sent out to spot for monitor firing after dark. She got in touch with monitor, and was able to observe the first few rounds—these were "overs," but gradually coming down approaching "Goeben" as result of observation, when the atmosphere became hazy, and no further spotting could be carried out. This machine observed that the monitor was engaged by shore batteries, but their shooting was wild.

H.M.S. "Empress" arrived at 1305 on the 24th January 1918 with only forty-four 16-lb. bombs and forty-nine 65-lb. bombs, and the newly arrived pilots were immediately given the benefit of information obtained by local pilots during previous raids.

A raid from her by two Short seaplanes on "Goeben" was carried out from 2220 to 0120 on the 24th/25th January, and dropped four 65-lb. bombs. One bomb made a direct hit on the bow of the "Goeben." No craft were observed alongside her or in the vicinity, and she was in complete darkness. Three searchlights were seen on the Asiatic coast. Heavy anti-aircraft fire and machine-gun fire experienced. Atmosphere slightly misty.

Soon after dark a raid was made by five B.E. 12 machines piloted by the R.F.C., and three bombers. They attacked "Goeben" at intervals of 10 minutes, and dropped 22 bombs. They made one direct hit. All the machines returned safely.

H.M.S. "Manxman" arrived at 0620 on the 25th January, bringing a useful reinforcement of bombs, viz., two hundred and eighteen 112-lb. bombs, eighty 100-lb., ten 200-lb., and forty-five 65-lb.

The number of flights made from 0800 on the 24th to 0800 on the 25th January was 34, and the weight of bombs dropped three tons.

Four R.F.C. machines left Salonica on the morning of the 25th January to reinforce, but only two arrived, as, owing to the stiff north-easterly wind, one had to land at Stavros and another at Ikiros in the Athos Peninsula. There was also a French machine at Salonica ready to proceed, but the last three machines did not arrive until the 28th January.

A raid from Mudros was made on the "Goeben" from 0820 to 1000 on the morning of the 25th by five D.H. 4's. Four reached the objective, and one returned with engine trouble. Each of the four machines dropped two 112-lb. bombs from a very considerable altitude, on account of the accurate anti-aircraft fire. No hits were observed. One of our machines was attacked by two hostile machines, one being a very fast land machine, but they broke off the engagement before coming to close quarters. They reported that, as regards the "Goeben," her situation seemed unaltered, and no further damage could be observed. Smoke was seen coming from one funnel only. There was a vessel of about 2,000 tons some 20 feet away, off the starboard bow.

These machines reported a strong wind from the north-east, making it difficult for them to attain their object.

Five R.F.C. B.E.'s and a Sopwith Bomber, escorted by six "Camels," left Imbros at 0830 to carry out an attack on "Goeben." Clouds were encountered at 7,000 feet, and the formation was broken up. One machine dropped her bombs at sea on account of engine failure, and crashed in a field near the aerodrome in trying to land. Two other machines experienced engine trouble and dropped their bombs on gun positions at Gaba Tepe. No results of the bombs dropped on the "Goeben" could be seen.

The Sopwith Bomber and a "Camel" passed over Galata Aerodrome on their way back. No machines were seen on the ground, and no activity was evident.

The number of flights during the 24 hours, from 0800 on the 25th to 0800 on the 26th January 1918, was 23, and the weight of bombs dropped 1 ton.

Owing to strong north-easterly winds no flying was possible from 0800 on the 26th to 0800 on the 27th January.

Preparations had been made to make an attack with torpedoes from seaplanes on the 24th January. The "Ark Royal" had a Short machine ready fitted for dropping a 14-inch torpedo, but the tests were too unsatisfactory to send her away that night, and on the 25th the "Manxman" brought up two seaplanes fitted with 18-inch torpedoes, so this method of attack was turned over to the "Manxman," but the change in the weather already reported prevented the attacks being made. The "Ark Royal" commenced experiments for fitting a machine to drop 300-lb. depth charges and 18-inch warheads with the machine previously fitted with 14-inch torpedo.

The R.F.C. at Salonica took over the work of the Stavros R.N.A.S. station during the attacks on the "Goeben," as Stavros was emptied of pilots.

On the news of the "Goeben–Breslau" raid on the 20th January all the Greek pilots at Thasos also flew over to Mudros to take part in the operations.

On the 27th January a strong wind continued throughout the day until about 2000, when it dropped and by midnight was quite calm.

Early in the morning of the 27th January a "Camel" was ordered to proceed from Imbros to reconnoitre the Straits. Owing to the air conditions the machine was blown over on to one wing tip and wrecked in starting. A second "Camel" was thereupon sent over and this machine reported that there was a 90-knot wind at 10,000 feet and low cloud, through which she could not see the "Goeben." At midday a third "Camel" was sent and reported the "Goeben" still in position.

A raid was made in the afternoon by five D.H. 4's, but it was found impossible to make headway against the wind, and they landed at about 1330 with nothing to report.

A machine was sent up during the afternoon of the 27th to practise spotting for Monitor, but had to return owing to the W/T being out of action. A further test was carried out at 1700, when satisfactory signals were received at headquarters at

N. 5 W/T station from the aeroplane, the signals often being of strength R. 8 when Monitor was reporting them as N. 2.

At 1630 a D.H. 4 with special passenger left Mudros for Imbros. This machine also was damaged on landing owing to weather conditions. Shortly afterwards the R.F.C. Squadron attempted to proceed to Imbros, but were recalled, as it was impossible for them to make Imbros before dark with the rising wind.

A seaplane raid by three machines from "Ark Royal" and one from "Empress" left shortly after midnight, but only one machine, a Short seaplane flown by Flight Commander Malet, and fitted with an 18-inch warhead, got over the Straits, two of the others having to return owing to the weather conditions. The Short machine came down to 1,600 feet and was subject to severe anti-aircraft fire. He could not see the "Goeben," although he saw small boats close at hand. He dropped his warhead on the estimated position of the "Goeben" just off the point. There was a tremendous explosion and all anti-aircraft fire at once ceased. He was not prepared to state definitely that the "Goeben" was not there, as visibility was poor.

The "Empress" machine, Short seaplane 1582 (Flight Lieut. C. C. Bronson and observer Lieut. Pakenham Walsh), did not return, and although search was made for her on the 29th and 30th January 1918, no news of this machine could be obtained. An English submarine, E 14, had also been sent out during the afternoon of the 27th January to attack the "Goeben," and the night bombing operations already described were timed to act as a diversion, but no news was heard of this submarine, except that about 1120 on the 28th January, Flight Commander Hicks, flying a "Camel," reported that he saw a submerged object resembling a submarine in the entrance to the Dardanelles, between Helles and Kumkale, and that shore batteries and a torpedo boat in the Straits were firing at the surface. He harried them as far as he was able with his machine guns, and then went straight back to Imbros to report. A bomber with escort were immediately sent out, but by the time they got there, no activity was apparent at the entrance to the Dardanelles.

No further news of either the seaplane or the submarine were obtained until the intercepted Turkish official of the 31st January 1918, which stated:—

> "In the Dardanelles near Kum Kale an English submarine, 'E 4,' was sunk by fire of the shore batteries—seven of the crew were saved. A second English submarine, 'E 82,' appeared near Nagara, and was subjected to very heavy fire from the shore batteries. Although no actual hits were seen, a large patch of oil was observed after she dived, and it is most probable that she was destroyed. An English seaplane was forced by machine-gun fire to land near Nagara, and the crew were captured uninjured."

During the earlier period, before the "Camel" report already mentioned, *i.e.*, at 0415 on the 28th January, Flight Lieut. Woodward and observer Lieutenant Palmer carried out a reconnaissance up the Straits, between 3,000 and 4,000 feet, to 5 miles beyond Nagara Point. They reported :—

> "The 'Goeben' has disappeared. There were two torpedo boat destroyers 5 miles south of Nagara on watch, but not moving. Two other craft were seen at Nagara not in motion. There was no sign of any wreckage where 'Goeben' was. Clouds were at between 3,000 and 4,000 feet. Anti-aircraft fire severe and machine was hit twice."

This report was corroborated by a D.H. 4 (Flight Lieut. Grigson and observer Sub-Lieut. Gayford) and also by the pilot of a "Camel" from Imbros Air Station. The report of the D.H. 4 is as follows :—

> "Cloud was encountered at varying heights between 4,000 and 5,000 feet. Considerable but not very accurate anti-aircraft fire experienced from Nagara and Maidos, tail plane and elevator only hit by a few splinters.
>
> "The 'Goeben' was not in position, neither was there any wreckage floating around the spot where she had been. Visibility under water was good and the bottom for a considerable distance around Nagara Point visible. There was a curious lightish patch on the water about a mile S.S.W. from the Point, over which two torpedo boats were patrolling; there were also two torpedo boats tied up to the jetty just north of the seaplane sheds and a dredger anchored just off shore. A seaplane was patrolling between Chanak and the Point at a height of about 500 feet. Nothing beyond the usual small craft was seen in Chanak. In Square 105 S. 8 three masts were showing up above the water and a caique was standing by; this would probably be the repair ship sunk a few days ago. Off Galata another seaplane was patrolling, steering a southerly course. Nothing of importance was in Gallipoli and there were no signs of activity. Only a few caiques were visible in the Sea of Marmora, and when Marmora Island was reached we turned back and returned down the whole length of the Dardanelles. Another seaplane was seen patrolling just south of Lapsaki. The only shipping seen south of Chanak were two motor boats patrolling between Kum Kale and Sedd el Bahr. These were fired on by a machine gun from a height of 4,000 feet. Two mines were seen floating just inside the entrance."

At 1235 on the 29th January, as ordered by R.A.E., a special reconnaissance was made into the Sea of Marmora, two D.H. 4's being sent off from Mudros. These machines encountered a high wind and took an hour to reach Imbros, where they filled up with fuel in order to get as far into the Marmora as possible. One machine subsequently returned to Imbros with engine trouble. The other went on until well into the Marmora, encountering a high wind during the whole journey, and when in the Marmora having practically no visibility on the water, as the sea was covered with low cloud and fog. The machine accordingly returned to Mudros, arriving just before dark.

A D.H. 4 started as soon as the first report that the "Goeben" had left was received, and proceeded into the Marmora as far as the Panderma-Rodosto line, but could see no trace of her.

The usual dawn reconnaissance of the Dardanelles was made from Imbros on the 29th January, and it was reported at 0645 that no submarine nor wreckage was seen at Nagara. The Straits were clear of shipping.

The following is a report of the reconnaissance of Constantinople area to locate "Goeben" made on the 29th January, 1918 :—

Machine D.H. 4, N. 6420, with 200 b.h.p. engine, pilot Flight Commander L. Hervey, R.N.A.S., observer Sub-Lieut. S. Chryssidy of the Greek Navy.

The machine left Mudros at 1220 L.T., and pursued a course to the westward of Imbros to the head of the Gulf of Xeros, continuing on the same course unttl just south of Rodosto. At Rodosto a fairly large troopship or transport was observed alongside the pier, with one T.B.D. standing by. Course was then altered due east, crossing the heads of Big and Little Checkmejeh to the north of the German air base at San Stefano, which was reached at 1530. Three machines were seen to leave the aerodrome, but none got nearer than 3,000 feet of the D.H. 4. Course was again altered to the north-east, keeping to the western outskirts of Constantinople.

At this point the "Goeben" was first identified. She was seen to be lying near the inner of the two bridges spanning the Golden Horn by the arsenal, and stretcheng half-way along that bridge. Her exact position was one cable northward of s.s. "General," which also lies inside the old harbour bridge, "Goeben" being off Petit Champ des Morts.

A large ship, probably the "Torgud Reis," lay at the 8-fathom mark at the western end of Admiralty Basin, and a number of T.B.'s and T.B.D.'s, about ten in all, were lying between the two ships. Another fairly large merchant ship was lying off the cold stores at the western end of the inner bridge.

The largest of the arsenal dry docks was seen to be flooded and open, and appeared to be larger than the dimensions given in Chart 1198 of 4th March 1905. The smaller dry dock contained a ship which could not be identified.

Both pilot and observer are absolutely positive that the ship lying in the position described is the "Goeben."

After passing over the western edge of Constantinople, the aeroplane proceeded N.N.E., keeping inland from the Bosphorus. She turned just to the north of Stenia Bay, one large ship only being observed in Buyuk Dere Bay to the northward. Stenia Bay contained no warships, but a floating dock lay on the northern side of the bay. There are no nets at present at the entrance to Stenia Bay.

Just south of Stenia Bay, lying close to the European shore, two ships were seen having the appearance of T.B.D.'s or light cruisers. In the Bosphorus only one ship was seen. She was a large two-funnelled troopship, with a distinct stagger to funnels and mast. She did not appear to be under way, but at anchor off Kuru Bank.

The aeroplane proceeded down the Bosphorus, passing close over the eastern end of Constantinople, where another view of "Goeben" was had. The harbour was seen to be in a fairly active condition, a number of small steamboats being under way.

Subsequently the machine passed over San Stefano Aerodrome, where there was seen to be one Bessonneau in addition to the permanent sheds. A railway line was seen to be made, branching off the main line towards the aerodrome.

No anti-aircraft fire was observed at any time during the flight. The gunpowder factory at Makrikeui was seen to be working.

On the return journey the course was pursued further to the southward of the outward course, throughout the whole journey.

The machine returned to Mudros, landing at 1735 L.T. having been 5 hours 15 minutes in the air.

The flight was made at between 6,000 and 7,000 feet; and while over Constantinople the machine rose to between 8,000 and 9,000 feet.

The total distance flown was 390 sea miles, or 449 English statute miles.

SUMMARY.

Number of flights - - - - - - 270
Approximate weight of bombs dropped - 15 tons 3 cwts.
 (This figure does not include the warhead.)
Direct hits - - - - - - - 16

Weekly Operations Report No. 98 (Week ending 3rd February 1918).

NOTE.—No Operation Report precisely No. 97 was sent in, as practically the whole work of the station was taken up in the "Goeben" operations, which have been fully described in the special reports forwarded.

Weather and Amount of Flying.—The first two days and the last three days of the week the wind was too high for flying, the only good days for aerial performance being Tuesday, Wednesday, and to a less extent Thursday.

THASOS AIR STATION.

"A" SQUADRON AND "Z" SQUADRON (GREEK).

Practically no work was done from this station, since machines and flying personnel at the beginning of the week were at Mudros or Imbros, for the continuation of operations against the "Goeben," and on their return to the station the weather became unsuitable.

STAVROS AIR STATION.

"D" SQUADRON.

Reconnaissance.—On the 31st January, the machines having returned on the 30th, there was an escorted reconnaissance over the front line. Two new gun emplacements were observed; elsewhere normal.

Photography—Hostile Aircraft Pursuit.—Again on the 2nd February there was an escorted photographic reconnaissance over the front line, which found the conditions normal. On this day, too, there was a hostile aeroplane over the aerodrome. A Sopwith was sent in pursuit, but failed to bring about an engagement.

KALLONI AIR STATION. MITYLENE.

"B" SQUADRON.

No work of importance was carried out.

GLIKI AIR STATION. IMBROS.

The particular work of this station is described in the concluding account of the operations against the "Goeben," which is attached; and also re-establishing the station on its normal footing, after those operations were carried out.

MUDROS.

Result of Reconnaissance.—Similarly, the work at Mudros is described in the "Goeben" operations, and the re-arrangement of units necessary to their conclusion; but concerning both Mudros and Imbros, an important reconnaissance to Panderma was carried out from Mudros on January 29th by an Imbros D.H.4, Flight Commander Sorley, and observer Sub-Lieut

Smith. They left Mudros at 0935, and steered east for the coast, and headed across country for Karabigha.

Near Mount Dideh large barracks were observed.

At Karabigha there was a large amount of traffic on the road running south from the town. The machine then followed the coast eastward and passed Bigha, where there is a two-span steel girder bridge 200 feet long.

At Edinjik a good road runs into the interior, on which there was considerable traffic, the general trend of which was southward. There was also traffic on the Edinjik-Panderma road.

At Panderma there was a 2,000-ton ship unloading at the pier, three other small steamers, and about 50 caiques in the harbour. There was a camp on the seashore, and another on the eastern border of the town, and a good deal of rolling stock in the station, which is near the harbour.

At Ezine there was a large shed, which appeared to be a Zeppelin shed, but no activity was observed near. No traffic was seen on the railway.

The machine returned to Mudros at 1305.

BRITISH ADRIATIC SQUADRON.

(SUMMARY OF FLYING AND INTELLIGENCE REPORTS FOR
WEEK ENDING 29TH JANUARY 1918.)

MALTA.

(*For Week ending 26th January* 1918.)

Remarks.—During this period a total of 17 hours 25 minutes flying has been carried out, covering a distance of 960 miles. This includes anti-submarine patrols, escorts, and test flights. There has been considerable submarine activity in the vicinity of Malta during the week, but the weather and sea conditions, however, prevented regular escorting patrols. No submarines were actually sighted by aircraft during the week; but on one occasion a seaplane on escort patrol sighted submarine oil tracks, but was forced to return to the base owing to engine trouble. Another seaplane left to continue the patrol, but failed to pick up the oil tracks.

OTRANTO.

(For Week ending 29th January 1918.)

Amount of Flying.—During this period a total of 13 hours flying (18 flights) have been carried out. This includes anti-submarine patrols, bomb dropping, and armament practice and test flights.

January 24th.

Attack on Submarine.—A submarine was sighted on the surface by a drifter, and attacked at a range of about 300 yards.

The submarine was hit three times below the conning tower, upon which it heeled over and disappeared. Seaplanes patrolled the area until forced to return to the base, owing to adverse weather conditions, without, however, locating the submarine.

January 28th.

Two hostile aeroplanes were reported by the look-out station at Saseno, but nothing was seen or heard of them at Otranto.

General.—H.M.S. "Manxman" returned to Taranto on February 5th from Mudros, where she had been employed in connection with operations against the "Goeben."

Febrvary 3rd.

An Austrian seaplane was picked up off Manfredonia by the Italians, the three occupants being made prisoners. The machine was in perfect condition, and was flown to Brindisi next day by Italian pilots. The machine has been visited by British experts from Otranto, and a written report of the examination will be forwarded in due course.

ROYAL FLYING CORPS COMMUNIQUÉS.

ROYAL FLYING CORPS COMMUNIQUÉ.—No. 125.

During the period under review (January 29th to February 4th, inclusive) we have claimed officially 27 enemy aircraft brought down (three of which fell in our lines) and twenty-five enemy aircraft driven down out of control. Two hostile balloons were destroyed. Five of our machines are missing.

Approximately 33 tons of bombs were dropped and 64,816 rounds fired at ground targets.

January 29th.

The weather was fine all day but the visibility bad.

Twelve reconnaissances were carried out, four of which were long distance photographic reconnaissances by No. 25 Squadron (Ninth Wing), Second Lieuts. C. Pike and O. Hinson reaching Namur and exposing 32 plates.

Seventy hostile batteries were successfully engaged for destruction with aeroplane observation; two gun-pits were destroyed, 42 damaged, 27 explosions, and 22 fires caused. Forty zone calls were sent down.

On the 28th, balloons registered seven targets, six of which were by balloons of the Second Brigade, and one active hostile battery was located by a balloon of the First Brigade.

Two hundred and ninety-seven 25-lb. and ninety-three 112-lb. bombs were dropped during the night of the 28th-29th, 1,880 photographs taken, three hundred and forty-three 25-lb. and ten 112-lb. bombs dropped, and 13,685 rounds fired at ground targets during the day as follows :—

Night, 28th-29th.

First Brigade.—No. 2 Squadron dropped fifty-three 112-lb. bombs on Meurchin, Annœullin, Carvin, and Haubourdin; No. 5 Squadron dropped sixty 25-lb. bombs and fired 250 rounds on Brebières, Izel, Vitry, and Quiery-la-Motte; No. 16 Squadron dropped forty 112-lb. and forty-one 25-lb. bombs on Annay, Pont-à-Vendin, Billy Montigny, Drocourt, Henin-Liétard, a train and a hostile battery.

Fifth Brigade.—No. 8 Squadron dropped eight 25-lb. bombs on Bohain.

Ninth Wing.—No. 102 Squadron dropped eighty-seven 25-lb. bombs and six 2-lb. H.E. shells, and fired 500 rounds on Marquain, Gontrode, and Cruyshautem aerodromes, Hoogte, and Seclin.

(No. 101 Squadron were unable to leave the ground owing to thick mist enveloping their aerodrome.)

Day 29th.

First Brigade.—Three hundred and six photographs. First Wing dropped twenty-nine 25-lb. bombs. No. 18 Squadron dropped twenty 25-lb. bombs, and Tenth Wing fired 3,150 rounds.

Second Brigade.—Four hundred and fifty-two photographs were taken and 3,981 rounds fired. No. 57 Squadron dropped sixty-two 25-lb. bombs on Gulleghem ammunition dump, and Second Wing dropped eighty-two 25-lb. bombs.

Third Brigade.—Four hundred and three photographs were taken, sixty-one 25-lb. bombs were dropped, and 1,785 rounds fired.

Fifth Brigade.—Five hundred and fifty-five photographs. 15th Wing dropped fifty-seven 25-lb. bombs and fired 4,369 rounds, and 22nd Wing dropped twelve 25-lb. bombs and fired 400 rounds.

Ninth Wing.—No. 25 Squadron dropped ten 112-lb. bombs on Marquain Aerodrome.

Enemy Aircraft.—There was considerable activity, especially opposite the Second Brigade. Eight hostile machines were brought down and four driven down out of control.

Second Lieut. Lindsay, No. 54 Squadron, brought down a hostile balloon in flames.

Flight Sub-Lieut. Day, Naval Squadron No. 8, attacked one of five Albatross Scouts at close range and drove it down out of control. Flight Commander Munday attacked one enemy aircraft scout at close range and fired about 150 rounds. Tracers were seen to enter the enemy aircraft's fuselage, which turned practically over and fell down in a vertical dive completely out of control. A general engagement between a patrol of this squadron and six enemy aircraft scouts resulted in one of the latter being shot down completely out of control by Flight Sub-Lieut. R. Johns and two others being driven down.

A patrol of No. 70 Squadron attacked some enemy aircraft scouts, and in the combat that took place Captain Quigley followed an Albatross down to 6,000 feet, firing all the way. The enemy aircraft went down in flames. Lieutenant E. Peverell dived on an enemy aircraft and got in a long burst with both guns. The enemy aircraft turned completely over and went down in a spin obviously out of control.

Lieutenant Seth-Smith attacked an Albatross Scout nose-on at about 30 yards' range, and the enemy aircraft fell out of control. Second Lieut. A. Koch attacked two enemy aircraft, one of which was driven down out of control. Captain F. Hobson attacked an Albatross Scout which had dived on one of our artillery machines. The enemy aircraft went down out of control in a series of slide-slips.

Two patrols of No. 29 Squadron attacked 15 Albatross Scouts. Captain W. Molesworth, after a short engagement, drove down one which turned east and burst into flames.

Captain E. Meek dived on one enemy aircraft after firing 50 rounds into it from 60 yards' range. It zoomed up sharply, one wing crumpled up, and the enemy machine burst into flames. Second Lieut. L. Tims got on to the tail of one enemy aircraft and drove it down out of control.

Second Lieut. C. Howsam, No. 32 Squadron, after a short combat with one enemy aircraft scout, drove it down out of control, and it was seen to crash.

Second Lieut. T. Williams, No. 65 Squadron, attacked an enemy aircraft scout at point blank range, and it went down out of control with smoke coming out of its fuselage. Lieutenant C. Matthews attacked an enemy aircraft from close range. The enemy aircraft went down completely out of control and was confirmed by another pilot to break up in the air. Captain J. Gilmour dived on a large two-seater and followed it down to 5,000 feet, firing at it at very close range. The enemy aircraft was eventually observed to crash. Lieutenant H. Symons drove down one enemy aircraft scout completely out of control. He then immediately engaged an enemy aircraft two-seater, which went down completely out of control and was still diving when last seen very near the ground.

Lieutenant R. Fagan and Second Lieut. A. Matt, No. 82 Squadron, whilst on photography, were attacked by six Albatross Scouts, one of which was shot down and seen to crash in the French lines. The A.W. was badly shot about. Second Lieut. E. Clear was forced to leave his patrol owing to engine trouble. On his way home he saw two two-seater enemy aircraft and attacked one of them. After firing a burst at the hostile machine the observer was seen to fall forward over his gun. A second burst was fired into the enemy aircraft, which went down in flames. Second Lieut. Clear was then attacked by five Albatross Scots, but in spite of a failing engine managed to regain his aerodrome.

Second Lieuts. W. Henney and A. Wright, No. 27 Squadron, while on photography were attacked by three enemy aircraft. Second Lient. Wright fired two drums into one enemy aircraft, which went down out of control.

On the night of the 28th/29th, machines of Nos. 2, 5, and 16 Squadrons carried out very successful bomb raids, several of the pilots making three trips.

Lieutenant Hayter and Captain Beadon, No. 12 Squadron, ranged the 281st Siege Battery; 65 observations were given and two O.K.'s obtained.

Lieutenants Belway and Booth, No. 13 Squadron, ranged the 231st Siege Battery; 70 observations were given, and a hostile position was severely damaged.

Lieutenants McCall and Andrew, No. 13 Squadron, ranged the 184th Siege Battery; 44 observations were given, one pit was damaged, and one large explosion caused.

Lieutenant Worthington and First Air Mechanic Livingstone, No. 13 Squadron, ranged the 179th Siege Battery. Four pits were damaged, one fire and one explosion caused.

Lieutenants Douglas and Senior, No. 15 Squadron, ranged the 56th Siege Battery; 66 observations were given and four O.K.'s obtained. All four pits of a hostile battery were damaged.

Lieutenants Hobbs and Gibbs, No. 15 Squadron, ranged the 278th Siege Battery; 49 observations were given, one fire caused, and the hostile battery position considerably damaged.

Captain Stadden-Lea and Lieutenant Upfill, No. 59 Squadron, working with the 44th Siege Battery, destroyed one gun-pit and damaged two others.

Lieutenants Marten-Smith and Smith, No. 59 Squadron, working with the 126th Siege Battery, obtained one O.K., two pits being damaged and one fire caused.

Captain Wolton and Lieutenant Warren, No. 35 Squadron, ranged the 19th Siege Battery, destroying three pits, damaging one, causing two explosions and one fire.

Lieutenants Norton and Briggs, No. 35 Squadron, ranged the 24th Siege Battery, destroying one pit and causing one explosion.

On the 28th, 12 machines of No. 55 Squadron attempted a raid on Kreuznach. The lines were crossed at 10,000 feet, but owing to the fog and mist getting thicker the raid was abandoned. Nine plates were exposed. All machines returned.

January 30th.

The weather was fine but misty all day.

Twelve successful reconnaissances were carried out—three by the Second Brigade, five by the Third Brigade, three by the Fifth Brigade, and one by the Ninth Wing. Captain D. Jardine and Lieutenant H. Ashton, No. 25 Squadon, completed the Namur reconnaissance, taking 36 photographs.

Fifty-two hostile batteries were successfully engaged for destruction and two neutralised; three gun-pits were destroyed, 18 damaged, 24 explosions and 16 fires caused. Fifty-three active hostile batteries were reported by zone call.

Lieutenant Hayter and Captain Beadon, No. 12 Squadron, ranged the 231st Siege Battery. Sixty-four observations were given, four O.K.'s being obtained, and two pits damaged.

On the 29th, balloons of the Second Brigade ranged on 10 targets, one of which was a hostile battery.

During the night of the 29th/30th, 306 bombs were dropped and 525 rounds fired, and during the day 303 bombs were dropped and 10,652 rounds fired, and 1,384 photographs taken as follows:—

Night 29th–30th.

First Brigade.—No. 2 Squadron dropped one hundred and twenty-five 25-lb. bombs on Provin and one hundred and five 25-lb. bombs on Fournes; No. 4 Squadron dropped forty-five 25-lb. bombs on Wicres, Salome, Marquillies, Lomme, and La Bassée; No. 4 Squadron fired 525 rounds; No. 16 Squadron dropped ten 112-lb. and thirteen 25-lb. bombs on Noyelle, Auby, Beaumont, and Esquerchin, and No. 35 Squadron dropped eight 25-lb. bombs on Bohain.

(Nos. 101 and 102 Squadrons were unable to leave the ground owing to a thick mist over their aerodromes.)

Day 30th.

First Brigade.—One hundred and eighty-one photographs. First Wing dropped thirty-five 25-lb. bombs; Tenth Wing fired 2,250 rounds and No. 5 Squadron 75 rounds.

Second Brigade.—Three hundred and forty-four photographs. No. 57 Squadron dropped forty-four 25-lb. bombs on Iseghem Dump, and Second Wing dropped seventy-one 25-lb. bombs and fired 2,005 rounds.

Third Brigade.—Three hundred and eighty-seven photographs were taken, thirty-seven 25-lb. bombs dropped and 1,300 rounds fired.

Fifth Brigade.—Three hundred and eighty photographs were taken, and Fifteenth Wing dropped seventy-eight 25-lb. bombs and fired 5,022 rounds.

Ninth Wing.—Ninety-two photographs. No. 25 Squadron dropped eight 112-lb. bombs on Scheldewindeke Aerodrome, and No. 27 Squadron dropped four 112-lb. and sixteen 25-lb. on Courtrai railway sidings.

Enemy Aircraft.—Activity was not so marked as on previous days.

Second Lieuts. S. Oades and S. Bunting, No. 22 Squadron, attacked an enemy two-seater. The enemy aircraft went down in flames and was seen to crash.

Second Lieut. W. Casson, No. 43 Squadron, shot down out of control an enemy aircraft two-seater, which he followed down to 4,000 feet, firing all the time.

Lieutenant J. Coombe, No. 29 Squadron, whilst on offensive patrol attacked one of nine Albatross scouts. He fired 200 rounds at it and it went down in a spin.

Lieutenant J. Hewett, No. 23 Squadron, attacked an Albatross Scout, diving on it out of the sun. After a long burst, the enemy aircraft went down out of control, falling from side to side.

Second Lieutenants D. McGoun and C. Agelasto, No. 20 Squadron, dived on an Albatross Scout, the pilot firing about 100 rounds and the observer 200 rounds at 30 yards' range. The enemy aircraft went down completely out of control and was seen to crash.

Lieutenant R. Bennett and second Air Mechanic B. Matthews, of the same squadron, were attacked by an Albatross Scout, which they shot down completely out of control.

Lieutenant Junor, No. 56 Squadron, dived on two enemy scouts and opened fire from about 100 yards. One enemy aircraft went down in a series of sharp dives and at 8,000 feet it burst into flames and crashed. Captain G. Bowman led a patrol against seven Albatross Scouts; he himself fired 50 rounds at 30 yards' range at one enemy aircraft, which dived almost vertically and crashed. Captain J. B. McCudden attacked four enemy aircraft scouts, into one of which he fired a short burst from both guns at 50 yards' range, when pieces of what appeared to be three-ply fell off the enemy aircraft. Turning over to the left the enemy aircraft went down in a vertical dive, absolutely out of control. He then flew on behind a Phalz and fired a short burst from both guns. The enemy aircraft went down in a spiral, finally stalling and side-slipping and was last seen at 6,000 feet still out of control.

A patrol of No. 84 Squadron, led by Captain Leask, attacked six enemy aircraft scouts and one two-seater. The enemy were eventually reinforced by six more machines, and in the fighting which ensued two enemy scouts were driven down completely out of control, one by Captain Leask and one by Second Lieut. McCudden.

January 31st.

The weather was fine but thick mist prevailed all day, with the exception of a few hours on the 2nd Brigade front.

Two reconnaissances were carried out by the 2nd Brigade.

Six hostile batteries were successfully engaged for destruction by the 3rd Brigade and one by the 2nd Brigade; four gun-pits were damaged, two explosions and one fire caused. Four zone calls were sent down.

Seventy-nine 25-lb. bombs and twenty 112-lb. bombs were dropped during the night of the 30th/31st, and 41 photographs were taken, one hundred 25-lb. and two 112-lb. bombs were dropped and 750 rounds fired during the day as follows:—

Night 30/31st.

1st Brigade.—No. 5 Squadron dropped forty-eight 25-lb. bombs on Esquerchin, Quiery-la-Motte and Vitry. No. 16 Squadron dropped fifteen 25-lb. bombs on Menin, Courcelles, Dourges, Sallaumines and Billy Montigny.

5th Brigade.—Nos. 8 and 35 Squadrons dropped four 112-lb. and sixteen 25-lb. bombs on Fontaine Uterte.

Day 31st.

1st Brigade.—No. 2 Squadron dropped two 25-lb. bombs on Wingles.

2nd Brigade.—No. 57 Squadron dropped sixty-eight 25-lb. bombs on Deerlyck Ammunition Dump (north-east of Courtrai), and two 25-lb. bombs were dropped and 50 rounds fired at various targets.

3rd Brigade.—Fourteen 25-lb. bombs were dropped and 700 rounds fired.

9th Wing.—No. 27 Squadron dropped two 112-lb. and six 25-lb. bombs on Ingelmunster and eight 25-lb. bombs on Wynghene Aerodrome.

On the 30th, balloons of the 2nd Brigade registered 16 targets, seven of which were hostile batteries; five active hostile batteries were located, and a successful shoot on a hostile balloon was carried out with cross observation by two balloons (Nos. 9 and 13 Sections).

Enemy Aircraft.—No fighting took place at all.

February 1st.

Thick mist all day on all Brigade fronts prevented any service flying being carried out.

February 2nd.

The weather was fine but mist and ground haze prevailed.

Twelve reconnaissances were carried out—four by the 1st Brigade, and one, a long distance photographic reconnaissance of the line Valenciennes—Busigny, when 31 plates were exposed, by Second Lieuts. Wright and Hobbs, No. 25 Squadron (9th Wing).

One thousand two hundred and twenty-four photographs were taken; two hundred and eighty-five 25-lb. and twelve 112-lb. bombs dropped and 13,285 rounds fired on ground targets as follows:—

1st Brigade.—Two hundred and twenty-six photographs, sixty-four 25-lb. bombs on miscellaneous targets dropped by 1st Wing, and four 25-lb. bombs on Fournes dropped by No. 43 Squadron. Four thousand six hundred rounds were fired.

2nd Brigade.—Two hundred and twenty-two photographs were taken and 3,210 rounds fired. No. 57 Squadron dropped seventy-two 25-lb. bombs on sidings at Roulers, and Corps Squadrons dropped forty-seven 25-lb. bombs.

3rd Brigade.—Three hundred and fifteen photographs were taken and 500 rounds fired. Twelfth Wing dropped twenty-eight 25-lb. bombs.

5th Brigade.—Three hundred and ninety photographs were taken and 4,955 rounds fired. No. 8 Squadron dropped thirty-four 25-lb. bombs, No. 35 Squadron fourteen 25-lb. bombs,

No. 52 Squadron eight 25-lb. bombs, and No. 48 Squadron sixteen 25-lb. bombs.

9th Wing.—No. 25 Squadron dropped twelve 112-lb. bombs on Valenciennes and took 71 photographs.

Enemy Aircraft.—Enemy aircraft activity was normal.

Lieutenant McElroy, No. 40 Squadron, shot down one enemy aircraft out of control.

Flight Commander Compston, Naval Squadron No. 8, attacked an Albatross Scout at point blank range and shot it down completely out of control. He then attacked a two-seater and fired about 60 rounds at very close range. The enemy aircraft went down in a side-slipping dive absolutely out of control and was seen to crash.

While on roving commission, Sergeant Gay and Second Lieut. Flavell, No. 57 Squadron, were attacked by five Albatross Scouts and one two-seater. The observer fired 200 rounds at 250 yards' range, and one of the scouts was seen to fall enveloped in a large cloud of smoke.

Captain Gorringe, No. 70 Squadron, attacked one of two enemy aircraft two-seaters, and after firing about 100 rounds, the enemy aircraft was last seen going down in a steep dive, and was later seen to crash (confirmed by anti-aircraft battery).

Captain McCudden, No. 56 Squadron, attacked an L.V.G. at 100 yards' range. He fired a long burst from both guns, after which the enemy aircraft went down vertically, then fell on to its back, and the enemy aircraft gunner fell out. The machine finally crashed in our lines.

Captain Chappell, No. 41 Squadron, fired about 60 rounds at very close range at an Albatross Scout. The enemy aircraft stalled, side-slipped and spun to earth, and finally crashed. Captain Chappell was immediately attacked by six enemy aircraft scouts. He put his machine into a spin, and on coming out, observed one enemy aircraft in front of him and five still above. He attacked the single enemy aircraft, which did a long side-slip, and was last seen about 2,000 feet from the ground, still spinning and completely out of control.

Second Lieut. Jones, No. 41 Squadron, dived on one enemy aircraft and fired a short burst from about 100 yards' range; he then zoomed up and got on to the enemy aircraft's tail, and when at about 20 yards got off a burst of 50 rounds, whereupon the enemy aircraft side-slipped for a considerable distance and spun down. When last seen it was still spinning about 4,000 feet below.

Lieutenant Cuthbertson, No. 54 Squadron, attacked an Albatross Scout which was attacking a Sopwith Camel. The enemy aircraft fell out of control and then broke up in the air.

Captain Shelton, No. 54 Squadron, descended to an altitude of 50 feet and fired on a balloon which was then on the ground. The balloon was seen to burst into flames. He then attacked troops which were in the vicinity of the balloon from the same height, causing considerable consternation.

Two machines of No. 35 Squadron, whilst on photography, were attacked by five Fokker triplanes. A patrol of No. 54 Squadron and several more enemy scouts joined in. A general combat ensued as a result of which two Fokker triplanes were driven down and forced to land.

Captain Child, No. 84 Squadron, attacked a large two-seater D.F.W., and apparently hit the observer, who disappeared into his cock-pit. Owing to gun trouble Captain Child was unable to carry on the combat.

Artillery Co-operation.—Lieutenant MacPherson and Lieutenant Hurr, No. 35 Squadron, ranged No. 24 Siege Battery, firing 270 rounds, destroying two pits and causing three explosions. In the middle of this shoot they were attacked by six enemy aircraft triplanes and driven down to 1,000 feet. They also dropped four 25-lb. bombs, fired 650 rounds on ground targets, and brought back some useful information. This flight lasted from 11 a.m. to 3.20 p.m.

February 3rd.

The weather was fine all day but visibility bad owing to mist.

Nine reconnaissances were carried out, four of which were by the 2nd Brigade.

Second Lieut. R. Pohlmann and Second Lieut. Creek, No. 25 Squadron, carried out a successful reconnaissance of hostile aerodromes, exposing 32 plates.

Sixty-six hostile batteries were successfully engaged for destruction, 12 gun-pits were destroyed, 60 damaged, 18 explosions and 16 fires caused. Fifty-four zone calls were sent down.

Captain Green and Lieutenant O'Kill, No. 59 Squadron, ranged the 244th Siege Battery; 300 rounds were fired, seven O.K.'s obtained, and two pits damaged.

Lieutenant Perfect and Corporal Gray, No. 13 Squadron, ranged the 258th Siege Battery; 56 observations were given with good results, the hostile position being badly damaged.

Lieutenants Douglas and Senior, No. 15 Squadron, ranged the 57th Siege Battery, giving 28 observations and damaging the hostile position generally.

On the 2nd, balloons of the 2nd Brigade engaged four targets, two of which were hostile batteries.

One thousand one hundred and seventy-three photographs were taken, four hundred and fifty-one 25-lb. and twenty 112-lb. bombs dropped, and 14,418 rounds fired at ground targets as follows:—

Night 2nd/3rd.

5th Brigade.—Fifteenth Wing dropped six 112-lb. and sixteen 25-lb. bombs on Fresnoy-le-Grand.

9th Wing.—No. 102 Squadron dropped twenty-four 25-lb. bombs on miscellaneous targets and sixteen 25-lb. bombs on Scheldewindeke, and No. 58 Squadron dropped fifty-seven 25-lb. bombs on Rumbeke Aerodrome.

Day.

1st Brigade.—One hundred and eleven photographs. First Wing dropped forty 20-lb. and 10th Wing dropped twenty 20-lb. bombs on miscellaneous targets, and 5,010 rounds were fired.

2nd Brigade.—Four hundred and seven photographs were taken and 3,674 rounds fired. No. 57 Squadron dropped sixty-four 25-lb. bombs on railway sidings at Lichtervelde, and Corps Squadrons dropped seventy-three 25-lb. bombs on various targets.

3rd Brigade.—Three hundred and thirty-eight photographs were taken; 12th Wing dropped twenty-six 25-lb. bombs and 13th Wing dropped nineteen 25-lb. bombs.

5th Brigade.—Corps Squadrons dropped sixty-two 25-lb. bombs and No. 48 Squadron dropped eight 20-lb. bombs, and 5,124 rounds were fired.

9th Wing.—No. 27 Squadron dropped twelve 25-lb. and four 112-lb. bombs on Ingelmunster, and No. 25 Squadron dropped ten 112-bombs on Melle Sidings.

Enemy Aircraft.—Enemy aircraft activity was about normal. Five enemy aircraft were destroyed and nine driven down out of control.

Captain O'Hara-Wood, 4th Squadron A.F.C., attacked at point-blank range an enemy two-seater, which fell out of control and was seen several thousand feet lower down still out of control.

Captain O. Horsley, No. 40 Squadron, whilst on patrol, attacked one of seven Albatross Scouts. He fired bursts from both guns at exceedingly close range, and the enemy aircraft fell down completely out of control, first spinning and then commencing to go down first on one wing tip and then on the other.

Flight Commander Compston, Naval Squadron No. 8, attacked a D.F.W., firing about 200 rounds at point-blank range. The enemy aircraft fell over on its side and went down vertically out of control. Flight Commander Compston then attacked another enemy aircraft, firing about 150 rounds at point-blank range. Other pilots fired 400 rounds at this enemy machine, which was observed to fall completely out of control and crash. Flight Commander Munday attacked an Albatross Scout, firing over 250 rounds, the latter part of the burst at very close range. The enemy aircraft suddenly went down vertically out of control and was last seen to be still falling in the same manner. Flight Sub-Lieut. White fired 100 rounds at an enemy aircraft at close range and it turned over on one wing and fell into a steep dive. Flight Sub-Lieut. Cumming fired about 200 rounds at an Albatross Scout, which was seen to stall slowly and then to spin down out of sight.

Second Lieutenants Green and Gros, No. 57 Squadron, while on photography were attacked by two Albatross Scouts. Second Lieutenant Gros fired half a drum into one of these at 50 yards' range, and the enemy aircraft was seen to fall completely out of control, first in a vertical nose-dive and then alternately side-slipping and stalling until it was lost to view. The second enemy aircraft was engaged and driven off.

Second Lieutenants W. Beaver and H. Easton, No. 20 Squadron, while on offensive patrol dived on an Albatross Scout. The pilot fired about 150 rounds at close range and the enemy aircraft was seen to fall completely out of control and burst into flames when near the ground.

Second Lieutenant H. Lewis, No. 23 Squadron, shot down an enemy aircraft out of control, but was unable to follow it down as he was immediately engaged with three other enemy aircraft.

Captain J. Gilmour, No. 65 Squadron, attacked one of 12 Albatross Scouts, firing at 20 yards' range, and the enemy aircraft went down out of control. In the same flight, Second Lieutenant G. Knocker attacked another Albatross Scout, firing about 60 rounds. The enemy aircraft went down out of control.

A patrol of No. 41 Squadron observed two enemy aircraft two-seaters. Captain D. MacLean got under the tail of the higher enemy aircraft and fired about 40 rounds into it at from 15 to 20 yards' range. The enemy aircraft then turned on to its right side and at the same time Second Lieut. G. Lipsett dived from above and fired 60 rounds at 30 yards' range at it, and it spun slowly down completely out of control.

Captain H. Maddocks, while leading a patrol of No. 54 Squadron, encountered five enemy scouts; he dived at the nearest enemy aircraft, which went down 2,000 feet and then burst into flames. Captain Maddocks then attacked another enemy aircraft and after a short engagement got in a burst at very close range. The enemy aircraft immediately burst into flames and went down. Lieutenant G. Cuthbertson attacked one of the enemy aircraft, and shot it down out of control and it was seen to crash on the ground by another pilot.

Captain E. Pennell, No. 84 Squadron, attacked an enemy balloon. The observer was seen to jump out in a parachute. Captain Pennell could see Buckingham enter the balloon, but it did not catch fire, so he again flew over the balloon to enable Lieutenant Proctor to make another attempt to fire it. The balloon when last seen was descending quickly but not on fire.

February 4th.

The weather was fine all day, though overcast, and the visibility was very bad owing to mist.

Seven successful reconnaissances were carried out, one by the 1st Brigade, three by the 2nd, and three by the 5th.

Twenty-one hostile batteries were successfully engaged for destruction and five neutralised; one gun-pit was destroyed, four damaged, 11 explosions and 11 fires caused. Seventy-five zone calls were sent down.

On the 3rd, balloons of the 2nd Brigade engaged four targets, one being a hostile battery, which was successfully engaged for destruction.

Three hundred photographs were taken, 275 bombs dropped, and 11,521 rounds fired at ground targets as follows:—

1st Brigade.—Thirty-six photographs. 1st Wing dropped 137 and the 10th Wing dropped sixty 25-lb. bombs and fired 8,440 rounds.

2nd Brigade.—Two hundred and forty-four photographs. No. 57 Squadron dropped sixty-eight 25-lb. bombs on a dump at Heule; Corps Squadrons dropped fifty-two 25-lb. bombs and 2,341 rounds were fired.

3rd Brigade.—Eighteen photographs; fourteen 25-lb. bombs were dropped (six of which were on a battery in action near Dury), and 300 rounds fired.

5th Brigade.—No. 35 Squadron dropped four 25-lb. bombs on miscellaneous targets and fired 440 rounds.

Enemy Aircraft.—Enemy aircraft activity was slight all day, except on the 2nd Brigade front. Five enemy machines were brought down, one of which fell in our lines, and eight driven down out of control.

Second Lieut. A. Atkey and Lieutenant C. Ffolliott, No. 18 Squadron, when returning from a photographic and bombing expedition, were attacked by about 10 enemy scouts. Lieutenant Ffolliott fired a burst at the leader which went down out of control, a portion of his tail plane detaching itself. A burst was then fired at another enemy aircraft, which went down out of control. The remainder of the formation then broke off the combat. Second Lieutenant Atkey's machine was badly shot about, the magazine gun and the observer's drum being shot through and one of the elevator control wires shot away.

Second Lieut. H. Hegarty and Lieutenant H. Crompton, No. 60 Squadron, whilst an offensive patrol, both attacked an Albatross Scout. The enemy aircraft spun down out of control and crashed in our lines. Lieutenant W. Duncan and Second Lieutenant J. Priestley, of the same Squadron, both attacked one of a formation of Albatross Scouts. One of the planes fell off the enemy aircraft and the enemy machine burst into flames.

An offensive patrol of No. 20 Squadron engaged 20 Albatross Scouts. Lieutenant Leigh-Pemberton and Captain Taylor fired at one, which burst into flames. Second Lieuts. Weston and Noble attacked a second enemy aircraft, Second Lieut. Noble firing two drums, and the enemy aircraft went down in a slow spin. Lieutenant Bennett and 1st Air Mechanic Mather fired 200 rounds at a third enemy aircraft, which went down out of control. They were then attacked by three Scouts, and first Air Mechanic Mather fired a drum into one of these and it burst into flames and fell to pieces in the air. Second Lieuts. Cook and Agelasto attacked a fifth enemy aircraft, which they shot down out of control. Second Lieuts. Lindup and Dougall attacked a sixth enemy aircraft with the back gun and the enemy aircraft went down completely out of control. Second Lieut. Colville-Jones and Captain Hedley attacked another enemy aircraft into which the pilot fired 100 rounds, and the enemy aircraft fell out of control and crashed. Second Lieut. L. Roberts and Lieutenant M. Farquharson-Roberts attacked an Albatross Scout, which went down out of control after a burst of 100 rounds at close range had been fired by Lieutenant Farquharson-Roberts.

Lieutenant Colville-Jones and Captain Hedley, No. 20 Squadron, dived on a hostile balloon, firing 100 rounds. The balloon was seen to crumple up and fall to the ground.

Honours and Awards.

The Military Cross.—Captain M. E. Gonne, Second Lieut. G. R. Housam, Captain R. K. Kirkman, Captain R. T. O. Windsor, Lieutenant R. S. Larkin, Captain T. Grant.

ROYAL FLYING CORPS COMMUNIQUÉ.—No. 126.

During the period under review (February 5th to 11th, inclusive) we have claimed officially seven enemy aircraft brought down and five driven down out of control, and one hostile balloon brought down. Nine of our machines are missing. Approximately 13 tons of bombs were dropped, 49,966 rounds fired at ground targets, and 1,261 photographs taken.

February 5th.

The weather was again misty except on the 2nd Brigade front, but in spite of bad visibility 17 successful reconnaissances were carried out, 10 of which were by machines of the 5th Brigade.

Seventy-seven hostile batteries were successfully engaged for destruction and 10 neutralised; nine gun-pits were destroyed, 23 damaged, 50 explosions and 17 fires caused. Eighty-seven zone calls were sent down.

Eight hundred and sixty-six photographs were taken (464 of which were by the 2nd Brigade), 516 bombs dropped, and 21,099 rounds fired at ground targets as follows :—

Night 4th–5th.

9th Wing.—No. 58 Squadron dropped twenty-four 25-lb. bombs on Menin Station; No. 101 Squadron dropped one hundred and eight 25-lb. bombs on Etreux Aerodrome and fired 2,250 rounds into hangars on the aerodrome.

Day 5th.

1st Brigade.—Two hundred and seventy-seven photographs were taken and 9,730 rounds fired. 1st Wing dropped 70 and 10th Wing dropped fifty-four 25-lb. bombs on miscellaneous targets.

2nd Brigade.—Four hundred and sixty-four photographs were taken and 3,039 rounds fired. Corps Squadrons dropped eighty-five 25-lb. bombs on miscellaneous targets and No. 57 Squadron dropped ten 112-lb. bombs on Roulers sidings.

3rd Brigade.—Sixty photographs were taken and 1,220 rounds fired. Corps Squadrons dropped thirty-five and 13th Wing dropped fourteen 25-lb. bombs on miscellaneous targets.

5th Brigade.—Thirty-six photographs were taken and 6,710 rounds fired. Corps Squadrons dropped 53 and 22nd Wing dropped sixteen 25-lb. bombs.

9th Wing.—Forty-nine photographs were taken; No. 27 Squadron dropped thirteen 25-lb. and ten 112-lb. bombs on Dechy Station, and No. 25 Squadron dropped twelve 112-lb. bombs on Deynze Station.

Enemy Aircraft.—Lieutenant G. McElroy, No. 40 Squadron, while on offensive patrol, singled out a D.F.W. and when within about 100 yards' range fired 100 rounds. Pieces were seen to fall from the enemy aircraft's tail and fuselage, and the enemy aircraft went down in a slow spin and finally crashed. After this encounter Lieutenant McElroy found himself separated from his patrol. He observed a D.F.W. which was pointed out to him by anti-aircraft fire; he dived and fired about 200 rounds, and the enemy aircraft burst into flames.

A patrol of Naval Squadron No. 8 attacked two Albatross Scouts. Flight Lieut. McDonald fired 300 rounds at one from fairly close range, and Flight Sub-Lieuts. Day and Fowler also engaged the same enemy aircraft, which went down completely out of control and crashed.

An offensive patrol of No. 20 Squadron engaged 12 Albatross Scouts. Second Lieuts. Cooke and Agelasto dived on one of the enemy aircraft, firing 100 rounds at close range, and the enemy aircraft was seen to go down completely out of control. Shortly afterwards they were attacked by an Albatross Scout from behind and slightly below. Second Lieut. Angelasto fired two drums into this enemy aircraft, which went down completely out of control in a slow spin. Second Lieuts. Beaver and Easton dived on an enemy aircraft Scout, firing 200 rounds, and the enemy aircraft went down out of control. They then attacked another enemy aircraft which was on their tail, and which they also drove down completely out of control after 300 rounds had been fired at it by Second Lieut. Easton.

Captain Molesworth, No. 29 Squadron, attacked an enemy aircraft at 100 yards' range, and after 100 rounds had been fired into it the enemy aircraft turned on its back and fell into the clouds completely out of control. Second Lieut. F. Williams fired a drum into another enemy aircraft, and after a few seconds this enemy aircraft behaved in a similar manner, turning completely over on its back and falling into the clouds quite out of control.

Major J. Cunningham, No. 65 Squadron, attacked an Albatross Scout which was diving on another member of his patrol and fired a burst with both guns at 50 yards' range. The enemy aircraft fell completely out of control, its tail plane folding up, and it was observed to crash.

Second Lieut. E. Peacock attacked another Albatross Scout, firing at about 150 yards' range and tracers were seen to enter the fuselage, and the enemy aircraft went down in a vertical dive apparently out of control.

Second Lieut. A. Leitch, No. 65 Squadron, attacked an Albatross Scout, which he shot down out of control. He was then attacked by other enemy aircraft and was forced to cross the lines at about 1,200 feet.

Lieutenant J. Aldred, No. 70 Squadron, attacked one of eight enemy aircraft and drove it down out of control. Lieutenant E. Peverell engaged an enemy aircraft two-seater and followed it down to about 1,000 feet, firing all the way. The enemy aircraft finally went down side-slipping and diving out of control, but owing to machine gun-fire from the ground, Lieutenant Peverell was obliged to turn away and was not able to watch the enemy aircraft crash.

Captain F. Soden, No. 60 Squadron, attacked an Albatross Scout over Gheluvelt, which he drove down out of control. Two other hostile machines then attacked Captain Soden, and he was driven down from 15,000 to 50 feet, eight miles over the lines. He came back zooming and banking round trees, and saw the leading enemy aircraft crash into a tree. He outdistanced the remaining enemy aircraft and crossed the lines at 50 feet.

Lieutenant G. Shaw and Sergeant F. Hopper, No. 25 Squadron, when returning from a bomb raid, were attacked by a formation of Albatross Scouts. A drum was fired at the nearest enemy aircraft, which went down out of control.

Miscellaneous.—Captain J. Gilmour, No. 65 Squadron, attacked a hostile balloon. The occupants descended by parachute, and the balloon went down with black smoke issuing from it.

Second Lieut. Lindsay, No. 54 Squadron, attacked an enemy balloon and fired about 200 rounds into it. The observer jumped out and the balloon was hauled down.

Captain Vickers and Lieutenant Smith, No. 101 Squadron, dropped their bombs on Etreux Aerodrome (night 4th–5th) from 1,500 feet and obtained three direct hits on some hangars on the east side of the aerodrome, and afterwards fired 400 rounds into the hangars, &c.

February 6th.

Weather.—Low clouds and mist in the morning, improving in the afternoon.

Eight successful reconnaissances were carried out, all by machines of the 5th Brigade.

Six hostile batteries were successfully engaged for destruction (five by the 1st Brigade) and four neutralised, two gun-pits were damaged, three explosions and one fire caused, and 18 zone calls were sent down.

On the 5th, balloons of the 1st Brigade located three active hostile batteries, one of which was silenced, a fire being caused in one of the gun-pits. Six targets were engaged by balloons of the 2nd Brigade, three being hostile batteries, one of which was successfully engaged for destruction.

One hundred and five photographs were taken, 262 bombs dropped, and 9,405 rounds fired as follows:—

Night 5th/6th

5th Brigade.—Corps Squadron dropped twenty-four 25-lb. and two 112-lb. bombs on Ribemont.

9th Wing.—No. 101 Squadron dropped one hundred and thirty-two 25-lb. bombs on Etreux Aerodrome and fired 2,000 rounds into hangars on the aerodrome, and No. 102 Squadron dropped eight 25-lb. bombs on Courtrai.

Day 6th.

1st Brigade.—Thirty-six photographs. 1st Wing dropped fifty-three 25-lb. bombs and fired 300 rounds, and 10th Wing fired 4,200 rounds.

2nd Brigade.—3rd Squadron A.F.C. dropped two 25-lb. bombs and fired 2,220 rounds.

3rd Brigade.—Forty-two photographs. Corps Squadrons dropped thirteen 25-lb. bombs and fired 900 rounds.

5th Brigade.—Twenty-seven photographs. Corps Squadrons dropped twelve 25-lb. bombs, 22nd Wing dropped sixteen 25-lb. bombs, and 1,785 rounds were fired.

Enemy Aircraft.—A patrol of No. 3 Squadron attacked six Albatross Scouts, and Lieutenant G. Alderson and Second Lieut. Kent each shot down one enemy aircraft, which are reported by anti-aircraft to have crashed. In this fight Captain Sutton collided with one of the enemy aircraft and had his fin taken off, and was forced to retire from the combat.

February 7th.

Mist, rain, and strong wind interfered with operations.

One hostile battery was successfully engaged for destruction, and nine zone calls sent down.

On the 6th, balloons of the 1st Brigade carried out two shoots, successfully engaging one hostile battery for destruction and neutralising another. Balloons of the 3rd Brigade successfully engaged one hostile battery for destruction.

Honours and Awards.

Bar to the Distinguished Service Cross.—Flight Commander G. W. Price, D.S.C.; Flight Lieut. W. L. Jordan, D.S.C.

The Distinguished Service Cross.—Flight Sub-Lieut. E. G. Johnstone.

Bar to the Military Cross.—Captain W. E. Molesworth, M.C.

The Military Cross.—Captain J. H. Tudhope; Lieutenant G. E. H. McElroy; Captain K. M. St. C. G. Leask.

February 8th.

Low clouds, high wind, and rain made flying practically impossible.

One hostile battery was neutralised by machines of the 1st Wing, one other target engaged for effect, one fire was caused, and seven active hostile batteries reported by zone calls.

Ten 25-lb. bombs were dropped on miscellaneous targets by machines of the 1st Wing.

Three plates were exposed by the 12th Wing.

Enemy aircraft activity was nil, except on the 1st Brigade front, where a few two-seaters were seen in the afternoon. No combats took place.

February 9th.

In spite of low clouds and a strong wind, a certain amount of flying was done.

Eight successful reconnaissances were completed (five by the 5th Brigade and three by the 3rd Brigade).

Five hostile batteries were successfully engaged for destruction and two neutralised; two gun-pits were destroyed, three damaged, three explosions and two fires caused. Seven zone calls were sent down.

Fifty-two photographs were taken (all by the 5th Brigade), 138 bombs dropped, and 8,057 rounds fired at ground targets as follows:—

Night 8th/9th.

9th Wing.—Forty-four 25-lb. bombs on Courtrai, lights near Bisseghem, Menin, Moorslede, billets at Heule and St. Denis Westrem by No. 102 Squadron.

By Day.

1st Brigade.—1st Wing dropped thirty 25-lb. bombs on miscellaneous targets and fired 4,090 rounds.

3rd Brigade.—Twenty-three 25-lb. bombs were dropped and 870 rounds fired.

5th Brigade—15th Wing took 52 photographs, dropped thirty-seven 25-lb. bombs and fired 2,597 rounds, and 22nd Wing dropped four 25-lb. bombs.

Enemy Aircraft.—Enemy aircraft activity was very slight and only one decisive combat took place.

Second Lieut. Hartley and Lieutenant Herring, No. 48 Squadron, shot down one enemy aircraft completely out of control, and it was last seen at a height of 2,000 feet still in the same condition. It was impossible to see the enemy aircraft crash owing to clouds.

February 10th.

The weather was very overcast with a high wind and little flying was carried out.

Five successful reconnaissances were completed (four by the 5th Brigade).

Three hostile batteries were successfully engaged for destruction and nine neutralised; two gun-pits were damaged, three explosions and two fires caused. Twenty-two zone calls were sent down.

Thirty-five photographs were taken, 50 bombs dropped, and 4,327 rounds fired at ground targets as follows:—

1st Brigade.—1st Wing dropped eighteen 25-lb. bombs and fired 800 rounds.

3rd Brigade.—12th Wing took 10 photographs and dropped four 25-lb. bombs on trench targets.

5th Brigade.—15th Wing took 25 photographs, dropped twenty-eight 25-lb. bombs, and fired 3,527 rounds.

Enemy aircraft activity was very slight and no combats took place.

8th Brigade.—During the night of the 9th/10th, six machines of No. 100 Squadron left the ground to bomb the railway station and junction at Courcelles-les-Metz (S.E. of Metz). The weather conditions were by no means good, the night being very dark and misty, but all the pilots reached the objective. Twelve 112-lb., twenty 25-lb., and two 40-lb. (phosphorus) bombs were dropped with good results. The leaders dropped phosphorus bombs, the bursts of which guided other pilots to the objective. The results of the bursts were unobserved owing to mist. Seven hundred rounds were fired at anti-aircraft guns and searchlights.

One machine failed to return.

Honours and Awards.

Second Bar to the Distinguished Service Cross.— Flight Commander R. J. O. Compston, D.S.C.

The Military Cross.—Second Lieut. A. B. Whiteside.

February 11th.

Clouds, mist, and a strong wind interfered with flying, the weather being somewhat better on the 5th Brigade front.

One hostile battery was neutralised, 14 registrations carried out, and a fire caused. Fourteen zone calls were sent down.

One hundred and forty-four photographs were taken, 102 bombs dropped, and 4,376 rounds fired at ground targets as follows:—

1st Brigade.—Fourteen 25-lb. bombs on miscellaneous targets by the 1st Wing.

3rd Brigade.—12th Wing dropped ten 25-lb. bombs and fired 500 rounds on various targets.

5th Brigade.—One hundred and forty-four plates were exposed and 3,876 rounds fired. 15th Wing dropped sixty-six 24-lb. bombs and 22nd Wing dropped twelve 25-lb. bombs.

Enemy aircraft activity was very slight. No combats took place.

L. A. K. BUTT, Captain,
Staff Officer.

Headquarters,
  Royal Flying Corps,
      13th February 1918.

No. 52.

CONFIDENTIAL.

ROYAL NAVAL AIR SERVICE.

OPERATIONS REPORT

(with Royal Flying Corps Reports attached).

15th to 28th FEBRUARY 1918.

NAVAL STAFF,
  AIR DIVISION.
   28th February 1918.

ROYAL NAVAL AIR SERVICE.

REPORT OF OPERATIONS

(Completed from Reports during period
15th to 28th February 1918.)

CONTENTS.

	PAGE
HOME STATIONS	2
DUNKIRK	4
BRITISH ADRIATIC SQUADRON	14
EASTERN MEDITERRANEAN	14
ROYAL FLYING CORPS COMMUNIQUÉS	21

HOME STATIONS.

SUBMARINE PATROL WORK.

February 20th.

Yarmouth.—Large American Seaplane No. 8666 left on a special submarine patrol at 1240 and at 1303 when flying at a height of 450 feet in position, 5 miles north of Smiths Knoll Pillar Buoy, and steering north, a submarine was sighted steering south, with the conning tower above water. Another submarine was seen steering southward about one mile astern of the first one, but this one submerged immediately afterwards and only a slight wash could be seen.

At 1305, two 230-lb. bombs were dropped at the first submarine. One dropped in the swirl made by the conning tower, and directly astern of it, the other dropped within 30 feet of the conning tower, and slightly abaft abeam. The first bomb either failed to explode, or crashing right through the submarine exploded inside or directly underneath it.

The second bomb exploded and a column of water was thrown in the air, and black deposit was afterwards visible on the surface.

When the bombs were released the submarine was submerging at an angle of from 15 to 20 degrees from the horizontal, but immediately after the dropping of the bombs the stern of the submarine was seen to rise out of the water, turn over and disappear at an angle of fully 60 degrees.

The seaplane was put about and circled round the spot where the submarine was sunk, and a large patch of thick oil 50 feet in diameter was observed on the surface. Owing to the low visibility and the fact that the seaplane was almost uncontrollable on account of the extremely bumpy weather, the patch of oil was soon lost sight of. A course was then made for the base.

The concussion from the explosion of the two 230-lb. bombs from a height of 450 feet endangered the safety of the seaplane, but the local weather conditions made it imperative to fly at this height to carry out an effective attack.

Names of crew :—

Flight Commander Leckie.
Flight Lieutenant Fetherston.
A. M. Grant (Engineer).
P. O. Thomson (W/T).

February 16th.

Night Attacks by Hostile Aircraft. — A bombing raid of approximately 2½ hours' duration was carried out by four "Riesen" (Giant type) aeroplanes over the area, Thames Estuary, Essex, Kent, and London. The four machines crossed the coast between the river Crouch and Shoeburyness shortly before 2200 and proceeded towards London along the River Thames. Two of the machines were engaged and turned back by the Chatham defences at about 2215.

The third penetrated into London via Belvedere, Woolwich, Blackheath and Chelsea. One bomb was dropped in front of the Garrison Church, Woolwich, killing a soldier and a woman; a second bomb which fell in Artillery Place demolished one house and damaged another. It is reported that two bombs were dropped at Beckenham.

A bomb fell on the officers quarters at Chelsea Hospital demolishing a house and burying an officer, his wife, and five children in the ruins.

Another enemy machine attacked Dover about 2245, but was driven off by gunfire after dropping seven or eight bombs near St. Margarets.

Royal Flying Corps pilots engaged the enemy and it is reported that one enemy machine fell in the sea off Folkestone, but it is not known whether this was the result of an action or not. The raiders left the coast in the vicinity of Dover about midnight.

February 17th.

A bombing raid of approximately three hours duration was carried out by, probably one Giant type, and four or five other aeroplanes, the type of which it is not possible to establish definitely but which were possibly Gothas. The area involved was the Thames Estuary, Essex, Kent and London.

The Giant aeroplane was first reported off the North Foreland at 2145 and avoiding the defences on the Isle of Thanet it steered along the Thames Estuary till it reached the River Medway when it altered course across Grain, being heavily engaged by the guns of the Chatham defences. It was next reported from Tilbury, Greenhithe, Dartford, Woolwich and the Tower at 2245 and was possibly followed into London at a few minutes interval by two other machines.

High explosive bombs were dropped in the following places, resulting in considerable damage to property, and a number of persons being killed and injured:—

Lewisham, Old Kent Road, New Kent Road, St. Pancras Hotel, Southwark and Bow Street.

The enemy machines proceeded out of London along the line of the River Thames.

The other enemy machines crossed the coast between the Crouch and the Thames, between 2215 and 2230.

The last of the raiders left the coast in the vicinity of Dover 0015.

DUNKIRK.

WEATHER.

During this period the weather has been fair generally, but on several days clouds have hindered flying operations.

RECONNAISSANCE.

No. 1 Wing, Nos. 2 and 13 Squadron.

Reconnaissance and W/T patrol operations have been carried out almost daily during this period by machines of the above squadrons. These include a number of special coastal reconnaissances during which good shipping information was obtained.

PHOTOGRAPHIC RECONNAISSANCE.

February 16th.

No. 1 Wing (2nd Squadron).—A photographic reconnaissance was carried out, and plates were exposed along the Canal between Zeebrugge Mole and Bruges Harbour.

February 17th.

Photographs were taken over Maria Aalter Aerodrome which shows no change. A new medium-sized battery is in course of construction a little to the south of Uytkerke.

February 18th.

A reconnaissance was carried out and plates were exposed over Zeebrugge Mole, Darse, and Lock.

February 18th.

A reconnaissance was carried out, and plates were exposed over Aertrycke and Varssenaere Aerodromes.

February 21st.

A photographic reconnaissance was carried out over Ostende, during which 43 plates were exposed and good results obtained.

OFFENSIVE PATROL—ENGAGEMENTS WITH ENEMY.

February 16th.

No. 1 Wing (13th Squadron).—Whilst on patrol at 17,000 feet, Flight Commander Day (Sopwith Camel No. 6363) observed a great deal of anti-aircraft fire over Nieuport, and upon investigation saw three enemy aircraft (two sections) a few miles out to sea.

The Camel manœuvred up sun, and dived on the enemy aircraft, firing two long bursts at 100 to 70 yards range. At this point pressure gave trouble, and the engine had to be changed over to gravity, thus losing distance. About 100 more rounds were fired at 100 to 150 yards range, and the combat was broken off Westende.

The machine which was attacked was last seen gliding slowly along the beach very low.

The Sopwith was hit in several places, including one explosive bullet in the cowl, and one bullet through a main spar.

February 17th.

No. 4 Wing (3rd Squadron).—Whilst on patrol over the Middlekerke–Houthulst Forest line a formation of five Sopwith Camels encountered a formation of eight Albatross Scouts just west of Roulers going south, and a number of engagements took place.

Flight Lieut. A. T. Whealy attacked one of the enemy machines, and diving on his tail fired a burst of 25 to 30 rounds from each gun at a range of from 400 to 300 feet. The enemy machine did three or four almost vertical turns going down steeply, and carried on down out of control.

The pilot then attacked another machine which prevented him observing the final result of the first attack. The engagements between other pilots and enemy machines were indecisive.

February 18th.

No. 4 Wing (3rd Squadron).—A formation of five Sopwith Camels left to carry out a patrol over the Middlekerke-Houthulst Forest line, during which a formation of 27 enemy aircraft were encountered over Thourout – Dixmude, and several engagements took place.

Flight Lieut. Bawlf observed one machine a little way behind the others, which he attacked with about 50 rounds at close range. The enemy machine turned over on its back and started spinning completely out of control, but the final result was not observed.

The same pilot attacked several other machines, but with no decisive results.

Flight Lieut. Ireland dived on one of the enemy machines, and got off a good burst of about 100 rounds from 100 yards range. The pilot then had to abandon the attack on account of being attacked from above, and climbed towards Dixmude and observed an enemy machine coming from that direction and about 500 feet below. The Sopwith pilot dived on him, getting in 300 rounds, and then had to pull off owing to both guns missfiring. This machine was last seen to go over on its side and go down towards Thourout.

Flight Commander F. C. Armstrong attacked one enemy machine just east of Dixmude, and after firing about 100 rounds from close range it went down in a spin but levelled up again.

The same pilot attacked a second enemy machine, and after firing about 200 rounds, had to break off on account of being attacked from above.

February 18th.

No. 4 Wing (10th Squadron).—A patrol of five Sopwith Camels encountered a formation of five Albatross Scouts, and engaged them at 15,000 feet over Menin.

Flight Lieut. Manuel fired 100 rounds into one of the enemy machines from very close range. This machine stalled, spun for a short distance, then nose-dived, and finally crashed on the ground to the southward of Menin. The same pilot attacked another enemy machine, firing about 300 rounds without any decisive result.

Flight Sub-Lieut. Hall got into a good position on the tail of another of the enemy machines, and after firing 200 rounds at very close range it was observed to side-slip, and went down absolutely out of control, eventually crashing on the ground to the southward of Menin, close to the first machine which had crashed.

Flight Sub-Lieut. Hall then attacked another machine, but after a short indecisive engagement his machine spun down to about 2,000 feet, then flattened out and got away.

February 19th.

No. 1 Wing (13th Squadron).—A patrol of five Sopwith Camels sighted an enemy aeroplane, at 200 feet over Ostend proceeding towards Wenduyne. The patrol manœuvred up sun and dived on the seaplane, which turned back towards Ostend over Wenduyne.

The Sopwiths attacked one mile from Wenduyne, and 100 yards from the beach, and the seaplane went down striking the water twice, 80 yards from the beach, and one mile east of Ostend. It then turned sharply towards the beach and burst into flames. The machine sank almost immediately, and neither the pilot or observer were seen to leave the wreckage.

February 19th.

No. 4 Wing (10th Squadron).—Whilst on patrol a formation of six Sopwith Camels encountered four enemy scout machines at 13,000 feet east of Roulers. One of these was engaged by Flight Lieut. Manuel, who got into a good position and fired

400 rounds at a range of 150 to 100 yards range. The enemy machine went into a stall to the right and dived vertically.

The Sopwith was then attacked by another enemy machine, which prevented him observing the result of the attack, but when last seen the enemy machine was still diving apparently out of control.

February 19th.

No. 4 Wing (10th Squadron).—Whilst on patrol a formation of eight Sopwith Camels observed four enemy scout machines above them and approaching the lines south-east of Ypres.

The Sopwith formation climbed above them, and several combats took place.

Flight Lieut. Carter attacked one machine over our lines at 8,000 feet, and obtained a good position on his tail. He followed this machine down to 80 feet, firing short bursts into it, and saw it crash and burst into flames.

Other combats took place, but without decisive results.

February 21st.

No. 4 Wing (3rd Squadron).—Whilst on patrol, a flight of four Sopwith Camels observed a large formation of about 20 enemy machines coming towards the line from the direction of Menin.

Flight Commander L. H. Rochford picked out an Albatross Scout and fired a burst of about 30 rounds into him from 20 yards range.

The enemy machine reeled over to the right and slipped underneath Flight Commander Rochford's machine, and was lost sight of, but it appears probable that it was badly hit and went down out of control.

February 28th.

No. 4 Wing (10th Squadron).—Whilst on patrol, a flight of four Sopwith Camels encountered a formation of 12 Albatross Scouts in the locality N.E. of Ypres. A general engagement ensued, during which Flight Lieut. Mellings got into position at close range on the tail of one of the enemy machines and fired 100 rounds.

Tracers were observed entering the fuselage, and the enemy machine passed from a steep dive right over on his back, and appeared quite out of control.

The other engagements were without decisive results.

ATTACK ON ENEMY TRENCHES.

February 19th.

No. 1 Wing (13th Squadron).—Whilst returning from a patrol five Sopwith Camels fired about 100 rounds at trenches near Dixmude from 8,000 feet.

ATTACK ON ENEMY SHIPPING.

February 23rd.

No. 1 Wing (2nd Squadron).—While returning from a coastal reconnaissance, escorting machines fired on an enemy motor boat and a small steam vessel. Ostende and Zeebrugge Mole were attacked with machine-gun fire from 2,000 yards range. A train running from Zeebrugge to Ostende was also attacked.

An enemy steam trawler steering towards Blankenberghe was attacked with about 80 rounds of machine-gun fire.

BOMB ATTACK ON ENEMY DESTROYERS.

February 24th.

No. 1 Wing (13th Squadron).—A bombing attack was carried out by three Sopwith Camels on three enemy destroyers seven miles north, north-west of Zeebrugge. Six bombs were dropped in a bunch, 50 to 75 yards from the ships from a height of 600 feet.

BOMB ATTACKS.

(Carried out during the period between the dates given.)

*Bruges Docks	Feb. 16th	2,688 lbs.	H.P.
Mariakerke Aerodrome	Feb. 16th–17th	8,288 ,,	,,
*Zuidwege Dump	Feb. 16th	1,604 ,,	D.H. 4.
*Uytkerke Aerodrome	,, 17th	1,040 ,,	,,
Zeebrugge Docks	Feb. 17th–18th	3,240 ,,	H.P.
Zeebrugge Lock Gates	,, ,,	1,672 ,,	,,
Bruges Docks	,, ,,	4,592 ,,	,,
East and West Bassins	,, ,,	3,024 ,,	,,
*Varssenaere Aerodrome	Feb. 18th	1,280 ,,	D.H. 4
St. Denis Westrem Aerodrome.	Feb. 18th–19th	1,080 ,,	H.P.
Bruges Docks	,, ,,	3,136 ,,	,,
*Aertrycke Aerodrome	Feb. 19th	1,460 ,,	H.D. 4
*Engel Dump	,, ,,	64 ,,	,,
Abeele Aerodrome	Feb. 26th–27th	128 ,,	S. Camel
Bruges Docks	,, 25th–26th	6,376 ,,	H.P.
Oostacker Aerodrome	,, ,,	6,272 ,,	,,
*Engel Dump	Feb. 26th	952 ,,	D.H. 4
	Total -	56,896 lbs.	

* Daylight raid.   (A) Aeroplanes.

February 16th–17th.

No. 5 Wing (7th and 14th Squadrons).—A night bombing attack was carried out by six Handley Page machines on Mariakerke Aerodrome, during which seventy-four 112-lb. bombs were dropped principally on the western group of sheds. Low visibility prevented accurate observations of results, but many bombs were seen to burst close to and among the principal group of sheds and hangars on the aerodrome.

Two machines attacked Bruges Docks with twenty-four 112-lb. bombs. These were dropped in several good straddles over the principal bassins and buildings in between; a small fire was started close to the West Bassin.

Anti-aircraft fire was heavy and very accurate; one machine crashed on landing, but none of the crew were hurt.

February 16th.

No. 5 Wing (5th Squadron).—A bombing attack was carried out in Zuidwege Dump by seven D.H. 4 bombing machines with two escorting machines, at about noon, and twelve 50-lb., forty-seven 20-lb., and four 16-lb. bombs were dropped on the objective from heights varying from 15,000 to 17,000 feet. The target was well straddled from north to south, and many bombs were observed to burst on the dump. A fire was caused in the centre on the target by two 50-lb. bombs, but no other direct hits are reported.

February 17th.

No. 5 Wing (5th Squadron).—Engagement with Enemy.— Five D.H. 4 bombing machines, accompanied by two escorting machines, left at 1021 to carry out an attack on Uytkerke Aerodrome. One escort machine was compelled to return on account of trouble with the rear gun mounting, and one bomber which could not attain the height of the formation.

The other five machines reached the target, on which eight 50-lb. and thirty-two 20-lb. bombs were dropped at 1140 from heights of from 15,000 to 16,400 feet.

The target was straddled from north-west to south-east, and many bombs were seen to burst close to the sheds and on the aerodrome, but no direct hits were observed.

Two photographic plates were exposed, one over the objective and one between the objective and Uytkerke Village.

Flight Lieut. E. Dickson, D.S.C. (D.H. 4 N. 6000), when picking up the formation between Ostend and Blankenberghe, observed three enemy machines coming from the direction of Ostend. A. G. L. Naylor (observer) opened fire on one of them at about 500 feet range, firing three double pans, after which the hostile machine spun and dived, apparently out of control.

The D.H. 4 was then attacked by another hostile machine, on account of which the first machine was lost sight of.

Visibility was good, and anti-aircraft fire moderate; all machines returned safely.

February 17th–18th.

No. 5 Wing (7th and 14th Squadrons).—Two Handley Page machines from No. 7 Squadron were despatched during the night to carry out a bombing attack on Zeebrugge Docks, and four 250-lb. and twenty 112-lb. bombs were dropped on the objective. Visibility was good, and bombs were seen to fall in a good line between the North and South Lock Gates and along side the submarine shelter near Darse No. 1.

A second trip was made by one Handley Page, which left at 2140, and the Lock Gates were again attacked with four 250-lb. and six 112-lb. bombs, which were seen to burst in a good line over the gates.

Four Handley Pages from No. 14 Squadron left at 1919 to attack Bruges Docks; one had to return owing to engine trouble. The other three reached the objective, on which forty-one 112-lb. bombs were dropped from heights of 5,000 to 6,800 feet. Good shooting was made, and many bombs were seen to burst on the quays adjacent to the East and West Bassins. From the western quay of the Eastern Bassin a cloud of smoke, and what appeared to be blue electric flashes, were seen after the attack.

A second attack was carried out by two Handley Page machines, and twenty-seven 112-lb. bombs were dropped at the East and West Bassins.

The visibility was good, throughout all the attacks above described, and it is estimated that considerable damage must have been done. Anti-aircraft fire was very heavy and accurate, but all machines returned safely.

February 18th.

No. 5 Wing (5th Squadron).—Engagement with Enemy.— Six D.H. 4 bombing machines, accompanied by two escorting machines, left at 1103 to carry out a bombing raid on Varssenaere Aerodrome. Of these, one escorting machine had to return owing to engine trouble, and one bomber which could not attain height. Ten 50-lb. and thirty-nine 20-lb. bombs were dropped over the target from heights of from 15,500 to 17,000 feet. The principal group of sheds were straddled, and several hits are reported on or close to a group of hangars.

Many other bombs were seen to explode along the line of sheds at the east side and the group of hangars at the north-west corner of the aerodrome, also on the landing ground itself.

The D.H. 4's were heavily attacked by enemy aircraft, and several were considerably shot about. A cut wire on Flight Sub-Lieut Mason's machine jammed his ailerons, and he returned using the rudder only.

D.H. 4 N. 6000 (pilot, Flight Lieut. E. Dickson, D.S.C.; observer, A. G. L. Naylor) had an engagement with a single seater Albatross, resulting in the enemy machine going down out of control in a vertical dive.

The D.H. 4 was badly shot about, but returned safely.

February 18th–19th.

No. 5 Wing (7th and 14th Squadrons).—Engagement with Enemy.—A raid was carried out during the night on St. Denis Westrem Aerodrome by two Handley Page machines during which four 250-lb. and twenty 112-lb. bombs were dropped on the objective. Good visibility allowed an excellent sight of the sheds, and two direct hits are claimed in the southern position of the Aerodrome.

During the return journey Handley Page 3119, (Pilot, Flight Lieut. Barker, D.S.C., Observer, Sub-Lieut. Hudson) met an enemy machine and attacked it under very favourable conditions.

The Handley Page attacked from 50 feet behind and 20 yards above, when a burst of 10 rounds was fired, and bullets were seen to penetrate the front portion of the fuselage near the pilot's seat.

The enemy machine was then seen to stall and another 10 rounds was fired when the machine was at its stalling point.

The machine then nose-dived until lost to sight against a dark background.

It is assumed that the pilot must have been badly wounded or killed, and that the machine was destroyed.

Four Handley Pages from No. 14 Squadron left to carry out a raid on St. Denis Westrem Aerodrome, and fifty-six 112-lb. bombs were dropped over the target. The sheds in the south-west corner and on the southern side of the Aerodrome were well straddled, but no definite results could be observed.

One machine carried out a second raid on the same objective and dropped fourteen 112-lb. bombs. A line from south-west to north-east was taken over the target, straddling the sheds in the north-east corner, but no results were observed.

Bruges Docks were attacked by two Handley Pages, and twenty-eight 112-lb. bombs were dropped.

A good line was taken by both machines and the Eastern and Western Bassins were straddled.

Owing to the glare of the enemy searchlights no observations of results could be made.

February 19th.

No. 5 Wing (5th Squadron).—Seven D.H. 4 bombing machines, accompanied by two escorting machines, left to carry out a bomb attack on Aertrycke Aerodrome, and ten 50-lb. and forty-eight 20-lb. bombs were dropped on the objective at 1240 from heights of 15,000 to 17,000 feet. The sheds and hangars along the eastern boundary of the Aerodrome were well straddled, and hits were reported on two sheds, one at the north end and the other in the south-east corner. Several other bursts were seen in the proximity of the hangars, and on the landing ground.

One of the escorting machines failed to pick up the original objective, and dropped its four 16-lb. bombs on Engel Dump, where a direct hit is reported on a small shed in the south-east corner. Visibility was fair, and anti-aircraft fire light and accurate; several enemy aircraft were seen but did not attack.

Three photographs were taken over Engel Dump.

February 25th–26th.

No. 5 Wing (7th and 14th Squadrons).—A bombing raid was carried out during the night on Bruges Docks, by four Handley Page machines, in which four 250-lb. and forty-eight 112-lb. bombs were dropped, and a number of explosions were observed on the quays adjacent to the East and West Bassins.

Oostacker Aerodrome was attacked by four machines and fifty-six 112-lb. bombs were dropped, and the principal groups of sheds and hangars on the southern portion of the Aerodrome were well straddled.

February 29th.

No. 5 Wing (5th Squadron).—Eight D.H. 4 bombing machines accompanied by three fighters left at 0858 to carry out an attack on Wynghene Aerodrome, with Engel Dump as an alternative objective. Owing to the high wind the original target was not attacked and the machines proceeded to carry out an attack on Engel Dump.

Two bombing machines returned before crossing the lines owing to engine trouble, and two other bombing machines were forced to return owing to not being able to keep up with the formation. One of these crashed on landing.

One photographic machine experienced engine trouble over Zaren and had to return after exposing one plate over the railway in the vicinity. One bomber was attacked by an enemy triplane and shots were exchanged. The D.H. 4 was forced to break off the engagement owing to a pierced petrol tank.

The remaining machines dropped thirty-eight 20-lb. and twelve 16-lb. bombs over the target from heights of from 16,000 to 17,200 feet.

The target was well covered, numerous bombs being seen to burst on the Dump and sidings, causing a fire in the centre of the Dump.

Visibility was good and anti-aircraft fire was light.

February 26th–27th.

No. 4 Wing (10th* Squadron).—A bombing attack was carried out during the night on Aheele Aerodrome by Flight Lieut. Hinchliffe (Sopwith Camel B. 7190) and Flight Sub-Lieut. McKelvey (Sopwith Camel B. 6391). The latter pilot descended to 400 feet, and dropped his four 16-lb. bombs on a line of sheds on the Aerodrome. He was held by searchlights for some time and subjected to heavy machine-gun fire. The effect of the bombs was not observed.

Flight Lieut. Hinchliffe descended to about 200 feet over a line of hangars on the Aerodrome, and observed his first 16-lb. bomb fall about 50 yards short of the hangars, the next two burst amongst them, and the fourth among some huts, about 50 yards beyond the last of the hangars. This pilot also was caught in the searchlights and heavily fired on by machine guns. After dropping his last bomb, the pilot turned and fired about 20 rounds into a number of men running about among the huts. Both machines returned safely in company.

HONOURS AND AWARDS.

Name.	Unit.	Awarded.
Acting Flight Commander W. A. Curtiss.	No. 10 Squadron	Bar to D.S.C.
Acting Flight Commander M. J. G. Day	No. 13 ,,	D.S.C.

BELGIAN HONOURS.

Name.	Unit.	Awarded.
Flight Commander G. M. T. Rouse	Late No. 5 Squadron.	Chevalier de la Couronne, Croix de Guerre.
Flight Commander R. B. Munday	No. 8 Squadron	Croix de Guerre.

CASUALTIES.

Name.	Unit.	Date.
Missing.		
Flight Commander M. J. G. Day, D.S.C., died of Wounds.	No. 13 Squadron	27.2.18.
Flight Sub-Lieut. R. E. Burr	No. 10	18.2.18.

BRITISH ADRIATIC SQUADRON.

MALTA SEAPLANE BASE.

February 8th

Attacks on Enemy Submarine.—Short Seaplane N. 1491 (pilot, Flight Lieut. Nunn, observer, A. C. Hosken) left on a routine patrol at 0640 and at 0850, when about 1,000 yards from a French battleship, escorted by two destroyers, the pilot observed a submarine submerged about 60 feet proceeding across the bows of the battleship. The seaplane immediately got into position, and one 230-lb. bomb (delay action) was dropped, which exploded about 30 feet behind the submarine. At this moment a torpedo track from the submarine was seen travelling in the direction of the ships. After the explosion, bubbles, oil, and a certain quantity of what appeared to be wreckage appeared on the surface. The pilot reserved his second bomb in case the submarine came to the surface, and a calcium flare was dropped to mark the position of the attack.

The observer then signalled to the battleship "Have bombed enemy submarine submerged," after which he observed one of the two destroyers making for the position where the bomb had exploded, and signalled to her, "Use your hydrophones." After signalling to the base by W/T the seaplane continued to encircle the position, and afterwards escorted the battleship, then signalled to three drifters and one motor launch to the effect that a submarine had been bombed.

EASTERN MEDITERRANEAN STATION.

(Compiled from Weekly Reports, Nos. 100 and 101, dating from February 10th to 24th, 1918.)

NOTE.—W. O. R. No. 99 has not yet come to hand, and will be included in the next number.

March 10th–16th.

Weather.—Until Thursday, the weather was fine and suitable for operations. On Friday there was a southerly wind up to 40 miles per hour in some parts of the Ægean, particularly at Imbros and towards the Dardanelles, where there were intermittent showers and low heavy clouds. On Friday evening a strong north-easterly wind sprang up and continued with heavy rain until Saturday evening, rendering all flying impossible.

THASOS AIR STATION.

"A" Squadron and "Z" (Greek) Squadron.

March 10th–16th.

Only test and practice flights were carried out during this period.

March 17th–24th.

Weather.—Up till Friday, in the Northern Ægean, a north-easterly wind made flying impossible. Friday and Saturday were fine. On Sunday the 17th, and Monday morning, the gale was very severe, and caused damage to air sheds.

March 17th–24th.

The gale of the 7th wrecked the Bessoneau of "A" Squadron, and two baby seaplanes were badly damaged. In "Z" Squadron two Bessoneaux were stripped of canvas, and the sides and curtain carried away.

Only test and practice flights were carried out.

STAVROS AIR STATION.

"D" Squadron.

March 10th–16th.

Reconnaissance.—On the 11th, 12th, and 13th escorted reconnaissances were carried out over the front lines. Nothing unusual was observed.

Spotting.—On the 11th an escorted spotting flight was carried out for H.M.S. "Abercrombie" and Monitor No. 18 on to battery positions.

Reconnaissance and Photography.—On the 12th an escorted reconnaissance to Angista. Photographic flights took 72 photographs of the Karcoltafel Kop.

March 17th–24th.

Reconnaissance.—On the 18th, 19th, 20th, 22nd, and 23rd reconnaissances were made of the front line trenches.

The report of the 18th states that the front line roads were covered with snow, and did not look as if they had been used much.

On the 20th, reported at Drama that there were 10 hangars, one tent and three sheds. No machines seen. There was a train of 20 trucks leaving Angista station.

Nothing of any special importance in the other reconnaissances.

Bomb Attack on Stavros Aerodrome.—At 2300 on the 20th three hostile machines dropped 12 bombs in the vicinity of the aerodrome. No damage was done.

Hostile aircraft were over the aerodrome during the morning of the 21st.

GLIKI AIR STATION (IMBROS).

"C" SQUADRON.

March 10th–16th.

Reconnaissance.—Daily reconnaissances (excepting Saturday) of the Dardanelles were carried out. Nothing special to report.

On the 10th a special reconnaissance of our own mines ordered by R.A.E. was completed.

About noon on the 12th two Camels were sent to the Dardanelles to ascertain if the enemy made any attempt to intercept the Constantinople reconnaissance, but no hostile machines were seen to rise from the aerodromes.

A special search for hostile mines was made.

March 17th–24th.

The first part of the week the aerodrome was too soft for machines to get up.

Reconnaissance.—On the 21st and 22nd, morning and evening, reconnaissances were made of the Straits, and reported all clear. On the 21st two hostile aircraft were sighted, but not engaged.

Special Reconnaissance.—On the 21st also a special reconnaissance was made by a D.H. 4, but a detailed report has not yet been received owing to communication being out of action.

KALLONI AIR STATION (MITYLENE).

"B" SQUADRON.

March 10th to 16th.

On the 12th, a D.H. 4 landed here at 1215 on its return from a long reconnaissance to Constantinople, reported under Mudros. This machine left Mitylene for Mudros at 0130. It had been escorted during the last part of its flight to Mitylene by two Camels from this station.

Reconnaissance.—A report was received from Mitylene too late to include in last week's report, of a reconnaissance of Smyrna and Vourla by three machines in formation. This was ordered by S.N.O., as he had received news that a large ship had been seen at 0500 on the 7th, south of Kalloni harbour bearing E. by S., and as no such ship had entered into our harbours in that area during the previous 24 hours, it was thought that she might have slipped into harbour at Smyrna or Vourla. The reconnaissance proved that the shipping in Smyrna was normal, and nothing unusual was to be seen in the Gulf.

March 17th–24th.

Nothing of importance to report.

Reconnaissance.—On the 22nd two Camels were sent out at midday to endeavour to find our long distance reconnaissance machine from Constantinople. At 1300 (L.T.) Mitylene reported that this machine had not landed there.

MUDROS.

Mine Patrol on the 14th.

March 10th–16th.

Anti-Submarine Patrol.—On every day until Saturday, dawn patrols were carried out to search for submarines. Frequently these patrols were continued throughout the day.

On the 15th a submarine was sighted, full details being given in the submarine report.

A final long patrol on the 15th by a Short, ended in engine trouble on the return journey, about 15 miles from Kondia, while changing tanks at 1550. The pilot managed to attract the attention of a trawler at 1730 and was towed into Kondia harbour, which was reached at 1930. Machine was undamaged.

Special Flight.—On Sunday 10th, a special flight was carried out to enable Commander Long of R.A.E. staff to gain some idea of the difficulties of observers in reporting on and photographing men-of-war.

Photographic Reconnaissance of "Goeben" at Stenia Bay.—On the 12th a long reconnaissance of Stenia Bay ordered by R.A.E. was carried out, to report if the "Goeben" was still in position, and to obtain photographs of the starboard side of the ship, to try to discover if her trim was even. Flight Lieutenant Hoskins, and Observer Lieutenant G. E. Wright, in a D.H. 4 (B.H.F.) left the repair base at 0700, and returned via Mitylene as already reported at 1215.

The "Goeben" was found in exactly the same position as previously photographed, riding on an even keel. Smoke was issuing from both funnels, which rendered photography difficult, the wind being south-west ; but both photographs and the report of the observer tend to show that she was not down by the stern.

On the way up at 0820, 12 miles south-east of Rodosto, this machine observed a large submarine steering eastward at a high speed.

Although they flew at a height of not over 4,000 feet over Constantinople, the only aircraft fire experienced was after leaving Haidar Pasha, when after proceeding south-west and about two miles out to sea, heavy anti-aircraft fire was observed about a mile astern. No hostile aircraft were sighted.

Every preparation had been made to carry out another dawn reconnaissance of Stenia on the 15th, but weather reports were so unfavourable that this was abandoned.

To verify the weather reports a machine was sent up from Mudros to 10,000 feet, flying in the direction of the Dardanelles. The direction of the wind being southerly, was the worst possible for such an expedition.

Mine Patrol.—On the 15th a special reconnaissance was carried out around the island to search for enemy mines. Nothing was observed.

March 17th–24th.

Loss of D.H. 4, No. 6410.—No flying was possible until the 22nd. On that morning the weather being favourable, D.H. 4 No. 6410, Flight Commander T. R. Hackman and Observer Lieutenant T. H. Piper, left at 0522 to go to Stenia to locate and photograph the "Goeben," with orders to return via Mitylene or whatever route they deemed the best. They failed to return.

The Turkish official of the 23rd contains the following:—

"In the region of Keshan an enemy aeroplane was shot down. The occupants were made prisoners before they could destroy the machine."

It is believed that this was the route they intended to take on the outward journey. (From wireless interception it is fairly well established that the approach of our machines to Constantinople is signalled long before they reach their destination.)

This reconnaissance was ordered by the R.A.E., and another reconnaissance is to be made when machines are available.

Spotting.—Throughout the morning and part of the afternoon of the 22nd seaplanes and aeroplanes were engaged in escorting H.M.S. "Lord Nelson" at target practice, and in spotting for her long distance firing. The wireless of the spotting machine was not able to communicate direct with the "Lord Nelson," but her signals were distinctly taken at R.N.A.S. headquarters, and forwarded the same evening to the ship.

Every opportunity is now being taken to practice Aldis lamp and wireless communication between planes and ships at target practice, and destroyers.

Reconnaissance.—On the 22nd, S.O. 2nd D.S. asked for reconnaissance of the Straits to be carried out from Mudros, and if the gun which was then firing at Mavro could be spotted. A D.H. 4 was ordered out to do this, but had to return with engine trouble, and before another machine could be sent, Imbros reported that their aerodrome had dried, and that they had carried out the reconnaissance.

The Short seaplane which was reported last week as being towed into Kondia harbour was safely towed round to the "Ark Royal." She was undamaged except for the engine trouble which brought her down in the first place.

Reconnaissance.—On the 23rd a careful reconnaissance was made round the island by seaplanes and aeroplanes to search for any trace of hostile mines. Nothing was observed.

In the gale on Sunday the 17th, the doors at both ends of the Airship shed were carried away, and some injury was done to several of the Bessoneaux, but working parties were able to save the machines.

At 0900 on the 23rd Tenedos reported an hostile seaplane flying in the direction of Mudros. Mavro made a similar report at 0917. Camels were sent up, one to 10,000 feet, but nothing was observed of the hostile aircraft. It is thought that these hostile seaplanes were reconnoitring our minefields, and R.A.E. directed that Imbros should endeavour to interrupt such reconnaissances. Instructions were given accordingly.

It is regretted that only one D.H. 4 is in action at Imbros, and only Camels are available for this purpose.

The D.H. 4's at Mudros are being fitted with extra tanks to enable them to make long distance reconnaissances.

KASSANDRA AIRSHIP STATION.

March 10th–16th.

Patrol Work.—The airship was put into commission and did a satisfactory trial trip on the 11th, and did regular patrols for the remainder of the week, Saturday excepted.

March 17th–24th.

The airship has been in action during the week and two flights were made, one of nine hours.

SUDA BAY SEAPLANE STATION.

March 10th–16th.

Anti-Submarine Patrols. — Submarine patrols of the approaches, &c., were carried out practically every day.

March 17th–24th.

Patrols.—Submarine patrols of the approaches were made on the 20th and 22nd.

SYRA.

March 10th–16th.

No reports to hand. Work is being done here in repairing the slipway.

March 17th–24th.

Have been unable to carry out reconnaissances on account of the bad weather, and defective slipway.

H.M.S. "PEONY."

March 10th–16th.

Anti-Submarine Patrols.—On the 8th a submarine patrol was carried out of the islands to the south of Samos. Nothing was observed.

March 17th–24th.

Reconnaissance.—Made a submarine reconnaissance of the channel between Stampalia and Kos.

ROYAL FLYING CORPS COMMUNIQUÉS.

ROYAL FLYING CORPS COMMUNIQUÉ No. 127.

During the period under review (February 12th–18th inclusive), we have claimed officially thirty-nine enemy aircraft brought down and nineteen driven down out of control. Eleven of our machines are missing. Approximately 26 tons of bombs were dropped, 43,000 rounds were fired at ground targets, and 6,657 photographs taken.

February 12th.

Little flying was possible owing to the bad weather continuing, although in the afternoon it cleared somewhat, particularly in the south, but at no time was work with the artillery really possible.

Four hostile batteries were neutralised, three targets registered, and seven zone calls sent down.

Eighty-seven photographs were taken, 45 bombs dropped, and 2,035 rounds fired at ground targets as follows:—

First Brigade.—10th Wing dropped eight 25-lb. bombs and fired 500 rounds.

Second Brigade.—2nd Wing dropped two 25-lb. bombs.

Third Brigade.—12th Wing took 36 photographs, dropped two 25-lb. bombs, and fired 625 rounds.

Fifth Brigade.—15th Wing dropped ten 25-lb. bombs, and fired 910 rounds.

Eighth Brigade.—Fifty-one photographs. Five 230-lb., four 112-lb. and four 40-lb. phosphorus bombs were dropped by No. 55 Squadron on barracks and railway station at Offenburg (Germany).

Enemy aircraft activity was very slight. No combats took place.

Bombing.—Eighth Brigade.—Twelve machines of No. 55 Squadron carried out a raid into Germany—the barracks and railway station at Offenburg being the objectives. As the results of bomb bursts, two large fires were caused, one in the north and one in the south of the town. Several direct hits were obtained on the railway station and on the line, and one on a railway workshop. Several bursts were seen around the barracks, and a direct hit was obtained on a house just beside the building. Four enemy aircraft were seen over the objectives, but these did not attack. Thirty-three photographs were taken. All our machines returned.

Miscellaneous.—A machine of No. 55 Squadron carried out a successful photographic reconnaissance of hostile aerodromes in Germany, exposing 18 plates.

Honours and Awards.

The Military Cross.—Second Lieut. A. J. Wright, Second Lieut. R. W. Hobbs.

February 13th.

Practically no flying was done owing to rain and mist.

Fifth Brigade was able to carry out three reconnaissances, and machines of this Brigade also dropped bombs.

February 14th.

The weather was again very misty and the sky completely overcast, but a machine of the First Brigade dropped four 25-lb. bombs on Lorgies, and fired 200 rounds from a height of 50 feet into a convoy of troops on the Henin Liétard–Douai Road.

Honours and Awards.

The Distinguished Service Order.—Captain G. H. Bowman.

The Military Cross.—Captain R. N. Welton, Second Lieut. R. A. George.

February 15th.

The mist experienced in the previous days still continued, but showed signs of clearing in the afternoon, and a certain amount of work was carried out.

A machine of the First Brigade dropped four 25-lb. bombs on Haubourdin, and a machine of the Fifth Brigade dropped four 25-lb. bombs on various targets behind the enemy's lines. A total of 2,350 rounds were fired into the enemy's trenches and at ground targets.

A "Friedrichshafen" landed in the Third Army area.

February 16th.

The weather was very fine and the visibility good.

Thirty-three reconnaissances were carried out, eight of which were long-distance photographic flights by machines of the Ninth Wing.

Eighty-three hostile batteries were successfully engaged for destruction and six neutralised: nine gun-pits were destroyed, 33 damaged, 29 explosions and 26 fires caused. Eighty-eight zone calls were sent down.

A total of 2,547 photographs were taken, this being a record. Over seven tons of bombs were dropped and 10,410 rounds fired, as follows:—

First Brigade.—On the night of the 15th/16th, No. 58 Squadron dropped forty-three 25-lb. bombs and fired 277 rounds at Menin Railway Station, and No. 102 Squadron dropped thirty-two 25-lb. bombs and fired 400 rounds at Marquain Aerodrome and aerodromes in the Lys Valley.

During the day, Nos. 2, 4, 4a, 5, 16 and 18 Squadrons dropped six 230-lb., thirty-three 112-lb. and twelve 20-lb. bombs on a hostile gun position near Courrieres; No. 18 Squadron dropped two 112-lb. and fourteen 25-lb. bombs on billets; First Wing dropped fifty-three 25-lb. bombs on miscellaneous targets, and Tenth Wing fired 1,350 rounds.

Second Brigade.—Two thousand six hundred and forty-one rounds were fired at various targets, and No. 57 Squadron dropped ten 112-lb. bombs on Iseghem ammunition dump.

Third Brigade.—Thirty-three 25-lb. bombs were dropped and 510 rounds fired at various objectives.

Fifth Brigade.—Five thousand two hundred and thirty-two rounds were fired; Fifteenth Wing dropped seventy-four 25-lb. bombs and Twenty-second Wing dropped thirteen 25-lb. bombs.

Ninth Wing.—Six 112-lb. and twenty-four 25-lb. bombs were dropped on Inglemunster Railway Station by No. 27 Squadron.

Enemy Aircraft.—Captain H. H. Balfour, No. 43 Squadron, while leading a patrol observed two enemy aircraft formations. He attacked one enemy aircraft at point-blank range, and drove it down out of control. He then got on the tail of another enemy aircraft, which went down in a spin and was seen to crash.

Second Lieut. G. Bailey, No. 43 Squadron, saw an Albatross Scout attacking an R.E. 8. He dived on to the tail of the enemy aircraft and opened fire: the enemy aircraft went down in flames and crashed.

Major C. Miles, No. 43 Squadron, attacked a hostile scout at very close range and drove it down completely out of control.

Second Lieut. C. King, No. 43 Squadron, followed a hostile down to 3,000 feet, firing continuously, and when last seen the enemy aircraft was still diving vertically out of control.

Captain J. Trollope, No. 43 Squadron, attacked a hostile machine and continued fighting it down to 5,000 feet, and the enemy aircraft was seen to go down in a series of side-slips and stalls and eventually crashed.

Lieutenant G. McElroy, No. 40 Squadron, attacked a hostile machine which was pointed out to him by anti-aircraft fire. After a short burst from both guns had been fired into it, the enemy aircraft turned over and went down in a slow regular spin obviously out of control.

Captain G. Lewis and Lieutenant A. Usher, No. 40 Squadron, attacked an enemy aircraft scout which went down completely out of control.

Second Lieut. P. Clayso.., No. 1 Squadron, attacked an enemy scout which was flying low down over our lines. He dived and opened fire from close range, and the enemy aircraft went down and turned over in a ploughed field in our lines.

Second Lieuts. W. Beaver and H. Easton, No. 20 Squadron, attacked an enemy two-seater, which they shot down completely out of control.

The following is an account of combats by Captain J. B. McCudden, No. 56 Squadron, who brought down four enemy machines, one of which fell in our lines :—

> "Left aerodrome at 0940 and crossed lines over Bantouzelle at 16,000 feet at 1025. Many enemy aircraft scouts about, mostly above us, who withdrew north and east. At 1035 saw a Rumpler getting height over Caudry at 16,500. I secured a good position and fired a long burst with both guns, after which enemy aircraft went down in a vertical dive, and then all four wings fell off and the wreckage fell south-west of Caudry. At about 1045 saw a D.W.F. south of Bois de Vaucelles at about 15,000 feet. I secured a firing position at 100 yards range, and after firing a long burst from both guns enemy aircraft went down in flames, after which it fell to pieces, the wreckage falling just north-east of Le Catelet.
>
> "Now engaged an L.V.G., which went down damaged with water coming from radiator after being fired at by Lieutenant Junor and self. At 1105 I fired a green light as one of my elevators was out of action and my Aldis and wind-screen were covered with ice, due to a radiator leak.
>
> "On recrossing lines I engaged a Rumpler at 15,500 feet over Hargicourt at 1110. After firing a long burst from both guns, enemy aircraft went down fairly steeply south-east emitting smoke, and was then seen by Captain Fielding Johnson to go into a right-hand spiral dive, apparently out of control."

(This machine was afterwards confirmed as having burst into flames near the ground.)

> "Left aerodrome at 11.45 a.m., and at 12.30 engaged a Rumpler at 15,500 feet as it was recrossing the lines over Lagnicourt. I secured a good position, but enemy aircraft immediately turned. However, I got into position again and fired a short burst from both guns, after which enemy aircraft went down vertically and fell to pieces, and the wreckage fell in our lines in the vicinity of Lagnicourt. Returned at 1.20."

Second Lieut. J. McCudden, No. 84 Squadron, attacked a two-seater Rumpler and fired a good burst from both guns. The enemy aircraft dived, and Second Lieut. McCudden followed it down to 1,000 feet, firing from time to time. The enemy aircraft was seen to crash, and this was confirmed by Second Lieut. Sorsoleil, of the same patrol.

Second Lieut. Sorsoleil, No. 84 Squadron, was attacked by five Albatross Scouts who were escorting the machine shot down by Second Lieut. McCudden. Second Lieut. Sorsoleil attacked one of the enemy aircraft, which burst into flames.

Lieutenant J. Larson, No. 84 Squadron, attacked an enemy scout. The pilot appeared to be hit, and the machine stalled and fell over on its back, and was last seen falling out of control.

Captain F. Brown, No. 84 Squadron attacked one of four enemy aircraft scouts, which he shot down completely out of control. He then attacked a second scout, and tracers were seen to enter the hostile machine, which fell out of control. Captain Brown's engine then started to give trouble, and he made for our lines. On the way back he encountered a two-seater L.V.G. and fired 150 rounds into it at 30 yards' range, after which the enemy aircraft fell out of control, and was seen to crash by another member of the patrol.

Lieutenant G. Johnson, No. 84 Squadron, attacked an Albatross Scout and fired bursts into it with both guns. The enemy aircraft fell out of control and was seen to crash.

Captain J. Ralston, No. 24 Squadron, attacked an Albatross Scout, firing a drum into it and the enemy aircraft fell out of control. Captain Ralston had not time to change his drum before he was attacked by a second Albatross Scout, and though wounded he managed to regain his aerodrome.

Major Bowman, No. 41 Squadron, fired a short burst from both guns at an enemy aircraft, which was diving at him. The enemy aircraft went down in a steep left-hand turn, completely out of control

Captain G. Thomson, No. 45 Squadron, dived at an enemy aircraft two-seater and fired 70 rounds. The enemy aircraft went down vertically, giving out smoke, and was confirmed by anti-aircraft as being out of control.

A "Friedrichshafen" was brought down by anti-aircraft gunfire in the First Army area.

An enemy machine landed at Catigny.

February 17th.

The weather was fine throughout the day and the visibility good.

Twenty-seven successful reconnaissances were carried out, six of which were long-distance photographic flights by machines of Nos. 25 and 27 Squadrons.

On the 16th, 25 targets were registered by balloons, 21 of which were by those of the Second Brigade. Eleven active hostile batteries were located.

On the 17th, 87 hostile batteries were successfully engaged for destruction with aeroplane observation and eight neutralised ;

18 gun-pits were destroyed, 46 damaged, 54 explosions and 32 fires caused. Fifty zone calls were sent down.

Lieutenant Brown, No. 7 Squadron, carried out two successful shoots with the 145th Siege Battery; in the first, two gun-pits of a hostile battery position were destroyed and two damaged, while a fire was caused in an ammunition dump which continued for half an hour; in the second, two pits were completely destroyed, two damaged, and a fire and an explosion caused.

Second Lieutenants Mayoss and Haddow, No. 15 Squadron, observing for the 431st Siege Battery, badly damaged a hostile battery position, completely destroying one gun-pit.

Second Lieutenants Muirhead and Scott, No. 15 Squadron, with the 57th Siege Battery, destroyed two gun-pits in a hostile battery position and damaged one other.

Lieutenants Williams and Crow, No. 35 Squadron, during a flight of 4 hours 25 minutes, observing for the 228th Siege Battery, caused a fire in a hostile battery position and completely destroyed one pit.

In a flight of 4 hours 15 minutes' duration, Lieutenants Pybus and Cave, No. 35 Squadron, with the 91st Siege Battery destroyed two gun-pits and caused two fires in a hostile battery position.

Two thousand two hundred and fifty-six photographs were taken, of which 643 were by the 3rd Brigade and 103 were of hostile aerodromes in the enemy's back areas by the 9th Wing.

Twelve-and-a-half tons of bombs were dropped and 17,034 rounds fired at ground targets as follows:—

Night 16th–17th.

First Brigade.—No. 2 Squadron dropped forty-eight 25-lb. bombs on Lesquin, Wicres and Fournes; No. 4 Squadron dropped twenty-five 25-lb. bombs on Lommes, Don, La Bassée and Mouveaux Aerodrome, and No. 16 Squadron dropped eight 112-lb. bombs on Meurchin.

Second Brigade.—No. 10 Squadron dropped thirty-eight 25-lb. bombs on Menin.

Third Brigade.—No. 13 Squadron dropped twenty-four 25-lb. bombs on a dump at Oisy-le-Verger; No. 12 Squadron, dropped twelve 25-lb. bombs on Iwuy Dump, and No. 59 Squadron dropped eighteen 25-lb. bombs on an ammunition dump.

Fifth Brigade.—Four 112-lb. and sixteen 25-lb. bombs on Villers Outreaux, and twenty-nine 25-lb. bombs on Beaurevoir were dropped.

Ninth Wing.—No. 101 Squadron dropped ninety-six 25-lb. bombs on Vivaise Aerodrome; No. 58 Squadron dropped fifty-six 25-lb. bombs on Rumbeke Aerodrome and fifty-two 25-lb. bombs on Marquain Aerodrome; and fired 1,462 rounds;

No. 102 Squadron dropped twenty 25-lb. bombs on Scheldewindeke, thirty-one 25.lb. bombs on Marquain, fourteen 25-lb. bombs on Gontrode, eight 25-lb. bombs on Worteghem Aerodrome, ten 25-lb. bombs on trains and twenty-nine 2-lb. shells and 900 rounds were fired.

By Day.

First Brigade.—No. 18 Squadron dropped four 112-lb. and eight 25-lb. bombs on Ascq Aerodrome; three 112-lb. and four 25-lb. bombs on Marquain Aerodrome; two 112-lb. bombs on Lezennes, and thirty-two 25-lb. bombs on billets; 1st Wing dropped seventy-two 25-lb. bombs and fired 200 rounds, and 10th Wing fired 6,850 rounds.

Second Brigade.—No. 57 Squadron dropped seventy-two 25-lb. bombs on Bisseghem ammunition dump; 11th Wing dropped thirty 25-lb. bombs, and 3,375 rounds were fired.

Third Brigade.—Eighty-eight 25-lb. bombs were dropped and 840 rounds fired.

Fifth Brigade.—Fifteenth Wing dropped eighty-five 25-lb. bombs and fired 3,407 rounds, and No. 84 Squadron dropped eight 25-lb. bombs.

Ninth Wing.—No. 27 Squadron dropped nine 112-lb. and twenty-four 25-lb. bombs on Marquain Aerodrome.

Eighth Brigade.—On the night of the 16th/17th, in addition to the above, five machines of No. 100 Squadron bombed the railway station and sidings at Conflans (15 miles west of Metz) from a height of 1,000 feet. Two 230-lb., four 112-lb., one 40-lb., and fourteen 25-lb. bombs were dropped, and 600 rounds fired at ground targets. Two 112-lb. bombs burst on the station, and eight others in the sidings. All machines returned.

Enemy Aircraft.—Second Lieut. W. Casson, No. 43 Squadron, whilst leading a patrol, fired a long burst at the nearest machine of four hostile two-seaters. The left-hand bottom plane crumpled up, and the machine went down completely out of control and crashed.

Second Lieuts. S. A. Oades and S. W. Bunting, No. 22 Squadron, brought down a hostile scout after firing a burst of 100 rounds into it at close range.

Lieutenant G. McElroy, No. 40 Squadron, whilst on escort duty, opened fire from close range at a hostile scout, which went down out of control and was seen to crash on the outskirts of Lille. Later in his flight, he observed an enemy aircraft approaching our lines near Lens. This he attacked and drove down, and finally saw it crash to the ground and catch fire.

Second Lieut. R. Wade, No. 40 Squadron, fired several long bursts into a hostile scout, which went down in flames and was seen to crash.

Second Lieut. E. Lindup and Corporal M. Mather, No. 20 Squadron, whilst on offensive patrol with 12 Bristol Fighters, engaged one out of a formation of hostile scouts, firing 50 rounds into it from close range. The enemy aircraft was seen to hit the ground and burst into flames by other members of the patrol.

Sergeant F. Johnson and Captain J. Hedley, No. 20 Squadron, in formation with 11 Bristol Fighters, fired 100 rounds into one of 16 enemy aircraft encountered. The hostile machine went down completely out of control and crashed west of Moorslede.

Lieutenant K. Junor, No. 56 Squadron, when at 14,000 feet, was attacked by a single Albatross Scout, which fired a short burst and then dived away east. He dived after it, and opened fire with both guns from 100 yards range. The hostile machine burst into flames and crashed in a field.

Lieutenant M. Mealing, No. 56 Squadron, fired a burst from very close range at one of five hostile scouts, and the enemy aircraft crashed to the ground.

Second Lieut. J. McCudden, No. 84 Squadron, attacked two hostile triplanes, one of which he followed down to within 600 feet of the ground, firing all the time, and finally saw it dive straight into the ground.

Hostile machines were driven down out of control by the following:—Captain D. Flockart, 4th Squadron, A.F.C.; Lieutenant F. Woolhouse, 4th Squadron, A.F.C.; Captain J. Trollope, No. 43 Squadron; Second Lieut. H. Daniel, No. 43 Squadron; Second Lieut. H. Highton, No. 43 Squadron; Second Lieut. A. Doble, No. 43 Squadron; Captain H. Balfour, No. 43 Squadron; Second Lieut. R. Wade, No. 40 Squadron; Second Lieuts. D. McGoun and Masding, No. 20 Squadron; Sergeant F. Johnson and Captain J. Hedley, No. 20 Squadron; Lieutenant R. Bennett and Corporal F. Archer, No. 20 Squadron; Captain J. Hamilton, No. 29 Squadron; Captain W. Fielding Johnson, No. 56 Squadron; Captain J. B. McCudden, No. 56 Squadron; Second Lieut. D. Judson, No. 3 Squadron; Second Lieut. A. Proctor, No. 84 Squadron; and Second Lieut. G. Travers, No. 84 Squadron.

February 18th.

The weather was again fine but the visibility only fair.

Twenty reconnaissances were carried out, six of these were successful long-distance photographic reconnaissances on which 22 hostile aerodromes were photographed by machines of Nos. 25 and 27 Squadrons.

On the 17th balloons, of the 2nd Brigade registered 16 targets, three of which were hostile batteries.

On the 18th, 58 hostile batteries were successfully engaged for destruction with aeroplane observation and two neutralized;

seven gun-pits were destroyed, 30 damaged, 25 explosions and 14 fires caused. Twenty-eight zone calls were sent down.

Lieutenant Hayter and Captain Beadon, No. 12 Squadron, during a flight lasting 4 hours 15 minutes, ranged the 324th and 203rd Siege Batteries on to two hostile batteries simultaneously; in one case two O.K.'s were obtained and one gun-pit damaged.

Lieutenants Pybus and Cave, No. 35 Squadron, with the 233rd Siege Battery, destroyed two pits, damaged another and caused an explosion in a hostile battery position.

A total of 1,797 photographs were taken, six tons of bombs dropped, fifty 2-lb. shells and 10,799 rounds fired at ground targets as follows:—

Night, 17th–18th.

First Brigade.—No. 16 Squadron dropped twelve 112-lb. bombs on Henin-Liètard, Auby and Blanc Maison: No. 5 Squadron dropped eight 112-lb. and forty-five 25-lb. bombs on Douai, Vitry, Beaumont, Bois Grenier, Esquerchin and Quiery, and No. 2 Squadron dropped sixteen 25-lb. bombs on Fournes.

Fifth Brigade.—No. 82 Squadron dropped eight 25-lb. bombs on Bohain.

Ninth Wing.—No. 152 Squadron dropped eight 25-lb. bombs on Gontrode Aerodrome, fourteen 25-lb. bombs on Scheldewindeke Aerodrome, sixteen 25-lb. bombs on trains, and fifty 2-lb. shells and 1,000 rounds were fired.

By Day.

First Brigade.—Four hundred and forty-eight photographs. No. 18 Squadron dropped thirty-six 25-lb. bombs on Faumont Aerodrome and twelve 25-lb. bombs on various targets; 1st Wing dropped seventy 25-lb. bombs; No. 4a Squadron fired 100 rounds and 10th Wing fired 2,510 rounds.

Second Brigade.—Three hundred and thirty-seven photographs and 3,132 rounds. No. 57 Squadron dropped seventy-two 25-lb. bombs on Harlebeke Dump and 11th Wing dropped fifty-five 25-lb. bombs on various targets.

Third Brigade.—Fifty-six 25-lb. bombs were dropped and 570 rounds fired.

Fifth Brigade.—Fifteenth Wing dropped seventy-nine 25-lb. bombs and fired 3,467 rounds.

Ninth Wing.—No. 27 Squadron dropped four 112-lb. and fifteen 25-lb. bombs on Dechy.

The following bomb raids were carried out by the 8th Brigade:—

Night 17th–18th.

Six machines of No. 100 Squadron dropped three 230-lb., six 112-lb., thirty 25-lb. and two 40-lb. bombs from a height of

1,000 feet on the railway station and sidings at Conflans (15 miles west of Metz). Four bursts were observed in the sheds and on the edge of the sidings where a large fire was started. Seven hundred rounds were fired at ground targets. All machines returned.

By Day, 18th.

Five machines of No. 55 Squadron dropped ten 112-lb. and thirty 40-lb. bombs from 12,500 feet on the barracks and railway station at Treves (on the Moselle). Three bursts were seen in the gasworks, one near the post office, one in the railway workshops, and two near the barracks. Two houses were left blazing.

Four machines of the same squadron dropped eight 112-lb. bombs and one 40-lb. bomb from 13,500 feet on the station and steel works at Thionville. Bursts were seen on the railway track. Anti-aircraft fire was considerable and accurate, two machines being hit. All machines returned.

Enemy Aircraft.—Enemy aircraft activity was about the same as on the previous day.

Captain J. Allport and Lieutenant A. Hammond, No. 2 Squadron, whilst on photography were attacked by six hostile scouts. The observer opened fire as one of the scouts dived vertically at his machine, and the enemy aircraft burst into flames and was seen to crash. The observer then engaged one of the scouts that was flying parallel to his machine, and after a burst the scout was seen to crumple up and fall to pieces. The second combat was confirmed by ground observers.

A patrol of three machines of No. 22 Squadron encountered four hostile scouts and two two-seaters near Seclin. A long combat took place, during which one of the two-seaters was brought down by Second Lieut. S. Wallage, and two others were seen to go down out of control.

Captain F. Gorringe, No. 70 Squadron, when in formation was attacked by one of several Albatross Scouts. He managed to obtain a position under the hostile machine's tail and fired a burst, when the latter burst into flames and crashed to the ground.

Captain Hamersley, Second Lieuts. Clark, Evans, and Kent, No. 60 Squadron, engaged four enemy triplanes. One of these was brought down by Captain Hamersley and seen to crash from 12,000 feet; another was driven down to about 300 feet by Lieutenants Evans and Clark, and finally crashed into a tree. Lieutenant Kent drove down another and saw it crash to the ground.

Captain J. B. McCudden, No. 56 Squadron, when leading a formation, dived on four enemy scouts. He fired a short burst into the leader, whose machine burst into flames, the pilot falling out. Captain McCudden then fired a long burst into another of the enemy's scouts from a range of 100 yards, and it went into a steep dive and was seen to crash.

Hostile machines were also driven down out of control by Lieutenant R. Howard, 2nd Squadron, A.F.C.; Captain F. Huxley, 2nd Squadron, A.F.C.; Captain G. McElroy, No. 40 Squadron; Flight Lieut. Jordan, Flight Sub-Lieuts. Johnstone and Walworth, and Flight Commander Compston, all of Naval Squadron No. 8; Captain H, Balfour, Second Lieuts. King, Orcutt, and Grandy, of No. 43 Squadron; Second Lieuts. Oades and Bunting, No. 22 Squadron; Second Lieuts. Roberts and Noble, No. 20 Squadron; Second Lieut. J. Todd, No. 70 Squadron; Captain R. Rusby, No. 29 Squadron; Second Lieuts. Cowper, Mark, and Richardson, of No. 24 Squadron; Second Lieut. Saunders, No. 84 Squadron; Lieutenant Wensley and Second Lieut. Creek, No. 25 Squadron.

R. J. BARTON, Major,
Headquarters,   General Staff.
   Royal Flying Corps.
      20th February 1918.

ROYAL FLYING CORPS COMMUNIQUÉ No. 128.

During the period under review (February 19th–25th inclusive) we have claimed officially 58 enemy aircraft brought down and 22 driven down out of control. Twenty-two of our machines are missing. Approximately $58\frac{1}{4}$ tons of bombs were dropped and 9,290 photographs taken.

February 19th.

The weather was fine but the visibility bad.

On the 2nd Brigade front, no work was possible by corps squadrons owing to the haze.

Six successful long-distance photographic reconnaissances, on which 228 photographs were taken, were carried out by the 9th Wing and seven reconnaissances by machines of other brigades.

Twenty-two hostile batteries were successfully engaged for destruction with aeroplane observation and one neutralised; two gun-pits were destroyed, 13 damaged, seven explosions and eight fires caused. Twelve zones were sent down.

Lieutenants Brown and Selby, No. 13 Squadron, gave 72 observations for the 328th Siege Battery, which badly damaged four gun-pits of a hostile battery position.

Captain Dash and Lieutenant Fenton, No. 8 Squadron, observed for 145 rounds with the 33rd Siege Battery. One gun-pit was damaged and one explosion caused.

A total number of 1,190 photographs were taken, and 4½ tons of bombs dropped as follows:—

Night 18th-19th.

1st Brigade.—No 2 Squadron dropped thirty-two 25-lb. bombs on Fournes and Wicres, and No. 5 Squadron dropped twelve 112-lb. and twenty-four 25-lb. bombs on billets.

5th Brigade.—Nos. 8, 35, and 52 Squadrons dropped two 112-lb. and thirty-two 25-lb. bombs on Bohain.

9th Wing.—No. 102 Squadron dropped sixteen 25-lb. bombs on Comines.

By Day.

1st Brigade.—One hundred and two photographs. No. 18 Squadron dropped two 112-lb. and twenty-four 25-lb. bombs on large calibre gun at Courrieres, and on Vitry and Douai railway stations.

2nd Brigade.—No. 57 Squadron dropped seventy-two 25-lb. bombs on Mouscron ammunition dump, and No. 21 Squadron and 3rd Squadron, A.F.C., took 252 photographs and dropped twelve 25-lb. bombs.

3rd Brigade.—Two hundred and forty-eight photographs were taken and forty-nine 25-lb. bombs dropped.

5th Brigade.—15th Wing took 360 photographs, dropped forty-five 25-lb. bombs, and 22nd Wing dropped eight 25-lb. bombs.

9th Wing.—Two hundred and twenty-eight photographs. No. 27 Squadron dropped twenty-six 25-lb. bombs on Phalempin Aerodrome.

In addition to the above, the following bomb raids were carried out by the **8th Brigade** :—

Night 18th-19th.

Eight machines of No. 100 Squadron dropped four 230-lb., eight 112-lb., one 40-lb., and fourteen 25-lb. bombs from a height of 1,500 feet on the railway station and barracks at Treves. Five bursts were seen in the station, which at once burst into flames. Three fires were blazing when the machines left. One machine failed to return.

Two machines of No. 100 Squadron dropped two 230-lb, one 40-lb., and six 25-lb. bombs from 1,800 feet on the railway and gas works at Thionville. A large fire was started, which was seen by the pilots attacking Treves. Both machines returned.

A total of 3¼ tons of bombs were dropped on the above raids.

By Day.

Eleven machines of No. 55 Squadron dropped one 230-lb., eighteen 112-lb. and six 40-lb. bombs from 15,000 feet on the railway station and barracks at Treves. Eleven bursts were observed on the station and six on the buildings round about. Three good fires were started. Thirty-seven plates were exposed, some of which show these fires. One machine is missing.

Enemy Aircraft.—Enemy aircraft was not as active as on the preceding days, though a number of scouts were encountered.

Lieutenant R. Mackenzie and Lieutenant L. Benjamin, Second Squadron, A.F.C., attacked a hostile scout, which went down out of control, and was seen by ground observers to crash near Vendin-le-Vieil.

Second Lieut. R. Owen, No. 43 Squadron, whilst on offensive patrol, was attacked by five Albatross Scouts. He fired a burst of 20 rounds at the nearest enemy aircraft, which went down out of control, and was observed by anti-aircraft to fall in flames near the Bois du Biez.

Second Lieut. W. Kent, No. 60 Squadron, fired with both his guns at a hostile scout from a range of about 400 yards. The enemy aircraft burst into flames and crashed in our lines near Hollebeke.

Second Lieuts. A. Cowper, R. Mark, R. Hammersley, and P. McDougall, No. 24 Squadron, each fired about 100 rounds into a hostile two-seater which burst into flames, and fell into Servais village.

Captain R. Grosvenor, No. 84 Squadron, dived on a large formation of hostile scouts escorting a two-seater, which dived away in an easterly direction. Captain Grosvenor turned and followed the two-seater which stalled right in front of him and enabled him to get in a good burst; the enemy machine went down and crashed into a wood south of St. Quentin.

Second Lieuts. J. Sorsoleil, No. 84 Squadron, whilst on patrol attacked one of 10 hostile scouts. This machine started to spin and finally crashed near St. Gobain Woods. He was then attacked by one of the other scouts, but after some manoeuvring managed to get on its tail and fired a burst from both guns. The enemy aircraft dived vertically and crashed in the same wood as the previous machine.

Second Lieut. J. McCudden, No. 84 Squadron, was attacked by several enemy aircraft scouts. Into one of these he managed to fire a good burst, and the enemy scout went down out of control and crashed in the Forest of St. Gobain.

Second Lieut. A. Proctor, No. 84 Squadron, engaged one of several hostile scouts at a height of about 15,000 feet. The hostile machine stalled, fell over sideways out of control and was seen to crash by Second Lieut. McCudden.

Lieutenant J. Hewett, No. 23 Squadron, attacked one of two enemy two-seaters. He dived at this machine and zoomed up under it three times, firing bursts from both guns at each dive. The two-seater went down in a slow glide and was seen by Lieutenant Faulkner to crash into a house at Crecy.

Second Lieut. A. Lindsay, No. 54 Squadron, whilst on offensive patrol encountered five enemy scouts escorting a two-seater. Whilst observing one enemy aircraft going down, he heard another firing behind him and half rolled under it and turned back on to the enemy aircraft's tail, when he fired a short burst. The machine fell vertically and crashed into the ground near Monceau.

Lieutenant N. Clark, No. 54 Squadron, attacked one of the hostile scouts encountered by Second Lieut. Lindsay. He followed it down to a height of 3,000 feet, firing short bursts, when a part of the hostile machine broke off, the remainder crashing to the ground near Monceau.

Hostile machines were drven down out of control by the following :—

Captain Jarvis, No. 56 Squadron; Second Lieuts. A. Cowper, P. McDougall, R. Hammersley, and R. Mark, No. 24 Squadron; Captain Grosvenor, No. 84 Squadron (two); Second Lieut. J. McCudden and Lieutenant Larson, No. 84 Squadron.

Feburary 20th.

During the morning the sky was overcast with mist, which turned to rain in the afternoon.

Five reconnaissances were carried out by the 5th Brigade, and a total of 97 plates exposed. Twelve hostile batteries were successfully engaged for destruction with aeroplane observation; eight gun-pits damaged, three explosions and one fire caused.

Lieutenants Bell and Settle, No. 12 Squadron, gave observations for the 223rd Siege Battery and the 129th Siege Battery simultaneously on two hostile batteries. The 223rd Siege Battery succeeded in damaging two gun-pits.

Lieutenants Philcox and Wisnekowitz, No. 8 Squadron, observed 105 rounds fired by the 33rd Siege Battery, which damaged four pits of a hostile battery position.

Major Snow and Lieutenant Spencer, No. 2 Squadron, during a flight of three hours 40 minutes, in mist and rain, successfully engaged a hostile battery with the 71st and 73rd Siege Batteries.

Enemy Aircraft.—No combats took place all day.

Bombing.—Three and a half tons of bombs were dropped as follows.

Night 19th–20th.

1st Brigade.—No. 5 Squadron dropped six 112-lb. and four 25-lb. bombs on Quiery-la-Motte and Izel, and No. 16 Squadron dropped six 112-lb bombs on Carvin and Bois de Phalempin.

5th Brigade.—Two 112-lb. and twenty-four 25-lb. bombs were dropped on Bohain by Nos. 8, 35, and 52 Squadrons.

9th Wing.—No. 101 Squadron dropped two 112-lb. bombs and one hundred and eight 25-lb. bombs on Bohain, and

No. 102 Squadron dropped fifteen 25-lb. bombs on Carvin and Provin.

By Day.

1st Brigade.—No. 2 Squadron dropped twenty-six 25-lb. bombs.

2nd Brigade.—Two 25-lb. bombs were dropped.

3rd Brigade.—Thirty-seven 25-lb. bombs were dropped.

5th Brigade.—2nd Wing dropped thirty-three 25-lb. bombs.

The following bomb raids were carried out by the **8th Brigade** :—

Night 19th–20th.

Two machines of Naval Squadron No. 16 (Handley Pages) dropped twenty-six 112-lb. bombs on the railway station at Thionville. Two large fires were started and a large explosion caused.

By Day.

Eight machines of No. 55 Squadron dropped two 230-lb., ten 112-lb., and eight 40-lb. bombs on the factories and stations at Pirmasens in Germany from a height of 15,000 feet. Bursts were observed near the factories in the centre and the south end of the town and on the railway near the station. Bombs were also dropped close to the gas works. One hundred and thirteen plates were exposed. All machines returned.

Photographic reconnaissances of hostile aerodromes were also carried out, 20 plates being exposed.

February 21st.

The weather was fine all day with excellent visibility.

Twenty-one reconnaissances were carried out by Brigades and six reconnaissances by No. 25 and No. 27 Squadrons on which 154 photographs were taken.

Seventy hostile batteries were engaged for destruction with aeroplane observation and seven neutralized. Eleven gun-pits were destroyed, 30 damaged, 41 explosions, and 22 fires caused. Fifty zone calls were sent down.

Captain Watts, No. 7 Squadron, ranged the 185th Siege Battery on to a hostile battery position which appeared to be totally destroyed. Several fires were caused. During the shoot our battery was shelled, but continued firing with its rear section.

Lieutenant Francis, No. 9 Squadron, observing for the 117th Siege Battery on a M.G. shoot, caused three explosions in a hostile battery position.

Captain Milton and Lieutenant Davis, No. 8 Squadron, with the 156 Siege Battery, during a flight lasting four hours ten minutes, caused two fires and one explosion in a hostile battery position. Lieutenants Jefferies and Dell, of the same squadron, continued the shoot with the same Siege Battery, causing two more explosions and a fire in a hostile position and damaging one gun pit.

A total of 1,216 photographs were taken and $4\frac{1}{2}$ tons of bombs dropped as follows :—

First Brigade.—Two hundred and thirty-three photographs. No. 18 Squadron dropped four 112-lb. and eight 25-lb. bombs on Dechy and twelve 25-lb. bombs on La Bassée and Illies. Sixty-four 25-lb. bombs were dropped by machines of the First Wing.

Second Brigade.—Four hundred and thirty-seven photographs. Twelve 112-lb. bombs were dropped on Ledeghem Railway Station by No. 57 Squadron, and forty-eight 25-lb. bombs dropped by machines of the Second Wing.

Third Brigade.—Three hundred and twenty-nine photographs taken and forty-seven 25-lb. bombs dropped.

Fifth Brigade.—Sixty-three photographs. Four 25-lb. bombs were dropped by No. 48 Squadron, and seventy-nine 25-lb. bombs dropped by machines of the 15th Wing.

Ninth Wing.—One hundred and fifty-four photographs. No. 27 Squadron dropped forty-four 25-lb. bombs on Courtrai Railway Sidings.

Enemy Aircraft.—Enemy aircraft were fairly active all day, the activity being most marked in the afternoon.

Second Lieut. W. Adams, No. 4 Squadron, A.F.C., was attacked by two hostile scouts. He managed to get above them and dived on one, firing a long burst at short range. The hostile machine spun down and was observed to crash.

Lieutenant G. Jones, 4th Squadron, A.F.C., whilst on offensive patrol, attacked one of five or six hostile scouts which attacked the patrol. He followed this machine from 15,000 to 10,000 feet, firing about 100 rounds at point blank range. One wing of the hostile machine broke off, and the machine crashed to the ground.

Lieutenant A. Clark, 2nd Squadron, A.F.C., when leading his patrol, fired about 50 rounds from a range of 40 yards into a hostile machine which was diving at him. It fell over on its left wing, dropped vertically, and was seen to crash.

Captain W. Molesworth, No. 29 Squadron, chased a hostile two-seater which he saw being "archied" over Ypres. He managed to get on its tail, and after 20 rounds being fired, it burst into flames and fell in our lines between Hooge and Gheluvelt.

Lieutenant R. Bennett and Corporal Veale, No. 20 Squadron, whilst on offensive patrol with eight Bristol Fighters, dived at an enemy two-seater and fired a burst from the front gun at about 200 yards range. The hostile machine side-slipped and was seen to crash on the ground.

Captain J. McCudden, No. 56 Squadron, attacked a hostile two-seater at a height of 9,000 feet over Acheville. After four shots had been fired from each gun, the hostile machine burst into flames and crashed on the railway line just south of Mericourt.

Captain G. Hughes and Captain H. Claye, No. 62 Squadron, whilst leading a formation at 13,000 feet, saw a large hostile two-seater flying south over Armentières at a height of 7,000 feet. The pilot dived to within 200 feet of the hostile machine, then "zoomed" up to within 50 yards under its tail, the pilot firing 50 rounds with his front gun. The hostile machine turned east, and the pilot again fired a burst of 50 rounds, after which it broke to pieces in the air.

Hostile machines were driven down out of control by the following :—

> Lieutenant Benjamin, 2nd Squadron A.F.C.; Flight Commander Munday, Naval Squadron No. 8; Captain H. Symons, No. 65 Squadron; Second Lieut. F. Martin and Second Lieut. W. Venmore, No. 57 Squadron; Captain G. McElroy, No. 24 Squadron.

Honours and Awards.

The following is an extract from Fifth Supplement to "London Gazette," dated 8th February 1918 :—

> "The undermentioned officers have been brought to the notice of the Secretary of State for War, by the Army Council, for very valuable services rendered in connection with the war up to 31st December 1917 :—
>
> Pitcher, Maj., and Bt.-Lieut.-Col. (temp. Brig.-Gen.) D. Le G., Ind. Army."

February 22nd.

The sky was covered with low clouds and there was occasional rain.

Four successful reconnaissances were carried out by machines of the 5th Brigade.

Sixteen hostile batteries were successfully engaged for destruction with aeroplane observation; 12 of these were by pilots of the 3rd Brigade, who destroyed one gun-pit, damaged 12 others, caused eight explosions and one fire. They also reported 13 active hostile batteries.

Lieutenants Kirk and Wyre, No. 59 Squadron, ranged D/293 Battery on to a hostile battery position in which five gun-pits were badly damaged and a fire caused.

The 86th Siege Battery, with observation by Second Lieuts. Muirhead and Scott, No. 15 Squadron, destroyed a gun-pit and generally a hostile gun position.

On the 21st instant, balloons of the 1st Brigade registered 11 targets, eight of which were hostile batteries, and those of the 2nd Brigade 21 targets, five of which were hostile batteries. Two fires and one explosion were caused in hostile battery positions and 15 active hostile batteries located. Three of the shoots carried out by the 2nd Brigade were in conjunction with aeroplanes.

A total of 89 photographs were taken and 7¾ tons of bombs dropped as follows:—

Night 21st–22nd.

1st Brigade.—No. 2 Squadron dropped one hundred and seven 25-lb. bombs on Fournes and Wicres, and No. 4 Squadron dropped thirty-six 25-lb. bombs on Lomme, Fournes, and Haubourdin.

2nd Brigade.—No 10 Squadron dropped eight 25-lb. bombs on Menin.

9th Wing.—No. 58 Squadron dropped sixty 25-lb. bombs on Marquain Aerodrome, direct hits being obtained on hangars and sheds, twelve 25-lb. bombs on Gontrode Aerodrome and sixty 25-lb. bombs on various objectives.

No. 101 Squadron dropped two 112-lb. and three hundred 25-lb. bombs on Etreux Aerodrome, obtaining 19 direct hits on hangars. Twelve pilots and observers made two trips during the night.

No. 102 Squadron dropped thirty-five 25-lb. bombs on Marquain Aerodrome, eight 25-lb. bombs on Scheldewindeke Aerodrome and fifty-two 25-lb. bombs on various objectives.

By Day.

1st Brigade.—Sixty-two photographs.

3rd Brigade.—Twenty-seven photographs were taken and eight 25-lb. bombs dropped.

5th Brigade.—15th Wing dropped eighteen 25-lb. bombs.
There were no combats all day.

February 23rd.

The weather was bad most of the day with very short clear intervals.

Seven reconnaissances were carried out, seven hostile batteries engaged for destruction with aeroplane observation and three neutralized; four gun-pits were damaged and eight explosions caused. Twelve active hostile batteries were reported by zone call.

In spite of very bad visibility, the 226th Siege Battery, with observation by Lieutenant Burdick, No. 10 Squadron, engaged a hostile battery, causing a large fire and several small ones in the battery position.

Enemy Aircraft.—No combats took place.

On the 19th inst., Captain W. Fielding Johnson, M.C., No. 56 Squadron, drove down a hostile scout out of control, which has since been confirmed by anti-aircraft observers as having crashed.

Bombing. — 1st Brigade. — Twenty-eight 25-lb. bombs dropped.

2nd Brigade.—Twenty-four 25-lb. bombs dropped.

3rd Brigade.—Eight 25-lb. bombs dropped.

5th Brigade.—Fourteen 25-lb. bombs dropped.

February 24th.

The sky was covered with low clouds, but there were a few short bright intervals.

Nine reconnaissances were carried out and 25 plates exposed.

Twenty-nine hostile batteries were engaged for destruction with aeroplane observation and 12 neutralized. Three gun-pits were destroyed, 12 damaged, 16 explosions, and 13 fires caused. Sixty zone calls were sent down. Of the hostile batteries engaged, 12 were by machines of the 1st Brigade, 16 by those of the 2nd Brigade and one by those of the 3rd Brigade.

The 145th Siege Battery, with observation by Lieutenant Brown, No. 7 Squadron, blew up a gun-pit and hit another twice in a hostile battery position. A large explosion was also caused.

The 290th Siege Battery, with observation by Captain Hilton, No. 9 Squadron, started such a large fire in a hostile battery position that further observation by the aeroplane was impossible.

Captain Sayers and Lieutenant Spencer, No. 13 Squadron, obtained a direct hit on an active hostile gun, which at once ceased fire.

Two hundred and three bombs were dropped as follows :—

Night 23rd–24th.

9th Wing.—No. 58 Squadron dropped twelve 25-lb. bombs on Moorseele Aerodrome, nine 25-lb. bombs on Menin Station, twenty-two 25-lb. bombs on Bavichove Aerodrome and twenty-four 25-lb. bombs on Oyghem.

Day 24th.

1st Brigade.—Thirty-four 25-lb. bombs were dropped by machines of the 1st Wing. 4th Squadron, A.F.C., dropped ten 25-lb. bombs on transport, hitting one waggon.

2nd Brigade.—Thirty-four 25-lb. bombs were dropped by machines of the 2nd Wing. Five 25-lb. bombs were dropped on an anti-aircraft battery by No. 70 Squadron.

3rd Brigade.—Twenty 25-lb. bombs were dropped.

5th Brigade.—Thirty-three 25-lb. bombs were dropped by machines of 15th Wing.

Enemy Aircraft.—Enemy aircraft activity was very slight, only a few indecisive combats taking place.

February 25th.

There were low clouds most of the day.

Four reconnaissance were carried out by machines of the 5th Brigade and five photographs taken.

Six hostile batteries were successfully engaged for destruction with aeroplane observation and six neutralized; two gun-pits destroyed and two explosions caused. Forty zone calls were sent down.

On the 24th instant, balloons of the 1st Brigade registered nine targets, five of which were hostile batteries, and those of the 2nd Brigade, five targets, three of which were hostile batteries. One explosion and one fire were caused and 17 active hostile batteries located.

A total of four tons of bombs were dropped as follows:—

Night 24th–25th.

9th Wing.—Seventy-six 25-lb. bombs on aerodromes in the Lys Valley including Ingelmunster, Bisseghem, Bavichove, Dries, and Oostroosebeke Aerodromes by No. 58 Squadron.

Eight 25-lb. bombs on Ennetieres by No. 102 Squadron.

Two 40-lb. and one hundred and sixty-four 25-lb. bombs on Mont Brehain by No. 101 Squadron.

Day 25th.

1st Brigade.—Fourteen 25-lb. bombs by 1st Wing.

2nd Brigade.—Two 25-lb. bombs.

3rd Brigade.—Thirty 25-lb. bombs by 15th Wing and thirteen 25-lb. bombs by No. 48 Squadron.

9th Wing. — Forty 25-lb. bombs on Menin by No. 27 Squadron.

Honours and Awards.

Bar to the Military Cross.—Lieutenant G. E. H. McElroy, M.C.

Military Cross.—Second Lieut. J. A. McCudden, Lieutenant F. E. Brown, Second Lieut. G. McPherson, Second Lieut. D. F. Hurr.

R. J. BARTON, Major,
General Staff.

Headquarters,
 Royal Flying Corps,
  27th February 1918.

ROYAL FLYING CORPS COMMUNIQUÉ.—No. 128a.

During the period under review (February 26 to March 4th inclusive), we have claimed officially 15 enemy aircraft brought down and three driven down out of control. In addition to this, three enemy aircraft were brought down by anti-aircraft fire. Ten of our machines are missing. Approximately $29\frac{1}{4}$ tons of bombs were dropped and 4,333 photographs taken.

February 26th.

The weather was fine with a very strong west wind in the morning; squalls and rain in the afternoon.

Eleven reconnaissances were carried out by brigades, and five successful long-distance photographic flights by No. 25 Squadron and one by No. 27 Squadron.

Eighty-two hostile batteries were successfully engaged for destruction with æroplane observation and 11 neutralized; 16 gun-pits were destroyed, 37 damaged, 39 explosions and 13 fires caused. Forty-eight zone calls were sent down.

During a fight of four hours, five minutes, the 140th and 96th Siege Batteries were ranged on to a hostile battery by Captain Twist and Lieutenant Rosborough, No. 16 Squadron; explosions, lasting about half an hour, were caused in one of the pits, and a bridge over the canal in the vicinity of the target was also badly damaged.

One gun-pit was destroyed and a large explosion caused in a hostile battery position by the 37th Siege Battery, with observation by Captain Glenny, No. 7 Squadron.

The 152nd Siege Battery, with observation by Lieutenant Hughman, No. 9 Squadron, caused four fires and three explosions in a hostile battery position and destroyed two gun-pits.

Lieutenants Hayter and Binns, No. 12 Squadron, ranged the 262nd Siege Battery on to a hostile battery position, causing a fire. They then ranged the 133rd Siege Battery on to another battery position in which two gun-pits were damaged.

The 276th and 46 Siege Batteries were ranged on to separate hostile batteries by Lieutenant Worthington and First Air Mechanic Rose, No. 13 Squadron. In the latter shoot three explosions were caused and the position badly damaged.

A hostile battery position was badly damaged, one gun-pit completely destroyed, and one fire caused by the 57th Siege Battery, with observation by Lieutenants Price and Atkinson, No. 15 Squadron.

Lieutenants Walker and Jones, No. 35 Squadron, during a flight of 4 hours 25 minutes, working with the 23rd Siege Battery, destroyed two gun-pits in a hostile battery position and caused one explosion.

The 91st Siege Battery carried out two successful shoots with observation by Lieutenants Pybus and Cave, No. 35

Squadron; one gun-pit was destroyed, three damaged, one explosion, and one fire caused.

Enemy Aircraft.—Enemy aircraft were active on the whole front.

Second Lieut. A. Double, No. 43 Squadron, attacked an enemy two-seater which nose-dived into ground and was seen to crash by several pilots.

Second Lieut. C. King, No. 43 Squadron, drove down a hostile two-seater from 12,000 to 6,000 feet, firing about 160 rounds at close range. He then drove three hostile scouts down to the ground, and while contour chasing saw two Albatross Scouts above him. One of these he attacked and drove down completely out of control, it was seen to crash by other pilots and an anti-aircraft battery.

Sergeant E. Elton and Sergeant C. Hagan, No. 22 Squadron, whilst in formation were attacked by 10 Albatross Scouts. Sergeant Hagan got a burst into one enemy aircraft which was diving on his tail; the pilot was seen to collapse over the fuselage and the enemy machine crashed to the ground. They then dived on another enemy aircraft which was below, and after firing a burst from short range the enemy machine collapsed in the air and fell to pieces.

Second Lieuts. S. Oades and S. Bunting, No. 22 Squadron, attacked one of five Albatross Scouts encountered near Douai. The enemy machine burst into flames and fell to pieces.

Captain W. Molesworth, No. 29 Squadron, whilst leading a patrol, fired two drums at a hostile two-seater, which was diving east; it went into a vertical dive and was seen to crash south-east of Becelaere by No. 10 Squadron.

Sergeant E. Clayton and Second-Lieut. L. Sloot, No. 57 Squadron, whilst taking photographs were attacked by three enemy scouts. The observer fired 20 rounds at the leading machine, whose wings fell off and the machine burst into flames. The result of this combat was confirmed by Naval Squadron No. 1.

Captain J. B. McCudden, No. 56 Squadron, attacked an enemy two-seater at 17,000 feet as he was recrossing the lines after two indecisive combats. He opened fire at 200 yards and kept on firing until the hostile machine burst into flames and fell to pieces. He then went south and attacked a hostile scout doing escort duty, at which he opened fire at a range of 200 yards, continuing until the hostile machine fell to pieces, the wreckage falling near Cherisy.

Second Lieutenant A. Cowper, No. 24 Squadron, was dived on by a hostile scout which overshot him on our side of the lines, allowing him to get on to its tail and fire a long burst. The enemy aircraft dived down to 500 feet, and Second Lieut. Cowper kept east, heading it off whenever it tried to recross the lines. The hostile machine flew west at a height of 200 feet, Second Lieut. Cowper finally forcing it to land intact at No. 52

Squadron's aerodrome. Another hostile machine, on being attacked by Second Lieut. Cowper, broke up in the air and fell in pieces.

Whilst on patrol Captain G. McElroy, No. 24 Squadron, attacked a triplane, getting in several good bursts at close range. The enemy machine burst into flames and crashed about four miles from Laon.

Second Lieut. P. McDougall, No. 24 Squadron, on patrol with Captain McElroy, attacked another triplane from above. After an engagement of about 10 minutes the hostile machine spun, and was seen to crash on the ground.

Second Lieut. J. McDonald, No. 24 Squadron, drove a hostile triplane down to 4,000 feet, firing short bursts from close range; it went down completely out of control and was seen to crash. He then saw a triplane being attacked by other pilots of his control; he joined in and after a long fight at a height of about 200 feet, drove the hostile machine into the wood east of Samoussy, into which it crashed.

Hostile machines were driven down out of control by the following:—Second Lieut. M. Peiler, No. 43 Squadron; Second Lieut. S. Oades and Second Lieut. S. Bunting, No. 22 Squadron; Sergeant C. Noel and Corporal T. Hodgson, No. 57 Squadron; Major G. Bowman, No. 41 Squadron; Lieutenant K. Junor, No. 56 Squadron; Second Lieut. R. Hammersley and Second Lieut. H. Richardson, No. 24 Squadron.

Bombing.—A total of 2,507 photographs were taken, and 15½ tons of bombs dropped, as follows:—

Night 25th/26th.

First Brigade.—No. 5 Squadron dropped thirty-two 112-lb. and forty-six 25-lb. bombs on billets; No. 4 Squadron dropped forty-five 25-lb. bombs on billets, and No. 16 Squadron dropped eleven 112-lb. bombs on billets.

Second Brigade.—No. 21 Squadron dropped forty-eight 25-lb. bombs on Menin, and No. 10 Squadron dropped twenty-four 25-lb. bombs on Menin.

Ninth Wing.—No. 58 Squadron dropped forty-three 25-lb. bombs on Gontrode Aerodrome; twelve 25-lb. bombs on Bavichove Aerodrome on which one direct hit was obtained; thirty-eight 25-lb. bombs on Oyghem Aerodrome when bursts were observed among the hangars; thirty 25-lb. bombs on Bisseghem Aerodrome (bursts seen on hangars); four 25-lb. bombs on Marcke Aerodrome, and nine 25-lb. bombs on sidings and trains.

No. 102 Squadrons dropped thirty-seven 25-lb. bombs on Marquain Aerodrome when bursts were seen among the hangars; forty-one 25-lb. bombs on Scheldewindeke Arerodrome; eight 25-lb. bombs on Lezennes Aerodrome; eight 25-lb. bombs on Ramegnies Chin Aerodrome, and fourteen 25-lb. bombs on sidings and trains.

No. 101 Squadron dropped twelve 40-lb. and three hundred and seventy-eight 25-lb. bombs on billets in the woods east of Fontaine Uterte. All the bombs fell in the wood, but it was impossible to say if they hit the huts. A large fire was caused in one of the woods. All the pilots made two raids and one pilot succeeded in making three.

By Day.

First Brigade.—Four hundred and thirteen photographs, No. 18 Squadron, dropped two 112-lb. and twenty-four 25-lb. bombs on Faumont Aerodrome; six 25-lb. bombs on Flines Aerodrome, and two 112-lb. and eight 25-lb. bombs on billets; No. 2 Squadron dropped twenty-one 25-lb. bombs on billets; No. 4 Squadron dropped twenty 25-lb. bombs; No. 5 Squadron dropped fourteen 25-lb. bombs, and No. 4A Squadron dropped four 25-lb. bombs.

Second Brigade.—Six hundred and twenty-two photographs. No. 57 Squadron, dropped eight 112-lb. bombs on Courtrai railway sidings, and 2nd Wing dropped forty-four 25-lb. bombs.

Third Brigade.—Six hundred and sixteen were taken, and forty-four 25-lb. bombs dropped on various targets. No. 46 Squadron dropped ten 25-lb. bombs.

Fifth Brigade.—Six hundred and sixty-four photographs. 15th Wing dropped sixty-five 25-lb. bombs, and No. 48 Squadron dropped fifteen 25-lb. bombs.

Ninth Wing.—One hundred and ninety-two photographs. No. 27 Squadron dropped forty 25-lb. bombs on Somain sidings.

February 27th.

The sky was overcast all day with rain in the afternoon.

Seven reconnaissances were carried out; 18 hostile batteries successfully engaged for destruction and three neutralized with aeroplane observation; four gun-pits destroyed, eight explosions and five fires caused. Nineteen zone calls were sent down.

On the 26th inst., balloons of the First Brigade registered seven targets, four of which were hostile batteries, and located four active hostile batteries, and those of the 2nd Brigade registered eight targets, of which five were hostile batteries. Four of the shoots were carried out in conjunction with aeroplanes.

Enemy Aircraft.—Enemy aircraft activity was very slight, only a few combats taking place.

Second Lieut. G. Howsam, No. 70 Squadron, attacked an enemy two-seater near Warneton at 500 feet. He fired two bursts at a range of 100 yards, when the enemy aircraft fell out of control and crashed into a hedge south-east of Comines.

Bombing.—A total of 83 photographs were taken, and 138 bombs dropped as follows:—

First Brigade.—Thirty-two photographs. Nos. 2, 4, and 5 Squadrons dropped twenty-six 25-lb. bombs.

Second Brigade.—Second Wing dropped twenty 25-lb. bombs.

Third Brigade.—Fifty-one photographs and eleven 25-lb bombs.

Fifth Brigade.—Fifteenth Wing dropped twenty-one 25-lb. bombs.

Ninth Wing.—No. 27 Squadron dropped sixty 25-lb. bombs on Ascq Railway Station.

In addition to the above, the following raids were carried out by the **8th Brigade**:—

Night 26th–27th.

One machine of Naval Squadron No. 16 dropped twelve 112-lb. bombs on the barracks and railway station at Treves. Eight bursts were seen on the railway station and sidings, and four on a factory with a furnace. The pilot on approaching the target found it very misty, and had difficulty in locating it. He flew away for a short distance and waited 30 minutes, when the lights of the town were lit up (the "all clear" presumably having been given). He thereupon returned and dropped his bombs.

Nine machines of No. 100 Squadron dropped four 230-lb., nine 112-lb., nine 40-lb. and thirty-two 25-lb. bombs on Frescaty Aerodrome; 36 rounds from the pom-pom gun and 2,100 from machine guns were fired at various ground targets. The first three machines to arrive at the targets found sixteen pairs of lights lined up on the aerodrome, which on descending lower they identified as machines. Bombs were dropped amongst them from 1,000 feet and 30 rounds from the pom-pom fired into them. One hostile machine taking off was bombed and caused to crash. Several direct hits on the hangars and hutments were obtained. On the homeward journey a hostile machine passed about 30 feet under one of our machines; 100 rounds were fired at a range of 50 feet which sent the hostile machine down vertically out of control. All our machines returned.

Honours and Awards.

The Military Cross.—Second Lieut. W. M. Blackie.

February 28th.

The weather was bad, but there were occasional bright intervals.

Five reconnaissances were carried out by the 1st, 2nd, and 5th Brigades.

Twenty hostile batteries were successfully engaged for destruction with aeroplane observation and twelve neutralized. Fifteen of the batteries engaged for destruction were by machines of the 1st Brigade. Six gun-pits were damaged, 16 explosions and five fires caused. Fifty-five zone calls were sent down.

Second Lieuts. Price and Atkinson, No. 15 Squadron, observed for the 57th Siege Battery on a hostile battery position in which two fires were caused, one gun-pit and the whole position badly damaged.

The 216th Siege Battery, with observation by Lieutenants McLean and Davies, No. 8 Squadron, damaged one gun-pit and caused one fire in a hostile battery position.

On the 27th inst., five targets (all of which were hostile batteries) were ranged by balloons of the First Brigade, and three (of which one was a hostile battery) by those of the Second Brigade. Sixteen active hostile batteries were located.

Enemy Aircraft.—Enemy aircraft activity was very slight all day.

Bombing.—A total of 194 photographs were taken and 246 bombs dropped, as follows:—

First Brigade.—Seventy-five photographs. No. 18 Squadron dropped two 112-lb. and twenty-eight 25-lb. bombs on dump at Annoeullin; six 112-lb. and twelve 25-lb. bombs on dump at Bauvin, and Nos. 2, 4 and 5 Squadrons dropped sixty-seven 25-lb. bombs on various targets.

Second Brigade.—One hundred and seven photographs. No. 57 Squadron dropped fourteen 112-lb. bombs on Courtrai railway sidings, and Second Wing dropped fourteen 25-lb. bombs.

Third Brigade.—Twenty-five 25-lb. bombs.

Fifth Brigade.—Fifteenth Wing dropped forty-six 25-lb. bombs.

Ninth Wing.—No. 27 Squadron dropped thirty-two 25-lb. bombs on Deynze Railway Junction.

March 1st.

There were low clouds throughout the day, with very short bright intervals.

Eighteen reconnaissances were carried out, nine of which were by machines of the Fifth Brigade.

Seventeen hostile batteries were successfully engaged for destruction with aeroplane observation and six neutralized; two gun-pits were destroyed, five damaged, four explosions and three fires caused. Twelve of the batteries engaged for destruction were with observation by machines of the First Brigade.

The 9th Siege Battery, with observation by Lieutenants Craig and Leighton, No. 59 Squadron, badly damaged an anti-tank position.

On the 28th February, balloons of the First Brigade registered six targets, five of which were hostile batteries, and located seven active hostile batteries, while those of the Second Brigade registered 11 targets (four being hostile batteries), and located two active hostile batteries. One of these shoots was carried out in conjunction with an aeroplane.

Enemy Aircraft.—Enemy aircraft activity was very slight.

Hostile machines were driven down out of control by Captain W. D. Patrick, Second Lieuts. F. McGoun and P. Clayson, No. 1 Squadron; Captain N. Millman and Second Lieut. H. Cooper, No. 48 Squadron (two); Captain J. Morris, No. 23 Squadron; Captain G. McElroy, No. 24 Squadron; Lieutenant G. Cuthbertson, No. 54 Squadron; and Second Lieut. A Proctor, No. 84 Squadron.

An enemy aircraft two-seater was brought down in our lines by anti-aircraft of the Third Army.

Bombing.—A total of 527 photographs were taken, and 6½ tons of bombs dropped, as follows:—

First Brigade.—No. 2 Squadron dropped eighty-five 25-lb. and sixteen 40-lb. bombs on Courrières and Estevelles; No. 4 Squadron dropped twenty-eight 25-lb. bombs on Bauvin, Don and Carvin, and No. 16 Squadron dropped sixteen 112-lb. bombs on Vitry, Quiéry-la-Motte and Billy Montigny.

Second Brigade.—No. 21 Squadron dropped twelve 25-lb. bombs on Oostnieuwkerke.

Ninth Wing.—No. 58 Squadron dropped three 112-lb. and forty-nine 25-lb. bombs on Grandglise Aerodrome (midway between Tournai and Mons), one 112-lb. and four 25-lb. bombs on Fresnes Railway Station; No. 102 Squadron dropped one 230-lb. and sixteen 25-lb. bombs on Grandglise Aerodrome; eight 25-lb. bombs on Seclin, and twelve 25-lb. bombs on trains.

By Day.

First Brigade. — Forty-seven photographs. First Wing dropped thirty-nine 25-lb. bombs.

Second Brigade.—Second Wing dropped thirty-three 25-lb. bombs.

Third Brigade.—One hundred and forty-six photographs, forty-five 25-lb. bombs.

Fifth Brigade.—Three hundred and thirty-four photographs, eighty-eight 25-lb. bombs.

Honours and Awards.

The Distinguished Service Cross.—Flight Commander R. B. Munday, R.N.A.S.

The Military Cross.—Captain G. H. B. Streatfield, Captain J. M. Allport, Lieutenant A. W. Hammond, Second Lieut. J. V. Sorsoleil.

March 2nd.

Clouds were low all day, with a very strong wind and snow at times.

One reconnaissance was carried out by machines of the Fifth Brigade.

Captain Carter and Captain Hyde, 4th Squadron, A.F.C., carried out a contact patrol over the area of the Portuguese front raided by the enemy during the night of the 1st/2nd inst.

Machines of the First Brigade successfully engaged four hostile batteries and neutralized one; one gun-pit was damaged, one explosion and one fire caused. Two zone calls were sent down.

Enemy aircraft activity was nil.

Twenty-two photographs were taken, and thirty-nine 25-lb. bombs dropped on various targets.

March 3rd.

Low clouds and mist throughout the day prevented all flying.

March 4th.

Low clouds, mist and rain on the whole front made flying practically impossible.

Two reconnaissances were carried out, and twelve 25-lb. bombs dropped on various targets, six by machines of the Third Brigade and six by those of the First Brigade.

Artillery co-operation was impossible but a few artillery and offensive patrols were carried out.

L. A. K. BUTT, Captain,
Staff Captain.

Headquarters,
Royal Flying Corps,
6th March 1918.

No. 53.

CONFIDENTIAL.

ROYAL NAVAL AIR SERVICE.

OPERATIONS REPORT

(with Royal Flying Corps Reports attached).

1st to 16th MARCH 1918.

NAVAL STAFF,
  AIR DIVISION.
    16th March 1918.

ROYAL NAVAL AIR SERVICE.

REPORT OF OPERATIONS

(Completed from Reports during period
1st to 16th March 1918).

CONTENTS.

	PAGE
HOME STATIONS	2
DUNKIRK	6
EASTERN MEDITERRANEAN	12
ROYAL FLYING CORPS COMMUNIQUÉS	19

HOME STATIONS.

SUBMARINE PATROL WORK.

March 6th.

   Calshot.—While on patrol Large America Seaplane N. 4340 (pilot, Flight Lieut. O'Brien) (observer, Sub-Lieut. Brice) sighted an enemy submarine at 1555 in position 50° 13′ N., 0° 27′ W. The submarine, which was on the surface and steering an easterly course, submerged, and was just under the surface when attacked. Two 230-lb. bombs (delay action) were dropped, the first of which exploded about 40 feet on the port side of the submarine, and the second about 100 feet ahead of where the submarine had dived. The seaplane remained in the vicinity until forced to return owing to darkness, but nothing further was sighted.

March 10th.

   "Campania."—Seaplane No. N. 1009 (pilot, Flight Sub-Lieut. Kerruish) whilst on patrol, shortly after 1600, sighted a wake about 8 miles ahead and turned to investigate. It soon became apparent that the wash was caused by the conning tower of a submarine just breaking surface. The seaplane proceeded at about 80 knots to attack, but before the objective could be reached the submarine began to submerge, and disappeared at 1615. Twelve seconds later two 100-lb. bombs were dropped from a height of 800 feet about 250–300 feet ahead of the swirl which was still discernible, but only one of the bombs exploded. The machine circled the vicinity at a height of less than 500 feet for a period of 40 minutes, but no oil or wreckage was observed, although it is considered the bomb exploded either directly over or very close to the submarine. Very's lights, indicating presence of a submarine, were then fired, but destroyer apparently did not see them, owing to the brilliancy of the sun. Directly after dropping the bombs communication was established with Destroyer G. 21 by Aldis lamp, informing her that submarine had submerged in a position approximately 59V steering east. The seaplane altered course for base at 1655. At 1705 another destroyer approaching from southward was informed of position of submarine, and the seaplane returned to base, landing there at 1824.

March 13th.

   Scapa.—Seaplane N. 1662 left at 1507 to carry out a search for an enemy submarine reported in position 59° 25′ N., 1° 45′ E.

After passing Anskerry visibility gradually decreased, but owing to a signal received by the seaplane stating that at 1448 the submarine was in a position S. by E. 17 miles from Ward Hill, steering S.E. by S. the pilot decided to carry on with the patrol. At 1554 it was estimated that the seaplane was in the vicinity of the submarine position, and courses were steered as requisite to search the locality on a line to the south-eastward. At 1615 course was altered to search to the north-westward, and at 1624 a submarine was sighted steering south-east, the conning tower just awash. The seaplane immediately turned to get into the wind, and the submarine having apparently sighted it immediately submerged. One bomb was dropped from 1,000 feet, which exploded about 100 yards ahead of the spot where the submarine submerged. The seaplane then circled the vicinity for a period of 15 minutes, and two red Very's lights were fired. A very large dark patch was observed in the vicinity of the explosion, but nothing further was seen of the submarine. Two destroyers were then observed to the W.N.W. and informed of the attack. The seaplane then altered course to return, but after steering this course for 60 minutes it was estimated that land should have been sighted. As the visibility was getting so low (5 miles) course was altered to S.W., and signal was made to ship reporting the pilot's doubt as regards his position. At 1810 H.M.S. "Campania" instructed the seaplane to steer W., and this was done until it was nearly dark and visibility was nil, the pilot then deemed it advisable to land and reserve the remaining petrol (about 1 hour's supply) until daylight. A good landing was made at 1845, the sea being calm, and a distress signal was fired and the remaining bomb released. Very's lights and Aldis lamp were used at intervals and about midnight the seaplane was sighted by the destroyer "Offa" and safely towed to Scapa.

ENGAGEMENTS WITH HOSTILE SEAPLANES.

March 12th.

Felixstowe.—Large America Seaplanes Nos. 8677, N. 4513, and N. 4510 left on patrol at 0742, and at 0847, when in position E. of the North Hinder, they were attacked in the rear by five enemy seaplanes—two single-seaters and three two-seaters. The Large Americas opened fire with their rear guns, and dropped their bombs to increase speed. At 0919 an enemy submarine was observed directly ahead, with three or four men on the conning tower. This was attacked with machine gun-fire. The enemy seaplanes continued to attack from close range until 0940, when the Large Americas were over five British trawlers, steering S., when they broke off the engagement and turned back. At 1004 Large America No. 8677 landed by the trawler with a burst petrol pipe, and the other two seaplanes circled round until repairs had been effected. Seaplanes

N. 8677 and N. 4513 landed safely at Felixstowe, and N. 4510 landed in the harbour at Orfordness.

Later in the day at 1300 Large America Seaplanes Nos. 4582, 8661, and N. 4510 left on patrol. At 1345 N. 4510 returned owing to engine trouble, and at 1400 the two remaining seaplanes sighted five enemy seaplanes resting on the water in position approximately 7 miles E. of the old position of North Hinder. The enemy seaplanes left the water and took a "V" formation, flying ahead of the Large Americas, which dived on them and opened a rapid fire, and, after some manœuvring, succeeded in breaking up the formation, compelling the enemy seaplanes to scatter haphazardly. During the action, which lasted for 30 minutes, one two-seater machine was shot down by W./T Operator Nicol in Seaplane 8661, and was seen to crash on the water. Another machine was driven down out of control and landed, but later it was seen to leave the water again and fly away.

Ensign Fallon, U.S.N., in Seaplane 4582 shot the gunner in an enemy two-seater, after which the machine nose-dived, but righted itself and broke off the engagement. During the action W/T Operator Grey in Seaplane 4582 was shot in the neck and collapsed. First aid was rendered by Ensign Fallon and Engineer Reid, who then returned to man their guns. Both seaplanes returned safely and landed at Felixstowe at 1540.

RAID BY HOSTILE AEROPLANES.

March 7th–8th.

A bombing raid by enemy aeroplanes of approximately three hours' duration was carried out during the night over the area, Thames Estuary, Essex, Kent, and London.

The raid appears to have been carried out by six giant aeroplanes, of which only two reached London.

This is the first occasion upon which an aeroplane raid on the capital has been attempted without the assistance of moonlight. The first raider approached the coast of Thanet about 2255. A few minutes later the guns on the coast came into action, and on encountering their fire the enemy machine turned and proceeded to sea again. A second machine passed along the Thames Estuary as far as Southend, where it was reported at 2355 after which it was lost sight of and apparently turned back. Meanwhile a third machine crossed the Essex coast near the mouth of the Crouch at about 2325 and proceeded due west. At 2345 it was reported at Ilford, and shortly afterwards the Tower gun was in action.

Shortly before midnight four high explosive bombs and one incendiary bomb were dropped in Maida Vale and St. John's Wood, demolishing a number of houses and starting a fire in one. A bomb was also dropped in Burland Road, Battersea, demolishing two houses A fourth machine which crossed the coast near Harwich was located at Luton at 2345, and some bombs were dropped between the latter place and Dunstable at about 2350. The machine then turned south and passed into North London, via Barnet and Palmer's Green. Bombs were dropped between 1220 and 1230 as follows :—

Whetstone, near Barnet, where one high explosive bomb partly demolished six houses, injuring several persons. Finchley and Hampstead, where two high explosive bombs were dropped, one of which demolished a house in the latter district.

Two other machines crossed the Essex coast, one of which passed from Harwich due south across the Thames into Kent, but does not appear to have dropped any bombs.

The movements of the other machine are obscure.

Three Royal Flying Corps machines which went up to engage the raiders crashed, and one pilot was killed.

ZEPPELIN RAIDS.

March 12th–13th.

A night bombing raid of approximately seven hours' duration was carried out over Yorkshire by two Zeppelins. Five airships were reported making for the coast of Yorkshire between 1800 and 1900, but only two of the five actually crossed the coast, one at Tunstall at 2030, and the other at Hornsea at 2116.

One of the Zeppelins attacked Hull at 2100, several bombs are reported to have been dropped in the vicinity, but only two on the city itself, where one house was demolished. The second airship reached the outskirts of York, then turned and proceeded east. Bombs are reported to have been dropped by her a few miles from Howden Airship Station. The country was declared clear of hostile aircraft at 0047.

March 13th–14th.

A night bombing raid of approximately five and a half hours' duration was carried out by one Zeppelin over the area of Durham and Yorkshire. Three airships were reported about 150 miles from Flamborough at 1745, but two of these turned back, taking no part in the raid. The third airship made the coast in the neighbourhood of Tynemouth and proceeding south dropped bombs near Seaham, and also at West Hartlepool, at which place a fair amount of damage was done to property, and several people killed and injured.

The country was declared clear of hostile aircraft at midnight.

DUNKIRK.

RECONNAISSANCE.

No. 1 Wing, 2nd Squadron.—W/T Fleet patrols and reconnaissances have been carried out almost daily, during this period, by D.H. 4 machines. On one occasion during the course of a patrol a number of rounds were fired at an armed patrol boat off Zeebrugge.

PHOTOGRAPHIC RECONNAISSANCE.

March 6th.

No. 1 Wing, 2nd Squadron.—A reconnaissance was carried out, and very good results were obtained from plates, exposed over Ostend Town and Seaplane Base.

March 8th.

A reconnaissance was carried out and plates were exposed over De Haan and the Mole, with good results. The hit on the Mole claimed by No. 10 Squadron was confirmed.

March 9th.

A reconnaissance was carried out over Bruges and Zeebrugge and Ostend Docks, also Zeebrugge-Bruges Canal, and De Haan, and the vicinity, 40 plates being successfully exposed.

March 11th.

A reconnaissance was carried out at noon, during which 20 plates were exposed over Bruges Docks, Zeebrugge Mole, Coolkerke Aerodrome, Dudzeel Dump, and De Haan Battery, with good results.

March 13th.

A reconnaissance was carried out between the Dutch frontier and Nieuport, and 49 plates were exposed with good results.

March 15th.

A reconnaissance was carried out and plates were exposed over Bruges Docks, Vlisseghen Aerodrome and hostile Torpedo Boat Destroyers.

OFFENSIVE PATROLS—ENGAGEMENTS WITH ENEMY.

March 6th.

No. 4 Wing, 10th Squadron.—A flight of five Sopwith Camels attacked four Albatross Scouts at 11,000 feet, south-east of Dixmude, during the course of which Flight Commander Alexander shot down one of the enemy machines completely out of control after a short engagement, at close range.

March 8th.

No. 1 Wing, 13th Squadron.—A formation of seven Sopwith Camels sighted a Rumpler two-seater machine over Conckeleare, and climbing up sun proceeded to attack. Flight-Lieut. Paynter engaged at close range after which the left lower wing of the enemy machine folded up and the machine fell near Conckeleare.

March 8th.

No. 1 Wing, 1st Squadron.—Eight enemy scout machines were attacked by a formation of five Sopwith Camels over Roulers, during which one of the enemy machines was driven down out of control by Flight Sub-Lieut. Findlay.

A giant aeroplane was seen on Ghistelles Aerodrome.

March 10th.

No. 1 Wing, 1st Squadron.—While on a special mission in Sopwith Camels, Flight-Lieuts. Kirkhead and Rosevear and Flight Sub-Lieut. Findlay attacked two enemy scouts and one two-seater machine. The two former pilots shot their opponents down out of control, and the latter saw his crash on the ground.

March 10th.

No. 4 Wing, 10th Squadron.—Flight Commander Alexander and Flight Lieut. Hinchcliffe in Sopwith Camels each brought down one enemy machine out of control.

March 11th.

No. 1 Wing, 1st Squadron.—Whilst on patrol a flight of Sopwith Camels encountered a formation of seven Albatross and Pfalz scout machines east of Armentieres. One of these was attacked by Flight Sub-Lieut. Wallace, and shot down out of control.

Whilst on a special mission by three machines, a formation of 12 enemy scout machines was observed south of Armentieres, and driven east. Flight Lieut. Rosevear engaged a two-seater and drove it down vertically out of control; it was still seen diving at 2,000 feet and probably crashed. While on a special mission Squadron Commander Dallas attacked an enemy two-seater near Dixmude, and after firing about 30 rounds at 40 yards into the enemy machine, the left wing folded up and the machine crashed in the floods.

March 11*th.*

No. 4 Wing, 4th Squadron.—After a running fight between a flight of Sopwith Camels and several enemy machines, Flight Commander Shook shot one down out of control. A number of indecisive engagements also took place.

No. 1 Wing, 13th Squadron.—A flight of Sopwith Camels returning from Fleet patrol engaged a two-seater Rumpler off Wenduyne, which was attacked by all machines of the Sopwith flight.

A small explosion occurred and the enemy machine burst into flames and spun into the sea.

March 13*th.*

No. 1 Wing, 1st Squadron.—A flight of Sopwith Camels on an early patrol encountered five enemy machines at 10,000 feet south-east of Dixmude. Flight Commander Minifie, who was leading the flight, fired about 75 rounds into one of these at 20 yards range, after which the enemy machine turned on its back and went down completely out of control.

The Sopwith pilot then attacked another and got 50 rounds in at close range, after which the enemy machine spun out of control and crashed into the floods. During the same engagement Flight Lieut. Rosevear, firing at point blank range, shot down an enemy scout machine, which was seen to crash in the floods.

March 13*th.*

No. 1 Wing, 1st Squadron.—An enemy kite balloon over Ypres was brought down by Flight Commanders Ridley and Rowley. It fell our side of the line and contained a dummy figure, filled with straw, probably as a decoy on which anti-aircraft guns were ranged.

Over 1,000 rounds were fired into enemy trenches.

March 15*th.*

No. 1 Wing, 1st Squadron.—A flight of Sopwith Camels encountered eight Pfalz Scouts east of Dixmude, two of which were shot down by Flight Lieut. Rosevear. One was seen to crash and the other went down completely out of control in flames.

Flight Sub-Lieut. Gates shot down one enemy scout machine which was probably destroyed. Several indecisive engagements took place.

ATTACK ON HOSTILE SUBMARINE.

March 13*th.*

No. 1 Wing, 17th Squadron.—D.H. 4 A. 7863 left on patrol at 1208 and when on a course north-east of Dunkirk and at

1,800 feet, the conning tower and a large portion of deck of a submarine was observed 800 yards distant on the starboard quarter.

The submarine which had two masts forward of the conning tower and one aft, dived on the approach of the aeroplane which altered course and dived to 400 feet to attack. One 230-lb. bomb (2½ seconds delay) was dropped which fell about 200 yards ahead of the swirl caused by the submarine submerging. No further signs of the submarine were observed.

BOMB ATTACKS.

Ostend Seaplane Base	March 3rd	434 lbs.	S. Camel.
Ypres-Thourout (railway building).	„ 5th	32 „	„
Zeebrugge Mole	7th	64	„
St. Pierre Capelle (billets and sidings).	9th	1,184	D.H. 9.
Giant aeroplane in field at St. Pierre Capelle.	9th	856	
Engel Aerodrome	10th	995	„
Engel Dump	10th	64	„
St. Pierre Capelle (billets and sidings).	12th	439	„
*Bruges Docks	12th–13th	6,264 „	H.P.
	Total -	10,332 lbs.	

* Night raid.

March 3rd.

No. 1 Wing, 13th Squadron.—A bombing raid by eight Sopwith Camels was carried out on Ostend Seaplane Base in the course of which one 50-lb. and twenty-four 16-lb. bombs were dropped at heights varying from 300 to 150 feet.

The 50-lb. bomb hit the seaplane sheds and eleven of the smaller bombs were seen to explode in the immediate vicinity. Three hits were also obtained on the anti-aircraft battery north of the Bassin de Chasse, Marc.

March 5th.

No. 4 Wing, 10th Squadron.—An attack was carried out by a Sopwith Camel on some buildings close to the Ypres-Thourout railway line, during which two 16-lb. bombs were dropped from 8,000 feet. One of the bombs was observed to explode close to the buildings. Owing to pressure failing the pilot was not able to descend lower to drop his bombs.

March 7th.

No. 4 Wing, 10th Squadron.—An attack was carried out by a Sopwith Camel on the Zeebrugge Mole at 0004 during which four 16-lb. bombs were dropped from a height of 500 feet.

Three of the bombs were observed to burst in the middle of the base of the Mole.

March 9th.

No. 5 Wing, 6th Squadron.—A bombing raid was carried out on billets and sidings at Saint Pierre Capelle by ten D.H. 9 machines during which thirty-two 25-lb. and twenty-four 16-lb. bombs were dropped. Direct hits were observed on three sheds and a fire started. On the return journey a "Giant" aeroplane which had made a false landing was observed. Six machines returned later to bomb it and twenty-four 25-lb. and sixteen 16-lb. bombs were dropped, but no direct hits were observed. Several soldiers and three motor cars which were in the immediate vicinity were attacked by machine-gun fire. On the return journey, D.H. 9 B. 7591, Flight Commander Le Mesurier, D.S.C. (pilot), Petty Officer A. G. L. Ryan (observer), was attacked by six "Albatross" Scouts from 100 to 50 yards range. After a running fight to the lines the gunlayer fired 50 rounds at one of the enemy machines and it was seen to go down in a spiral nose-dive and eventually crashed in the floods.

March 10th.

No. 5 Wing, 6th Squadron.—A bombing raid was carried out by D.H. 9 machines on Engel Aerodrome during which twenty-seven 25-lb. and twenty 16-lb. bombs were dropped many of which, were seen to burst close to the hangars. A direct hit is reported on a building south-west of the hangars. Four 16-lb. bombs were also dropped on Engel Dump and two fires were started.

March 12th.

No. 5 Wing, 6th Squadron.—An attack was carried out during the morning by D.H. 9 machines on Saint Pierre Capelle billets and railway sidings, on which fifteen 25-lb. and four 16-lb. bombs were dropped. The buildings and sidings were well straddled, and a fire was started which burnt for some considerable time.

March 12th–13th.

No. 5 Wing, 7th Squadron.—A bomb attack was carried out on Bruges Docks during the early hours of the morning by Handley Page machines and four 250-lb. and forty-seven 112-lb. bombs were dropped. Although no direct hits were observed good shooting appears to have been made.

SUMMARY.

Enemy machines driven down out of control - 11
    ,,   ,,   destroyed - - - - 7

Total - 18

Honours and Awards.

Name.	Unit.	Awarded.
Flight Commander R. B. Munday	No. 8 Squadron	D.S.C.

Belgian Honours.

Name.	Unit.	Awarded.
Flight Sub-Lieut. L. F. W. Smith (since killed).	Late No. 4 Squadron.	Croix de Guerre and Chevalier de la Couronne.
Flight Sub-Lieut. E. J. K. Buckley (since killed).	Late No. 4 Squadron.	Croix de Guerre and Chevalier de la Couronne.

Casualties.

Name.	Unit.	Date.
Missing, since reported Killed.		
Acting Flight Commander M. J. G. Day	No. 13 Squadron	27.2.18
Accidentally Killed.		
Flight Sub-Lieut. G. J. W. Goodwin	No. 12 Squadron	12.3.18
Flight Sub-Lieut. C. W. Emmett	No. 12 Squadron	15.3.18
Missing.		
Flight Sub-Lieut. H. R. Casgrain	No. 12 Squadron	8.3.18
Flight Sub-Lieut. C. G. Macdonald	No. 2 Squadron	11.3.18
A.M. 1 G. L. R. J. Capp, No. F. 7029	No. 2 Squadron	11.3.18
Wounded.		
Flight Sub-Lieut. A. M. Bannatyne	No. 6 Squadron	9.3.18
A.C. 1 G. L. R. A. Hollingsbee, O. No. L. 7595.	No. 6 Squadron	9.3.18

EASTERN MEDITERRANEAN STATION.

Weekly Operations Report No. 104,
Week ending March 17th, 1918.

NOTE.—Weekly Operations Reports Nos. 99, 102 and 103 have not yet come to hand, and will be included in the next issue.

Weather.—During this period a strong north-easterly wind, approaching a gale, has prevented much flying, Wednesday, 13th and the early morning of Thursday being the only days on which flying was possible at most stations.

THASOS AIR STATION.

"A" SQUADRON AND "Z" (GREEK) SQUADRON.

"A" Squadron did no flying, except when, on the 13th, a Short attempted a submarine patrol. It returned immediately with engine trouble.

On the same day this station was reinforced by two Baby seaplanes, one of which crashed on landing. The pilot was uninjured.

On the 13th a hostile machine was reported over Limena, and at 0825 an enemy seaplane was sighted approaching from that direction at a height of 10,000 feet. Anti-aircraft guns opened fire, and the enemy circled south out of range and disappeared north.

"Z" Squadron. Commander Moraitinis flew over from Mudros in a Camel on the 13th on a duty visit, and returned safely on the 14th in a very strong wind.

STAVROS AIR STATION.

"D" SQUADRON.

This station alone had weather which made daily flying possible.

Reconnaissance and Photography.—On the 10th, 11th, 12th, 13th, 14th, 15th and 16th, escorted reconnaissances of the front line were carried out, and photographs taken on three occasions.

On the 11th a hostile aircraft was sighted and pursued, but did not wait to be engaged.

Spotting.—On the 13th spotting was carried out for monitors firing, and three O.K.'s on a battery reported. During this spotting three hostile aircraft were observed by the escort, but there was no engagement.

On the 13th a reinforcement of two Camels was sent from Mudros. One of these crashed upon landing. The pilot, Flight Sub-Lieut. W. S. Anderson, was injured, breaking his thigh and receiving cuts and bruises on the head and body.

KALLONI AIR STATION, MITYLENE.

"B" Squadron.

Practically no work was carried out because of the weather.

Escort Work.—On the morning of the 14th two Camels were ordered out to escort back a D.H. 4 returning from Constantinople, which landed safely, *vide* Mudros report. The weather has prevented this machine from returning to Mudros, and only a W/T report that the "Goeben" was still in position and photographs taken, has yet been received.

GLIKI AIR STATION, IMBROS.

"C" Squadron.

Result of Reconnaissance.—The reconnaissance of Bashika Point mentioned in last week's report as taking place on the 3rd, reports a pile of recently excavated débris about half a mile west of Khatindermina village, and a small cloud of smoke was seen rising just north of the village. This reconnaissance was ordered because blasting had been reported here during the previous two or three days.

On the same day an attempt was made to reconnoitre the Adrianople-Constantinople railway, but on reaching Gremea the D.H. 4 had to return with engine trouble. When two to three miles N.N.W. of Kastro (Imbros) a small patch of oil was sighted. Two 100-lb. bombs were dropped from a height of 5,500 feet, which fell 40 and 50 feet away respectively. No other indication of a submarine was seen. Two T.B.D.'s were in the vicinity, and as probably there was no submarine the observer took the opportunity for releasing his bombs.

Reconnaissance.— A reconnaissance of the Straits was attempted on the 10th, but found impracticable, but successful reconnaissances were carried out on the 11th and at dawn on the 13th. Nothing of importance to report.

The station has been standing by all the week to carry out a reconnaissance of our own minefields as ordered by R.A.E., but there has been no favourable day.

On the 13th two D H. 4's were flown over to Mudros to bring pilots and observers for the long reconnaissance dealt with later in this report. It has not been possible to carry out a reconnaissance of the railway.

MUDROS.

The only suitable times for flying were the 13th and the early morning of the 14th. Advantage was taken of the fine weather on the 13th to get every available pilot, observer, and machine in the air, and reinforcing machines were sent to other stations.

Anti-Submarine Patrols.—An almost continuous submarine patrol was carried out, but no submarines were sighted.

Experimental Work.—On the morning of the 13th also the experiment of communicating between aircraft and patrol craft was continued. The towed buoy system having proved a failure, Captain D. ordered destroyers to rig out a spar with "R" international flag. The observer reported that this flag was visible at 1,000 yards distant and a height of 1,000 feet. It would be desirable to try this method a little further. Communication was readily made with the Aldis lamp and with W/T, so that no other methods seem necessary for communicating with destroyers, but the reason for the other experiments is to strive to obtain a system of communication with trawlers, &c., which may not be equipped with these appliances.

During the 13th also, preparations were made to carry out a "Goeben" reconnaissance at dawn on the 14th, should the weather prove suitable.

Reconnaissance.—At dawn on the 14th there was a slight north-easterly breeze, and the reconnaissance was made by two D.H. 4's proceeding in company.

The first machine (Flight Sub-Lieut. S. S. Flock, Observer Lieutenant W. R. Abbott) returned to Mitylene, and detailed report has not yet been received. The other machine (Flight Sub-Lieut. T. H. Blair and Observer Sub-Lieut. J. R. Young) left the repair base, Mudros, at 0436, and proceeded by Imbros to the Gulf of Xebros.

0516. Gulf of Xebros. Straits clear of shipping. Clouds low over Nagara and the Adriatic coast.

0538. Dorkhan, 9,000 feet. Crossed coast; anti-aircraft fire; five shrapnel bursts. Line of nine trenches, estimated three-quarters of a mile, not continuous, on crest of ridge north of Dorkhan.

0603. Merefte, 9,000 feet. Crossed coast of Marmora. Clouds at 4,000 feet, very dense. Steered E.N.E. by pilot's compass.

0643. Four miles E. of Rodosto. Three caiques on the W. side of Rodosto Harbour. Altered course to E.

0708. Three miles S. of Biyak Chekmeje. Six caiques on the W. side of the bay.

0715. Two miles S. of San Stefano, 9,000 feet. Train of 15 trucks going towards San Stefano, 1½ miles E. of the station.

Seven caiques sailing towards Biyak Chekmeje, approximately 1 mile off the shore.

0723. Constantinople, 9,000 feet. Clouds very dense at 4,000 feet; visibility very poor. Feneraki Station, Scutari, 80 trucks in sidings. One engine in station, apparently shunting trucks. Two cargo vessels, of about 800 tons, lying 800 yards off Scutari.

Constantinople Station. Forty or 50 waggons, one engine in siding.

Golden Horn. Two barges, and one cargo vessel of 800 tons lying below the lower bridge. Steam tug proceeding S. from the entrance of the Golden Horn. S.S. "General" above the upper bridge, and steamer on S. side of channel.

(*Note.*—The "General" at 0750 issued hostile aircraft warning, from which it would appear that they were taken by surprise.)

Fifteen caiques at the entrance to the Golden Horn. A 1,500-ton steamer in mid-channel of Bosphorus, 1 mile N. of the entrance to the Golden Horn.

0730–0735. Stenia Bay, 6,000 feet. "Goeben" was in the same position on the S. side of the bay as on previous occasions, the last being the 3rd March. No extraordinary activity was observed, and no anti-aircraft fire from the "Goeben" experienced. The supply ship which was alongside, shown in the photograph of the 3rd March, had been moved. No smoke observed from the funnels. Descended to 6,000 feet to take photographs. Exposed one plate. Thick clouds prevented further exposures. Except just at the moment when photograph was taken, visibility was very low and accurate observation difficult.

There was one barge outside entrance of bay, and two steamers of not more than 800 tons in Stenia Bay at the W. side.

0750. Patrolled one mile of Bosphorus at 7,000 feet. Train leaving San Stefano towards Chatalja, 15 trucks.

0750 to 0810. Sea of Marmora. Clouds at 4,000 feet, and dense to S.E. Steered to S.W.

0815. Panderma, 8,000 feet. Train leaving station, engine and 12 trucks, towards N.E. Twenty-five to 30 covered waggons, four-wheeled, on road leading to Panderma from S.W. about four miles from Panderma. Clouds very dense over the land, no observations possible until near the coast of the Ægean.

0900. N.E. of Elzine, 8,000 feet. Lost sight of D.H. 4 No. 6411. Last seen about half a mile astern, flying at 6,000–7,000 feet.

0905. Yukyere Bay, 7,000 feet. Crossed the coast heading for Tenedos, Mitylene appearing covered with clouds. Trenches about half a mile from the coast, extending 2 miles in a line

N. and S. from Kum Burnu, to the N. of Gheyikli. Double line of 9 trenches with communication trench to coast.

0915. Tenedos, 7,000 feet. Crossed Tenedos.

0946. Landed Repair Base, Mudros.

Visibility was poor over the Sea of Marmora, Bosphorus, and Asia Minor, owing to dense layer of clouds at 4,000 feet.

By the time this machine had returned the N.E. wind had increased considerably in force. A Short seaplane had been sent out at 0459 to proceed to Peristeri on submarine patrol. At 0630 it landed S of Khelidromi and spoke trawler No. 1609, and requested her to inform headquarters, which she did. At 0850 machine left Khelidromi and proceeded to S.W. of Skyropulon Island, where a convoy of seven colliers, three drifters, and one torpedo boat was sighted. Called up the torpedo boat with lamp for about 10 minutes, but received no reply. There was no wind here, but the wind at Mudros was increasing so much that a signal was sent for the machine to return immediately, or to land at Pelago Bay, should the wind become too strong. This was received correctly at 1010.

At 1045 the machine reported "engine giving trouble." At 1055 "engine all correct again." At 1130 spoke a light cruiser by Aldis lamp, about midway between Lemnos and Peperi, and returned safely to the base at 1214, after having been away for seven hours 14 minutes. Time in the air, five hours 15 minutes.

The strength of the wind can be estimated from the fact that the speed on the return journey was only 30 m.p.h. Nothing was seen in the swept channel, and no signs of mines or submarines.

The above details are given as a further illustration of the point made last week of the great advantages offered by a haven of refuge on one of these islands, which can be effected with little expense if supplies can be sent by trawler.

KASSANDRA AIRSHIP STATION.

Patrol Work.—A patrol of $9\frac{1}{2}$ hours was carried out on the 10th, and a patrol of $8\frac{1}{2}$ hours on the 11th. Detailed reports have not yet been received.

SUDA BAY.

Anti-Submarine Patrols.—Three anti-submarine patrols were carried out on the 10th, and three on the 13th. No detailed reports have been received.

SYRA.

No flying. Progress is being made with the slipway, and the lack of cement, which had delayed the work, has now been provided for.

"PEONY."

Anti-Submarine Patrol.—No report has been received, but on the 14th the Greek guard at Kuvelus reported sighting a submarine on the surface at 37.44 N.; 27.05 E., steering W., which turned, and was last seen going N.E. No trace of a submarine was seen three hours later by a searching seaplane.

ROYAL FLYING CORPS COMMUNIQUÉS.

ROYAL FLYING CORPS COMMUNIQUÉ.—No. 130.

During the period under review (March 5th–12th inclusive), we have claimed officially 50 enemy aircraft crashed (three of which fell in our lines) and 45 driven down out of control. Approximately 46 tons of bombs were dropped and 11,694 photographs taken. Thirteen of our machines are missing.

March 5th.

Low clouds and a strong wind prevailed, but the weather improved somewhat in the afternoon.

Twelve reconnaissances were carried out, eight of which were by machines of the Fifth Brigade.

Machines of the First Brigade were able to carry out a little artillery co-operation; one hostile battery was successfully engaged for destruction, one neutralized, two explosions and one fire caused. Two zone calls were sent down.

Seven hundred and ninety photographs were taken, and 77 bombs dropped as follows:—

1st Brigade.—Eighteen 25-lb. bombs on miscellaneous and trench targets.

2nd Brigade.—No. 57 Squadron dropped ten 112-lb. bombs on railway sidings at Mouscron.

3rd Brigade.—Twenty-one 25-lb. bombs on miscellaneous targets.

5th Brigade.—Twenty-eight 25-lb. bombs on miscellaneous targets, by 15th Wing.

Enemy Aircraft.—Enemy aircraft activity was below normal.

Captain J. L. Trollope, No. 43 Squadron, shot down one enemy aircraft out of control.

Second Lieut. C. W. Usher, No. 40 Squadron, attacked an enemy scout. After a short combat the enemy aircraft dived steeply, and was confirmed by anti-aircraft observers to have burst into flames 2,000 feet from the ground.

Second Lieuts. S. A. Oades and S. W. Bunting, No. 22 Squadron, attacked an enemy aircraft two-seater. On firing a burst into it the right wing of the enemy aircraft folded back, and the machine went down in a spinning nose-dive. They then attacked an enemy aircraft scout, which turned over and spun down completely out of control.

March 6th.

The weather was very fine, enabling much work to be done.

Twenty-five reconnaissances were carried out, four being long-distance photographic reconnaissances by machines of the 9th Wing.

Sixty hostile batteries were successfully engaged for destruction with aeroplane observation and five neutralized; eight gun-pits were destroyed, 23 damaged, 24 explosions and nine fires caused. Thirty-nine zone calls were sent down.

Two thousand five hundred and sixty-two photographs were taken, and over eight tons of bombs dropped as follows:—

Night, 5th–6th.

9th Brigade.—No. 58 Squadron dropped one 112-lb. and sixty-six 25-lb. bombs on Ingelmunster railway station; No. 101 Squadron dropped two 112-lb. and four 25-lb. bombs on Bohain, and twenty-two 112-lb. and fifty-two 25-lb. bombs on Siboncourt aerodrome.

Day, 6th.

1st Brigade.—Three hundred and twenty-three photographs. No. 18 Squadron dropped thirty-six 25-lb. bombs on dumps and billets, and the 1st Wing dropped ninety-seven 25-lb. bombs.

2nd Brigade.—Four hundred and ninety-two photographs. No. 57 Squadron dropped eight 112-lb. bombs on Tourcoing railway sidings, and the 2nd Wing dropped fifty-three 25-lb. bombs.

3rd Brigade.—Seven hundred and ninety-three photographs. Fifty-nine 25-lb. bombs.

5th Brigade.—Eight hundred and sixty-nine photographs. 15th Wing dropped one hundred and twenty-seven 25-lb. bombs, and No. 48 Squadron dropped twenty 25-lb. bombs.

9th Wing.—Eighty-five photographs. No. 27 Squadron dropped eight 25-lb. bombs on Cambrai.

Enemy Aircraft.—Enemy aircraft was very active, particularly on the 5th Brigade front.

Sergeant E. J. Elton and Second Lieutenant G. S. L. Hayward, No. 22 Squadron, shot down an enemy aircraft scout, which was seen to crash near Dechy.

Second Lieutenant R. J. Owen, No. 43 Squadron, whilst on patrol, was attacked by eight enemy aircraft scouts, one of which he shot down and was confirmed by "B" Battery A.A. to have crashed near the Bois du Biez.

Lieutenant F. J. Scott, 4th Squadron A.F.C., shot down a Rumpler two-seater, which was confirmed by an observer of No. 5 Squadron to have crashed near Lens.

Second Lieutenant F. Belway and First Air Mechanic F. Rose, No. 13 Squadron, whilst on artillery observation, shot down an enemy scout, which landed in our lines south of Feuchy.

Second Lieutenant H. P. Richardson, No. 24 Squadron, dived on one of five enemy aircraft scouts and after firing about 60 rounds both left planes broke off the enemy aircraft machine, which fell between Fontaine and Croin.

Lieutenants R. H. Little and L. N. Jones, No. 48 Squadron, attacked a formation of enemy scouts but were themselves attacked by an enemy aircraft formation from above. One enemy aircraft was shot down out of control and was seen to crash.

Captain G. E. H. McElroy, No. 24 Squadron, shot down one enemy scout which was seen to hit the ground north-east of Bellecourt. He then attacked an Albatross Scout and fired 200 rounds from close range. The enemy aircraft went down smoking and before reaching the ground burst into flames.

Captain K. G. Leask, No. 84 Squadron, whilst on offensive patrol, was attacked by a large number of enemy aircraft scouts, one of which he shot down out of control and was seen by an observer of another squadron to crash near Renansart.

Second Lieutenant D. M. Clements, No. 24 Squadron, succeeded in shooting down an enemy aircraft which collided with him in the air, and both machines crashed on our side of the lines.

Captain R. J. Tipton, No. 40 Squadron, whilst leading a patrol, observed seven Albatross Scouts. He singled out one of the enemy aircraft and opened fire with both guns; the enemy aircraft went down vertically and crashed on this side of the lines.

Second Lieutenant J. W. Wallwork, Second Lieutenant W. L. Harrison and Captain J. P. R. Napier, all of No. 40 Squadron, each attacked a hostile machine, and in each case shot it down out of control. All three enemy aircraft were reported by ground observers to have crashed—one west of Lens, one north of Lens and one just north of Mericourt.

Enemy machines were shot down out of control by the following:—Second Lieut. D. A. Stewart and Lieutenant H. W. M. Mackay, No. 18 Squadron (three); Sergeant E. J. Elton and Second Lieut. G. S. L. Hayward, No. 22 Squadron; Second Lieuts. H. F. Davison and J. L. Morgan, No. 22 Squadron; Second Lieuts. G. W. Bulmer and S. J. Hunter, No. 22 Squadron; Captain J. H. Tudhope, No. 40 Squadron; Second Lieut. W. L. Harrison, No. 40 Squadron; Captain A. G. Waller and Sergeant M. Kilroy, No. 18 Squadron; Sergeants W. McCleery and W. Dyke, No. 18 Squadron; Second Lieut. B. E. Sharwood-Smith and Sergeant J. C. Lowe, No. 57 Squadron; Captain R. W. Chappell, No. 41 Squadron; Captain G. E. Thomson, No. 46 Squadron; Second Lieut. D. R. MacLaren, No. 46 Squadron; Lieutenant G. D. Jenkins, No. 46 Squadron; Lieutenant F. R. McCall and Second Lieut. F. C. Farrington, No. 13 Squadron; Captain A. J. Brown, No. 24 Squadron; Second Lieut. A. K. Cowper, No. 24 Squadron; Second Lieut. E. Pybus and Lieut. T. W. Cave, No. 35 Squadron; Captain A. H. G. Fellowes, No. 54 Squadron; Second Lieut. P. A. MacDougall, No. 24 Squadron; Second Lieut. G. J. Dawe, No. 24 Squadron.

March 7th.

The weather was fine at first, but the visibility bad, the sky later being covered with clouds.

Fifteen reconnaissances were carried out, seven of which were by machines of the 9th Wing.

Six hostile batteries were successfully engaged for destruction with aeroplane observation, four gun-pits damaged and five fires caused. Two zone calls were sent down.

Two hundred and seventy-eight photographs were taken, and three and a half tons of bombs dropped as follows :—

Night, 6th–7th.

8th Brigade.—Six machines of No. 100 Squadron left to bomb Frescaty Aerodrome (just south-west of Metz). Owing to a thick mist coming up suddenly the machines were recalled, but one pilot, who failed to see the signal, reached the objective and dropped one 230-lb., one 40-lb., and five 25-lb. bombs from 1,500 feet.

Day, 7th.

1st Brigade. — One hundred and thirteen photographs. No. 18 Squadron dropped four 112-lb. and fourteen 25-lb. bombs on Salome, and two 112-lb. and four 25-lb. bombs on miscellaneous targets. 1st Wing dropped sixty 25-lb. bombs.

2nd Brigade.—Two 25-lb. bombs.

3rd Brigade.—Thirty-seven 25-lb. bombs.

5th Brigade.—15th Wing dropped seventy 25-lb. bombs, and Naval Squadron No. 5 dropped eighty-three 25-lb. bombs on Mont d'Origny Aerodrome.

Enemy Aircraft.—Enemy aircraft activity was very slight.

Captain J. F. Morris, No. 23 Squadron, attacked a Rumpler two-seater, which he shot down in flames. The enemy aircraft turned completely over, diving into the mist with black smoke and flames coming from its fuselage.

March 8th.

The weather was fine all day, but the visibility was indifferent.

Twenty-two reconnaissances were carried out by Brigades and six successful long-distance photographic flights by the 9th Wing.

Fifty-four hostile batteries were successfully engaged for destruction with aeroplane observation and six neutralized; 14 gun-pits were destroyed, 22 damaged, 24 explosions and 12 fires caused. Thirty-six zone calls were sent down.

Two thousand five hundred and thirty-four photographs were taken and 9½ tons of bombs dropped as follows :—

Night, 7th–8th.

9th Brigade.—No. 58 Squadron dropped one hundred and eleven 25-lb. bombs on Cambrai railway sidings; No. 101 Squadron dropped thirty 112-lb. and sixty-eight 25-lb. bombs on Busigny railway sidings, and one hundred and forty 25-lb. bombs were dropped on billets and active hostile batteries.

By Day.

1st Brigade.—Three hundred and seventy-five photographs. No. 18 Squadron dropped ten 112-lb. and twenty-two 25-lb. bombs on Salome, and 1st Wing dropped sixty-nine 25-lb. bombs.

2nd Brigade.—Five hundred and forty-nine photographs. No. 57 Squadron dropped two 230-lb. and four 112-lb. bombs on Menin, and 2nd Wing dropped thirty 25-lb. bombs.

3rd Brigade.—Eight hundred photographs were taken, and eighty-five 25-lb. bombs dropped.

5th Brigade.—Six hundred and fifty-four photographs. Naval Squadron No. 5 dropped forty-seven 25-lb. bombs on Guise railway sidings; 15th Wing dropped ninety-five 25-lb. bombs, and No. 48 Squadron dropped sixteen 25-lb. bombs.

9th Wing.—One hundred and fifty-six photographs. No. 27 Squadron dropped thirty-two 25-lb. bombs on Busigny railway station.

Enemy Aircraft.—Enemy aircraft were active but not abnormal, and a considerable amount of fighting took place. One hostile machine was brought down by anti-aircraft fire in the Third Army area.

Captain D. Flockart, 4th Squadron, A.F.C., whilst on offensive patrol, attacked the rear machine of two Albatross Scouts into which he fired a burst at 25 yards range. The enemy aircraft burst into flames and turning on its back started spinning; the wings were observed to fall off about 1,000 feet lower down.

Flight Lieutenant A. B. Ellwood, with Flight Sub-Lieuts. K. D. MacLeod and C. S. Devereux, Naval Squadron No. 3, attacked an enemy aircraft two-seater which immediately dived eastwards. They followed, firing at about 100 yards range; the enemy aircraft continued to dive, and a large trail of yellow smoke was observed to come from it. It was last seen on the ground on fire near Tortequesne.

Captain H. W. Woollett, No. 43 Squadron, shot down an Albatross Scout in flames.

Second Lieutenants H. F. Davison and J. L. Morgan, No. 22 Squadron, shot down an enemy aircraft scout, and the wing of the enemy machine was seen to break off in the air.

Sergeants E. J. Elton and S. Belding, No. 22 Squadron, shot down an Albatross Scout which crashed south-west of Lille.

Captain O. C. Bryson, No. 19 Squadron, attacked an Albatross Scout. The wings of this enemy aircraft folded back and the machine went down in a spin.

Captain E. R. Tempest, No. 64 Squadron, while leading his patrol, shot down an enemy aircraft scout, which was confirmed by anti-aircraft as crashed.

Lieutenant A. K. Cowper, No. 24 Squadron, attacked the leader of three enemy aircraft and fired 100 rounds at close range. The enemy aircraft dived, side-slipping right to the ground and was seen to crash.

Second Lieut. H. H. Hartley and Lieut. J. H. Robertson, No. 48 Squadron, attacked an enemy machine, which was firing at them from below. The enemy aircraft fell slowly spinning to the ground, and was observed to crash.

Captain G. H. McElroy, No. 24 Squadron, got on the tail of an enemy aircraft triplane, and fired bursts from both guns at very close range; pieces were seen to fall from the enemy aircraft, which was seen to crash in a field.

Lieutenant H. D. Barton, No. 24 Squadron, saw a triplane attack an S.E. He opened fire at 20 yards; the enemy aircraft did a half-stall and went vertically down, with black smoke issuing. This machine was observed 3,000 feet below still going down vertically, with large columns of smoke coming from it.

Enemy machines were driven down out of control by the following:—

Lieutenant G. Noland, 4th Squadron, A.F.C.; Captain O. Horsley, No. 40 Squadron; Second Lieuts. H. F. Davison and J. L. Morgan, No. 22 Squadron (two) (the pilot of one of the hostile machines was seen to fall out of the cockpit on to the centre section); Second Lieut. L. J. Sweeney and Lieutenant H. G. Burgess, No. 4 Squadron; Second Lieut. A. L. Paxton, 2nd Squadron, A.F.C.; Lieutenant L. H. Holden, 2nd Squadron, A.F.C.; Captain P. Huskinson, No. 19 Squadron; Captain F. G. Quigley, No. 70 Squadron; Second Lieut. G. R. Howsam, No. 70 Squadron; Captain J. A. Slater, No. 64 Squadron; Second Lieut. R. H. Topliss, No. 64 Squadron; Second Lieut. T. Rose, No. 64 Squadron; Captain G. E. Thomson, No. 46 Squadron; Lieutenant M. E. Mealing, No. 56 Squadron; Second Lieut. L. A. Payne and Lieutenant G. H. H. Scutt, No. 48 Squadron; Second Lieuts. E. S. Smethan-Jones and G. Dixon, No. 48 Squadron; Lieutenant W. A. McMichael and E. G. Humphrey, No. 48 Squadron; Second Lieut. H. H. Hartley and Lieut. J. H. Robertson, No. 48 Squadron; Lieut. J. E. Drummond and Second Lieut. N. Sillars, No. 48 Squadron; Captain G. E. McElroy, No. 24 Squadron; Captain N. C. Millman and Second Lieut. H. A. Cooper, No. 48 Squadron;

Second Lieut. J. Gray and Lieutenant J. A. McGinnis, No. 27 Squadron.

Miscellaneous.—No. 38 Balloon was shot down by enemy aircraft and destroyed. Both observers parachuted successfully.

March 9th.

The weather was fine all day but the visibility indifferent.

Thirty-two reconnaissances were carried out by brigades, and five successful long-distance photographic flights by the 9th Wing.

Forty-one hostile batteries were successfully engaged for destruction with aeroplane observation and five neutralised; seven gun-pits were destroyed, 11 damaged, 19 explosions, and four fires caused. Twenty-six zone calls were sent down.

On the 8th instant, balloons of the 2nd Brigade registered three targets, one of which was a hostile battery.

Two thousand and ninety-seven photographs were taken, and nine tons of bombs dropped as follows:—

Night, 8th–9th.

9th Brigade.—No. 58 Squadron dropped nine 25-lb. bombs on Courtrai railway station, and No. 101 Squadron dropped twenty-four 112-lb. and forty-eight 25-lb. bombs on the ammunition dump and station at Fresnoy-le-Grand, where a fire was caused as the result of three direct hits.

By Day.

1st Brigade.—Three hundred and fifty photographs. No. 18 Squadron dropped seventeen 112-lb. and forty 25-lb. bombs on dumps and billets, and 1st Wing dropped thirty-six 25-lb. bombs.

2nd Brigade.—Four hundred and ninety-eight photographs. No. 57 Squadron dropped five 112-lb. bombs; 11th Wing dropped forty-nine 25-lb. bombs, and 2nd Wing dropped fifty-eight 25-lb. bombs.

3rd Brigade.—Four hundred and seventy-four photographs. Seventy-seven 25-lb. bombs.

5th Brigade.—Six hundred and forty-eight photographs. 15th Wing dropped one hundred and six 25-lb. bombs; Naval Squadron No. 5 dropped sixty-five 25-lb. bombs on Mont d'Origny Aerodrome, and Nos. 23, 54, and 48 Squadrons dropped eighty-eight 25-lb. bombs on Bertry, Escaufort, and Busigny Aerodromes.

No. 9 Wing.—One hundred and twenty-seven photographs. No. 27 Squadron dropped fifty-seven 25-lb. bombs on Bohain railway station.

An attack on three hostile aerodromes was made by 61 machines of the 22nd Wing, 88 bombs being dropped. Squadrons were led by their Squadron Commanders, and the whole watched from above by the Wing Commander.

No. 23 Squadron covered by No. 24 Squadron dropped 14 bombs from a low altitude on Bertry Aerodrome. Four direct hits were obtained on hangars, and five bombs fell amongst machines which were out on the aerodrome. They flew back to the lines at a height of 100 feet, attacking horse transport on the roads, horses in an orchard (causing a stampede), a company of infantry, a group of officers on horses — two of whom were seen to fall off, and a balloon which was drawn down emitting smoke.

Busigny and Escaufort Aerodromes were attacked by machines of Nos. 48 and 54 Squadrons, covered by No. 84 Squadron. No. 54 Squadron dropped 22 bombs from a height of 500 feet, five direct hits being obtained on the hangars. Machines returned at a low height, firing on horse transport (causing a stampede), at troops at drill, cavalry and trains. Pilots of No. 48 Squadron dropped thirty-two 25-lb. bombs from 400 feet, obtaining direct hits on hangars, two of which were set on fire. They returned flying at a low altitude and engaged ground targets *en route*.

8th Brigade.—Eleven machines of No. 55 Squadron started off at midday to bomb Mainz in Germany—a distance of 132 miles from their aerodrome—and dropped two 230-lb., sixteen 112-lb., and seven 40-lb. bombs from a height of 13,000 feet. Bursts were seen on the barracks, railway sidings, and factories, and a large fire was started. Thirty-four photographs were taken. All machines returned.

One machine of No. 55 Squadron carried out a successful photographic reconnaissance of the railways south of Metz, and of hostile aerodromes.

Enemy Aircraft.—Enemy aircraft activity was great on the front of the 2nd Brigade, and about normal on the other brigade fronts.

Captain J. H. Tudhope, No. 40 Squadron, shot down an Albatross Scout, which was seen to crash and burst into flames.

Flight Lieut. J. A. Glen and Flight Sub-Lieut. Adam, Naval Squadron No. 3, attacked an enemy aircraft two-seater which they shot down in flames.

Second Lieut. G. R. Howsam, No. 70 Squadron, attacked one of five Albatross Scouts which he shot down, the enemy aircraft being observed to go to the ground.

Captain F. G. Quigley, No. 70 Squadron, attacked an Albatross Scout, firing three bursts at close range, the enemy aircraft went down in a steep spiral and on fire. He then engaged an Albatross two-seater which he shot down, the enemy aircraft crashing in a field.

Captain G. M. Cox, No. 65 Squadron, attacked a Fokker triplane, which stalled and went down in a spin with one of its planes folded up.

Captain P. Huskinson, No. 19 Squadron, shot down a Pfalz, which crashed and burst into flames S.E. of Wervicq.

Captain H. A. Hamersley, No. 60 Squadron, shot down an enemy aircraft scout out of control. When at about 2,000 feet from the ground the wings fell off and the enemy aircraft crashed near Dadizeele.

Captain J. F. Morris, Lieutenant J. F. N. Macrae and Second Lieut. G. W. R. Poisley, No. 23 Squadron, all fired bursts at an enemy aircraft, which they drove down, the enemy aircraft crashing in a field near Walincourt.

Lieutenant H. V. Puckridge, No. 19 Squadron, attacked an enemy aircraft, which spun down for several thousand feet, and was eventually observed to burst into flames by another pilot of the same squadron.

Enemy machines were shot down out of control by the following :—

Second Lieut. W. L. Harrison, No. 40 Squadron; Second Lieut. H. S. Wolff, No. 40 Squadron; Second Lieut. W. E. Warden, No. 40 Squadron; Second Lieut. J. W. Wallwork, No. 40 Squadron (two); Captain R. J. Tipton, No. 40 Squadron; Lieutenant R. E. Bion, No. 40 Squadron; Second Lieut. G. A. Lingham, No. 43 Squadron; Second Lieut. H. Daniel, No. 43 Squadron; Lieutenant A. G. Clark, No. 2 Squadron, A.F.C.; Captain R. W. Howard, No. 2 Squadron, A.F.C.; Second Lieut. L. H. T. Capel and Corporal M. B. Mather, No. 20 Squadron (two); Second Lieut. G. R. Howsam, No. 70 Squadron; Second Lient. H. L. Whiteside, No. 70 Squadron; Second Lieuts. D. G. Cooke and J. J. Scaramanga, No. 20 Squadron; Lieut. J. A. Duncan, No. 60 Squadron; Captain H. D. Crompton, No. 60 Squadron; Second Lieut. E. J. Blyth, No. 19 Squadron; Second Lieut. J. S. Griffith, No. 60 Squadron; Captain F. G. Quigley, No. 70 Squadron (two); Second Lieut. G. Brenridge, No. 65 Squadron; Lieutenant H. W. Soulby, No. 70 Squadron; Second Lieut. D. C. M. Brooks and Lieutenant H. R. Kincaid, No. 11 Squadron; Sergeants D. W. Beard and H. W. Scammell, No. 11 Squadron; Second Lieuts. W. F. Mayoss and W. Haddow, No. 15 Squadron; Flight Sub-Lieut. C. E. Siedle and Acting Gunner L. Middleton, Naval Squadron, No. 5; Captain G. E. H. McElroy, No. 24 Squadron; Lieutenant H. V. L. Tubbs, No. 24 Squadron; Second Lieuts. J. Baird and F. Keith, No. 48 Squadron; Second Lieut. H. H. Hartley and Lieut. J. H. Robertson, No. 48 Squadron; Captain N. C. Millman and Second Lieut. H. A. Cooper, No. 48 Squadron.

Miscellaneous.—Captain H. J. Hamilton, No. 1 Squadron, attacked and destroyed a hostile balloon.

March 10*th.*

The weather was fine all day, but the visibility was very bad.

Twenty reconnaissances were carried out by brigades, and six photographic reconnaissances by the 9th Wing.

Thirty-two hostile batteries were successfully engaged for destruction with aeroplane observation and six neutralised; three gun-pits were destroyed, 10 damaged, 12 explosions and five fires caused. Thirty-four zone calls were sent down.

On the 9th instant three targets were registered by balloons of the 2nd Brigade.

One thousand five hundred and thirty-three photographs were taken and $5\frac{1}{2}$ tons of bombs dropped as follows:—

1st Brigade.—Four and forty-eight photographs. No. 18 Squadron dropped six 112-lb. and forty-two 25-lb. bombs on ammunition dumps and railway stations; 1st Wing dropped fifty-four 25-lb. bombs, and No. 57 Squadron dropped eleven 112-lb. bombs on Menin, Roulers, and Ledeghem.

2nd Brigade.—One hundred and eighty-three photographs. 2nd Wing dropped twenty-four 25-lb. bombs and 11th Wing dropped four 25-lb. bombs.

3rd Brigade.—Five hundred and eighty-four photographs were taken and sixty-eight 25-lb. bombs dropped.

5th Brigade.—One hundred and twenty-six photographs. 15th Wing dropped fifty-four 25-lb. bombs, No. 48 Squadron dropped thirty-two 25-lb. bombs, and Naval Squadron No. 5 dropped forty-eight 25-lb. bombs on Premont ammunition dump.

9th Wing.—One hundred and ninety-two photographs. No. 25 Squadron dropped ten 112-lb. bombs on Cambrai railway station, and No. 27 Squadron dropped fifty-two 25-lb. bombs on Solesmes railway station.

8th Brigade.—Eleven machines of No. 55 Squadron attacked, in broad daylight, the Daimler Works at Stuttgart in Germany (150 miles from their aerodrome). Two 230-lb., sixteen 112-lb., and seven 40-lb. phosphorus bombs were dropped from a height of 12,500 feet, and bursts were seen on the railway station and the works alongside it, three on a munition factory south-east of the town, one near the gasworks, and several on the Daimler Works. A stationary train in the station was hit and set on fire. Eighteen plates were exposed. The formation was attacked by three enemy aircraft, but the enemy aircraft withdrew on being attacked. All our machines returned with the exception of one, which evidently had engine trouble on the homeward journey, just before crossing the lines, as the pilot fired a green light and went down under control.

Enemy Aircraft.—Enemy aircraft activity was very slight owing to the mist. In addition to the enemy machines brought down by our aeroplanes, one low-flying enemy aircraft was brought down by the infantry.

Second Lieut. D. A. Stewart and Sergeant C. Beardmore, No. 18 Squadron, whilst on a bomb raid, were attacked by several formations of enemy aircraft scouts. They shot one down out of control, which was reported by anti-aircraft to have crashed.

Flight Lieut. A. T. Whealy, Naval Squadron No. 3, shot down an enemy aircraft scout, which was observed by other pilots of the squadron to crash.

Second Lieut. D. R. MacLaren, No. 46 Squadron, shot down an enemy aircraft scout, the tail of which was seen to fall to pieces.

Second Lieut. E. A. Clear, No. 84 Squadron, shot down an enemy aircraft two-seater, which crashed in a field near Estrees.

Captain M. Le Blanc-Smith, No. 73 Squadron, shot down a Fokker triplane, which is reported by another pilot of the same squadron to have crashed.

Captains G. F. Hughes and H. Claye, No. 62 Squadron, shot down an Albatross Scout, which fell in flames.

Enemy machines were shot down out of control by the following:—Captain A. G. Waller and Sergeant M. V. Kilroy, No. 18 Squadron; Second Lieut. G. Darvill and Sergeant A. Pollard, No. 18 Squadron; Captain R. W. Howard, No. 2 Squadron, A.F.C.; Flight Sub-Lieut. A. B. Ellwood, Naval Squadron No. 3; Flight Sub-Lieut. F. J. S. Britnell, Naval Squadron No. 3; Flight Lieut. W. H. Chisam, Naval Squadron No. 3; Captain R. S. C. McClintock, No. 64 Squadron; Second Lieut. W. H. Brown, No. 84 Squadron; Second Lieut. D. Gardiner, No. 80 Squadron; Captain St. C. C. Taylor, No. 80 Squadron (two); Lieutenants C. W. Robinson and C. D. Wells, No. 62 Squadron (two); Captains G. F. Hughes and H. Claye. No. 62 Squadron; Second Lieut. C. Allen and Lieutenant J. M. Hay, No. 62 Squadron; Second Lieut. M. H. Cleary and Lieutenant N. T. Watson, No. 62 Squadron.

Miscellaneous.—Second Lieut. F. P. Magoun, No. 1 Squadron, attacked a hostile balloon which went down in a deflated condition.

Captain G. B. Moore, Lieutenant H. A. Rigby and Second Lieut. A. E. Sweeting, No. 1 Squadron, all attacked a hostile balloon which crumpled up and went down deflated, the observer jumping out.

Second Lieut. J. C. Bateman, No. 1 Squadron, attacked a hostile balloon which was last seen disappearing below the clouds in a very deflated condition. Shortly afterwards smoke was seen issuing from the locality where the balloon went down.

March 11th.

The fine weather continued, but the visibility was again bad.

During the night of the 10th–11th instant, reconnaissances were carried out by a machine of No. 2 Squadron and one of No. 58 Squadron.

On the 11th, 20 reconnaissances were carried out by Brigades and six successful photographic reconnaissances by the 9th Wing.

Seventeen hostile batteries were successfully engaged for destruction with aeroplane observation and three neutralised. Eight zone calls were sent down. Three gun-pits were destroyed, 13 damaged, 19 explosions and two fires caused.

One thousand eight hundred plates were exposed and eight tons of bombs dropped as follows :—

1st Brigade. — Two hundred and fifty-five photographs. Twenty-two 112-lb and thirty-four 25-lb. bombs on billets and dumps by No. 18 Squadron, and sixty-two 25-lb. bombs by the 1st Wing.

2nd Brigade.—Two hundred and twenty-eight photographs. No. 57 Squadron dropped thirteen 112-lb. bombs on Mouscron, Ledeghem and Menin ; 2nd Wing dropped twenty-two 25-lb. bombs, and 11th Wing dropped sixty-five 25-lb. bombs.

3rd Brigade.—Six hundred and sixteen photographs. No. 49 Squadron dropped nine 112-lb. bombs on Dury Dump, and sixty-two 25-lb. bombs were dropped on various objectives.

5th Brigade.—Five hundred and twenty-one photographs. Naval Squadron No. 5 dropped fifty-nine 25-lb. bombs on Elincourt Ammunition Dump. No. 48 Squadron dropped twenty-two 25-lb. bombs, and 15th Wing dropped forty-four 25-lb. bombs.

9th Wing.—One hundred and eighty photographs. No. 25 Squadron dropped seven 112-lb. and forty 25-lb. bombs on Aulnoye Station and Dump, and No. 27 Squadron dropped four 112-lb. and forty 25-lb. bombs on Beaudignies Ammunition Dump (7 miles south of Valenciennes).

Enemy Aircraft.—Enemy aircraft were very active in the vicinity of Lens and Lille.

Sergeant E. J. Elton and Second Lieut. G. S. L. Hayward, No. 22 Squadron, in a general engagement with enemy aircraft scouts, shot down one which was seen to crash at Faches.

Flight-Commander F. C. Armstrong, Naval Squadron No. 3, shot down an Albatross Scout, the tail of the enemy aircraft falling off in the air.

Second Lieut W. L. Harrison, No. 40 Squadron, shot down an enemy aircraft two-seater, which was being fired at by our anti-aircraft guns. The enemy aircraft crashed near the canal, west of La Bassée.

Captain J. A. Slater, No. 64 Squadron, attacked an Albatross Scout which he shot down in flames.

Second Lieuts. F. H. Davies and E. M. Cleland, No. 13 Squadron, while on artillery patrol, were attacked by five Albatross Scouts, one of which they shot down and observed to crash near Sailly.

Captain F. E. Brown and Lieutenant G. O. Johnson, both of No. 84 Squadron, attacked an enemy aircraft scout which finally crashed into the ground near Lavergies.

Second Lieut. E. R. Varley, No. 23 Squadron, attacked one of two enemy aircraft and fired a good burst at close quarters with both guns. The enemy aircraft rolled over on its back, and was seen to crash. (Confirmed by anti-aircraft.)

Second Lieut. S. W. Symons and Sergeant W. N. Holmes, No. 62 Squadron, brought down an enemy aircraft triplane, which burst into flames near the ground.

Second Lieut. G. S. Hodson, No. 73 Squadron, attacked an enemy aircraft triplane, which he shot down, the wings of the enemy machine finally breaking off in the air.

Captain T. S. Sharpe, No. 73 Squadron, attacked an enemy aircraft triplane at very close range. The enemy machine went down out of control, and was seen to crash near Hancourt.

Enemy machines were shot down out of control by the following:—Lieutenant L. H. Holden, No. 2 Squadron, A.F.C.; Captain H. H. Balfour, No. 43 Squadron; Captain H. W. Woollett, No. 43 Squadron; Captain J. L. Trollope, No. 43 Squadron; Second Lieut. R. J. Owen, No. 43 Squadron; Sergeant E. J. Elton and Second Lieut. G. S. L. Hayward, No. 22 Squadron; Second Lieut. S. H. Wallage and Sergeant J. H. Jones, No. 22 Squadron, two; Captain J. A. Slater, No. 64 Squadron; Captain D. J. Bell, No. 3 Squadron; Captain D. H. Oliver and Second Lieut. W. H. Eastoe, No. 59 Squadron; Captain A. J. Brown, Second Lieut. P. Nolan, Second Lieut. R. T. Mark, Second Lieut. H. T. Richardson, and Second Lieut. E. W. Lindeberg drove down one enemy aircraft out of control; Second Lieut. E. J. Smetham-Jones and Lieutenant A. C. Cooper, No. 48 Squadron; Second Lieut. H. H. Hartley and Lieutenant J. H. Robertson, No. 48 Squadron; Captain H. F. S. Drewitt, No. 23 Squadron; Captains G. F. Hughes and H. Claye, No. 62 Squadron; Second Lieut. R. G. Lawson, No. 73 Squadron; Second Lieut. W. a'B. Probart, No. 73 Squadron.

Miscellaneous.—Captain F. G. Quigley, No. 70 Squadron, attacked an enemy balloon and fired two long bursts into it, and smoke was observed coming out of its side. Second Lieut. A. Koch, Lieutenant K. A. Seth-Smith, and Second Lieut. W. M. Carlaw, of the same squadron, then attacked it and the balloon went down in flames. Two men were seen in the basket when the balloon was set on fire.

Corrections.—R.F.C. Communiqué for the period February 26th to March 4th inclusive, *should* be numbered 129 *not* 128.

Captain Carter and Captain Hyde, who carried out a contact patrol on March 2nd, belong to No. 4A Squadron, and not as mentioned in the last number of this Communiqué.

L. A. K. BUTT, Captain,
Staff Officer.

Headquarters,
Royal Flying Corps,
13th March 1918.

ROYAL FLYING CORPS COMMUNIQUÉ.—No. 131.

During the period under review (12th March to 18th March, inclusive) we have claimed officially 98 enemy aircraft brought down and 46 enemy aircraft driven down out of control. Approximately $95\frac{1}{4}$ tons of bombs were dropped, 10,441 photographs taken, and 163,567 rounds fired at ground targets. Thirty-six of our machines are missing.

March 12th.

The weather was fine, and there was a considerable improvement in the visibility.

A machine of No. 2 Squadron carried out a reconnaissance on the night of the 11th–12th.

Twenty-seven reconnaissances were carried out by brigades, and two photographic reconnaissances by the 9th Wing.

Eighty-six hostile batteries were successfully engaged for destruction with aeroplane observation, and seven neutralised; 13 gun-pits were destroyed, 29 damaged, 50 explosions and 32 fires caused. Forty-seven zone calls were sent down.

On the 11th instant, balloons of the 2nd Brigade registered two targets.

Two thousand one hundred and thirty-four photographs were taken and $15\frac{1}{2}$ tons of bombs dropped as follows :—

Night, 11th–12th.

5th Brigade.—No. 101 Squadron dropped one hundred and eighty 25-lb. and fifteen 15-lb. bombs on the ammunition dumps at Brancourt-le-Grand.

By Day, 12th.

1st Brigade.—Three hundred and eighty-eight photographs. No. 18 Squadron dropped twenty-six 112-lb. and fifty-four 25-lb. bombs on Haubourdin, and two 112-lb. and four 25-lb. bombs on billets at Sallaumines and Moisnil. Fifty-four 25-lb. bombs were dropped on various objectives.

2nd Brigade.—Two hundred and seventy-five photographs. No. 57 Squadron dropped thirteen 112-lb. bombs on Tourcoing,

Ledeghem, and Wervicq; 2nd Wing dropped seventy-seven 25-lb. bombs, and 11th Wing dropped ninety-nine 25-lb. bombs.

3rd Brigade.—Five hundred and twenty-one photographs. No. 49 Squadron dropped fourteen 112-lb. and fifteen 25-lb. bombs on Dury, and one hundred 25-lb. bombs were dropped on various targets.

5th Brigade.—Eight hundred and twenty photographs. 15th Wing dropped one hundred and twenty-two 25-lb. bombs; Naval Squadron No. 5 dropped ninety-nine 25-lb. bombs on Etreux ammunition dump, and No. 48 Squadron dropped sixteen 25-lb. bombs.

9th Wing.—One hundred and thirty photographs. No. 25 Squadron dropped nine 112-lb. and thirty 25-lb. bombs on Mons railway sidings, and No. 27 Squadron dropped eight 112-lb. and thirty-two 25-lb. bombs on Bavai railway junction.

8th Brigade.—No. 55 Squadron carried out a long distance bomb raid, this being the third within the last four days. Nine machines dropped one 230-lb., ten 112-lb., twenty-eight 25-lb., and ten 40-lb. bombs on the railway station, factories, and barracks at Coblenz (a distance of 130 miles). Two fires were started, and bursts were seen on the objective. A very large explosion was caused, a building in the south-west corner of the town being hit. Seventy-two plates were exposed. All machines returned.

Enemy Aircraft. — Enemy aircraft were active, and a considerable amount of fighting took place.

Lieutenant L. H. Holden, No. 2 Squadron, A.F.C., fired a burst of about 50 rounds at one enemy aircraft, which immediately fell out of control, and is reported by "A" Battery, Anti-Aircraft to have gone down in flames near Wingles.

Lieutenant R. W. Mackenzie, No. 2 Squadron, A.F.C., on the same patrol dived on an enemy aircraft two-seater; smoke was seen issuing from the enemy machine which fell out of control and was reported by "A" Battery, Anti-Aircraft, to go down in flames.

Captain H. H. Balfour, No. 43 Squadron, attacked a two-seater; the observer was seen to collapse in the cock-pit. After Captain Balfour had fired several more bursts the enemy aircraft suddenly dived vertically, then spun slowly with clouds of black smoke coming out of the fuselage, finally catching fire.

Lieutenant J. W. Aldred, No. 70 Squadron, shot down an enemy aircraft scout completely out of control; the enemy aircraft was seen to crash by another pilot of the patrol.

Captain F. G. Quigley, No 70 Squadron, fired three bursts into one of four enemy aircraft scouts. The enemy aircraft immediately dived, leaving a trail of blue smoke. This machine was shortly afterwards seen smoking on the ground near Dadizeele. Captain Quigley shot down another enemy aircraft scout which burst into flames at about 4,000 feet.

Second Lieut. H. L. Whiteside, No. 70 Squadron, attacked an Albatross Scout and followed it down to a height of 5,000 feet, the enemy aircraft being finally seen to crash into the ground.

Lieutenants H. W. Sellars and C. C. Robson, No. 11 Squadron, while returning from a reconnaissance, attacked an Albatross two-seater which fell in flames in our lines near Doignies.

Second Lieuts. J. P. Seabrook and C. Wrigglesworth, No. 11 Squadron, whilst on offensive patrol, engaged one of a large number of enemy scouts which they shot down, the enemy aircraft crashing in a field south-east of Cambrai.

Captain A. P. Maclean and Lieutenant F. H. Cantlon, No. 11 Squadron, engaged one enemy aircraft with their rear gun at 100 yards range; the enemy aircraft burst into flames.

Lieutenant M. E. Mealing, No. 56 Squadron, attacked an enemy aircraft two-seater over Ribecourt. He fired a good burst from both guns at close range; the enemy aircraft dived steeply and finally hit the ground in our lines.

Captain J. F. Morris, No. 43 Squadron, was attacked by five enemy aircraft. He dived on the nearest and fired about 150 rounds at close range; the enemy aircraft dived away and was seen to crash by A/177 Battery, R.F.A.

Captain H. F. S. Drewitt, No. 23 Squadron, shot down an enemy aircraft scout which was attacking an S.E. 5. The enemy aircraft eventually crashed near the canal just east of Bellenglise.

Second Lieut. N. Roberts and Corporal W. Lawder, No. 48 Squadron, shot down a Fokker triplane which was observed to crash in a wood at St. Claude, north-north-east of St. Quentin.

Second Lieuts. P. A. MacDougall and W. Selwyn, both of No. 24 Squadron, each attacked an enemy aircraft two-seater which dived away east. It was followed by Second Lieut. MacDougall who shot it down.

Captain A. J. Brown, No. 24 Squadron, got in a burst of 50 rounds at close range at an enemy aircraft which went down vertically and crashed near the enemy's front lines.

Captain T. E. Withington, No. 65 Squadron, and Major J. A. Cunningham, of the same squadron, each shot down an Albatross Scout completely out of control, but were unable to observe the result owing to the presence of other enemy scouts. These two machines were reported by pilots of Naval Squadron No. 23 to have been shot down east of Ypres.

Enemy machines were shot down out of control by the following:—Second Lieut. A McN. Denovan, No. 1 Squadron; Flight Commander L. Rochford, Naval Squadron No. 3; Second

Lieut. A. K. Lomax, No. 43 Squadron; Captain W. B. Tunbridge, 4th Squadron, A.F.C.; Captain H. J. Hamilton, No. 1 Squadron, and Second Lieut. P. J. Clayson, of the same squadron, one; Captain F. G. Quigley, No. 70 Squadron, Lieutenant K. A. Seth-Smith, No. 70 Squadron; Second Lieut. J. Todd, No. 70 Squadron; Second Lieut. W. M. Carlaw, No. 70 Squadron; Second Lieut. J. S. Chick and Lieutenant P. Douglas, No. 11 Squadron, five; Captain A. P. Maclean and Lieutenant F. H. Cantlon, No. 11 Squadron; Captain C. C. Haynes and Lieutenant J. L. Smith, No. 11 Squadron; Captain G. E. Thomson, No. 46 Squadron; Captain A. J. Brown, No. 24 Squadron, two; Second Lieut. H. T. Richardson, No. 24 Squadron; Captain L. D. Baker, No. 23 Squadron, Second Lieut. C. A. Hore and Corporal J. Cruickshank, No. 48 Squadron, two; Flight Commander A. M. Shook, Naval Squadron No. 4; Lieutenant G. E. Gibbons and Lieutenant S. A. W. Knights, No. 62 Squadron; Second Lieut. P. R. Hampton and Second Lieut. L. Lane, No. 62 Squadron.

During the night of the 11th–12th instant, a "Freidrichshafen" landed in our lines in the Third Army area, the four occupants being taken prisoners.

Miscellaneous.—Second Lieut. F. J. Williams, Lieutenant W. E. Durant, and Second Lieut. H. R. Uttley, No. 29 Squadron, made a combined attack on an enemy balloon. After many bursts had been fired into it the balloon was seen to go adrift in a south-west direction over our lines.

March 13th.

On the 13th the weather was fine and the visibility fair.

Thirty-one reconnaissances were carried out by day by brigades, and three photographic flights by the 9th Wing. Ten night reconnaissances were carried out by brigades.

Fifty-nine hostile batteries were successfully engaged for destruction, 12 neutralised; nine gun-pits were destroyed, 29 damaged, 28 explosions and 16 fires caused. Forty-seven zone calls were sent down.

On the 12th instant balloons of the 2nd Brigade registered 18 targets, eight of which were hostile batteries, and balloons of the 5th Brigade registered 12 targets.

One thousand five hundred and forty-seven photographs were taken and 17 tons of bombs dropped as follows :—

Night, 12th–13th.

1st Brigade.—No. 2 Squadron dropped eight 25-lb. bombs on Marquillies dump.

9th Brigade.—No. 58 Squadron dropped one hundred and seventeen 25-lb. bombs on rest billets opposite the front of the First Army. A direct hit was obtained on a bridge over the canal south-west of Haubourdin.

No. 102 Squadron dropped five hundred and fifty-two 25-lb. bombs on billets opposite the front of the Third Army.

Day, 13th.

1st Brigade.— One hundred and ninety-one photographs. Fourteen 112-lb. and sixteen 25-lb. bombs were dropped on Pont-à-Vendin, Wavrin, and Fournes by No. 18 Squadron, and sixty-four 25-lb. bombs were dropped by machines of the 1st Wing.

2nd Brigade.—Three hundred and ninety-four photographs. No. 57 Squadron dropped ten 112-lb. bombs on Courtrai railway sidings, and six 112-lb. and twenty-two 25-lb. bombs on Ledeghem, Staden, and Wervicq. Seventy-two 25-lb. bombs were dropped by 11th Wing and forty-three 25-lb. by 2nd Wing.

3rd Brigade.—Four hundred and fifty-two photographs. No. 49 Squadron dropped twelve 112-lb. and sixteen 25-lb. bombs on Cantin. Eighty-eight 25-lb. bombs were dropped on miscellaneous targets.

5th Brigade.—Three hundred and seventy-six photographs. Sixty-eight 25-lb. bombs were dropped on Étreux Aerodrome and twelve 25-lb. bombs on huts east of St. Quentin by Naval Squadron No. 5; one hundred and fifty-four 25-lb. bombs were dropped by the 15th Wing, and thirty-one 25-lb. bombs by No. 48 Squadron.

9th Wing.—One hundred and thirty photographs. Six 112-lb. and sixteen 25-lb. bombs were dropped on Denain railway station by No. 25 Squadron, and seven 112-lb. and twenty-four 25-lb. bombs on the same objective by No. 27 Squadron.

8th Brigade.—On the afternoon of the 13th instant, nine machines of No. 55 Squadron left to bomb the railway station and barracks at Freiburg (Germany). Eight machines reached the objective and dropped two 230-lb., twelve 112-lb., two 40-lb., and four 25-lb. bombs from 14,000 feet. Bursts were seen round the power station, in the railway station, and on the railway north of the town. Forty-one photographs were taken. After the formation dropped the bombs it was attacked by 16 hostile machines. Three of our machines are missing.

A machine of the same squadron carried out a photographic reconnaissance, exposing 29 plates.

Enemy Aircraft.—Enemy aircraft were active all day on all the Army fronts, large formations being encountered east of Cambrai and east of La Bassée.

Captain F. E. Brown, No. 84 Squadron, whilst on patrol, attacked an enemy aircraft scout which he shot down, and it was seen to crash on Homblieres village.

Second Lieut. P. K. Hobson, No. 84 Squadron, on the same patrol, attacked an enemy aircraft scout which broke to pieces in the air, the top and bottom left hand planes breaking away.

Captain D. J. Bell, No. 3 Squadron, attacked an Albatross two-seater at very close range. The left plane of the enemy aircraft came off, and the wreckage of the machine crashed near Villers.

A patrol of No. 1 Squadron attacked an enemy aircraft scout which they shot down completely out of control. This machine was confirmed as crashed by signals, 49th Division. The following officers of No. 1 Squadron took part in the combat :— Captain W. D. Patrick, Captain C. B. Moore, Captain H. J. Hamilton, Second Lieut. A. Hollis, Lieutenant H. Rigby.

Second Lieut. M. F. Peiler, No. 43 Squadron, dived on one of 12 enemy aircraft which were attacking three A.W.s. The enemy aircraft went down completely out of control and was seen to crash. Second Lieut. C. F. King, No. 43 Squadron, attacked one of two enemy aircraft scouts, which went down in a slow spin and finally crashed. Second Lieut. A. K. Lomax, No. 43 Squadron, attacked a third enemy aircraft, which he shot down south-east of Bois du Biez. Second Lieut. C. A. Lingham, of the same squadron, also attacked one of the enemy aircraft scouts, the enemy aircraft going down completely out of control and crashing near La Bassée. Captain H. W. Woollet, No. 43 Squadron, whilst leading his patrol, attacked two of the enemy aircraft scouts, one of which he shot to pieces, the machine collapsing in the air and falling to bits.

Lieutenant R. W. McKenzie, No. 2 Squadron, A.F.C. dived on an Albatross Scout which he shot down, the enemy aircraft crashing between Wingles and Meurchin.

Second Lieut. G. S. Hodson, No. 73 Squadron, dived on an enemy aircraft scout which went down completely out of control and crashed near Wambaix, south-east of Cambrai.

Captain A. H. Orlebar, No. 73 Squadron, dived on a Fokker triplane, opening fire at close range. The enemy aircraft instantly nose-dived, its top plane coming off.

Captain C. C. Taylor, No. 80 Squadron, attacked an enemy aircraft scout which was diving on another member of his patrol. Captain Taylor fired two long bursts, and the enemy aircraft went down, breaking up before it reached the ground.

Captain F. L. Luxmoore, No. 54 Squadron, attacked an enemy aircraft two-seater and fired several bursts at close range. This machine was also attacked by Second Lieut. J. R. Moore, of the same squadron, who got in several bursts. The enemy aircraft was seen diving down, and it eventually crashed.

Second Lieut. H. F. Davison and Second Lieut. J. L Morgan, No. 22 Squadron, opened fire on one enemy aircraft at about 100 yards range and continued firing until the enemy aircraft turned over and burst into flames. This machine eventually crashed near Annoeullin.

Lieutenant F. G. C. Weare and Second Lieut. S. J. Hunter, No. 22 Squadron, whilst on patrol, dived on one of seven hostile scouts and fired a burst at very close range. The enemy aircraft's ring wing came off, and it crashed between Seclin and Houplin.

Lieutenant W. L. Wells and Second Lieut. P. S. Williams, No. 22 Squadron, fired about 150 rounds into an enemy aircraft scout which turned over sideways and went down spinning, and continued until it crashed just west of Emmerin.

Sergeant E. J. Elton and Second Lieut. G. S. L. Hayward, No. 22 Squadron, attacked one enemy aircraft which they shot down out of control. They followed it down and, after they fired another burst, the enemy aircraft broke to pieces, the wings falling off. They then attacked another machine which crashed near Herrin.

Captain G. F. Hughes and Captain H. Clay, No. 62 Squadron, in a general engagement between his patrol and a very large formation of enemy aircraft scouts, shot down one enemy aircraft triplane, which was confirmed by other members of the patrol to have crashed. He then attacked one of three triplanes which were diving on his tail. This enemy aircraft went down vertically; the top plane was seen falling away in pieces. Captain Hughes was then attacked by at least six other Albatross scouts and triplanes. The observer's gun was out of action, and he found it impossible to keep the enemy aircraft off his tail, but he finally out-distanced all the enemy aircraft except one Fokker triplane which was handled remarkably well. Captain Hughes managed to eventually out-manœuvre this machine by diving with the engine full on, and succeeded in recrossing the lines at 3,000 feet.

Hostile machines were driven down out of control by the following:—Captain A. J. Brown, No. 24 Squadron, 1; Lieutenant R. T. Mark, No. 24 Squadron, 1; Second Lieut. A. K. Cowper, No. 24, 1; Second Lieut. C. L. Stubbs, No. 84 Squadron, 1; Lieutenants H. W. Sellars and C. C. Robson, No. 11 Squadron, 1; Second Lieut. J. S. Chick and Lieut. P. Douglas, No. 11 Squadron, 1; Captain C. C. Haynes and Lieutenant D. S. Allison, No. 11 Squadron, 1; Captain A. Roulstone and Lieutenant D. F. V. Page, No. 57 Squadron, 1; Second Lieuts. D. Latimer and J. J. Scaramanga, No. 20 Squadron, 1; Second Lieut. E. Lindup and Corporal F. Archer, No. 20 Squadron, 1; Captain G. M. Cox, No. 65 Squadron, 1; Lieutenant A. C. Dean, No. 43 Squadron, 1; Second Lieut. H. S. Montgomerie and Lieutenant W. H. Wardrope, No. 2 Squadron, 1; Second Lieut. M. F. Peiler, No. 43 Squadron, 1; Captain H. W. Woollett, No. 43 Squadron, 1; Captain A. H. Orlebar, No. 73 Squadron, 1; Lieutenant B. Balfour, No. 65 Squadron, 1; Second Lieut. G. L. Ormerod and Sergeant A. Burton, No. 22

Squadron, 1; Lieutenant A. R. James and Lieutenant J. M. Hay, No. 62 Squadron, 1; Second Lieut. W. E. Staton and Second Lieut. H. E. Merritt, No. 62 Squadron, 2; Captain S. W. Symons and Sergeant W. N. Holmes, No. 62 Squadron, 1.

Miscellaneous.—The work done by No. 102 Squadron on the night of the 12th-13th constitutes a record as regards the number of bombs dropped by one squadron in one night. All pilots, except three, made three trips, four pilots made four trips, and two made five trips. The first flight started at 1944 and the last machine landed at 0410. Over 11,600 rounds were fired at ground targets.

March 14th.

Low clouds and mist and rain in the morning prevented flying, though the weather improved a little in the afternoon.

Seventeen reconnaissances were carried out by brigades; 36 hostile batteries successfully engaged for destruction and one neutralised. Two gun-pits were destroyed, 21 damaged, 18 explosions and 14 fires caused; 38 zone calls were sent down.

On the 13th, 15 targets were registered by balloons, seven of which were hostile batteries, balloons of the 2nd Brigade registering 11 of the total number of targets. Four active hostile batteries were located.

Four hundred and thirty-six photographs were taken, and $4\frac{1}{2}$ tons of bombs dropped as follows:—

1st Brigade.—One hundred and twenty-six photographs. Eight 112-lb. and twenty-eight 25-lb. bombs were dropped on La Carnoy by No. 18 Squadron, and nineteen 25-lb. bombs were dropped by the 1st Wing.

2nd Brigade.—One hundred and twenty-six photographs. Three 25-lb. bombs were dropped on Perenchies by machines of the 11th Wing, and forty-seven 25-lb. bombs were dropped by those of the 2nd Wing.

3rd Brigade.—Twenty-six 25-lb. bombs were dropped on miscellaneous targets.

5th Brigade.—One hundred and eighty-four photographs. Naval Squadron No. 5 dropped sixty-two 25-lb. bombs on Etreux Aerodrome and six 25-lb. bombs on Manneruet Aerodrome. A direct hit was obtained on a hangar.

Fifty-six 25-lb. bombs were dropped by the 15th Wing and one hundred and ten 25-lb. bombs by the 22nd Wing.

An attack on Mont d'Origny Aerodrome was carried out by 19 machines of Nos. 24, 48, and 84 Squadrons; 42 bombs were dropped on and 4,760 rounds fired at hangars on the aerodrome and other favourable targets. No. 24 Squadron dropped 12 bombs from 100 to 2,000 feet. One hangar was set on fire, and at least two others were damaged; 100 rounds were fired into the nose of a Pfalz Scout which was seen protruding through a hangar; 910 rounds were fired into horse transport, troops, &c., on the way back.

No. 48 Squadron dropped 16 bombs from 1,000 to 2,000 feet on various targets and fired over 3,600 rounds at troops on the road, billets, and lorries, driving the troops to cover.

No. 84 Squadron missed the objective and got four bombs on barges at Bernot from 500 feet; one of the barges was hit. Fifty rounds were fired into the barges, and on the way back 200 rounds were fired at motor cars on the road.

Enemy aircraft activity was very slight and no combats took place.

March 15th.

On the 15th the weather was fine with a strong east wind.

Twenty-four reconnaissances were carried out by brigades and two long distance photographic flights by the 9th Wing.

Thirty-four hostile batteries were successfully engaged for destruction with aeroplane observation and two neutralised. Twenty-one gun-pits were destroyed, 12 damaged, 42 explosions and 17 fires caused. Twenty-three zone calls were sent down.

One thousand six hundred and forty-eight plates were exposed, and 12 tons of bombs dropped as follows:—

1st Brigade.—Three hundred and twenty-four photographs. No. 18 Squadron dropped five 112-lb., twenty 25-lb., and four 40-lb. bombs on Avelin Aerodrome, and four 112-lb. and twelve 25-lb. on billets; forty-one 25-lb. bombs were dropped by machines of 1st Wing.

2nd Brigade.—Two hundred and seventy-three photographs. No. 57 Squadron dropped twelve 112-lb. and seventy-two 25-lb. bombs on Menin, and eight 112-lb. and one hundred and forty-three 25-lb. on rest billets; sixty-one 25-lb. bombs were dropped by machines of 2nd Wing.

3rd Brigade.—Three hundred and eighty-six photographs. No. 49 Squadron dropped four 112-lb. and nineteen 25-lb. bombs on Oisy-le-Verger Ammunition dump; ninety-four 25-lb. bombs were dropped on miscellaneous targets.

5th Brigade.—Five hundred and ninety-three photographs. Naval Squadron No. 5 dropped fifty-two 25-lb. bombs on Bohain Aerodrome and thirty 25-lb. bombs on Bohain Dump. No. 48 Squadron dropped thirty-six 25-lb. and 15th Wing one hundred and twenty-four 25-lb. bombs on miscellaneous targets.

9th Wing.—Seventy-two photographs. No. 25 Squadron dropped ten 112-lb. and forty-eight 25-lb. bombs on Hirson Railway Station, and No. 27 Squadron dropped six 112-lb. and thirty-two 25-lb. bombs on the same objective.

Enemy Aircraft.—Enemy aircraft were very active up to noon; after that time the activity decreased.

Captain W. Fielding Johnson, No. 56 Squadron, shot down an enemy aircraft scout out of control This enemy aircraft was reported by another pilot to have burst into flames.

Lieutenant M. Mealing, No. 56 Squadron, attacked an enemy aircraft scout at very close range. This enemy aircraft went down at a terrific speed in a spin and was seen to crash by another pilot of the same patrol. Later, an enemy aircraft two-seater was encountered south-east of Inchy. Lieutenant Mealing engaged it first and fired a good burst from both guns. He left the enemy aircraft as he observed some water and a small stream of flame come out of the cowling of the engine. Captain Fielding Johnson then attacked, firing at very close range, and the enemy aircraft got into a steep dive and was seen to crash by the whole patrol.

Second Lieut. J. S. Chick and Lieutenant P. Douglas, No. 11 Squadron, shot down an enemy aircraft in flames which was attacking them from behind.

Sergeant D. W. Beard and Sergeant H. W. Scarnell, No. 11 Squadron, attacked one enemy aircraft and fired about 20 rounds at 40 yards range. The enemy pilot fell forward in his seat; the machine immediately nose-dived and shortly afterwards broke up in the air.

Captain H. F. S. Drewitt, No. 23 Squadron, dived on an enemy aircraft two-seater and continued to fire with both guns until almost on top of the enemy aircraft. The enemy aircraft went down in a steep glide, and was then followed by Captain Drewitt and Lieutenant G. G. Macphee, both firing into it. Lieutenant Macphee followed the enemy aircraft down and saw it crash in a field.

Second Lieut. A. W. B. Proctor, No. 84 Squadron, saw an enemy aircraft attacking a S.E. 5. Second Lieut. Proctor got beneath the enemy aircraft and opened fire at 200 yards range. At 100 yards he opened fire with both guns, and after a short burst the enemy aircraft started to spin down slowly and crash in our lines south of Villeret.

Second Lieut. E. A. Clear, No. 84 Squadron, attacked an Albatross Scout which he observed crashing into the ground near Mesnil St. Laurent.

Second Lieut. C. T. Travers, No. 84 Squadron, attacked one of three enemy aircraft scouts. After he had fired 150 rounds the enemy aircraft started to dive, smoke and flames coming out of its fuselage. The other enemy aircraft then attacked Second Lieut. Travers, but he succeeded in driving them east and he returned to the lines.

Second Lieut. A. K. Cowper, No. 24 Squadron, dived on one of two Rumplers, firing about 100 rounds from 50 to 10 yards range. The enemy aircraft started going down steeply, and Second Lieut. R. T. Mark got on its tail and fired 100 rounds at 60 yards range. The enemy aircraft continued to dive and was finally attacked by Second Lieut. H. B. Richardson, and it was seen to crash into the wood north of Premonte.

Second Lieut. F. P. Magoun, No. 1 Squadron, attacked an enemy aircraft and fired a long burst up to within 20 to 30 yards. This enemy aircraft was also attacked by Second Lieut. L. W. Mawbey who fired a burst of 50 rounds. The enemy aircraft stalled, went down in a vertical dive and crashed south of Ledeghem.

Captain W. D. Patrick, No. 1 Squadron, got on the tail of an Albatross Scout and fired a long burst from both guns. The enemy aircraft nose-dived and was observed by the rest of the patrol to crash.

Major A. D. Carter, No. 19 Squadron, fired several bursts from very close range from both guns at an enemy aircraft scout. The enemy aircraft appeared to be out of control and finally, after Major Carter had fired another burst, it went down in a spin, the right wings folding back.

Second Lieut. D. A. Stewart and Sergeant A. O. Pollard, No. 18 Squadron, whilst returning from a bomb raid, were attacked by five Pfalz Scouts from underneath. They fired at one of the enemy aircraft at about 30 yards range, and it proceeded to spin down and crash.

Enemy aircraft were shot down out of control by the following:— Lieutenant M. Mealing, No. 56 Squadron, 1; Second Lieut. H. J. Walkerdine, No. 56 Squadron, 1; Captain L. R. Wren and Second Lieut. E. Gilroy, No. 11 Squadron, 1; Lieutenant H. W. Sellars and Lieutenant C. C. Robson, No. 11 Squadron, 1; Second Lieut. J. S. Chick and Lieutenant P. Douglas, No. 11 Squadron, 1; Sergeant D. W. Beard and Sergeant H. W. Scarnell, No. 11 Squadron, 2; Captain J. A. Slater, No. 64 Squadron, 1; Second Lieut. J. F. T. Barrett, No. 64 Squadron, 1; Second Lieut. H. B. Redler, No. 24 Squadron, 1; Captain F. M. Kitto, No. 54 Squadron, 1; Lieutenant J. F. Larson, No. 84 Squadron, 1; Major A. D. Carter, No. 19 Squadron, 1; Captain P. Huskinson, No. 19 Squadron, 1; Second Lieut. N. W. Hustings, No. 19 Squadron, 1; Captain J. Leacroft, No. 19 Squadron, 2; Lieutenant A. W. Adams, No. 4 Squadron, A.F.C., 1; Lieutenant J. C. Courtney, No. 4 Squadron, A.F.C., 1; Captain A. G. Waller and Lieutenant J. Brisbane, No. 18 Squadron, 1; Lieutenants A. R. James and J. M. Hay, No. 62 Squadron, 1.

Honours and Awards.

Under authority granted by His Majesty the King, the Field-Marshal, Commanding-in-Chief, has made the following awards :—

Bar to the Military Cross.—Captain H. H. Balfour, K.R.R.C. and R.F.C.

The Military Cross.—Second Lieut. C. F. King, General List, R.F.C.; Lieutenant G. C. Cuthbertson, General List, R.F.C.

March 16th.

On the 16th the weather was fine.

Thirty-eight reconnaissances were carried out by Brigades, one photographic reconnaissance by the 9th Wing, one night reconnaissance by the 1st Brigade and one by the 9th Brigade.

Twenty-seven hostile batteries were successfully engaged for destruction and eight neutralized; one gun-pit was destroyed, 11 damaged, 14 explosions and eight fires caused; 39 zone calls were sent down.

On the 15th instant three targets were registered by balloons of the 5th Brigade, and two active hostile batteries were located.

One thousand five hundred and sixty photographs were taken and $21\frac{3}{4}$ tons of bombs dropped as follows:—

Night, 15th–16th.

1st Brigade.—No. 2 Squadron dropped two 40-lb. phosphorus bombs during a night reconnaissance.

9th Brigade.—No. 58 Squadron dropped one hundred and ninety-five 25-lb. bombs and fired two 2-lb. shells on Comines, Wervicq, Roncq, Halluin, Linselles and Menin.

No. 101 Squadron dropped five 230-lb., six 112-lb. and eight 25-lb. on Poncheaux Ammunition Dump, and three 230-lb. bombs on a railway bridge south-west of Le Cateau.

No. 102 Squadron dropped four hundred and seventy 25-lb. bombs on Bourlon, Tilloy, and Fontaine Notre Dame. Four large fires were started. Nearly all pilots carried out three consecutive trips.

Day, 16th.

1st Brigade.—Two hundred and twenty photographs. No. 18 Squadron dropped twenty-seven 112-lb., eight 25-lb. and eighteen 40-lb. bombs on Haubourdin, Sallaumines and Wavrin. One 40-lb. and fifty-four 25-lb. bombs were dropped by the 1st Wing.

2nd Brigade.—Three hundred and sixty-four photographs. No. 57 Squadron dropped twenty-eight 112-lb. and two hundred and eleven 25-lb. bombs on Halluin, Comines, Wervicq, Roncq. Forty-seven 25-lb. bombs were dropped by machines of the 2nd Wing.

3rd Brigade.—Five hundred and thirty-nine photographs. No. 49 Squadron dropped four 112-lb. and eighteen 25-lb. bombs on Tilloy Ammunition Dump; other squadrons dropped sixty-eight 25-lb. bombs.

5th Brigade.—Three hundred and seventy-six photographs. Naval Squadron No. 5 dropped one hundred and four 25-lb. bombs on Etreux Aerodrome. One hangar was hit and a Gotha which attempted to get off the ground was seen to crash. This squadron also dropped twenty-eight 25-lb. bombs on Busigny Aerodrome and sixty-five 25-lb. bombs on Busigny Ammunition Dump. No. 48 Squadron dropped thirty-two 25-lb. bombs, and machines of 15th Wing one hundred and three 25-lb. bombs on miscellaneous targets.

9th Wing.—Sixty-one photographs. No. 25 Squadron dropped ten 112-lb. and fifty 25-lb. bombs on Etreux Aerodrome. No. 27 Squadron dropped four 112-lb. and sixteen 25-lb. bombs on Bohain and two 112-lb. and sixteen 25-lb. bombs on Etreux Aerodrome.

8th Brigade.—Ten machines of No. 55 Squadron, left to bomb military objectives at Mannheim. Three machines returned, two with engine trouble and one shot through the petrol tank by enemy aircraft. The remaining seven machines were unable to reach their objective, as they ran into thick clouds, but they attacked the barracks and railway station at Zweibrucken from 12,500 feet, dropping fourteen 112-lb., six 25-lb., and four 40-lb. phosphorus bombs. Bursts were seen on the barracks and all round the station. Four enemy aircraft attacked the formation, but were driven off. All machines returned.

Enemy Aircraft.—Enemy aircraft were again active, especially in the morning.

Captain D. J. Bell, No. 3 Squadron, dived and got on the tail of an enemy aircraft and fired a short burst of 10 rounds at about 15 yards range. The enemy aircraft went down in a spin, and was confirmed by another pilot to have broken up in the air. Captain Bell then observed an enemy aircraft which was 2,000 feet below him. He just got below the enemy aircraft's tail and fired a short burst at very close range, when the left wing of the enemy aircraft immediately broke off.

Captain G. E. Thomson, No. 46 Squadron, attacked an enemy aircraft two-seater and fired 60 rounds at about 50 yards range. The enemy aircraft stalled and then went down completely out of control in flames.

Captain R. W. Chappell, No. 41 Squadron, attacked one of three enemy aircraft two-seaters, firing a burst from both guns at about 125 yards range. A large cloud of smoke and a sheet of flame came from the enemy aircraft's cockpit and it went down in a spin.

Lieutenant W. L. Wells and Second Lieut. G. S. L. Hayward, No. 22 Squadron, fired a long burst at very close range at one of three Albatross Scouts. The enemy aircraft immediately turned upside down and fell several thousand feet completely out of control, crashing near Beaumont.

Second Lieut. H. L. Christie and Sergeant S. Belding, No. 22 Squadron, dived on several enemy aircraft scouts which were attacking another formation of Bristols of their squadron. They fired at several machines, eventually bringing one down in flames, which crashed in a wood at Carvin. Sergeant E. J. Elton and Second Lieut. R. Critchley, No. 22 Squadron, in the same engagement, fired a short burst at one enemy aircraft, which went down in flames.

Lieutenant F. G. C. Weare and Second Lieut. S. J. Hunter, No. 22 Squadron, singled out one of three Pfalz Scouts and fired about 150 rounds into it. The enemy aircraft went down completely out of control and crashed south-west of Esquerchin.

Flight Lieut. W. H. Chisam, Naval Squadron No. 3, fired a burst of 50 rounds into an enemy aircraft two-seater. Tracers were seen entering the enemy aircraft, which dived vertically and was seen to crash from "C" Battery observation post.

Flight Commander L. H. Rochford, Naval Squadron No. 3, attacked an enemy aircraft two-seater with Flight Lieuts. Glen and Ellwood, the enemy aircraft finally going down on fire.

Second Lieutenant E. R. Varley, No. 23 Squadron, attacked a two-seater enemy aircraft which was flying north over Lehaucourt. Second Lieut. Varley opened fire with both guns at about 100 yards' range. The enemy aircraft went down out of control emitting smoke, and was seen to crash by another pilot of the same patrol.

Captain H. F. S. Drewitt, No. 23 Squadron, attacked an enemy aircraft two-seater which he shot down in flames and which he observed to crash. (Confirmed by anti-aircraft.)

Lieutenant N. Clark, No. 54 Squadron, followed an enemy aircraft two-seater down to 200 feet which had been driven down by his patrol. Lieutenant Clark continued firing at close range; the enemy aircraft spun into the ground and burst into flames.

Lieutenant G. O. Johnson, No. 84 Squadron, attacked an enemy aircraft two-seater which he drove down into a steep dive, and at 2,000 feet he observed smoke coming from the enemy aircraft's cockpit. The smoke then ceased and Second Lieut. P. K. Hobson attacked the enemy aircraft and fired a burst into it, following it down to 1,000 feet, the enemy aircraft finally crashing into the ground between Villers Outreaux and Serain. Other members of the patrol saw the crashed machine on the ground.

Flight Lieut. Dickson and Sub-Lieut. Scott, Naval Squadron No. 5, when returning from a bomb raid, went to the assistance of one of their machines which was being attacked by four enemy aircraft. They shot down one enemy aircraft, which was seen to crash by other pilots. Then they went to the assistance of another of their machines which was being attacked by no less than 12 enemy aircraft of various types. A front gun of their machine ran out of ammunition, the back gun jammed several times, and they finally ran out of ammunition altogether. Their machine was very badly shot about, bullets entering the petrol tanks, the fuselage in a number of places, planes and tail.

Flight Lieut. Watkins and Squadron Commander Goble, Naval Squadron No. 5, when returning from a bomb raid, shot down one of five enemy aircraft scouts. The enemy aircraft fell over sideways and started spinning and was observed by other members of the formation to crash into the ground.

Second Lieut. H. B. Richardson, No. 24 Squadron, dived on an enemy aircraft scout which was attacking Lieutenant Cowper. Lieutenant Richardson was then attacked by several other enemy aircraft and he broke off the combat. Finding himself above the first enemy aircraft scout, he dived and followed it down to 5,000 feet, firing short bursts. The enemy aircraft was diving so fast that, although Lieutenant Richardson's pilot was showing 80 m.p.h. on the second revolution, he was left behind. Lieutenant Richardson pulled out and saw the enemy aircraft crash into a wood.

Enemy machines were also driven down out of control by the following:—Sergeant C. W. Noel and Second Lieut. L. L. T. Sloot, No. 57 Squadron, 2; Flight Lieut. Mellinge, Naval Squadron No. 10, 1; Second Lieut. C. E. Mayer, No. 3 Squadron, 1; Captain L. W. Jarvis, No 56 Squadron, 1; Second Lieut. H. J. Walkerdine, No. 56 Squadron, 1; Captain G. E. Thomson, No. 46 Squadron, 1; Captain S. P. Smith, No. 46 Squadron, 1; Lieutenant W. L. Wells and Second Lieut. G. S. L. Hayward, No. 22 Squadron, 2; Second Lieut. W. F. J. Harvey and Sergeant A. Burton, No. 22 Squadron, 1; Sergeant E. J. Elton and Second Lieut. R. Critchley, No. 22 Squadron, 1; Second Lieut. G. W. Bulmer and Second Lieut. P. S. Williams, No. 22 Squadron, 2; Lieutenant G. F. Malley, No. 4 Squadron A.F.C., 1; Second Lieut. A. W. Adams, No. 4 Squadron A.F.C., 1, Captain J. L Gordon and Second Lieut. J. C. O'Reilly King, No. 25 Squadron, 1; Lieutenant P. Burrowes and Second Lieut. R. S. Herring, No. 48 Squadron, 2; Flight Lieut. Watkins and Squadron Commander Goble, Naval Squadron No. 5, 1; Lieutenant H. V. L. Tubbs, Second Lieut. J. J. Dawe, No. 24 Squadron, 1; Lieutenant F. H. Taylor, No. 41 Squadron, 1.

March 17th.

On the 17th the weather was fine and the visibility good.

Eighteen reconnaissances were carried out by brigades and two photographic flights by the 9th Brigade.

One hundred and six hostile batteries were engaged for destruction and 13 neutralised. Thirteen gun-pits were destroyed, 49 damaged, 63 explosions and 50 fires caused. Eighty-five zone calls were sent down.

On the 16th 21 targets were registered by balloons, of which 20 were by balloons of the 2nd Brigade. Five active hostile batteries were located.

One hundred and thirty-four photographs were taken, and 13¼ tons of bombs dropped as follows :—

Night 16th/17th.

One hundred and sixteen 25-lb. bombs and seven 2-lb. shells on billets opposite the Second Army front by No. 58 Squadron.

One hundred and thirty-four 25-lb. bombs on rest billets opposite the Third Army front by No. 102 Squadron.

Day 17th.

1st Brigade.—One hundred and eighty-eight photographs. No. 18 Squadron dropped four 112-lb., six 25-lb., and two 40-lb. bombs on La Bassée, and eight 112-lb., two 25-lb., and six 40-lb. bombs on Avelin Aerodrome. 1st Wing dropped sixty-three 25-lb. bombs.

2nd Brigade.—Four hundred and eight photographs. No 57 Squadron dropped thirteen 112-lb. and seventy-two 25-lb. bombs on Menin and Halluin. 11th Wing dropped twenty-five 112-lb. and ninety-one 25-lb. bombs on billets, and 2nd Wing dropped eighty-three 25-lb. bombs on miscellaneous targets.

3rd Brigade.—Four hundred and twenty-one photographs. Sixty-one 25-lb. bombs were dropped.

5th Brigade.—Three hundred and sixty-six photographs. Naval Squadron No. 5 dropped fifty-two 25-lb. bombs on Busigny Aerodrome. No. 48 Squadron dropped twenty-nine 25-lb. bombs on miscellaneous targets and one hundred and fifty-five 25-lb. bombs were dropped by the 15th Wing.

9th Wing.—Fifty-one photographs. No. 27 Squadron dropped six 112-lb. and thirty 25-lb. bombs on Saultain (Valenciennes) Aerodrome, and one 112-lb. and twenty-eight 25-lb. bombs on Somain Sidings.

8th Brigade.—On the morning of the 17th instant 10 machines of No. 55 Squadron left to bomb military objectives at Mannheim. One returned with engine trouble and the remainder ran into thick clouds, which prevented them from reaching their objective. Twenty 112-lb., nine 25-lb., and three 40-lb. bombs were dropped from between 13,000 and 15,000 feet on the factories and railway station at Kaiserslautern. Two direct hits were obtained on the station, one truck being set on fire, and a large fire started. Sixteen enemy aircraft attacked the formation but were driven off. Twenty-seven photographs were taken, showing excellent results. All machines returned.

Enemy Aircraft.—Enemy aircraft were very active, and a considerable amount of fighting took place.

Captain L. J. Trollope, No. 43 Squadron, attacked one of four enemy aircraft at close range and fired about 40 rounds. The enemy aircraft dived vertically with clouds of brown smoke issuing from it, and later burst into flames and broke up in the air.

Lieutenant M. R. N. Jennings, No. 19 Squadron, attacked an enemy aircraft, which was diving on the tail of another machine of his patrol. The enemy aircraft did a half roll and dived away and is confirmed to have crashed by another member of the same patrol.

Lieutenant A. B. Fairclough, No. 19 Squadron, fired two bursts at close range into an enemy aircraft scout. This enemy aircraft was also attacked by Second Lieut. E. Oliver, and it went down in flames.

Captain J. Leacroft, No. 19 Squadron, attacked one of many enemy aircraft and after a few shots from both guns, the enemy spun down out of control, burst into flames and crashed. This was confirmed by other members of the same patrol. Lieutenant N. W. Hustings, No. 19 Squadron, got on the tail of an enemy aircraft scout, which went down completely out of control. Lieutenant Hustings then lost this machine, but shortly afterwards saw it crashed on the ground.

Captain P. Huskinson, No. 19 Squadron, dived on one of a large formation of enemy aircraft scouts, followed it down to 3,500 feet, and saw it crash near Roulers.

Major J. A. Cunningham, No. 65 Squadron, attacked an enemy aircraft scout, which immediately turned east and dived. Major Cunningham followed and fired about 50 rounds from each gun at close range. The enemy aircraft kept on diving and eventually crashed at Zuidhoek.

Lieutenant J. K. V. Peden, No. 3 Squadron, whilst on low bombing, engaged one of two enemy aircraft. He fired a burst of about 50 rounds into the enemy aircraft from below at 70 to 50 yards range. The enemy aircraft immediately went into a vertical dive and flattened about 1,000 feet below. Lieutenant Peden again attacked, putting in about three bursts of about 50 rounds each. The enemy aircraft then went down into a vertical dive and crashed.

Second Lieut. A. A. M. Arnot, No. 3 Squadron, whilst on offensive patrol, got on to the tail of an enemy aircraft scout and fired a long burst at about 10 yards' range. The enemy aircraft immediately caught fire, and went down in a steep dive with flames and smoke pouring from its fuselage.

Captain E. R. Tempest, No. 64 Squadron, whilst leading his patrol, dived on a formation of five enemy aircraft scouts, one of which he shot down in flames.

Captain W. H. Park and Second Lieut. H. J. Greenwood, No. 11 Squadron, engaged the leader of four enemy aircraft scouts; after about 100 rounds being fired, the enemy aircraft went down completely out of control and was observed to crash by another observer. Captain Park afterwards saw the enemy aircraft burning on the ground.

Second Lieut. A. W. B. Proctor, No. 84 Squadron, in a general engagement, managed to get on the tail of an enemy aircraft scout, and fired about 100 rounds. The enemy aircraft did a steep dive, followed by a zoom and a quick left-hand turn, whereupon the bottom left-hand plane gave way, and the whole left wing crumpled up against the fuselage.

Second Lieut. C. L. Stubbs, No. 84 Squadron, dived on one enemy aircraft scout and fired a burst with both guns. The enemy aircraft nose-dived vertically and Second Lieut. Stubbs followed him down to 5,000 feet, continually firing. The enemy aircraft was seen to crash in a village.

Second Lieut. J. V. Sorsoleil, No. 84 Squadron, dived on an enemy aircraft and fired a long burst with both guns. The enemy aircraft went down vertically and crashed one mile east of Moretz.

Lieutenant N. Clark, No. 54 Squadron, attacked an enemy aircraft two-seater, which caught fire in the pilot's seat whilst in the air and burst into flames on hitting the ground.

Lieutenant J. R. Rodger, No. 80 Squadron, dived on the rear machine of four enemy aircraft scouts. Tracers were observed passing through the seat of the enemy machine, and Lieutenant Rodger watched this machine falling completely out of control. The enemy aircraft fell so slowly that Lieutenant Rodger rejoined his formation, without wating to see any definite result. Anti-aircraft report that this machine burst into flames.

Captain H. A. Whistler, No. 80 Squadron, whilst on offensive patrol, engaged an enemy aircraft scout and was immediately attacked from the rear by three other enemy aircraft. Captain Whistler zoomed up and came down behind the last machine, firing about 100 rounds at close range. The enemy aircraft immediately fell and turned over and over, finally crashing into a wood.

Lieutenant R. A. Preeston, No. 80 Squadron, whilst flying in formation, dived on one enemy machine of a large number which were attacking his formation and was immediately attacked by three more enemy aircraft which he managed to shake off. Finding himself alone, he turned west and climbed to 12,000 feet and he was attacked by 12 enemy aircraft. He fired a short burst into one which overshot him in a dive, and then, being outnumbered, he spun and dived to about 2,000 feet. He succeeded in reaching our side of the lines after a running fight the whole of the way.

With reference to the above combat, the 66th Division report that at 11.10 a.m. one British scout put up a wonderful fight with eight enemy aircraft and No. 35 Squadron report one enemy aircraft still falling out of control 300 feet from the ground at the same place and time. A pilot of No. 35 Squadron confirms this. The enemy aircraft was one of a large formation which were fighting one Camel.

Second Lieut. A. K. Cowper, No. 24 Squadron, attacked an enemy aircraft which immediately went down in a dive. He followed the enemy aircraft for 1,000 feet, still firing at it. The enemy aircraft went into a slow spin and finally crashed in a field south-west of Ramicourt.

Second Lieut. E. A. Clear dived on a triplane which was attacking another machine of his patrol. After Second Lieut. Clear had fired a few rounds, the enemy aircraft made a sharp turn to the left. At the same time an enemy aircraft "V strutter" also turned round a bank of clouds and crashed into the enemy aircraft triplane practically end-on. The planes of both machines folded back, and they both dropped like a stone.

Enemy machines were brought down out of control by the following:—Captain L. J. Trollope, No. 43 Squadron, 1; Flight Lieut. A. T. Whealy, Naval Squadron No. 3, 1; Major A. D. Carter, No. 19 Squadron, 1; Captain A. Roulstone, No. 57 Squadron, 1; Second Lieut. A. E. Venmore, No. 57 Squadron, 1; Second Lieut. H. E. Stewart, No. 3 Squadron, 1; Second Lieut. W. C. Dennett, No. 3 Squadron, 1; Captain G. E. Thomson, No. 46 Squadron, 1; Captain E. R. Tempest, No. 64 Squadron, 1; Second Lieut A. W. B. Proctor, 2; Second Lieut. J. Loupinsky and Sergeant A. Remington, No. 25 Squadron, 1; Lieut. G. E. Gibbons and Second Lieut. S. A. W. Knights. No. 62 Squadron, 1; Captain H. A Whistler, No. 80 Squadron, 1; Second Lieut. R. T. Mark, No. 24 Squadron, 1; Second Lieut. H. B. Richardson, No. 24 Squadron, 1; Second Lieut. W. H. Brown, No. 84 Squadron, 2; Captain F. E. Brown, No. 84 Squadron, 2.

March 18th.

On the 18th fine weather continued, enabling a considerable amount of work to be done.

Fourteen reconnaissances were carried out by Brigades and three photographic reconnaissances.

Ninety-six hostile batteries were successfully engaged for destruction with aeroplane observation and 15 neutralised. Twenty gun-pits were destroyed, 33 damaged, 67 explosions and 41 fires caused. One hundred and four zone calls were sent down.

On the 17th 63 targets, of which 37 were hostile batteries, were registered by balloons. Of these, 20 were by the First Brigade, 22 by the Second Brigade, 16 by the Third, and 5 by the Fifth. Thirty seven active hostile batteries were located.

One thousand six hundred and eighty-two photographs were taken, and 14 tons of bombs dropped as follows:—

Night, 17th–18th.

Ninth Brigade.—No. 58 Squadron dropped one hundred and twenty-six 25-lb. bombs on Mouchin Aerodrome, two fires being started amongst the hangars and one hut burnt. This squadron also dropped twenty-eight 25-lb. bombs on Don, Seclin and Haubourdin.

No. 101 Squadron dropped two 230-lb., six 112-lb. and four 25-lb. bombs on Premont Ammunition Dump; seven 250-lb., six 112-lb. and twenty-four 25-lb. bombs on a railway bridge S.W. of Le Cateau.

No. 102 Squadron dropped fifty 25-lb. bombs on Emerchicourt Aerodrome and one hundred 25-lb. bombs on billets.

Day, 18th.

1st Brigade.—Two hundred and seventy-five photographs. No. 18 Squadron dropped twelve 112-lb., ten 25-lb. and six 40-lb. bombs on Fournes and La Carnoy railhead. Sixty-five 25-lb. bombs were dropped by 1st Wing.

2nd Brigade.—Two hundred and forty-nine photographs. No. 57 Squadron dropped twelve 112-lb. bombs on Zarren. Seventy-nine 25-lb. bombs were dropped by 2nd Wing, and thirty-three 25-lb. bombs by 11th Wing.

3rd Brigade.—Four hundred and fifty-three photographs. No. 49 Squadron dropped eleven 25-lb. bombs on Iwuy Dump, six 25-lb. bombs on Oisy-le-Verger and six 112-lb. bombs on Aubencheul.

Seventy-one 25-lb. bombs were dropped on miscellaneous targets.

5th Brigade.—Five hundred and forty-eight photographs. Naval Squadron No. 5 dropped sixty-eight 25-lb. bombs on Busigny Aerodrome. One hangar and one shed were hit. No. 48 Squadron dropped twenty-three 25-lb. and 15th Wing one hundred and sixty-eight 25-lb. bombs on various targets.

9th Wing.—One hundred and fifty-seven photographs. No. 25 Squadron dropped four 112-lb. and thirty 25-lb. bombs on Busigny railway station. No. 27 Squadron dropped five 112-lb. and thirty-two 25-lb. bombs on Etreux Aerodrome, and two 112-lb. and sixteen 25-lb. bombs on Busigny railway station.

8th Brigade.—Ten machines of No. 55 Squadron left to bomb military objectives at Mannheim on the Rhine. Nine machines reached the target and dropped eighteen 112-lb., ten 25-lb., and two 40-lb. bombs from an average height of 13,500 feet. As a result, bursts were seen as follows :—Direct hits on the *Badische-Aniline und Soda Fabrik*, causing a huge cloud of black and white smoke to ascend, four direct hits on the docks, one on and one alongside the Sulzer Factory and many others round the objective. The bombing machines were attacked by two formations of enemy aircraft scouts (14 machines) over the objective. A combat ensued, as a result of which two enemy aircraft were driven down out of control, but owing to the fighting and to the fact that there was a certain amount of mist, these machines were not actually seen to crash. They were, however, followed down for 5,000 feet and were then completely out of control. A total of 36 plates were exposed with good results. All our machines returned safely.

Enemy Aircraft.—Enemy aircraft were very active, and the fighting throughout the day was intense.

Sergeant E. J. Elton and Second Lieut. R. Critchley, No. 22 Squadron, dived and fired a burst at an enemy aircraft, which went down in a vertical dive; the top plane of the enemy aircraft came off, and the machine was seen to crash.

Second Lieut. W. F. J. Harvey and Second Lieut. J. L. Morgan, No. 22 Squadron, fired a long burst at an enemy aircraft, which immediately dived and fell in flames.

Flight Sub-Lieut. S. Smith, Naval Squadron No. 3, whilst on offensive patrol, attacked one of five enemy scouts and fired about 300 rounds into it. The enemy aircraft fell out of control and was observed to crash by everyone in the patrol.

Flight Lieut. E. T. Hayne, Naval Squadron No. 3, dived on an enemy aircraft two-seater and fired a burst of 100 rounds at point blank range. The enemy aircraft dived below him, and was immediately attacked by Flight Sub-Lieut. Berlyn, Naval Squadron No. 3, at close range. The enemy observer was seen to fall on his gun, and the enemy aircraft crashed alongside houses about a mile east of Henin Lietard.

Captain H. W. Woollett, No. 43 Squadron, attacked an enemy aircraft two-seater, and followed it due east until he got to close quarters. He then fired about 90 rounds into it. The enemy aircraft spun down and was seen to crash and immediately went up like an explosion, clouds of black smoke appearing from it.

Second Lieut. W. L. Harrison, No. 40 Squadron, attacked an enemy aircraft two-seater and fired about 150 rounds into it. The enemy aircraft went down in a steep dive and burst into flames when near the ground.

Captain R. W. Howard, No. 2 Squadron, A.F.C., dived and fired about 60 rounds into an enemy aircraft two-seater; smoke immediately issued from the fuselage, and two other pilots of Captain Howard's patrol saw this machine diving steeply out of control and in flames.

Captain W. E. Molesworth, when leading a patrol of No. 29 Squadron, encountered a patrol of enemy aircraft. He engaged the leader, and fired about 20 rounds at 100 yards range. The enemy aircraft turned on its back and fell completely out of control, crashing south-east of Rumbeke. In the same patrol, Second Lieut. F. J. Williams, No. 29 Squadron, fired a drum into another enemy aircraft at about 50 yards range, the left wing of the enemy aircraft being completely shot away, and it was seen to fall off.

Captain H. A. Hammersley, No. 60 Squadron, engaged one of several enemy aircraft scouts over Roulers. He attacked one and the right hand bottom plane of the enemy aircraft came off. The enemy aircraft then went down in a spin and the top plane collapsed. The enemy aircraft was seen to crash just east of Rumbeke Aerodrome.

Second Lieut. W. H. Brown, No. 84 Squadron, in a general engagement, was attacked by an enemy aircraft triplane. The triplane fired at him from a stalling position. Second Lieut. Brown dived on the enemy aircraft, firing with both guns. The enemy aircraft immediately dived away under Second Lieut. Brown's machine. He continued to dive after the enemy aircraft firing a long burst from short range. The triplane immediately started spinning, and, after doing a few turns, went into a vertical dive which continued until it hit the ground.

Second Lieuts. E. R. Varley and H. A. F. Goodison, No. 23 Squadron, saw anti-aircraft bursts east of Urvillers. They dived down and attacked an enemy aircraft which endeavoured to make away east, but they succeeded in cutting it off, firing at it as occasion offered, and eventually forced the enemy aircraft to land in our lines near Essigny-le-Grand.

Flight Sub-Lieut. G. B. McBain and aerial gunlayer W. Jones, Naval Squadron No. 5, engaged one of five enemy aircraft scouts and fired about 80 rounds into it. Tracers were seen to enter the fuselage of the enemy aircraft by the cockpit. The enemy aircraft then went into a dive, but later seemed to lose control, turned into a nose-dive and the tail plane dropped off.

Second Lieut. E. A. Richardson, No. 54 Squadron, during an engagement between Camels, S.E.-5's, and a large formation of enemy aircraft attacked one enemy aircraft triplane. He got in a long burst at a range of about 50 feet. The triplane nose dived and burst into flames, later breaking up in the air.

A patrol of No. 84 Squadron saw several enemy aircraft north of Busigny. Second Lieut. E. A. Clear singled out one red triplane and fired a burst from his Lewis gun. The enemy aircraft immediately went down in a spin, and after about five or six turns flattened out. Second Lieut. Clear expected this and followed the enemy aircraft down and fired another burst at 30 yards range. The enemy aircraft stalled, and then fell completely out of control, and was followed down to 9,000 feet by Second Lieut. Clear who was then compelled to leave the enemy aircraft owing to gun stoppages. This machine is confirmed as crashed by No. 54 Squadron.

Major C. M. Crowe (attached to No. 56 Squadron), observed an enemy aircraft two-seater over Inchy. Major Crowe attacked, firing both guns at close range. The enemy aircraft immediately fell out of control and was seen to crash.

Captain W. S. Fielding Johnson, No. 56 Squadron, saw about 10 enemy aircraft attacking a patrol of Camels. He attacked one enemy aircraft scout, firing a burst at short range. The enemy aircraft immediately went down out of control and crashed. He then attacked another which did a left-hand spin and crashed into the ground on its back. Second Lieut. H. J. Walkerdine, No. 56 Squadron, in the same engagement, shot down one enemy aircraft scout, which was seen to crash. He then attacked a second, which he shot down in a spin, and which also crashed. The latter enemy aircraft was confirmed by Captain Fielding Johnson.

Lieutenant F. H. Taylor, No. 41 Squadron, whilst on a test flight, saw five enemy aircraft two-seaters over Lecluse. He dived on the enemy aircraft, firing about 100 rounds, and the enemy aircraft dived through the clouds and was lost to sight. This enemy aircraft is confirmed crashed by two anti-aircraft batteries.

Enemy machines were also driven down out of control by the following :—

Captain F. C. G. Weare and Second Lieut. G. S. L. Hayward, No. 22 Squadron, 1; Second Lieut. H. L. Christie and Sergeant R. Pritchard, No. 22 Squadron, 1; Flight Lieut. E. T. Hayne, Naval Squadron, No 3, 1; Lieutenant A. G. Wingate-Grey, No. 29 Squadron, 1; Captain J. G. Coombe, No. 29 Squadron, 1; Second Lieut. F. J. Davies, No. 29 Squadron, 1; Second Lieut. C. F. Cunningham, No. 60 Squadron, 1; Second Lieut. J. S. Griffiths, No. 60 Squadron, 1; Lieutenant J. F. Larson, No. 84 Squadron, 1; Captain F. E. Brown, No. 84 Squadron, 1; Second Lieut. W. H. Brown, No. 84 Squadron, 1; Flight Lieut. E. Dickson and Sub-Lieut. W. H. Scott, Naval Squadron No. 5, 1; Flight Commander C. P. Bartlett and Aerial Gunlayer Naylor, Naval Squadron No. 5, 1; Second Lieut. N. M. Drysdale, No. 54 Squadron, 1; Captain B. P. G. Beanlands, Second Lieut. H. B. Redler, No. 24 Squadron, 1; Lieutenant A. K. Cowper, No. 24 Squadron, 1; Captain K. G. Leask, No. 84 Squadron, 1; Lieutenant G. O. Johnson, No. 84 Squadron, 1; Captain E. R. Tempest, No. 64 Squadron, 1; Lieutenant H. W. Sellars and Lieutenant C. C. Robson, No. 11 Squadron, 1; Major C. M. Crowe, attached to No. 56 Squadron, 1; Second Lieut. C. A. Bridgland and Second Lieut. E. R. Steward, No. 55 Squadron, 1; Captain S. B. Collett and Lieutenant G. Breyer-Ash, No. 55 Squadron, 1.

Miscellaneous.—Naval Squadron No. 5 (5th Brigade) again bombed Busigny Aerodrome with a view to drawing up hostile machines, which were to be attacked by Nos. 54 and 84

Squadrons. The plan was successful, a fierce fight taking place, in which four enemy aircraft were brought down, and eight driven down out of control.

L. A. K. BUTT, Captain,
Staff Officer.

Headquarters, R.F.C.,
20th March 1918.

www.ingramcontent.com/pod-product-compliance
Lightning Source LLC
Chambersburg PA
CBHW060452300426
44113CB00016B/2565